THE PURSUIT OF PLEASURABLE WORK

Morris's Garden, ink drawing. © Jenn Law, 2021.

THE PURSUIT OF
PLEASURABLE WORK

Craftwork in
Twenty-First Century England

Trevor H.J. Marchand

berghahn
NEW YORK · OXFORD
www.berghahnbooks.com

First published in 2022 by

Berghahn Books

www.berghahnbooks.com

© 2022, 2024 Trevor H.J. Marchand
First paperback edition published in 2024

Library of Congress Cataloging-in-Publication Data

Names: Marchand, Trevor H.J., author.
Title: The Pursuit of Pleasurable Work: Craftwork in Twenty-First Century England /
 Trevor H.J. Marchand.
Description: New York: Berghahn Books, 2022. | Series: New Anthropologies of
 Europe; volume 4 | Includes bibliographical references and index.
Identifiers: LCCN 2021040492 (print) | LCCN 2021040493 (ebook) | ISBN
 9781800732742 (hardback) | ISBN 9781800732759 (ebook)
Subjects: LCSH: Woodworkers—England—London—History—21st century. |
 Woodwork—England—London—History—21st century. | Meaning (Psychology)—
 England—London—History—21st century.
Classification: LCC HD8039.W62 G763 2022 (print) | LCC HD8039.W62 (ebook) |
 DDC 331.7/6840809421—dc23
LC record available at https://lccn.loc.gov/2021040492
LC ebook record available at https://lccn.loc.gov/2021040493

British Library Cataloguing in Publication Data
A catalogue record for this book is available from the British Library

ISBN 978-1-80073-274-2 hardback
ISBN 978-1-80539-313-9 paperback
ISBN 978-1-80539-426-6 epub
ISBN 978-1-80073-275-9 web pdf

https://doi.org/10.3167/9781800732742

New Anthropologies of Europe: Perspectives and Provocations

Series Editors:
Michael Herzfeld, *Harvard University*
Melissa L. Caldwell, *UC Santa Cruz*

The anthropology of Europe has dramatically shifted ground from its emergence in descriptive ethnography to the exploration of innovative theoretical and methodological approaches today. This well-established series, relaunched by Berghahn Books with a new subtitle, invites proposals that speak to contemporary social and cultural theory through innovative ethnography and vivid description. Topics range from migration, human rights and humanitarianism to historical, visual and material anthropology to the neoliberal and audit-culture politics of Schengen and the European Union.

In dedication to Jim O'Brien, John Appleton and Michael Montague-Smith: three gentlemen whose untiring commitment to craft gave countless young men and women the opportunity to pursue fulfilling careers.

CONTENTS

❦

FIGURES

༄

ACKNOWLEDGEMENTS

My father had strong, oversized hands. His palms were wide and his fingers thick as Cumberland sausages. Any lack in nimble dexterity he made up for in strength and perseverance. One year, Santa Claus brought my younger brother and me our first tool chests, stocked with tiny saws, hammers and screwdrivers. As a boy I regularly assisted my dad with home repairs. I learned about materials and assembly, and I sometimes learned by example how best *not* to go about a task. When I bought my first flat in London, Dad travelled from Montreal to lend a hand with renovations. For six weeks we shared a mattress on the floor at the centre of the main room, surrounded at night by carefully stacked piles of timber, plaster board and my faithful Black & Decker workhorse. A few years later, my partner and I moved into a country house in Gloucestershire. My dad visited each spring to help repair outbuildings. Our final project together was reconstructing a shed roof with its original double-roman tiles. By that time, Dad's pace had slowed and his energy ebbed, but he kept me entertained with chitchat and occasional guidance from where he sat comfortably in a lawn chair. Shortly after, a rapid deterioration in Dad's health led to an excruciating year in hospital, where he died with exemplary courage and dignity. His memory accompanies me always when I practise or write about carpentry.

The research for this book would not have been possible without the generous support of the Economic & Social Research Council (RES-000–27–0159) and the British Academy (Mid-Career Fellowship). I thank Jacqui Arrol-Barker and Rob Whiting in the SOAS Research Office for their support throughout the application processes, and to all my dear colleagues at SOAS for their encouragement and the genuine interest they expressed in my research. In writing this, I also pause to remember SOAS Director Paul Webley, whose support I cherished.

I owe tremendous gratitude to the Building Crafts College, where my main fieldwork was carried out in 2005–7 and 2012–13. I thank first and foremost the cohorts of fine-woodwork students with whom I trained and researched. Each of the men and women enriched my life in unique ways, and I am proud to enjoy continuing friendships with many. I also thank the dozen or so Modern Apprentices at the College who sat down with me in the library to be interviewed about their working lives and training experiences. I extend heartfelt thanks to Director John Taylor and his successor Len Conway, who welcomed me to the College and lent my studies their fullest support. Thanks, too, to all the remarkable people who worked at the College during those years, with special mention of the inspiring woodworking instructors and technicians: Cornelius Lynch, David Wheeler (who kindly contributed several illustrations for the book), John Wilkie, Cheryl Mattey, Kate Payne, Jim O'Brien, John Appleton, Errol Boswell and Colin Eden-Eadon. I am grateful to stonemasons Nina Bilbey, Nigel Gilkison and Max Lawson for sharing expertise about their own fascinating craft. I also thank filmmakers Pete Durgerian and Michel Bewley for their assistance with my 'brain, hand and tool' study at the College, and Pete for his marvellous contribution to the making of my documentary film *The Intelligent Hand* (2015).

I am indebted to London's Worshipful Company of Carpenters, and especially to Chairman of the College Committee Michael Montague-Smith and the extraordinary Archivist Julie Tancell, who provided kind assistance throughout the project. I pay thanks to Executive Director of the Crafts Council Rosy Greenlees, with whom I share both concerns and great hopes for the future of craftsmanship in Britain, and to Betty Norbury for a most enlightening interview over tea in Cheltenham. I am highly appreciative of the insights of the designer-makers of bespoke furniture who I interviewed over the years. They include the talented David Gates, Phil Koomen, Anna Williams, Nick Gutfreund, James Verner, Anna Hoare, Johnny Hawkes, Rupert Williamson, Fred Baier, Emma Leslie and Rhiannon Wilkey. Sadly, I was not able to represent all of their individual voices in the chapters, but I hope that the spirit of my book does justice to the great passion they have for their trade.

I thank my family, friends and colleagues who read drafts of various chapters and offered invaluable feedback. These include Parvathi Raman, Roy Dilley, Thomas Kirsch, Tim Ingold, Elizabeth Hallam, Richard Fardon, Regina Bendix, Dorothee Hemme, Lorraine Daston, anonymous committee members of the International Association for the Study of Traditional Environments (IASTE), Keith Marchand, Linda Marchand and Eric Vallée. Very special thanks goes to lifelong friend, artist and anthropologist Jenn Law, who not only commented on the full script, but also created the sumptuous artwork for the front cover, and to the two anonymous reviewers of the manuscript for their heartening feedback. Finally, I owe deep gratitude to John Heywood for his unswerving support and belief in me, and to our dog Rusty, dozing on the grass beneath the garden table where I sit reflecting on those enjoyable years of fieldwork and writing these words of thanks.

PROLOGUE
Toiling to Live

My reasons for writing this prologue were twofold. First, I felt it imperative to offer the reader a brief historical account of the structural changes and resulting crises in British higher education that affected me as a university academic, and that motivated the present study and, ultimately, my own pursuit of pleasurable work. Second, the prologue presents a picture of core changes to the delivery of vocational education and training in England and Wales that took shape in parallel with those being made by the government to mainstream schooling and universities. The period covered spans the early 1980s to the starting point of my apprentice-style fieldwork with carpenters in 2005. By conveying that history here, the preface sets the context for the curriculum of learning I underwent as a trainee at the Building Crafts College in London's East End.

* * *

> Worthy work carries with it the hope of pleasure in rest, the hope of the pleasure in our using what it makes, and the hope of pleasure in our daily creative skill. All other work but this is worthless; it is slaves' work [*sic*] – mere toiling to live, that we may live to toil.
>
> —William Morris[1]

I tucked a bookmark between the pages, dropped the book gently to the floor at the side of my bed and switched off the light. I lay on my back, agitated and peering wide-eyed into the darkness. The chapter I was reading by William Morris set my mind into oscillation between hope and despair, between a yearning for fulfilment and the stark awareness that my cherished vocation was being systematically hollowed out by bureaucracy, standardisation and the commodification of the things I create. My thoughts wrestled and my body perspired, twisting and tangling with the sheets. There had to be another way: a way to keep my long pursuit of purposeful and pleasurable work from being reduced to a 'toiling to live'.

William Morris – the prolific Victorian designer, maker and social activist – first delivered his lecture on 'Useful Work versus Useless Toil' on 16 January 1884 to the Hampstead Liberal Club. True to his socialist convictions, Morris chastised the moral bankruptcy of a capitalist system built upon institutionalised inequality and he condemned industrial Britain for shackling its labouring population to a lifetime of hopeless drudgery. Morris' fiery prose warned of the dire, even bloody consequences of inaction. By the 1880s, however, industrial processes had already become deeply rooted in Britain, Western Europe and North America, and were triumphantly infiltrating nearly every sector of manufacture. In the quest for efficiency, economy of scale and profit, mechanisation had transformed nearly all manner of artisan and craftsperson, smallholder farmer and semi-skilled labourer into mill or factory worker.

How did this history affect me? Why were worries of 'useless toil' robbing me of sleep? It was 2004, not the nineteenth century, and I was a lecturer at an esteemed London university, not a labourer or factory worker. In fact, Morris' message did take explicit account of a changing university life in England: 'Even at the ancient universities', he pronounced, 'learning is but little regarded unless in the long run it can be made *to pay*.'[2] University education, to his mind, had given way to the 'pressures of commercial exigencies'.[3] This resonated with my own growing experiences of quantification and auditing of 'outputs' – whether it be publications, presentations, citations, 'impact' or student numbers – and of a cold, callous bureaucratisation creeping into all levels of higher education.[4] The new breed of university managers wielded performance metric measures to control, reward or punish what they did not understand.[5]

German sociologist Max Weber expressed similar worries in his early twentieth-century writings on 'The Alleged "Academic Freedom" of the German Universities'.[6] The logic of industrial capitalism and the intrusion of government in relation to the autonomy of the academy, Weber argued, were contaminating the organisational principles of universities and academic disciplines with a means-end rationality. This in turn made universities compliant instruments of political policy and transformed them into marketplace actors. In addition to the threat this posed to scholarly ethics and the moral authority of faculties, Weber was troubled by what he saw as an institutional change of mindset: the professoriate had come to actively participate in turning knowledge and learning into a quantifiable good.[7] This was part and parcel of 'the relentless march of bureaucratic rationality in capitalist societies', which was 'leaving organisations and cultural activities devoid of freedom and empty of meaning'.[8]

At the turn of the millennium, concerns in British universities echoed those of Weber, and resistance and vocal opposition to a bloating 'audit culture' were on the rise.[9] The origins of the current malaise in academia, however, stretch back to the early 1980s, following the election of the first Thatcher government in 1979. The Conservative Party agenda was to shrink the state's role in public-sector services and unleash neoliberal market forces that would overhaul them, making them leaner, competitive, enterprising, more flexible, dynamic and efficient – the alleged virtues of the private sector.

Prime Minister Margaret Thatcher, like American President Ronald Reagan, was a devout proponent of economist Friedrich Hayek's worldview that all reality can be structured on the model of market competition, and of economist Milton Friedman's ideas that economics is an objective science and is in principle independent of any ethical position or normative judgements.[10] Tried and tested in Augusto Pinochet's Chile, the neoliberal ideology embraced by the United Kingdom and the United States during the 1980s was soon after pedalled by the International Monetary Fund in the structural adjustment programmes implemented throughout Latin America and Sub-Saharan Africa, and it served as the cornerstone of new international trade treaties. The impact has been global and lasting. The Tory agenda succeeded in framing the political discourse and economic policies of future governments, from New Labour onwards – and, to a great extent, it shaped popular belief, values and behaviour.[11]

The National Health Service (NHS) and local authorities across the United Kingdom were targeted for reform, but the education sector would receive particular attention from Thatcher and her chief architect, Keith Joseph,[12] and his successor, Kenneth Baker.[13] In contrast to Thatcher's purported goal to retract the state from people's lives, central government under her premiership took unprecedented control over schools, colleges and universities. Questions earlier posed by Labour Prime Minister James Callaghan in his Ruskin College speech (1976)[14] on the needs for standards, accountability and economic responsiveness in the United Kingdom's education system were to be bluntly answered by the Tories' market-driven reforms.

In short, the reforms spelled a dramatic demotion of the authority of those on the frontlines of education, namely the teachers, headteachers, schools and Local Education Authorities. Lasting results included the establishment of a National Curriculum for primary and secondary schools,[15] which, incidentally, marked the vanishing of woodwork and metalwork shops from many schools, as well as the disappearance of other hands-on crafts and technical drawing from syllabi; the Office for Standards in Education (Ofsted), whose inspections are carried out in accordance with a National Framework;[16] and tighter coordination between schools, parents, professional bodies, industry and government in efforts to improve accountability and to inculcate in students the values of economic liberalism and social conservatism.[17] Treatment of the universities, however, was especially pernicious, being 'an almost total usurpation, a dissolution of the university system, comparable to the dissolution of the monasteries'.[18]

Journalist Alex Preston noted that:

> Thatcher – the only prime minister to have been secretary of state for education – made the universities the exception in her neo-liberal drive to decentralise. She asserted more government power over the universities in an attempt to strong-arm them into complying with her vision of an entrepreneurial, vocational education system.[19]

Like mainstream education, the vocational routes that prepare young men and women for work as craftspeople, tradespeople or technicians were reconfigured through far-reaching government intervention.[20] Decades of decline in the United Kingdom's general manufacturing sector had resulted by the early 1980s in a dramatic drop in the take-up of traditional apprenticeships,[21] deterioration of the related training programmes, unacceptably high levels of youth unemployment, and social unrest and rioting.[22] In response, the Conservative government initiated the Youth Training Scheme (YTS) in 1983 as a manpower creation programme designed to supply on-the-job training primarily for sixteen and seventeen-year-old school-leavers and thereby improve their employment prospects.[23]

However, the success rates were mixed and criticism was levelled against the scheme for its high dropout rate.[24] It was also denounced because the majority of attendees achieved no credible certificate upon leaving,[25] and young men in particular gained no privileged access to employment.[26] Some believed that the YTS was 'little more than a means of reducing the unemployment figures'[27] and others accused it of inadvertently creating opportunity for employers to exploit a cheap source of unskilled and low-skilled labour.[28] Notably, the YTS (later renamed Youth Training) also struggled against being stigmatised as 'a low-status scheme for the less able, the less motivated, and the less employable'[29] – tragically, a recurring slur in the United Kingdom against vocational education, including apprenticeships in craftwork or any kind of physical handiwork.

From the mid-1980s, the emphasis shifted somewhat from the quantitative dimension of youth unemployment to skills and the quality of training.[30] The National Council for Vocational Qualifications (NCVQ) was set up in 1986 to achieve the first coherent framework for vocational qualifications in England and Wales. Hitherto, some 300 different (and sometimes overlapping) bodies awarded qualifications, the largest of which were the City &

Guilds of London Institute, the Royal Society of Arts, and the Business and Technician Education Council.

The launch of National Vocational Qualifications (NVQs) in 1988 coincided with the Education Reform Act and the advent of a common examination at the end of compulsory schooling. The objectives of the NVQ framework, with its five progressive levels, were to alleviate the persistent shortage of intermediate-level skills and better ensure that trainees in craftwork, construction, engineering, manufacturing, business services and other sectors were achieving skill competency relevant to the needs of the nation's industry and commerce.[31] By the mid-1990s, however, the structure and purported values of the NVQ system remained opaque to many trainees and employers in terms of its expectations, criteria and assessment; take-up remained low and popular perceptions of NVQs being 'Mickey Mouse' qualifications persisted.[32] The combination of a lack of prescribed syllabi and a stress on competence-based outcomes (i.e. observable performances) fomented arguments that the NVQ framework 'neglected the general purpose of education for personal development and citizenship in a modern society'.[33] Frustratingly, such lines of reasoning went largely unheeded by the government, as Thatcher had already grandiloquently declared the nonexistence of 'society'.[34]

In order to create more sustainable education and training 'markets' linked to the nation's industry and commerce, a publicly funded 'Modern Apprenticeship' (MA) scheme was inaugurated in 1994 (and later renamed simply 'Apprenticeships').[35] Designed for school-leavers, but allowing entry to women and men who would complete before the age of twenty-five, the MA frameworks addressed the development of core skills (i.e. communication, numeracy and IT skills), broad occupational knowledge and job-specific skills, leading to NVQ Level 3 or above.[36] Whilst aiming to create a modern workforce in possession of the flexible, transferrable skills demanded by an ever-changing work environment, MAs also aspired to retain select qualities of traditional apprenticeships, including formal training agreements to foster mutual commitment between trainees and employers. As noted by educationalists Alison Fuller and Lorna Unwin, 'the concept of apprenticeship was synonymous in many people's minds with high standards of workplace training'.[37]

Just a few years into its existence, it was already evident that large numbers of apprentices enrolled on the MA scheme were quitting before having finished training. A report published in 1998 by the Centre for Economic Performance recommended, among other things, that there be expanded government financing for the scheme and that the apprenticeships be reformed to include a strengthening of their educational content, which they remarked was 'well below levels expected in apprenticeships in other European countries'.[38] The NVQs that underpinned MAs were censured by other experts for prioritising competency-based 'outputs' (and outcomes) at the expense of structural 'inputs' (i.e. content), such as regulated training processes and prescribed syllabi,[39] and the MA framework itself was critiqued for the absence of mechanisms to ensure integration of on-the-job and college-based learning.[40] Still others slated the government and its agencies for their negligence in systematically vetting employers that enrolled apprentices on MAs and the conditions under which apprentices were working.[41] Uptake of the training scheme by business and industry was, in any case, sluggish, especially among small and medium-sized enterprises that shared concerns over the proportion of enrolment costs to any benefits they might possibly derive.

Indeed, the reluctance displayed by employers reflected an historical and general absence of a 'training culture' in Britain compared to other European countries, such as Germany.[42] Britain's failure to train stemmed (and continues to stem) from the short-term perspective held by most companies, pressure on managers to maximise immediate profits and shareholder value, and a business orientation towards low-cost, low-quality production.[43] In effect, a pervasive laissez-faire liberal attitude to vocational education and training trapped the country in a 'low-skills equilibrium'.[44] As opposed to being defined 'solely in terms of its value to the economy', Lorna Unwin advocated that vocational education should be supporting 'people's need to create artefacts, to improve their surroundings, to fight against becoming deskilled consumers, to feel part of the natural world, and to demonstrate the true extent of their capabilities'.[45] An exploration of these empowering factors is at the core of this book about woodworkers.

I return at this point to my account of the parallel plight of universities. Funding to higher education was slashed during the Thatcher era and academics lost security of tenure. In 1986, the University Grants Committee (UGC, a government advisory body) introduced the Research Selectivity Exercise, which would determine the disbursement of limited funds for university research. An important component of the UGC mandate was to make annual contracts with universities to provide student places in line with national needs for, once again, qualified 'manpower'. The powers of the UGC were transferred in 1989 to the Universities Funding Council (UFC), a body directly answerable to Parliament and on which academic representation was reduced to a minority. The 1989 Research Selectivity Exercise overseen by the UFC subjected a far greater number of academic disciplines and 'units of assessment' to bureaucratic scrutiny.

From the early 1990s onwards, the accountability of both higher education institutions and individual academics was increasingly regulated not by government directly, but by intermediary agencies that were established by government, including the Higher Education Funding Councils (HEFC, which replaced the UFC in 1992)[46] and the Quality Assurance Agency for Higher Education (QAA). The Tory mantra of 'performance management' and the accountancy mentality of its agencies progressively percolated into the operating systems of the universities. Because of its resource allocation powers, there was growing concern that the research assessment exercises were 'determining rather than measuring the ways research is conducted in universities'.[47]

With the passing years, the tables turned on academics. Swelling ranks of administrators, many brandishing MBAs and armed with corporate business models, were now running the nation's institutions of higher education. They not only oversaw the finance and balance sheets, but were also increasingly vested with authority to chair committee meetings, set 'targets' and 'benchmarks', develop 'corporate identities' and 'marketing strategies', structure departments and faculties for greater economy and efficiency, and shape academic programmes and course curricula to raise 'completion rates' and produce more readily readable, routinised 'data'. With the exception of some institutions (including my own),[48] rises in senior management pay would soon outpace that of academics by obscene ratios.[49] Neoliberal justifications were offered in defence of the high executive salaries, despite the fact that British universities are formally charities, not private enterprises with dividend-demanding shareholders. Paradoxically, in an era branded by faith in free market capitalism, managers conveniently relied on the 'passionate commitment' of academics to do their work primarily for the 'satisfaction' they gain and not for the money.

In 1992, the same year that the distinction between universities and polytechnics was abolished, the nationwide Research Assessment Exercise (RAE) was launched with the aim to carry out a more robust and rigorous audit than its predecessors. Subsequent RAEs were carried out in 1996 and 2001 under Tony Blair's New Labour government, each time with the exercise criteria modified and the goalposts changed in response to vehement complaint and criticism from the sector, but also according to the government's neoliberal strategies and ambitions for distributing available funding among select and 'deserving' institutions.

The Association of University Teachers (AUT), in its sustained opposition to the RAE, reported in 2002 to the Select Committee on Science and Technology that the 'balance between the need, on the one hand, to ensure accountability and "value for money" in the use of public funds, and, on the other, to encourage creative enquiry and flexibility' had 'gone too far in the direction of audit, assessment and instant evaluation'. The AUT made plain that its members' 'experience of research selectivity in the context of funding cuts has been overwhelmingly one of divisiveness, unfairness and demoralisation'.[50] It urged that if there were to be another RAE,[51] then it should be streamlined to reduce the burden of bureaucracy and workload on staff, that its appropriateness for all subject areas should be carefully considered, and that peer review of research quality should replace the current emphasis on quantitative performance indicators and bibliometric analysis. Discouragingly, this had little or no effect on future Whitehall policy-making.[52]

Peer review, qualitative assessment and ranking are practices that lie historically at the heart of academia and have long been upheld by researchers, lecturers and students as both necessary and beneficial. British universities had exercised autonomy under royal charter to set their standards, monitor quality, and promote the best research and thinking.[53] The new market-driven audit culture, by contrast, was eroding traditional academic values, work practices and morale. Those affected by it also found themselves ensnared by its logic. Like Weber, but in the language of Michel Foucault, anthropologists Chris Shore and Susan Wright exposed not merely the corrosive effects that nearly two decades of managerial culture and government-inflicted accountability was having on higher education, but also the 'disciplinary technologies that impel subjects [i.e. academics] to actively contribute to authoritarian and coercive practices of accounting'.[54] In a nutshell, academics were being saddled with a vast and ever-growing responsibility to account for what they and their colleagues did, while at the same time being divested of control and professional autonomy over their labours and the things they created.

It was these conditions that impelled me on that sleepless night in 2004 to chart an alternative path. As much as I wished for it, I would never awaken in a house on the River Thames, like the protagonist in *News from Nowhere*, and stroll outdoors into a transformed utopian England.[55] I therefore took my chances and seized what control I could to reinvigorate my work with intellectual curiosity and a sense of exploration. The next morning, with a budding plan in mind and buoyancy of spirit, I sat down with the director of the university's research office. This was the start of what would be my most gratifying study yet, and in many ways my most challenging. In a year's time, I would be training alongside carpenters, delving into questions about human skill and creativity; the indissoluble relationship between mind, body, the tools that we use and the things that we make; and, perhaps most importantly, the human impulse to seek pleasure and autonomy in the work that we do.

Trevor H.J. Marchand
West Gloucestershire

NOTES

1. Morris, 'Useful Work', 289. Given Morris' consistent emphasis on the value of pur-poseful, pleasurable and fulfilling forms of work, I interpret his employment of the term 'slave's work' to be metaphorical here, referring not specifically to the labour of enslaved people, but rather more generally to modes of monotonous labouring at machines or in factories, mass-producing inferior-quality goods for the Victorian consumer market.
2. Ibid., 20, italics in original. On Morris and transformations in universities in the late nineteenth century, see Bennett, 'Educating for Utopia'.
3. Morris, 'The Aims of Art', 85. Morris originally published this essay in 1915.
4. Likewise, anthropologist Michael Herzfeld draws an analogy between the de-skilling of the contemporary artisan and the current threat to academic and intel-lectual autonomy. See Herzfeld, 'Deskilling, "Dumbing Down" and the Auditing of Knowledge'.
5. As Stefan Collini noted: 'Metrics are frequently used in an attempt to replace in-trinsic motivation with extrinsic motivation, that is, in trying to create a situation in which people are responding to a uniform [and, for administrators, more "efficient"] system of rewards and penalties, usually financial, rather than being driven largely by the satisfaction that comes with the exercise of skill, the enjoyment of respect, the achieving of shared purpose and so on.' He concludes that 'metrics – the moral code of a sourly reductive managerial culture – are the means to make sure that pro-fessionals' working conditions [i.e. those of university academics] should more and more correspond to the alienated, insecure, hollowed-out working conditions of so many other members of society' (Collini, 'Kept Alive', 36 and 38).
6. In Weber, *Max Weber on Universities*, 14–23.
7. See also Samier, 'Weber on Education and Its Administration'.
8. Murphy, 'Bureaucracy and Its Limits', 683–84.
9. For example, see Strathern, 'The Tyranny of Transparency'; Strathern, *Audit Cul-tures*; Collini, 'HiEdBiz'; Brehony and Deem, 'Challenging the Post-Fordist/Flex-ible Organisation Thesis'; Strathern, 'A Community of Critics?'; and Herzfeld, 'Deskilling, "Dumbing Down" and the Auditing of Knowledge'.
10. Friedman, 'The Methodology of Positive Economics'.
11. For a comprehensive account of the ways in which neoliberalism shaped and con-tinues to frame politics as well as popular thinking and behaviour, see Harvey, *A Brief History of Neoliberalism*; and for a briefer but erudite discussion, see Metcalf, 'Neoliberalism'.
12. Keith Joseph was author of the pamphlet *Why Britain Needs a Social Market Econ-omy* (1975), a publication that was hugely influential in shaping Tory policy from the Thatcher era onwards. As Secretary of State for Education and Science, Joseph was first to propose a levying of university tuition fees (a feat ultimately realised by Labour under Tony Blair) and to advocate a paternalistic inspectorate system to assess the quality of university research and output, with the emphasis on the sec-tor's responsiveness to the changing industrial and commercial circumstances of the nation. On Joseph and tuition fees, see *House of Commons Hansard*, 14 November 1984; and Ward, 'Tough Choices'. On the need for appraisal of research in higher education, see Keith Joseph's '1985 Speech Higher Education', which he defended in the House of Commons.

13. Kenneth Baker served as Secretary of State for Education from 1986 to 1989. He instituted the highly controversial Education Reform Act 1988, the most significant education act since 1944. Among the numerous structural changes introduced were the creation of a national core curriculum, the devolution of financial control of primary and secondary schools to heads and governors, the creation of City Technical Colleges that were partly financed by private enterprise, the severe weakening of local education authorities with the alleged aim to create 'choice' for parents, and the establishment of two new funding bodies for higher and further education, whose members would be appointed by the Secretary of State. See Gillard, 'Thatcher and the New Right'.

14. Callaghan, 'A Rational Debate'. This speech is widely regarded as having initiated 'The Great Debate' on the nature and purpose of public education.

15. The National Curriculum for England and Wales was first introduced by the Education Reform Act of 1988.

16. Ofsted came about through a reconstitution of His or Her Majesty's Inspectorate (HMI) under Prime Minister John Major's government's Education (Schools) Act 1992.

17. Dale, 'The Thatcherite Project in Education'.

18. Atlas, 'Oxford versus Thatcher's England', quoting John Griffith, Professor of Public Law at LSE.

19. Preston, 'The War against Humanities'.

20. Regarding craftwork specifically, it is noteworthy that already by the early twentieth century, Charles R. Ashbee, architect and prominent craftsman of the Arts and Crafts movement, advocated for direct government legislation alongside voluntary associations and the 'greater union and organisation of arts and craftsmen', to 'provide general regulation of industry [i.e. standards] in the interest of the whole community [of craftspeople]' (Ashbee, *The Guild of Handicraft*, 91).

21. The numbers enrolled on traditional apprenticeships reached an all-time low by the early 1980s, with the exception of those in high-technology areas of work.

22. Towns and major cities across England experienced serious riots in 1981. Though popularly labelled 'race riots' at the time, the root causes extended well beyond racial tensions to include the highest rates of unemployment since the 1930s, a sense of social marginalisation and economic abjection (especially among young men), decrepit housing conditions, the instituting of stop-and-search powers for police (disproportionately applied to Black communities) and a general distrust of authority.

23. Prior to 1977, there were no government training schemes. James Callaghan's Labour government introduced the Youth Opportunities Programme (YOP) in 1978. This was expanded under Thatcher's government and replaced in 1983 with the YTS, which was renamed Youth Training (YT) in 1989.

24. Oulton and Steedman, 'The British System of Youth Training', 64–65.

25. Ibid., 74.

26. See Dolton, Makepeace and Treble, 'The Youth Training Scheme'.

27. Gray and Morgan, 'Modern Apprenticeships', 124.

28. See *The Independent*, 'Youth Training Scheme a Failure'; and Fergusson and Unwin, 'Making Better Sense of Post-16 Destinations'.

29. Steinmann, 'The Vocational Education and Training System', 34.

30. Ibid., 31. However, Gray and Morgan wrote that 'training in the UK was still reactive and focused on unemployment . . . rather than proactive and concentrating on skills

development for the future' and that the UK is struggling to move toward an emphasis on quality ('Modern Apprenticeships', 131).

31. NVQs would remain the standard awards for trainees in vocational fields until 2015, at which point they were replaced with the Regulated Qualifications Framework (RQF). General National Vocational Qualifications (GNVQs) were introduced in 1990, offering a combination of academic, general vocational and vocational education, and thereby creating a bridge between Britain's long-entrenched academic/vocational divide. GNVQs lasted until 2007.

32. Gleeson et al., 'Reflections on Youth Training', 605.

33. Steinmann, 'The Vocational Education and Training System', 38. See also Evans, 'Competence and Citizenship'.

34. Prime Minister Margaret Thatcher in an interview for *Woman's Own* with Douglas Keay, 23 September 1987. Retrieved 20 May 2021 from https://www.margaretthatcher.org/document/106689.

35. Training frameworks for the MAs were 'developed on a sector-by-sector basis by employer-led partnerships between Industry Training Organisations (ITOs) and Training and Enterprise Councils (TECs)' (Steinmann, 'The Vocational Education and Training System', 34).

36. Gray and Morgan, 'Modern Apprenticeships', 125. NVQ Level 3 was listed by the government as being equivalent to AS and A levels in the Regulated Qualifications Framework.

37. Fuller and Unwin, 'Reconceptualising Apprenticeship', 153.

38. Steedman, Gospel and Ryan, *Apprenticeship: A Strategy for Growth*, 8.

39. See Gray and Morgan, 'Modern Apprenticeships', 128; Steinmann, 'The Vocational Education and Training System', 45 and 49; Fuller and Unwin, 'Reconceptualising Apprenticeship', 161; and Unwin, 'Twenty-First Century Vocational Education', 176.

40. Fuller and Unwin, 'Reconceptualising Apprenticeship', 164.

41. Unwin, 'Twenty-First Century Vocational Education', 184–85.

42. See Steinmann, 'The Vocational Education and Training System', 49; Unwin, 'Twenty-First Century Vocational Education', 185–86; Finegold and Soskice, 'The Failure of Training in Britain'. For a direct comparison of the apprenticeship systems in England and Germany, see Deissinger, 'Apprenticeship Systems in England and Germany'.

43. Finegold and Soskice, 'The Failure of Training in Britain'.

44. Ibid., 22.

45. Unwin, 'Twenty-First Century Vocational Education', 176–77.

46. HEFCs were set up for England, Scotland, Wales and Northern Ireland by the Further and Higher Education Act 1992.

47. Bence and Oppenheim, 'The Evolution of the UK's Research Assessment Exercise', 140.

48. Professor Paul Webley, the Director of SOAS, set a commendable example by maintaining a reasonable differential between his salary figure and the salaries of senior academic staff. Regrettably, many other directors and vice chancellors of British higher education institutions did not adopt his ethical standard.

49. In 2015, after resigning in protest from her post at the University of Essex, Marina Warner reported that the differential in pay between the lowest paid at a university and the highest was approximately 14:1, and that the average salary for vice chancel-

lors was more than £250,000 (Warner, 'Learning My Lesson'); £250,000 was more than three times the salary of an average British professor in 2015. In 2018, it was reported by the BBC that the vice chancellor of the University of Bath, Professor Dame Glynis Breakwell, had been receiving an annual salary of £468,000 (BBC, 'University of Bath').

50. Association of University Teachers, 'Memorandum'.
51. There was indeed another RAE in 2008. In 2014, the RAE was replaced by the Research Excellence Framework (REF). At the time of this publication, the REF continues to operate and it has been supplemented in England (from 2020) with a Teaching Excellence Framework (TEF), the results of which will determine whether state-funded providers are permitted to raise their tuition fees. Both audit exercises consume considerable resources and divert the energies of academics from what are meant to be the core practices of their work – namely, research and teaching.
52. With the introduction of the first REF in 2014, the guidelines setting out the criteria and procedures to be followed ran to 789 numbered paragraphs, plus 23 pages of annexes. Stefan Collini, Professor of English Literature and Intellectual History at the University of Cambridge, remarked in his 2012 book *What Are Universities For?* that 'compelling and often devastating criticisms appear to have had little or no effect on policy-making. The arguments have not been answered; they have merely been ignored' (quoted in Warner, 'Learning My Lesson', 9)
53. Shore and Wright, 'Audit Culture and Anthropology', 563.
54. Ibid., 571.
55. The reference here is to the protagonist and narrator William Guest in William Morris' *News from Nowhere*, originally published in 1890.

INTRODUCTION
A Pursuit of Pleasurable Studies
with Woodworkers

A CRAFT RENAISSANCE IN BRITAIN

Craft was undergoing a renaissance when I began this study. At the turn of the millennium, there was growing evidence that the value and potential benefits of things 'handmade' were on the radar of both producers and consumers in Britain and elsewhere in the post-industrial world.[1] By 2006, there were an estimated 32,000 self-identified craftspeople – or, in contemporary language, 'designer-makers' – living and working in England and Wales alone, and 5.6 million original crafted items were being purchased annually at an estimated total value of nearly £900 million.[2] While writing this introduction, the Crafts Council jubilantly reported that craft sales in the United Kingdom exceeded £3 billion in 2019.[3] Clearly, craft survived the 2008 financial crisis and seemingly thrived during the messy aftermath of government-imposed austerity.[4] In fact, over a brief two-decade period, Britain's craftworld underwent rapid diversification and massive transformation in terms of the sheer number of practitioners, skill growth, innovations in materials, product quality, improved cultural status, marketing savvy and public outreach.

Already during the early years of the 'renaissance', *The Observer* reported:

> Village fayres may still peddle brown pots and woven wall hangings, but in the galleries there is a whole other scene in which craft means aesthetically exciting, skilfully executed objects made of ceramic, glass, metal and wood that are every bit as desirable – and collectible – as contemporary painting and sculpture.[5]

Alongside the thriving 'traditional' craft sector that produces architectural components, functional items and aesthetic objects,[6] new craft disciplines emerged during the first decade of the 2000s that innovatively combined handwork technologies with mechanical and digital ones to create cutting-edge works. Some of these products provocatively blurred the age-old 'functional versus conceptual' divide that has distinguished craft from fine art since the Quattrocento,[7] while others fruitfully engaged with an array of scientific fields, including engineering, material sciences, biotechnology and communications – and the onward march continues.

The dynamism of craft renders it notoriously difficult to define and contain. As a concept, it continually spills over into new realms of practice, materials and technologies, and the term is increasingly usurped by industry to construct affective, marketable narratives around mass-produced consumables. Nevertheless, craft seemingly retains a set of immutable, yet enigmatic core properties – at least in the popular imagination. For this reason, I have classified craft as a 'polythetic' category, which I will describe later in this introduction.

In juxtaposition to Britain's ever-diversifying and expansive craftworld, this book tells a more intimate story: one about a small community of fine woodworkers training at a vocational college in East London, and set during the early years of this most recent and continuing renaissance of craftsmanship.[8] It is a colourful account of personal and shared experiences, achievements and challenges, and an anthropology of skill and knowledge, the deep desire to create with our hands, and the persistent human longing to find pleasurable and purposeful work. The stories of these young men and women speak volumes to the vast field of contemporary craft, as well as to craft's past and its possible futures in a troubled world.

THE 'THIRD WAVE'

There have always been and always will be craftspeople and markets for the things they make. However, periods of flourishing activity and widespread enthusiasm for craft have tended to come in cycles, typically as a counter-cultural response to the prevailing modes of production or the governing economic models of a given era.

The Arts and Crafts movement that flourished from the late Victorian period until the end of the First World War was, in the eyes of its founder William Morris, a socialist critique of the hegemonic capitalist culture that arose with and was sustained by industrialisation, mass production and the progressive mechanisation of human labour. It is highly noteworthy that the elaboration of an antithetical relation between handwork and machine-made by Morris, and earlier by John Ruskin,[9] gave rise to a modern and persisting concept of 'craft' as both practice and social ideology. Morris also contravened rigid social and gender conventions of his day, which relegated manual labour to the lower classes and divided craft occupations between the sexes. Being an upper middle-class gentleman who put his hand to a wide range of craftwork, including tapestry weaving (which was typically associated with women's mill and factory work),[10] Morris 'broke an important barrier . . . and gave handwork a classlessness that survives to this day'.[11]

Stirred by Morris' socialist vision and by John Ruskin's writings on the plight of crafts and craftspeople, a number of arts and crafts organisations were founded during the final decades of the nineteenth century. Among the most celebrated of these were the Century Guild, founded by Arthur Heygate Mackmurdo,[12] the Guild and School of Handicraft, set up by Charles Robert Ashbee,[13] and the Art Workers' Guild in central London.[14] These organisations shared the 'ethos of collective solidarity and a vision of the importance of beauty, aesthetics and the ethical treatment of the craftsperson in society', and they served as a model for craft organisations that evolved during the next century.[15] In 1907, May Morris (daughter of William Morris) and Mary Elizabeth Turner founded the Women's Guild of Arts in reaction to women being barred from joining the aforementioned and to achieve professional identity and status for women artists and craftswomen.[16]

In the 1960s and 1970s, the Craft Revival movement similarly coalesced around anti-establishment sentiments and boundary-pushing issues. During the socially conservative decades following the Second World War, Fordism reached its florescence, powering an economic boom grounded in assembly-line manufacturing, standardised production, the further deskilling of labour, lower prices and mass consumption. Craftwork therefore offered its practitioners and patrons sanctuary from encroaching technologies and modes of production that threatened human autonomy, creativity and purpose. It also promised an alternative way of being to the one shaped by homogenising forces of consumer culture, faceless modernism, sprawling suburbia and capitalist-driven governance.[17]

Hastened by the momentum of that second wave in craft, the Craft Advisory Committee (CAC) was formed in 1971 to sponsor improvements in craft production, while keeping alive the relevance and value of craft in the minds of the British public and representing the needs of craftspeople to successive governments. To do so, the CAC launched a Development Award in 1973 to support those whom it judged to be the most innovative and influential makers in establishing their practices.[18] It also staged public markets, including the *Chelsea Crafts Fair*, which became a long-running and fondly remembered annual event from its inception in 1974 until its closure in 2000. The CAC was renamed the Crafts Council in 1979 and received its Royal Charter three years later, with a clear but demanding mandate 'to advance and encourage the creation and conservation of works of fine craftsmanship and to foster, promote and increase the interest of the public in the works of fine craftsmen and the accessibility of those works to the public in England and Wales'.[19]

Outside the capital, other key initiatives that supported craft in the post-war era through to the present day included the Gloucestershire Guild of Craftsmen, which was an outgrowth of the vibrant Arts and Crafts tradition of that county, and the Devon Guild of Craftsmen, set up in 1955 by a local furniture maker and fellow artisans. Both staged public exhibitions, as did a handful of dedicated galleries dotted around the country. A noteworthy newcomer to the scene was the Birmingham-based charity Craftspace. Established in 1986, its remit is to develop and promote contemporary craft and design through national and international touring exhibitions, lifelong learning projects and pioneering action-research partnerships.[20]

By the late 1990s, with considerable infrastructure already in place, the so-called 'third wave' in craft arrived in Britain, North America and numerous other regions around the world. Established craftspeople were attracting fresh audiences and profiting from an expanding clientele with deeper pockets, while a new generation of makers were opening workshops and setting up studios and boutique galleries. With the passing years, growing numbers of makers harnessed the new digital and social media technologies not only to disseminate images of their finished works, but also to create and share narratives about their craft identities, and reveal the complex processes and duration of their creative production.[21] These efforts augmented and connected craft communities at home and abroad, and they cultivated deeper public understanding and appreciation for the 'art of craft'.

In 2004, the Crafts Council launched *Collect*, an international fair of craft-inspired artworks that was first hosted at the Victoria and Albert Museum;[22] and, two years later it staged *Origin* at Somerset House – a grand successor to the *Chelsea Crafts Fair*.[23] New craft award schemes were inaugurated with laudable aims to raise the status of handwork and reward the leading makers, promising recruits and daring innovators in the sector.[24]

Craft as a way of doing, with emphases on process, materials and embodied engagement, was being steadily incorporated into the practices of fine artists and designers.[25] Previously, artists typically regarded craft as 'mere skill', and the artworld harboured 'contempt for the way most craft objects are designed to be used in a domestic setting or the way they are frequently employed in the non-monetary economy of gift-giving'.[26] This perspective has changed. Malcolm Ferris, creator and coordinator of the vibrant *Making Futures* craft conferences,[27] remarked that budding interests among fine artists and designers in craft's ethical and activist practices had come 'after a period of feverish global capitalism in which contemporary art and design both came to be seen as characteristic of conspicuous consumer excess'.[28]

Somewhat earlier, artist, wood joiner and political activist Roger Coleman had already concluded that, for artists who adopted a craft ethos:

> Doing and making things well, with care and concern for how and why they are made, brings real quality into everyday life ... a quality which takes us beyond material wealth, and gives us a truer way of measuring value than a market economy does.[29]

At a more popular level in UK society, special exhibitions at the V&A and the British Museum astonished visitors with displays of meticulously crafted objects and fuelled curiosity about how the everyday objects that surround us are made and how they work.[30] These shows were especially poignant during this digital epoch that has vanquished material and mechanical understandings of the things we use and consume, thereby engendering feelings of detachment, disembodiment and impotence. Achieving even wider-reaching impact, trendy television serials about home renovation and self-build projects spurred the growth of DIY (do-it-yourself) culture, empowering viewers to take up the tools and give it a try.[31] As a result, some enrolled on short courses to further their skills, while those more profoundly inspired set out on career paths into the trades or crafts.

In the realm of training and education, the Labour government and the industry training boards were promoting Modern Apprenticeship programmes to school-leavers and young adults (albeit in the shadow of the Prime Minister's vociferous drive for 'fifty per cent in higher education').[32] The main impetuses were the perennial need to reduce Britain's staggering skills gap and to create a workforce better prepared to meet the commercial and industrial demands of the twenty-first century.[33] The National Heritage Training Group (NHTG), formed in 2003,[34] was tasked with coordinating the development and delivery of traditional building crafts training and qualifications in the heritage sector of the United Kingdom's construction industry. The objective was to safeguard the preservation and sustainability of the estimated five million historic (i.e. pre-1919) buildings that existed in England alone.[35] However, to train trainees requires trainers with the necessary skills. Master Crafts qualifications were thus created, exceeding the criteria of the National Vocational Qualifications (NVQs) that underpinned the Modern Apprenticeships and centrally included a mentoring component.[36]

Several of the London livery companies (i.e. guilds), including the Gunmakers, Goldsmiths, Farriers, Stationers, Newspaper Makers and Saddlers, had reinvigorated the binding of working apprentices to learn the 'misteries' (i.e. the skills and art) of their respective trades.[37] The Worshipful Company of Carpenters (i.e. the Carpenters' Livery), which I discuss at length in Chapter 2, had long maintained an active interest in the wood occupations in the capital and further afield. The Livery Company was the patron of the vocational college in East London where I carried out the core fieldwork for this book and where Modern Apprenticeships in wood occupations took place. The apprenticeship route into various kinds of craftwork also garnered firm support from the Prince of Wales and the Prince's Trust.[38] In an interview with the BBC, Prince Charles declared:

> I am a huge believer in the importance of craftsmanship, [and] in encouraging young people into professions which are not necessarily desk-bound and management-orientated – and actually using their unfulfilled vocational talents.[39]

The Heritage Crafts Association (HCA), on which the Prince sat as President, was founded six years after the NHTG to promote and advocate for heritage crafts. This came in response to the Crafts Council's apparent redirection of its energies into supporting the more artistic, aesthetic and innovative crafts,[40] and promoting ideas of postdisciplinarity, postfunction and postmaterials in craftwork.[41] The HCA's wide umbrella of heritage crafts included such occupations as blacksmithing, basketry, wheelwrighting and coach-building, as well as crafts classified as 'endangered', such as scissor-making, bell founding, piano-making and watch-making. Wood turner and HCA Trustee Robin Wood alleged that: 'Almost every country in the world [was] doing more to support these crafts than [the United Kingdom]'. Help is needed, he continued, to 'maintain them as real, thriving, evolving businesses, not just objects in a museum'.[42] Indeed, the HCA was unique among the United Kingdom's craft advocacy groups in adopting the UNESCO Convention on intangible heritage and backing the conservation of the specialised ways of knowing that go into making crafted objects, and of their mastery by younger generations.[43]

Scholars, too, were turning their minds to craft from the start of the third wave. There was already a long history of anthropologists studying material culture, handmade objects and even skill-learning and processes of production,[44] but the predominant focus had been on non-Western preindustrial societies. It was historians and economists who shone the narrower spotlight on Britain, documenting the activities of London's livery companies and the plight of the old craft trades and apprenticeship regimes, while educationalists and sociologists (several of who are cited in later chapters) scrutinised the government's ever-changing vocational training schemes and associated funding regimes.

There was, however, an emergent scholarship that made 'craft' its primary subject of study and that critically engaged with craft's history, meaning, identity/identities, practices, materials, technologies and contested boundaries.[45] Some of the seminal publications that mark the beginnings of the third wave include Tanya Harrod's unrivalled tome on twentieth-century crafts in Britain, and illuminating edited volumes by Peter Dormer, Jean Johnson and Paul Greenhalgh.[46] These were followed shortly afterwards by a string of celebrated books by academics Glenn Adamson, Howard Risatti and Richard Sennett, all of which reached wide reading audiences and dialogued with my own musings on the nature of craft while researching and writing about my woodwork colleagues.[47]

Given the hive of activity around craft in the twenty-first century, the obvious question that arises is: 'What were the drivers that propagated the third wave and fuelled widespread intrigue with the "handmade" among such a diverse set of actors?' Insightful responses emerge in the narratives and experiences of my fellow woodworkers documented in the forthcoming chapters. It becomes clear that a multitude of factors and concerns – some harmonising, others diametrically opposed – animated their individual moves into craftwork at the start of the new millennium. To an extent, their motivations resonated with those that incited the Arts and Crafts movement and the Craft Revival of the 1960s and 1970s, but the woodwork trainees, instructors and established makers who I interviewed also expressed uniquely contemporary concerns, sometimes with animated urgency. In short, craft served as a vehicle for pondering the state of our world and contemplating alternative paths that might lead to more sustainable, more fulfilling and more pleasurable ways of living and working.[48]

Looking back upon the pre-2008 years of the new millennium, Malcolm Ferris neatly speculated that 'the rehabilitation of the value of craft in society ... constituted a shared utopian narrative that mobilised what became in effect a molecular ethical-communitarian revolt against the febrile pre-crash epoch of futures-financed consumption'. More than a century earlier, William Morris penned something not entirely dissimilar in spirit:

> For some time past there has been a good deal of interest shown in [handicraft] ... People interested, or who suppose that they are interested, in the details of the arts of life feel a desire to revert to methods of handicraft for production in general; and it may therefore be worth considering how far this is a mere reactionary sentiment incapable of realisation, and how far it may foreshadow a real coming change in our habits of life as irresistible as the former change which has produced the system of machine-production, the system against which revolt is now attempted.[49]

Perhaps rather than conceiving of today's revolt as a unique and bounded episode of our time, we might more beneficially understand it as the current phase in a timeless grassroots quest for a utopian society that is more humane, more just, peaceful, deferential to beauty, ecologically respectful and, above all, ethically purposeful.

A NOTE ON 'CRAFT'

'Craft has always been a supremely messy word', observed curator and author Paul Greenhalgh.[50] I likewise qualified craft as a 'polysemous, ambiguous, and often-contested term'.[51] Wisely perhaps, Tanya Harrod resolved not to attempt a definition and got on with telling its fascinating history through objects and the people who made them.[52] Richard Sennett ventured that craftsmanship 'names an enduring, basic human impulse, the desire to do a job well for its own sake',[53] while for Glenn Adamson, craft is 'not a classification of objects, institutions or people', but rather 'a way of doing things . . . an active, relational concept', embodied most powerfully in skill.[54]

Their contemporary, Howard Risatti, adhered to a more conventional but equally illuminating concept of craft, premised on the mastery of specific techniques and materials in the creation of objects that have 'practical physical functionality'.[55] Furthermore, he noted, 'because craft objects are by their very nature intended to be physiologically functional, they are objects made for the body and bodily "action"; therefore they must accommodate the body and be somatically oriented'.[56] Critical questioning of 'functionality' as a defining attribute of craft emerged during the Craft Revival and Studio Craft movements of the 1960s,[57] and debates around 'post-functionality', as well as 'post-disciplinary practice',[58] among makers, benefactors and scholars of craft gathered greater momentum during the third wave.

Attempts at staking boundaries around what craft is and what it is *not* do have valuable purpose. It is important, I contend, to safeguard the word against being used to define any and every creative endeavour that involves some level of skill – or, more problematically, being usurped by manufacturers to market mass-produced wares with auras of exclusivity and suggestions of hands-on attention to detail. Left unclaimed and undefended, the term 'craft' risks being rendered vacuous – and, so too, what craftspeople do and what they make.

In taking an inventory of the various attributes or defining features of craft that were identified by contributing authors to my book *Craftwork as Problem Solving*, I arrived at a list of twenty-two items. In alphabetical order, they were apprenticeship, attitude (qualified by commitment and patience, among other virtues), autonomy (over one's production), bespoke, the body (in motion), design-and-making, economic precarity (i.e. vulnerability to fluctuating economies and markets), expertise, focus, functionality, identity (in terms of qualifications and professional status), innovation, locality (i.e. place-based), materials, problem solving, social politics, risk (in handwork), the (perceptual) senses, skill, standards, tools and technologies, and tradition.[59]

In reviewing the substantial literature on craftwork from different times and places around the world, it is striking that the members of any given craft community employ varying combinations of the above attributes in defining themselves, their practices and the objects they make. Some attributes may be especially emphasised and others disregarded or even unrecognised as belonging to their tradition of craftwork.[60] Indeed, each feature forms part of an overarching and ever-shifting discourse on craft that no longer has clear-cut national or regional boundaries. For this reason, and in acknowledging the 'messiness' of the term, I propose that craft be framed as a 'polythetic category'.

A polythetic category is one in which any of its members possess some, but not necessarily all of the properties attributed to that category. Most conveniently, polythetic categories possess an inherent capacity and flexibility to shed and absorb new 'defining' criteria; thus, the polythetic nature of craft licenses the inclusion of further attributes or the removal of existing ones as craft practices and craft identities evolve and transform. The power of a polythetic category lies in the fact that although no single property is essential for membership, popular belief maintains that the category is stable, and is so more or less across time and space.[61] Thus, while it may be impossible to conclusively define craft or to reach any final consensus on its constituents, engaging with its polythetic nature does make the anthropological, historical or sociological task of determining what is *not* craft in a given context far more practicable.

Despite differences in the ways that craftspeople might define themselves and what they do, there are, to my mind, two seriously injurious experiences shared by large numbers of contemporary makers around the world, including fine woodworkers and furniture makers in the United Kingdom. First, whether practising in Europe, Asia, Africa, the Americas or elsewhere, craftspeople are operating in a surplus global economy in which the combination of mass production, cheaper prices and throwaway culture has steadily diminished demand for handcrafted wares and rendered bespoke production redundant or, at best, an inessential luxury – or poses an imminent threat to do so.[62] The surplus economy is coupled with the serial displacement of production, whereby companies producing handmade wares transfer or outsource operations to factories and workshops in countries with lower labour costs – and, typically, with less stringent health and safety policies. As noted by economic sociologist Wolfgang Streeck: 'The hellish Manchester of early industrialisation still exists, but on the global periphery.'[63] The combination of these phenomena has exacerbated an already precarious economic existence that countless artisans endure, most acutely in the Global South.[64]

Indeed, while affluent countries of the Global North, or what is conventionally categorised as 'the West', have witnessed an upswing over the past two decades in the reskilling of local craftspeople and growing patronage for bespoke and handmade items, many nations in the Global South have experienced rapid deskilling as an effect of industrialisation, economic development and international trade deals that unleash floods of inexpensive, mass-produced imported (plastic) goods into local economies.[65] Of the women and men who continue to eke out a living as craftspeople, significant numbers have been compelled to turn their hands to producing folk crafts for tourist markets and collectors. Not only are those markets highly unpredictable and subject to volatile global politics, economic recessions, pandemics and changing aesthetic trends, but what makers make is also disconnected from original purposes and functions, and decontextualised from local values. In his study of the predicament of Cretan craftsmen, anthropologist Michael Herzfeld shrewdly observed that:

> Artisans face a chilling choice among accepting their role as the picturesque bearers of an obsolescent tradition, becoming merchants in a rat race that most of them are destined to lose, or joining an international labour force in which the price of modernity is to lose one's identity as a skilled and individual personality.[66]

The second widely shared experience, and one that this book scrutinises at closer range, is the persistently low social status borne by craftspeople, even by many who profited from the third wave. Though British makers in several craft disciplines have benefited from increases in income and greater public recognition and appreciation for what they create, handwork continues to be stigmatised as a 'second-track' for those lacking academic aptitude. Two years after the 2008 financial crisis, the senior conservator for the Royal Household commented: 'The crafts have survived in the UK but they need support and a much better attitude towards technical skills because there is still the deep-seated view that working with your hands is somehow a second-rate career.'[67] This issue resurfaced repeatedly during my research.

For craftwork in Europe, the roots of its often low (and sometimes denigrated) status relative to that enjoyed by 'intellectuals', white-collar workers and the merchant classes can be traced back to ancient Greece. In *Nicomachean Ethics*, Aristotle distinguished between *techné*, translated as 'craft', and *epistemé*, translated as 'scientific' knowledge, which at that time referred specifically to geometry, mathematics and logic. For Aristotle, *techné* is concerned with contingent reality, or the bringing into existence of things that can either exist or not, such as the artefacts produced by a craftsman (*technitae*). *Epistemé*, by contrast, is concerned with necessary 'truths' that stand apart from (and presumably above) the world of everyday contingencies. The philosopher supplied a straightforward example of their differences:

> A carpenter's interest in the right angle is different from the geometrician's: the former is concerned with it only so far as it is useful for his work, but the other wants to know what it is or what its properties are, because his gaze is set on the truth.[68]

This ancient Greek distinction supplied foundations for the modern-day conceptual split between theory and practice, which has in turn buttressed a hierarchy of value between work of the mind and that of the hand – and, correspondingly, between university education and vocational training. The divide, along with its colossal social and economic ramifications, was exported around the globe with European colonialism and seeded by imperialist policies in the thinking, social-class politics, constructed ethnicities and educational systems of the Other.

In England and Wales, the divide between classroom learning at a desk (or computer terminal) and embodied practices of 'making knowledge' in handwork became further entrenched with the introduction of the National Curriculum in 1988. The aftermath of the Education Reform Act witnessed the further closure of woodworking and metalworking shops in schools, and their replacement in some cases with courses in design technology.

The forthcoming chapters make it plain that learning to relate directly to and create with materials entails a profound immersion in problem solving. Without access to that in schools, children are being denied the opportunity to develop an essential skillset: one that enables them simultaneously to conceptualise, emotionally respond to and physically engage with complex situations. This knowhow can be carried by them into adulthood and into whatever line of work they enter or career they pursue. The current curriculum, with objectives to prepare students for a narrow spectrum of the job market, is in fact equipping girls and boys with specific occupational skills that presently have a half-life of 'about five years, and quickly shortening'.[69] In 2016, the World Economic Forum reported that an estimated '65% of children entering primary school today will ultimately end up working in completely new job types that don't yet exist'.[70] It is therefore both a failure and an injustice on the part of government, educational institutions and society more generally to forgo more rounded forms of learning that unify body and mind in tasks of critical, exploratory thinking and that incite passion for creating and problem solving.

This book is a retort to the dehumanising trend of deskilling. My goal, as both an academic and a maker, is not merely to promote global appreciation for the learning, skill and knowledge at the heart of craftwork, but also to ignite a positive revaluation of creative handwork as a vehicle for individual fulfilment and wellbeing.

MY MOVE TO WOODWORKING

Over a period of thirteen years, I carried out anthropological fieldwork with teams of masons on building sites in West Africa and Arabia, studying their apprenticeship systems and the ways in which skilled trade knowledge was learned and practised in predominantly Islamic urban contexts. Two of the cities in which I worked were UNESCO World Heritage sites. That international status, with its accompanying rules, regulations and expectations, had a significant bearing on what was built in terms of materials, structure, scale and architectural expression, and, on who was deemed qualified to build the buildings. While practices were framed by local and international discourses on 'tradition' and continuity, the master masons I laboured alongside tactically improvised and strategically innovated.[71] This was part and parcel of everyday problem solving on site, but it also served to meet the changing needs and tastes of a contemporary clientele and, on occasion, to satisfy masons' personal ambitions to concoct hallmark solutions or features and establish reputations.

To more fully consider the tensions between modernity and tradition, between the processes of globalisation and the politics of place, and between 'useless toil' and worthy work, it became necessary to include a Western case study of craft training and practice within the scope of my comparative research. A grant application to Britain's Economic and Social Research Council in 2004 secured me a three-year Research Fellowship,[72] which included two years of fieldwork at the historic Building Crafts College in Stratford, in London's East End.

Since its founding in 1893, the Building Crafts College has been governed by the Worshipful Company of Carpenters, one of the oldest liveries (i.e. guilds) in the City of London and one of the few to keep an active hand in craft training, the awarding of qualifications, and the regulation of standards and practice.[73] The Livery's objective in opening the trade school was to safeguard traditional building crafts against sweeping changes wrought by industrialisation and mass production. The college remit has changed over time, but when I began fieldwork there in the autumn of 2005, it retained a strong sense of its founding spirit, committed to fostering craft excellence and perpetuating building-craft traditions in wood, stonemasonry and leadwork. Like an English woodcarver's training in the seventeenth-century workshop of Grinling Gibbons or the contemporary apprenticeship systems I studied in West Africa and Arabia, learning at the Building Crafts College was first and foremost practice-based.

Although all of my fieldwork to date had been with masons, I chose to sign up to the College's two-year City & Guilds-accredited programme in fine woodworking, which included tuition in both architectural joinery and furniture making. At the time, a number of other colleges in England had well-established and well-reputed programmes in furniture making: notably Buckinghamshire Chilterns University College, London Metropolitan University and Rycote College. Despite the decades-long erosion of Britain's manufacturing sector, the furniture-making industry survived and there remain many thousands of companies and workshops, big and small, producing furniture in a variety of materials. The near-mythical Parnham College, founded and run by renowned furniture maker-in-wood John Makepeace, had shut its doors in 2000, but short courses in 'fine furniture making' were being offered in the refined grounds of West Dean College in West Sussex and other such places around England. Established makers, too, were offering private training and tuition in their own workshops, thereby enriching learning with a modicum of work experience in a commercial environment.[74]

The Building Crafts College, however, was of special interest for a number of reasons. For practical purposes, I lived in London and the College presented an easily accessible field site. For scholarly reasons, I was intrigued by the College's long history and its strong links with the ancient Carpenters' Livery Company and thus with the ever-fascinating Square Mile. The small student numbers on the fine woodworking programme suited my field methodology, which I will describe in more detail in Chapter 1 – and, close to my heart, the course prioritised hand tools and focused exclusively on timber.

The affinity I have for timber as a material has always been strong, and definitely stronger than that for stone or brick. I appreciate the warmth of timber and the endless variety of hues, figure and textures that it presents, and I relish its comforting smell when freshly cut or planed. Additionally, the process of assembling in carpentry is more appealing to my architectural sensibilities than the subtractive nature of woodcarving, woodturning or banker masonry (i.e. banker masons typically work in a workshop, shaping blocks of stone with tools). This point perhaps demands further explanation.

The primary objective of the one-year full-time banker masonry course at the College was to train students in traditional techniques, which included cutting stone, squaring-up, boning and dressing, and then to progress them to architectural stone carving, comprising the production of individual building components. All of these tasks entailed bringing a predefined and measured three-dimensional form out of a homogeneous block of raw material through meticulous processes of subtraction. These processes were mainly carried out in the time-honoured manner of the trade, wielding a mallet, chisels, a metal straight edge and a square.

A trainee might work at a single block of stone for many weeks or longer, cutting, chipping and tapping in highly controlled ways and continually making small adjustments to the angle of the chisel and force of their mallet. A stonemason's skill is therefore qualified by their ability to proficiently employ a set of unchanging technical principles in the precise execution of a prefigured form. In their study with conservation stonemasons working on Glasgow Cathedral, anthropologists Thomas Yarrow and Siân Jones remarked that the mason's skill is 'in explicit opposition to creativity', while their pride as a craftsperson is instead vested in 'the discipline and patience required to actualise a tradition which remains fundamentally unchanged'.[75]

Students at the College also learned about setting out masonry structures, which involved complex geometric calculations, technical drawing, and the production of templates and moulds. A cohort of trainees might collectively plan and create, for example, a Romanesque arch or the tracery of a Gothic-style window over the course of a year. The principal task of the individual student, however, was to produce one or more of the solid components for these collaboratively produced architectural assemblages.[76]

The fine woodwork trainees, by contrast, individually produced full units of architectural joinery (in progression, a casement window, frame-and-panel door and staircase) and then, at the end of year one and throughout year two, pieces of furniture, culminating in a bespoke designed chair. All such carpentry projects naturally involved the subtractive processes of trimming, planing, cutting and possibly shaping planks of timber, but they also involved assembly, which was generally achieved by each trainee on their own using traditional joinery techniques (e.g. lap, bridle, mortise-and-tenon, dovetail and tusk-tenon joints). However, students also had licence to improvise and devise novel techniques for assembling their creations, as will be discussed in Chapters 4 and 10. In the additive process of assembling the finished components of, for example, a tool chest or a bedside cabinet, spatial relations were explored, solid planes and voids were juxtaposed, and interiors and exteriors came into existence.

Like my earlier overseas studies with masons, signing up to a community of woodworkers in London allowed me to engage directly and regularly in the very regime of training and social politics of craftwork that I had set out to investigate. Term commenced in mid-September and ended in early July, and the weekly schedule emulated the average full-time working week in the building trades. At the bench, with tools and timber in hand, I, like my fellow trainees, could at once dwell in creative contemplation, coordinated (and sometimes not-so-coordinated) physical movement and the dynamic social interactions that transpired among workshop instructors and students. Both individual learning and collaborative forms of knowledge-making were realised in the recurrent intersections between these three activities.

The instructors and their assistants imparted trade-related theory in dedicated lecture rooms or during impromptu 'toolbox' discussions in the workshop. As trainees, we regularly collaborated to complete our workbook assignments, either in the College library or after hours, huddled around a table in the nearby Builders Arms pub. We made fieldtrips, including one to the botanical gardens at Kew where we learned about the growth cycles of trees, the differences between hardwoods and softwoods, the choice species used in carpentry and the properties of their timber. We were taught to systematically mark the face and edge of our timber with a soft-lead pencil and, little by little, we acquired the rich vocabulary for the component parts of the architectural joinery and furniture that we made and the hardware they required. We were tutored in technical drawing, preparing cutting lists and calculating project costs. We were introduced to a vast array of traditional hand tools in succession, as well as to a more limited number of power tools that we were permitted to use and to the deafening machinery in the mill. We dismantled wood planes and machines to maintain and repair them and to sharpen their blades. We were drilled in health and safety regulations, disciplined in timekeeping and etiquette, and obliged to sport appropriate attire and personal protection equipment when necessary. We became practised in taking up good posture at our workbenches, in lifting and moving heavy loads, and in executing our tool-wielding tasks with economy and rhythmic efficiency. We also learned to look and to touch in more discerning ways, which enabled us to critically evaluate our own work in progress and the work of our fellow trainees. The target was to achieve perfection in joinery, with tolerances of less than a millimetre.

Over the intensive two-year period, we gave shape and direction to our ambitions for becoming craftspeople and we discovered personal potential and limitations. Each of us came to realise that 'patience' was the essential ingredient to success in fine woodworking. Frustrations over making mistakes were gradually reframed as opportunities for practice, which in turn built confidence in our abilities to repair and make good. We learned the challenges of teamwork and the benefits of sharing best practice. Despite differences in age and in our social and cultural backgrounds, the members of the cohort formed strong social bonds and even friendships that extended beyond the bounds of the training college and, in some cases, well beyond the duration of the programme.

My cohort was made up of nine trainees, all of whom were male. Despite College ambitions for gender diversity in its programmes, only one woman had applied that year to the fine woodworking department and she ultimately declined the offer of a place. Four of the men in my cohort were teenagers and recent finishers of secondary education with GCSE (General Certificate of Secondary Education) qualifications. The remaining trainees were mature students, ranging in age from their early twenties to their late thirties. I was the eldest, at thirty-nine years old. The four teenagers had taken wood-shop classes at school, but prior experience 'in the tools' varied considerably among the older students, ranging from nearly none to possessing intermediate skills in joinery.

All the mature students had abandoned other lines of employment and the security of steady wages in their quest for a new and what they hoped would be a more satisfying way of living and working. In my writing, I coin them collectively as 'vocational migrants' and not 'career changers', which is the more conventional term.[77] I use this term because each one had made a deliberate decision to pursue carpentry as a practice to which they would dedicate their whole person – heart, mind and body. The life experiences they brought to their learning and the thoughtful aspirations they had for the future made their contributions to my study especially rich.

The first and second-year cohorts of fine woodworkers shared a bright and airy workshop. There was ample social interaction between them at the bench, in the canteen and at the pub, and there was occasional overlap in their curricular activities. This allowed me to expand my community of study to include the trainees from the cohorts ahead of and behind my own. Out of a total of twenty-four trainees over three cohorts, just two of the students were women, both of whom were 'vocational migrants'.[78] The fine-grained study of woodworking practices that I carried out was complemented by a series of recorded in-depth interviews with each student at progressive stages of their training. The interviews explored social backgrounds and career motivations, and they documented changes in the students' thinking about both the programme structure and their personal development as craftspeople – or 'designer-makers' or 'artist-craftsmen', as some alternatively labelled themselves.

I also recorded lengthy interviews with a handful of recent graduates of the programme to discover where their training and qualifications were taking them, and with the instructors and shop assistants of the fine woodwork and bench joinery courses to learn about their backgrounds, expertise and teaching philosophies. In parallel with my research at the College, I met with and interviewed established furniture makers in England and other individuals in the industry who illuminated my thinking about contemporary trends, green agendas, politics and economies in the trade.

THE MINDFUL BODY IN WOODWORKING

A distinct but equally important line of inquiry of my research was to investigate the role that the motor domains of our cognition play in learning, simulating, rehearsing and communicating skilled practice. The aim was to contribute to a theory of human knowledge that begins from the premise that 'knowing' is an emergent state of mind-body engaged in and with the immediate social and physical environment. My thesis on the embodied ways that hand skills are communicated (and thereby learned) is grounded in a model of interactive alignment and shared utterance in dialogue and in the theory of Dynamic Syntax, both of which were developed in the field of linguistics.[79]

In brief, the model of interactive alignment that I adopted describes how the mental representations of a speaker and a listener are individually and incrementally constructed on-line (i.e. in the real time of dialogue), word-by-word, over the course of an utterance, and how parity in their mental representations is achieved (or not). Furthermore, it elegantly models the event of shared utterance, whereby the listener makes a cognitive 'leap' to complete their own context-dependent mental representation before the speaker has finished their utterance, and the listener interrupts by supplying the final word(s). If, however, the mental representation constructed by the listener is incongruous with that which the initial speaker had in mind to communicate, then the conclusion to the shared utterance supplied by listener-cum-speaker has the potential to either derail the dialogue or, more interestingly, take the dialogue in a new or different direction, and so on. The latter possibility makes plain that dialogue is not an articulation of fixed things already known, but rather is a kind of 'knowing in progress'. The state of knowing is one of constant flux, update and transformation.

With these seminal ideas and with a focus on craftwork, I explored the occurrence of what I coined 'shared performance' between interacting craftspeople. In an earlier publication, I summarised my background thinking on this subject and the questions it spawned as follows:

> [In] playing sports, dancing, working, or making things together, practitioners regularly co-ordinate their activities, and at some point, mid-action, one may intervene and successively complete the motions of another's goal-directed sequence. In other words, co-practitioners swap roles as observers and generators (or parsers and producers, respectively) in performing tasks. We all regularly do so in the co-ordinated (and sometimes not-so-co-ordinated) tasks and activities that we do together, and that we have been doing since our days in the childhood nursery. Probing this seemingly mundane, everyday occurrence unleashes a multitude of questions concerning the ways that shared activity, and consequently shared productions of knowledge, is achieved. What are the processes (cognitive, motor and otherwise) that enable an observer to leap to the conclusion of what their co-practitioner has in mind to do, intercept the activity, and complete the task? How, as in shared utterance, do parser-cum-producers introduce new directions to the motor-based interpretations that co-practitioners are simultaneously constructing as they work together, and thereby introduce change to skilled practice? And, what role, too, does the environment of tools, materials, fellow actors, artefacts, and physical setting play in the interpretation and generation of activity?[80]

My further thinking about these questions was supported by the theory of Dynamic Syntax. Dynamic Syntax foregrounds a model of incremental, on-line parsing to describe the cognitive processes involved in both interpreting *and* generating an utterance. During the first decade of the twenty-first century, researchers employing Dynamic Syntax theory focused almost exclusively on spoken dialogue, with more recent excursions into the performance of free improvisation music.[81] My own research, however, explored its possible applications to the communication of hand skills between two or more craftspeople working together in close proximity or on a shared task, and with a minimal exchange of words. Drawing inspiration from emerging theories and findings in the cognitive sciences and neurosciences, I considered how complex imitation, like that performed by an apprentice learning a new skill alongside their master, involves parsing the master's display into a composite of familiar actions and sequences that can be (re)produced, honed and transformed. Parsing and generating movement, I contended, occur principally in our motor domains of cognition and are grounded in motor-based concepts; in other words, the activities of interpreting, understanding and mentally rehearsing a skilled activity are seated in the very same neural networks that spring us into action.

Dedicated accounts of my research using Dynamic Syntax theory have been published separately.[82] However, the interest in nonverbal communication percolates through much of the ethnography and anthropological thinking in this book – albeit in a more gentle manner and with fewer detours into the deep theory.

THE CENTRALITY OF PROBLEM SOLVING IN CRAFTWORK

Ongoing developments in my explorations of embodied ways of thinking and knowing returned me to the Building Crafts College in 2012 and 2013 to conduct new research, this time supported by a British Academy Mid-Career Fellowship. The field-based project (which, on this occasion, did not involve an apprentice-style methodology) investigated the intertwined relationship between our brains, our hands and the tools that we use. Over the duration of an academic year at the College, I spent a full day each week with the first-year cohort of fine woodworkers conducting one-on-one interviews and, with a smaller selection of willing trainees, making frequent digital video recordings of their practices at the workbench. Video recordings were made each week with the same individuals while they used chisels, wood planes and handsaws to complete course assignments.

A professional cameraman assisted with the visual recording exercises. By positioning our two cameras at 90° to one another – one in front and the other to one side of a student's workbench – we simultaneously captured their tool-wielding activities from both angles. The complementary recordings enabled me to take stock of and examine the grasps, postures and gestures that comprised a trainee's tooling actions on their timber. More importantly, by comparing and contrasting an entire series of video footage made with a single student over the year, I was able to observe and analyse progressions (or their absence) in the economy and efficiency with which they employed a particular tool, as well as developments of individual tactics and of a personal style or 'signature' in their movements. Ultimately, my objective was to systematically document the microphysics of skill learning.

Additionally, data capture with the first-year cohort allowed me to scrutinise solo and collaborative problem-solving sessions at the workbench. Collaborative sessions between a student and the instructor typically entailed a mix of spoken discourse, hands-on exploration and experimentation, and practical demonstration. The recordings were therefore richly laden with information to mine. The models of shared utterance and shared performance that I had previously explored and developed were especially helpful for deliberating upon and accounting for the making of knowledge between the two parties as they collaboratively addressed and conquered challenges.

Creative problem solving is integral to every stage of carpentry production: from design and making to marketing and pricing, to delivery and installation.[83] Solving a problem draws heavily on past learning and practical experiences that are directly or tangentially related to the challenge at hand. At the same time, it relies on the ability to imagine options, forecast outcomes, weigh choices and strategise a plausible way forward. To do so in a manner that appears effortless is a defining trait of mastery. Like all makers who work with natural materials and hand tools, carpenters must be open to risk when experimenting with new solutions or with variations on old ones, and be amenable to backtracking or even starting all over again. Again, the esteemed virtue of patience is indispensable.

Because of the array of skills and the many kinds of intelligence called upon in problem solving, this activity features throughout this book and constitutes the central theme of Chapter 8. The ability to solve problems and overcome challenges in the flow of work is empowering. Crafting solutions builds confidence, motivates the desire to reach further, and heightens the sense of agency that makers have over their production and the contribution they make to society. Put simply, it is a vehicle to self-discovery, fulfilment and pleasurable work.[84]

RUMINATIONS ON THE 'PURSUIT OF PLEASURABLE WORK'

In discussing the title of this book with an academic colleague, she challenged me to define what I meant by 'pleasure'.[85] The search for an answer returned me to foundational texts in ancient Greek philosophy and took me to current debates on the concept. I therefore take pause to offer explanation of the title and share my ruminations on the meaning of 'pleasurable' with the curious reader.

I settled on the book title at an early point in my study, when the motivations of fellow trainees on the woodworking programme were becoming clearer to me.[86] In individually interviewing them and during tea-break exchanges, I was struck by the degree to which the sociopolitical perspectives they articulated and their aspirations for life and work resonated in diverse ways with the spirit of William Morris' socialist utopian writings. Notably, this was despite the fact that few were aware at the time of the great Arts and Crafts figure, much less the politically charged speeches he delivered in London and elsewhere.

The wording of the title pays tribute to the style of Morris' prose and draws inspiration from ideals powerfully expressed in his socialist utopia *News from Nowhere* (1890) and his essays 'Useful Work versus Useless Toil' (1884) and 'The Relations of Art to Labour' (1884).[87] In 'Useful Work', Morris posed the following question: 'What is the nature of the hope which, when it is present in work, makes it worth doing?' The answer, he believed, is threefold: 'the hope of pleasure in rest, the hope of pleasure in our using what it makes, and the hope of pleasure in our daily creative skill'.[88]

In English, 'a pursuit' can refer to the engagement in an activity of a specific kind, typically one that is done for leisure, outside the regular work schedule. In this sense, woodworking qualifies as 'a pursuit' for the hobbyist. A pursuit, however, may also be the defining activity of an individual in their vocation: for example, a lifelong pursuit of justice, truth, God, wealth, knowledge or mastery of an art, craft or trade. The intended signification of 'pursuit' in the title corresponds to the latter. More specifically, 'the pursuit of' denotes the attempt at attaining a goal, often entailing duration and demanding considerable effort, and possibly a measure of discomfort or sacrifice on the part of the pursuer.

All of my fellow fine-woodwork trainees were in pursuit of new trade skills and knowledge, as well as the official certifications that would clear the way to new job opportunities. Additionally, and perhaps more saliently, the majority, and especially those with previous experience in other employment sectors, were in pursuit of alternative ways of working and living that would be more integrative of the whole person and bring pleasure to being.

Before grappling with 'pleasurable', I first define 'work'. The word 'work' operates in the title as both a noun and verb. In its noun form, work refers to the compilation of mental and physical operations involved in doing 'the job' of, in this case, fine woodworking. As a verb, it stands for the activity of bringing a desired quality, consistency and shape to not only the timber (i.e. to work the material) but also, importantly, to the personhood of the carpenter. In other words, the pursuit of woodworking for the majority of those I trained with was not merely to work with wood in order to 'make a living'; it was also about engaging in an activity that would foster those values, ethics

and worldviews to which they aspired and would thereby lead to self-fulfil-
ment. A sense of fulfilment is entwined with that of pleasure.

Evidently, 'pleasurable' is the key word here. Derived from the Old French
plaisir, the root, pleasure, is conventionally defined as the 'feeling of happy
satisfaction and enjoyment' or as 'an event or activity from which one de-
rives' such a feeling of happy satisfaction. Pleasure can also refer to 'sensual
gratification' that is experienced with any of the body's stimulated senses.[89]
However, the signification of 'pleasure', and consequently 'pleasurable', has
proven far more complicated for philosophers, novelists and poets, psychol-
ogists, political agitators and even neuroscientists. In her investigation into
its meaning in the works of eighteenth-century intellectuals, Rowan Boyson
pinpoints the 'weird difficulty' that pleasure presents.[90] Philosopher Laura
Sizer observes that: 'Philosophers disagree over whether it's a feeling, an attitude, or something else; whether it is the excitement that accompanies the
pursuit of certain activities, or the contentment that marks the satisfaction of
desire.'[91] The history of thinking about the concept is fascinating, but equally
enormous and unwieldy. I therefore attempt only to introduce a few of the
most seminal ideas about pleasure and stake my position in the debates.

Hēdonē (ἡδονή), translated from the ancient Greek as 'pleasure', was an
important subject in the philosophical investigations of Plato, Aristotle and
Epicurus into what motivates us as humans. I ground my exploration of pleasure in these three because, in large measure, they framed the thinking that
has persisted around the concept to the present day.

To begin, Plato's *Philebus* is a Socratic dialogue dedicated to describing
the good life (i.e. the life of the philosopher) and the way people ought to
live.[92] Pleasure and knowledge take prominence in the dialogue between
Socrates, Protarchus and Philebus, the latter of whom espouses hedonism or
the pursuit of pleasure for its own sake. Like many of the great thinkers who
preceded and followed him, Plato holds that the relation between pleasure
and pain is as oppositional correlates along a continuum,[93] and claims that
pleasure is remedial of pain and replenishing of lack. In doing so, he squarely
refutes hedonism by exposing its inherent contradiction: in desiring to maximise both the quantity and intensity of their (bodily and sensual) pleasure,
Plato deduces that the hedonist must also desire to maximise the quantity
and intensity of their pains. Pain – certainly in its extreme forms – is not a
desirable element in the 'good life' idealised by Plato.

While acknowledging that pleasure of certain kinds and in moderate intensity does have a place in the good life,[94] Plato was wary of its latent potential to interrupt the mind at work. Indeed, pleasure in itself is conceived as
being deceptive, in that it appears to be good when it is not. In scrutinising
Plato's distrust of pleasure, present-day philosopher Jessica Moss concludes
that: 'When we devote ourselves to pleasure, we accept a counterfeit reality

and fail to seek out the true world that lies beyond appearances.'[95] Plato accordingly consigned pleasure to operations of the irrational in humankind, and in opposition to the rational aim of knowledge. Notably, however, pleasure and knowledge were not conceived as being mutually exclusive, but Plato did believe that 'admissible' pleasures should remain merely the means to attaining the real goal, which for him is knowledge. More concisely, pleasure should not be mistaken as a goal in itself.

Epicurus, in contrast to Plato and his exaltation of reason over the senses, was an ardent empiricist, believing that the sensations we perceive, including pleasure, are a reliable source of information and truth about the world. According to Epicurus, pleasure was indeed a 'good', and even the highest good in that: 'It is the starting point of every choice and of every aversion, and to it we come back, inasmuch as we make feeling the rule by which to judge of every good thing.' 'Choice-worthy' pleasure (distinct from prodigal pleasure or abandon to sensual delights) is 'the absence of pain in the body and of trouble in the soul' and is thus a fundamental component of a good life. For Epicurus, a good life – one defined by the virtues of prudence, honour and justice – is also a life of pleasure, and vice versa: 'For the virtues have grown into one with a pleasant life, and a pleasant life is inseparable from them.'[96] It should be noted that the Epicurean take on pleasure comes a long stride closer than Plato to my interpretation of the pleasure that can arise *in* craftwork.

Of additional significance to my exploration, Epicurus distinguished between pleasure experienced in motion and activity, such as joy and delight, and that experienced during a state of rest, such as peace of mind and freedom from pain.[97] Philosophers often refer to these as kinetic and katastematic forms of pleasure respectively. Thus, kinetic pleasure may be found while engaged in the pursuit of satisfying a desire (e.g. drinking water when thirsty), and a katastematic one experienced in the state of having already satisfied it (e.g. having quenched one's thirst).[98] For Epicurus, both kinds of pleasure can occur in the body and the soul (mind); however, he considers the absence of pain or deficiency (or the replenishment of lack) in the soul (mind) to be the highest good, and thus the ultimate goal: for, once 'free from pain and fear . . . the tempest of the soul is laid'.[99]

Although Epicurus characterised katastematic pleasure as a static one, associating it with a state of rest and peace of mind, it does not preclude experiencing such pleasure while engaged in an activity. In the words of philosopher Julia Annas, Epicurus' category of static pleasure is experienced 'when functioning without interference . . . the pleasure of normal untrammelled activity'.[100] While an example of such activity might be mindful contemplation, it might also be a physical activity, such as carpentry. Psychologist Mihaly Csikszentmihalyi uses the term 'flow' to describe that optimal state of pleasure and happiness experienced by athletes or artisans, for example, when fully absorbed in a challenging but achievable task in which action and awareness are seamlessly merged.[101] Repetition, too, can give rise to katastemic pleasure, whereby the metrical reiteration of micro-gestures and actions that lead toward a desired goal induces a trance-like state of channelled concentration. In the same manner that athletes often describe the pleasure of being in full, unimpeded flow as being 'in the zone', so too did my fellow woodworkers when they found that 'sweet spot' of serene focus: body moving in controlled rhythm with the tool in hand and in harmonious exchange with the timber being worked.

It is important to acknowledge that pain, in a real physical sense, is a regular part of such pleasure-inducing activities. Aching muscles, inflamed joints or strained eyes may result from long hours of intense activity at the potter's wheel, the loom or the carpenter's bench. Artist Jenn Law noted that: 'Many artisanal pursuits result in repetitive strain injuries, and that is certainly the case for me when printmaking and paper-cutting. I have worked so many consecutive hours on some paper cuts that I've lost feeling in my hand for days.' But she qualified the pain by adding: 'While engaged in that detailed, repetitive labour, there is definitely something deeply pleasurable about it. I think it has to do with "losing yourself" in the labour and the materials.'[102] The relationship between pleasure and pain is therefore more nuanced than the ancient Greek's model of a linear continuum suggests. Rather, a maker – or for that matter a musician or athlete – may simultaneously experience enrapture and the discomforts instantiated by being 'in the zone'.[103]

Returning to Julia Annas, she also pointed out the similarity between Epicurus' notion of pleasure experienced in 'normal untrammelled activity' and that of Aristotle, for whom pleasure is the 'unimpeded' activity of our natural state.[104] For Aristotle, however, it is 'happiness' (Greek εὐδαιμονία, *eudaimonia*) that is the final overall good to which our actions should be directed. This is because, when achieved, happiness is complete and self-sufficient. He distinguishes happiness from pleasure in a conceptually helpful way. The state of happiness, in contrast to pleasure, is 'complete' (or 'final') because it is sought for its own sake and not sought for the sake of attaining some other state. In other words, the pursuit of (choice-worthy) pleasure or even of good qualities, such as intelligence and honour, is for the sake of achieving happiness; yet, one does not pursue 'happiness for *their* sake, or in general for any other reason'. Similarly, a state of happiness is 'self-sufficient' because happiness by itself 'makes life desirable and in no way deficient'.[105]

I would have described many of my fellow woodwork trainees, several of the college instructors and most of the established furniture makers I encountered during my research as 'happy people'. However, I had no grounds for believing that any existed in an Aristotelian state of 'completeness', whereby they had achieved happiness as a 'final good'. In reality, I question the mortal likelihood of such achievement full stop. To greater or lesser degrees, quotidian worries impinged upon the lives of the woodworkers, as they do for everyone. Worries were experienced variously over finances, health, personal relationships, global issues, deficiencies in skills or knowledge, or future prospects. Consequently, they experienced periods of sadness and sometimes grief, and, in a few cases, depression. While presumably all wished to be 'happy', carpentry was just one activity (albeit a weighty one) of the many they pursued in their individual quests of that goal. When describing to me their aspirations for becoming fine woodworkers, some trainees in fact mentioned 'happiness'. However, they more often spoke of engaging in work in which they could 'take pride', that produced 'useful' and 'enduring' things, that licensed 'autonomy' and 'control' over all stages of production, that would be embedded in a web of 'meaningful' (i.e. of worthy quality) social and professional relations with their suppliers of materials, their clients and a mutually supportive community of craftspeople, and, ultimately, that would be experienced as 'pleasurable'. I therefore expound the relation of pleasure to work a little further.

Aristotle held that just as there is pleasure to thought and contemplation, there is also a pleasure corresponding to each of the senses, and that the perceptual activities (seeing, hearing, touching, etc.) are most pleasurable when each of the senses is directed towards the 'worthiest of its objects'.[106] This notion he extended to encompass activity more generally, declaring that 'pleasure does not occur without activity . . . and every activity is perfected by its pleasure'.[107] As pointed out by philosopher Talbot Brewer, Aristotle does not explain how pleasure perfects or completes an activity, but it appears that he held pleasure 'to involve lively attentiveness to what we are doing' in a way that renders it 'wholehearted'.[108] In Aristotle's words, 'the mind is stimulated and exercises itself vigorously upon the object [of its activity]'.[109]

The connections Aristotle drew between activity, attentiveness and pleasure were taken up by the mid-twentieth-century Oxford philosopher Gilbert Ryle in his cogitations on the nature of 'pleasure' (a term he uses interchangeably with 'enjoyment').[110] Ryle contested the traditionally held account that pleasure is 'an agreeable feeling' in favour of the thesis that pleasure is a kind of 'attention': a wholehearted attending to the activity or object that is the source of pleasure. Such attending is characterised by being 'so absorbed in an activity . . . that [one] is reluctant to stop, or even to think of anything else'.[111] According to Ryle's account, an individual's engagement in an activity is, notably, 'not a vehicle for their pleasure';[112] pleasure is not a concomitant (i.e. a naturally accompanying phenomenon) of the activity. In other words, to take pleasure is not taking pleasure alongside one's activity, but rather it is instantiated *in* one's wholehearted engagement in that activity.[113]

Ryle's idea here corresponds closely with my findings about woodworking, namely that pleasure is not something separable from the activity that is being experienced as pleasant. When a carpenter experiences pleasure in planing an evenly figured plank of pungent yellow pine (*Pinus jeffreyi*), for example, they are not engaged in two separate activities: planing *and* having a pleasant experience. Rather, the pleasant experience is *in* planing; in the fully attentive, sensual and embodied engagement in the activity. I would add that pleasure can be instantiated not only in *doing* wood planing but also in the activity of contemplating it: in meditating on planning or preparing to do it, in rehearsing and simulating it in the motor domains of cognition, and in dwelling in the memory of having done it.

Over the millennia, scholars, religious leaders and political scientists have questioned whether pleasure is merely a selfish pursuit. Is it an indulgence that leads us astray? An experience whose only value is in and of itself? Or, conversely, can it possess a moral dimension? Can pleasure serve a wider good? Guided by Talbot Brewer's thoughtful reflections on the matter, I conclude by briefly addressing the positive potential in pleasure for both personal development and as an engine for social change.

Brewer's thinking builds on Ryle and, by turn, Aristotle, in that 'taking pleasure in an activity is tantamount to engaging in the activity while fervently desiring to do it and it alone'.[114] But what is it, he asked, that drives such engagement to be 'wholehearted'?

In the preceding discussion, I cited the enduring idea that pleasure and pain constitute opposite poles on a continuum.[115] Brewer contended that the duo also comes into play in qualifying our sense of self. We may be 'pained', for instance, when engaging in activities that give rise to a sense of our being 'at odds with ourselves', often manifested as thoughts that 'we ought to be other than we are'.[116]

Vocational migrants to the College's woodworking programme articulated clear examples of this when recounting their life journeys that had taken them to craftwork. They spoke of the painful misfit between the jobs they had been previously doing and the values, worldviews and aspirations they held, and the latent abilities they believed they possessed. One, a graduate in philosophy who delighted in putting his intellectual grasp of logic to hands-on repair and the creation of things, had found himself discontentedly working as a real-estate broker. Another, with an MPhil in social science and a resounding commitment to green issues, had pleasingly landed a position in an environmental agency, but soon discovered that realising effective green policy and legislation was repeatedly hampered by intractable bureaucratic mechanisms and competing financial priorities. In these two cases and many others, the 'pain' beneficially moved them onward in their quests to do something differ-ent: namely, work that promised fulfilment far beyond merely meeting basic necessities and that they perceived as having intrinsic social value.[117]

When we have a sense of the value or moral worth in a 'genuinely good activity', writes Brewer, the pleasure derived while engaging in it is instanti-ated not only when discovering that 'sweet spot' in the embodied work, as I described earlier, but also from the 'harmony' that we achieve as 'agents': agents with capacity to perceive 'our actions, and ourselves manifest in those actions, as good'.[118] When the latter arises, Brewer astutely observed that: 'It alters the activity itself and enhances its value by making it . . . whole-hearted.'[119] Thus, engaging in activity or work of this nature provides 'a valu-able respite from the distractions and unwarranted doubts that so often leave us at odds with ourselves and alienated from our own doings',[120] and, I would add, from the creative endeavours of others.

More than a century earlier, William Morris captured the spirit of that message when he wrote:

> To all living things there is a pleasure in the exercise of their energies . . . A man at work, making something which he feels will exist because he is working at it and wills it, is exercising the energies of his mind and soul as well as of his body. Memory and imagination help him as he works. Not only his own thoughts, but the thoughts of the men of past ages guide his hands; and, as a part of the human race, he creates.[121]

It is hopefully clear by this point why the pursuit of pleasurable work lies at the heart of my book. It is my 'wholehearted' conviction that, as a society, we must ardently strive to make pleasure the basis for all work. The starting point, however, is to put pleasure at the heart of learning and enskilment at every level and in every branch of our educational system, from nursery schooling to higher education in all its varieties. Pleasure is, after all, the most essential ingredient in the making of a happier, healthier, purposeful, ethical and creative society – in short, a good one.

THE RIGHTS TO RESEARCH

Before concluding with an outline of the contents of this book, I offer a note on consent and representation.

The college director and instructors were fully informed about the nature of my anthropological study before I applied for a place on the fine wood-work programme in 2005, and again when I returned in 2012 to carry out the second project. Consent was generously granted for both and I benefited from the full cooperation of college administrators and teaching staff. At the very start of both fieldwork periods, I explained in detail my respective research methods and objectives to fellow trainees and to the subjects of my 'brain, hand and tool' study. Consent was freely given by all involved in the research to publish my findings, to share their engrossing stories as crafts-people-in-the-making and to use their names. I have chosen to use the real names of the instructors and established furniture makers, but to change the names of the college trainees to protect their identities.

Throughout both periods of fieldwork, my invitations to interview were enthusiastically accepted by instructors and students alike, and I was regularly engaged by my peers in conversation during workshop hours and at break times about the issues I was exploring and the things I had observed. The Building Crafts College and the grand Hall of the Carpenters' Company in the City of London have been among the many venues where I have delivered lectures on my woodworking research. In delivering my professorial inaugural lecture at the School of Oriental and African Studies (SOAS, University of London) in 2010, one of the most gratifying experiences that evening was having the support of close carpentry colleagues in the audience. I can only hope that my published accounts of their learning, skilled practice and dreams of satisfying work do them proud.

OUTLINE OF THE CONTENTS

In this final section, I summarise the remaining contents of the book. Although the progression of chapters loosely maps a timeline of events, it is possible to read them in any order and independently of one another, since each chapter grapples with a specific topic of investigation. For the reader less concerned with the histories of London's Carpenters' Company, the Building Crafts College and England's apprenticeship system(s), and more interested in the ethnographically grounded study, you may wish to progress from Chapter 1 directly to Chapter 4. Notably, earlier versions of several chapters were published either as journal articles or as chapters in edited volumes, but all were substantially revised, elaborated and updated with new material for inclusion in this monograph.[122]

As a prelude to the book's core study of becoming a carpenter at a London vocational college, Chapter 1 offers a candid personal account of my journey into the anthropology of craftwork and deliberations on the apprentice-style method that I have developed and employed in the field. Training alongside the craftspeople I study has been key to my discoveries about the ways we as humans learn and become enskilled (and deskilled). The chapter revisits the main findings from earlier fieldwork projects in West Africa and Arabia, and examines the evolving array of research questions that defined not only what I was seeking but also how I went about finding it.

Chapters 2 and 3 furnish vital and fascinating histories of the carpentry trade in London, England's evolving apprenticeship system, and my chosen field site. In doing so, the two chapters also present an historical review of the British government's mix of neglect and intervention in skill training in step with changing economic ideologies and political ambitions. Chapter 2 begins with the colourful history of the Worshipful Company of Carpenters, reviewing its main functions and activities as a London livery from the thirteenth century to the late nineteenth century. This includes discussion of the seminal role played by the Company, its fellow liveries and the Crown in structuring apprenticeships and vocational training. Chapter 3 follows chronologically, taking its starting point in 1893 with the Carpenters' establishment of the Trades Training School in West London and concluding in 2001 when the institution, now known as the Building Crafts College, was relocated to Stratford, East London. It is there that I trained for two years, earning National Vocational Qualifications (NVQs) in wood occupations and a City & Guilds diploma in fine woodwork. It is also where I later returned to carry out dedicated studies on the relation between brain, hands and tools, and on problem solving at the bench.

The next seven chapters are grounded in my ethnographic observations and experiences of training and socialising at the College and in my anthropological analyses of skill, teaching, learning, problem solving, and individual pursuits of pleasurable and meaningful work. The stories and voices of my fellow students, our instructors and the established furniture makers who I interviewed take centre stage throughout. Their daily dialogue and the responses they offered to my open questions squarely challenge widely held misconceptions that craftspeople are good with their hands, but struggle to verbalise what they know. These men and women vividly recount their journeys into craftwork and thoughtfully articulate opinions, positions, hopes and concerns, at times with poetic insight and profound wisdom. Their ideas and reflections contribute directly to the theory and analysis I offer in the chapters. This book is therefore intended for a broad readership with shared interests in skill and making, including craftspeople themselves.

Chapter 4, 'Getting Started', supplies the backdrop to my initial two-year fieldwork project at the Building Crafts College. It begins with day one and progresses rapidly through the first term of the programme, introducing my fellow trainees, the college facilities at our disposal, and the curriculum of study and practical projects that we followed. The early relationships that formed between trainees quickly established a tight community, which in turn gave rise to a strongly (but not universally) shared ethos about craft, the value of handwork and our responsibility as makers to the natural environment. The tenor of the community was a significant factor in shaping the learning environment, as were the differences in social background, experience and expertise that individuals brought to the course. The chapter concludes with an account of the annual prize-giving ceremony at Carpenters' Hall, which both strengthened the sense of community and imputed a hierarchy of competency and achievement within it.

A medley of college woodwork instructors is formally introduced in Chapter 5, 'Crafting Craftspeople'. All came to teaching with an abundance of practical, on-site experience, and their recollections of becoming carpenters and working in urban and rural England provide fascinating historical illustrations of the transformations undergone by the wood industries. Reflections on years of teaching reveal critical changes and continuities in the country's vocational education framework. The passion they share for timber and the tools, and their dedication to passing that enthusiasm on to successive generations, comes through powerfully in their narratives. The importance of nurturing both physical and mental dexterity in trainees is underscored, and so too is the spiritual dimension of craftwork, which is positively manifested as confidence in oneself and pride in the things that one creates.

Chapter 6, 'Vocational Migrants to Craftwork', explores the motivations that propelled a majority of the mature trainees on the fine woodwork programme to abandon careers that afforded financial security in order to take up the tools and the risks involved in becoming craftspeople in the present era of mass consumerism and 'throwaway' culture. Each articulated their own reasoning, but all shared a longing to engage in work that they believed was meaningful, over which they felt they had control, and that promoted an authentic and aesthetic way of living in the world. In many respects, their aspirations were utopian. The chapter therefore begins with a survey of the roots of the socialist utopia in England, from the writings of Thomas More to William Morris, before examining its contemporary interpretations among craftspeople. For the vocational migrants featured in this chapter, and for some already established furniture makers, utopian narratives simultaneously encompass ideals about the nation's rural past and a post-industrial future that embraces an ethical green agenda for production and consumption.[123] What emerges, however, are the real political and marketplace challenges to achieving those ambitions. Indeed, following the thesis of sociologist Ruth Levitas,[124] the chapter reveals that utopias are not strategic plans for realising revolutionary ideologies or 'real worlds', but rather their key functions are to educate desire and direct human longing towards a future of more pleasing and enriching possibilities.

The desires expressed by vocational migrants in Chapter 6 to engage in work that fosters a greater sense of unity between mind and body, and between the maker, their tools and the natural materials they use, is further explored in Chapter 7, 'The Intelligent Hand'. The underlying message is that engagement in skilled handwork can be an important conduit to emotional and spiritual wellbeing. The chapter considers how carpenter and tool reciprocally form one another and, more particularly, the way that hand tools become an extension of the body during the course of practical training and with use. With illustrations from the workshop, I show how mastering a tool modifies and expands both our conceptual and motor cognition, and strengthens the neural networks that bind them. In navigating the intricate connections between brain, hands and tools, my arguments draw upon related literature on skill and craft, and on research from the cognitive and neurosciences. Ultimately, it is hoped that the chapter encourages further thinking about our embodied relations to the material objects and implements with which we interact on a daily basis.

Nearly half a century ago, David Pye, Professor of Furniture Design at the Royal College of Art, declared that risk was inherent to handwork.[125] Trainee and seasoned craftsperson alike make mistakes, especially when experimenting with tools, techniques or new materials. The ability to correctly identify the source of an error and to make the necessary adjustments or repairs is essential to a maker's skillset. Chapter 8, 'Problem Solving at the Workbench', carries out a meticulous investigation into the ways that mistakes are identified and problems resolved by fine woodwork trainees in the workshop. My analysis adopts a 'situated cognition' approach, whereby problems of any kind are recognised as being anchored in concrete settings and resolved by reasoning in situation-specific ways.[126] The description and analysis focus on a one-on-one workbench tutorial session between the fine woodwork convenor and a first-year trainee with no previous woodworking experience. The complexity and density of the exchange that unfolds between the two in collaboratively resolving a practical carpentry problem is made apparent. While providing insights into the trainee's educational background, their preferred ways of learning and their motivations for becoming a woodworker, the chapter captures the dynamics of teaching and learning, and of communicating and interpreting techniques in language, and with the body.

Chapter 9, 'Managing Pleasurable Pursuits', revisits the theme of utopia. I consider how pastoral visions of work and life, and a strong emphasis at the College on practical bench time over classroom learning deflected efforts to acquire basic business skills as part of the curriculum. Additionally, a 'cult of the hand tool' emerged, most strongly amongst the vocational migrants. This was fuelled in large part by an active ignoring of the merits of machinery and downplaying the degree of skill involved in deftly and safely operating (the 'noisy') power tools. In combination, a perceived incompatibility between the ethics of craftwork and those of business, and an aversion to mechanised forms of practice curtailed chances of succeeding as a sole trader in the real world of furniture making and architectural joinery. By considering some of the contradictory attitudes and desires expressed by trainees, the chapter probes the arts of ignoring and 'not knowing' that were employed to shield utopian ideals of 'true' craft and craftsmanship from corruption. At the end of the woodwork programme, when graduates confronted the enormity and sheer competitiveness of the design world beyond the College, many of the ideals and convictions that had been cultivated in the workshop became untethered. Gaps in knowledge that had been conveniently put to one side while training could no longer be ignored. The final section discusses how this awakening also tested the social bonds within the formerly tight-knit community of fine woodworkers.

Woodworking offers its practitioners constant challenge, and mastering the craft demands a persistent willingness to learn and develop. As revealed by the previous chapters, a carpenter's skill is measured by their ability to creatively improvise, solve problems and incorporate new techniques and information into their working processes. However, skill-based knowledge does not merely grow and develop. Like the organic properties of the timber they work, a woodworker's skill is susceptible to deterioration and decline. Chapter 10, 'Skill and Ageing', explores the development and the deterioration of craft skill over a human lifespan by bringing together narratives about work and life from four generations of carpenters. The generations are represented by a teenage trainee and an older vocational migrant who were enrolled on the College's fine woodwork programme, an established middle-age designer-maker of furniture, and a retired carpenter who had been active in the trade for more than seventy years. By weaving their stories with findings from the neurosciences on brain plasticity, the chapter provides an ethnographic account of the kinds of transformation that occur in the nervous system as the body grows, practises and ages. It also conveys the need for craftspeople to reskill and to reorganise their working environments when injured or as they age so that they may stay active in their cherished trade.

In the 'Epilogue', I revisit several of the book's main themes, beginning with an interview that a fellow woodworking student conducted with me about my personal experiences as a trainee. The interview was conducted at the midpoint of the fine woodwork programme and reveals my contemplations at the time about joining the vocational migrants to become a furniture maker. The Epilogue concludes with a reaffirmation of my longstanding convictions that skilled handwork be conferred greater status in all societies and that craft training be made an integral part of a rounded education that nurtures muscles, morals and mind. In order to advance in that direction, popular cultural definitions of 'intelligence' or 'intellectual' must be challenged and expanded to include, as a minimum, the skilled body at work and play. After all, it is with bodies, and not merely words, that people communicate, interpret, improvise and negotiate – in a word, 'craft' – their ways of knowing and living in the world.

NOTES

1. See, for example, Adamson, *Thinking through Craft*, 166–67; Adamson, 'Section Introduction: Contemporary Approaches', 587; Luckman, *Craft*. At this same moment in history, anthropologist Rudi Colloredo-Mansfeld stated in his study of artisans in non-Western contexts that artisans had proliferated in the global cultural economy, 'perhaps no more strongly than in places that have embraced premarket reforms and global integration', such as Mexico or Senegal ('An Ethnography of Neoliberalism', 115 and 124). Relatedly, artist and curator Ingrid Bachman observed that Western collectors tend to 'fetishize the product of excessive and often skilled labour from an individual in the developed world, but disregard similar labour originating from the developing world' ('New Craft Paradigms', 46).
2. Morris, Hargreaves and McIntyre, *The Market for Craft*, 6–8. See also Morris, Hargreaves and McIntyre, *Making It to Market*.
3. Morris, Hargreaves and McIntyre, *The Market for Craft*, 2.
4. See Crafts Council et al., *Craft in an Age of Change*, 44.
5. Abrahams, 'Hands That Do Dishes'.
6. This sector broadly comprises makers working in the disciplines of ceramics, glass, stone, wood, iron, smithing of precious metals, jewellery-making, graphic crafts, heritage and traditional crafts (e.g. wheelwrights, broom-makers, thatchers, etc.), taxidermy, textiles, leather, musical instrument making, toys and automata (Creative & Cultural Skills and Crafts Council, *The Craft Blueprint*, 14).
7. For a fuller discussion about the history of the division made between art and craft, see Marchand, Introduction: Craftwork as Problem Solving', 3–10. For discussions of the high-level debates during the 1980s concerning competing definitions of 'crafts' and the commitments of the Crafts Council to the 'artist craftsperson' as opposed to the vernacular crafts, see Harrod, *Crafts in Britain*, 409, 411–14, 421 and 460–61.
8. A 2011 survey of nearly 2,000 makers (which excluded hobbyists and makers of traditional and heritage craft) found that 10 per cent of makers in the UK worked in wood (excluding furniture making) and a further 5.9 per cent were makers of furniture in wood. Interestingly, 23.8 per cent of all male makers in the UK worked in wood and a further 15.4 per cent made wood furniture, while 4.7 per cent of all female makers worked in wood and a further 1.5 per cent made wood furniture (Crafts Council et al., *Craft in an Age of Change*, 24).
9. See, for example, Ruskin, 'The Nature of Gothic'.
10. Morris established a tapestry factory at Merton Abbey in Surrey.
11. Metcalf, 'Contemporary Craft', 15.
12. Mackmurdo, an architect and designer, set up the Century Guild of Artists in 1882.
13. Ashbee, an architect and designer, set up his Guild in 1888 in East London, but it was later moved to the Cotswold town of Chipping Campden in Gloucestershire.
14. The Art Workers' Guild was set up in 1884 in Central London by a group of architects, including W.R. Lethaby, who opposed the distinction made between fine arts and the applied arts. The Guild is still in operation.

15. Thomas, 'Modernity, Crafts and Guilded Practices', 66–67.
16. The Art Workers' Guild and the Guild of Handicraft only began admitting women in the 1960s.
17. Marchand, Introduction: Craftwork as Problem Solving', 5. See also Harrod, *Crafts in Britain*, 242.
18. In 2001, the Crafts Council with support from Arts Council England launched 'Next Move', which aimed at providing selected graduates with financial, business and professional development support in setting up their creative businesses.
19. Retrieved 24 May 2021 from https://www.craftscouncil.org.uk/about/history.
20. To note, I had the pleasure of taking up a Craftspace research action partnership in 2015 to work with Ugandan-British craftsman-artist Andrew Omoding and document his creative processes and problem-solving strategies while engaged in making. For more information, see https://craftspace.co.uk/radical-craft-explora tions-in-creativity (retrieved 24 May 2021). See also my film, *Art of Andrew Omoding*, and my publications from that research: Marchand, 'Explorations in Creativity'; 'Ducks and Daughters'; 'Toward an Anthropology of Mathematizing' and 'Dwelling in Craftwork'.
21. In 2012, it was reported that 57 per cent of makers in the UK were using digital technology in practice or production, and it was allowing them to reach an entirely new customer base (Crafts Council et al., *Craft in an Age of Change*, 8 and 39).
22. *Collect* shows featured the works of over 350 artists, many for whom craftwork is integral to their processes.
23. *Origin* was started in 2006, drawing exhibiting designer-makers from across the United Kingdom and around Europe.
24. Examples include the Wood Awards, launched in 2003 and replacing the earlier Carpenters' Award (1971–2001) and the Timber Industry Award (2001–2003). The annual Wood Awards recognise excellence in all areas of design, craftsmanship and installation in buildings and furniture in the twenty-first century. The Wesley-Barrell Craft Awards began in 2006, at a time when crafts were enjoying a well-deserved revival. They are organised in association with the Crafts Council, with the aim of supporting British craftsmanship and recognising the quality of home-grown mid-career talent, including a category for furniture. In the same year, the magazine *Country Living* launched the Balvenie Artisan Award to recognise excellence in the heritage crafts sector and those passing on their skills to future generations.
25. See Adamson, *Thinking through Craft*, 166–67; Hung and Magliaro, *By Hand*, 11–12; and the collection of chapters in Buszek, *Extra/Ordinary*.
26. Metcalf, 'Contemporary Craft', 22.
27. Beginning in 2009, this popular biennial conference series has been organised by the Plymouth College of Art, attracting participants from around the world to present on, discuss and advance current agendas in the craftworld and beyond.
28. Ferris, 'Making Futures'.
29. Coleman, *The Art of Work*, 37.
30. In 2007, the V&A hosted *Out of the Ordinary: Spectacular Craft*, which featured eight artists 'who place meticulous craftsmanship at the heart of their work', and, in 2011 the museum hosted the blockbuster show *Power of Making* that celebrated the role of making in our everyday lives and exhibited a diverse range of skills and imaginative uses of materials. In 2007, the British Museum hosted the astonishing *Crafting*

Beauty in Modern Japan exhibition, which showcased some of the very best works produced in that country during the previous half-century.

31. For example, the well-known American serial *This Old House* was launched in 1979 and is still running at the time of writing; Channel 4's *Grand Designs* was launched in 1999; and in 2003, BBC launched a set of television series called *Renovation*.

32. The '50 per cent' target had been controversial from the start, being viewed as further prioritising higher education over vocational education and training, as well as exacerbating the existing skills gap in the United Kingdom. The objective was dropped in 2010 by the Conservative-Liberal Democrat coalition government.

33. These points were emphasised, for example, by Sir Michael Latham in a speech delivered on behalf of ConstructionSkills to the Construction Liveries Group at Carpenters' Hall, 24 March 2004.

34. The NHTG was formed with support from ConstructionSkills, the Sector Skills Development Agency and English Heritage.

35. This demanded substantial increases to the present numbers of skilful bricklayers, roofers (including thatchers), leadworkers, stonemasons, dry-stone wallers/masons, millwrights and earth-wall builders. See NHTG, *Traditional Building Crafts Skills*.

36. In 2006, the Conference on Training in Architectural Conservation (COTAC) developed Master Crafts National Occupational Standards and was devising a mentoring programme for helping individuals to progress to Master Crafts status and thereby have qualifications to train others. In carpentry, a total of eighty-nine Master Carpenter Certificates had been issued by 2008, recognising 'excellence in the art, craft, science and practice' in the wood trades (Institute of Carpenters, *Annual Report* 2008, 11).

37. Corporation of London, *The Livery Companies*, 17. Notably, the Livery Companies Skills Council was started in 1993 to establish a forum within the Livery to promote vocational training. The objective of the Council's sixty-two liveries, which included the Carpenters, Furniture Makers, Joiners and Ceilers, Shipwrights and Turners (all of which represent wood occupations), was to encourage government to channel funding to small and medium-sized businesses and to sole traders in specialised disciplines linked to ancient and modern livery companies.

38. The Prince's Trust, founded in 1976, works to support vulnerable young people to get into training and work.

39. BBC, 'Charles Promotes Apprenticeships'.

40. Jakob and Thomas, 'Firing up Craft Capital', 499. Notably, the three studies conducted by McAuley and Fillis between 2002 and 2006 excluded hobbyists and those who described the 'subject or style' of their work as 'traditional' (Crafts Council et al., *Craft in an Age of Change*, 189–90).

41. Marchand, 'Introduction: Craftwork as Problem Solving', 8.

42. Henley, 'Heritage Crafts at Risk'.

43. The Convention for the Safeguarding of the Intangible Cultural Heritage is a UNESCO treaty adopted by the UNESCO General Conference on 17 October 2003, which came into force in 2006.

44. Concerted anthropological interest in material culture arguably begins with Franz Boas (1858–1942) and his students in the late nineteenth and early twentieth centuries. The early focus on the step-by-step processes of making, as well as using (and disposing of), artefacts is exemplified in anthropological studies that employ

the 'chaîne opératoire', a methodology pioneered by French archaeologist André Leroi-Gourhan (1911–86), who was a student of Marcel Mauss.

45. Notably, this coincided with reinvigorated interest in the ideas of David Pye, Professor of Furniture Design at the Royal Academy of Art, who trained some of the leading Craft Revival furniture makers. During the 1960s, Pye authored two works of considerable importance to the study of craft: *The Nature of Design* and *The Nature of Art of Workmanship*.

46. In order of mention: Harrod, *Crafts in Britain*; Dormer, *The Culture of Craft*; Johnson, *Exploring Contemporary Craft*; and Greenhalgh, *The Persistence of Craft*.

47. In order of mention: Adamson, *Thinking through Craft*; Risatti, *A Theory of Craft*; and Sennett, *The Craftsman*.

48. The term 'Craftivism', which succinctly captures this sentiment, was popularised by American writer and maker Betsy Greer in 2003.

49. Morris, 'The Revival of Handicraft', 331.

50. Greenhalgh, 'Craft in a Changing World', 1.

51. Marchand, 'Introduction: Craftwork as Problem Solving', 8. This section of the Introduction presents in summarised form the key issues and ideas pertaining to the definition of craft that I explored in pages 3–10 of 'Introduction: Craftwork as Problem Solving'.

52. Harrod, *Crafts in Britain*, 9.

53. Sennett, *The Craftsman*, 9.

54. Adamson, *Thinking through Craft*, 3–4.

55. Risatti, *A Theory of Craft*, 16–18.

56. Ibid., 108–9.

57. See ibid., Chapter 27, 281–302. The Studio Craft movement began in the United States after the Second World War and is characterised by the works of 'craft artists' who experiment with nontraditional materials and techniques.

58. See Adamson, *Thinking through Craft*, 6.

59. Marchand, 'Introduction: Craftwork as Problem Solving', 9–10.

60. Ibid.,10.

61. Ibid., 8.

62. Ibid., 6. See also Metcalf, 'Contemporary Craft', 13.

63. Streeck, 'Through Unending Halls', 30.

64. For example, see Clifford Collard, 'Crafting Livelihood'.

65. By contrast, in her study of seamstresses in Trinidad, anthropologist Rebecca Prentice found that changing demands in the neoliberal economic environment forced these women to be 'opportunist, flexible and self-reliant'. Their ongoing accumulation of new sewing skills and abilities to produce the latest fashions 'prepare them for fragmented livelihoods that will see them seizing opportunities, withstanding economic uncertainties, and finding pleasure in what otherwise could be grinding and tedious work' (Prentice, '"No One Ever Showed Me Nothing"', 411).

66. Herzfeld, *The Body Impolitic*, 60.

67. Lightfoot, 'Pencil, Ruler, Fretsaw', 49.

68. Aristotle, *Nicomachean Ethics*, Book 1, Chapter vii, 1098a: 25–30.

69. Sharp and Kinder, 'The New Workforce'.

70. World Economic Forum, 'Chapter 1'.

71. Marchand, 'Process over Product'; 'Negotiating License and Limits'; and 'Negotiating Tradition'.

72. Research Fellowship number RES 000-27-0159.
73. London's Worshipful Company of Goldsmiths also plays an active role in the City's jewellery industry by supporting apprenticeships in the trade, and its assay office hallmarks precious metals.
74. Examples include David Charlesworth, who had been teaching the craft since 1977 and offering courses at Harton Manor in Devon; David Savage, the experienced cabinet maker and furniture designer who offered courses in North Devon; and the famous Edward Barnsley Workshop in Hampshire, which has been training apprentices since 1980.
75. Yarrow and Jones, '"Stone Is Stone"', 265–66.
76. I thank Max Lawson, graduate of the stonemasonry course at the Building Crafts College, for verifying my description and supplying key information.
77. In 2011, 27.5 per cent of makers in the UK were categorised as 'career changers', and they were often in mid-life (Crafts Council et al., *Craft in an Age of Change*, 5).
78. By contrast, it was reported that the United Kingdom's craft sector is 'heavily female'. The percentage of Black, Asian and minority ethnic (BAME) individuals in the craft sector remained low (3.5 per cent), while representation of foreign-born and dyslexic/disabled people were above the national averages (ibid., 7).
79. On interactive alignment in dialogue, see Purver and Kempson, 'Incrementality'. On Dynamic Syntax, see Kempson, Meyer-Viol and Gabbay, *Dynamic Syntax*; and Cann, Kempson and Marten, *The Dynamics of Language*.
80. Marchand, 'Making Knowledge', 12–13.
81. Orwin, 'Dynamic Syntax'. Though not using Dynamic Syntax, G. Novembre and P.E. Keller make a fascinating exploration of a 'general grammar of action' in the goal-directed actions and motor-based predictions of skilled musicians (Novembre and Keller, 'A Grammar of Action'). Their findings resonate in numerous ways with my own (Marchand, 'Making Knowledge').
82. Marchand, 'Crafting Knowledge'; 'Embodied Cognition, Communication and the Making of Place & Identity'; 'Making Knowledge'; and 'Embodied Cognition and Communication'.
83. Geographer Nicola Thomas claims that it is also important to understand such activities as part of a craftsperson's embodied practice 'if we are to appreciate a rounded understanding of the geographies of making' (Thomas, 'Modernity', 64).
84. On the nature of problem solving, see Marchand, 'Introduction: Craftwork as Problem Solving'.
85. I thank Dr Jenn Law for this productive challenge.
86. I first used the title for a lecture delivered in 2008 to the Archaeology and Anthropology Society at the University of Bristol, and it stuck as the title for this book.
87. The first two are published in Morris, *News from Nowhere* and the third in Morris, *The Relations of Art to Labour*. Other seminal essays by Morris that gave shape to my thinking are: with Webb and SPAB, 'Manifesto'; 'How We Live' (1896); 'Revival of Handicraft' (1888); 'Art and Its Producers', (1888); and 'The Arts and Crafts of Today' (1889).
88. Morris, 'Useful Work', 289.
89. *New Oxford Dictionary*.
90. Boyson, *Wordsworth*.
91. Sizer, 'The Two Facets', 215. In this essay, Sizer convincingly brings studies in the natural and neurological sciences to bear on some of the philosophical questions about pleasure.

92. Plato, *Philebus*.
93. It is not possible to include a full list in an endnote, but prominent figures include Scottish Enlightenment philosopher David Hume, who wrote: 'There is implanted in the human mind a perception of pain and pleasure as the chief spring and moving principle of all its actions' (*A Treatise of Human Nature*, Book 1, Part 3, section 10); and English utilitarian philosopher Jeremy Bentham, who wrote: 'Nature has placed mankind under the governance of two sovereign masters, pain and pleasure. It is for them alone to point out what we ought to do, as well as to determine what we shall do. On the one hand the standard of right and wrong, on the other the chain of causes and effects, are fastened to their throne' (*An Introduction to the Principles of Morals*, Chapter 1, 'Of the Principle of Utility', opening paragraph, p. 1). Another important example is the founder of psychoanalysis Sigmund Freud, whose theory of the 'pleasure principle' describes the basic motivating force of the id as being the instinctive drive to seek pleasure and avoid pain, with the function of reducing psychic tension ('Beyond the Pleasure Principle').
94. A great deal of dialogue in the *Philebus* is dedicated to discerning between sensual pleasures, pleasures derived from being respected and pleasures had in intellectual activity, and to categorising pleasures as pure or impure, true or false. In *The Republic*, Plato further separates out appetites (i.e. the desire for pleasures for pleasure's sake) from desires for truth or honour, which yield their own kinds of pleasure when attained (Plato, *The Republic*, 206–17).
95. Moss, 'Pleasure and Illusion', 533.
96. Laërtius, 'Epicurus', passages 129–32.
97. Ibid., passage 136.
98. See Annas, 'Epicurus on Pleasure', 8–10; Rosenbaum, 'Epicurus on Pleasure', 23–24; and Sizer, 'Two Facets', 228–29.
99. Laërtius, 'Epicurus', 128.
100. Annas, 'Epicurus on Pleasure', 9.
101. Csikszentmihalyi, *Flow*.
102. Personal communication, May 2020.
103. A number of (Counter-Reformation) Baroque artists succeeded in capturing in their works this dual experience of pleasure and pain. A prime example is Gian Lorenzo Bernini's statue of *Ecstasy of Saint Teresa* (1647–52).
104. Annas, 'Epicurus on Pleasure', 9; and Aristotle, *Nicomachean Ethics*, Book VII, Chapter xi, 1153a. Like Plato, however, Aristotle held pleasure to be an 'apparent' good (i.e. with the potential to deceive), but he contended that there is something correct in the appearance that pleasure is good. After all, as an empiricist and champion of the perceptual senses as our instrument for knowledge, he maintained that, in general, there is something correct in appearances. For a discussion of this, see Moss, 'Pleasure and Illusion', 530 and footnote 56.
105. Aristotle, *Nicomachean Ethics*, Book I, Chapter vii.
106. Ibid., Book X, Chapter iv, 1174b: 20–24.
107. Ibid. Book X, Chapter iv, 1175a: 20–21.
108. Brewer, 'Savouring Time', 149.
109. Aristotle, *Nicomachean Ethics*, Book X, 1175a.
110. Ryle, *The Concept of Mind*, Chapter 4, 'Emotion', part 6 'Enjoying & Wanting', 91–94; and Ryle, 'Pleasure, Part I', 135–46.
111. Ryle, *The Concept of Mind*, 92. Though C.C.W. Taylor was in general agreement with Ryle's analysis of 'pleasure as attention . . . for pleasures in activities which

themselves require the direction of attention', he provocatively noted its limits in explaining 'pleasures where the element of attention in minimal' (Taylor, 'Pleasure', 4).

112. Ryle, *The Concept of Mind*, 93, emphasis added.
113. Coming at the problem from an entirely different angle, namely a phenomenological one, Aaron Smuts' 'feel good theory' of pleasure arrives at a conclusion somewhat commensurable with that of Ryle, in that 'pleasure is not distinct from the experience' of an activity. According to Smuts, what makes something pleasurable is simply the way the experience feels (Smuts, 'The Feels Good Theory').
114. Brewer, 'Savouring Time', 143–44.
115. However, it should be noted that Ryle made a distinction between a physical sensation of pain and a sense of being pained by, for instance, a thought or recollection: '"pain", in the sense in which I have pains in my stomach, is not the opposite of "pleasure". In this sense, a pain is a sensation of a special sort, which we ordinarily dislike having' (Ryle, *The Concept of Mind*, 93). See W.B. Gallie's retort to Ryle's argument (Gallie, 'Pleasure, Part II', in Ryle and Gallie, 147–64).
116. Brewer, 'Savouring Time', 157.
117. See also philosopher Hannah Arendt's distinction between 'work' and 'labour' (*The Human Condition*, especially Parts III and IV).
118. Brewer, 'Savouring Time', 157–58.
119. Ibid., 158.
120. Ibid., 144. Coming at the issue from a somewhat different angle, Laura Sizer similarly concludes that what she defines as the 'pleasure system' can imbue 'goals . . . and activities with incentive salience making them wants – objects of striving in their own right, and can mark our achievements with satisfaction, giving us a sense of progress and accomplishment' (Sizer, 'Two Facets', 232).
121. Morris, 'Useful Work', 288–89.
122. In numerical order, an earlier version of Chapter 6 was published (2007) as 'Vocational Migrants and a Tradition of Longing'; an earlier version of Chapter 7 as 'Knowledge in Hand'; an earlier version of Chapter 9 as 'Managing Pleasurable Pursuits'; and an earlier version of Chapter 10 as 'Skill and Ageing'. Synopses of the edited volumes in which the earlier versions of 'Managing Pleasurable Pursuits' and 'Skill and Ageing' appear at the beginning of the endnotes for Chapters 9 and 10 respectively. This is for the benefit of readers who wish to further explore the themes of either 'ignorance and not knowing' (Kirsch and Dilley, *Regimes of Ignorance*) or 'making and growing' (Hallam and Ingold, *Making and Growing*).
123. In her book *Contemporary Crafts*, Imogen Racz explores the underlying philosophies that link craft and making to place, society and environment, and she specifically addresses the ways that concepts of nature, feelings for the land, the rural idyll and contemporary green agendas have informed craft and craft identities in England, from the Arts and Crafts movement to the present.
124. Levitas, *The Concept of Utopia*.
125. Pye, *The Nature and Art of Workmanship*.
126. Kirsch, 'Problem Solving'.

CHAPTER 1

AN ANTHROPOLOGIST'S JOURNEY INTO CRAFTWORK AND APPRENTICESHIP

One summer day each year, acres of green open fields along the banks of the River Wye are transformed into the Monmouth Show. The prime attraction of this bustling agricultural fair is the main ring, where immaculately groomed horses, show dogs and scrubbed sheep and cattle are paraded, and where the action-packed equestrian events take place. A sea of marquee tents shelter sellers of sturdy country clothing and host competitions for the tastiest cakes and pies, flower arrangements and prize vegetables. Displays of tractors lure the farmers, while children excitedly play organised games and take part in contests. Fanciers display perfectly preened poultry and fine plump pigs in pens, and wildlife conservationists man educational displays on honeybees, otters and our indigenous birds of prey. Local craftspeople, too, exhibit their wares and some supply entertaining spectacles of their artisanal skills.

I recall a team of blacksmiths from the neighbouring county of Herefordshire who had one year set up an outdoor smithy on a grassy patch at the edge of the fairground. A coke-fuelled forge blazed near the anvil and all manner of tools – callipers, hammers, chisels, tongs, punches and drifts – were laid out, ready to hand for hammering, bending and twisting lengths of mild steel into coiling and sinuous forms. The smiths had suspended a thick rope between wooden posts to demarcate their workspace and to keep the steady stream of onlookers at a safe distance from the heat. When I arrived at the display, a five or six-year-old boy was standing at the front of the gathering. His two tiny hands gripped the rope barrier that swayed just beneath his chin and he stared wide-eyed at the smith who rhythmically hammered the glowing metal with his ball-peen hammer. 'Tang-tang-tang!', it rang. The boy stayed put, mesmerised by the smith's magic that transmuted a mundane rod of mild steel into an elaborate medieval-style candlestick with a barley-twist stem.

I left the smiths to visit other nearby displays and to watch a parade of handsome shire horses decorated with shiny, glittering tack. Retracing my steps an hour or so later, I passed again by the forge and anvil. The little boy was still there, unmoved from his position, but now chattering away to the blacksmith who cheerfully partook in the exchange. Hundreds of other children had witnessed the blacksmith's work that day, but clearly, this boy had been entranced. The experience sparked his imagination and would possibly colour what he dreamed of becoming.

The wonderment in that boy's eyes was immediately recognisable to me. Since childhood, I have had a passion for making things and, from the start of my career as an anthropologist, that interest has steered my inquiry.

This opening chapter is a prelude to the book's core study of becoming and being a carpenter at the Building Crafts College. It offers the reader a personal account of my journey into the anthropology of craftwork while deliberating upon the apprentice-style field method that I adopted and adapted over a period of many years. The journey took me to successive studies with masons, first in northern Nigeria, then Yemen and finally Mali. All of these men were practised in the vernacular style of architecture that characterised their town or city, employing either mud or kiln-baked brick and local building technologies to create distinctive building forms and decorative elements.

The sections of the chapter revisit some of my key findings about craftwork on the West African and Arabian building sites, as well as some of the shortcomings identified in each of those studies. Significantly, reflection on the shortcomings fine-tuned my line of questioning, which in turn progressed my field methods. Learning to sustain focused attention and inquisitiveness as an anthropologist while labouring and apprenticing on busy building sites prepared me for the even more intense immersion I would experience as a full-time trainee within a community of fine woodworkers in London's East End.

Importantly, the shift from studies on building sites to one at a vocational training college allowed me to carefully scrutinise the nature of the dialogue between design and making. As a labourer, I had executed the designs conceptualised by the West African and Arabian master masons. Though I was permitted to inquire about their design practices, I had no direct involvement in them. By contrast, my study of craft as a fine-woodwork and furniture-making trainee was enriched by first-hand experience in both activities.

Observations and analyses of the dynamic processes that unfold between design and making are therefore shared throughout the book.

The move to a Western educational institution also enabled me make a comparative study of craft training in diverse social and cultural contexts.[1] Unlike the lengthy apprenticeships on the African and Arabian sites, the college training period was condensed into two short years. Because contemporary British vocational qualifications in the building crafts involve written examinations and keeping logbooks in addition to practical components, students must be literate and numerate. This reflects the division made in the European educational context between practice and theory, which was far less prevalent on the sites of my earlier studies, and where gaining qualifications was more singularly dependent on what one could accomplish with materials and the tool in hand. My fellow college trainees enjoyed greater licence to pose questions and challenge doctrine, and they had easier access to technical information, but, unlike the Nigerian, Yemeni or Malian apprentices, they were exposed to a far narrower range of professional, on-the-job experiences. As a result, their future as carpenters was, in some ways, less secure. The sources and effects of this precarity are explored in later chapters.

Finally, a few general remarks on my field method. Apprenticing as a technique of anthropological inquiry is well suited to the study of learning and knowing in practice-based contexts where talking is upstaged by doing. It also equips anthropologists with first-hand experience – and possibly some level of expertise – in the practices that they theorise and write about.[2] At a personal level, while apprenticing and training in craftwork, I could pursue the pleasure that I experience in collectively making things with others while indulging my curiosity about the ways that we, as humans, think, calculate, communicate and create. In the process, confidence in my own abilities to make and repair things and to problem solve in the flow of the task was bolstered, and that has positively enhanced my sense of self.

However, apprenticing as an anthropological method also has its challenges, which I discuss here and in the Epilogue. It is hoped that this chapter will not only resonate with fellow researchers who employ similar methodologies, but will also prompt deeper contemplation among craftspeople, tradespeople and all who work with their hands on what it is that they do, how they have come to do it and how their ways of doing are constantly changing.

THE STARTING POINT

My parents firmly believed that there was more fun to be had with a box of crayons, a stack of paper and a roll of tape than with store-bought toys.

Consequently, my trove of Lego pieces and miniature Canadian Logs was pitifully small. Villages and cityscapes had to be assembled with discarded cardboard packaging, toilet-paper-roll tubes, aluminium foil, swatches of fabric and other found bits. I would work for days on end constructing these models that quickly spread across my bedroom floor, and then dismantle and rebuild again with 'improvements'. By the age of five, I was determined to become an architect.

I took the science route through secondary school, my strengths in maths and physics offset by lacklustre performances in chemistry class. I continued with pure and applied sciences at college,[3] but the majority of my college elective courses were in art history, taught by the luminous Lenore Krantz, whose erudition ranged from Greek and Roman art through to the modern period. The disciplinary blend of science and art earned me a place at McGill University's School of Architecture, which, pleasingly, was a sanctuary of creative expression within the solemn faculty of engineering.

During the final years of my undergraduate studies, I was fortunate to secure several design commissions for new houses in greater Montreal. Alongside that independent work, I was employed during the summer months as a municipal building inspector. The combination allowed me to hone my design and technical drawing skills while gaining practical construction knowledge and first-hand experience of site operations. I learned much through observing, conversing, negotiating and sometimes debating with the contractors and tradespeople who erected the buildings I inspected and the houses I designed. Discrepancies between the creation of buildings with architectural graphic standards on paper and the actual ways they are realised in timber, bricks and mortar became increasingly apparent to me. Attending to the methods of tradespeople not only deepened my appreciation for their skill, but also instigated a seismic shift in my intellectual curiosity.

On site, I was frequently struck by the way that the carpenters, in particular, carried out often-complicated assignments and calculations with a Spartan economy of words and, unnervingly, with only brief and infrequent reference to my fastidiously prepared plan drawings. Novice carpenters would shoot sidelong glances at senior colleagues for clues about executing new tasks or estimating measurements and spacing. The dearth of verbal instruction spawned numerous questions in my mind: what did communication between carpenters consist of? How was parity of understanding established? How did novices translate visual information into motor skills? What combinations of activities, circumstances and environmental stimuli gave rise to learning? And how did problem solving unfold in the joint physical activities undertaken by the work crew? These fundamental queries about human cognition and communication eventually drove me to social anthropology, and I have worked and studied ever since alongside craftspeople, learning about their lives and their skills while endeavouring to 'learn about learning'.

THE MASONS OF ZARIA

I had my first taste of fieldwork in the early 1990s, as a precursor to formal training in anthropology. A grant from the Canadian International Development Agency (CIDA) made it possible for me to travel to northern Nigeria and to carry out six months of fieldwork in the Hausa Emirate town of Zaria.[4] The principal aim of my study was to document layouts, spatial configurations, building structures and flamboyantly decorated façades of the vast extended-family residential compounds in the ancient walled town (Birnin Zaria).[5] I also examined the extent to which the associated mud-masonry practices had changed, if at all, since the publication of Friedrich Schwerdtfeger's classic study on *Traditional Housing in African Cities*.[6]

In contrast to Schwerdtfeger's dire warning of the imminent disappearance of Zaria's remarkable mud architecture, I found traditional building practices to be thriving. Nigeria's economic slump in the 1980s (due in large part to declining production and prices of crude oil and a weak Naira) had hobbled the spread of breezeblock construction and compelled poorer folk to source cheaper, locally available materials for their building needs. But, furthermore, a handful of wealthy title-holding families in the old walled town continued to patronise local masons and the traditional building styles because of their enduring symbolic associations with Hausa heritage and Zaria's famous royal palace.

A ceremonious audience with the Emir at his palace secured the official permission needed for my fieldwork. I surveyed twenty-six family compounds in Birnin Zaria and several outside the walls with reliable assistance from a small team of local male and female university students. Detailed scale drawings were made of each compound (some the size of small villages), including all building outlines and their reflected ceiling plans. Lengthy interviews were conducted with household men and women to record family histories and to gather demographic data and information about gender and age-set practices and household economies. This information allowed me to get a sense of the ways that compounds grew and contracted over time with fluctuations in family fortunes, changing kinship arrangements and new lifestyle choices.

I was especially keen to hear from Zaria's famous mud masons who built, repaired and maintained the family compounds that I was documenting. On several occasions, I met with the Sarkin Magina (Master of Builders) and his retinue of officials and other title-holding masons. A rigid hierarchy existed among Zaria's masons and the community abided by an unwritten code of conduct and etiquette. The Sarkin Magina himself was now too elderly to engage physically in construction, but he continued to delegate work among his dependants in the trade community, organise project schedules and supervise sites. Like most royal office holders, he received a small allowance from the Emir, which he supplemented with income from ongoing building activities and subsistence farming. He was always impeccably dressed in a flowing, exquisitely embroidered *baban riga* (voluminous gown) and a conical white turban with an extending veil that draped beneath his chin and framed his chiselled facial features and dark shimmering eyes.

Following the lengthy protocol of formal greetings, we sat together on woven mats laid out on the earthen floor of his magnificent *zauré*. This was where the Sarkin Magina customarily received male guests to his home and negotiated building contracts ('always verbal, never written') with clients. The circumference of the *zauré's* generous central space was defined by eight evenly spaced piers, the inside faces of which arched gracefully from floor level to ceiling, joining together in a flat circular boss at the apex. The smoothly rendered structural elements were painted white with geometric patterns picked out in bright blue and orange, and the surface of the boss was decorated in relief with a six-petal rosette surrounded by a chain of curlicues. When sitting in that space, I had the distinct sense of sheltering beneath the abdomen of a giant mythical spider.

The Sarkin Magina was a gifted storyteller and I listened attentively. He spoke with pride about Zaria's architectural history and, with long fine fingers, he drew building plans and construction details in the earth floor at the front of his mat. I filled the pages of my notebook with anecdotes and with the names, lineages and tales about the mystifying feats of his ancestors. The Sarkin Magina was a direct descendant of Mallam Mikhaila 'Babban Gwani', the 'Great Expert' and nineteenth-century builder of Zaria's (once iconic) Friday Mosque. 'Babban Gwani', he recounted, 'had ordered his labourers to prepare the mud bricks and mortar during the daytime and to leave them on the site. Upon returning the next morning, the labourers discovered that Babban Gwani had single-handedly constructed the mosque during the night!' The legendary mason demonstrated his supernatural powers on another occasion, while settling a dispute with Emir Abdulkarim (r. 1835–46) over the correct orientation of the mosque's *mihrab* (prayer niche): 'Babban Gwani invited the Emir to stand behind him and to gaze in the direction he was pointing. Upon doing so, the Emir had a vivid vision of the pilgrims circumambulating the Kaaba in Mecca, and was thus convinced of his mason's authority on this matter.'[7]

The Sarkin Magina declared that master builders, including himself, have mystical powers like those possessed by Babban Gwani: 'If, for example, an-

other mason has a dispute with me,' he cautioned, 'then that mason's structures will collapse!' A decade later, I would hear the very same claim made
by mud masons in Mali. There was evidently a great deal more to becoming a
master craftsman in West Africa (and elsewhere) than merely procuring technical proficiency. My learning about craft knowledge was only just beginning.

While in Zaria, I absorbed much about the history of the place and about
daily life in the walled town. I also learned something about the livelihoods
and social positions of Zaria's masons. However, my insights into the everyday politics of work and social interactions on a building site, the jostling
for rank, and the criteria by which competence and expertise were evalu-
ated and contested were extremely limited. I did leave with some knowledge
about continuity and change in the vernacular style of the town's architecture, but with little understanding of how changing aesthetics were socially
negotiated or why some innovations in form and structure were made part
of the canon and others were not.

I watched buildings being built and listened carefully to explanations
about standard construction methods, but gained no feeling for the embodied techniques and gestures that were employed in laying the conical *tubali*
bricks or constructing *bakan gizo* vaults. Likewise, the mental and physical
operations that constituted on-site improvisation or problem solving within
the flow of work remained opaque. I was told repeatedly 'We never use plan
drawings', but I had only meagre knowledge of the ways that new buildings
were measured out in strides and in relation to the body, how spatial arrangements evolved in the process or how the elaborate configurations of
palm-timber ceilings were determined.

I recorded the names given to the various mixtures of laterite soil, clay
and natural binders that were used for specific purposes and for particular
components of a building, but I had no clue as to how to mix them. I diligently photographed the stages in producing relief decoration on exterior
walls, but without knowing how masons, without drawings, conceptually
and manually organised the complex geometries to cover entire wall surfaces with a resulting sense of balance, proportion and dazzling beauty.

Masons claimed there was growing demand for their services and that
more and more young men were taking up apprenticeships in the trade.
However, my study failed to shed light on the ways that technical knowhow,
trade secrets, supernatural powers, and correct social and moral comportment were taught to, and learned by, a younger generation. I did not know
in any detail what an apprenticeship consisted of, what apprentices experienced during training, what drove them to the trade (or away from it) or
what they aspired to become.

These gaping holes in my understanding signalled a need to shift more
fully from a focus on architecture as the object of study to examining the

human interactions and hands-on processes that create it. The prospects for future research as a foreign scholar in northern Nigeria, however, were bleak. Ethnic and religious tensions were rising and the security situation was deteriorating. Disappointingly, I was obliged to identify an entirely different field site for my inquiries.

MINARET BUILDING IN YEMEN

Two years prior to the fieldwork in Nigeria, I had backpacked across Yemen. That extraordinary 'Land of Builders' indelibly marked my imagination and I was determined to return there. I embarked on a research degree in social anthropology at London's School of Oriental and African Studies (SOAS) in 1994 and studied Arabic in preparation for doctoral fieldwork in Yemen's architecturally unique capital, Sanaa.[8] I was eager to seek answers to my many questions about the nature of building-craft knowledge in a context where formal technical schooling and drawn plans were irrelevant, and where master masons were both designer and maker. Progression in my understanding of skill, I reckoned, would be contingent on my becoming fully and physically engaged in my subject of study.[9]

The end of the Civil War in North Yemen (1962–70) between royalist partisans of the Mutawakkilite Kingdom and the victorious pro-republican forces ushered in a period of relative peace and prosperity in what was now called the Yemen Arab Republic. The unification in 1990 between North Yemen and its southern neighbour, previously the People's Democratic Republic of Yemen, was not without its challenges, but it eventually delivered a degree of stability to the entire region – albeit that this was short-lived.[10] Eased access for foreigners to Yemen from 1970 until the early 2000s attracted not only global business ventures and development initiatives, but also the arrival of an international community of scholars who made the country's archaeology, ancient history, rich culture and diverse architecture the focus of their various forms of research.

Improved economic prospects, an expanding infrastructure of roads and communication networks, and the provision of healthcare and other basic amenities stoked rapid population growth, urban migration and massive development. When I arrived in the capital Sanaa in 1996 to begin fieldwork, the construction boom was in full swing. The surrounding rural villages were being swiftly absorbed within the ever-extending city limits, and farm fields, vineyards, orchards and pasturelands were being carpeted over with concrete villas and tower blocks. The art of building with traditional methods and locally sourced materials nevertheless persisted. There was a burgeoning appreciation among Yemenis for their architectural heritage, spurred in part by international interest and the inscription of the old city of Shibam in Wadi Hadhramaut on UNESCO's World Heritage list in 1982, followed by Sanaa's old walled city four years later.

During my stay in Sanaa, masons told me bluntly that traditional kiln-baked brick and local stone was more durable than concrete block and cast-in-place concrete. Some added that brick and stone could be 'controlled', in that individual masonry units could be removed, replaced and modified with relative ease and without undermining the overall structure. To do so required the kind of knowhow that could only be had through long practical experience. These masons conceived of themselves as heirs to a precious legacy: in maintaining and reproducing Sanaa's ornate stone and brick façades, they perpetuated a noble craft dating to the building of the legendary Ghumdan Palace in the third century CE, if not earlier.[11] During my stay at the close of the twentieth century, that 'noble craft' continued to garner cultural prestige and was in fact experiencing a renaissance of sorts.

Sections of Sanaa's immense defensive walls were being resurrected in stone and thick horizontal layers of rammed earth (*zabur*),[12] and the streets and twisting laneways of the Old City were being paved in chunky blocks of basalt. Ancient *samsaras* (caravanserais) and monumental tower houses in the medieval quarters were being restored, conserved and extended skyward, while outside the walls brand new tower houses, boutique hotels and public baths were being assembled in traditional masonry with stained-glass *takhrim* fanlights and elaborately carved interior plasterwork. The spike in patronage for traditional Sanaani-style buildings also included the construction of new mosques, the refurbishment (or rebuilding) of historic ones and, notably, the raising of lofty freestanding minarets – mostly financed by charitable trusts set up by the city's established families and its new moneyed classes of industrialists and merchant-traders.

A series of fortuitous events resulted in my admittance as a labourer by a team specialised in the rather unique trade of minaret building. The family business was headed by brothers Muhammad and Ahmad al-Maswari, who had apprenticed under their father and now, as recognised masters of the craft, employed their sons, grandsons and a squadron of labourers. I worked alongside these men for a year, mainly hauling armloads of clay bricks and buckets of mortar up the spiral staircase. Once I had proven my mettle, I was permitted on occasion to take up an adze and carve the bricks that composed the angular patterns of the minaret's exterior relief decoration. The first of two minarets that I worked on with the Maswaris was for the Addil Mosque in the old Ottoman quarter of Bir al-Azab, and it is that experience that I summarise below.

Mosque minarets in Sanaa were constructed from the inside out, so to speak, and without external scaffolding. The structure's central column, its staircase and its exterior walls were raised in tandem, all resting on deep foundations of dense, impervious basalt stone. While a small group of labourers prepared building materials outside at ground level, a larger team relayed them upward, hand to hand, along the counterclockwise spiral of the dark and dusty staircase. The apprentice stationed on the top stair stacked the incoming materials as safely as possible in his cramped space, located just a metre or so below the working masons. On cue, he supplied what they demanded, cleaned their trowels and circulated glasses of sugary tea. The masons squatted perilously on the top of the narrow walls, flanked on one side by a drop into the steep staircase and on the other by a far more menacing plunge to the street. Seemingly unperturbed by their location, they busily laid units of masonry in fresh beds of mortar, pausing regularly to check the evenness of the coursework with a water level and the verticality of their rising structure with a plumbline.

Like the ancient freestanding minarets of the Old City, those that Muhammad and Ahmad built were composed of three parts: a high four-sided plinth that supported a multifaceted round tower capped by a dome. The Maswaris characteristically constructed their plinths in black volcanic stone and their towers and domes in kiln-baked brick (a few exceptions were built entirely in stone). Once the minaret's plinth was completed, the masons suspended a giant brass emblem from an iron chain over the ground-level doorway. Its fine calligraphic script read 'ma shaa Allah' (What God Wills), invoking God's protection for all who entered and worked on these dangerous building sites.

It was a gruelling six-day workweek, starting early morning and finishing before the sunset call to prayer. We had a short break in the morning for tea and breakfast and a longer one for lunch, which regularly involved sharing a stone bowl of bubbling-hot *saltah* and flatbread. After eating, we ventured into the *suq* to buy bundles of *qat* (*Catha edulis*, a mild stimulant) and the masons and labourers masticated cheekfuls of the bitter leaf all afternoon while working. As the hours wore on, the lively chatter, banter and rhythmic choruses of *hajl* work songs gave way to silence and introspection. The calm was periodically shattered by sharp commands from above for 'more bricks and mortar' or by cries of warning that empty buckets were being hurled down the staircase for refilling.

Muhammad, the elder of the two Maswari brothers, assumed responsibility for the bespoke design of each minaret. The patron's budget determined the height that could be feasibly built, but the mason resolved the dimensions and relative proportions of the three component parts, the exterior expression of decorative patterns and the style of dome. Muhammad did not produce measured drawings, but instead claimed that his designs, ornamented with interlocking diamonds and chevrons, were concocted in his mind's eye while sitting relaxed, chewing *qat*. Indeed, many Yemeni artisans and poets professed that the leaf roused their creative juices and focussed their thinking.[13]

Concerning the minaret's overall proportions, the master mason (*usta*) judged them to be correct when the tower, he said, 'fills my eye', animating his proclamation by slowly crossing his thumb and index finger in front of his right eyeball. When asked by members of the public to explain his skilled knowhow and designs, Muhammad responded by pressing forefingers to his temples and pronouncing: 'It is all in my head.' Such performances re-inforced commonly held beliefs that the city's building traditions were somehow conserved as mental templates by master craftsmen, making them living repositories of cultural heritage and Yemeni identity.

As an anthropologist, I took an interest in the social significance of these events for constructing professional personas, asserting expertise and bol-stering status. I quickly realised, however, that soliciting verbal descriptions of skills from fellow builders yielded little insight into their knowing-as-doing (or, equally, their doing-as-knowing). It was thus imperative that I supplement conversation and observation with assiduous reflection on my own embodied learning and on-site practices. To be clear, the purpose of that exercise was not to produce a 'reflexive autoethnography', but rather it served as an 'ethnographic tool' in my explorations of embodied learning.[14]

As the slender brick tower rose, the geometries of its exterior circum-ference were transformed, alternating between being perfectly circular, octagonal and hexadecagonal (sixteen-sided). The diameter of the internal stairwell remained constant from bottom to top, but the thickness of the tower walls was reduced by a full brick-width above the level of the pro-jecting calling platform. The radius of the stairs and the various radii of the minaret's changing external dimensions and geometries were measured out and repeatedly verified with a nylon cord that was either knotted or pierced with a nail at fixed points along its length. One end of the cord was fastened to an axial steel post upon which its length could be pivoted, like the arm of a giant compass. The vertical post was securely embedded at the core of the minaret's central masonry column, and its threaded ends allowed for it to be incrementally extended through the entire height of the tower, ultimately piercing the apex of the dome to support an enormous brass *hilal* crescent moon.

The Maswari brothers employed Muhammad's son Majid and another mason, Abdullah as-Samawi. Abdullah was not a family member, but, like Majid, he had trained under the Maswaris and was valued as a loyal and reli-able colleague. As the most junior in rank among the four, he was delegated the task of neatly infilling the thick masonry walls. Majid built the interior staircase wall and, with assistance from Abdullah and the site apprentice, he was also in charge of constructing the central column and assembling the masonry stair treads that were supported on spans of tamarisk timber. Muhammad and Ahmad executed the finely detailed brickwork of the minaret's public face, all the while orchestrating the team's activities and managing the business of building.

The head labourer and apprentice during the Addil minaret project was Saat, an earnest and somewhat dour young man who, when asked, guessed that he might be seventeen years of age. Intriguingly, no mason I encountered in Sanaa used *al-ghulaam al-mumahan* or any other standard Arabic term (or phrase) to label the role of 'apprentice'. The titleless role, with its associated privileges and responsibilities, was nevertheless recognised as the gateway to becoming a mason and was thus fiercely competed for amongst the highly motivated labourers. With no formal contract or training agreement, holding on to that position was a challenge. If and when the top labourer-cum-apprentice transgressed the rules of comportment or displeased the masons in any way, he risked being swiftly demoted and replaced – as would be Saat's fate at the next minaret-building project. The precarious nature of the role, I reckoned, contributed significantly to the young man's anxiety and hostility towards fellow labourers.

Saat hailed from Dhamar, like Abdullah as-Samawi and the other workers, and after nearly five years of dedication to the Maswaris, he rose to become – quite literally – the top labourer on the minaret. From his post on the uppermost stair, Saat brusquely relayed the masons' commands to the rest of the labourers distributed along the staircase below and he methodically regulated the upward flow of materials. He was vested with authority to rebuke his underlings when their rhythm of work faltered or if they fell out of line, and he did so with flair. Discipline was a defining feature of work with the Maswaris, at all levels of the hierarchy. Mastering self-discipline and the ability to subjugate others to one's control were essential competencies for moving up the chain of command.

It was also from Saat's coveted spot that he enjoyed privileged access to learning the craft and the trade. Working right next to the masons exposed the young trainee to techniques for trowelling mortar, laying stones and bricks, checking levelness and verticality, reinforcing walls with horizontal inlays of timbers, assembling stairs of equal risers and even treads, building up the central column, and using the nylon cord to produce and verify the tower's geometries. In cleaning, preparing and passing the tools, Saat got a first-hand feel for their physical properties, and, by repeatedly watching them in use, he developed a sense of their individual purpose and function. If there was a lull in the masons' activities or the men had abandoned their station for a break or to attend other business, then Saat seized the opportunity to pick up their tools and have a go – wisely on an inconspicuous patch.

From time to time, he was directed to assist Abdullah and Majid in their tasks or to chisel bricks for Muhammad's decorative work, thereby being sanctioned to learn and develop.

Repeatedly carving bricks into a fixed array of polygonal shapes with accurate dimensions and sharp edges was, I discovered, foundational to a mason's education. In creating those smallest units of the building assembly, Saat was not only engaging with the tools and the physical properties of the materials, but he was also learning about geometry, composition and spatial relations at a manageable, immediately graspable level. Practice and experimentation on units of that scale was also both safe and economically viable: making mistakes posed no threat to the structure of the minaret or to the project budget.

While working alongside Abdullah to infill the wall between its outer and inner surfaces, Saat was typically engaged in selecting fragments and pieces of broken bricks to fit the empty spaces, like a jigsaw puzzle. The apprentice was thereby gaining a hands-on understanding of assemblage in the horizontal planes of the brickwork. Aiding Majid to construct the spiral stairs further exercised Saat's thinking and practical problem solving in three dimensions and expanded his understanding of complex interconnecting geometries as well as structure.

Saat's progression from acquiring self-discipline as a labourer to handling and carving bricks, and onward to participating in the making of larger and increasingly complex structural components was all part of a broader training regime that would one day equip him with the ability to conceptualise and organise a minaret project in its entirety and at all scales of its assemblage. However, graduating to masonhood involved much more than mere technical proficiency; it required a command of social politics, economics and the managerial responsibilities of operating a building site. The masons did not forthrightly educate Saat in these matters, nor did they entertain questions or solicit his views when chatting together or with their clients or suppliers of materials. The apprentice was therefore obliged to 'steal' that knowledge by hanging about, vigilantly observing and listening, and covertly imitating his mentors.[15]

From the top stair, Saat was privy to the masons' talk of budgets, current prices, salaries, schedules and supply chains, as well as to their praise for and condemnation of individual team members and their often-harsh appraisals of competitors in the trade. He was also witness to the masons' conduct, postures and ways of speaking, which he awkwardly endeavoured to imitate. Muhammad al-Maswari, for example, played the patriarchal disciplinarian with the workers and could be sharp-tongued when issuing directives and reprimands. By contrast, when conversing with clients, suppliers or visitors to the site, Muhammad eloquently peppered his speech with Quranic verse and Islamic idioms, and he strictly observed midday prayer. Those outward displays of piety and moral comportment beneficially reinforced in the minds of clients and the general public a connection between the master mason and the religious structures that he and his family had come to specialise in making.

After an apprentice was declared a fully fledged mason, as Abdullah as-Samawi had been, his mentoring continued under the yoke of his master(s), sometimes for many years. This arrangement was typical of the building teams that I knew in Sanaa. During my twelve months there, both Majid and Abdullah were delegated growing responsibility and were periodically dispatched to oversee projects that were running in parallel with the minaret, including a new house for the Yemeni President's brother and a miniature five-metre-high minaret in a hamlet outside the city. For these junior masons, the licensed autonomy was instrumental to their developing confidence and prestige. Without the blood connections to his employers that Majid enjoyed, Abdullah's next hurdle would be to establish a separate clientele and thereby a modicum of professional and financial security to start up a business of his own. In the meantime, he would continue to earn and learn with the Maswaris.

Late one morning, sitting on the walls at the top of the Addil minaret and surveying the city's mushrooming modern skyline with Muhammad and Ahmad, I invited them to share their thoughts about the new office towers. Ahmad shrugged his eyebrows and dismissed them as 'no good', and then proceeded to sip his tea from a tin can. Muhammad turned his gaze towards the half-a-dozen or so concrete structures rising from nearby Zubeiry Street. After a drawn-out silence, he replied: 'This [the minaret] will be here for a long time after they [the concrete towers] have crumbled and disappeared. Our construction is *qaweey jidaan* [very strong] . . . We use brick and stone, and we don't need architects and their plans.'

Through direct physical engagement in masonry, Muhammad both realised and conceptualised form and space. In effect, ideas and planning took shape in the coordinated activities of his eyes, ears, hands and tools with the materials. The master craftsman derived immense satisfaction from his hands-on work and problem solving, and from the autonomy and control he exercised over the design and engineering of his creations. Muhammad also exuded a kind of spiritual pride, knowing that what he and his team built was for posterity.

A significant threat to small-scale enterprises like that of the Maswaris and other 'traditional builders' – or *bunaat al-taqleedeeya*, as they self-proclaimed in distinction to 'modern' contractors – was, and continues to be, reinforced concrete construction. When I visited one year after completing my fieldwork, the Maswari brothers confidently assured me that they would win the contract for erecting the minarets of the city's planned congregational mosque. When the gargantuan project finally did get under way, construction of the opulent Saleh Mosque (named for the sitting President) was managed by Western-style building contractors, and, like the prayer hall, its six soaring minarets were, lamentably, erected in cast-in-place concrete and dressed in a veneer of brick.[16]

For other Sanaani masons, and especially for those employed in carrying out conservation work on the Old City monuments, the thorniest challenge to their role and identity as craftspeople was the radical change to the pecking order among practitioners. In my review of a colleague's book on Sanaa's architectural heritage, I wrote:

> Traditional master masons, who for centuries presided unchallenged over both design and construction, were progressively side lined [during the 1990s and early 2000s] by the new 'paper professionals', including foreign and local architects, engineers, conservationists and contractors. The hands-on masters of building materials and technique were rendered 'unskilled' in the current operational setting, which demanded higher levels of literacy and numeracy than was possessed by the vast majority of masons. Project sponsorship demanded formal bidding procedures and came with requirements for a designated contractor (with a business bank account, which most masons did not have). Drawn plans, written specifications, and a scientific approach to managing heritage and the past became the norm. Consequently, the status of master masons on many sites was reduced to that of a contracted labourer.[17]

The passage testifies to a dismal truth that the deskilling of artisans is a phenomenon confined not strictly to industrialised nations and post-industrial societies. In fact, as discussed in the Introduction to this volume, while affluent countries, including the United Kingdom, witnessed a 'renaissance in craft' during recent decades, many communities of craftspeople in the Global South, including Yemen, have experienced growing marginalisation and faced economic peril as a consequence of the deluge of cheaper, mass-produced imported goods reaching their marketplaces. Reading William Morris reminds us that this state of affairs had already begun to unfold in the late nineteenth century. Assessing the impact of industrialisation and factory production on South Asia and its artisans, he wrote:

> So far-reaching is this curse of commercial war that no country is safe from its ravages; the traditions of a thousand years fall before it in a month; it overruns a weak or semi-barbarous country, and whatever romance or pleasure or art existed there, is trodden down into a mire of sordidness and ugliness.[18]

Military conflict, too, lays waste not only to the extant material culture and heritage of a place, but also to the histories and practices that produced it. At the turn of the millennium, political stability and security in Yemen steadily deteriorated, resulting by 2015 in a devastating civil war of unprecedented consequences and intensified by the brutal intervention of rival international alliances. Prior to that chain of catastrophic events, I had been immensely privileged to enjoy such a rich experience of hands-on work with the minaret builders. This laid the groundwork for an apprentice-style field method that I would employ in subsequent studies with craftspeople in other parts of the world, including the city of London, where I resided.

REFINING AN APPRENTICESHIP METHOD IN DJENNÉ, MALI

As a labourer in Sanaa, I gained access to a unique community of practice[19] and was thus able to engage and collaborate more closely with my subjects of study. That role also allowed me to occasionally indulge in the creative handwork of carving bricks while being immersed in activities that provoked ruminations on the nature of skill and on the widely shared human aspiration to do work that is at the same time challenging, useful, fulfilling and pleasurable.

In this section, I offer a brief account of my fieldwork in Djenné, Mali, with further comparative reflections on my research in Yemen, before more fully expounding the benefits and opportunities that training and working alongside the subjects of my study offered, as well as the challenges and drawbacks it posed.

A grant from the British Academy returned me to a town in Mali that I first visited when backpacking solo across West Africa in the 1980s. Nestled in a weave of gentle waterways along the Bani River, Djenné was once a powerful centre of trade and Islamic scholarship. During the annual rains, the town becomes an island, naturally defended by a riparian landscape where local residents fish and cultivate fields of rice and vegetables. Annual deposits of alluvial silts are rich in organic materials that act as binders and soil stabilisers. The deposits are therefore ideal for manufacturing the mud bricks, mortar and plasters of Djenné's world-renowned architecture.

The town's equivalent to the Eiffel Tower is its grand mosque, reputed to be the largest single mud-brick building in the world, and famously depicted on postage stamps and postcards printed since the earliest years of French colonial administration.[20] The mosque sits at the centre of the old town, surrounded by densely populated urban quarters of one- and two-storey mud-brick houses built in the historic Tukolor and 'Moroccan' styles. The integrity of the historical ensemble made Djenné an icon of UNESCO's World Heritage programme. Its status was granted in 1988, but regrettably Djenné was moved on to the list of World Heritage in Danger in 2016. Four years earlier, the political stability and security of that once-enchanting country dissolved in the violence of a coup d'état, a renewed Tuareg insurgency, escalating ethnic tensions and the jihadi activities of competing Islamist terror cells.[21] At the time of this publication, the troubles in central Mali continue unabated. Like my experience in Yemen, I was privileged to spend time in Djenné during a period of political stability, national pride and cultural exuberance.

Between 2000 and 2002, I spent two fieldwork seasons constructing, repairing and plastering mud houses with an esteemed team of local masons. That and subsequent annual visits to Djenné enabled me to carefully consider the intricate combination of handiwork and social knowledge, and the ways in which craft skills were communicated on site and across generations.[22] Their professional community was organised through the centuries-old guild-like *barey ton* (literally, masons association). The *barey ton* was chaired by the *barey bumo* (chief of masons), who was elected by senior members of the trade. Masons claimed that each household in the old town was contractually bound to an individual mason or family of masons for all of its major building works, and that these ties of patronage endured over many decades and longer. When masons retired or died, they willed their client list and related responsibilities to select disciples whom they mentored, and who may or may not have been kin.

Like Zaria and Sanaa, a mason's tuition in Djenné was grounded in a practical apprenticeship as opposed to an institutional training. My separate bodies of research in these places point to the fact that apprenticeship is not a unitary, unchanging system. Programmes of training and learning, trade hierarchies and social relations between actors, and opportunities and trajectories for professional progress are all conditioned by the prevailing environmental, economic and political conditions of a time and place. Despite variations in form and content, the apprenticeship systems I documented supplied a rounded education. They honed managerial and business skills, and inculcated professional ethics and correct comportment, while endowing young men with the complex set of technical skills for creating dwellings, monuments and urban landscapes to which residents of the respective towns attached shared meaning and a sense of ownership.[23]

Typically, the first major test for a masonry apprentice in Djenné was to construct a brick wall that was perfectly vertical and structurally sound. If there were flaws, then he had to dismantle the wall and begin anew, but if he succeeded and could do so repeatedly, then his master presented him with a plumbline. This elementary tool heralded the young man's rising status towards masonhood. If and when the master judged his apprentice to be competent in all undertakings on a building site, he then announced his decision to make the mentee a mason at a meeting of the *barey ton*. He could safely rely on receiving unanimous endorsement for his verdict. In fact, the decision concerning the young man's qualifications will have been a shared one. Throughout their training, apprentices were seconded to other masons and so, in effect, the members of this close-knit community collectively contributed to the formation of the young man's skill and conduct. Learning was therefore not restrained within a one-on-one master–apprentice relationship, but was embedded in a rich social and professional network through which apprentices circulated.

In addition to basic construction techniques, masons also taught trusted apprentices to recite benedictions that protected the building team and worksites from harm and that warded off curses cast by powerful rivals. Their benedictions comprised a mix of *bai quaré* (Quranic-based knowledge) and *bai bibi* (literally 'black-skin' knowledge, referring to animist powers), and they sometimes employed amulets and objects blessed by *marabouts* (Muslim holy men) in laying foundations and constructing walls. Over the course of his career, a master mason accumulated a cache of secret rites to exorcise the land and buildings of evil *djinn* spirits and to guarantee the integrity of the edifices he erected. Magic was therefore deemed to be as vital to making sturdy buildings as the mortar between bricks.

Perhaps more than in any other Malian town, Djenné's architectural heritage displayed a strong sense of historical continuity. But like any place, tradition and continuity were necessarily entangled in relationships with modernity and change. Through training and practice, the town's masons learned to respond creatively to the changing aspirations and lifestyle choices of the inhabitants and to diminishing supplies of full-length Borassus palm timbers. As a rule, their individual creativity did not react against Djenné's traditional architectural styles, but rather was responsive to it. Improvisations and small innovations in structure, layout or decoration expanded and embellished the repertoire of architectural expression by producing its own articulation within the discursive boundaries of 'tradition'. The creative ingenuity of Djenné's most prominent masons therefore grasped tradition as a dynamic resource, not a static code of predetermined possibilities.

Over the course of two building seasons, I worked with two different teams, both headed by talented men of the Kouroumansé family. With them, I built a two-storey extension to an historic house, reconstructed a second historic house in the old city and erected a new spacious two-storey residence outside of town, located at a tranquil spot on the banks of the Bani River. Like my fieldwork in Sanaa, my role for the most part was assisting the labourers to relay materials to the masons and their apprentice, including woven baskets of thick, oozing mud mortar, hefty sun-dried mud bricks and lengths of prickly palm timbers that were used for constructing ceilings and staircases.

Also as in Sanaa, I elected to work unsalaried so as not to deprive a local man of the wages that I might have received. There were tactical motives, too, behind that choice. First, my voluntary labour allowed me to negotiate a somewhat more flexible work schedule when my aching body demanded rest or when I needed time to quietly contemplate what I had observed and experienced on site and flesh out my fieldnotes. Importantly, it also gave me the chance to pose questions from time to time; in short, to engage in an exchange of toil for ethnographic knowledge. In Yemen, the Maswari brothers entertained my curiosity insofar as it did not interrupt the rhythms of work, but if any other labourer had solicited information, the masons would have interpreted it as a challenge to their authority and chided the young man. By comparison, the hierarchy in Djenné was less rigid and social interaction was generally more affable. The enquiries that I put to the Kouroumansé brothers frequently generated wider discussion and competing commentary among all present. That, of course, was invaluable to forming nuanced anthropological understandings of key issues.

I never petitioned to be, nor was I officially ordained, an apprentice. Had I been, I would likely have robbed someone of a prized training opportunity and a future livelihood. It was clear in the minds of the masons that I was there, on site, for a fixed period. My labour was offered without guarantees of long-term dedication to the trade, except for the publications or other forms of representation that I would produce about it and its practitioners.[24] I was thus unworthy, for the most part, of the masons' full investment of training time and technical resources.

Exceptionally, however, one of the Kouroumansé brothers, al-Haji, did take me under his wing as an apprentice of sorts. He regularly made time to instruct me in handling the trowel and overtly demonstrated the more complex tasks he performed, which were occasionally accompanied by explanation. Al-Haji was a born teacher and was determined that I learn the trade thoroughly in order to represent it accurately. So, although I was not a trade apprentice in the full sense, my fieldwork did constitute a dedicated apprenticeship in the daily procedures and routines and in learning about the working lives of the masons and their labourers.[25]

A decade later, when al-Haji and I met in the Netherlands to make a documentary film together,[26] he proudly presented me with masonry tools and traditional mason's garb. In the presence of his accompanying colleagues, he declared me a 'mason'. This, he said, was not because I was an accomplished practitioner of the craft, but because I had succeeded in publishing a book that promoted international awareness and respect for what they did.

In Sanaa, by comparison, the security of my status as a trainee and labourer had been altogether different. Intrigues circulated among residents of the Bir al-Azab quarter concerning my true motivations for working on a minaret. One morning, several months into my fieldwork, the masons tersely denied me access to the construction site. I soon discovered that I stood accused by neighbourhood gossipmongers of spying on government buildings from my perch on top of the minaret walls. An astute intervention by a Yemeni official on my behalf resolved the matter quickly, but traces of uncertainty lingered.

Notably, the Maswaris also harboured suspicions that I might export my learning to London, where I would profitably build brick minarets in imitation of theirs. After all, in reproducing their skillset in others, master craftspeople run the real risk of proliferating their own competition.[27] It was therefore essential for masons in Yemen, and in Mali, to scrutinise those admitted to apprenticeships and to strategise as to what trade knowledge to reveal and when. In addition to the objective of striking a favourable balance between their investment in training and the return in productivity from trainees, masons also needed to regulate apprentice numbers in light of fluctuating market demand for the trade skills. In Chapters 2 and 3, I will discuss the ways that carpenters similarly regulated apprenticeships in medieval and early modern London.

On the Djenné building sites, steady participation in the daily grind resulted in my being swiftly absorbed into the community of practice, thereby minimising the impact of my presence on the behaviour, language and interactions of my fellow workers and trainees. Working closely alongside the men over long periods also allowed me to monitor and scrutinise my evolving role within the team dynamics and to take account of that in my analyses. While generating plentiful and varied data, continual physical engagement did demand speedy methods for scribbling notes between arriving basketloads of mud or bricks. It also presented obstacles to making sketches, sound recordings and photography. I therefore scheduled periodic interludes in the workday to record with my camera and I reserved ample quiet time at the end of each afternoon to turn hastily made records and fresh memories into detailed longhand accounts and measured drawings.

Crucially, labouring while learning gave me a 'real' role: one that was immediately understandable and valued by my fellow builders, and that tangibly enhanced the resources and capacity of the team. In effect, I was transformed from 'foreign outsider' to team member and, in the process, established relations of mutual trust and long-term friendships. Insights into the experiences of co-workers were vastly enriched by reflecting on my own learning challenges, mistakes and progressions; by dwelling in the exhilaration of physical work or in the monotony and the physical pain that many of our collective tasks entailed; and by enduring bone-chilling mornings, intense afternoon heat, dehydration and pangs of hunger, and the blinding, stinging dust storms that blanket the West African Sahel during winter months. Occasional bouts of illness or bodily injuries were evidently best avoided, but those experiences, too, provided windows onto the hazards of the trade.[28]

Labouring also supplied direct access to everyday conversation, lively banter, playful competition, social jousting and heated disputes, as well as to moments of shared laughter or the giddy euphoria that erupts in overcoming a group challenge or completing a task together. Equally, it rendered me subject to the hierarchies of authority on site and to being disciplined, which, aside from being humbling, directly exposed me to the relations of power and techniques of coercion. All of these fluid exchanges revealed views, opinions, temperaments and ways of being that often differed to those encountered in my formal interviews with the very same men. I could thus come to know my individual colleagues as rounded persons, with all their human complexities and contradictions as well as their charms, charisma and humour.

In Mali, I became closely acquainted with the men's social circles beyond the workplace, including their families, friends and neighbours. While meeting and interacting with masons' wives was permissible in Djenné, it was not so in Sanaa where the separation of male and female social spheres was highly regulated. Construction work in both places was a strictly male occupation, and thus my ethnographies contain detailed accounts of competing masculinities, but, admittedly, offer a dearth of insights into the lives of Malian or Yemeni women.[29]

A shortcoming in working tightly with small cohorts of masons was that it curtailed opportunities to survey the broader spectrum of practitioners in either Djenné or Sanaa. This means that my ethnographic accounts of site dynamics and individual lives cannot claim to be representative of the entire mason communities of those places. In point of fact, that was never my objective. My goal as an anthropologist was to better understand the ways that learning and making unfold in direct relation to the immediate given context and environment.[30] The same holds true for the study with carpenters at London's Building Crafts College, which is the central focus of Chapter 4 onwards.

The long training with British fine woodworkers further expanded my thinking about skill learning, but it also reinforced much of what I had gleaned during previous studies in Nigeria, Yemen and Mali about the relationship craftspeople have with their work. Characteristically, masons in all three locations were focused individuals, keenly observant, deliberate in their execution and adept at critically assessing the fruits of their labour. They could also be fastidious, obsessive, sometimes short-tempered, judgemental, somewhat guarded and (entertainingly) cynical. But, most prominently, they shared an enthusiasm for their trade, took pride in their creations, and readily assumed responsibility for the integrity and durability of their structures.

It does not follow that the pleasure these men experienced in making things is universally felt among craftspeople. Some anthropological studies in other social and cultural contexts in fact convey the overwhelming sense of drudgery and dissatisfaction that artisans experience in their working lives,[31] or the denigrated positions they occupy in their societies.[32] In exposing the 'Luddite fantasy' of America's artisanal golden age, Donovan Hohn speculated that:

> Homespun textiles required endless, mind-numbing cottage industry. Likewise the churning of butter, the curing of meat, the hewing of beams and chiselling of mortises. No wonder so many of our agrarian forebears fled to cities at the first chance they got, or else bet the farm on motorised combines and harvesters.[33]

While my mason colleagues did grumble about aching muscles and sore backs, about monotonous, repetitive tasks and about mediocre wages, their complaints were outweighed by the autonomy they enjoyed as sole traders (i.e. self-employed tradesmen) and by the authority and control they wielded over seeing projects through from start to finish. All of the masons I had the privilege of working with were inquisitive men by nature, and their craft offered scope for continuous experimentation, learning and development. It was that opportunity, more than the prospect of financial gain, that propelled them towards attaining and sustaining self-actualisation.

My own learning and development as both craftsman and anthropologist continued closer to home, with full-time training alongside fine-woodwork students at the Building Crafts College in East London. The next two chapters supply rich historical background, first to the ancient Worshipful Company of Carpenters and next to the college that they founded in 1893. These chapters also tell the captivating story of apprenticeship training in England and the many major transformations that this system of learning underwent between the thirteenth century and the dawn of the new millennium.

NOTES

1. See Marchand, 'Muscles, Morals and Mind'.
2. Ibid., 249. See also Coy, *Apprenticeship*. In reviewing the 'sensorial revolution' that followed the 'corporeal turn' in anthropology, David Howes intriguingly suggested that the new fieldwork is grounded in a methodology of '"participant sensation" as opposed to "observation"', which promises to reveal 'alternative psychologies of perception' (Howes, 'Charting the Sensorial Revolution', 121).
3. In fact, I attended what is called CEGEP (Collège d'enseignement général et professionnel). CEGEP is a publicly funded pre-university college system unique to the Canadian province of Québec.
4. In addition to CIDA, I also thank the Emir of Zaria for his kind permission to carry out fieldwork, colleagues at Ahmadu Bello University for the academic support they lent, and Dr Shaibu Garba for his warm hospitality and friendship throughout my stay in Nigeria.

5. Marchand, 'Gidan Hausa'.
6. Schwerdtfeger, *Traditional Housing*.
7. Interview with the Sarkin Magina of Zaria, 5 November 1992.
8. This abridged account is based on Marchand, *Minaret Building*; Marchand, 'Muscles, Morals and Mind', 245–71; and Marchand, 'Minarets of Sanaa'.
9. Anthropologist François Sigaut noted in 1993 that up until that time, good ethnographic studies of apprenticeship were 'few and far between'. This he thought 'strange' given that so many anthropologists/ethnologists whose 'works were meant to be useful for preserving *les savoir-faire menacés*' (threatened kinds of knowhow) failed to make apprenticeship a central 'topic of interest in their fieldwork' (Sigaut, 'Learning, Teaching, and Apprenticeship', 105 and 110).
10. The foiled attempt of Yemen's security forces to rescue kidnapped tourists in 1998 and the bombing two years later of the *USS Cole* in Aden's harbour signalled a major shift in the country's stability. From 2000, headlines about Yemen were increasingly dominated by news of hijackings, militarised cells of Islamic extremists, a coup d'état, political turmoil and, from March 2015 to the time of writing, the atrocities of a Civil War that has decimated livelihoods and heritage, and generated one of the world's worst humanitarian crises in modern history. See Marchand, 'Review Essay'.
11. Medieval sources allege that the renowned Ghumdan Palace was 20 storeys high and was built for the Sabaean King Ilsharah Yahdub (Lewcock, 'Early and Medieval Sanaa', 32).
12. See Marchand, 'Walling Old Sanaa'.
13. On the social and ritual uses of *qat* in Yemen, see Weir, *Qat in Yemen*.
14. For a discussion of this issue, see Wacquant, 'Habitus as Topic and Tool'. See also Downey, Dalidowicz and Mason, 'Apprenticeship as Method', 195. All three authors employed an apprentice-style method in their anthropological fieldwork.
15. See Michael Herzfeld on Cretan apprentices 'stealing' knowledge (Herzfeld, 'It Takes One to Know One').
16. The mosque was inaugurated in 2008 and built at a staggering cost of US$60 million. The UN reported that same year that 37 per cent of Yemen's population was malnourished and nearly 50 per cent were living below the poverty line.
17. Marchand, 'Review Essay', 52.
18. Morris, 'How We Live', no pagination.
19. Lave and Wenger, *Situated Learning*.
20. See Marchand, 'The Djenné Mosque'.
21. See Marchand, 'For the Love of Masonry'.
22. See Marchand, *The Masons of Djenné*.
23. Marchand, 'Muscles, Morals and Mind'.
24. In addition to the numerous publications I produced on the masons of Yemen and Mali, I also curated museum exhibitions dedicated to them and their work. These include: *Djenné: African City of Mud* at the Royal Institute of British Architects, London (2010); *Mud Masons of Mali* at the Smithsonian National Museum of Natural History, Washington DC (2013–present); and *Buildings That Fill My Eye: Architectural Heritage of Yemen* at the SOAS Brunei Gallery, London (2017), the Museum of Oriental Art, Turin (2017) and the Pergamon Museum, Berlin (2018). I also produced/directed documentary films, including *The Future of Mud* (2007, with S. Vogel and S. Sidibé) and *Masons of Djenné* (2013, for the Smithsonian National Museum of Natural History).

25. Similarly, Downey, Dalidowicz and Mason note: 'We hope to achieve, not mastery, but a more intimate knowledge of the paths that lead to mastery.' ('Apprenticeship as Method', 185).

26. Due to the sudden eruption of troubles in Mali in 2012, five masons of different rank were flown to the Netherlands, where I directed a series of four short documentary films for the Smithsonian National Museum of Natural History with assistance from the Rijksmuseum voor Volkenkundé in Leiden. See https://www.youtube.com/watch?v=XiHOqxo5tpc (retrieved 25 May 2021). For an account of the filmmaking process, see Marchand, 'Diary of Filmmaking'.

27. On this point, see also Lancy, '"First You Must Master Pain"', 114.

28. In Djenné, membership dues were paid to the *barey ton*, which managed a collective fund to support (in a small way) ill, injured or aged masons. Such financial security did not extend to apprentices or labourers.

29. See Downey, Dalidowizc and Mason, who likewise comment that, while apprenticing: 'Whole portions of the local population may be excluded from the ethnography because the community of practice specifically insulates training from outsiders' ('Apprenticeship as Method', 187).

30. See Downey, Dalidowicz and Mason for a discussion of this issue on 'representativeness' in their own choices of field sites and communities of study (ibid., 186–87).

31. See, for example, Venkatesan, 'Learning to Weave'.

32. See for example Herzfeld, *The Body Impolitic.*

33. Hohn, 'A Romance of Rust', 46.

CHAPTER 2

THE CARPENTERS' COMPANY AND EARLY LONDON APPRENTICESHIPS

The contemporary boundaries of the 'City' define the 'Square Mile',[1] a densely urban and endlessly intriguing area that marks the place of London's Roman beginnings on the River Thames and its subsequent growth into one of the wealthiest and most populous cities of the medieval world. Today, international banking and finance generate the City's fortunes, but historically its riches were rooted in the brisk trade of local wares and imported merchandise, and, notably, in the bustling enterprises of London's craftspeople.

This first of two historical chapters delves into London's past to describe the emergence of the powerful livery companies in combination with the formalisation of apprenticeships. The liveries, as corporate associations of craftspeople, arose in the late medieval period from humble beginnings as fraternities, whose members plied a common trade.[2] My story naturally centres on the City's carpenters. The opening historical account, spanning the thirteenth century to the Great Fire of London, supplies a backdrop to my subsequent discussions about the activities of the Carpenters' Company during the early modern period, which extended well beyond regulating the trade. These included property acquisitions, charitable endeavours and a growing active interest in education and vocational training, especially from the nineteenth century to the present day. The significant role played by the Company in education and its establishment in 1893 of the Building Crafts College – the site of my long fieldwork – is the subject of Chapter 3.

THE EMERGENCE OF THE LIVERIES

'The Square Mile' is a distinct polity and administered in a unique fashion. In 1215, King John granted the commune of the City of London a royal charter to elect its own mayor each year,[3] with the requirement that the mayor travel from the City to Westminster to swear loyalty to the Crown.[4] A court of aldermen and a court of common council underpin the City's political structure, and, since the early fifteenth century, Guildhall has served as its ceremonial and administrative centre. Annually, senior members of the City's 'Worshipful Livery Companies' elect fellow high-ranking liverymen to the highest offices of Lord Mayor and Sheriff.[5] In so doing, the electoral powers of liverymen have for centuries guaranteed the political representation and status of their respective companies.

The term 'livery' refers to both the distinctive uniform worn by members, servants or officials of a worshipful company and to the collective members of that association. Liveries are the descendants of earlier craft and trade guilds (or 'misteries'), which had evolved from parish fraternities. The early dividing lines between fraternities and guilds were in fact often ambiguous. The more clearly defined liveries arose in the late medieval period as corporate companies under royal charters.

Royal charters bestowed legal rights upon the liveries as well as responsibilities for regulating apprenticeship training, wages, business and standards in their respective industry. These privileges and duties were exercised within the boundaries of a defined territory, which included the entire City and an adjacent peripheral region. The latter variously extended between one and four miles (1.6 and 6.4 kilometres) beyond the walls and gates, depending on the dictates of the prevailing charter at the time.

From the thirteenth century onwards, the craft misteries-cum-liveries formulated rules and compiled ordinances for orderly governance and for ensuring that practising members upheld standards. The early ordinances empowered the company master and its wardens to 'oversee, search, rule, and govern to commonality and mistery, and all men occupying the same, their servants, stuffs, works and merchandizes' within the City of London and its suburbs and precincts.[6] On being approved by the mayor and aldermen, craft ordinances became City ordinances, and thus the means of control within the livery companies figured prominently in City law and custom.[7] In essence, the liveries of the late medieval and early modern eras were integral to the making of the City of London.[8]

Counted among the earliest of London's liveries, though not ranked as one of the so-called 'Great Twelve',[9] is the Worshipful Company of Carpenters. The first known study of the Great Twelve Livery Companies of London was carried out by William Herbert, Librarian to the Corporation of London (1828–45), and was published in 1836–37.[10] The earliest detailed history of a particular livery, however, was that published in 1848 about the Carpenters by the Company's clerk, Edward Basil Jupp.[11] The next major history of London's Carpenters appeared in 1968, authored by historians Bernard W.E. Alford and Theodore Cardwell Barker,[12] and that was followed in 1995 by Jasper Ridley's historical biography of the Company.[13] A recent major contribution to historical studies of London's Carpenters is that of Doreen Sylvia Leach, which investigates the organisation of the trade and the lives and livelihoods of its practitioners in the Late Middle Ages.[14] *The Carpenters' Company Broadsheet*, published biannually since 1991, has regularly included historical essays by archivist Julie Tancell, as well as current updates on the Livery's activities and its involvement in education and the wood trades.

These publications along with City records and other historical documents and a most informative interview with Liveryman, former Master (2002) and Chairman of the Building Crafts College Committee, Michael Montague-Smith,[15] served as key resources for constructing my account of the Carpenters in this chapter and my story of the College and twentieth-century vocational training regimes in Chapter 3.

THE CARPENTERS: EARLY BEGINNINGS

London's Worshipful Company of Carpenters received its first Royal Charter of Incorporation in 1477. The Charter officially validated the Livery as a legal body with jurisdiction over the trade in the City of London, and in its suburbs and precincts. However, a professional association of carpenters seemingly existed at a far earlier date.

The earliest suggested year for their association is 1271,[16] though this proposal was ostensibly extrapolated from the mention of a 'Master Carpenter' in the City of London records of that same year. It is clear from the London records, however, that two carpenters and two masons were sworn to the Office of City Viewer in 1301, by which time trade experts were increasingly called upon to assist the mayor and aldermen in dealing with citizen disputes concerning buildings, boundaries and obstruction of ways.[17] London was by now densely populated with some 80,000 inhabitants and established as England's greatest city and one of the most affluent in Europe. Because half-timbering was the dominant form of construction, the City provided a steady and busy schedule of lucrative work for carpenters, who in turn accrued capital and held influential positions.

In comparison with stone, timber was readily available from nearby forests and easier to transport and to work, thereby making it the more affordable building material. Half-timber framing with wattle-and-daub infill also supplied greater flexibility for modifying structures and adding upper storeys, which could be cantilevered over streets and alleyways to maximise the area of floor plates. Structural components, including posts, beams and roof trusses, were hewn from massive timbers and assembled with a variety of joints, as well as with nails and pegs. Large timbers were also used for making hoists, scaffoldings and temporary centrings for the construction of masonry arches.

Carpenters and their close cousins, the joiners (who belonged to a separate livery),[18] made gates, doors, window frames, staircases and other elements of architectural joinery, as well as most items of household furnishing, components for tools and weaponry, and even coffins. Carvers produced all manner of decorative elements in wood; wheelwrights made spoke wheels for wooden carts; coopers produced barrels; luthiers made wooden string instruments; and turners crafted musical wind instruments as well as vessels, wooden measures for victuals and drink, and cylindrical components for tables, chairs and railings.[19] For large-scale and public projects, the City and the Crown contracted carpenters to construct mills, bridges, wharves, city gates, stockades, wooden drainage gutters, gallows and spectator stands for tournaments and pageants.[20] In short, the medieval woodworker was in high demand, and the regularity with which fires occurred meant a steady stream of commissions.

Fourteenth-century London also threw up numerous challenges to entrepreneurial aspirations. On the heels of the Great Famine (1315–17) were recurring outbreaks of bubonic plague. The decimation of London's population in the grip of the Black Death, which peaked in the mid-fourteenth century in Europe, would presumably have had significant impact on the livelihoods of carpenters. At the same time, a high mortality rate created opportunities for those who survived and for skilled incomers (referred to as 'forrens') arriving mainly from the counties closest to London, but also from further afield in England and exceptionally from Ireland, Scotland, Wales and northern European countries.[21] As Leach noted, the Black Death was also 'a major impetus for the formation of fraternities and liveries', whose main function was to pray for deceased members and to ensure that they were 'buried with appropriate rites'.[22]

The first concrete evidence of the existence of a Brotherhood of the Carpenters of London is their *Boke of Ordinances*. This record of the rules and regulations by which the association was governed was allegedly drawn up in 1333.[23] The Brotherhood was made up of 'good men carpenters' and, typical of fraternities of the time, included their related women, some of whom participated in the running of family businesses or in managing them when widowed.[24] The Carpenters' *Boke* provided directives mainly for religious observances and burials, and for mutual help in poverty and sickness,[25] rather than rules and standards of carpentry practice. Although carpenters were obliged to present a potential apprentice to the master and wardens of the Company for their approval of the young man's fitness for the trade and future livery membership, only three of their thirty ancient ordinances specifically addressed apprentices.[26]

In 1388, the Carpenters submitted their *Boke* to King Richard II as part of a return to a writ made in compliance with the Crown's investigation into the foundation dates, organisational structure, social events and properties held by the guilds and fraternities of the country. This official submission may have marked an important point in the Carpenters' transition from their organisation as a fraternity to a professional association.[27]

There is no surviving evidence prior to 1438 that the Carpenters sent representatives to the City's Common Council at Guildhall and there are no extant craft records from before that year.[28] Nevertheless, other sources in addition to evidence of their 1388 submission do indicate that the carpenters were established and recognised as a professional association by at least the late fourteenth century. In *The Canterbury Tales* (1387–1400),[29] for instance, Geoffrey Chaucer described the following liveried members among the party of pilgrims who travelled from London to the shrine of St Thomas Becket in Canterbury Cathedral:

An Haberdasshere and a Carpenter
  [A haberdasher and a Carpenter]
A Webbe, a Dyere, and a Tapycer, –
  [A Weaver, a Dyer, and a Carpet/Tapestry-maker]
And they were clothed alle in o lyveree
  [And they were all clothed in one livery]
Of a solémpne and a greet fraternitee.
  [Of a solemn and a great fraternity (parish guild)]

Chaucer's inclusion of a carpenter supports the idea that practitioners of this trade, like other London craftspeople of the era, were not only organised as a fraternity but also enjoyed the status of a professional craft association.[30] Presumably many craftspeople and those entering the trades also enjoyed a certain level of financial privilege and social standing. The fees paid by apprentices in the thirteenth century for their training were considerable and 'could only have been paid by well-to-do families, which were able to set up their sons in business'.[31] Apprenticeship was, after all, the main route to a practical occupation or trade qualifications throughout the medieval and early modern periods.

In addition to technical instruction, a carpenter's trusted apprentice might be granted access to insights about managing the workshop, pricing the work or services, doing the accounting, and negotiating with timber merchants, ironmongers and glaziers, and he would learn to conduct himself in a satisfactory manner with patrons and clients. Apprentices received no wage,[32] but the master could be expected to sustain his mentee with food, lodging and clothing, and possibly offer a modicum of Christian moral guidance. Religious education would have also involved the young man's regular attendance at the local parish church.

In the late fourteenth century and first quarter of the fifteenth century, it is probable that the carpenters' association was based at the Hospital of St Thomas of Acre (or Acon) on Cheapside. Cheapside was the birthplace of St Thomas Becket and a popular venue in London for public gatherings, civic ceremonies and royal processions. The Hospital itself was a beneficiary of numerous endowments and chantries from eminent Londoners, and it served as a meeting place of professional associations. These included the Mercers (dealers in fine textile fabrics, or traders more generally), who established links with the Order of St Thomas and developed close relations with the Hospital.[33]

Unlike the Mercers, the Carpenters were not ranked among the Great Twelve, but they did come to possess one of the City's most substantial livery halls.[34] In 1429, the Carpenters moved to a site in Broad Street Ward, located at the northern edge of the City and within London Wall.[35] The site, formerly the possession of the Priory of St Mary Spital (also known as the Priory of the Blessed Virgin Mary-without-Bishopsgate), was developed with a great half-timbered hall together with three houses on the east side and one on the west.[36]

The Hall provided livery members with a place to meet, hold court and store records,[37] ceremonial regalia and material wealth, generally in the form of gold, silver and pewter plate.[38] Livery meetings were where the business of the craft was discussed, disputes settled, and penalties and punishments for misconduct meted out in the presence of the Company's Court.[39] The Carpenters were in a minority of liveries to have their own hall at such an early date. This they rented out to other associations that did not possess their own dedicated buildings for meetings, and thereby generated an income for the Company.

The property in Broad Street Ward has remained the site of Carpenters' Hall to the present day. The length of the Hall lies along London Wall (street) and has a prestigious address on Throgmorton Avenue, a private and gated street developed and shared with the Drapers' Company. The building and its surroundings, not surprisingly, underwent substantial modifications and reconstructions during the almost 600 years since they first settled there, some of which will be recounted in the following sections.[40]

The nearby church of All Hallows-on-the-Wall became the Carpenters' principal place of worship.[41] According to Jupp, the Company's annual election day of masters and wardens began with a high mass in the church, which was attended by all the fraternity. Mass was followed by voting at the Hall and a feast, during which the election results were announced and the new master and wardens were crowned. Festivities and entertainment reportedly continued into the evening with performances by minstrels and a 'monkish' play.[42]

CONSOLIDATION, FIRE AND CHANGING FORTUNES

The second half of the fifteenth century witnessed the Carpenters' official consolidation as a Worshipful Livery Company.

Like other liveries, the Carpenters paid contributions to a number of civic institutions and schemes, which included Guildhall, the periodic initiatives to feed London's poor, a fund for the City's protection against external threats and internal disorder, and England's military campaigns.[43] In the tradition of the fraternities, the Livery provided its members with a measure of social and financial security in times of sickness, injury or old age. It also conferred a schedule of responsibilities upon individual carpenters, including payment of quarterage fees and attendance at mass, social events and livery meetings. Together, these benefits and rules served as the social glue that bonded the community of craftsmen and their kin over many generations.[44]

Unlike the Brotherhood's fourteenth-century ordinances, those compiled by 1455 were less concerned with religious affairs and were more attentive to the everyday work of carpenters, exerting control over exclusionary rights for practising in the City and, notably, over apprenticeship training.[45] Taking up and successfully completing an apprenticeship was one of three ways to gain the 'Freedom' of the City of London, the others being patrimony and redemption through payment to a livery company. The Freedom, believed to have been first presented in 1237,[46] guaranteed freedom from serfdom and the right to carry on one's craft or trade in the Square Mile, to take on apprentices, to earn money and to own land.[47] As noted earlier, the Freemen of the Carpenters' Company played a leading role in the physical building of the City. Throughout the late medieval and early modern periods, the London carpenter, not the mason, was the master craftsman in the realm of domestic construction.[48] The trade accrued status.

In 1466, the Livery received its Grant of Arms – an exquisite document of fine calligraphic script on vellum with the coat of arms illuminated on the left.[49] Eleven years later, in 1477, King Edward IV granted the Carpenters their first Royal Charter of Incorporation.[50] The Charter defined the association as 'a body Corporate and Politic by the name of the Master, Wardens and Commonalty of the Mistery of Freemen of the Carpentry of the City of

London'.[51] While granting the Carpenters a monopoly and judicial powers over the practice of their trade within a delimited territory, as well as the right to receive bequests and gifts of property, the Charter also restricted them from engaging or meddling in the work of other craft and building trades.

All liveries were obliged to renew their royal charters on occasion, predictably with a change of monarch. The cost of renewal was dear and thus their issuance provided an important source of revenue to the Crown.[52] The Carpenters had theirs reconfirmed on a number of occasions between 1477 and 1944,[53] and these included new or updated clauses. The Charter bestowed in 1607 by King James I, for example, extended the Carpenters' jurisdiction to two miles around the City,[54] and that of Charles I in 1640 expanded it to a four-mile radius beyond the City walls.[55]

The Company's ordinances and bye-laws, too, were revised, first in 1487 and again in 1607.[56] Like the charters, these reaffirmed their rights and privileges over the trade as decreed, for example, in the latter:

> No person within the City, its suburbs and precincts, or two miles thereof, to exercise the trade of Carpentry unless he should have first been bound apprentice to the same trade, and served in the same by the space of seven years at the least, or otherwise orderly admitted to the fellowship, under a penalty of £3, one moiety to the use of the King and the other moiety to the Company.[57]

It is worth noting that the stipulation in the above clause that apprenticeships be a minimum of seven years is a reinforcement of the historically important Statute of Artificers.[58] The Statute was enacted by Parliament in 1563, under Queen Elizabeth I, to regulate prices, wage inflation,[59] labour mobility and the apprenticeship system itself. It represents a formative moment in the state's attempt to appropriate the liveries' jurisdiction and masters' powers over both trade business and education.[60] By restricting workers' abilities to move between employers and places, and by limiting exclusionary practices, Parliament's aim was to ensure a steady and adequate supply of skilled and qualified labour, especially during recurring periods of social unrest or epidemic. At the same time, the Statute also entrenched social-class divisions by stipulating a hierarchy of apprenticeship fees by trade. This restricted entry to the 'superior trades', such as the Mercers, Grocers or Drapers who worked in commerce, to the sons of wealthy and established families.[61] Carpenters, like masons, bricklayers, plasterers and other building craftsmen who performed manual work, were socially and economically relegated to the middling ranks of tradespeople.

In most towns and cities outside London, the nature and duration of craft training had been hitherto regulated by the local guilds, as were wages and prices. The Elizabethan Act, however, made it illegal to 'exercise any art, mistery or occupation now used or occupied within the realm of England and Wales except he shall have been brought up therein seven years at the least as an apprentice'.[62] The seven-year timeframe became reified and, to a certain extent, mythologised over the following centuries. Indeed, the idea that a 'proper' apprenticeship be seven years persists in the minds of some UK craftspeople to the present day – not unlike the magical thinking behind the belief that becoming a skilled craftsperson can be measured in '10,000 hours of practice'.[63]

In London, however, a handful of guilds had already enforced a minimum seven-year training, or longer, by the thirteenth century.[64] Apprenticeship in London was, after all, a means to gaining the much-coveted Freedom, and thus the city authorities, Guildhall, and the masters and wardens of the individual misteries had vested interest in regulating the duration and contractual obligations, and in limiting the number of apprentices a master craftsperson could train at any one time.[65] Apprentices, or more likely their families, paid a premium for the indentured training, and a price was also paid at Guildhall for enrolling the covenant made between the two parties.[66]

Evidence from the records shows that trade apprentices in early modern London were generally bound in their mid to late teens.[67] By the mid-sixteenth century, apprenticeship had become the principal route to the Freedom. The vast majority of apprentices were not native Londoners, but 'forrens': young men (and women)[68] hailing from all corners of the kingdom and small numbers coming from the continent.[69] Once they secured their indentures, apprentices had high stakes in protecting their rights to training and future paid work, and they played an active and, at times, a violent part in policing the activities of other forrens who illegally worked within the City limits or accepted lower wages.[70]

By the late sixteenth century, the average age of a carpentry apprentice in London was 19.5 years.[71] This may have been older than the norm for craft apprentices because of the strenuous physical demands of carpentry work.[72] It does mean that diligent carpenters could fulfil their legally binding indentures by their mid to late twenties and, according to City ordinances, they were eligible to gain the Freedom at the age of twenty-four. With this combination of qualifications a young carpenter could, in theory, join the Carpenters' Company, open a workshop and employ his own apprentices. In practice, however, this was near-impossible for the majority, who lacked the financial means and the full complement of business skills, social capital and clientele.

As England's largest city, London was also the country's most important single site of training.[73] Apprentices once constituted a significant proportion of London's 'mob'.[74] During the seventeenth century, for example, it is estimated that anywhere from 10 to 40 per cent of the City's adult male population were apprentices, and by the end of that century, it is believed that some 6.5 per cent of English teenage males journeyed to London to enlist in training with a master.[75] The ordinances of the crafts and trades therefore needed to be explicit in order to retain social and administrative order, limit new competition,[76] safeguard the stream of incomes derived from the existing system, and maintain standards of workmanship. The Carpenters 1607 ordinances, for example, confined its members to their own discipline and enforced a clear-cut division of labour among the building crafts:

> No person of the fellowship using the trade of Carpentry to take upon himself to intromitt or meddle himself with any bargain of the occupacions of Plumary [plumbers], Masons, Dawbinge [plasterers], Tilinge [tilers] or any other occupacion except yt be vppon his owne proper houses & vpon his owne Dwellinge house, under penalty of 20s more or less at the discretion of the Master and Wardens.[77]

Individual craftsmen, too, were motivated to protect their individual business interests and hedge against surplus competition. They did so by limiting the number of apprentices they took on or, more rarely, by admitting only kin or the sons of close acquaintances.[78] Masters also retained the authority to prolong or cut short the training period or to restrict a young man's access to the full skillset needed in order to one day set up independently. Some masters were also guilty of abusing their apprentices, depriving them of sustenance or misappropriating their labour, and thereby diminishing their chances of fulfilling their indentures and gaining the Freedom.

As previously mentioned, the freemen of the Carpenters' Company played leading roles in the physical building of the late medieval and early modern City. Though most could be categorised as being in a middle-income bracket, some men became prosperous and experienced upward social mobility.[79] From the late fifteenth century, the Carpenters' Livery was firmly established. They profited from a steady stream of quarterage payments and they enjoyed the prestige of having their own Great Hall, which, along with the adjacent houses, earned rents. A past master of the Company secured the freehold for the land on which the Hall sat in 1519–20 and soon after endowed it to the Carpenters in his last will and testament.[80] Their assets were further supplemented by bequests (especially of plate of precious metals) and endowments of property.

Rising levels of wealth allowed the Carpenters to carry out repairs and major redecoration of their Hall in 1561–62. According to Jupp, these works included the creation of four wall paintings, three of which survive and are prominently displayed in the contemporary Hall on Throgmorton Avenue. They were painted with distemper on a thick layer of straw-reinforced mud, which was supported on wooden laths and prepared with lime plaster. The four paintings depicted biblical scenes from the Old and New Testaments that feature carpentry: Noah and his sons building the Ark; Josiah, King of Judah, enthroned and ordering the rebuilding of the Temple (2 Kings 22); Joseph at work as a carpenter while the child Jesus gathers sticks of wood in a basket and Mary sits spinning at a wheel; and Jesus as a young man teaching in the synagogue, which is accompanied by the question posed by his fellow Nazarenes: 'Is not this the carpenter's son?' (Matthew 13:55, King James Bible).[81] The wall paintings were probably concealed at some point in the seventeenth century when, as noted by Jupp, Puritans condemned representations of 'persons of the Trinity or of the Virgin' as being superstitious. The artworks were rediscovered in December 1845 by workmen carrying out repairs to the Hall.[82]

Fortunes began to ebb for the Carpenters during the last decades of the sixteenth century, as new construction became increasingly regulated for reasons of overcrowding, moral decline, disease control and, ultimately, to safeguard the monarch. In 1580, in an attempt to curb the rampant growth of London, a proclamation was issued from Nonsuch Palace by Queen Elizabeth I against the erection of any new building within three miles of the City gates. This garnered the support of the Lord Mayor, aldermen and other 'grave wise men' of the City. Without mincing its words, the proclamation:

> doth charge and straightly command all manner of persons, of what qualitie soever they be, to desist and forbeare from any new buildings of any house or tenement within three miles from any of the gates of the said citie of London, to serve for habitation or lodging for any person, where no former house hath bene knowen to have been in the memorie of such as are now living.[83]

Any person found to be contravening the law, including the workmen, would 'be committed to close prison'. Enforcing the proclamation proved difficult and many supplementary efforts were needed. In 1583, William Fleetwood, the Recorder of London, declared in a speech that in accordance with the law of the realm, houses would be pulled down to avoid 'the rages of fire'.[84]

The threat of fire was constant, and London had already by that point experienced devastating citywide blazes. Fire swept through London in 1087, destroying much of the Norman city, including St Paul's Cathedral (and that being the second time in just over 125 years). Much of the city lying between St Paul's and St Clement Danes in Westminster was ravaged by fire in 1135–36. Later that century, under King Richard I, the first known fire protection act in London was introduced by the City's first Lord Mayor, Henry fitz Ailwin. The measures aimed to regulate the height of partition walls between neighbouring buildings to prevent the spread of flames.[85] Regardless, in 1212, the most catastrophic blaze, known as the Great Fire of Southwark, spread from that borough and crossed the River Thames to the City on strong southerly winds, killing many trapped between the two banks on London Bridge.

For centuries to come, the outbreak of fire in houses, workshops, factories and stableyards continued to pose a serious menace to London.

By the early seventeenth century, more exacting measures promoting the use of masonry over timber were announced. Under King James I, it was decreed in 1605 that 'all persons henceforward' must 'build their forefronts and windows either of brick or stone'.[86] According to Jupp, this provoked struggles between the Carpenters and the Bricklayers 'involving merits of their materials'.[87] The proclamation, however, was made not merely to improve housing conditions and for the prevention of fire in the capital. Its parallel motive was to strategically protect timber supplies for other needs: 'by reason all great and well-grown woods are much spent and wasted; so as timber for shipping waxed scarce'.[88] The European Age of Exploration was flourishing, and English galleons plied the seas for trade and plunder, and naval fleets defended state interests. The building of these sailing vessels required tremendous quantities of timber, the supplies of which were dwindling. Notably, it was not the Carpenters' Livery but a corporate body of London Shipwrights and their main competitors, the Shipwrights of Redriff (i.e. Rotherhithe), who regulated the construction of galleons.

Like that of Elizabeth I, the edict of James I had little effect, and so the King issued further proclamations in 1607 and 1614 that included more stringent penalties for noncompliance. It may be argued that it was at this time that reformation of London's architecture and building fabric began, with more fire-resistant materials replacing the traditional use of wood in new and prominent buildings.[89] In 1630, King Charles I released a similar proclamation for the use of masonry,[90] but with additional prescriptions that wall thickness be a minimum of one and a half bricks, and that bricks be a uniform size, measuring 9 by 4⅜ inches (approximately 23 x 11 centimetres). These royal proclamations, however, could not be effectively enforced; meanwhile, London continued to attract 'hordes of migrants', many of whom resided in cramped and substandard dwellings.[91]

Insalubrious urban conditions contributed to periodic outbreaks of bubonic plague, which was endemic in seventeenth-century London. The plague reached its climax in the mid-1660s, killing an estimated 20 per cent of the City's population by the end of 1665, undoubtedly including many practising carpenters among the dead. In the second half of that year, just one apprentice was bound as a carpenter.[92] The Great Fire that broke out the following September was popularly believed to have eradicated bubonic plague from the capital,[93] but it also destroyed 80 per cent of the City's buildings: an estimated 13,200 houses, eighty-nine churches and fifty-two guildhalls, as well as civil administration buildings. The Carpenter's Livery Hall was fortuitously spared. As one of the few substantial buildings left standing, it was in demand by other liveries (including the Drapers, Goldsmiths, Feltmakers and Weavers) for their meetings and by four successive lord mayors.[94] These rents generated income for the Company until 1670.

The Great Fire of 1666 brought about enormous change to the construction industry and sparked a long decline in the status and authority of the City's working carpenters. As shrewdly noted by economic historians Alford and Barker, without its established property interests, it is unlikely that the Carpenters' Company would have survived. Already in 1630, the Carpenters purchased an estate on Hog Lane (now Worship Street), in the liberty of Norton Folgate. This was added to a growing portfolio of real estate. Hog Lane was managed by trustees drawn from the Company, and the rents received were used to assist the Poor of the Company and thereby ease the Livery's taxes.[95] By necessity, the Company underwent transformation after the Fire from a craft organisation to a modern livery, which meant a shift in focus from matters of the trade to matters of financial and property investment.[96]

Instrumental in forcing this change was the Rebuilding of London Act, drafted after the Great Fire and passed by Parliament in February 1667. The Act prohibited wooden buildings and required that all exteriors be constructed in brick or stone with the exception of door cases, window frames and shop fronts, the latter of which were 'left to the discretion of the Builder to use substantiall Oaken Timber instead of Bricke or Stone for conveniency of Shopps'.[97] Indeed, prohibitions against timber buildings in London remained in effect until 1999.[98] Overall, the new and detailed building regulations set out in the 1667 Act greatly profited masons, bricklayers and tilers for centuries to come at the expense of carpenters.[99]

The impact of diminished building contracts for carpenters was compounded by yet other adverse factors. The enormous demand for skilled and unskilled labour during the post-Great Fire period for rebuilding London brought a flood of forrens into the City, ultimately resulting in declining wages by the early 1670s.[100] Article XVI of the Rebuilding of London Act declared that all building craftsmen who were not Freemen could exercise their trade for the next seven years or until the rebuilding of London was completed. During that time, they would enjoy the same liberties as Freemen, and those who had spent seven years in that work would be made Freemen and could practise in the City indefinitely.[101] In several legal cases brought to the London Court by forren craftsmen, their indentures of apprenticeship to masters outside London were upheld, which materially and politically affected the Carpenters and other liveries.[102] Despite protests from liveries, including the Carpenters, Joiners, Bricklayers, Masons and Plasterers, the authorities refused to expel the forrens, who bolstered both the workforce and the City's dwindling population.[103]

After the last lord mayor vacated Carpenters' Hall in 1670, the Livery continued to lucratively lease its premises. Between 1673 and 1715, it was let to a 'Turkey Merchant' (i.e. a member of the Turkey Company, formed in 1581 to conduct English trade with the Ottoman Empire and the Levant)[104] and afterwards to 'a Citizen and Skinner, one Mr. James Fordham' for a term of 41 years.[105] The Hall was leased in 1850 to printers, who used it as a machine room and warehouse.[106] Already by 1739, the Carpenters' Company had ended its futile attempt to control the trade in London, and turned its attention to growing its prosperity as a livery and to charitable enterprises.[107]

THE CARPENTERS AS CHARITABLE BENEFACTORS

One of the original objectives of trade guilds was to provide relief for poorer brethren and sisters of the fraternity. Funds for this charitable activity were drawn from membership dues and from bequests of money, goods and property made by benevolent individuals.[108] In that same Christian spirit, the Carpenters' fourteenth-century *Boke of Ordinances* bound its members to making annual contributions of a fixed sum to be used for alleviating hardship of ill, injured or aged fellows of the Brotherhood. It also compelled carpenters to employ their fellow craftsmen who were without work.

The first recorded endowment of property was that gifted to the Company by one Thomas Warham in the fifteenth century. It comprised a house and four gardens in Lime Street, located south of Leadenhall Street in the heart of the City.[109] Changing religious attitudes during the sixteenth-century Reformation meant that fewer individuals were inclined to leave legacies to the Church, and so the Carpenters, like other secular associations, benefited from a rise in the number and size of endowments received.[110]

In 1618, timber merchant and three-times Master of the Company Richard Wyatt bequeathed a property at Henley-on-Thames, with the condition that the rents be used to pay allowances to thirteen poor women. On his death the following year, Wyatt left £500 for the building of almshouses and a chapel near Godalming, Surrey, for ten 'respectable' poor men from five local parishes.[111] The Wyatt Almshouses were built in 1622 and, having undergone refurbishments in 1958, operate to this day under the trusteeship of the Carpenters. Although the post-Great Fire era was financially challenging for the Carpenters, they nevertheless continued to pay pensions and make charitable donations.[112]

In 1767, the Company made one of its most important long-term investments: the freehold purchase of a sixty-three-acre rural estate in the Parish of West Ham, northeast of the City and close to the River Lea. At that time, the adjacent farming village of Stratford supplied London markets with fresh produce, and the Carpenters earned £126 per annum from rents on their land. The Stratford Estate was expanded in the early nineteenth century with the purchase of more acreage. Shortly afterwards, in the 1830s, the Carpenters sold parcels of the estate to railway companies. The profits reaped were considerable.[113]

Likewise, the aforementioned estate on Hog Lane, which had been purchased in 1630 for £660 and had yielded considerable income in rents, was sold in the early nineteenth century to railway companies. The substantial profits from that sale would eventually form the basis of one of the Company's chief charitable endowments. The Carpenters' Norton Folgate Trust, as named, was established in 2005 and the majority of its earnings are directed to education, including vocational training in carpentry and other building trades.[114]

New wealth enabled the Livery in 1840 to purchase land in Twickenham (which now forms a part of the Borough of Richmond) for building almshouses to accommodate ten 'poor' of the Company.[115] The Carpenters also rebuilt their Great Hall to replace the earlier structure, which had become dilapidated, further weakened by fire in 1849[116] and, in the estimation of Edward Jupp, 'devoid of all artistic or antiquarian interest'.[117] The old Hall and adjacent small houses on the property were demolished and the cornerstone for the new building was laid in 1876.[118] Both the Twickenham almshouses and the grand neo-Italianate Hall were built to the designs of liveryman William Wilmer Pocock, who was later elected Master of the Company. The new Hall incorporated various decorative timber fittings from its medieval predecessor and it contained one of the largest banqueting halls in the City, which was used for lectures and exhibitions as well as entertainment.[119] Another late-nineteenth-century Master, Henry Harben, founded the Rustington Convalescence Home in West Sussex and bestowed its governance to the Company upon his death in 1911.

Over the centuries, the Carpenters' Company thus came to manage properties in and outside London, administer almshouses and convalescence homes, make charitable donations and, notably, support education.[120]

In the next chapter, I explore the Carpenters' involvement in education, the establishment of their Trades Training School-cum-Building Crafts College, and the evolution of that unique institution over the course of the twentieth century in tandem with national developments in vocational training, and challenges to creating and sustaining a skilled labour force of British craftspeople.

NOTES

1. In fact, the colloquially named 'Square Mile' measures 1.12 square miles.
2. The Corporation of London speculates that the livery companies in England originated before 1066 (Corporation of London, *The Livery Companies*, 5).

3. Notably, the second elected Mayor, William Hardel, supported the rebellious barons and played a role in bringing King John to the negotiating table in 1215. He was one of the twenty-five signatories to the Magna Carta, which importantly includes clause 13: 'And the city of London is to have all its ancient liberties and free customs, both on land and water. Moreover we wish and grant that all other cities, boroughs, towns and ports are to have all their liberties and free customs.'

4. By the sixteenth century, the annual procession of the newly elected Lord Mayor had become an immensely popular event, and in 1937 it was one of the earliest outdoor events to be broadcast live on British television.

5. The title of Lord Mayor was first used in 1354, bestowed on Thomas Legge by King Edward III. The Lord Mayor is distinct from the more recent office of Mayor of London, which directs the entirety of Greater London. For a brief discussion of the roles of Lord Mayor, Alderman, Sheriff and Councilman, and the election process for these offices, see Kennedy Melling, *Discovering London's Guilds*, 23–26.

6. Jupp, *An Historical Account*, 134. The Charter granted by King James I in 1607 extended the powers of the Company with 'the oversight, search, correction, government, and reformation of all works, stuffs, things and merchandizes, concerning the art or mystery of Carpentry, and of their Measurers and Scantlings [timber beams of small cross section], to be put to sale within the prescribed limits, and also of all edifices, reparations, and buildings'. Powers were also granted to the Master and Wardens 'to enter into the premises of any freeman of the Company, or of anyone following the trade of a carpenter, to see if buildings and works were skilfully made, to seize and dispose of all improper stuffs, punishing the offenders; and upon application of any party grieved, to reform and correct the building works and reparations, or cause the same to be done' (ibid., 146).

7. Thomas, 'Introduction: Apprenticeship'.

8. There are presently 110 livery companies in the City of London and nearly forty livery halls.

9. As established in 1515, the Great Twelve Liveries of the City of London (also referred to as the 'Twelve Great') include in descending order of precedence the Mercers, Grocers, Drapers, Fishmongers, Goldsmiths, Merchant Taylors, Skinners, Haberdashers, Salters, Ironmongers, Vintners and Clothworkers. Based on economic and political influence, the Carpenters were ranked twenty-sixth out of the forty-eight Liveries in existence at the time.

10. Herbert, *History of the Twelve Great Livery Companies*.

11. Jupp, *An Historical Account*.

12. Alford and Barker, *A History of the Carpenters' Company*.

13. Ridley, *A History of the Carpenters' Company*.

14. Leach, 'Carpenters in Medieval London'.

15. Died 4 August 2017, aged eighty-three.

16. Jupp, *An Historical Account*, 8 and 187. See also http://www.carpentersco.com/history (retrieved 26 May 2021)

17. Chew and Kellaway, 'Introduction'. The regulations for building and property were set out in the *Assisa de Edificiis* (also known as *The Assize*), the earliest version of which is traditionally dated to the mayoralty of the goldsmith Henry fitz Ailwin (1189–1212). Chew and Kellaway note, however, that it is 'not possible, with one notable exception, to establish which parts of the *Assize* belong incontestably to a period earlier than the 1270s' (ibid.). Regarding the status of masons, the meticulous

research of D. Knoop and G.P. Jones suggests that a guild of masons probably did not exist in London much before 1376 (Knoop and Jones, 'Masons and Apprentices', 366) and that there are no extant Company records for the Masons prior to 1619 (Knoop and Jones, 'The Impressment of Masons', 58).

18. The Worshipful Company of Joiners and Ceilers was formed in 1375 and was granted its Royal Charter of Incorporation in 1571. Historically, they were separate from the Carpenters because they attach wood with glue, whereas carpenters use nails and pegs. The two companies had disputes over which should control what parts of the wood trade, and an especially extensive and expensive dispute took place in the seventeenth century (Alford and Barker, *A History of the Carpenters' Company*, 78–81). For Company records of the Carpenters' pleas to the Court to intervene and settle the disputes between them and the Joiners, as well as the Shipwrights and Sawyers, see Jupp, *An Historical Account*, Appendices B–F, 295–308.

19. The Worshipful Company of Wheelwrights was granted its Royal Charter in 1630, that of the Coopers in 1501 and that of the Turners in 1601. All three, however, existed as organized trade associations at much earlier dates.

20. Notably, the office of the King's Carpenter was established perhaps as early as 1256, during the reign of Henry III (Leach, 'Carpenters in Medieval London', 189), though Jupp suggested 1484, during the reign of Richard III (*An Historical Account*, 165). Humphrey Cooke was King's Carpenter to Henry VIII and was responsible for erecting the Field of Cloth and Gold in 1520 for the King's meetings with King Francis I in France (Worshipful Company of Carpenters, *The Carpenters' Company*, 2).

21. Leach, 'Carpenters in Medieval London', 71–75.

22. Ibid., 83.

23. *The Boke of the Ordinances of the Brotherhood of Carpenters of London, 7 Edward III (1333)*, transcribed and edited from the original in the Public Record Office by C. Welch, London, 1912. If the date of 1333 CE is correct, then the Carpenters would have been one of the earliest craft associations formed in London. However, based on some of the terminology used in the document, Leach queries the date, suggesting that it is too early and that the *Boke of Ordinances* was more likely created closer to 1388, when it was submitted to the Crown ('Carpenters in Medieval London', 82–83).

24. See Leach, 'Carpenters in Medieval London', 87 and 148–49; and Tancell, 'Women', 18.

25. The 1333 *Boke of Ordinances* required each member to pay 12 pence per annum to assist those who became sick or injured during work (Worshipful Company of Carpenters, *The Carpenters' Company*, 1).

26. Leach, 'Carpenters in Medieval London', 133 and Appendix 3, 252–257 (see paragraphs 19, 22 and 23). The source is Marsh, *Records of the Worshipful*, Vol. 2, 'Wardens' Accounts, 1438–1516'.

27. Leach, 'Carpenters in Medieval London', 81.

28. Ibid., 80.
    Jupp states that the Carpenters' Company was 'exercising usual functions as a trade mystery' by 1438 (*Historical Account*, 133). Leach notes that early fifteenth century wills and the City's administrative records supply evidence of the carpenters being organized as an association with 'officers, ordinances and livery' before that year ('Carpenters in Medieval London', 94). The Company records indicate that by 1442 there were ten freemen, and two years later the Company lists fifty members. The

first mention of a Master of the Company is 1458 and of a Clerk in 1470 (Jupp, *An Historical Account*, 133–34).

29. Chaucer, 'General Prologue', lines 363–66.

30. See McCutchan, 'A Solémpne'.

31. Thomas, 'Introduction: Apprenticeship', no pagination. Parish apprenticeships were established in 1692 for training 'pauper children'. Boys and girls of poor families were apprenticed to households to learn and perform mainly menial labour skills. Until 1767, such apprenticeships for boys lasted until they reached the age of twenty-four and for girls until they reached the age of twenty-one or married. An Act for the Better Regulation of the Parish Poor Children came into effect that year, limiting the duration of parish apprenticeships to seven years and designed to put checks on abuse by masters.

32. An exception to this rule was when the apprentice was taken to work on an outside job, under the direction of another master craftsman (see Leach, 'Carpenters in Medieval London', 134–35).

33. See Page, 'Houses of Military Orders', 491–95. The Mercers were incorporated under a Royal Charter of 1394 and their Hall is still located on Cheapside.

34. The Hall was a half-timber construction with wattle-and-daub infill and a tiled roof. For a detailed account of the acquisition of land and description of the construction, maintenance and decoration of the Hall based on the Carpenters' fifteenth-century *Accounts*, see Leach, 'Carpenters in Medieval London', 95–101.

35. The land on which the Hall was built had once been a tributary of Walbrook stream, which flowed toward the Thames and was a main source of water supply for Roman London. The Upper Walbrook silted-up from the twelfth century and became the property of St Mary Spital in 1197 (Clark, *Carpenters' Hall*, 2)

36. Jupp, *An Historical Account*, 217. Jupp records that 'in 1428, Roger Jordan, the Prior of the Hospital and the Convent, granted a lease of five cottages and a waste piece of ground in the Parish of All Hallows by the London Wall, to Richard Aas, Peter Sextein and Richard Puncheon, citizens and carpenters of London, for a term of ninety-eight years at the rent of 20s' (ibid.). Twelve months later, the cottages were pulled down, the Hall and houses were erected, and the lease was assigned to twenty-nine members of the Company. Leach notes that the lease was carefully passed along from one generation of Company members to the next, thereby ensuring that it remained in the hands of the Carpenters. The freehold for the land on which the Hall was built was formally acquired in 1519/20 by Thomas Smart, a former Master, and bequeathed to the Company in his will (Leach, 'Carpenters in Medieval London', 96 and fn. 18).

37. Among the numerous documents, records and charters stored in the archives at Carpenters' Hall, the Guildhall Library (manuscript section) and the National Archives are the Company accounts. The Court minutes form an almost unbroken series from 1438 and 1533 respectively to the present day. Registers of apprentices date from 1654 and of Freemen from 1673 (Carpenters' Company, *The Carpenters' Company*).

38. All livery companies have plate, consisting of cups, staves (rods), dishes, basins and loving cups (a shared two-handled drinking container used at weddings or, in the case of livery companies, at banquets). For a brief inventory of the material wealth stored and displayed in Carpenters' Hall, see http://www.carpentersco.com/history/collections (retrieved 9 June 2021).

39. Jupp, *An Historical Account*, 138–42.

THE CARPENTERS' COMPANY AND EARLY LONDON APPRENTICESHIPS

40. Jupp notes that the Hall was extensively repaired and decorated in 1561, with further alterations in 1572 and additions in 1588, 1595 and 1664 (ibid., 222–26). Repairs and refurbishments were carried out again in 1668 and modifications were made in 1718 (ibid., 231–32). An entrance hall and main staircase that led to the court rooms were erected in 1780, and the entrance hall was decorated with emblematic figures and implements used in the trade, and with heads of Vitruvius, Palladio, Inigo Jones and Christopher Wren (ibid., 232–33). The Hall was rebuilt to the designs of W.W. Pocock in 1876–80 and again in 1956–60 (preserving Pocock's Italianate-style exterior facades). For a concise overview of the history of the alterations to the Hall, see Clark, *Carpenters' Hall*, 2–12.

41. The Carpenters maintained lights in St Mary Spital and in All-Hallows-on-the-Wall, both of which were in the vicinity of the Hall. Their patron saint may have been the Virgin Mary or All Saints (Jupp, *An Historical Account*, 19), or possibly Joseph, husband of the Virgin and carpenter by trade (Leach, 'Carpenters in Medieval London', 85).

42. Jupp, *An Historical Account*, 209.

43. For example, the Carpenters took part in the Midsummer Watch, an annual procession that 'formed part of the ordinary system of surveillance by which London's rulers controlled the city' and for which 'marchers were supplied mainly by the guilds' (Lindenbaum, 'City and Oligarchy',173). The Carpenters also made contributions toward the following: Henry VII's wars with France (Jupp, *An Historical Account*, 36); the importation of grain during times of scarcity (the 'Corn Custom') and generally the prevention of famine (ibid., 58–61); the nation's protection against the Spanish Armada in 1588 and subsequent offensives (ibid., 63–65); the erection of city gates during the reign of King James I, which involved the participation of eighty joiners, sixty carpenters and two master carpenters (ibid., 70–71); the colonisation of Virginia in the early seventeenth century (ibid., 78) and the colonisation of Ireland (Ulster) by 'planters' during the reigns of James I and Charles I (ibid., 90–91); and the City's collections for the poor in 1665 during the Great Plague. Notably, the Hall was used for billeting parliamentary troops during the English Civil War (1642–51) (ibid., 105–7).

44. Regarding family generational connections within trades, however, careful analysis of the indenture records of the period 1600–1749 concluded that 'parental connections to the London trades do not appear critical: remarkably few apprentices were training in a company linked to their father's occupation – perhaps ten per cent of metropolitan apprentices, and five per cent of migrants' (Leunig, Minns and Wallis, 'Networks in the Premodern Economy', 435).

45. Further ordinances were drawn up in 1487 and 1607 (Carpenters' Company, 'Administrative/Biographical History', no pagination)

46. See 'Freedom of the City' on the *City of London* webpage: https://www.cityof london.gov.uk/about-us/law-historic-governance/freedom-of-the-city (retrieved 9 June 2021).

47. The tradition of the Freedom still exists in the City of London. Although the privileges and practicalities originally associated with the Freedom are no longer relevant, it continues to confer status and it serves as the basis of the liveries and of the City's municipal democracy. The Freedom is no longer restricted to men and women of Britain or the Commonwealth. Since 1996, it may be conferred upon citizens of any nation who are nominated or presented by a livery company.

48. Alford and Barker, *A History of the Carpenters' Company*, 28. Knoop and Jones note that 'mediæval houses were generally constructed of wood and clay; stone and brick came into use gradually for chimneys and floors, but the almost exclusive use of these materials in domestic architecture is a relatively modern phenomenon. Town walls were doubtless constructed of stone and likewise certain churches, bridges and halls, but the principal stone buildings of the Middle Ages were abbeys, cathedrals and castles, which often lay outside towns ... [thus] the number of masons for whom regular employment could be found in a town must have been strictly limited' ('Masons and Apprentices', 346–47).

49. The Carpenters' Company coat of arms is described as 'A felde silver a Cheveron sable grayled iii Compas of the same'. The 'Cheveron' is probably symbolic of the French term *chevron*, meaning 'roof rafter', and the three compasses represent an important tool of the trade. The most important tool, however, for the medieval carpenter was the axe, which was used for everything from felling trees to shaping timbers and making joints for half-timber constructions.

50. Jupp, *An Historical Account*, 12–15.

51. Carpenters' Company, 'Administrative/Biographical History'.

52. Renard, *Guilds*, 12.

53. The Carpenters' Charter was confirmed and renewed in 1558 (Queen Mary and Philip of Spain), 1560 (Queen Elizabeth I), 1607 (King James I), 1640 (King Charles I), 1674 (King Charles II), 1686 (King James II; however, the charter was made null and void by William and Mary's Act of Reversal in 1689) and 1944 (King George VI). The constant extortion of money by the Tudor and Stuart monarchs, who called in company charters and sold them new ones at high prices, was a source of decline for the City liveries. In 1640, the City companies finally refused attempts by Charles I to coerce them into providing large sums and 'so eventually helped Parliament to win the Civil War' (Corporation of London, *The Livery Companies*, 10–11).

54. Jupp, *An Historical Account*, 145.

55. Ibid., 154.

56. The Ordinances of 1486–87 were reprinted in Jupp and Pocock, *An Historical Account*, 44–353. Pocock comments that the fifteenth-century ordinances were so well 'adapted to their purpose' that they were again embodied in those of 1607 with but few alterations except in their religious observances' (at 353).

57. Jupp, *An Historical Account*, 146–47. The term of seven years was the legal minimum, but apprenticeships could also last up to ten years.

58. The full name of the statute is 'The Statute of Artificers, Labourers, Servants of Husbandry, and Apprentices'. Later, it was referred to simply as the 'Statute of Artificers' or the 'Statute of Apprentices'. Note that 'artificer' means a 'skilled craftsman'.

59. Wage rates were set each year at the Court of Chancery. For a discussion of the factors prompting the Statute of Artificers, see Woodward, 'The Background to the Statute of Artificers'.

60. It has been argued that rather than being a constructive piece of statecraft, the Statute of Artificers should be regarded as an attempt by statesmen to address the social situation and industry of the mid-sixteenth century. See, for example, Daniels, *The Early English Cotton Industry*, 48–49; and Woodward, 'The Background to the Statute of Artificers', 32–33.

61. The Statute decreed: 'None to be received as an apprentice except his father spend 40s. od. a year of freehold, nor to be apprenticed to a merchant except his father

spend £10 a year of freehold, or be descended from a gentleman or merchant' (Woodward, 'The Background to the Statute of Artificers', 34)

62. Quoted in Dewey, 'The Rise, Fall, Rise, Fall and Rise Again of Apprenticeships', 47.

63. See, for example, Ericson, Krampe and Tesch-Romer, 'The Role of Deliberate Practice'. Their findings were popularised in Gladwell, *Outliers*.

64. The London Loriners (makers of small iron objects), for example, ordained in 1260–61 that apprenticeship in their trade be a minimum of ten years. The Fishmongers made seven years the minimum. This soon became the model for other misteries, and in some instances the duration served to protect masters against too much competition from former trainees (Thomas, 'Introduction: Apprenticeship').

65. For example, it was decreed by the Fishmongers in 1278–79 'that no one shall take more than two or three apprentices at most, and then only if he is able to support them, nor shall he take an apprentice for less than seven years. The master and apprentice must bring the covenant to be enrolled at Guildhall, and at the end of his term the apprentice shall be presented again by his master, or if his master be dead, by four reputable men of the mistery, after which he may be allowed to engage in trade' (ibid.).

66. To become a legal document, indentures had to be signed by the Justice of the Peace. Two copies were made, one of which was kept by the parents (or parish) on behalf of the child and the other by the master. For a list of the information included in the indentures of carpenters, see Marsh, 'Introduction', ix–x.

67. Wallis, 'Apprenticeship and Training', 846.

68. For a comprehensive discussion of the history of women in the building trades in Britain, including carpentry, see Clarke and Wall, 'Omitted from History'. Hanawalt, in her discussion of female apprentice in London, writes that the experience of apprenticeship was very different for women than for men. There were no female guilds. For women, apprenticeship was not perceived as a vehicle to the Freedom of the City, and for women of modest means, the skills acquired in apprenticeship could be expected to be used at home to supplement household incomes. Their contracts could be quite different from those of male apprentices, with payment of lower bonds and the duration shorter, or in some cases much longer, than the standard seven years (Hanawalt, *Growing up*, 142–44). Writing about the gendering of work in the eighteenth century, Simonton contends that: 'Apprenticeship was a period when the role of the male apprentice moved from lad to man . . . [and its close identification] with sexual development helps to identify the role of the institution in defining masculinity and conversely femininity and in excluding females from the system' (Simonton, 'Gendered Work', 34). In the case of carpentry, Leach's research found that during the medieval period to 1540, 'carpentry work in London was almost wholly a male occupation. There is no evidence that women attended any of the feasts in the fifteenth century or played any role in the Company, and there is little evidence that they became involved in the carpentry business at all' (Leach, 'Carpenters in Medieval London', 233). By contrast, high numbers of women attended the Brewers' feasts, but again, none, it seems, were directly involved in the running of that guild (ibid., 152). Although it was a well-established civic custom for widows of London citizens to take over responsibility for their late husband's apprentices (at least until they completed their training), Leach found just one mention in the *Carpenters' Account Book* of a woman doing so (ibid., 148–49). Leach's study identifies only one possible female carpentry apprentice: Katherine Gy was

specifically mentioned in the will of William Togood (d. 1467) as 'my apprentice', and the carpenter requested that she serve his wife, Alice. Leach reports that: 'There are no further details so it is not possible to know whether Katherine was an apprentice carpenter or whether Togood had another trade, such as brewing, to which she was apprenticed. It is even possible that Katherine was employed as a household servant rather than an indentured apprentice' (ibid., 149). Between 1654 and 1694, '21 women were bound apprentice at Carpenters' Hall to members of the Company who either themselves or with the assistance of their wives followed trades that admitted female workers, such as sempster, milliner or childs-coat-seller' (Marsh, 'Introduction', x–xi).

69. From the perspective of the City companies and Free craftsmen, those who had not apprenticed in London but had nevertheless been granted the Freedom of the City had no right to work in the city or the surrounding regions under its authority.

70. In 1517, during the early reign of Henry VIII, a group of London apprentices (and other citizens) viciously attacked 'forrens' (at that time, these were mainly Flemish inhabitants of the City). The event became known as 'Evil May Day', and the rioters were convicted of treason and some of them hanged (see Bloom, *Violent London*; and Rappaport, *Worlds within Worlds*).

71. See Rappaport, *Worlds within Worlds*, 295–96, who gathered evidence about the Carpenters' Company and apprenticeships for the period between 1572 and 1594.

72. Wallis, Webb and Minns, 'Leaving Home', 6 and 14.

73. Ibid., 4.

74. The term 'London mob' was first coined in the late seventeenth century and was popularly used during the eighteenth century to describe the chaos and violence of early Georgian London (for a fuller discussion, see Shoemaker, *The London Mob*).

75. See Wallis, Webb and Minns, 'Leaving Home', 4.

76. For individual master carpenters, however, training apprentices was in most cases a means to producing future rivals, not long-term employees. (cf. Wallis, 'Apprenticeship and Training', 845).

77. Jupp, *An Historical Account*, 147–48.

78. By contrast, Leunig, Minns and Wallis conclude that personal ties did not shape apprenticeship recruitment, grounding their argument in evidence from indenture records across a wide range of trades, spanning 1600 to 1749 ('Networks in the Premodern Economy', 413–33). Leach also notes that 'in common with a number of other city companies son-to-father apprenticeships seem to have been rare amongst carpenters' (Leach, 'Carpenters in Medieval London', 146).

79. Leach, 'Carpenters in Medieval London', 208–13.

80. See the Carpenters' Company webpage: http://www.carpentersco.com/carpenters-hall (retrieved 9 June 2021). See also Leach, 'Carpenters in Medieval London', 96, fn. 18.

81. For a detailed history of these paintings, made by an unknown artist, see Tancell, 'The Carpenters' Tudor Wall Paintings', 12–14; and Jupp, *An Historical Account*, 236–42.

82. Jupp, *An Historical Account*, 241–42. At some time around 1850, when the Hall was leased out to a printing company, the paintings were again covered over. They were removed from the building before the first hall was demolished in 1876, but Tancell has suggested that the one of Noah and his sons was too fragile and was lost. She goes on to recount: 'In 1933 they were loaned to the London Museum for conservation,

where they remained during WWII, avoiding the fire that burnt the Hall in May 1941. In 1959 they were built into the wall of the new Hall on their original wattle and daub ground' (Tancell, 'The Carpenters' Tudor Wall Paintings', 14).

83. Noorthouck, 'Appendix', 799–811.
84. Walford, 'Fires and Fire Insurance', 352.
85. This was introduced in 1189 (Walford, 'Fires and Fire Insurance', 350).
86. Walford, 'Fires and Fire Insurance', 352.
87. Jupp, *An Historical Account*, 275.
88. Aikin, *Memoirs of the Court of King James the First*, 302.
89. Elmes, 'History of Architecture', 209.
90. Wade, *History of the Middle and Working Classes*, 59.
91. Sharpe, *The Personal Rule of Charles I*, 408.
92. Marsh, 'Introduction', xi.
93. This claim is dubious because some of the London neighbourhoods worst affected by plague, such as Whitechapel, Clerkenwell and Southwark, were not directly impacted by the Fire, and Londoners continued to die of plague until 1670.
94. Tancell, 'Plague, Fire and the Carpenters' Company', 20–22. See also Jupp, *An Historical Account*, 248, who states that three successive Lord Mayors rented space in Carpenters' Hall. It became tradition that each newly elected Lord Mayor dines first at Carpenters' Hall after taking office.
95. Tancell, 'Carpenters' Company Charities 1333–1700', 11.
96. Alford and Barker, *A History of the Carpenters' Company*, 128.
97. Raithby, 'Charles II', 603–12.
98. Michael Buckley noted that wooden construction was 'virtually banned by building regulations for the next three centuries'. Until recently, it was impossible to obtain a bank loan in Britain for any home not built in bricks and mortar. The 'turning point came in 1999 when the Building Research Establishment built a six-storey building and burned it under test, reporting to the Timber Frame Association that the fire was contained. As a result regulations prohibiting wooden structures were relaxed' (Buckley, 'Burning Issues', 7–8).
99. Jupp, *An Historical Account*, 280.
100. See Marsh, 'Introduction', xi.
101. Raithby, 'Charles II', 603–12.
102. Jupp, *An Historical Account*, 280–82.
103. Alford and Barker, *A History of the Carpenters' Company*, 114–16.
104. Sir Gabriel Roberts was a merchant who traded with Smyrna and the Ottoman Empire.
105. Jupp, *An Historical Account*, 249. Clark noted that James Fordham used the Hall as a warehouse for carpets in 1758 (*Carpenters' Hall*, 3).
106. Tancell, 'The Carpenters' Tudor Wall Paintings', 14.
107. Alford and Barker, *A History of the Carpenters' Company*, 138. Notably, the Carpenters' Company of the City and County of Philadelphia was established at this time (1724). The Carpenters are unique among London liveries for having an offshoot in the United States. The President in Philadelphia and the Master in London are honorary members of each other's Company.
108. Jupp, *An Historical Account*, 251.
109. The property, developed in the nineteenth century and again in the twentieth, remains in the ownership of the Carpenters' Company. The original date that the

Lime Street property came into the Carpenters' ownership is uncertain. According to the Carpenters' Company, it may have been in either 1454 or 1481 (*Estates, Charities and Gifts of the Carpenters' Company*); or, according to Tancell, the bequest was made in 1447 ('Carpenters' Company Charities', 9).

110. Tancell, 'Carpenters' Company Charities 1333–1700', 9.
111. Jupp, *An Historical Account*, 251–53.
112. Tancell, 'Carpenters' Company Charities from 1700', 16.
113. Tancell, 'The Stratford Estate', 18. The Company paid 3,000 guineas (£3,150) for the estate in 1767.
114. Tancell, 'Carpenters' Company Charities 1333–1700', 11.
115. The Company was obliged to sell the property in 1947 to Twickenham Borough Council. See Carpenters' Company, *Estates, Charities and Gifts of the Carpenters' Company*.
116. In October that year, a fire broke out at the adjacent building, which was occupied by a firm of wool merchants and brokers. The fire did extensive damage to Carpenters' Hall (Clark, *Carpenters' Hall*, 7).
117. Jupp, quoted in ibid., 8.
118. Construction of the new Hall was completed in 1880.
119. Clark, *Carpenters' Hall*, 8–9.
120. The Livery's Archivist, Julie Tancell, records that: 'Today the Company administers five charitable trusts: the Rustington Convalescent Home, the Carpenters' Company Charitable Trust, Wyatt's Almshouses, the Norton Folgate Trust and the Building Crafts College. The numerous charities accumulated by the Company over centuries have largely been amalgamated into the CCCT and NFT as the result of major restructuring in the 1990s' ('Carpenters' Company Charities from 1700', 18). The Company is also closely associated with the Carpenters & Dockland Centre, which is a youth, community and social facility in Stratford (East London) and Carpenters Primary School in East London. Additionally, the London Carpenters retain close ties with the Carpenters' Company of the City and County of Philadelphia, and sponsor a biannual Exchange Lecture. The Livery is also a founding member of the Lord Mayor's Big Curry Lunch, which raises funds for the Current Operations Fund of the Army Benevolent Fund. The Company has strong affiliations with both HMS Daring, first in Class of the Type 45 air-defence destroyers built for the Royal Navy, and with 4th Battalion, The Rifles, based in Aldershot, Hampshire.

CHAPTER 3

THE BUILDING CRAFTS COLLEGE
A History

The previous chapter recounted the rise of London's Worshipful Company of Carpenters from its medieval beginnings to its pinnacle of control over trade activities in the seventeenth century, and the subsequent diversification of the Livery's financial, real estate and charitable interests following the Great Fire in 1666. Entwined with that history were descriptions of the substantial developments in London's apprenticeship system and its codification in the Elizabethan Statute of Artificers in 1563, which prevailed for some 250 years.

The Carpenters' investments in education also began during the Elizabethan period, growing substantially during the eighteenth and nineteenth centuries, and culminating with the founding of the Trades Training School in London's West End. This chapter supplies an historical overview of that pioneering vocational training institution, from its start in 1893 on Great Titchfield Street in West London to its expansion and move to Stratford in East London in 2001. Renamed the Building Crafts College in 1993, this was the site of my own training as a fine woodworker and of my anthropological study of embodied learning and the politics of skilled handwork in the twenty-first century.

My telling of the College history is accompanied by a schematic review of the complex developments in apprenticeships and vocational training in England since the late Victorian period. Although the fine-woodwork programme on which I enrolled was not an 'apprenticeship', the history of that course is deeply entangled with that of college-based technical training for apprentices in various building trades, beginning with the foundation of the College.

In the mid-1990s, the government launched a new 'Modern Apprenticeships' scheme and the Building Crafts College became a training centre, providing instruction in shop fitting, carpentry and joinery on behalf of the Construction Industry Training Board (CITB). Shortly before arriving to begin my training and my study, the Building Crafts College had earned full accreditation as a Centre of Vocational Excellence (CoVE) in traditional building crafts and its intake of Modern Apprentices was growing at a substantial rate. It is therefore imperative to tell that story, and in so doing enrich the description of my field site context before moving on to concentrate on the personal experiences and enskilment of the fine woodworkers in the remaining chapters.

PATRONS OF TECHNICAL EDUCATION

The Company's investment in education began during the Elizabethan era with offers of funding to 'poor scholars' attending Oxford and Cambridge. The Carpenters' bursary programme for students at those universities continues, with additional grants available to young men and women attending other institutions of higher education. In 1711–12, merchant, philanthropist and politician Sir John Cass was concurrently Company Master and Sheriff of the City.[1] On his death in 1718, Cass left a substantial legacy that, thirty years later, was established as a major foundation in support of education.[2] However, it was not until the nineteenth century that the Carpenters' Company itself became directly invested as a benefactor in technical education in the wood trades.

Until the late seventeenth century, Britain was essentially a 'one-way technological debtor', importing most of its industrial and manufacturing processes from the continent. This situation began to reverse and, by 1750, premodern England was transformed from 'a technological and under-urbanised periphery to the most technologically innovative and urbanised country in the West'.[3] Rapid technological development, industrialisation, changing labour relations and rampant urbanisation would characterise the new era, persisting well into the twentieth century.

The seismic changes to the ways that things were produced brought dramatic transformations to the lives and livelihoods of craftspeople, including woodworkers. Economies of scale and standardisation became deeply ingrained in all aspects of manufacture and construction. That rationale is exemplified in the plethora of late eighteenth-century trade publications for woodworkers, such as the highly successful *Mr. Hoppus's Measurer*,[4] which systematically categorised, graded and priced all trade materials required by the carpenter-builder; William Pain's *Practical Builder* and his later *Car-*

penter and Joiners' Repository, both containing illustrations of structural carpentry details;[5] and Peter Nicholson's *Carpenter and Joiner's Assistant*, which
offered a scientific approach to the design of structural members.[6]

The history of liberal thinking in Britain, from John Locke to John Stuart
Mill, also had a profound impact on the fate of the old trade order and the
transformations of artisan to labourer and workshop to factory. With their
emphases on economic freedom and opposition to state intervention in
commercial practice, liberal philosophers, economists and political thinkers
generally regarded preindustrial livery apprenticeships as a hindrance to the
'wealth of nations'.[7] Adam Smith insisted on major reform to the apprenticeship structures of his time, arguing that:

> The exclusive privilege of an incorporated trade [i.e. one controlled by the guilds]
> necessarily restrains the competition, in the town where it is established . . . The bye-
> laws of the corporation regulate sometimes the number of apprentices which any
> master is allowed to have, and almost always the number of years which each appren-
> tice is obliged to serve. The intention of both regulations is to restrain the competition
> to a much smaller number than might otherwise be disposed to enter into the trade.[8]

Many of London's traditional livery-controlled apprenticeships were, in
fact, already in decline by the late eighteenth century,[9] and wage labour was
becoming increasingly common. The average age at which boys and young
men commenced their indenture had also changed across the centuries in
step with changing social conditions, supply and demand, and the shifting
fortunes of the City and the country. By the nineteenth century, the average
starting age of London apprentices was 15.5 years old, down a full 2.5 years
from that in the Elizabethan era.[10] This trend presaged the expanding role
that child labour would play in the Industrial Revolution.

A multitude of changes to the structure and regulations of apprenticeship
during this period were made in response to the liveries' weakening grip on
both the (sometimes abusive) conditions of apprenticeship training and the
(sometimes disorderly) conduct of apprentices themselves. The rash of new
statutes also reflected the wider social and economic transformations ignited
by the advent of large-scale machine production.[11] Mills and factories necessitated a new division of labour, whereby vast numbers of unskilled and
semi-skilled workers operated the machines and a more select (and exclusively male) cohort of skilled workers designed, built and maintained them.[12]
The latter grouping, comprising engineers and machinists, typically received
their training via the new kinds of apprenticeships that emerged in the industrial economy.

Responding to revolutionary changes in the mode of production and the
concerns of liberal economists and entrepreneurial industrialists, Parliament passed an Act in 1814 to repeal the Elizabethan Statute of Artificers.[13]

The 1814 Act did not abolish apprenticeship per se, but instead legalised the rights of individuals to practice a trade without having been indentured or having served seven years. Apprenticeship nevertheless remained popular among those entering trades, including engineering and machining, the building craft occupations, and craft industries more generally, all of which demanded practical hands-on skills.

Craft learning and practice was most noticeably affected in the nation's urban centres. Industrial progress not only endangered the kinds and quality of things that had been produced for centuries, but more potently it also jeopardised a whole system of learning grounded in hand skill, finely attuned perception, informed judgement and incessant hands-on problem solving. These occupational-specific ways of knowing had unfolded between generations of masters and apprentices in workshop and on-site settings. The skills and expertise were not documented, but rather preserved in the ongoing physical engagement of craftspeople in their trades and with one another.

The likes of John Ruskin and William Morris pitched impassioned attacks on the laissez-faire capitalism of the factory, its mechanised mode of production and its impact on the human spirit. Although the power of the guilds had been weakened, the Arts and Crafts movement spawned 'a revival of guild ideals through [its] anti-industrial critiques and [its] spirit of new-medievalism'.[14] The appeals issued by Ruskin and Morris for a return to traditional small-scale artisanal work drew much-needed public attention to the plight of British craft:[15]

> And the great cry that rises from all our manufacturing cities, louder than their furnace blast, is all in very deed for this – that we manufacture everything there except men; we blanch cotton, and strengthen steel, and refine sugar, and shape pottery; but to brighten, to strengthen, to refine, or to form a single living spirit, never enters into our estimate of advantages.
>
> —John Ruskin[16]

> They are called 'labour-saving machines' – a commonly used phrase which implies what we expect of them: but we do not get what we expect. What they really do is to reduce the skilled labour to the ranks of the unskilled, to increase the number of the 'reserve army of labour' – that is, to increase the precariousness of life among the workers and to intensify labour of those who serve the machines.
>
> —William Morris[17]

Craft unions were eventually formed in the mid-nineteenth century, mainly to control recruitment and uphold the quality of workmanship through the implementation of rigorous, collectively bargained apprenticeships. The craft unions grew in strength by leveraging the scarcity of skilled workers to achieve better employment conditions. Thus, as the century progressed, vocational training was systematically transferred from traditional small-scale artisan workshops to factories or to institutional settings.

As the promotion of domestic industry came to dominate the agendas of Europe's mercantile states, the correlation drawn between technological advancement and economic progress strengthened, and competition between nations to develop new and more efficient methods of production intensified.[18] By the late nineteenth century, Britain's hard-won position as industrial leader and the 'workshop of the world'[19] was threatened by the rising prowess of other manufacturing nations, most notably France, Belgium, Prussia, Austria and Switzerland – all of which invested more heavily in technical education.[20] In contrast, the British government's laissez-faire approach to vocational training saw responsibility delegated to employers, the workplace and the factory. These, however, lacked a global, linked-up strategy for educating and qualifying the working classes.[21] Rising concern among British industrialists that the nation was losing its competitive edge incited the Carpenters and other City liveries to sponsor the development of formal technical education in London.[22]

The growing sense of responsibility for providing formal technical education emerged in tandem with the sweeping educational reforms that were taking place in late nineteenth-century Britain.[23] Parliament's Elementary Education Act of 1870, also known as the Forster Act, demonstrated commitment on a national scale to the provision of free, universal and compulsory education for all children between the ages of five and thirteen.[24] This did not go unchallenged, as a welfare-state attempt to establish a national system of education and training was in conflict with 'the standpoints and interests of the industrial middle class', who financially benefited from the employment of children and young people in the factories.[25] Nevertheless, in promoting his bill, Liberal MP William Forster explained to Parliament:

> Upon the speedy provision of elementary education depends our industrial prosperity. It is no use trying to give technical teaching to our artisans without elementary education; uneducated labourers – and many of our labourers are utterly uneducated – are, for the most part, unskilled labourers, and if we leave our workfolk any longer unskilled, notwithstanding their strong sinews and determined energy, they will be overmatched in the competition of the world.[26]

This excerpt from Forster's parliamentary speech underscores the perceived links at the time between schooling, technical skills and the performance of the national economy. Challenging this, Thomas Henry Huxley, the eminent Victorian biologist, anthropologist and educator, cautioned that if the direction of education were steered by such political and commercial concerns, schooling would be rendered 'a process of manufacturing human tools'.[27]

Full implementation of the principles of the Forster Act required the legislation of additional reform acts over the next decade and longer.[28] Together,
these set the groundwork for Britain's modern systems of schooling and
technical education. The Technical Instruction Act was eventually passed in
1889, promoting the establishment of technical colleges run by local governments, and, during the 1890s, practical subjects including drawing, cooking
and woodworking were introduced into elementary school curricula.

In 1876, a number of livery companies met at Mansion House and resolved that:

> It is desirable that the attention of the Livery Companies be directed to the promotion
> of Education not only in the Metropolis but throughout the country, and especially
> to technical education, with the view of educating young artisans and others in the
> scientific and artistic branches of their trades.[29]

As a result, the Corporation of the City of London and the liveries, including the Carpenters, established the City & Guilds of London Institute
(C&GLI) for the Advancement of Technical Education in 1878, which was
incorporated two years later.[30] The C&GLI served as a joint central body
for the promotion of technical and scientific learning,[31] and for conducting a
system of qualifying examinations in technical subjects.[32] Its foundation was
a major milestone in improving the training of craftspeople in the building
trades, not only in London but also nationwide. With generous support
from the livery companies, the Finsbury Technical College opened in 1883
and the Central Technical College (also known as the Central Institution),
designed by architect Alfred Waterhouse,[33] opened in South Kensington in
1884. Teaching began there the following year.[34] The Central Technical College was renamed City & Guilds College in 1907 and was incorporated as
part of Imperial College London in 1910.

Sharing in the Victorian enthusiasm for exhibitions, the Carpenters, in
conjunction with the Joiners, hosted the first annual carpentry show at their
Hall in 1884. The Company adopted a more active role at this time in promoting building-craft education and establishing recognised qualifications and
trade standards. Banister Fletcher, Professor of Architecture at Kings' College
London and vocal advocate for technical schooling, was the chief initiator behind the Carpentry and Joinery technical examinations that were first administered by the Company in 1888.[35] The three-day exam comprised theory and
practical components, and was mainly targeted at those aspiring to become
foremen or clerks of work. The trade 'theory' was progressively collated and
methodised in textbooks – for example, in the Fletcher brothers' *Carpentry
and Joinery* (1897) and Ellis' seminal *Modern Practical Joinery* (1902).

Eleven craftsmen who had achieved first-class passes in 1890 founded
the Incorporated British Institute of Certified Carpenters (renamed the In-

stitute of Carpenters in 1976). The Company's examination continued to serve as means of entry to the Institute until 1956.[36] The Institute's mission was, and continues to be, the promotion of the wood trades and traditional hand skills and milling practices. Its members oversaw training regimes for carpenters and joiners, and worked to disseminate and maintain high professional standards in those crafts. A member who joined in 1898 later reflected: 'There was enthusiasm and hope that the Institute would become to the craft a great and inspiring head to revive the nobility of the craft which it was said existed in some past age.'[37]

Meanwhile, to the east of the City, the Parish of West Ham and its once-tiny village of Stratford were being transformed by industrialisation, like many formerly rural regions that lay at London's peripheries. After parcels of the Carpenters' Stratford estate were sold to the railways in the 1830s, the market gardens soon gave way to factories and housing. Tancell noted that the change of land use in Stratford was spurred on by the 1844 Metropolitan Building Act. In addition to its concern with the thickness of party walls and the use of fire-resistant materials in London proper, the Act also prohibited the setting up of noxious and dangerous businesses within 50 feet of other buildings. Many such industries that had been located in East London migrated east of the River Lea (which was London's eastern boundary), and with this relocation came a population explosion and insalubrious living conditions for the labouring classes.

On the remaining land of the Carpenters' estate, for example, leases were taken up from the early 1860s onwards by brick makers, matchmakers, linen manufacturers, chemical processors and distillers.[38] In an attempt to improve employment options and livelihoods for the local population, the Carpenters' Company opened a Technical Institute in 1886, offering tuition to boys and young men in the trades of carpentry, joinery, plumbing, geometry, mechanical drawing and cooking.[39]

Five years after launching the Carpentry and Joinery technical examination, the Company founded a dedicated Trades Training School in West London. Renamed the Building Crafts Training School in 1948 and then the Building Crafts College in 1993, the institution constitutes the Livery's primary education and charitable commitment. Until 2012, when the Goldsmiths' Company opened the Goldsmiths' Centre on Britton Street in Farringdon, the Carpenters were unique among the liveries in funding their own dedicated craft school.[40]

The next section is dedicated to the history of the College, its changing operations and its relocation to a parcel of Carpenters' land in Stratford, which, at the time, was one of the most deprived neighbourhoods in the capital. This story is interwoven with an account of the momentous transformations in vocational education and training in twentieth-century England.

AN EVENTFUL TWENTIETH CENTURY:
TRAINING SCHOOL-CUM-COLLEGE

The Trades Training School (TTS) opened in 1893 on Great Titchfield Street, in East Marylebone, a district of London's West End that underwent substantial urban development during the second half of the eighteenth century.[41] By the late nineteenth century, the area was rapidly changing again, with many of its Georgian residential dwellings being demolished and replaced with large blocks of flats and business premises sporting late Victorian and Edwardian-style frontages.[42] The Carpenters' Company's new School at 153–55 Great Titchfield Street was a three-storey red-brick building with a smart Queen Anne-style façade of eight generous window bays. A broad Dutch gable at either end of the long roof emphasised the pleasing symmetry of the school building.

The Carpenters' operated the School in collaboration with seven other London liveries,[43] offering young men courses in a variety of building-related trades, including carpentry and joinery, wheelwrighting (i.e. wooden wheel making), masonry, stone carving, brickwork and tiling, plasterwork, painting and plumbing. Its first director was Herbert Phillips Fletcher, a Fellow of the Royal Institute of British Architects (RIBA) and partner in his father's practice, Banister Fletcher and Sons.

The Fletchers were well connected and the father and both sons played significant roles in the history of the Company and its School well into the twentieth century. Banister Fletcher (senior), mentioned earlier, had served as a Liberal Member of Parliament and as Master of the Carpenters' Company (1889). He and another son, Banister Flight Fletcher, authored the renowned tome *A History of Architecture on the Comparative Method*, which was published in revised editions numerous times over the next century and remains a standard reference today.[44] During the First World War, Major Herbert Phillips Fletcher was killed in action and directorship of the Trades Training School was taken up by his brother, Banister Flight Fletcher, who was later knighted, elected President of the RIBA, and served as Master of the Carpenters' Company (1936).[45]

The Company, like most London liveries and business establishments across Britain, faced enormous financial challenges during the First World War, due in large measure to increased taxation for funding the war efforts. Nevertheless, Carpenters' Hall was used to entertain troops and the Company retained all of its charitable functions and almshouses, including Rustington, which was transformed into a convalescence home for discharged soldiers and munitions workers. However, the Carpenters' technical examinations were temporarily cancelled because of the lack of men to sit them during the War. Though the Trades Training School managed to remain open, it operated with fewer and younger students.[46]

Numbers attending the School grew again after the War and by the mid-1930s, while still under the Directorship of Sir Banister Flight Fletcher, an average of ninety-three students were attending evening classes.[47] Activities at the Company's Livery Hall flourished, including the hosting of the technical examination as well as lectures and exhibitions on woodworking and joinery. However, the start of the Second World War would seriously impact both the Company and the School.

On the night of 10 May 1941, during the most devastating Luftwaffe air raid on London, a 'landmine' (i.e. parachute bomb)[48] was dropped in London Wall (street), igniting a gas main and resulting in a fire that ravaged the Hall.[49] The Company was offered temporary accommodation by the adjacent Drapers' Company and by the Cutlers' to conduct its business. On its estate in Stratford, heavy bombing destroyed nearly a third of the cottages.[50] The School, too, suffered bomb damage on four separate occasions, but continued to function, making its facilities on Great Titchfield Street available to government for the training of servicemen as carpenters, sheet-metal workers and blacksmiths.[51]

In 1944, the government's Education Act created a tripartite system of secondary education, comprising academically selective grammar schools, secondary moderns and selective technical schools. The purpose of the latter was to train the next generation of scientists, technicians and engineers, but the remit of technical schools was never entirely clear. Few actually opened owing to insufficient funding for the necessary equipment, and those that did were turned into grammar schools by 1960. However, apprenticeships during the postwar period remained outside the system of mainstream education and under the control of employers, trade guilds (cum trade unions) and craft unions.[52]

Despite the absence of a national strategy for vocational training, the number of apprentices increased during the late 1940s and the 1950s in sync with the surge in British manufacturing. In the case of the building trades, many apprentices were receiving supplementary off-site instruction at institutions like the Trades Training School. In 1947, the School's name was changed to the Building Crafts Training School. In addition to evening classes, it now offered day classes for demobilised servicemen and for apprentices on block release from their employers, and modifications were made to the curriculum to reflect the changing needs of Britain's modernising construction industry.[53]

However, the number of entrants for the Carpenters' technical examination declined steadily after the Second World War. The Company therefore decided to replace the examination in 1956 with an annual Carpenters' Craft Competition, which was intended to encourage excellence in traditional woodworking methods.[54] The student competition in executing a challenging set piece (e.g. a linen-fold panel or complex curved sign bracket in hardwood) continues to the present day, and since 1972 it has been run in collaboration with the Institute of Carpenters.[55] In the same year as the launch of the competition, rebuilding of the Company's Livery Hall commenced. The nineteenth-century Italianate-style stone façade that had survived the fire was conserved, but the new interior boldly displayed modern woodwork, employing some eighteen different species of timber in its grand reception chambers.[56]

In the face of growing criticism that the institution of apprenticeship was a 'medieval survivor inappropriate to the systematic teaching of skills in modern technologies'[57] and that it 'focussed on time-serving rather than on the attainment of standards',[58] the number of apprentices actually continued to grow. By the mid-1960s, apprenticeship in Britain had reached its 'high water mark' with an estimated one-third of male school-leavers between the ages of fifteen and seventeen pursuing this training route.[59]

Conversely, student numbers at the Building Crafts Training School were dropping, due in part to its worn and antiquated facilities.[60] This prompted the Company to rebuild the School in 1968 on the same Great Titchfield Street site. Guided by the goals of the 1964 Industrial Training Act to 'develop new modular methods of training and set new standards for apprenticeship',[61] the School 'developed as a centre for advanced training' in woodwork and stone masonry.[62] Regardless, student enrolment remained low during the early 1970s, reflecting challenges in the wider national economy spawned by a decline in manufacturing, industrial unrest, widespread strikes, a worldwide energy crisis, rising costs of living, a recession and high unemployment. Later that decade, student enrolment at the School gradually rose again and staff numbers increased.[63]

Vacillations in the economy were not the sole challenge to traditional liveries and trade schools. Changing architectural styles and an exponential increase in the use of reinforced concrete, steel, glass and prefabricated elements in the postwar decades equated to shrinking demand for the traditional building crafts, including carpentry, joinery and shop fitting. In an effort to rekindle interest in the wood occupations, the Carpenters inaugurated the Carpenters' Award in 1971 to recognise 'the very best work in joinery or other woodworking'. The prestigious annual prize was renamed the Wood Awards in 2003, celebrating 'excellence in all areas of design, craftsmanship and installation in buildings and furniture' made with timber.[64]

Nevertheless, many forms of artisanal production and their associated apprenticeships, including woodworking, declined precipitously during the

1980s, in tandem with the collapse of Britain's heavy manufacturing sector and its once-colossal fleet of apprenticeships.[65] Artisan Roger Coleman accurately observed that 'the reduction of human labour in modern industrial processes [had created] not leisure for all but rather massive unemployment ... and a growing sector of the population [was] ... looked on as useless because it was not involved in material production' of consumer goods.[66]

From its high point in 1966, the number of apprentices in Britain fell from 243,700 to 53,000 by 1990.[67] The apprenticeship route into a craft, trade or profession was being adversely affected by, among other factors, changes in the nature of work, the high costs of apprenticeship training to employers,[68] and a growing proportion of school-leavers opting for the academic track into higher education. Many young people, growing numbers of whom lacked any skills training or educational qualifications, could not find work. By the late 1970s, the nation was being increasingly characterised by high unemployment, the disaffection of its working classes and its Black, Asian and minority ethnic (BAME) communities, and social unrest, which together would ignite riots in cities around England in the early 1980s.[69]

In attempt to remedy the situation, James Callaghan's Labour government introduced Britain's first state-funded and coordinated vocational training programme in 1978. The aims of the Youth Opportunities Programme (YOP), as it was named, were 'to enhance the skills and personal development of unemployed young people and to compensate for any deficiencies in their education by offering them remedial training in basic and social skills'.[70] Some believed that the YOP actually functioned as 'an instrument for the social control of the workforce'[71] and operated primarily as a 'palliative' in the contractual relation between the Labour government and the trade union movement.[72]

The YOP continued operating for three more years following the election of Margaret Thatcher's Conservative government and was replaced in 1983 with the Youth Training Scheme (YTS). Participants in that scheme 'were not apprentices with an employment status but trainees with a government allowance'.[73] As already discussed in the Prologue, the YTS was criticised for a number of serious shortcomings, including its being driven by an agenda to massage unemployment figures rather than to educate and improve skills. The scheme suffered a high dropout rate, lack of credibility in equipping young men and women with meaningful qualifications, and a bruising stigmatisation as a low-status scheme for society's underachievers.[74] These failings only widened the gulf in status between academic and vocational education streams.

The Tories, who in the main 'mistrusted apprenticeship training as an instrument of trade union influence in the workplace',[75] repealed the interventionist 1964 Industrial Training Act in 1982 and demobilised most of the Industrial Training Boards (ITBs). The ITBs had previously provided an opportunity for private-sector industries to operate a levy-grant system for training activities and thereby spread the costs,[76] and had organised training curricula in coordination with related occupational bodies.[77] With their disappearance, vocational training passed increasingly into the control of an employer-led system of locally based Training and Enterprise Councils (TECs) that operated as private limited companies and were largely unaccountable.[78]

Another game-changing move by the Tories was the rationalisation of vocational qualifications and the plethora of nearly 300 different bodies that awarded them. In 1986, the government set up the National Council for Vocational Qualifications, whose remit was to establish and promote a framework for National Vocational Qualifications (NVQs).[79] Rolled out across England, Wales and Northern Ireland two years later,[80] the system further undermined trade union involvement in the defining of training criteria, assessment and qualifications, and it created a framework of standards based on job-specific 'competencies' rather than time-serving measures.

Though some regarded the NVQ framework as an improvement over the past muddle of accreditation frameworks, its critics disparaged NVQ standards for being low and the range of skills narrow, for separating out theory from practice, and for there being no compulsion on employers to partake in the system and improve the skills of employees. Educationalists Alison Fuller and Lorna Unwin observed that 'large companies, often with their own in-house training schools, either stopped employing school leavers or became involved on a smaller scale with the government-led youth training schemes', which were underpinned by the new NVQs.[81]

In sum, the YTS (renamed Youth Training in 1990) and the NVQ framework did little to revitalise the apprenticeship route or to attract school-leavers into vocational training. Sociologist Ken Roberts remarked that 'a great deal of the new further education and training created in the 1980s was "warehousing"',[82] which unsurprisingly diminished the status of vocational education training and young people's motivations to enrol.[83] The low and, in fact, tumbling uptake on the YTS was further exacerbated by the economic recession in the early 1990s that hammered the construction industry with particular force. Correspondingly, the skills gap continued to widen, both within the national workforce and in comparison to Britain's economic competitors.[84] At this point, the Conservatives were coerced into rethinking apprenticeships and formulating a more robust national programme of training that would raise skill levels among craftspeople, technicians and people in supervisory posts.

Pilots for the so-called 'Modern Apprenticeship' (MA) scheme were launched in 1994 in fourteen sectors and in forty TECs around England and

Wales.[85] By 1996, the scheme was expanded to cover fifty-four sectors, including the building trades. MAs were rooted in work-based training with periods of block-release for college training. Like traditional apprenticeships, a written agreement was signed between employer and apprentice; however, unlike them, MAs were not structured around time-serving, but rather on the competencies defined by NVQs, up to Level 3 (i.e. 'intermediate skills'). The MA frameworks, devised by government-licensed and employer-led Sector Skills Councils, comprised a competence-based component, a knowledge-based component and 'key skills', namely in literacy, numeracy and communication.

Tony Blair's Labour Party (also known as 'New Labour') came to power in 1997 with a mantra of 'Education, Education, Education'.[86] By 1998, 225,000 young people had embarked on MAs in England and Wales, half of whom were women.[87] Though vocational education and training (VET) were on Labour's radar, promotion of MAs lagged far behind its promotion of university education. From September 1999 onwards, newspaper headlines were dominated by the Party's ambitious target to get 50 per cent of all people under the age of thirty into university by 2010.[88] That target, in turn, was heavily scrutinised by the press, industry, educationalists and a raft of other experts who claimed that the goal was misguided, that it failed to address the real skills gap in Britain and that too many 'school leavers [were] being shoe-horned onto academic courses to which they are unsuited' and that had 'little bearing on the environment in which they [would] be working'.[89]

While the MA scheme was retained by Labour as the star component in its commitment to closing the skills gap,[90] the *Cassels Report*, published in 2001 by the Department of Education and Skills, concluded that MAs were 'marginal to national life' because they were 'inconsistently delivered; poorly managed; and poorly known about and understood'.[91]

Meanwhile, the Carpenters' Company had recognised the potential for growing enrolment in what was now named the Building Crafts College with Modern Apprentices,[92] but facilities at the College on Great Titchfield Street had again fallen below the standards of the day and were deemed unsuitable for technical training in the twenty-first century. Noise levels were high, the dust extraction mechanism was insufficient, the amenities for female students were makeshift and, perhaps most problematically, there was no possibility for physical expansion of the premises.[93] By the turn of the millennium, there were only six staff and the average admission was about thirty students, which occasionally included small numbers of women.[94] In the estimation of its then director, John Taylor, 'the whole operation lacked critical mass'.[95]

The lease on the Great Titchfield Street property was expiring, prompting the Company to take a bold decision and relocate the College to a purpose-built facility located on a parcel of their remaining Stratford estate in East London.[96] Modern, spacious, flexible and light-filled, the new Building Crafts College on Kennard Road opened its doors in 2001 and instruction commenced that autumn.[97] Cherished as the 'jewel in its crown',[98] the Carpenters continued to operate the College under its governance and to endow it with charitable and management support.[99] The Building Crafts College offered its flagship City & Guilds diploma courses in fine woodworking and stonemasonry, as well as three-year training courses for Modern Apprentices on behalf of the CITB. MAs in bench joinery, shop fitting, banker masonry, architectural stone carving and other occupations in construction, conservation and restoration led to Advanced Construction Awards and NVQs Levels 2 and 3. The College also nurtured its existing links and forged new ones with key national organisations involved in construction skills training, as well as in the conservation, repair and maintenance of Britain's built heritage.[100]

The opening year saw fifty students enrol,[101] but that number would rise exponentially over the next decade. By 2010, there would be 750 enrolments on an array of programmes (including industry training courses), some of which were homed in new and additional buildings, and staff numbers would reach nearly sixty.[102] While capacity on the apprenticeship programmes multiplied during the 2000s, student numbers on the College's flagship courses remained steady, with small dips and moderate increases during the first decade. Female students, as well as Black and Asian ones, remained a minority, in spite of efforts on the part of the College, the government and CITB-ConstructionSkills to recruit a more diverse training and labour force. By 2003 (predominantly white) men still accounted for 99 per cent of the Modern Apprentices in construction occupations.[103] Whiteness and masculinity in the construction sector is explored further in the next chapter, and gender in the wood trades is addressed in several of the upcoming chapters.

The government's MA programme inherited many of the problems that plagued previous youth training schemes, including 'difficulties in attracting "suitable" young people', ongoing employers' concerns about its capacity 'to contribute to the future supply of employees with intermediate-level skills'[104] and a 'one-size-fits-all approach that fail[ed] to provide adequate flexibility'.[105] Michael Montague-Smith, Chair of the Building Crafts College Committee, acknowledged the challenge confronting training providers 'to reconcile the individual requirements of firms with the rigid requirements of the NVQ curriculum'. In conversation, he offered the example of a small and specialised bench joinery firm that would 'want its apprentices to become highly skilled in making windows and doors', but 'in order to get the NVQ qualification needed, they'll need to tick a box on "site work experience" or "experience in a delivery bay" – things that the firm probably doesn't do'.[106] In general, the MA curricula were judged too broad and lacking in content in comparison to those for apprenticeships in other European countries,[107] and only 24 per cent of participants completed all requirements.[108]

It is important to note that the process of institutionalising apprenticeship over the course of the twentieth century – a process in which MAs were merely the latest phase – served to further reify the old divide made between trade theory and practice. In the case of the building crafts, the partial transfer of learning from operational workshops and construction sites to college classrooms necessitated a codification of trade knowledge in the form of manuals, textbooks and course study packs, which, unsurprisingly, bear little resemblance to the risk, complexity and choices that real-life working situations present. It also created overreliance on standardised and generic examinations for conferring qualifications. MAs were indeed critiqued for being primarily 'a vehicle for delivering qualifications',[109] and thereby depriving trainees of the longer, necessary time period that had been integral to 'traditional' apprenticeships, and that supported deeper learning and development of a more rounded skillset, centrally including personal development.[110]

Certainly, not all training providers failed to foster personal development in their trainees. The instructors convening the MAs in carpentry, joinery and shop fitting at the Building Crafts College excelled in modelling responsibility, diligence and sound judgement, and in teaching the value of good social skills when communicating with clients and when interacting with fellow tradespeople. Chapter 5 introduces two of the College's most authentic personalities and highly talented MA instructors, Jim O'Brien and Cheryl Mattey, both of whom also had a hand in forming the fine woodworking students.

MAs continued to undergo numerous reforms in the early 2000s. These included a greater say from employers regarding their content.[111] However, 'the design, delivery and assessment of apprenticeships [was still] largely determined by government-funded bodies'.[112] The scheme did raise its game in promoting the training and education route to a greater spectrum of young men and women over the age of sixteen, including high academic achievers. Interest in the MA scheme and in employing apprentices was also beginning to take hold in industry and business. Nonetheless, the Leitch Review of Skills, commissioned by the government in 2004 and published two years later, was damning in its statement that 'the quantity and quality of necessary vocational skills' in the UK trailed behind those of France, Germany and the nation's other main competitors. Leitch recommended in the strongest terms that there be 'radical change right across the skill spectrum' and that the nation 'begin a new journey to embed a culture of learning' through greater awareness and investment by 'the State, employers and individuals'.[113] To eventuate the 'risks of increasing inequality, deprivation and child poverty [and] . . . a generation cut off permanently from labour market opportunity', the report called for an urgent increase in the number of Apprentices, to reach 500,000 per year by 2020,[114] and for a larger, more highly qualified workforce who shared 'a commitment to continue progression'.[115]

In 2003, the Livery Companies Apprenticeship Scheme (LCAS), in partnership with City & Guilds, had already taken the enlightened decision to introduce the Master Craft Certificate. This was awarded not only in recognition of craft excellence, but also for the recipient's 'commitment to continue the progression' of others in their craft occupation.[116] The scheme acknowledged the long-neglected but vital role that mentorship played in the formation of craftspeople, and in the sustainability and adaptability of trade knowledge over the long term. It appeared that apprenticeship, albeit greatly altered from its past forms, was being revived in some pockets of British work and industry with renewed appreciation for the learning and employment opportunities that it provided. The Carpenters' Building Crafts College was an active contributor to this process.

In the same year that the Leitch Review was commissioned, the popularity of construction-based apprenticeships was actually growing, with more than 12,000 young people starting them each year, and competition for a placement on the scheme was becoming keener. According to an article in *The Independent*, the construction industry was intent on debunking the enduring myth that construction is an exclusively male preserve. CITB-ConstructionSkills' 'efforts to attract more young women into the industry [were] bearing fruit, aided by the gradual reduction in the number of jobs that require physical strength'.[117] As for the Carpenters, the Company had already begun by the late twentieth century to grant the Freedom to women who were professional carpenters and woodworkers,[118] and it finally admitted the first women to the Livery in 2004.[119] In 2017, the Carpenters would elect their first female Master.[120] The Company was changing and not only in terms of gender diversity; it had also abolished patrimony in 2002 and adopted a positive policy to recruit active craftspeople to the Livery, who hitherto had constituted a tiny minority of its membership.[121]

Though the remit of the Building Crafts College had also changed and expanded enormously since its nineteenth-century beginnings, it retained the kernel of its founding spirit. More specifically, the institution remained firmly committed to fostering craft excellence and to meeting the ever-present challenge of perpetuating the craft traditions in wood and stone masonry. In the next chapter, I introduce daily life at the College and my immersion, and that of fellow trainees, in a rich and challenging learning environment defined by hand tools, soft woods and hard woods, the timber mill and a whole new set of bodily practices prescribed by an ancient wood-working tradition.

NOTES

1. Cass later switched from the Carpenters' to the Skinners' Company (which is one of the Great Twelve) and became its Master in 1714. The Skinners, like the Carpenters, are associates of the Sir John Cass Foundation.
2. Today, the Sir John Cass Foundation is one of the oldest and largest educational charities in London. Its remit includes the offer of bursaries to students at the Building Crafts College.
3. Epstein, 'Transferring Technical Knowledge', 30.
4. *Mr. Hoppus's Measurer Greatly Enlarged & Improved*, published by E. Hoppus, 1790. The first edition was published in 1736 and numerous editions appeared during its first hundred years of publication. It 'became the standard manual of its kind and continued to be printed into the [twentieth century]' (Yeomans, 'Early Carpenters' Manuals', 16).
5. W. Pain, *The Practical Builder or Workman's General Assistant* (1774); *The Carpenter and Joiners' Repository: or a new system of lines and proportions* (1778). For further discussion and details, see Yeoman, 'Early Carpenters' Manuals', 24–27.
6. P. Nicholson, *The Carpenter and Joiner's Assistant* (1797). See Yeoman, 'Early Carpenters' Manuals', 28.
7. Deissinger, 'Apprenticeship Systems', 34.
8. Smith, *An Inquiry*, Book I, Chapter X, Part 2, 148. On both moral and practical grounds, Adam Smith also maintained in *The Wealth of Nations* that the apprenticeship system was oppressive and exploitative of the apprentice's labour, and that the lack of financial incentive for apprentices while labouring for their masters made them idle (ibid., Book I, Chapter X, Part I, 124–25 and 152). Smith also argued that apprenticeship constrained the potential of the apprentice, and inhibited the free flow of the labour market: 'The patrimony of a poor man lies in the strength and dexterity of his hands; and to hinder him from employing this strength and dexterity in what manner he thinks proper without injury to his neighbour, is a plain violation of this most sacred property. It is a manifest encroachment upon the just liberty both of the workman and of those who might be disposed to employ him' (ibid., 151). Contemporary historian Emma Griffin argues in her book that with the repeal of the Statute of Artificers in 1814 – due in large part to lobbying by liberal reformers, in-dustrialists and factory owners – greater opportunities opened up to larger numbers of men to be trained through informal arrangements, enter trades and benefit from higher wages (Griffin, *Liberty's Dawn*).
9. See Snell, *Annals of the Labouring Poor*, 228–31. However, despite a decline in the number of formal livery-based apprenticeships, parish and pauper apprenticeships remained important for poorer segments of the population in London because of its 'ties to ideals on poverty prevention, settlement acquisition, and training in skills'. Parish apprenticeships, in fact, served both traditional and industrialising sectors of the economy simultaneously by readying a young labour force. (Levene, 'Parish Apprenticeship', 919).

10. Wallis, Webb and Minns, 'Leaving Home', 12.
11. For a summary of changes to apprenticeships in the eighteenth century, see Lane, *Apprenticeship in England*, 4–7.
12. In their study of the age of London apprentices, economic historians Wallis, Webb and Minns note that 'the fall in age of entry into service' over the two centuries to 1780 and London's growing population of young people attracted by the capital's booming economy resulted in an expansion in the supply of skilled and semi-skilled, as well as unskilled labour in the run-up to industrialisation, thus contributing significantly to the genesis of England's Industrial Revolution ('Leaving Home', 24).
13. Officially called the Apprentices Act 1814 (repealed). Deissinger notes that: 'Parliamentary debate revolved around the clauses in the Statutes of Apprentices which prescribed a seven-year training period and those intended to protect craft trades from the practices of "free employment" that were adopted in cottage industries and factories. The apprentice campaign failed for want of political support and was formally ended by laws passed in 1814 and [the Municipal Corporations Acts of] 1835' (Deissinger, 'Apprenticeship Systems', 33).
14. Thomas, 'Modernity, Crafts and Guilded Practices', 65.
15. More than 400 years earlier, Thomas More's *Utopia* also promulgated the social importance of every person participating in a trade as well as in agricultural production (More, *Utopia*, 55).
16. Ruskin, 'The Nature of Gothic', 19.
17. Morris, 'Useful Work', 304.
18. Epstein, 'Transferring Technical Knowledge', 29.
19. The expression 'Workshop of the World' to describe industrial Britain was used by future Prime Minister Benjamin Disraeli in the House of Commons in 1838, when he was still a backbencher.
20. This observation was made by scientist, Liberal politician and juror at the Paris Exhibition of 1967 Lyon Playfair, and was shared by British manufacturers. See Northrop, *Education Abroad*, 147.
21. Deissinger, 'Apprenticeship Systems', 36.
22. Alford and Barker, *A History of the Carpenters' Company*, 158.
23. The state's first direct involvement in education in England and Wales was in its funding for the building of schools for poor children in 1833.
24. The 1870 Elementary Education Act was largely a result of the Second Reform Act of 1867 and the government's objective to have an educated electorate. Changing attitudes towards education, and growing positive valuation, began much earlier, starting with Samuel Whitbread's 1807 Bill for reforming the Poor Law, as well as the Factory Acts of 1833, 1844 and 1867, which imposed restrictions on child labour and opened the possibility for national education. The year 1869 saw the establishment of the secular Education League and the more conservative and Anglican National Education Union, both of which played an important part in Britain's adoption of the Education Act the following year. A further Education Act in 1891 established free elementary education.
25. Deissinger, 'Apprenticeship Systems', 35.
26. Quoted in Middleton, 'The Education Act of 1870', 167.
27. Huxley, 'Professor Huxley's Inaugural Address', 146.
28. This included the Elementary Education Sandon Act of 1876, which made it the legal duty of parents to ensure that their children received basic education; the 1880

Elementary Education Act (or Mundella Act), requiring school boards to enforce compulsory education for children between the ages of five and ten; and the 1891 Elementary Education Act, which made primary education free of charge.

29. Glynn, 'The City of London', 131–32.
30. City & Guilds was granted a Royal Charter in 1900.
31. Thorogood, *One Hundred Years*, 21.
32. The system of qualifying examinations had been established by the Society of Arts in 1873 and was taken over by C&GLI in 1879.
33. Waterhouse (1830–1905) is perhaps best known for his design for the Natural History Museum in Kensington, a splendid example of Victorian Gothic Revival style.
34. Finsbury Technical College was set up as a feeder for the Central Institution. It is recognised as the first technical training college in England. It closed in 1929.
35. Thorogood, *One Hundred Years*, 3.
36. Wilson, 'The Institute of Carpenters Examinations', 10.
37. Sweett, 'Commentary', no pagination.
38. Tancell, 'The Stratford Estate', 18–20.
39. The Institute became a day school for boys in 1891 and was closed in 1905 when the local Borough Council opened its own school.
40. Lancaster, 'Message from the Master', 1.
41. Great Titchfield Street was developed by the Duke of Portland and already appears in its current complete form on the Richard Horwood Map of 1793. The street is located in East Marylebone, within a district that became informally known as Fitzrovia sometime before the Second World War.
42. London Department of Planning and City Development, *East Marylebone*, 10.
43. The original six other Liveries included the Joiners and Ceilers, Wheelwrights, Plaisterers, Painter-Stainers, Tylers and Bricklayers, and Plumbers. The Glaziers Company introduced a new class after the First World War (Tancell, 'Company History', 33).
44. The sixth edition, published in 1921, was heavily revised by Sir B.F. Fletcher, and his father's name was dropped. The twenty-first edition of the book was published in 2019.
45. The Sir Banister Fletcher Award is made to the 'student of the year' at the Building Crafts College.
46. Tancell, 'The Carpenters' Company in World War One', 16–17.
47. Tancell, 'Company History', 33.
48. These were sea mines that were transformed into 'landmines' (also known as parachute bombs or parachute mines) that could be dropped by the Luftwaffe and made to detonate once they reached the roof level of buildings, before impact. Their effect was powerful and devastating.
49. Most of the Company's treasures were saved, including the three surviving sixteenth-century wall paintings. The paintings were reinstated on the walls of the reception hall of the new and present Hall.
50. Tancell, 'The Stratford Estate', 20. Between 1945 and 1965, West Ham Borough Council 'carried out redevelopment and slum clearance schemes, building more than 9500 dwellings, including on the Carpenters' estate' (ibid.).
51. Tancell, 'Company History', 33.
52. Unwin, 'Employer-Led Realities', 60.
53. Tancell, 'Company History', 34.

54. Thorogood, *One Hundred Years*, 16. The Carpenters' Craft Competition is the only national one of its kind open to students of carpentry, joinery and shop fitting.

55. The Institute of Carpenters also administered an exam, but the number of entrants began dropping in the 2000s because of the removal of national public funding for its Intermediate Examination. Funding for the its Foundation and Advanced examinations was terminated in 2009. The cessation of funding was alleged to be 'a deliberate government policy to stop the funding of "development" examinations and to concentrate on the basic skills in the form of the Construction Awards and the NVQ system recognized by ConstructionSkills [i.e. the Sector Skills Council for Construction]' (Institute of Carpenters *Annual Report*, 10).

56. The new Hall was built according to the designs of architects Whinney, Son & Austen Hall. A pedestrian arcade was introduced at ground level so that London Wall (street) could be widened; a bridge was built over Throgmorton Avenue to accommodate the new banqueting hall, and two additional storeys were added, set back from the façade. Construction was completed in 1960 and the Hall reopened on 4 May.

57. Barnett, *The Verdict of Peace*, 465. Also quoted in Harris, *Modern Apprenticeships*, 14.

58. Recorded in Harris, *Modern Apprenticeships*, 15. See also Gospel, 'Whatever Happened to Apprenticeship Training?', 7.

59. Harris, *Modern Apprenticeships*, 14.

60. Tancell, 'Company History', 34.

61. Gospel, 'Whatever Happened to Apprenticeship Training?', 8.

62. See Tancell, 'Company History', 34.

63. Ibid.

64. Carpenters' Company. *Carpenters' Company*. Promotional pamphlet, no date/pagination.

65. Harris, *Modern Apprenticeships*, 15.

66. Coleman, *The Art of Work*, 97.

67. Fuller and Unwin, 'Does Apprenticeship Still Have Meaning in the UK?', 103.

68. 'Apprentice wages in relation to adult earnings were much higher in Britain than elsewhere, with the result that training costs were correspondingly greater.' For example, British apprentice wages were 60 per cent of those of adults compared to 17–25 per cent in Switzerland and Germany (Harris, *Modern Apprenticeships*, 15 and fn. 45).

69. See the Prologue in this book.

70. Raffe, 'Education, Employment and the Youth Opportunities Programme', 211.

71. Ibid., 220.

72. Edwards, 'The History and Politics of the Youth Opportunities Programme', 136.

73. Gospel, 'Whatever Happened to Apprenticeship Training?', 8.

74. See the supporting references for these criticisms of the YTS in the Prologue to this book.

75. Harris, *Modern Apprenticeships*, 16.

76. See Gospel, 'Whatever Happened to Apprenticeship Training?', 9. Most of the twenty-one Industrial Training Boards were wound up after the passing of the 1982 Industrial Training Act and were replaced by voluntary employer-led training organisations that assumed much the same responsibilities, but operated without statutory levies. The ITBs in Construction (CITB) and Engineering Construction

(CITB) nevertheless survived, and raise most of their funds through training levies and various commercial activities.

77. Fuller and Unwin, 'Reconceptualising Apprenticeship', 156.

78. TECs were disbanded in 2001.

79. In 1985, the government launched the *Review of Vocational Qualifications in England and Wales*. The recommendations for substantial reform were accepted in the 1986 White Paper, *Working Together – Education and Training* (Cmnd 9832), which called for the setting-up of the National Council for Vocational Qualifications (NCVQ) for England, Wales and Northern Ireland. The NCVQ was an independent company limited by guarantee that was established and initially funded by the government. Government funding ceased once the NCVQ became financially viable. Its remit was to create and promote the NVQ framework (NCVQ Working Party, 'The National Council', 145–47).

80. Scotland operated the Scottish Vocational Qualifications framework.

81. Fuller and Unwin, 'Reconceptualising Apprenticeship', 156.

82. Roberts, 'Career Trajectories', 236.

83. Ibid., 155; and Senker et al., 'Working to Learn', 194.

84. For example, in a 2003 White Paper, it was reported that just 28 per cent of the British workforce had qualified to intermediate skill levels (i.e. apprenticeship, skilled craft and technician level) compared to 51 per cent in France and 65 per cent in Germany (Department for Education and Skills, *21st Century Skills*, 12).

85. Mirza-Davies, 'Apprenticeships Policy', 5.

86. Blair, 'Leader's Speech, Brighton 1997'.

87. Mirza-Davies, 'Apprenticeships Policy', 6.

88. BBC, 'Education: Blair Wants Student Boom'. It is noteworthy that in 1980, just 15 per cent of young people over the age of eighteen stayed in full-time education, whether this was vocational training, further or higher education, including universities and polytechnics. This figure rose to 25 per cent by 1990. Labour's 50 per cent target was finally achieved in 2019 (50.2%), and 57 per cent of that population were women (Coughlan, 'The Symbolic Target').

89. A quote from Lewis Sidnick, the education and skills policy advisor for the British Chambers of Commerce, which represented more than 135,000 firms. Quoted in Crace, 'Business Lament Lack of Bright Trainees'. See also, for example, BBC, 'Increase in Student Numbers Not Needed'. Notably, at this time in 2004, Labour was also trying to get its Higher Education Bill through its final reading, which proposed variable tuition fees of up to £3,000 per annum. This fee increase came into effect in England in 2006 and later in Wales and Northern Ireland. In 2012, university fees trebled to £9,000 per annum – a watershed moment for higher education in England, Wales and Northern Ireland.

90. Labour's 2003 White Paper on *21st Century Skills* reaffirmed the government's commitment to the Modern Apprenticeship scheme as the 'primary work-based vocational route for young people', and set a target for getting 28 per cent of the population below the age of twenty-two to participate by 2004 (Department for Education and Skills, *21st Century Skills*, 79).

91. Cassels, *Modern Apprenticeships*, 13.

92. The Building Crafts Training School was renamed the Building Crafts College in 1993.

93. Taylor, 'Building Crafts College', 4. See also Tancell, 'Company History', 35.
94. Instructor and Vice Principal David Pearham, who had been employed by the Building Crafts College since 1993, recalled that there had been women students at the College at the time he started (personal communication through Principal Len Conway, 16 June 2020). There were no available records to confirm the year that the first female students attended either the Trades Training School or Building Crafts College.
95. Taylor, 'Building Crafts College', 4.
96. This required bringing back under Company control a number of outstanding leases in its Stratford estate. Plans for a Channel Tunnel Rail Link and Stratford International rail station had already been approved, and it was apparent that this area of London would be undergoing massive redevelopment, in which the College and Company might find new opportunities (Taylor, 'Building Crafts College', 5). The estate at the time was still heavily industrialised. In 2003, 19.5 acres of the estate was sold to the London Development Agency as part of the Olympic Land Bid for London 2012 and was used most notably for the building of the Aquatics Centre. The Carpenters' Company retains six sites outside the Olympic Park, including the Building Crafts College (Tancell, 'The Stratford Estate', 21).
97. Tectus designed the new college building and Rooff Ltd. acted as the main building contractor. Michael Montague-Smith recalled that the Carpenters' Company was not entirely confident that the move to Stratford would be successful and there were doubts that people would want to travel out so far for training. The building was therefore designed in such a way that if the College failed in that location, then it could be converted into a community workshop (interview with Montague-Smith, 7 July 2008).
98. Matthews, 'Message from the Master', 1.
99. The Building Crafts College Committee was comprised of the Master of the Carpenters' Company, the Middle Warden, three other members of the Company Court, the Chairman of the Craft Committee and up to four co-opted members of the Livery. The Principal of the College attended the regular College Committee meetings. The College is constituted as an educational charity. Approximately 60 per cent of its income is derived from public sources, 25 per cent from student fees and 15 per cent from charitable sources, being mainly the Carpenters' Company Charitable Trust. Tancell reported that a tradition continues whereby each liveryman donates £150 annually to the College (Tancell, 'Carpenters' Company Charities from 1700', 18). The Company's Norton Folgate Trust provides support for students in need who are engaged in education or craft training. Its biggest commitment (10 per cent) is to students at the College. In recent years, the Company has sponsored a student attending the Edward Barnsley Workshop in Petersfield and students on the Building Crafts Apprentices course at the Prince's Foundation.
100. These included Sector Skills Councils, BOSS (Building One Stop Shop), the Let's Build Programme for youngsters, and the adult training scheme with East Thames Housing, the National Heritage Training Group (NHTG), the Society for the Protection of Ancient Buildings (SPAB) and the Conference on Training in Architectural Conservation (COTAC) (Taylor, 'Building Crafts College', 10; and interview with M. Montague-Smith, 7 July 2008).
101. Sennitt, 'Message from the Master', 1–2.

102. Conway, 'Building Crafts College' (2010), 3–4. Examples of the College expanding remit include its operation of a 'Let's Build' vocational education training centre for year 10 and 11 pupils, created in 2004 in Canning Town. In 2006, the Carpenters Craft Company Limited was set up 'as a wholly owned subsidiary of the College to undertake training and to manage externally funded projects beyond the scope of core craft activities', which enabled 'the College to diversify its income base'. The College also took on the role as a lead partner 'in promoting construction training in East London and ensuring that local communities derive[d] maximum benefit from the unprecedented levels of construction', including the Thames Gateway project and 2012 Olympic site in Stratford (Taylor, 'Building Crafts College', 9–10). Notably, a new extension to the Kennard Road campus was completed in 2008, increasing college floor space by 30 per cent. An annex was also established at Anchor House in Canning Town and, in 2009, the College opened its Gibbins Road Campus, allowing it to extend construction training to an even larger number of disciplines.
103. BBC, 'Where Next for School-Leavers?'.
104. Maguire, 'Modern Apprenticeships', 172–73.
105. Harris, *Modern Apprenticeships*, 10.
106. In interview with Montague-Smith, 7 July 2008.
107. Senker et al., 'Working to Learn', 193; and Fuller and Unwin, 'The Content of Apprenticeship', 33.
108. Harris, *Modern Apprenticeships*, 10.
109. Fuller and Unwin, 'The Content of Apprenticeship', 33.
110. Fuller and Unwin, 'Learning as Apprentices', 424. See also Bynner, who states that 'the English [Apprenticeship] system sees no links between the preparation for employment and citizenship' (Bynner, 'Youth Transitions', 24).
111. Notably, the National Union of Students feared that a greater say from employers would be at the expense of trainees' individual development (BBC, 'Promise of a Skills Revolution'). Similarly, policy consultant Tess Lanning noted that 'too often a focus on meeting employers' immediate skill needs means that the role of vocational education is largely restricted to assessing competence in specific job roles … In other European countries, aims go beyond, for example preparing young Germans for active and responsible citizenship' (Lanning, 'Why Rethink Apprenticeship?', 8).
112. Lanning, 'Why Rethink Apprenticeship?', 15.
113. Leitch, *The Leitch Review of Skills*, 2.
114. In response to the *Leitch Review*, the National Apprenticeship Service was launched in 2009, and a number of funding and incentive schemes were introduced during the following years. The *Apprenticeship Statistics* Briefing Paper for England published in August 2020 explains that 'it wasn't until 2007/08 that apprenticeship [started to exceed] 200,000 per year. Between 2009/10 and 2011/12 there was a large increase in starts, and since then there were generally around 500,000 starts each year, before the large decrease in starts in 2017/18'. The Briefing Paper notes that: 'The number of starts fell following the introduction of a new apprenticeship funding system in May 2017 [i.e. the Apprenticeship Levy scheme]. This led to a large fall in starts in the final quarter of 2016/17, and the lower number of starts continued in 2017/18. The number of starts … increased by 17,600 in 2018/19,

but [was] still below the number in 2016/17.' It goes on to state that: 'In the first three quarters of the 2019/20 academic year (August to April), there were 275,900 apprenticeship starts. This was a drop of 13% from the same period in 2018/19, with around 43,000 fewer starts.' The greatest fall in starts was among the under-nineteen age cohort, which fell by 17 per cent from the previous year (Foley, *Apprenticeship Statistics*, 6–10).

115. Ibid., 3. Five years after the publication of the *Leitch Review*, eleven employees per 1,000 in England had done an apprenticeship. England trailed far behind Austria (39 per 1,000), Germany (40) and Switzerland (43). 'Fewer than 1 in 10 employers in England offered apprenticeships compared to at least 1 in 4 in these countries' (Lanning, 'Why Rethink Apprenticeship?', 9). Also, the average time to complete an apprenticeship in England was just one year compared to an average of four in German-speaking countries (ibid., 11).

116. The purpose of the Master Certificate Scheme is to encourage career progression in areas of skills identified with the City of London Livery Companies, including the Carpenters.

117. McCormack, 'Rewards for Early Starters'.

118. For centuries, women had been granted the Freedom by the Company, but this had been through patrimony and not because they were practitioners in the wood occupations. Regarding the rules of patrimony that applied to women, see Ridley, *A History of the Carpenters' Company*, 182–83. The first woman to receive the Honorary Freedom from the Company was Mary Woodgate Wharrie in 1917. She was the daughter of liveryman and insurer Sir Henry Harben and a benefactor to Rustington convalescent home. In 1954, Queen Juliana of the Netherlands was the second woman to receive an Honorary Freedom (ibid., 133).

119. Jasper Ridley writes that 'admission of women to the Freedom and the Livery, and their participation in social events' was a 'matter of controversy' for the Company Court (ibid., 181). For a more detailed discussion of women's participation in Company social events and their admission to the Livery, see ibid., 181–83.

120. See Tancell, 'Women and the Carpenters' Company', 19–20. Master Rachel Bower (2017–18) had working ties to the building and construction industry and had been Education Officer for the Society for the Protection of Ancient Buildings (SPAB).

121. Michael Montague-Smith, in interview 7 July 2008. The Carpenters' Company was the first livery to abolish the Patrimony.

CHAPTER 4

GETTING STARTED

DAY-ONE INTRODUCTIONS

'Don't let them give you a swirly', cautioned my brother-in-law teasingly. He had worked as a site carpenter in the past and knew the 'tricks' of the trade. 'A swirly', he explained to my naïve self, 'is when two guys bigger than you pick you up by the ankles, hang you over an open toilet bowl, lower your hair to the scum-line, and flush.' That repulsive imagery played in my mind on the long tube journey eastward across London on the first morning of term.

I had initially visited the Building Crafts College nearly one year earlier. I had arranged a meeting with its Director to explain my proposed research in the hopes of winning his consent and being offered a place on the fine wood-work programme. Guided by the map in my well-fingered *London A–Z*, I navigated my way on foot from Stratford tube station along a drab, desolate road running alongside the railway tracks, and then up a flight of stairs and over a narrow footbridge. The iron structure rumbled with each passing train on the six busy lines beneath. Halfway along the footbridge, a small patch was cordoned off with black and yellow tape, flapping and twisting in the breeze. On the pavement within the protected space, and thickly outlined in white chalk, was the silhouette of a body, arms spread above the contours of the head and shoulders. I paused there, deferentially, allowing an oncoming pedestrian to pass, and then hurried along, descended the steps and, with relief, found the college directly before me.

The college exterior of red brick and silver steel cladding was unremarkable and industrial in appearance – not at all what I had anticipated for such an historic institution. However, inside, beyond the threshold, was an entirely different world: orderly, light-filled and scented by freshly cut timber.

A reception desk of simple design in unstained oak was positioned directly in front of the three glass entry doors. The small lobby opened onto a long and airy two-storey atrium of pleasing angular geometries. Crisp white wall surfaces were punctuated by plain oak doorways; the flooring was polished oak planks, and a broad staircase of open risers, also constructed in oak, led to a mezzanine, off of which the administrative offices were located. The atrium was bathed in natural light, flooding in from the uninterrupted strip of skylights that stretched along the entire length of the space. At the far end was the college canteen and, on the left-hand side, a set of double doors provided access to the vast workshops.

On the first morning of term, the College buzzed with a freneticism all too familiar from my experiences of university registration week – a ritual that filled my stomach with butterflies, whether I was a student or a lecturer. As a kid, the smell of new school supplies stacked high on drugstore shelves triggered a queasy realisation that summer was over and it was back to classroom confinement.

After queuing to sign in at the reception desk, registered trainees on the fine woodwork and stonemasonry courses were directed to the canteen to await further instruction. Alex was the first classmate I met. He was a big and powerful guy who, if he had wanted, could have given me that dreaded 'swirly' single-handed. Instead, he politely asked if he could join me at the small round table to drink his coffee. Like all the men in the canteen – and it was exclusively men at that point – Alex was clean-shaven with a recent haircut and sported new work clothing and steel-toe boots. He was just a little younger than me and was similarly apprehensive about what lay ahead for the next two years. He told me that he had been a lorry driver and a quality inspector for BMW, but now, at thirty-seven years of age, he wanted a trade that would offer a satisfying challenge and the promise of autonomy. Alex lived in Swindon, some 150 kilometres west of Stratford, and so the daily rail commute in itself demonstrated serious commitment to his goals.

At 9:00 AM, all students were summoned to a spacious lecture hall where we were asked to be seated while the Director graciously welcomed us and introduced key administrators and the course instructors in turn. Afterwards, we were taken on a guided tour of the College facilities, first visiting the sprawling ground-floor workshop where the Modern Apprentices in wood occupations came to train on a rotational basis. This was followed by cursory introductions to the 'large' and the 'small' timber mills before continuing our tour with a circuit through the stonemasonry workshop.

We then climbed a wide metal staircase to a long and spacious mezzanine, which had been recently extended to span the full length of the workshop building.[1] The high mezzanine overlooked the Apprentices and the stonemasons on the ground floor. One end of the mezzanine was home to the small number of leadwork trainees. The first and second-year cohorts of fine woodworkers shared a generous-sized workshop at the opposite end, located directly above the concrete ceiling of the large mill. Like the college atrium, the workshops were brightly illuminated by a wide strip of skylights that extended perpendicularly across the building's gently arching metal roof, as well as by numerous windows and large overhead lamps.

After the morning tea break, the first-year fine woodworkers reconvened in the college library, where the course instructors, Con and David, more fully introduced themselves and the structure of the programme. The students then made a round of brief personal introductions. We were nine all-male trainees. In addition to Alex, there was Jens, who had previously worked as a researcher for BBC radio programming, Robert, who held an MPhil and had worked for an environmental conservation agency in London, and Tony, who was unique among us in that he possessed actual carpentry experience as a joiner. Tony had been employed by a door-and-window manufacturer in Potters Bar, but had also put his hands to arboriculture, grafting fruit trees during extended travels in New Zealand. The combination had endowed him with enviable knowledge of timber species and their Latin classifications.

Alex, Jens, Robert and Tony were mature students, ranging in age from mid-twenties to late thirties. Each had a colourful history of education, employment and life experiences that had circuitously taken them to the Building Crafts College. As described in the Introduction to this volume, I coined these men, and individuals like them, 'vocational migrants', because of the thoughtful deliberations they had made to leave jobs and careers in order to pursue woodworking as a lifestyle choice as much as a livelihood.

The four remaining trainees of our cohort were school-leavers, aged sixteen and seventeen, and still residing at home with their parents. Darren's family were in Aldersbrook, where his secondary schooling had included a taste of bench carpentry. Tariq and Abdul both lived in Whitechapel and knew one another from school, where, like Darren, they had gained elementary woodworking experience. In the coming months, Tariq, with his quiet, gentle nature and hands like bear paws, would prove to be a highly talented craftsman. It was clear from day one, however, that Abdul lacked the necessary drive. The same was true for Liam, who, along with two chums in the second year of the programme, came from London's southeast borough of Bromley. Liam boasted that he would become a futures trader, like his dad, and that he was at college 'killing time' until he turned eighteen, at which point he could begin a trader's training. Liam's father had learned carpentry during a spell behind bars and believed that the hands-on training would provide his son with focus and discipline.

Con and David kindly allotted extra minutes during my personal introduction so that I could describe my intended research as a participating
trainee and an observer of our collective skill learning and development at
the College. This generated interest, several questions and unanimous consent from my fellow students and the two instructors. It was the start of good
friendships, exhilarating learning challenges and two of the most pleasurable
years of my career as an anthropologist.

The social dynamics within the community were significant in shaping
the learning environment, as were the different values and perspectives that
individuals brought to the course. This chapter tells the story of the first term
of fine woodworking, supplying the backdrop to themes revisited in successive chapters and introducing some of the key people who populated my
field site and shared a passion for craftwork. It concludes with an account of
the annual prize-giving ceremony at Carpenters' Hall, which simultaneously
fortified the bonds between trainees while generating greater competition
and imputing hierarchy amongst us.

WOODWORKING CURRICULA

For prospective trainees, discovering the existence of the Building Crafts
College was in itself an accomplishment. Despite its position as the oldest
institution of its kind in the country, the College kept a low profile. Its two
advanced craft courses, namely fine woodworking and stonemasonry, preserved small student numbers, and information posted on the College website was rudimentary at best.[2] When I arrived in 2005, there were roughly
210 students enrolled across all courses. The vast majority (more than 80 per
cent) were Modern Apprentices who came for short periods on block release
from their places of work in order to earn National Vocational Qualifications
(NVQs).[3] Enrolment of Modern Apprentices had nearly quadrupled since
2001, when the College moved from its former location on Great Titchfield
Street to the newly built premises in Stratford,[4] and their numbers would
continue to grow year on year. This represented an imported revenue stream
for the College. Its direct involvement in the government's youth training
scheme also allowed administrators to enjoy greater influence in England's
construction industry.

Growth, however, was often in tension with the institution's proud claims
to being 'rooted in the past'. According to some instructors, the enormity
of the Apprenticeship programme threatened to overshadow the College's
much smaller craft-intensive courses and thereby disfigure its distinct character and identity. Efforts to counter that eventuality and preserve the College traditions of hands-on training and craftsmanship were channelled into

the steadfast promotion of its flagship diploma courses in stonemasonry and fine woodworking.

Fine woodworking is a two-year, full-time course. In 2005, when I started, tuition fees were a steep £5,375 per annum, but numerous trainees who could demonstrate need for financial assistance received charitable grants from the Carpenters' Company. The course was advertised as being:

> Practically based and designed to equip students with the craft skills and management expertise necessary to enable them to set up a small independent business. Students learn traditional carpentry and joinery skills before progressing to woodturning, hand veneering, inlaying/marquetry, French polishing and business start-up instruction.[5]

More precisely, the curriculum promoted sound understanding and competent handling of tools, conceptual planning of the progressive stages of woodworking projects, development of critical judgement of one's own work and creative approaches to practical problem solving. In combination, ample bench time, a well-stocked timber rack and normally patient instruction afforded the chance to make mistakes and to learn from them, and to repeat procedures until the logic made sense and the execution became incorporated into a more-or-less fluid choreography of stances, postures, gazes, grasps and movements. The rigour of the 'business start-up instruction' was somewhat lacklustre, however. Discussion of that deficiency and the complicated dynamics that perpetuated it will be taken up in Chapter 9.

The first year supplied a foundation in architectural joinery equivalent to NVQ Level 2 requirements, allowing students to earn an Intermediate Construction Award (ICA) in Wood Occupations. The daily schedule of activities at the Building Crafts College concentrated on practical assignments that were carried out in the workshop. Relevant theory or underpinning knowledge was shared in impromptu 'toolbox sessions' around the workbench, while more formal lectures were delivered in classrooms or in the library, where students also completed written assignments and filled out their mandatory logbooks.

In chronological sequence, the set-piece carpentry projects in year one included a casement window with glazing bars, a small dovetail-jointed tool cabinet, a frame-and-panel door, and a half-scale staircase with banister and newel post, all made in Redwood pine. High levels of accuracy were emphasised, with tolerances of ±2 millimetres. Trainees learned to produce scale drawings, full-size rod drawings and cutting lists, which included the quantities and dimensions of components needed for a set piece. They selected their own planks from the timber racks and were closely supervised in the mill until they successfully completed the machining course and passed the Construction Industry Training Board (CITB) health and safety test.

Figure 4.1 View of the fine-woodwork workshop at the Building Crafts College, 2007. © David Wheeler

In the second year, students progressed to advanced hardwood projects and to the design and making of handcrafted furniture,[6] with acceptable tolerances of a maximum of ±1 millimetre. Notably, the softwood-hardwood classification refers not to the hardness of the wood, but rather is a botanical classification that distinguishes respectively between gymnosperms whose seeds are 'naked' and whose leaves are needle-like or scale-like and often evergreen, and angiosperms that belong to the flowering plant group and produce 'covered' seeds. Nevertheless, the European oak, American or English walnut, cherry, ash and beech that were most frequently used in the college workshop for making furniture were indeed much 'harder' than the Redwood pine used in year one, and therefore allowed for cleaner cuts and chops, but demanded more frequent sharpening of tool blades.

Year-two students progressively assembled a portfolio of projects, which included a bedside cabinet, coffee table, chair, dovetail box or chest with inlay or marquetry, and other items if term time permitted. Trainees were encouraged to produce design sketches as well as maquettes (i.e. scale test models) in softwood to explore jointing details and proportions. As in year one, they produced scale drawings, rod drawings and cutting lists before commencing the final piece, which might entail the additional design and making of router jigs, formers and templates. Candidates who successfully completed the course earned joint City & Guilds and Carpenters' Company Diplomas.

By the time they reached graduation, many trainees had hopes of becoming designer-makers of bespoke furniture and running small businesses from dedicated workshops. In North America, the more familiar term for such craftspeople is 'studio furniture makers', referring to the small studio settings in which they typically operate. Like their British counterparts, most acquire the necessary skills at a college or are self-taught and 'experience a longer, self-directed, and less constrained learning process' than wage-based furniture makers employed in mass manufacturing, who are often task-specialised.[7] The aspirations of college trainees to be autonomous designer-makers are explored in detail in Chapter 6 and the formidable impediments to realising those dreams are addressed in Chapter 9.

Unlike the fine-woodwork students, the Modern Apprentices who trained on the ground floor were already employed in work. A critical history of the government's numerous youth training schemes, including Modern Apprenticeships (MAs), was presented in Chapter 3. Although the Modern Apprentices were not the subject of my study, their outsized presence at the College merits a brief description of their programme.

Apprentices attended the College over three years on periods of block-release training that was run by the College on behalf of the CITB.[8] The MA scheme was originally intended for school-leavers and young adults who would complete their training by the age of twenty-four. A complementary scheme was later introduced for those twenty-five years and older,[9] but mature trainees remained a tiny minority on the college course. Block-release periods were of two or three weeks in duration, totalling twelve weeks in year one, eleven weeks in year two and ten in the final year. The course covered carpentry, joinery and shop fitting leading to NVQ Levels 2 and 3 and Advanced Construction Awards (ACA).

Time at the College was structured for Apprentices to absorb the theory and underpinning knowledge of wood occupations, and to hone their trade skills. Under the ever-watchful eyes of convenors Jim and Cheryl, students learned not only to operate safely and efficiently with tools, but also to measure-up projects, produce technical drawings, estimate quantities, compile cutting lists, machine sawn stock, mark-out timber, cut joints, assemble components and finish the surfaces. Jim and Cheryl, along with fine-woodwork instructor David, share colourful accounts of their teaching experiences and philosophies in the next chapter.

To earn NVQs, Apprentices completed log books and made full-scale storm-proof windows, frame-and-panel doors with doorframes, staircases, wall units and traditional oak wall panelling, which was attractively installed in the college meeting rooms and along its corridors. Apprentices took their learning back to the workplace or building site, where, ideally, the new knowledge was integrated into their experiences of daily operations. Some might build careers within the same companies that invested in their training, while others might progress to shop-fitters' firms specialised in high-end interiors or, more rarely, to advanced craft studies. Instructors Jim and Cheryl hoped that today's trainees might one day hire and mentor apprentices of their own.

CORNELIUS: APPRENTICE TO MENTOR

Term-time began in mid-September and ended in early July. The Monday to Friday schedule at college was modelled on full-time work, starting at 8:45 AM and finishing at 4:45 PM. There was a 45-minute lunch break and short tea breaks in the morning and afternoon. Year-one convenor Cornelius – better known to all as Con – enforced a strict regime of punctuality and required his trainees to sport proper attire, be courteous, abide by the health and safety regulations, keep bench tops tidy and sweep-up work areas at the end of each day. Tending to tools was also heavily emphasised. Sharpening, oiling, cleaning, polishing and putting tools away in their proper place after use were institutionalised activities in Con's workshop.

Con had known since childhood that he wanted to be a carpenter. He grew up in Fulham Broadway's Irish community where 'plenty of men were carpenters of one sort or another', many of whom were 'musicians making their bread and butter labouring on London's building sites'. The Polish woodworking teacher at his local secondary school invented straightforward exercises for the pupils. 'Other students would go all wacky, but I always did them simply', he reminisced. 'My thinking was to get them over with and move onto the next exercise so I could learn new things.' That pragmatism would shape his approach as a workshop instructor.

Con's first job out of school was doing furniture repair for Harrods Department Store Company. The workshop was in the company's grand Victorian warehouse located along the Thames riverside in Barnes, now converted into luxury flats. The job also marked the start of a three-year apprenticeship. Con was sent one day each week by his employer to the esteemed London College of Furniture in Whitechapel for formal tuition in upholstery, cabinet making, woodturning, veneering and French polishing.[10] Later stages of the training included management studies, but accounting, paperwork and administrative tasks that took time away from the tools held little interest for Con.

In the final year of his apprenticeship, Con left Harrods to take up a position in the joiners' shop at the Victoria & Albert Museum. The in-house carpenters made repair works to the building and manufactured the exhibition showcases. As the youngest member of the team, he was taken under the wings of the older men. By their example, Con learned the responsibilities that came with mentoring apprentices: 'The craftsman serves as a role model for the youngster – not just in technical aspects, but, perhaps more importantly, in behaviour and conduct.'

Upon completing his apprenticeship, Con decided against establishing an independent workshop. 'You could be a great craftsperson, but going into business on your own is another thing', he cautioned. 'You have to have business acumen or else you'll wind up working for nothing and have all the stress.' After the V&A, he took positions in various workshops in Knightsbridge, Hammersmith and Camberwell, participating in challenging heritage projects that included making a bookcase for an eighteenth-century Robert Adam's room in Syon House, and the removal of fittings from the original Lyric Hammersmith and their meticulous reinstallation in the newly built theatre that opened in 1979.

While employed in Jackson's workshop in Hammersmith, Con was promoted to foreman of joinery operations and was delegated the task of training up a new apprentice. 'He was sixteen or seventeen', Con recounted, 'and it took some initial effort to teach the young man the importance of punctuality.' He repeatedly stressed the necessity of good timekeeping and completing commissions to deadline in order to survive and thrive in the world of work. 'When things were slack', he said, 'I gave him little jobs so that he'd push himself and learn new things. He'd be proud when he finished, and I also felt the satisfaction. That's where I discovered my interest in teaching.'

Con applied for a position at the Building Crafts College in 2001, at the time when the College was transferring from West London to Stratford. He was appointed convenor of fine woodworking, covering the instruction for both years of the programme. 'The paperwork that came with the job was exactly what I didn't want to be doing. But', he recalled with a jolly smile, 'the teaching side of it was great!' Total numbers on the course in the early 2000s fluctuated between eleven and twelve students. Training began with a brief excursion into architectural joinery before moving rapidly on to furniture. Con's broad carpentry experience made him query the emphasis on turning out furniture makers. He progressively increased the proportion of architectural joinery projects in order 'to broaden the scope of what people could learn' and thereby expand their employment prospects after graduation. 'If someone doesn't have the aptitude for fine woodwork', he reasoned, 'then timber-frame building offers another alternative. It's a different discipline but the accuracy is still there. And, some people cope better working with larger things than with small and fine ones.'

By 2005, total student numbers on the course had increased to seventeen, and so the College appointed a new convenor, David Wheeler, to administer the full programme and oversee the progression of year-two trainees in particular. Pleasingly for Con, this alleviated much of his paperwork duties and allowed him to dedicate his full energies to forming the new students.

BUILDING RAPPORT WITH A BENCH PLANE

On day two, Con introduced us to a variety of bench planes, including the fine smoothing plane, the longer, general-purpose jack plane, and the even-longer try or jointer plane, which is used for levelling the surfaces of wide panels or the seams of jointed boards.[11] The indispensable bench plane has traditionally been the first tool to which novices are introduced, forming the basis for all subsequent hand skills in the craft. Hand planes have been essential to the carpenter's toolkit since at least Roman times[12] and have changed little in design since then. It has been logically suggested that the constancy in form and design of many basic hand tools is straightforwardly due to the configuration and limitations of our human anatomy, the properties of the material being worked and the laws of physics.[13]

In the not-so-distant past, all carpentry workshops kept an assortment of dedicated hand planes for producing rebates, grooves and a multitude of profiles for skirting boards and mouldings. All of these tasks can now be accomplished with speed and accuracy using either a handheld router or stationary spindle moulder with changeable blades. Already beginning in the late eighteenth and early nineteenth centuries, most classic woodworking tools were being progressively mechanised.[14] The work of the mortise chisel was supplanted by mortising machines; the tenon saw and bevelled chisels by tenoning machines; brace-and-bit augers by the drill press or electric drills; dovetail saws by the dovetail machine; and the array of other specialised handheld saws by the chop saw, circular saw, panel saw, band saw, radial arm saw and electric jig saw. Smoothing planes were moved aside by the thicknesser and the over-hand planer, and, with the advent of electrical transmission, by the power sander as well.

However, even those woodworkers who have largely mechanised their production and rely on the speed and efficiency of power tools keep a hand plane conveniently at the ready for smoothing edges and finely finishing surfaces. Wielding a plane with competence takes practice. Carpenter and author Jeff Taylor vividly noted that: 'A dull and maladjusted plane is brutally uncooperative; it shaves stomach lining and peace of mind, but not wood.' By contrast, a well-kept plane in the hands of an expert can slowly sculpt a rough or winding board 'into square shapes of buttery smoothness'.[15] American furniture maker and instructor Jeff Miller correctly observed that planes can be 'the source of both the most frustration and the most pleasure' in woodworking. Until a carpenter achieves an understanding of the parts, mechanics and function of the plane, learns to correctly sharpen the blade, understands how wood behaves and embodies the basic techniques of wielding the tool, 'a plane may seem like an instrument uniquely suited for torturing wood'. Once these various elements are brought together, however, 'the plane is a tool that can do amazing things'.[16]

Our very first task was to take apart and reassemble a bench plane and to sharpen its cutting iron on a diamond stone. Con gathered the nine new trainees around Jens' workbench to demonstrate the dissection of a sturdy Stanley smoothing plane. He began by lifting the lever on the 'lever cap' in order to slide the cap off the 'locking screw', and he then removed the 'cap iron' and the 'blade' that lay below. With a large flat-headed screwdriver, the instructor loosened the locking screw to separate cap iron from blade. He named and explained the anatomy of the tool beginning with the wooden knob and wooden handle located at the 'toe' and 'heel' of the plane respectively, and then proceeded to the levers and screws of the 'frog' that adjust the depth and lateral positioning of the blade in relation to the plane's 'mouth' (or 'throat'). Following the lesson, we returned to our individual benches to disassemble and reassemble a smoothing plane and experiment with the effects produced by its levers and screws.

Con soon summoned us back to show how a cutting iron is sharpened. Good tool sharpening is a skill in its own right, demanding concentration, controlled hands, firm wrists and repeated practice. It also requires understanding of the ways that the sharpened steel blade will interface with a timber surface. Con first flattened the back of the cutting iron, progressing from medium to finer grades of oilstone to achieve a mirror shine. He then clamped the blade into a honing guide to sharpen the grinding bevel at 25 degrees, and, by adjusting the guide, he made a narrow secondary honing bevel at 35 degrees along the cutting-iron edge. The steel 'burr', formed by honing the bevelled edge, was removed by lapping the back of the cutting iron on the fine-grade stone. Con finished the demonstration by polishing the cutting edge on a leather strop. He and David were unrelenting in their insistence on caring for tools, and so during the next two years, we would regularly exercise these sharpening procedures with our planes and chisels.

After the lunch break, a milled block of pine was distributed to each trainee. We would work nearly exclusively during year one with softwood and, more specifically, with pleasantly aromatic Redwood pine (*Pinus sylvestris*), also popularly known as Scots pine. Its straight and rapid growth habit, combined with mechanised harvesting, standardised milling practices and an air-drying time that is typically half that for hardwoods, has made Redwood pine abundant in British lumberyards at comparatively affordable prices. Availability and price explain its widespread use on carpentry courses, as well as in building construction, architectural joinery and the production of low to mid-range quality furniture. The resinous nature of Redwood, compounded by dead or encased knots, can pose a degree of challenge to the carpenter, but for the most part the timber is easily worked with hand tools and can be polished to a good finish.[17] For these reasons, it is ideally suited to learning and practising rudimentary hand-tool manoeuvres, and for executing design prototypes.

With our learning about smoothing planes still fresh in our minds, our first carpentry exercise was to mark a datum face and edge in pencil on our block of Redwood pine and to plane the opposite surfaces until the block was squared and measured exactly 107 millimetres wide and 45 millimetres thick. A lesson in technical skill, I believe it was also intended as a 'testosterone buster', assigned to exorcise excess energy and deflate any sense of machismo that young (and not-so-young) men have when embarking on a manual trade. I recorded in my logbook that: 'At first, using the plane felt like water-skiing over the surface of a choppy lake, but eventually I found the right stance, exertion of downward pressure, shooting angle and forward thrust. It was highly satisfying! But exhausting.' It also took us the rest of the afternoon and the better part of the next morning to complete the task.

Con told us that starting off with a lesson and exercise in planing hadn't changed since his own student days. Aside from acquainting trainees with the archetypal tool of the trade, the instructor also thought that the exercise made plain individual levels of drive and commitment. 'You can actually tell straight way', he said with a knowing grin, 'those who are going to try [on the course], because they're the ones who are going to keep planing that plank of timber until they get it flat.'

Figure 4.2 A first-year trainee practising with a smoothing plane, 2013.
© Trevor H.J. Marchand

Correct use of a bench plane, like any hand tool, does not involve brute force. By contrast, it is a matter of technique and control. 'And, it's eyeing as well', Con added. 'It's using your eye, your body position, and a balanced stance.' To illustrate his point, he recounted:

> I get some women on the course, for example, who start off by saying, 'I'll never be able to do that.' I tell them, 'Well, you can try. Until you start trying, you're right.' And when they see a couple of the boys stuttering with a plane across the surface of a plank, they think, 'Hmmm, wait a moment!'

Con's former trainee-turned-teaching assistant, John W., backed up that insight: 'If you're using muscle to move a tool through wood, then either the blade isn't sharp or you're using it the wrong way.' In writing on the topic, Jeff Miller clearly explained the force and control exerted when planing as a division of labour between the lower and upper body respectively:

> Most of the time, the power behind the plane comes from the lower body, all the way down to the toes. The planing motion is almost like a lunge in fencing ... [I]f you rely solely on throwing your arms forward to generate the bulk of the movement, you won't have much control. You'll also get really tired. Planing requires a very dynamic control over pressure [which comes primarily from the fingers, hands and lower arms].[18]

The lower body contains the larger muscle groups, which most effectively generate force behind a motion, while the elbows, hands and fingers exert greatest control over a tool, especially when contained in proximity to the torso. Though these activities can be conceptualised separately, applications of force and control are nevertheless interdependent.[19] Hand planing entails a flowing and rhythmic coordination between numerous simultaneous movements that fulfil different functions in the overall movement. However, reaching the point at which the plane, the chisel and the saw were experienced as fluid extensions of the forces and mechanics of our bodies required continued guidance and monitoring from our instructors, and long practice. Chapter 7 more fully addresses the remarkable connections between brain, hand and tool.

GETTING TO GRIPS WITH THE BASICS

On day three, we cut our planed pine blocks lengthways in two with a rip saw and then further planed each piece down into a baton with a cross-section measuring 45 x 45 millimetres. Josh and Tariq were the first to finish, leaving the rest trailing behind. With the two batons, we produced a 'halving joint'. This elementary joint involves the use of four key tools: the marking gauge, tenon saw, smoothing plane and bevelled chisel. It was the starting point for learning a repertoire of more intricate wood joints, all of which would be essential to making our forthcoming projects. We proceeded from halving joints to making oblique joints, bridal joints and housing joints, and then haunched and straightforward varieties of mortise-and-tenon joints. In addition to the first four hand tools, mortise-and-tenon joints involved the use of a mortise chisel and wooden mallet. Next came dovetail joints, using the dovetail saw. John W. reasoned that: 'Each new joint progressively draws in all the core tools rather than introducing them all at once.'

Producing joinery with exact measurements, perfectly square cuts, comfortably tight fits and well-finished surfaces was the main prerequisite for progressing to fine furniture at the end of the year. Attaining these high standards was a trial at first for many of us, and Con's insistence on achieving minimal tolerances was not wholly appreciated until sometime later, once we began working with hardwood timber and actually assembling pieces of furniture. Unlike pine, there is no 'give' in oak, walnut or cherry, and so if a single joint is out-of-square or poorly fitting, then the entire piece may be compromised and the untold hours in producing it squandered.

Before starting on the casement window project, we made a small square practice frame with the kind of joinery typical of a window or panel-door frame. In addition to chopping and cutting haunched mortise-and-tenon joints, the task included making a rebate (a right-angle step-cut) and a chamfer (bevelled edge) along the inner edges of the frame's stiles and rails, and thereby added the 'rebate plane' to our toolkit. Con explained the project while producing drawings of the frame's components on the whiteboard. However, the interlocking geometries of the joints and the end points of the rebate and chamfer on the two stiles only began to make sense once we were engrossed in marking out the wood with our own implements and pencils and in experimentally laying out the stiles and rails in relation to one another on top of our workbenches at each stage of the project.

These activities exercised our dexterity in simultaneously manipulating the wood and implements, but, perhaps more crucially, they contributed to developing a 'carpenter's attitude' to our work. This meant patiently pausing to take stock, consider options, conceptually simulate each option and its consequences in the 'mind's eye' and with sketches on paper, select the most viable and then methodically plan the corresponding sequence of procedures prior to acting again with the tools.

In seeking understanding and solutions, we were actively encouraged to exploit all available resources, which included getting pointers from our more experienced second-year colleagues or observing good models of practice among our fellow first years. Tony was quickly identified as the 'go-to' guy. Deliberately taking time out to assess, reflect, calculate and plan in this

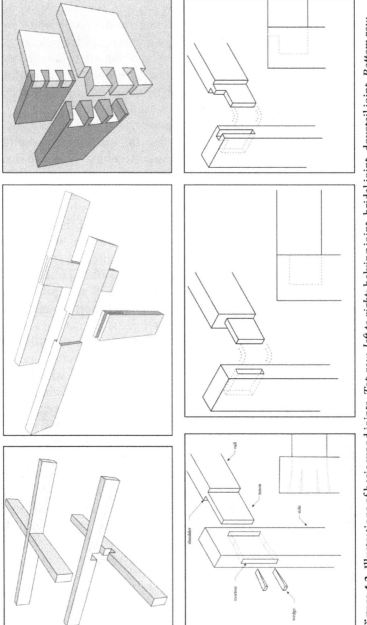

Figure 4.3 Illustrations of basic wood joints. *Top row, left to right:* halving joint, bridal joint, dovetail joint. *Bottom row, left to right:* through mortise-and-tenon joint, stopped or stub mortise-and-tenon, haunched mortise-and-tenon. All images sourced from Wikimedia. Images of halving joint and bridal joint © Crati. Image of dovetail joint © joinery-throughdovetail.gif. Images of all variations of mortise-and-tenon joints © Dave Dunford.

way reduced risks of making mistakes and wasting timber. It would also be an essential step until we reached the point where our conceptual thinking about the individual parts of a project, and of how the parts come together, had become more seamlessly integrated with the activities of tooling, which, too, called for mindful focus.

TRADE DEMOGRAPHICS

At the start of week two, the newly recruited woodworkers were inducted in health and safety and were given the rules for appropriate dress, footwear and personal protective equipment (PPE) for their eyes and ears. We were also introduced to regulations for working with hand tools, power tools and milling machinery, and for handling the toxic glues, oils and varnishes stored in the steel Control of Substances Hazardous to Health (COSHH) cabinet. Next was a practical session in correctly lifting the lengthy and weighty timber planks from the racks in teams of two and transporting them to the mill or upstairs to the workshop. Caring for the body was foundational to our instruction. Injury could postpone one's training or, worse yet, terminate a career.

On the following afternoon, a college administrator delivered a talk to all students on the institution's equal opportunities and harassment policies. He squarely addressed issues of gender, race, ethnicity and religion, but, conspicuously, made no mention of sexuality. In the world of construction and the building trades, heterosexuality was the presumed norm.

Gender representation in Britain's construction industry had in fact changed little since the late nineteenth century.[20] In 2005, approximately 3 per cent of construction trade trainees were women, the vast majority of whom were enrolled at further education colleges and not on Apprenticeships. Far fewer women, just 0.3 per cent, were actually employed in manual construction trades,[21] with slightly better representation in carpentry and joinery and in bricklaying and masonry, both standing at about 1 per cent.[22]

Of the four cohorts of fine woodworkers that I trained with or studied between 2005 and 2013, there were only four female students of the total thirty-eight (i.e. 10.5 per cent). Although stone masonry instructor Nina estimated that, in some years, her course attracted up to 40 per cent women, there were none enrolled in 2005 and no applications had been received. Nina believed that because stonemasons were among 'the lowest paid craftspeople', the incentive for women to undergo training was low. The drop-out rate from the programme was also higher among women than men, she explained, due to pregnancy and because a higher proportion of female students were in financially precarious positions.[23]

After leaving vocational college, obstacles for women only multiplied in the job market. A formal review commissioned to examine the place of women in the construction workforce cited 'inappropriate and poor working and employment conditions', 'discriminatory recruitment practices based on word of mouth rather than qualifications' and the 'persistence of a macho culture' as being among the major barriers to women's employment in the industry.[24] Predictably, College efforts to redress the gender balance amongst its instructors and students were countered by powerful, deeply entrenched structural forces at play in British society:[25] forces that perpetuated a construction industry dominated by men from working-class backgrounds, whose 'social networks in combination with corporeal ability' framed their 'social opportunities and buttressed their identities'.[26] The history and position of women in wood occupations and other building trades is explored more thoroughly in the next chapter, in combination with an account of instructor Cheryl's personal experiences.

In contrast to the grave imbalance in gender representation at the College, numbers of BAME people enrolled in the fine-woodwork programme, though low, corresponded more closely to the statistics for the general population of England and Wales. Within the same four cohorts previously described, there were two Black-African British, one African-Caribbean British and two South-Asian British trainees, all male.[27] None of the instructors at the time was from an ethnic minority background, but the College employed members of such communities in other capacities.

In Britain's construction industry more broadly, BAME representation did not fare significantly better than that of women. A report published by the Equality and Human Rights Commission stated that the sector was commonly perceived as being 'relatively low-status ... with hard and inflexible working conditions and a persistent "laddish" culture in a white, male-dominated environment'.[28] Some of the barriers to individuals of BAME communities correlated with those experienced by women, including the exclusionary effects of 'old' informal networks and word-of-mouth references. The report noted perceptions among BAME communities of an ingrained racism in the industry and, with the exception of larger firms, a failure on the part of employers to implement equality and diversity policies. Failings were also attributed to education services in British schooling, where there was a general lack of knowledge among careers counsellors regarding employment opportunities in the building trades.[29] This negatively impacted sector recruitment not merely from BAME communities, but also from successive cohorts of school-leavers across the board.

Michael Montague-Smith, Chairman of the Carpenters' Company College Committee, told me that: 'The biggest problem is changing people's perceptions about working as a craftsman in the industry, and getting them to realise that it can be wonderfully creative and a satisfying job for life.'[30] From experience, he concluded that the most effective way to achieve that change was by 'working on the kids and their parents through the school careers officers'. With the cooperation of the College Director, Michael organised for the College to take 'a road show around the schools' in the borough to explain and demonstrate to young students, teachers and advisors 'what it means to be a craftsman'. 'Changing perceptions in the East End, with its mix of ethnic minorities, can be challenging', he explained, 'because many immigrant parents hold strong aspirations for their children to pursue particular professional careers.'

In fact, biases against working in the manual trades were manifest nationwide in seemingly all communities. With a detectable note of exasperation, Michael added:

> The whole 'league tables' system is based on the number of A-levels that a school's students get, and the more kids that continue on to university, the higher the prestige of the school. So, the incentive for headmasters is to push more and more pupils down that route, irrespective of whether it's good for the kids.

The narrow definitions of 'worthy knowledge' with which we evaluate and operate neglect the rich diversity of intelligences in both children and adults, and leave latent aptitudes unattended and unformed. The exaltation of 'book smarts' has blinded our society to the kinds of complex skilled intelligence involved in craftwork. This blinkered system, with its sights set on academic achievement, has tragically diminished the range of desirable career options, constricted popular imaginings of success and undermined entire sectors of the nation's economy. These factors have contributed enormously to the 'skills gap' that has plagued Britain for the past half-century and, relatedly, to a widening socioeconomic disparity in the population. It was estimated in 2005 that a third of adults in the UK lacked a basic school-leaving qualification and five million adults had no qualifications at all.[31]

'England's building industry is being kept afloat by East European craftsman', observed Michael. 'They are invaluable, but the country cannot rely on them to always be here, available to work. They may decide to return home or move on elsewhere. We must, therefore, fill the vacuum.' The history of that 'vacuum' up to the early 2000s was recounted in Chapter 3. Given Michael's nod of appreciation to skilled East Europeans for building Britain's buildings, it is important to also take note of the parochial, nationalist rhetoric that was infiltrating official discourse on the skills gap at that time.

In 2007, under Gordon Brown's premiership, a scheme to create 120,000 new Apprenticeships, raise employability among Britain's unskilled workers and upgrade the skills of the workforce was launched with high-profile

speeches given at both the Labour Party and Trades Union Congress conferences.[32] 'A generation ago, a British Prime Minister had to worry about the
global arms race', stated Brown, but 'Today a British Prime Minister has to
worry about the global skills race'.[33]

The spirit of the government's scheme was far from new, but its objectives
were wholly legitimate. What was deeply problematic, however, was the accompanying mantra adopted by the government. 'British jobs for British
workers' was incendiary, feeding growing populist concerns over unbridled
immigration and "floods" of EU workers on UK shores, stealing jobs, driving
down wages, and sapping social services. 'Half of new jobs go to migrants',
read BBC news headlines in the autumn of 2007.[34] 'Immigration policy has
been out of control for a decade', claimed Shadow Home Secretary David
Davis.[35]

The volume of nationalist oratory only grew louder during the following
years. In a speech delivered in 2010, John Hayes, the Conservative Minister
for Further Education, Skills and Lifelong Learning, called for a 'new Arts
and Crafts movement for Britain in the 21st century . . . to serve national interest'.[36] A few months later, Chancellor George Osborne upped the ante,
melodramatically concluding his budget speech with the declaration that:
'We want the words: "Made in Britain" "Created in Britain" "Designed in
Britain" "Invented in Britain" to drive our nation forward. A Britain carried
aloft by the march of makers. That's how we will create jobs and support
families.'[37] Sociologist Doreen Jakob observed that in the years immediately
following the 2008 recession, craft was being 'increasingly singled out as
a political buzz word' in efforts to reinstate 'national pride and, above all,
dignity of labour and manual skills at a time when many western countries
bemoan[ed] their loss of manufacturing'.[38] As astutely remarked by educator
and promoter of craftwork Malcolm Ferris, craft was 'being reclaimed and
repurposed as a part of the radical right's political project'.[39]

With the gift of hindsight, the complicities of both major political parties
in the result of the UK's 2016 referendum on EU membership are all the
more apparent. Not only has Brexit staunched the influx of a much-needed
skilled workforce of builders, but opportunities for British craftspeople to
profit from international exchanges and advanced training programmes with
fellow European craftspeople and experts, and from employment prospects
on the continent, have also been detrimentally curtailed. In 2020, a study
commissioned by the Crafts Council and its partners reported on the concerns of makers regarding the effect of Brexit on their livelihoods. A quarter
of those surveyed stated that Brexit 'had already had an adverse impact on
their business' and a further quarter said they 'expected it to in the future'
in terms of rising costs of materials and shipping, and the loss of European
markets for their wares.[40]

LETTING-OFF STEAM

Early in term one, a meeting was convened between the fine-woodwork student representatives and the Director's right-hand man – a larger-than-life individual who had mastered both carpentry and the arts of mediation. The purpose was to review meeting minutes from the previous year and address arising student issues and concerns. Robert was our official year-one envoy, and I accompanied him to this and all future meetings in order to better understand college operations. The second-year trainees were represented by Angela, Shane and Russell, all of whom were mature 'vocational migrants' to the trade (and who are introduced more fully in Chapter 6).

I quickly learned that student requests for secure bicycle storage, healthier lunch options on the canteen menu, the replacement of disposable styrene with china crockery and stainless utensils, upgraded changing-and-shower-room facilities, more substantial college investment in its webpage profile, AutoCAD software for creating project designs and drawings, and a more formally structured programme of business start-up instruction were all recurrent grievances. However, the issue at the top of the students' agenda, and that which Robert pursued most vigorously, was the demand for assurances that college timber supplies were obtained from sustainable sources and were Forest Stewardship Council (FSC) approved. For numerous craftspeople, concerns about environmental degradation, the reckless exploitation of natural resources and climate change were, and continue to be, the driver behind the quest for greener practices. This subject is fleshed out in later chapters.

At the start of term, the convenors assigned mixed teams of first and second-year woodworking students to clean the large timber mill at the end of each day for weeklong periods on a rotating basis. On Fridays, in addition to the usual sweeping-up of wood shavings and vacuuming-down of machine surfaces, the job involved the more intensive task of cleaning the machine blades. During week two, Shane and I were on duty together. Shane showed me how to open the heavy cast-iron casings of the postwar-era conjoined thicknesser and over-hand planer to get access to the razor-sharp cutter heads inside, and how to safely access the teeth on the vertical blade of the bandsaw, the rotary components on the spindle moulder and tenoner, and the circular blades of the enormous panel saw and the radial-arm crosscut saw.

While getting on with his own end-of-week tasks, Errol, the wiry and spirited mill technician, scrutinised our procedures to ensure that we had shut down power supplies and were approaching the blades with care and keeping our bare hands at a safe distance. He also supplied fastidious supervision if we needed to change the blade on any of his beloved machines. Shane and I sprayed the blades of each in turn with mineral spirits and, using a nylon toothbrush and stick of softwood with a swatch of cloth tightly wound around one end, we removed any built-up resin or spots of rust and scrubbed the steel to a shine.

Cleaning the machines allowed trainees to become familiar with their parts and basic mechanics, as well as with the 'eccentricities' that some of the older ones had developed over the years. The task also helped to alleviate fears and anxieties about using these hulking, thunderous and potentially debilitating machines for our woodworking projects. However, we were also continually reminded by instructors that it was wise to *always* approach the machines with caution. Con knew first-hand, so to speak, how swiftly the rotating blades of a milling machine could remove a digit. On occasion, he recounted stories about debilitating injuries (or worse) incurred because a carpenter had fleetingly lowered their guard or strayed from the correct procedures. These anecdotes were not aimed at inciting fear, but rather at tempering our growing confidence in working with sharp blades with a healthy respect for the dangers they pose.

With the mill-cleaning mission accomplished and our instructors detained in a training session, the students were free to depart ahead of schedule. It was a splendid sunny September evening and so Jens, Tony, Alex and I took the Central Line into the West End. The plan was to shop for carpentry manuals and quite possibly enjoy our first pint together. Our book hunt began at the Building Centre on Store Street and we continued browsing at Foyles on Charing Cross Road. From there, I led my new mates to the nearby historic French House pub on Dean Street in Soho. The place was heaving, but the pub's tradition of serving only half-pints fell utterly flat with Tony and Alex. Alex was plainly outside his comfort zone in Soho and he began passing snide remarks about 'the trendies' and 'the mandy-pandies'. It was time to shuffle on elsewhere.

We crossed Charing Cross Road into Covent Garden, where I suggested we dip into one of my old locals, The Lamb and Flag. This venue went down much better with the guys and, by the time we had guzzled a second pint, the consensus was that we should stay put for the evening, on the broad pavement in front of the pub entrance. With each passing pint, Alex's talk became more hypermasculine, raucously divulging sexual conquests and fantasies while belligerently deriding 'gays'. He soon began goading each of us in turn to disclose the characteristics that most attracted us in a woman. Jens' stilted reply was made more in acquiescence than any real willingness to partake in the chauvinistic natter, while Tony's valiant efforts to divert Alex's train of thought and pacify his flaring bravado with good humour failed.

When Alex turned to me, he premised the invitation with: 'So, what about a smart, successful guy like you?' 'My partner's name is John', I replied candidly, staring Alex in the eyes and smiling. Alex's jaw dropped to his chest: 'You're fuckin' kidding! You?' 'Yep', I affirmed. 'But, you're not . . . "camp"', he scrunched his face quizzically. 'Nope, I'm just me.' Tony swiftly interjected to remind Alex that it was his round, and into the pub he went. 'Be careful, Trev', Tony cautioned. 'He's had a few and he's a live-wire, man.' In spite of The Lamb and Flag's historic notoriety as a bare-knuckle fighting venue, I was confident that the only consequences of my frank admission would be positive ones. I would be spending the next two years of my life training and learning alongside these men, and socialising with them as well. Individually, they would either accept me for who I was or would reject me because of fear, insecurity or ignorance. It was in my power and interests to placate and enlighten.

In his study of builders in London's construction industry, sociologist Darren Thiel observed that 'masculinity was tied up with notions of hetero-sexuality, physical strength and the associated roles of protector and pro-vider'.[41] Masculine posturing on the building site, especially when the men were in groups, was 'performed through tough stances and facial gestures, loud, deep voices, constant profanities, and in confrontational and often ag-gressive reactions to anyone who tried to "push them around" or "take the piss" too far'.[42]

Thiel's description of these performative acts corresponded strongly with the behaviour observed among a small proportion of Modern Appren-tices attending the College. When congregating socially in the canteen or library – and if Jim or Cheryl were out of earshot – cursing was rife and exaggerated tales of drunken exploits, illegal activities and violent weekend brawls were stridently recounted. By contrast, when encountered on their own, these same young men were normally polite and reserved. While en-gaged in workshop tasks, the banter bandied across Apprentices' benches was characteristically boisterous but harmless, and was routinely drowned out by the deafening drone of their power tools.

Across the four cohorts of fine woodworkers that I trained with or stud-ied, only Alex occasionally displayed extreme forms of masculine posturing. Certainly, competing masculinities were manifested in a variety of ways be-tween trainees, sometimes including between female fine woodworkers and their male counterparts. Most typically, this took the form of overtly com-petitive displays of knowledge, in particular about power tools; bantering duals that took jabs at one another's craft competency or, less frequently, their virility, and that imputed paternalistic hierarchies of seniority or de-pendency; and claims to prowess and stamina in extracurricular sporting activities (especially cycling and rock climbing) or, conversely, to heroic ca-pacities for alcohol consumption.

There are a number of interrelated explanations for the near-absence of overt macho swagger among the fine woodworkers in comparison with (some) college Apprentices. As already mentioned, a majority were mature career changers, many of whom held higher education qualifications and came from middle-class or cosmopolitan backgrounds. Almost unanimously, the move to fine woodworking had been a deliberate lifestyle choice as opposed to merely a job of 'being on the tools' to earn a living.[43] Fine woodworking was therefore unambiguously recognised as a 'craft' and not simply a 'trade'; in addition, it was conceptualised by many as a creative 'art' that centrally involves design. Craft, creativity, art and design are not typically classified in Britain as testosterone-fuelled activities.

Also, given the nature of the work, there was high probability that practising fine woodworkers would be working indoors, and very likely in solitude or in small teams, as opposed to labouring on a bustling, noisy construction site. Items of architectural joinery and, certainly, furniture are connected with the domestic sphere, with its associations to concepts of family, privacy, practices of nurturing and safe refuge. Relatedly, the scale of things made by fine woodworkers is generally smaller, meaning that they can be managed and manipulated without the 'shows of strength' that shifting structural components on a construction site might demand. Finally, many of my woodworking colleagues envisioned that their skills would one day serve high-end markets of both male and female patrons, and possibly worldwide, so keeping an open, liberal mindset was part of the deal.

Alex returned to the pavement outside the pub with four brimming pints of London Pride. 'I never!' he said chuckling and shaking his head, and then handed me a glass. Alex exhibited sincere effort to digest the fact and asked several questions in attempt to give it shape. Jens and Tony, on the other hand, remained entirely unfazed by my revelation. With yet more pints, the talk lightened, the conversation became ebullient and we stayed until closing.

Given that my upper limit is normally two pints, I heartily congratulated myself on the mere feat of getting home, but awoke the next day feeling gravely ill and completely mortified by incoherent memories of my inebriated state on the tube journey back. On returning to college on Monday morning, I learned that Tony and Jens had ventured afterwards for a late-night curry. Midway through the meal, Jens allegedly shut his eyes, slumped sideways to the floor and came to with a team of paramedics hovering over him. Alex missed his train stop altogether at Swindon and regained consciousness in distant Bristol. Our first social had been a powerfully bonding experience and one that we would recount repeatedly until it had achieved near-mythical status – but thankfully never again repeated with the same intoxicating quantities of ale.

THE POWER OF DEMONSTRATION

In past years, the panel-door project had been a set piece with a fixed composition and fully prescribed dimensions. But, heartened by the progress being made by our cohort, Con gave us free rein to alter the design if we so wished, as long as it contained all of the essential components and joinery challenges posed by the original exercise. The stages of the project were intended to simulate a real-life commission, requiring us to first measure up a doorway, as we would do on a site call. Based on those measurements, we produced 1:6 scale drawings and full-scale rod drawings of our door, which guided the preparation of timber cutting lists and order forms for the ironmongery that we intended to use. Only once the dimensions and detailing of the individual components and the overall assembly had been worked out on paper could we begin making our physical doors. Making in itself would introduce a whole new set of complications to be resolved, some of which would take us back to our drawings, and vice versa.

With hindsight, my Arts and Crafts-style door with its three dramatically projecting bevelled panels and stained-glass fanlights was perhaps overly ambitious. Given Con's inclination for straightforward design and joinery, he cautioned from the outset that its execution would take longer and require advanced milling techniques, thereby placing disproportionate demands

Figure 4.4 A woodwork trainee preparing a scale drawing, 2013.
© Trevor H.J. Marchand

on his limited supervision time. His resistance was entirely reasonable and I was happy to concede, at which point David, who appreciated my design and the challenges it presented, interceded by offering his mentorship. David initially encouraged me to make the door in European oak (*Quercus robur*) rather than Redwood pine, but the cost estimates from timber yards for the materials were prohibitively high and my calculations for the door's projected weight yielded a hefty figure. I would make the design, but would stick to Redwood.

'You've all got an awful lot of learning to get under your belts in two years', Con later said to me, reflecting on the syllabus and the diverse skillset demanded by fine woodwork. 'It's taken me a lifetime to gain that experience.' As an instructor, he was committed to passing on as much of that knowledge as possible, but he also recognised that:

> Students are bombarded by so much when they start off that it's best to slow things down a little in the first term. For the youngsters, especially, it's daunting enough to be at the start of a two-year course, which seems 'forever' to them, never mind having to learn the tools. And, it's not just about learning to use them, but how to sharpen them and look after them.

Con periodically advised students to adjust the height of their workbenches to avoid back pain, and he regularly monitored the postures that we took up and modified our tool-wielding gestures variously through patient instruction, critical commentary and demonstration. He felt an obligation 'to be there, constantly nagging, if you like, to wear students down and get them to do what I've asked them'. He was reconciled to the fact that: 'At the end of two years, if they don't want to do what I've asked, that's fine.' But his experience more commonly was that 'people finish the course and, after six months, come back to say, "You know, you were right!"' When students absorbed the logic of his lessons and made the reasoning their own, it gave Con 'a deep sense of satisfaction'. Yet more satisfying, he confided, 'is when I think a student has bitten off more than they can chew and I tell them, "You *can't* do that!", but they take me on and prove me wrong'.

For all trainees, including those with backgrounds in higher education, the preferred mode of carpentry instruction was demonstration. 'Demonstration, observation, imitation, correction and practice' succinctly summarises the one-to-one teaching and learning formula at the bench. Theoretical knowledge about such issues as the properties and behaviour of wood, the optimal angle and direction for plying a tool blade, or methods for calculating the width and depth of a tenon was integrated as best possible in the instructors' practical demonstrations. 'For some', explained John W., 'integrating theory in the practical tutorials works best because they don't see it as "theory" and therefore don't have as much animosity toward learning it.' As poetically stated by Ralph Waldo Emerson:

> [Words] cannot cover the dimensions of what is in truth. They break, chop and impoverish it. An action is the perfection and publication of thought. A right action seems to fill the eye, and to be related to all nature.[44]

In a previous journal publication,[45] I offered the example of Con's toolbox session on setting-out full-scale rod drawings, which were produced for the making of architectural joinery and furniture. The detailed example, which I reprint here, captures the fine combination of gestures, spoken language and resources to hand that the instructor employed in communicating both theory and practice to the gathering of trainees assembled around a workbench.

> Con had already cut a length of white paper from the roll and taped it down evenly to a sheet of MDF board. He steadily surveyed the faces around him and then, like a conductor, drew attention to his lesson with an upheld pencil. 'So, sharp pencil!' he announced audibly, drowning out the lingering murmurs. 'At the moment, uh, 2H pencils are sufficient, but if you want to invest in, you know, sort of drawing pens . . . or pencils, you can.'

> Con then picked up a bevel-edged chisel from the bench top and began sharpening the pencil tip. 'So, notice the chisel is pointing *away* from me . . . when I'm sharpen-

Figure 4.5 A fine-woodwork instructor offering students a toolbox session, 2006. © Trevor H.J. Marchand

ing it.' On emphasizing the direction of his action, he shot a sideways glance at Jens, who had negligently sliced his finger with a chisel the day before. The instructor's lips curled in a mocking grimace and the other trainees broke into a surge of chuckles. While Jens was self-consciously inspecting his wound with a bashful flush in his cheeks, Alex peered over his shoulder and, addressing Jens with a nickname, he sardonically offered condolences: 'Oh, I'm sorry Jannick my son!'

The instructor carried on with the lesson, now directing his gaze onto the open pages of a book to his left and signalling to the students to follow with renewed concentration. 'So I've ... I've got this book open. And this is, uh, *Building Craft Foundation*, levels one and two, at chapter 3 – *Communications*. It deals with scales. We'll be coming onto that when we do the second drawing; basically, the scale drawing.' Con shifted focus to the sheet of blank drafting paper laid out on the bench top before him. 'But it's a communication, and what you're drawing here, this rod, is a communication ... between other trades.' And then moving back to the book, he pointed to a series of diagrams and tapped them with his finger. 'Here we've got drawing symbols and abbreviations. And I'll just, I'll give you my sort of out... overview, really, of how drawings should be set out. And I'll be talking about that. I'll leave it on that page there, which is page 86.'

Con then held up a small wooden box with a long, narrow extension protruding through either end of its central axis. Scanning the assembly of students he asked, 'Okay, these are called what? Anyone know?' Liam, standing at the back of the small assembly, cautiously ventured a subdued response: 'Thumb ... thumb rules?'

The instructor's body suddenly stiffened and his face grew serious. The lesson was momentarily interrupted. He cast a cold stare across the workshop at Abdul, who had just arrived, and demanded abruptly, 'Twenty to ten. Is that right? Your ... your arrival time. You've just arrived? Twenty to ten.' 'No,' Abdul contested sheepishly, 'I saw you... before now.' 'Have you?' retorted Con curtly. 'Well the first time I've seen you! Could you get your diary, and put twenty to ten down? Yeah. I didn't really feel your diary times reflected your true arrival times last week.'

Con resumed the lesson and altered his tone accordingly. 'So the first line I'm going to put down... Sorry. What did we say this was?' he asked, while picking up the wooden box with the long extension and searching for a volunteer. Another student responded this time 'Thumb-rule ruler.' 'Yup, *thumb rule*,' agreed the instructor, reiterating the correct name. 'Who's got a combination square handy?' he asked as he proceeded to draw the measured construction lines for the rod, applying different degrees of pressure to the lead to produce lines of varying quality and thickness. After the session, a basic set of drafting equipment was distributed to each student and we returned to our respective workbenches to produce drawings based on the example provided.

Con structured his demonstration to reflect the sequence of stages involved in setting out a rod drawing, from preparing paper and tools to establishing a set of conventions and producing the measured pencil lines. He employed a combination of spoken language, visual material and bodily actions to communicate his lesson. The verbal content included statements of information and questions to elicit a response and promote interactive learning.

The teacher's tone and volume conveyed emotion and emphases, thereby providing the listening audience of trainees with additional context for interpreting his statements and drawing attention to the most essential content.

The visual materials Con used included diagrams contained in books, a display of the physical objects and implements required for the exercise, and a trail of pencil lines made on his own sample drawing. The lines of his rod drawing presented a set of instructions for making the item of architectural joinery and provided a benchmark for the students' work. Most pertinent to learning technical drawing, however, was not the example of the actual drawing *on paper*, but rather Con's demonstration of the drawing *in progress*. After all, woodworkers needed to acquire the skills for producing technical drawings, not merely for recognising and reading them. And, like learning any physical activity, this was achieved most effectively by observing and imitating the techniques of the body and the gestures of the hands.[46]

Although I had considerable drafting experience from my years of training and practice as an architect, the technical plans and elevations of buildings I had drawn were typically at a 1:50 scale, and occasionally I had produced architectural details at a 1:10 scale. However, in producing the full-scale rod drawings for my frame-and-panel door, I discovered that it was a highly effective procedure for systematically thinking through each component and its role in the assembly, for resolving joinery issues ahead of making them in timber, and for more clearly imagining every part of the project and 'rotating' it in my mind's eye. It also forced me to return to my 1:6 scale drawings to make amendments to the design and alter dimensions accordingly. Importantly, the rod drawings would be used for marking out our timber without the need for measuring tapes and straight rules, and they would serve as templates against which we could assess the accuracy of each finished component by laying it directly on the surface of the drawing.

In another toolbox session offered by David, he demonstrated the use of a marking gauge, which is used to accurately and speedily mark out shallow incised lines on a timber surface for guiding cuts or chopping operations. 'A correct grasp is key', he stressed. With deliberate gestures, he positioned his right thumb on the marking gauge stem, directly behind the pin, wrapped his index over the top of the fence and tucked his second finger firmly against the outer side of the fence. His third and fourth fingers were left free, making no contact with the tool. Then, holding a short length of timber in his left hand and bracing it lengthwise against the workbench, David moved the marking gauge into position by pressing the inside face of its fence against the edge of the timber. While rotating the tool counterclockwise until the tip of the pin met the board's face, he described it as 'an airplane readying to take-off from the runway'. Then, with a quick, fluid motion, David pushed the instrument away from his body and along the length of the board, all the while maintaining a steady angle with the pin and an even application of pressure with the fence against the board's edge. On reaching the opposite end of the timber, he simultaneously lifted and rotated the marking gauge upwards, with a 'taking-off' motion.

David regularly accompanied his physical demonstrations with an analogy in order to assist students in bridging the new information and practices he was introducing with their existing experiences and knowledge of the world. This promoted clearer conceptual, visual, haptic, motor and even emotional understanding of a tool and its associated tool-wielding actions. David underscored the importance of relying on our perceptual senses, including listening, for knowing when we were using a tool correctly or not. He also encouraged us to 'think of the tool in hand as an extension of our body and an instrument of our thinking'. This idea is revisited as the central theme of Chapter 7, and the role of analogy in teaching new skills is investigated in Chapter 8 during an intensive bench tutorial between Cheryl and a young trainee named Neil.

I had arrived at the point in my panel-door project for shaping the projecting bevelled features on the three timber panels. The assignment was progressing smoothly and I was enjoying the learning curve. The depth of each panel member had been built up by laminating planks of Redwood, and I would now need to use the spindle moulder – for the first time – to achieve the high 45-degree bevel profiles. David's input would be necessary for planning the logistics of the operation and I would also rely on him to monitor and assist with the machining.

It was early morning. David was not yet available and so I retrieved a newspaper from my rucksack, set it out on my workbench and began leafing through the pages, patiently waiting. Con was assisting Tariq at his bench and spied my (in)activity. An hour later, and with David now at my workbench drawing sketches and discussing machining options, Con marched over with a stern face. He took up position on the opposite side of my bench, planted both hands firmly on the top and then detonated. He belligerently chastised me for reading a newspaper in the workshop and ordered that I comport myself 'like a craftsman, not a "Joe" on a worksite'. I bit down firmly on my lower lip, keeping silent and erect. David took a stride back in bewilderment, all surrounding activity ground to a halt, and all eyes were cast in our direction.

The 'newspaper rule' appeared to be arbitrary, but had nevertheless provided a convenient opportunity to publicly discipline and bring me into line. One day later, all was forgotten. I never fully comprehended the nature of the event, but could only surmise that Con had been displeased with my decision to carry on with my original door design. I suspected, as well, that I had been caught in the crossfire between instructors who harboured two distinct philosophies to both teaching and craftwork, and who were wrestling to establish territory and dominance. After all, David had only arrived at the College a few months earlier to take up the position of programme convenor and mainly oversee the second-year students. The difference in their approaches will become clearer in the next chapter, which features David's reflections on woodworking.

I confess that my pride had been temporarily wounded in the match. As I stood there incensed and biting down on my lip, my emotions clasped onto my 'academic status', my 'seniority at the university' and the fact that I was a grown man in my late thirties. When the heat subsided, however, I recalled anew that none of those attributes had relevance here in the carpentry workshop. Like the labouring positions I had sought in Yemen and Mali, I had signed up at the Building Crafts College to learn and carry out fieldwork as a full member of that community of practice. From experience, I knew very well that discipline and periodic struggles over hierarchy were foundational to building-craft training, like most fields of practice.

A month later, with the frame-and-panel door completed, the cohort moved on to the small tool cabinet project. I was eager to get on with cutting my first-ever line of dovetails. 'Slow down!' Con barked loudly at me across the workshop. 'This isn't a sprint. It's more a marathon.' And right, he was.

ANNUAL PRIZE-GIVING AT CARPENTERS' HALL

On a Wednesday afternoon near the end of term, all first and second-year students were summoned to assist with bubble-wrapping the selected pieces of furniture that had been produced by last year's cohort of graduates. The next morning, the items were carefully loaded into the back of a truck and transported to the grand Carpenters' Hall on Throgmorton Avenue in the City. The graduates who had made the pieces unpacked and displayed them in the livery boardroom in preparation for the Building Crafts College End of Year Show. The walls of the luxuriant boardroom comprised walnut wainscoting and alternating vertical panels of burr-oak and burr-walnut veneer above.[47] Historic Company Charters and regal portraits of past Masters in heavy gold frames adorned the walls, and the dark-stained boardroom furnishings were made in elegant Chippendale style.

The College workshops closed on Thursday at lunchtime, giving everyone time to scrub up and get smartly attired for the prize-giving ceremonies that evening. The Company Beadle welcomed all arrivals and, after checking in coats and bags at the cloakroom, we ascended the broad staircase to the high-ceilinged reception room on the first storey, with its suites of Louis XVI-style chairs and French Canapé seats, ornately framed oversized mirrors and elaborate crystal chandeliers. The venue was worlds apart from the workshop.

From the reception room, the nearly 300 guests filed into the Banqueting Hall to take their seats, the front rows being reserved for the Company Clerk, the Wardens and their spouses, Court members, the Director of the College and distinguished guests from other London liveries. At the front of the Hall, on a raised platform, sat the Company Master, the guest of honour, Sir Michael Latham (the Chairman of CITB-ConstructionSkills), and Michael Montague-Smith. The large assembly of students comprised the presently enrolled fine woodworkers, stonemasons, leadworkers and Apprentices, and the recent graduates of those same programmes. The graduates would receive their diplomas this evening and a select few would be awarded prestigious prizes.

The spacious Banqueting Hall was housed in the bridge that spanned Throgmorton Avenue. The bridge building, inaugurated in 1960, had been designed by Clifford Weardon,[48] and its interior design was evidently influenced by the aesthetic of Weardon's former employer, Sir Basil Spence, architect of the postwar Coventry Cathedral. The high walls, both containing large triple-bay windows of stained glass, were panelled full height in elm and utile, the hardwood strip flooring was polished Rhodesian teak and the hexagonal ceiling panels were made from cedar.[49] On the walls hung portraits of nineteenth and twentieth-century liverymen who had served as lord mayors, sheriffs or aldermen of the City of London, or as Members of Parliament,[50] and at the head of the room, on the wall above the high table, was a large Tree of Life carved from Burma teak by former President of the Royal Academy, Charles Wheeler.[51]

The prize-giving ceremony commenced at 6:30 PM sharp. The Master welcomed the guests, and Michael Montague-Smith welcomed Sir Michael Latham, who presented the Building Crafts College prizes and the awards for the Carpenters Craft Competition. My mill-cleaning partner Shane received an award for having made exceptional progress during his first year of the programme. A graduate of fine woodwork, Nick, was the recipient of the coveted Sir Banister Fletcher Award for Best Student of the College. He would go on to win numerous commissions from the London liveries and establish his own fine furniture-making company in the West Country. Immediately following the prize giving, the Advanced Craft Diplomas were ceremonially awarded to the eight graduates of fine woodworking and nine of stonemasonry, after which the entire assembly retired to the reception room for refreshments.

Kitted-out in suits and ties and fine evening dress, the first and second-year fine-woodwork students and instructors clustered together with drinks in hand, remarking on the rarefied surroundings of the Hall and wittily differentiating themselves as 'salt-of-the-earth' artisans who would live by their hands from the so-called City 'suits' and posh guests in attendance. 'Carriages' were formally scheduled for 9:30 PM, meaning that we were hastily but graciously discharged from the Hall at that precise deadline.

The fine woodworkers, including young Darren, Liam and Tariq, reconvened at a nearby pub. Abdul, who had begun playing truant from the start, had by now disappeared entirely from the programme. The convivial evening of good-hearted banter and relaxed conversation fortified the communal ties among trainees and instructors. It was also an opportunity outside the daily college routine to exchange aspirations and imaginings of future life and work, thereby richly contributing to the craft narratives that each of us was constructing for ourselves.

As for the prize-giving ceremony, the public ranking of skill and the status awarded for achievement served to intensify the spirit of competition in the second-year cohort and to activate it among first years. Competition would grow once we began designing and making furniture, beneficially driving trainees to realise their fuller potential, and it would palpably intensify as we neared the finish line in year two.

NOTES

1. The extension of the mezzanine in 2004 had been financed by a bid for £200,000 of Centre of Vocational Excellence (CoVE) funding. This was the first of a series of physical expansions of the College in Stratford.
2. The Building Crafts College now has a much livelier web presence than it did when I undertook fine woodwork training there in 2005. The current site (http://www.thebcc.ac.uk) has been considerably developed and offers detailed information about its various training programmes, staff profiles and institutional history.
3. In 2004, 'Modern' was dropped from the title to become simply 'Apprenticeships'. I have nevertheless retained the older term in this book to make immediately clear to the reader the distinction between the UK government's programme and the references I make to apprenticeships in other countries where I studied craft training.
4. May, 'Message', 2.
5. Carpenters' Company, *Carpenters' Company*, pamphlet, no date.
6. Notably, there is a separate Furniture Makers' Company, which in 1963 became the 83rd London livery. However, the Furniture Makers' represent and promote all types of furniture and furnishings, and not strictly furniture in wood. For this reason, they have played no role to date in the fine-woodworking programme at the Building Crafts College.
7. Cooke, Ward and L'Ecuyer, *The Maker's Hand*, 13.
8. For construction or shop-fitting firms operating within the parameters of the CITB, the cost of new entrant training was paid by the CITB direct to the College. Firms should have also received various payments from the CITB towards the costs of administering the trainee. However, a serious problem with the scheme was that the

funding formula favoured large firms, making access for small and medium-sized enterprises (SMEs) difficult. Difficulties for SMEs in accessing the Apprenticeship scheme for their employees worsened in 2017 with the introduction of the apprenticeship levy (i.e. a percentage of an employer's pay bill), which once again favoured large firms with deeper pockets and more clout.

9. For trainees over the age of twenty-five, the CITB ran the Construction Apprenticeship Scheme, under which firms received a grant from the CITB and paid the College at a per-week rate.

10. The London College of Furniture had its beginnings in Shoreditch, which, historically, was an important centre of furniture production in East London. Originally called the Shoreditch Technical Institute for the Furnishing Trades, it was renamed Shoreditch Technical College in 1948, and renamed again the London College of Furniture in 1968. City & Guilds administered the examinations. The College moved to new premises on Commercial Road in 1970 and, twenty years later, it joined the City of London Polytechnic to become the Sir John Cass Faculty of Art, Design and Manufacture. The Polytechnic was given its charter in 1992 and became the London Guildhall University, which later merged with the University of North London to form London Metropolitan University. London Metropolitan offered a foundation degree in furniture making.

11. A large variety of planes exist in addition to the three bench planes mentioned in the text. These include, for example, the scrub plane for quickly removing wood; the rebate-and-fillister plane for cutting rebates; the shoulder plane for trimming tenon shoulders; the bullnose plane for trimming small joints or rebates; the low-angled block plane for trimming end grain; the compass plane with thin, flexible convex or concave blades for smoothing curves; the 'granny-tooth' (or plough) plane for cutting grooves; and the combination plane for producing beading. There are also a number of wooden-body Japanese planes that are pulled in towards – rather than pushed away from – the carpenter's body. For images of the various planes, see Jackson and Day, *Collin's Complete Woodworker's Manual*, 118–27.

12. See Garrett, *The Handplane Book*; and Taylor, *Tools of the Trade*.

13. Hohn, 'A Romance of Rust', 61.

14. See Ettema, 'Technological Innovation'.

15. Taylor, *Tools of the Trade*, 70.

16. Miller, *The Foundations of Better Woodworking*, 58.

17. The average dried density of Redwood pine is roughly 70% of that of popular European hardwood varieties like oak, beech, ash or walnut. This 'softer' quality means that cuts and mortises are easier to execute, and that plane and chisel blades require less frequent sharpening.

18. Miller, *The Foundations of Better Woodworking*, 65.

19. Ibid., 32–36.

20. Clarke et al., *No More Softly-Softly*, 6.

21. Clarke and Wall, 'Are Women "Not Up to" Working in Construction", 16–17.

22. In the 2011 census (Office for National Statistics, Standard Occupational Classification, 2010), women represented 1.4% of carpenters and joiners, and 1.5 % of bricklayers and masons (Clarke et al., *No More Softly-Softly*, 6).

23. Interview at the Building Crafts College, 20 October 2005.

24. Clarke et al., *No More Softly-Softly*, 4. Anthropologist L.K. Hart also reports 'machismo' as a characteristic of artisans in the West more generally (Hart, 'Work, Labor, and Artisans', 597).
25. In 2014, the College reported that eight out of thirty (27 per cent) frontline teachers and 12 per cent of students registered on its mainstream courses were women. Both proportions were significantly higher than industry averages at the time (Conway, 'Women at the College', 5).
26. Thiel, *Builders*, 155.
27. According to the 2011 England and Wales Census, people of South Asian origin (Pakistan, India and Bangladesh) represented 5.3% of the population; people of Black-African origin represented 1.8% and people of Black Caribbean represented 1.1% (https://www.ethnicity-facts-figures.service.gov.uk/uk-population-by-ethnicity/national-and-regional-populations/population-of-england-and-wales/latest#by-ethnicity, retrieved 1 June 2021).
28. Caplan et al., *Race Discrimination*, ii.
29. Ibid., 6.
30. In interview at Carpenters' Hall, London, 7 July 2008.
31. BBC, 'Skills Gap'.
32. BBC, 'Skills Drive'.
33. Brown, 'Speech on Expansion of Apprenticeships'.
34. BBC, 'Half of New Jobs'.
35. Ibid.
36. Hayes, '"The Craft So Long to Lerne"'.
37. Osborne, 'Budget 2011 Speech'.
38. Jakob, 'Crafting Your Way', 131.
39. Ferris, 'Making Futures', no pagination.
40. Morris Hargreaves McIntyre, *Market for Craft*, 37.
41. Thiel, *Builders*, 106.
42. Ibid., 107.
43. See ibid., 85.
44. Emerson, 'Nature 1836', 61.
45. Marchand, 'Embodied Cognition and Communication', S102–S103.
46. Ibid., S104.
47. Personal communication with Julie Tancell, 12 August 2020.
48. Tragically, Weardon is now more commonly associated with the notorious twenty-four-storey Grenfell Tower block of flats in North Kensington, which burned in June 2017, causing seventy-two deaths.
49. For a description of the materials used in the interior of the Banqueting Hall, see Tancell, 'The Tree of Life', 16–17.
50. Clark, *Carpenters' Hall*, 18–19.
51. Tancell, 'The Tree of Life', 16–17.

CHAPTER 5

CRAFTING CRAFTSPEOPLE
Introducing the Instructors

If you want knowledge, you must toil for it: if food, you must toil for it: and if pleasure, you must toil for it.

—John Ruskin[1]

Craftspeople shape and create not only artefacts; they also 'craft' successive generations of artisans. Institutions of vocational education and training, as well as workshops that supply on-the-job experience or formal apprenticeships, are prime sites for nurturing an interconnected array of skills, dispositions and ways of knowing, and, crucially, scaffolding processes of self-discovery.

A rounded craft curriculum includes, as a minimum, the history, lore, traditions and rituals of the particular craft occupation; an opportunity to grapple with the nature and behaviour of materials; first-hand acquaintance-ship with tools, their attributes and functions; repeated practice of technical procedures, postures, economic gestures and efficient movements; the honing of multiple kinds of perceptual awareness and nimble responsiveness; the education of aesthetic discernment; the formation of ethical judgement, with an accompanying sense of ownership and responsibility; and the acquisition of business acumen, appropriate ways of speaking and listening, and a disciplined comportment. In the fluid and sometimes-fraught exchanges between mentors and mentees, worldviews, value systems, identities, professional networks and a sense of community are forged, fostered, occasionally contested and often fortified.

I thus continue my exploration of craftspeople and their pursuit of pleasurable work by introducing some of those who made that pursuit possible in the first place.

INTRODUCING THE INSTRUCTORS

Con, the first-year instructor, was introduced in Chapter 4. Here, I present three others from the Building Crafts College who had a strong hand in crafting my skills and those of my fellow trainees on the fine-woodwork programme. Jim, David and Cheryl, like Con, came to the profession of teaching with a wealth of practical on-site experience in carpentry, joinery, heritage craft or furniture making. Jim had undertaken a London apprenticeship after leaving school; David set up his own workshop in the Chiltern Forest and Cheryl underwent training in Women's Workshops that had been established in boroughs across London. Their reflections on becoming carpenters and working in urban and rural England provide fascinating historical illustrations of the industry's transformations and its continuity, and their words on teaching offer profound insights into 'old-style' apprenticeships, contemporary craft education, funding regimes, gender politics, the role of banter in 'thickening skin', and the spiritual dimension of creative activity and newfound agency. These issues have resonance beyond the particularities of woodworking and speak to the history and experiences of numerous building trades and craft occupations in the United Kingdom. The personal and professional journeys of the three instructors differ in intriguing ways, but what they share is a passion for timber and the tools, and a devotion to passing that passion on.

In describing their respective philosophies and methods of teaching, the instructors featured here stressed the importance of cultivating both physical and mental dexterity, discipline, timekeeping, good manners and patience. As one instructor noted, teaching in the wood trades involves a 'holistic approach' that goes across the person. Some emphasised the role of hand tools in developing a direct and responsive relation between the body in motion and the timber being worked, and, in a similar vein, others underscored the need to attune students' sensory awareness – vitally, sight and touch – to the task at hand and to the workshop more generally. Safety also figures prominently in their narratives on good practice.

Together, the instructors sought to create a participatory learning environment in which trainees could be challenged – and challenge themselves – while feeling supported, and where making mistakes was intuitively grasped as an opportunity to explore solutions in an autonomous-but-guided manner. In pushing trainees to strive for professional standards, these instructors aimed to foster the confidence needed to critically engage with one's work balanced by a true pride in self and good workmanship.

In our recorded conversations, it is patently clear that the three derived a satisfaction from woodworking that was at once deeply intellectual, emotional and spiritual. That holistic satisfaction and the personal development it propels is voiced repeatedly throughout the book by the scores of trainees and practitioners whom I interviewed and worked alongside. Their collective perspectives squarely confute the low and demeaning status customarily attributed to manual vocations in Britain and in the ever-growing number of other nations that prize and prioritise academic over vocational learning. Individually, and in complementary ways, the featured instructors reinforced the idea that design and making entail constant improvisation, innovation and problem-solving strategies that tightly fuse mind and body at work.

Their words also awaken our appreciation for the 'craftwork' that exists in our everyday surroundings and that is thoughtlessly overlooked: the craftwork in frame-and-panel doors, sash windows, winding staircases, mouldings and embellishments, cabinetry, and the bespoke furniture we sit in, write at, eat at, store things in and sleep upon. In discussing these handmade objects together, the divide that is conventionally made by industry and training providers between carpentry and joinery as 'trades' and fine woodwork as a 'craft' is blurred.

The contents of the interviews and discussions speak mostly for themselves. Jim and Cheryl conversed vividly and at length about their personal journeys, experiences and convictions, while David tended to express his knowledge and passion for woodwork more eloquently in his actions and in briefer remarks made while teaching his students at the bench. For this reason, the three introductions to the instructors differ somewhat in style. I have left the narratives of Jim and Cheryl almost entirely in their words, while my account of David's ideas opens spaces for introducing key pedagogical objectives that I flesh out more fully in subsequent chapters.

Jim's reminiscences of his own apprenticeship, early jobs and discoveries about learning aptly provide an overarching framework for the themes raised by his two colleagues. David's philosophical reflections on the importance of creativity initiate investigation of the core intellectual and emotional qualities needed to thrive as a craftsperson. And finally, Cheryl's narrative brings many of the topics introduced by Jim full circle, and in doing so she broaches issues of gender, social class, pervasive discrimination against manual trades, and the future of craft skills in the United Kingdom.

JIM O.

The building trade is in transition in this country from the workmanship of risk to that of certainty, to the assembly of prefabricated components so made that neither care, knowledge nor dexterity are required for their assembly; and such trades as the joiner's are in decline. There are now too few good joiners.

—David Pye[2]

David Pye's observation on the state of joinery is as true today as it was forty years ago. Grave concerns about the nation's 'skills gap' have been flagged for decades by the government and the construction industry, and numerous schemes have been piloted with limited success.

A combination of issues continues to obstruct the sort of investment needed for seeding and nurturing a local skill base, improving the quality of building-craft education, and promoting the trades as desirable career trajectories over the long term. Arguably, the greatest obstruction is England's historic attachment to laissez-faire economics. This has curtailed any political will to commit wholeheartedly to industry training, and it panders to global market forces that promote the import of cheaper labour to the detriment of homegrown skill.

Another major deterrent keeping potentially talented woodworkers from pursuing the necessary vocational training is the persistent popular notion that the trades are a refuge for academic underachievers and members of the social 'underclasses'. Woodworking has been axed from the curriculum in many schools, allegedly for health and safety reasons and due to funding cuts and budgetary constraints. Career advisors and parents are either oblivious to, or prejudiced against, the manual trades as a possible career path for their children, and government targets to boost university graduate figures fuel peer pressure amongst youth to 'go to uni' in lieu of pursuing potentially more gratifying education routes (that, in the end, may also reap higher financial rewards).[3] Together, these factors gravely constrict recruitment to the building crafts in terms of the numbers, quality and diversity of candidates.

In 1970, at the age of sixteen, Jim O. underwent a four-year apprenticeship as a joiner with J.F. Nott Limited in London. He carried on in the wood trades, enjoying a long career restoring buildings of significant historic and architectural importance, which in turn opened up worlds of learning to him.

Following an injury, he earned a teaching certificate and joined the Building Crafts College in 2002 as Senior Tutor of the shop-fitting and bench joinery courses. These courses are taken by part-time students and by cohorts of young Apprentices coming from the construction industry on block release. Though Jim had no official involvement with the fine-woodwork programme, me and many of my fellow trainees garnered a great deal from his teaching during the two years. Jim frequently passed through our workshop, generously lending advice on technique, structure, and assembly, offering guidance on selecting the best timber from the racks, and earnestly issuing health and safety warnings in the mill.

In his own words, Jim colourfully describes being a London apprentice in the early 1970s and his site-work experience, drawing shrewd comparisons between on-the-job learning and college training. He also discusses his personal path into teaching and unswerving belief in the potential of his students. His devotion to the trade and the context he depicts for vocational education and employment, past and present, sets the scene for introducing the next two instructors featured in this chapter.

Learning the Trade

I can remember being six or seven and asking for a hammer and nails for my birthday. My father used to bring me home loads of bent nails. We straightened them out to make soapbox cars with bits of fallen tree. My father, uncles and older cousins were all navy men, and my ambition was to train as a ship's carpenter. I left school at fifteen with only a CSE in woodworking. A CSE was the lowest exam you could get: lower than a GCSE, lower than an O level. I took it just for the sake of leaving school with an exam. Not that I was thick or stupid. I hated school and I always knew I wanted to be a carpenter, so I didn't need to know anything else. It was 'go out and get an apprenticeship' and that's what I did. Unfortunate thing was, the year I left school in 1969, the navy stopped taking on apprentices to serve at sea.

A friend got me an apprenticeship at a local shop-fitting firm. The employer gave me £150 to buy tools and they deducted six pence a week from my salary until the debt was paid. I was instructed to make a box for my new tools. It took me two weeks. I was so proud of this bit of joinery with dovetail drawers, and all bits to put things in. I showed the guy I was working with and he took it, threw it on the furnace and burned it, and said: 'Now make the next one quicker.' It was to get me up to speed. But I never showed him the next one!

The first months are tough for anyone. There was one chap who would knock you about. He'd lay hands on you. And you'd expect it. He'd kick you up the ass if he caught you larking about or not paying attention. I spent my probation sweeping, sanding, and going down the road to get the rolls and tea. And you didn't just sweep your area; you did the whole place and took care of all their tools as well. It was a good way to see if you'd stick it out and if you could take the banter.

The guy I was working with, we were doing some veneering – huge veneering, and all hand-veneer. And once you did one side it tended to curl, so you damped the other side, turned it down and put a weight on it. So, Stan said to me: 'Go down to the machine shop, see Fred and ask him for the long weight.' So, I went down to the shop: 'Fred, Stan says can I have the long weight?' 'Yeah, alright', he said, and disappeared. Ten minutes, fifteen minutes ...Where's Fred? So I go and find him and he's having a fag and a cup of tea. 'What do you want?' Fred grumbled. 'The long weight', I said. 'You've *waited* long enough. Fuck off.'

I got caught on the 'long wait', but there're hundreds of them. Colleagues tell me about getting caught on the 'glass nail' and the 'skirting ladder', and things like that. Those are things you should never get caught on, but you do. Coming from school, you're green as cabbage. The firm's blacksmith told me that, while serving his apprenticeship, he was sent for a box of '5/8th holes'. Luckily for him, the bloke behind the counter was wise to that one, and gave him a box of 5/8th washers saying: 'Tell 'em to file the outsides off of them!' The technical terms are all new. If someone would have told me to go and get the '*wangdoo* with the 498 on it', I would have been off on the chase.

After six months' probation, my father came down to sign the apprenticeship contract with the master, Jack Knott, because I was under eighteen. A five-year apprenticeship was standard at that time, and I was also sent to college in Barking to learn site work and joinery. Every year I was put to work with a different joiner in the shop, and each had his own character and his own technique. I had one particular chap, Alf, whom everyone knew was slow. He'd have a go to show you, and then you'd have a go, and so on. He was given the jobs that took longer, so speed didn't matter. I learned early on to pay attention and watch carefully. It's difficult to say what exactly I was focusing on. The guys wouldn't tell you a lot because they had their own job to do, so you had to learn by close observation.

Another chap, Charlie, used to really make me laugh. Not so much his technique, but because he had a facial movement for every task he did. When he was sawing, his jaw would go side to side. When he was hammering, he went like *that* . . . [Jim flapped his jaw open and shut to demonstrate]. I'd first watch his facial expression; then I'd concentrate on what he was doing with his hands. Charlie rarely marked his timber, but by positioning his hands *just so*, he'd cut bang-on every time. I'd wonder 'How's he doing that?' 'What's he looking at?' This may sound fanciful, if you like, but Charlie could actually see the reflection of his cut line in the saw blade. His tools were pristine. The guy could determine by eye if it was square to what he was cutting. You know, I tried it and failed dismally, so I always work to the line.

I completed my apprenticeship on my twenty-first birthday. I was given back my indenture and explained the history, and [was] then told: 'You've got six months to go out and find another job.'[4] It was tradition to go off, pick up more skills and bring something back to the employer otherwise you would always be 'the boy'. They'd welcome you back as a man and you'd earn a man's wage. But they were equally happy to wave you away. That was standard practice, even though it doesn't stack up economically, so to speak. Some still work that way. I think it's altruistic. There's no money in it, but they do it because they want to carry on a trade and all the rest of it, you know. There's no money in training, especially for an employer. It takes years before a trainee starts earning any money for their employer, unless they're exceptional.

I didn't go back to the shop. I preferred site fitting, and the pay was fantastic. But you could work twenty hours a day, so I had no social life. After a year or so, I started to work on construction sites building houses, and even went out to France for a couple of years to work in Bordeaux.

Learning through Work

When I came back to London, I was asked to do work on a Tudor house in Cheyne Walk that was owned by Paul Getty, and by the end of the two-year project it was bought by the Sainsburys. I found myself having to explain to the SPAB [Society for the Protection of Ancient Buildings] architects on site about the repairs we were making, and that was the first time I had the chance to formally explain things, aside from giving the younger lads instruction.

The average Joe looks at a job and thinks: 'That's a fantastic building.' He might even think that the architect was brilliant, but he never thinks who the mason was, who the carpenter was, who did all the metal work and lead, and all of that. A part of the individual has gone into that building, and only that individual knows it. Architects put stuff down on paper and think: 'I'm not sure how that's going to work.' But a good tradesman can look at something on paper and actually visualise it – they can really see it. People don't appreciate our professional eye. The stuff that we do – all the twiddles and embellishments – wasn't originally put on by someone who wanted 'em. The joggles on the bottom of sash windows were put there as a strengthening piece for that joint. But it didn't have to be that shape: the carpenter done that. You look at things and think 'That doesn't look right', and so you skinny that bit and broaden that bit, and you do it until it's *just* right. That's what we do all the time.

From Cheyne Walk I picked up loads and loads of fantastic restoration work. Believe it or not, I went next to Broadmoor, the secure mental hospital in Berkshire. That was an early Victorian building built by the inmates and we were restoring some of the women's wing. It was a fantastic job and very bizarre. Although everything had to go back as near original as possible, it also had to be safe and secure so that the patients couldn't pull things off, access screws or something like that. From there I repaired a Hellfire Club gazebo in someone's back garden with a shell grotto below.[5] I also carried out considerable work in John Soane's house, restoring every window on the rear of the building, every door, and a lot of the flooring. The only part I didn't touch was downstairs [i.e. the ground floor] where the Hogarth paintings hang. Soane was an architect who built models of the things he designed. He understood what he was building.[6]

When you're working on old buildings, you start looking at things you never thought about before, and suddenly you find you're learning. What a joy!

When Miss Keller at school said 'One day this will come in useful', you went: 'Yeah, like hell it will!' But you suddenly realise that it does. You pick up history and geography while working, and sometimes you find out macabre titbits about a place, or why something's done one way in one part of the country and not in another. For instance, in the Suffolk, Norfolk and Lincolnshire fens, there's a lot of rivalry between them that you don't understand, and it goes back to when they used to fight over some bit of sheep or something. There's a certain fitting that we've always known as a 'thumb latch' that's fitted to a gate or a cupboard, and that you push and it lifts up. So in every part of the country, as far as I know, it's called a thumb latch, except in Suffolk where it's called a 'Norfolk', and in Norfolk it's called a 'Suffolk' – because they're like idiot things! It's all derogatory.

You learn bizarre stuff. I'd say to my dad, for instance: 'Ah Dad, we're working on a job where we're using Pitch pine.' And he'd say: 'Oh, I haven't seen that for years. You know that used to come in as dunnage on a ship.' That would mean a ship would go off to America and bring back a load of cargo, and to secure it they would buy all the Pitch pine they could. They'd use that as big boards and planks to jam everything in, to stop it moving around, and any repairs to the ship, they'd use that as they'd come along. And when they got to the London docks, they'd offload all the dunnage and flog it to the local Carpenters' Company. That's why Pitch pine was used in so many of the old buildings in London, even though it's one of the most flammable timbers there is. You try to get hold of it now and it's very hard. My dad actually told me about a company that was still working in the [Isle of] Dogs that dealt in dunnage, and they put me onto suppliers of timbers. So without mentioning that one timber, and my dad's history of working in the navy and the docks, I wouldn't have had that supply of Pitch pine.

It was coming up to one Christmas and I knew I'd tweaked my back at work. The doctor said: 'It's going to keep doing that so you'll have to learn a new technique for moving, sitting and walking, and it's going to limit your time on site.' I'm a 'hands-on' person, and I didn't want to just go around and price jobs, and waffle and waffle. The Beeb [BBC] was running a radio programme at the time about retraining, so I phoned up and started a teaching certificate at Epping College. When I finished, I did a PGCE [Postgraduate Certificate in Education] at Greenwich University. I applied for five or six jobs and got a reply from one – a small place, a bit like this [the Building Crafts College], called Canning Training Centre that specialised in construction. They had a bench joinery workshop, plumbing workshop, specialist techniques and a painting-decorating department. That was really good. I could still see myself there now if it wasn't for the fact that the financial director and the director were running a swindle, creaming the government, and not paying taxes, our insurance or pensions. So Inland Revenue closed it down and I was made redundant. Then the director [of the Building Crafts College] asked me to come and work here.

On the Building Crafts College

The ethos of this college, if you like, is the 'master and apprentice' – that's the way the [former] director definitely sees it. I wouldn't want to see it as anything as highfalutin as that, but I do think that any girl or boy working down here can see any instructor in a white coat. My own method of teaching is 'carrot and stick', and it starts more stick than carrot. They think I'm hard, and I like them to think I'm a hard nasty bastard. Those that are lazy, I'll push, and those that are capable, I'll push even harder. We don't teach to the lowest common denominator: we teach to the highest. Everyone's got to pull themselves up by the bootstraps.

When I started at Canning, a lot of people were there ticking over. They were there to get their £30 a week; they were there because they didn't want to be on the dole; they were there because their mum or dad made them do it. But that's not so much the case here. These guys are a bit different, and I treat them different. Yes, they're loud and leery, and some of them are probably quite street-wise as well. But most of these are polite young people who will hold the door for you and say 'please' and 'thank you'. We're teaching them personal formation. If you want to use the terminology, we're using a 'holistic' approach here. We don't just feed one sense; we're going across the whole person. When you get them in the first year, they're a pimply, sixteen, four-foot-nothing Lilliputian, and when the three years are up they're six-foot-two and wide as you like. And they've not just grown in body; they've grown spiritually and mentally as well. I'm not talking about 'religious' spiritual. The craft is spiritual, if you like. Our pride is a spiritual thing. It's a question of 'I done it'. I don't care who knows. I know. I know I done it. That's the spiritual bit.

Whenever possible in the workshop, I'll demonstrate, but you've got to be careful not to do the work for them. I'll show them how to hold the saw and how to manipulate their body, and let them go. And then I'll shout: 'Not like that! Across grain!' 'Hold your saw properly!' 'Hammers come with a free handle. Use it!' I don't understand people who hold a bit of wood to chisel when they can cramp it and have both hands free. In this trade, there are certain things where you have to be truly ambidextrous. It's not like an electrician. We're using both hands all the time. I walk around and show them [Jim holds both hands up in front and wiggles his fingers], and boast: 'I still got 'em.' I worked with a chap who used to say: 'That's the sign of a good tradesman. You've still got all your digits.' We all make silly foolish mistakes. We all cut ourselves. But if we're half-decent and our tools are properly sharp, it doesn't leave much of a scar. It's the ones that are blunt that, you know . . . That's why the students need those techniques and we have to develop them. But I can only demonstrate how to hold a chisel and pare. I can stand there with you, but I can't make you do it. It's a bit like learning to play a guitar. Someone can only position your fingers, but they can't make them move properly.

I prefer to demonstrate than explain. I try *not* to say to them: 'You're doing it like this because. . .' They're doing it like that because it's been done like that forever. Don't ask me the reason! I could tell them: 'Once upon a time in tenoning [i.e. cutting a tenon], everything was worked out in parts of a fifth – three-fifths and two-fifths. Now we go for thirds. . .' I just tell them we go for thirds because it's easier. It's been done that way for millennia. I'm damn sure when Joseph was showing Jesus, he done it like that. And when Noah was building the ark, his techniques were damn sure the same as the ones we're using now. Those things don't change. What does change is the quality of materials: in some cases far superior, and in others poorer. We've got better hand tools, better machinery. Those are the main differences; otherwise we're doing everything the same.

On Training Standards

I'm a composite of the four guys I trained with at the shop, plus the guys that taught me at college. The 'old boys' did their apprenticeship with one bloke for seven years, so they might have had a solid grounding in just that one discipline. It was highly specialised: you might be just a 'site carpenter', just a 'bench joiner', or just a 'shop fitter'. Directly after the War it went down to five years. I did bench joinery and site fitting, and went to college at the same time, so although I may not know as much in one little area, my knowledge is more rounded.

When teaching these guys, I'm conscious of showing them the different possible ways of doing things from the ways I learned. But for the young boys and girls today it's even more condensed. If they're doing three years in a site carpentry route, they'll probably learn a little bit about first fixing, a little about second fixing, and that's about it. They won't do any shuttering, and they probably won't do stair construction. They might do a bit of roof-truss construction, but they won't do any cut roofs.

We're told by the CITB [Construction Industry Training Board][7] – the driving force behind the NVQ [National Vocational Qualifications] – that the training programme is employer-led. It's the big construction companies who pay the bulk of the levy. They don't train their own apprentices, and they say to [the] CITB 'I want a guy who can hang a door' or, 'I want a guy who can fit architraves'. The small employer who puts someone through an apprenticeship and pays for all their training is saying: 'No! I want someone with a broader spectrum of training.' But, because they're not paying the major part of the levy, they've got less say. As a result, it's shaping the programme to minimum standards.

As far as the CITB technical requirements are concerned, it's a sort of 'box ticking' exercise. It's like telling them we've reached the targets – like the National Health [Service] being able to say that everyone can see a doctor within thirty minutes. 'We've put umpteen people through the training and 90 per cent have achieved.' So what? Big deal! How many have actually gone out and made something of themselves from what they learned from the CITB. None! It's what they learn from us, and what their employer is teaching them. In the three years, we get them through the minimum of what will earn them their ICA [Intermediate Construction Award], ACA [Advanced Construction Award] and NVQ Levels 2 and 3, and give them far more than that. For instance, we teach them machining aspects so that they learn to operate safely. And if the NVQ project calls for a straight flight of stairs, we require higher standards on the balustrade and we've reintroduced traditional features like the bull nosing [on stair treads].

One thing we do down here is drive them to speed up, and get them to motor on. When you're in here, you're in a very safe environment. When you're out there, you gotta be able to cut the mustard and earn the money. And then you've got to sort your clients out. You got to find out what the client wants. You've also got to be prepared to explain to the client why he or she can't always have what they want, and what's the best way to achieve what they want as close as possible in the most economic and safest way. So they need them skills. Sometimes it takes a long time for the penny to drop. It's like slow motion. But then, at some point, they come in with light in their eyes!

DAVID W.

At the end of the day, woodworking and furniture making is about having an idea and giving shape to it; and all the while working with the nature of the materials. That's the essence of it. There's no mystery to it; there's no secret. The inherent abilities are there in a person.

—David W.

David W. arrived at the Building Crafts College in 2005, the same year I began full-time training there. He had long experience as a practitioner in the trade and as a teacher in the furniture-making programme at what is now Buckinghamshire New University. During our long discussions together, we explored David's ideas about the importance of creativity to wellbeing, and the personal attributes that a craftsperson needs in order to grow and flourish. His inventory of core attributes included confidence, patience, critical perceptual awareness and an ability to constructively critique one's own practices and finished work. At the very root of each, David explained, is the learning that comes from making mistakes and making good of them.

In the views expressed below, David compares and contrasts the learning environments of the college workshop and the workplace, where making mistakes can have actual financial consequences. He also champions the usefulness of hand tools and critically ponders the historical introduction of power tools and machinery to the craft. David concludes with a strategy for preparing trainees for industry in the face of limited technological resources available at the College.

Walden in the Chiltern Hills

David's formative years were spent in the hilltop village of Penn, located twenty-five miles west of London. The surrounding forests of giant beech were his playground. David's father was a technical illustrator whom he described as possessing an 'engineer's pragmatism'. His paternal grandfather lived next door and worked as a carpenter out of a large shed at the bottom of the garden.

In 1965, following the eleven-plus exams,[8] David went to a technical training school where the focus was on engineering and vocational trades. The school's woodwork instructor inspired and nurtured David's talents. 'He was a Yorkshireman', said David, 'and he could be very stern. But there was no malice, or cruelty, or physical punishment. He was a proper old-style "gentleman" of good working-class stock, if you like.' David recalled how the instructor employed the 'magic of analogy' in his teaching to conjure powerful, enduring images in the mind that aided student learning and deepened their understanding of complex joinery tasks. The older man's sober patience and his nurturing approach would serve as a model for David in his later career as mentor and teacher.

At the age of eighteen, David left school to work for a small firm in High Wycombe, Buckinghamshire, which specialised in reproduction Chippendale and Victorian furniture. Three years of experience spurred ambitions to set up on his own. David did so initially in his late grandfather's shed and then hired a workshop in the Chiltern Hills. That space would become his 'Walden' for nearly two decades.

The town of High Wycombe and the surrounding Chiltern Hills has long been a renowned furniture-making centre, notably for the production of Windsor chairs, which flourished during the nineteenth and twentieth centuries. These distinctive chairs were manufactured using locally available timbers, typically elm or ash for the saddle seat and, occasionally, beech for the turned legs and spindle elements of the backrest and arms.[9] Historian and woodworker Harvey Green notes that 'Windsors were mass-produced by country carpenters and joiners who had easy access to small lumber' and who owned foot-powered lathes and a small assortment of basic hand tools.[10] Those who set up forest camps to turn legs and spindles from green wood on pole lathes were referred to locally as 'bodgers'. The decline of the chair-making industry from the 1960s onwards witnessed the closure of many furniture factories and a sharp rise in unemployment in High Wycombe, but quality woodworking and furniture making are still carried on by a handful of firms in the area.

David recounted how setting up a workshop in the nearby village of Little Kingshill, just five miles from his family home, gave him 'a foot in the region where [his] ancestors would have possibly indulged their craft and established their connection with the land'. Many years later, he would import the unique challenges involved in the Chiltern chair-making tradition to the college workshop curriculum. As he noted, 'making a chair entails a completely different type of thought process from making a cabinet or a table'. Designing and making chairs challenges the woodworker to draw upon and coordinate a broad spectrum of technical skills, and to enhance them in the process. It also calls for familiarity with the aesthetic history of chair design, and demands understanding of basic physics, structural loads and ergonomic principles.[11]

David's workshop, measuring just 37 square metres, occupied an old poultry unit. During the eighteen years he spent there, he honed his tool-sharpening skills and cultivated an intense curiosity in the art of wheelwrighting. The wheelwright all but disappeared with the advent of rubber tyre manufacture, surviving today solely as a speciality trade that furnishes wooden wheels for horse-drawn vehicles, collectors, museums and heritage centres. But the skill and precision involved in the craft continues to win the admiration of contemporary British and American woodworkers. George Sturt, an early twentieth-century wheelwright and writer on rural English crafts, correctly claimed that making 'a well-finished wheel . . . was a case for experts'.[12] David's small workshop space was suitable for experimenting with wooden wheels, but it was far too cramped for the growing number of cabinet-making commissions that earned him a living.

The isolation of working alone was also beginning to affect David's sense of wellbeing. Fortuitously, a friend and fellow woodworker who taught on the furniture-making course at Buckinghamshire College led a student field trip to David's workshop. While explaining to the young men and women how he was designing and making a large Welsh dresser, David had an epiphany, of sorts, that he 'was meant to be a teacher'. Shortly afterwards, he was offered part-time teaching at Buckinghamshire College, where he stayed for a decade. In 2005, David found full-time employment at the Building Crafts

College, convening their fine-woodwork programme and instructing the second-year students.

Building Confidence and Critical Awareness

'I try to fit the theory in at the bench', David explained while telling me about his teaching methods. 'The theory is *there*, in the practical. It's easy to distribute photocopied hand-outs or show an overhead projection and say, "That's that", but it's taking the longer journey through actually making a piece of furniture that really works.' He stressed the efficacy of experiential learning for transforming ways of thinking about, and approaching, a task. 'Experience-based learning', according to David, 'builds confidence'; and, 'as confidence grows, doubt falls away'. A woodworker's confidence as a craftsperson is conveyed in the ease with which they handle their tools and schedule procedures, in their calm resolve while working through challenges, in their willingness to experiment and expand their skillset, and in their capacity to be self-critical.

David believed that it wasn't necessary to tackle complex procedures and conquer elaborate projects in order to cultivate confidence at the workbench. Rather, mastering a succession of simple, straightforward assignments can prove invaluable: 'The simplicity of an idea can challenge many thought processes. The important thing is to work on that task; develop your understanding, and see what you come up with next.' For him, as for other instructors, instilling confidence in trainees in their technical and design abilities was synonymous with building self-reliance. This was incrementally achieved through the combination of immersing students in hands-on practice and fostering their individual capacities for independent reflection, reasoning and problem solving:

> My duty is to get students to realise that it's OK to make mistakes – as long as they do so without posing a threat to themselves or the safety of others – and to learn from them. It's to help students to believe in themselves as well as developing their understanding of how tools work and how timber behaves. It's ultimately about putting those elements of confidence and technical know-how together.

David conceived of the college workshop as a 'learning community' in which both instructors and trainees contributed to 'an element of growing and nurturing'. 'Some of the more advanced students might know more about certain things than even the teachers', he admitted, 'and that can pose a threat':

> But equally, that potential threat can be turned to advantage for the whole group by encouraging those individuals to share their knowledge or skills with the others. Younger students, too, who might be less confident, have a part to play in the com-

munity. Everyone is learning from one another the importance of interdependence. There's a dynamic. We all have our strengths and our weaknesses in certain areas, and so one student's strength can help turn another's weakness to a competency.

Reflecting on his role as instructor in that process, David acknowledged that he was 'only the messenger': 'The source of the energy isn't coming from me. The energy is coming from the students. My job is to disperse that energy as evenly as possible amongst them.' He conceded, however, that in doing so, 'energy does go from me. Instructors know that when we immerse ourselves in this kind of inclusive teaching and inclusive learning, we're going to expend a lot of effort in making it work.'

David routinely reflected on the correlation he drew between making things and fulfilling one's individual potential as a human. 'The philosophy of the craft', he shared, 'is rooted in our inherent need to be creative; to do things with our brain and our hands. And it's not Playstations, and it's not computers. It's actually making things.' David granted that computer programming could be a creative and satisfying endeavour and that computer programs could serve as effective tools in the design process. What he was referring to, however, was the addiction to digital technologies and social media that transform us into mere consumers of information, entertainment and commodities, and that numb our impulses to experience the world firsthand and respond to it and shape it as active agents. 'We all have abilities: "survival skills", if you like', he continued. 'Those skills came about by constructing crude shelters and making the sorts of things that our ancestors made to survive. It's intrinsic to the human psyche to be creative.'

In this age of mass manufacturing and highly specialised, infinitesimal division of labour, David conceded that the vast majority of us no longer have a need to make our own shelter, furnishings or implements in order to survive. But, those who do make things do so to satisfy 'an inherent need to express a sentiment'. 'If you're a painter', he stated, 'you do it with colour; if you're a carpenter, you do it with shape and form.' He pursued his thesis in earnest:

> We have a need to make things. It's a therapy. It is the answer to the world's problems: creativity, the antithesis to destruction. By example, the feeling of pushing a sharp chisel through wood: there is a balance there between destroying the plank of timber as it had existed while at the same time creating something new. I would caution that, where the outlet for creativity is taken away, where that experience is not allowed, where somebody is denied participating in that part of a community or society, the natural route is the opposite, toward the destructive.

David expounded further on the reciprocal relation between creative making and fostering a sense of self-control and agency. Through immersion in making and creating, he suggested, students were learning not only to physically control their technical manipulation of tools and the transformation of raw materials into functional and aesthetic objects; they were also learn-ing to temper their impatience; re-educate their desires and expectations for immediate results, and harness their emotions when confronted with a challenge or upon discovering a mistake. In short, students were cultivating self-discipline, and, in turn, self-discipline was channelled back into their creative approaches and technical practices. David complained of 'a general tendency' in today's society to be 'intolerant of the laborious, slow, steady ways of doing things. There's little popular demand for perfection'. Training in fine woodworking, by contrast, nurtures appreciation for perfection and insistence upon precision in one's own work.

College and Workplace: Continual Learning

Making and repairing mistakes is fundamental to learning to problem solve with growing efficiency and economy, as we will see in Chapter 8, and the ability to do so is the mark of mastery. While the college workshop provided the ideal safe environment for this kind of learning, it also limited trainees' learning about the real potential costs of making mistakes in the workplace. Depending on the nature of the error, a mistake can have serious financial implications in terms of person-hours and materials lost. Repeated mistakes might also result in the loss of a commission or of employment altogether.

'You've made a mistake. It's beyond repair. Let's have another go', said Da-vid, recapping the formula for college-based learning. 'Economically, that's okay here, but it's not really the way.' He compared the college training with the 'old-style' on-the-job apprenticeships that existed between the two World Wars and into the early 1970s, of the kind Jim O. had undergone. Trainees operated alongside experienced mentors, in real time and with the economic constraints of the marketplace. 'They were paid a small amount, but they *were* paid, and they *were* part of the economics of the company', David stressed. 'Therefore, there'd be the need to learn, but without casually saying, "Oh, I've messed up. I'll just get another piece of wood", like we do here.' The college workshop enabled students to acquire basic trade skills for launching their woodworking careers, but, according to David: 'The true learning goes on later, in the workplace.' This issue is explored more fully in Chapter 9.

In comparing past learning regimes with the new, David also lamented the diminishing array of hand skills acquired by contemporary carpenters and joiners. Echoing Walter Rose's reminiscences of the village carpenter in early twentieth-century England,[13] David believed that, in contrast to Jim's account of narrowly focused specialisation, apprentices of an earlier time had to be prepared to 'turn their hand to many facets of the craft', including tim-ber framing, carpentry, joinery, cabinet making, turning, carving, gilding, marquetry, parquetry, inlay and polishing. Each task had its corresponding kit of specialised hand tools and methods, which demand mastery to varying degrees. 'Few all-round carpenters of that sort exist today', declared David, 'though some still straddle several specialisations.' Woodworking is now divided into discreet occupations and subtrades, and the once vast variety of dedicated hand tools has been superseded by a far smaller number of power tools and compact machines, as was discussed in Chapter 4.

'The contemporary approach in furniture making', according to David, 'is highly machine-oriented. Modern trade journals are full of advertising by power-tool manufacturers.' Despite his great esteem for hand-tool skills, he accepted that power tools can speed up and simplify the production of quality pieces, and thus be cost-effective. 'Take for example the biscuit joiner', he added. 'Why go to the trouble of making hand-cut mortise-and-tenon joints if that piece of equipment gives you the results you need? Plus, it saves you time, energy and money. You would have to be a fool not to use it.'

Much of the furniture being produced by UK designer-makers and North American studio furniture makers, David noted, exhibits a 'certain minimalism', devoid of carving, marquetry or complex curvilinear geometries. Not wishing to undermine the skill and integrity of his fellow craftspeople, David volunteered that: 'Some work being produced is quite exciting, quite magical, but it does exhibit the limited range of hand-skill experience that today's fine woodworkers are getting, either at college or in the workplace.'

On the other hand, technologies such as computer-aided design (CAD) software and computer numerical control (CNC) machines are enabling furniture makers to produce pieces of fantastical form and complexity, pushing the boundaries of furniture design and construction. CAD, first developed in the 1960s, was already becoming a conventional tool in design studios by the 1990s. CNC woodworking machines are driven by CAD software and comprise a number of axes with rotary blades that accurately and speedily cut the contours of components for panels, windows, doors or furniture.

Independent designer-makers in the United Kingdom who employ such technologies remain a minority, for a variety of reasons. Some reject both CAD and CNC machines because, according to their philosophy, these technologies lay outside the craft tradition, with its focus on the hand. Designer-maker of furniture Peter Fleming noted that students of craft who are reluctant to draw and instead turn to CAD have failed to realise that this technology is merely a tool and 'a rather crude one at that, compared to the huge range of possibilities that a pencil can offer'.[14] CNC machines in particular have been demonised as a threat to hand skills, bespoke making, and even the future livelihoods of sole traders and craftspeople.[15] Such views evidently resonate with sentiments expressed by John Ruskin and William Morris, and in more extreme forms with those of the early nineteenth-century Luddite protests against 'labour-saving machinery'. In other cases, craftspeople have not (yet) identified clear economic or operational benefits for using this technology in their design and making. Most small to medium-sized furniture manufacturers cannot justify the very considerable financial outlay unless they are regularly engaged in large-batch production.

A perhaps more fundamental reason for the slow uptake of computer-aided technologies in carpentry workshops lies with the training programmes undergone by the majority of British woodworkers. At the time of my study, the Building Crafts College, for example, expressed ambitions to introduce CAD into the curriculum, but had not managed to do so during the period I researched there. As for CNC, it was a simple fact that, for most vocational colleges, the associated costs for the machinery and for training up in-house expertise were prohibitively high.

Though the College could not afford to keep pace with the latest technological advances in the industry, David believed that there were ways round this for preparing those trainees who were less interested in bespoke making, but aspired to create designs that lent themselves to mass production for retailers like Heals, Habitat, John Lewis or IKEA. He offered by way of example a design by Russell, a second-year fine-woodwork student. Russell wanted to create and market a modular table-cum-shelving unit of furniture with changeable, stackable components. The technology required to mass-produce the design was unavailable at the College, but David recounted how he and the student explored alternative available processes that 'paralleled the understanding of how the components would need to be designed and assembled for industry'. Before graduating from the programme, Russell displayed his innovation at the *New Designers* exhibition in Islington, where it attracted considerable interest.

'I would like to think that the majority of students will be employable', David told me, 'either in furniture making or architectural joinery, or in whatever their particular strength is. I'd like to be able to say, hand on heart, yes.' He recognised that many came to the Building Crafts College in pursuit of a career change, 'looking for something different, for a new direction. They're looking for some inspiration, and I think they find that here'. Some, he noted, would eventually go on to higher-level courses to further their design skills and develop expertise in new areas. 'I'm optimistic', he concluded, 'that most trainees will, in the end, find meaningful work.'

CHERYL M.

Lock up your libraries if you like; but there is no gate, no lock, no bolt that you can set upon the freedom of my mind.

—Virginia Woolf[16]

> Is not this the carpenter's son? Is not His mother called Mary, and His brothers, James and Joseph and Simon and Judas?
>
> —Matthew 13:55, King James Version

'I love wood as a material', Cheryl beamed. 'I guess I'm interested in what they call the "biblical trades".[17] It's going back to something that's natural – something of the earth. I couldn't give a toss about plastic or metal. I'm not interested in plumbing at all, or electrical stuff. And technology leaves me completely cold.' Pointing to a bespoke chair in the college library where we were speaking together, she added: 'What can you do that looks like *that* from any other material but timber?'

Cheryl M. was, for many years, an instructor on the carpentry and joinery (wood occupations) programme at the Building Crafts College, working alongside Jim and teaching the cohorts of Apprentices that came on block release from the construction industry. Aside from possessing profound carpentry knowhow, Cheryl had active interests in cabinet making, carving and historic building conservation. She undertook the Historic Building Conservation Foundation Degree course at the College between 2008 and 2010 as part of a Continuing Professional Development (CPD) initiative. When Con took voluntary redundancy in September 2012, Cheryl was an obvious choice for taking over the role of first-year convenor on the fine-woodwork course. She had long interacted with trainees on that programme, teaching letter carving to those interested and offering individual workbench tutorials when she passed through the workshop space.

Having taught on both programmes, Cheryl could make informed comparisons between them and she became acutely aware of the causes for the cool divide between both the students and faculty of the two programmes:

> Students upstairs [i.e. the fine woodworkers] aren't particularly aware of how privileged they appear to be to the Apprentices. They're able to have two years full-time education. Students downstairs are a bit jealous. They see students up here with nicer tools, in a nicer environment, producing better quality work, and maybe getting more attention. And, on the other hand, the students upstairs don't realise that there's a pool of talent downstairs. All they see are rowdy kids.

Cheryl learned from her many years of teaching 'to have no preconceptions about people: about what they've done before; what they're capable of doing, and what they're going to be in two years' time'. She insisted that: 'Nobody knows what's going to happen with each student, and that's what makes teaching exciting.' I probed more deeply to understand what motivated her to stay in teaching, given her potential to earn a good living as a site carpenter or bespoke maker:

Before this, I never stayed more than five years in a job. After five years there isn't anything interesting left there for me. But, with teaching it's different because it's 'people'. I'm not making a 'product'. I've learned everything there is to learn about making a product. The students aren't a product: they're a set of individuals that have come together quite by chance on the course, at a given moment in time. It's the interaction: what they learn from each other, and from us, and what we learn from them. All of that can't be replicated. It's a one-off! That's what keeps me in it.

The remainder of this fourth and final section is mostly in Cheryl's words. Through accounts of her personal experiences, she talks about the recent history of training opportunities and challenges for women in the building and carpentry trades. I have included additional text where I thought necessary to flesh out the broader historical context for the reader. Cheryl then discusses teaching at the Building Crafts College and the incongruity between what students ought to learn in order to become well-rounded woodworkers and the narrowly focused industry-led government curriculums. In conclusion, she shares animated reflections on the status of manual skills and the future of the woodworker's craft in the UK.

Women in the Trade

It's rare for women to leave school and know exactly what they want to do with the rest of their lives. I'm not sure that the same isn't true for blokes. Usually women make decisions about careers when they're in their late twenties, early thirties, but I don't think that women ever see woodwork as an option. It certainly never presented itself as a choice during my schooling. I came from a grammar school where the main options for successful students were becoming a secretary or a banker. You had to have five O levels to work in a bank, and that was seen as a good career move. Options were quite limited really.

The 1960s might have been a cultural revolution in swinging London, but in most people's homes it was still the 1950s. Things in schools have changed. Nowadays, they do a bit of craft and design. On the other hand, because schools have lost their workshop spaces and the tools and equipment they used to have, any craftwork is not likely to be woodwork.

The thing I loved most, and the thing I was best at, was art. But I had no idea what you could do with it in terms of employment. So I didn't go to art college, but instead went straight from school into the mundane sort of jobs that you get if you've got a mediocre qualification. I did a bit of office work, shop work and things like that. When I think back to working in a shoe shop, I was really lazy. In fact, I wasn't all that different from the guys that I'm teaching here at college. When you're young, the only reason to work is to make money to go clubbing at the weekend. I have to keep reminding myself of that. I so love woodwork and to me it's so important, but I'm teaching sixteen to nineteen-year-old boys now who might not have found the thing that interests them. Carpentry might be like the 'shoe shop' was for me.

Later on, I started working at holiday camps and travelling during the winter months. I eventually saved enough to travel a full year and when I came back I wasn't happy anymore with odd jobs. I was in my late twenties and I wanted more, but didn't really know what I wanted to do. I actually got into woodwork by accident. I picked up someone's newspaper on a bus and saw a picture of two women making rocking horses. I was interested, so I started looking into woodworking and found a short course at the Lambeth Women's Workshop. I then got onto a longer joinery course at Southwark Women's Workshop to learn more. Carpentry was the first thing that I had ever done that I could say, 'This feels like a career.' It wasn't something I was going to do just to make some money, and it was the first time that I felt I had a 'work ethic'.

In 1972, nearly a decade before Cheryl's search for a woodworking course began, the UK government's Department of Employment introduced the Training Opportunities Scheme (TOPS) with the (by now familiar) mandate to shrink the skills gap in the labour market. Although demand for places on TOPS courses increased exponentially year on year,[18] female trainees remained a small minority. The passing of the Sex Discrimination Act by the British Parliament in 1975 (which made it illegal to discriminate on gender grounds in education, training and employment, among other things) served as a major catalyst for growing women's participation on building trade courses, including carpentry. 'This route proved revolutionary', remarked scholars Linda Clarke and Christine Wall, '[in] being the first time that the acquisition of crafts skills was possible without the patronage of an employer through the apprenticeship system.'[19]

The Lambeth Women's Workshop, where Cheryl began training, opened five years after the Act was passed. This was one of a number of local authority initiatives launched in the early 1980s to establish women-only workshops. Provision of these training spaces widened access for women who aspired to enter the building trades, as did the Direct Labour Organisations (DLOs) financed by the European Social Fund for recruiting women into nontraditional areas of work, offering trainees direct and invaluable experience on building sites.[20]

Openings for women had occurred earlier in the twentieth century. Both were during the World Wars when severe shortages of skilled male labourers forced the hand of government, industry and the highly resistant trade unions to admit women to training schemes, workshops and building sites. These windows of opportunity were brief, however. The passing of the Res-

toration of the Pre-War Practices Act in 1919 led to widespread dismissal of
women who had taken up carpentry and joinery, bricklaying and labouring
to make vacancies for returning men from the First World War.[21] The pattern was repeated during the Second World War when, in 1941, the National
Joint Council for the Building Industry agreed terms for women's employment, but on discriminatory bases.[22] Women who helped to fill the enormous gap in the building industry workforce were paid a rate 20 per cent
lower than that for men performing equivalent tasks. The agreement also
required employers to first consult with the appropriate trade union before
hiring a woman to determine whether a man was available for the position,
and, if and when men did become available, then the number of women
could be reduced accordingly.[23] At the end of the War, the Minister of Labour 'refused to recruit any women into the skilled trades', though some
nevertheless managed to keep the jobs for which they had become enskilled
during wartime.[24]

Regrettably, the training schemes on which Cheryl enrolled managed
to thrive not much longer than those introduced during the World Wars.
Though immensely popular and having achieved some measure of both
gender and racial diversity within the almost exclusively white male building industry, squeezes in the late 1980s on local authority autonomy by the
Thatcher government included curtailment of their power to build new
houses, and thus many DLOs ceased operations.[25] The already precarious
situation of women and of BAME communities in the building trades was
further exacerbated by the economic recession at the start of the 1990s, as
Cheryl goes on to describe.

I was lucky to get on to an apprenticeship with Southwark Council. In the
1980s, local authorities had their own labour force that did mostly building
maintenance. The left-wing councils offered adult apprenticeships, and there
were small pockets of women working in the trade in places like Lambeth,
Lewisham, Southwark, Hackney and Haringey. So a lot of women got qualifications. It was a traditional three-year apprenticeship, and they sent you to
college to get your City & Guilds and Advanced Craft Certificate.

There was a sudden influx of adult women students into, what was then,
the Vauxhall College of Building, and this must have been quite a shock to the
teachers there. They were all old guys, a year or so from retirement, and they
had all gone to Brixton Boys Apprentice School. They had known each other
all their lives, gone out into the industry after their craft education, and then
returned to education as teachers in their forties or fifties. It was a boys' club.
They were so used to teaching sixteen-year-old boys who weren't really interested, came in late and messed about. And then all of a sudden they've got
these women who wanted as much as they could get out of the three years

and who wouldn't let them out of the classroom! They were a little bit fazed. They had spent their entire lives in an environment where women don't exist.

This was the same at Southwark Council. The manual workers there had all been men. They were considered the lowest of the manual trades, because council work is thought to be cheap and shabby. So, you know, they weren't the cleverest guys in the world, and they could not for the life of them understand why these women, who had a choice and any education, would want to do manual work for the council. That was a path they *had* to take. Their uncles and brothers had done it. But why would someone with a choice *choose* to do it?

It's true that it wasn't everyone's ideal apprenticeship. But you didn't have a pick of apprenticeships: you had only certain councils, in a certain era, and then it was gone. Soon the whole lot of them got made redundant. The left-wing councils were 'punished' by government in the late 80s. Cuts were made to the amount of money central government was feeding out and caps were put on local spending. New regulations meant that councils did not automatically get all the maintenance contracts for their own properties: they had to tender against private companies.

At that time, the construction industry was going through a bad patch in England and large companies, like Laing's, who had always been involved in new-build and never interested in maintenance, suddenly were. The councils had to accept the lowest bid. They were at a disadvantage because they had no experience of putting in competitive bids for tender, and their own programmes were expensive to run because they were very strict on health and safety, and what have you. They had to make redundancies. And a lot of the redundancies were handled pretty badly. The first people out of the door were the Black men, the women and trade unionists.

This was about twenty years ago now. I got a pretty good pay-off through the tribunal, so here was the start-up money for my own business. It takes a certain kind of woman to stick it out. There's a certain stubborn persistence that will help you become good at woodwork. I had the confidence to go out and do it. I had the tools as well as the experience in carpentry, joinery and maintenance. I had done fencing, kitchen fitting – you name it. So a lot of my redundancy money went on driving lessons and buying a car, which was the part of the picture that I didn't have.

Then, through a network of women friends, I got on to the approved list of contractors for Wandsworth Council to do repairs and maintenance in the blocks of council flats. New doors, frames, windows and kitchens made up the bulk of work I did, but I was also getting a few one-off joinery commissions for private clients. I was really quite excited about this area and obviously it didn't come up much in work for the council blocks. I was using Lewisham Women's Workspace to make these pieces because they had a scheme where women could use the machinery and have access to the power tools and workbenches – things I didn't have at home. They were also running courses at the workspace, and the women students would come to me for advice and guidance. And, before I knew it, I was falling naturally into a little bit of teaching. They eventually asked me to join the pool of tutors and gradually I was doing more teaching than working on the housing projects.

Teaching and the Building Crafts College

The students I taught at the workspace were long-term unemployed women in their late twenties, early thirties, who were coming in new to the trade. I had as many graduates as ex-offenders. A real mix, and I enjoyed it. It was really challenging because women didn't do any woodwork at school – at any stage, at any level. I understood their fears. It was about building up their confidence around machinery, using power tools, and in producing something that looks good. Quite often the first thing I had to teach them about routing was: 'Don't hold your breath … because if you do, you'll just have to work quicker and quicker in order to be able to breathe again.' That's what fear does, isn't it. Most sixteen-year old guys don't have that fear. So straight away there's a completely different teaching approach that I had to adopt when I took up the job here at the Building Crafts College. You're having to hold them back in there [Cheryl glances toward the workshop doors with raised eyebrows]. They can't wait to get on the machines and the power tools. But I want them to have some loving care over the hand tools. They're interested in the hand tools until they go blunt, and then they go: 'Tchsss … Bring on the power tools!'

What people do with their hands is fascinating. And I think we need more involved hand skills in the carpentry and joinery programme. After all, we're not a door-window-and-staircase factory. How many people do you know who can do wood carving? Shouldn't everybody who does woodwork have had a go at carving at some point in their training?

At the College, we try to bring in a creative element to the course when we can. And I think now's the time, more than ever, because the latest outline for the NVQ qualification is not so rigidly specified. Instead of being told exactly what needs to be done, we've now got categories – setting out, marking out, assembling, products – with some flexibility for interpretation. The 'products' category includes panels, staircases, doors, windows, frames and a unit. So what's a 'unit'? It could be anything you want, like maybe a writing desk. Who knows, though, how long this space for flexibility will last. The NVQs are employer-led and it's the large construction companies that have more clout than the smaller joinery firms. Every college has to abide by the NVQ scheme. If you want any funding, you have to be running a nationally recognised qualification. It used to be City & Guilds and there was nobody else, and now it's NVQ and they're the only show.

Most people would find woodwork *extremely* difficult, nigh impossible, to learn from the book. It's still difficult to learn from a video. Have you ever seen anyone make a mistake in a video? Never! CITB produce videos that cost £65 each. They're twenty minutes long and the bloke is perfectly clean, his tools are all pristine and he goes ahead and does a flawless job every time. How irritating is that for someone's who's just learning? What is it teaching them? It's just a show-off, isn't it? You can't watch a show-off for twenty minutes . . . not without wanting to hit him. The important thing is to learn from mistakes and difficulties. There'll be consequences from mistakes, and students will have to make decisions. Learning takes place when risks are taken: mistakes are made and solutions are found.

I tend to do a bit of demonstration. When you're used to doing things automatically, you have to stop and think 'Where am I standing?' or 'Where do my hands go?' because you don't look at yourself, do you? You just do it. I do physical demonstration on a one-to-one basis, so that they're very close. And I'll tell them to stand in different positions so that they can see where my thumb is, or how I'm standing. And while I demonstrate, I talk to them. Let's say I'm holding my chisel [Cheryl illustrates with an imaginary chisel]: I'll say: 'This is your "break", so you want to get that completely under your control. Grab it as near to the blade as you can. Sometimes you can put your finger underneath to give you a little bit extra. . .'

Like anything you do that involves your hands, woodworking means working with your whole body. So it is important how you stand. When sawing, the main mistake people make in the beginning is that they want to have one eye on this side [of the saw blade] and the other eye on that side, and so they're actually standing in the way of their own arm actions. They're making it so that the saw has to go like *that* to get around their body [Cheryl shows me the fumbled gesture]. They don't know they're doing that. They're not watching themselves. They're not body-conscious. Some of them say, for instance, that they don't know what a straight line looks like. Even though they've got a line drawn, they can't judge when they're going wonky. So I'll draw a horizontal line and I'll tell them: 'Take a vertical line off that. Now look. Is it 90 degrees?' And they know. All of them know. Your eyes are doing that all the time. When you walk into a room, if there's a wonky picture on the wall, you know it within seconds. Sometimes you have to point out to people that they actually know without knowing that they know.

I think one of the things that humans should do – but they don't – is rely on their senses. Just before you have an accident on a machine, you know it's going to happen, and it's so quick that you don't react to it. If you're tuned into that sense, though, you could actually adjust and save yourself. I think we've got an inbuilt safety mechanism and we don't trust that instinct. The same way that we don't trust our eyes and our fingertips because there's always an available tool for the purpose: there's a measuring tool, there's a marking tool, there's a squaring tool. When they're new students, you need to get them to *feel* bumps, to *feel* when the plane goes over a knot. You won't get that with power tools, which is a good reason for not going straight on to the power tools. A router goes 'tscccchhhh', and removes whatever it cuts. You're not going to know until after all the dust clears and you're finished: 'Oh no! It's ripped up the other side of the knot really bad!' But if you were planing something, you would feel if it were going over the knot. You'd feel if it were tearing. So you'd stop working and go at it from the other direction. But you have to be able to *trust* that you can feel that happen; *trust* when you feel the plane move slightly.

It's very difficult to teach somebody if you say to them: 'There's a millimetre gap on that joint' and they go 'Yeahhh…' without a care. If that doesn't bother them, how do you get them to change it? I get them to look at their own work at the end of a project and say what they are happy with and what they're not happy with. I ask: 'If somebody made that for you, would you pay for it?' So I try to teach them to be self-critical, but at the same time I want them to see that even if they've made a pig's ear of it, they can still learn something from it, and that they can possibly amend the problems. I think it's important that even if they can't achieve that level of quality, they're at least striving towards it, and they know the difference.

An Uncertain Future for the Craft?

The question of whether our craft has a future in the UK is difficult, isn't it? To me it's quite depressing to think about the [2012] Olympics. Stratford is one of the poorest boroughs in Britain and yet here we are cheering: 'The Olympics are coming to town!' It's almost as if you're a bit of a traitor if you're not excited. But what I see is that it won't include local craftspeople. It's going to be steel; it's going to be aluminium; it's going to be glass and plastic; it's going to be quick, and it's going to be as cheap as they can get away with without it looking cheap. It's going to be exhibition work. It's going to have a face value for the amount of time that the Olympics is on, and then after that Stratford can go back to being Stratford. It was summed up when they hung the baskets of flowers around Stratford Station for the Olympic committee visit, and the next day they took them all away. They didn't even give them away to people in Stratford! They didn't even leave them there until the flowers died! They just took them away. What's that saying to the people of Stratford? 'We don't care about you. We only care about you if someone's looking.'

So, you know, there's not going to be time and effort put into training people to use natural materials and to go into a craft for a month-long Olympics. That's not going to happen. It's going to take the same direction that the building industry's already headed: everything's going to be prefabricated in cheaper countries, flat-packed and assembled on site by semi-skilled people who might be one-trick ponies. That doesn't leave room for any crafts, does it? That doesn't leave room for anybody in Stratford to say 'See that bit on telly there, I made that' and to be proud of what they've done. In the past, craftspeople could point to a detail three storeys up on a building and say: 'I did that because I could ... and because I'm proud of it. I know it's there and that's enough.' The first things to go are all the trimmings, all the enhancements, and all the things that make a building beautiful in a hundred years' time. People are starting to think that the concrete monstrosities of the 1960s are worth saving ... that tells you how ugly buildings are now.

I actually don't know if we, as a society, haven't said: 'This isn't a trade that people here in the UK are interested in. Let's just let it go.' It's the same for nursing. You don't see much money going into their education. It's almost like the government have decided: 'We're not going to make this an attractive option for people in this country. It's a global market, so we don't really need to make an effort.' Parents, too, don't really want their boys going into construction work because of the lack of value placed on working with your hands.

That attitude is traditional, and it's been that way since at least the 1950s. If those who are less academically able are pushed into the industry, then it's a bit like wearing a dunce's hat, isn't it? Who wants to be a 'chippie' if a chippie is looked upon as someone who was just too thick to do maths? That stigma stays attached to manual trades – at least for boys. There isn't the same stigma for women because there's just no history of them in the trade at all.

Notably, economic historian Joyce Burnette writes that women did indeed participate in the 'guilded trades', including carpentry, in early modern England. This was often as 'wife or widow of a male member of the trade', and some were even admitted to the Freedom by the Company.[26] From early medieval times through to the early modern period, the workshop was an integral part of the home unit, and thus women had greater access to and, in some cases, a more direct hand in the running of the business. Citing evidence from the Carpenters' Company records, Burnette notes instances of women officially bestowed with responsibility to supervise apprentices, and, citing Dunlop and Denson's study of English apprenticeship, it appears that some women took up the trade themselves.[27]

In a study of the labouring poor, historian Keith Snell likewise discovered that, during the seventeenth, eighteenth and nineteenth centuries, small numbers of girls in English counties had undertaken parish (and nonparish) apprenticeships in carpentry and joinery, as well as in other traditionally male occupations.[28] However, he found that 'the wide range of trades seeing female apprenticeship in the early eighteenth century had disappeared' completely from the indenture records by 1800.[29]

As the wheels of the Industrial Revolution were set in motion, wage labour progressively replaced artisan labour, and thus the unity of workshop and home was sundered, and the gender division of labour became more deeply entrenched. As already discussed in Chapter 3, liberal reformers campaigned against the power of the livery companies and the old apprenticeship system they controlled, which industrialists and factory owners perceived as hindrances to the nation's prosperity. The Statute of Artificers, which had regulated apprenticeships since 1563, was repealed by Parliament in 1814 as a result. Clarke and Wall state that 'Without the protection of regulation, women were increasingly excluded' from apprenticeships with the result being that 'male trades became more male dominated [and female ones] more heavily female'.[30] This general erasure of women from the building trades and carpentry practice endured until brief windows of opportunity opened during the World Wars, as discussed earlier. It is therefore not surprising that Cheryl declared there to be 'no history at all' of women in carpentry.

Cheryl briefly pursued her challenge to popular stereotypes before concluding with wholehearted praise for college ambitions to promote gender equality in the building trades and raise levels of self-confidence and pride among its students:

> If you got a group of young kids to draw pictures of what 'brainy people' look like, they probably wouldn't be of women or of anybody who works with their hands. They would be of men in suits. But the wood occupations implicitly involve quite difficult geometry, maths and spatial awareness. To make a staircase is no small thing, but we're asking sixteen-year olds to make one and set it out!
>
> So you have to ask what the purpose of the Building Crafts College is aside from certificates and bits of paper. I think it's ultimately about giving the men and women a pride in making things and a sense of self-worth. The College itself isn't in the best area, but when you're in London you stop and look, and you think: 'My god, this place is important.' It's gorgeous and there are lovely buildings in London. It's a fantastic place, and it got that way because of people like the ones coming out of here. We're the Building Crafts College. We are probably the last place that can say: 'We uphold a century-plus tradition of pure skills.' And if it's not us, it's not going to be anybody.

NOTES

1. Ruskin, 'The Two Paths', 396.
2. Pye, *The Nature and Art of Workmanship*, 131.
3. In 1999, Prime Minister Tony Blair 'set a target of 50 per cent of young adults going into higher education in the next century' (Blair, 'UK Politics: Tony Blair's Speech in Full'). When pressured by the opposition to clarify the definition of 'higher education', Labour responded in 2002 that 'progress towards the 50% will be measured through the "Initial Entry Rate". The calculation will include "all courses of one year or more, above A-level and its equivalents, that lead to a qualification awarded by higher education institutions or widely recognised national awarding bodies (such as the Institute of Management)"' (BBC, 'Blair's University Targets'). Reviewing the results of Blair's 'Education, Education, Education' priority ten years later, Sean Coughlan of the BBC reported: 'The question of vocational education – always described as vital (for other people's children) – has remained unresolved, despite the chorus of warnings about skills gaps' (Coughlan, 'Education').
4. Jim showed me a copy of his indenture, which was a beautifully prepared formal document in calligraphic script. However, educationalists Fuller and Unwin, noted that: 'In the UK and contrary to the mythology that can surround apprenticeship, the provision of indentures only ever covered a minority of young males in training and an even smaller share of all young females . . . It was more common . . . for the apprenticeship arrangement to be covered by a verbal agreement between the two parties' (Fuller and Unwin, 'Learning as Apprentices', 419)
5. Hellfire Clubs were established in the eighteenth century for high-society rakes who indulged in morally improper activities. Some of the club pavilions, like that of Sir Francis Dashwood in West Wycombe, were architecturally noteworthy.
6. Sir John Soane (1753–1837) was a prominent architect and Professor of Architecture at the Royal Academy. His residence on Lincoln's Inn Fields has been a museum open to the public since 1837.
7. The CITB was set up in 1964 as the central coordinating body for training in the United Kingdom's construction industry. In 2003, the CITB became known as CITB-ConstructionSkills, but the name reverted to simply the CITB in 2013.
8. Created in 1944, the eleven-plus examinations streamed primary-school finishers into academic, technical or functional streams of secondary schooling based on examination results.
9. Miller, *Furniture*, 240.
10. Green, *Wood*, 103–4.
11. For a dedicated study of chairs, including the evolution and stylistic history of this item of furniture and the role of ergonomic design in its contemporary forms, see Cranz, *The Chair*.
12. Sturt, *The Wheelwright's Shop*, 95–96.
13. Rose, *The Village Carpenter*.
14. Fleming, 'Wood Practice', 66.
15. See ibid., 65.
16. Woolf, *A Room*, 63.
17. I frequently heard people in the building trades make reference to the 'biblical trades', which centrally includes carpentry and joinery because of their association with Noah, St Joseph and Jesus Christ. See, for example, Creasey, 'Training', 9–10.

18. Randall, 'The TOPS Preparatory Course', 7–10.
19. Clarke and Wall, 'Omitted from History', 51.
20. Clarke and Wall, 'Are Women "Not up to" Working in Construction', 15.
21. See Woollacott, *On Her Their Lives Depend*, 109.
22. See Wall, 'The Building Industry', 32–50.
23. Clarke and Wall, 'Omitted from History', 46–47.
24. Ibid., 49.
25. Cf. ibid., 52.
26. Burnette, *Gender, Work and Wages*, 235–36.
27. See Dunlop and Denman, *English Apprenticeship*, 151. For examples from the Records of the Worshipful Company of Carpenters, see Volume I, Apprentices' Entry Books, 1654–1694, Book 3: 1692.
28. Snell, *Annals of the Labouring Poor*, 276–93.
29. Ibid., 293.
30. Clarke and Wall, 'Omitted from History', 39.

CHAPTER 6

VOCATIONAL MIGRANTS TO CRAFTWORK

At the heart of this book is a particular craftworld: namely, one circum-scribed by the craft activities and interactions among a community of fine-woodwork trainees, instructors and practitioners in England at the turn of the millennium. Within that world, concepts of 'tradition' were in-vested in objects, materials, practices and ideas. These things included the woodworker's classic assortment of hand tools, which has stayed remark-ably constant through the ages; certain stylistic conventions in architec-tural joinery, cabinet making and furniture design; the use of select and, often, native species of timber; the reproduction of certain time-honoured skills, techniques and practices; and being part of a trade with ancient roots. For many of the fine woodworkers I worked alongside or inter-viewed, their engagement with those traditions roused varying degrees of nostalgia for an idealised past and hopes for a utopian future. In combi-nation, that nostalgia and those desires fuelled a sense of longing to be engaged in non-alienating modes of production and an authentic way of living and working. This state of being, in fact, has deep historical roots in England.

This chapter begins with an overview of the socialist utopia, with a focus on a few key works of English literature that progressively shaped this social, political and economic ideology. Thomas More's *Utopia* established a genre of utopian writing that is anchored in humanism and set in locations spa-tially or temporally displaced from the author's own. The culmination of the socialist utopia arrived centuries later with William Morris' *News from No-where*. Morris, like More, conjured up a future of fair economic distribution, social equality and, importantly, pleasurable work.

As the leading figure in the English Arts and Crafts movement, Morris' political vision had significant impact on the thinking and practices of makers throughout Europe and in North America, and his designs and his philosophy of 'honest' craftsmanship continue to resonate with contemporary craftspeople worldwide. Morris' writings emphasise the critical importance of an intimate connection between small-scale handicraft production, the workshop setting and the balanced working life of the craftsperson. This connection bestows a sense of control and autonomy, roots practice in place, and fluidly integrates the activities of mind and body in meaningful work that results in self-actualisation and contentedness. My discussion of utopian visions and the state of longing establishes a context for better understanding and situating the aspirations and the anxieties of those who participated in my study.

The next section of the chapter explores a contemporary spirit of craftwork articulated by Phil Koomen, one of Britain's renowned furniture makers. Koomen's practices embodied ideals of both the nation's rural past and a possible post-industrial future, and the language he used communicated a strong commitment to locality balanced with a sense of custodianship for the planet's natural environment. This bore resemblance to Morris' ecosocialist stance, expressed in the interconnections he perceived 'between the practices and discourses of art, beauty, socialism and ecological regeneration'.[1] A presentation of Koomen's vision sets the stage for a series of short illustrative case studies of 'vocational migrants', whose individual quests for something better took them to the Building Crafts College's fine-woodwork course.

Out of a total of thirty-eight trainees making up the four cohorts that participated in my two different periods of research, twenty-four (i.e. nearly two-thirds) were vocational migrants. As a demographic group, the vocational migrants comprised a mix of mainly white British men, two Black British men and four white British women. All were mature in age (early twenties and older), and the majority could be described socioeconomically as having middle-class backgrounds. They had completed secondary education and many held university degrees, after which they worked in a variety of fields, including business, banking, real estate, consultancy, healthcare, transport, the media and the fine arts. In coming to carpentry, they had either quit steady (and, in some cases, well-remunerated) jobs or professional careers, or had deviated from the usual trajectories dictated by the higher education qualifications they held. However, the most salient thing they shared in common was their search for a meaningful vocation and to participate in a more aesthetic way of living.

Long-term ambitions and the strategies deployed for achieving them varied among the vocational migrants, and sometimes conflicted. Regardless of their differences, a baseline of common values united most of these men and women in a struggle against the hegemony of late capitalism and, more specifically, the cheap, throwaway consumer culture it had spawned and the faceless corporate or institutional working environments than many had experienced first-hand. A good number had embarked upon personal missions to work in environmentally sustainable ways. Their hopes were to combine the sourcing of timber, the processes of making, and the customers for their creations with a strong sense of place or locality.[2]

The raw power of global market forces and a host of uncertainties and real risks threatened such utopian visions. Chief among these was, simply, that demand for high-quality joinery and cabinetry and for bespoke, hand-made furniture was tiny and patrons were geographically scattered. Competition among makers to win clients was therefore stiff, and the recipe for success extended beyond technical skill to include family connections, social networking, effective marketing strategies and good business acumen – circumstances and activities that many vocational migrants believed they had left behind at their former places of work. The hurdles to securing a livelihood in the artisanal wood trades would ultimately, and regrettably, deter many from their pursuit – or, at best, compel individuals to modify or dilute their original dream. However, while still immersed in the security of the College, all clutched tightly to a belief that, in the end, the obstacles looming outside were surmountable.

It must be noted at the outset that not all vocational migrants who came to fine woodworking at the College shared the utopian visions of those represented on the pages ahead. A few were driven by more purely financial goals or the need to attain qualifications for getting a toehold in the trade, while others merely enjoyed working with their hands without any drive to cultivate the 'craft' aspect of woodwork or its associated ethos and lifestyle. All three of these alternative perspectives were perhaps most strongly held by my fellow trainee Alex, who I introduced in Chapter 4 and who features in Chapter 9. The theme of utopia is revisited in that latter chapter, positioned within a complex matrix of binaries that contains utopia's antagonist, 'the real world'.

A TRADITION OF LONGING

Since we shall have to go through a long series of social and political events before we shall be free to choose how we shall live, we should welcome even the feeble protest which is now being made against the vulgarization of all life: first because it is one token amongst others of the sickness of modern civilization; and next, because it may help to keep alive memories of the past which are necessary elements of the life of the future, and methods of work which no society could afford to lose.

—William Morris[3]

Morris' prediction of a coming change never materialised. The spirit of his revolt nonetheless survives in the aspirations and manifestos of numerous twenty-first-century communities of craftspeople, as it did among many of the fine-woodwork trainees at the Building Crafts College.

In the British Isles, the longing for an alternative, more satisfying way of living and working perhaps finds its earliest literary manifestation in the fanciful early fourteenth-century poem *The Land of Cockaygne*.[4] Written in Hiberno-English, this poem of nearly 200 lines describes a fantastical earthly island paradise, where all good things are plentiful and life is pleasurable. A few selected lines (in translation) give a sense of the imagery of the medieval utopia:

> Far out to sea and west of Spain
> There is a country named Cockaygne.
> No place on earth compares to this
> For sheer delightfulness and bliss.
> Though Paradise is fair and bright,
> Cockaygne is a finer sight.
> . . .
> There are no quarrels and no strife,
> There is no death, but always life;
> Food and clothing are never short,
> You'll never hear a sharp retort,
> . . .
> But all is pleasure, joy, and bliss.
> Happy the man who has all this![5]

Marxist historian A.L. Morton suggested that *The Land of Cockaygne* 'anticipates some of the most fundamental conceptions of modern socialism' and is the 'beginning of a dialectical growth of the concept of utopia, which has its culmination in the greatest and the most fully socialist work of this type, William Morris' *News from Nowhere*'.[6] In the long interval separating these works, a number of seminal publications laid the groundwork for, and introduced diversity to, utopian thought and literature.

In 1516, during the reign of King Henry VIII, Thomas More published *Utopia*, a book that would establish a new and lasting genre for the expression of political will. *Utopia* (from Greek, meaning 'no-place')[7] is set, like *Cockaygne*, on a distant island. There, all citizens contribute to agricultural production and each is taught a special trade, including wool and flax processing, stonemasonry, blacksmithing and carpentry.[8] More believed that private property was the root cause of the inequitable distribution of goods,[9] the source of a dissatisfying organisation of human life and the reason why a handful of powerbrokers lorded over a vast majority of impoverished labourers. He argued that private property should therefore be abolished.

'Where money is the only standard of value', he wrote, 'there are bound to be dozens of unnecessary trades carried on, which merely supply luxury goods or entertainment.'[10]

By contrast, the main purpose of *Utopia*'s straightforward economy is to supply an abundance of time away from the drudgery of labour so that individuals may cultivate their intellect, which is the 'secret to a happy life'.[11] Pleasure and happiness, insisted More, should be sought in 'any state or activity, physical or mental, which is naturally enjoyable' and that serves basic human necessities without inflicting harm on others.[12] Notably, More was not advocating hedonistic pleasure like that depicted in *The Land of Cockagyne*, for he was a deeply religious and conservative man. Rather, for him, pleasure was to be found in noble and moral cultivations of mind and body – an idea with roots in both Aristotle and Epicurus,[13] and that would be taken up much later by John Ruskin and William Morris.

In the interim, philosopher and statesman Francis Bacon charted a different path from More's utopian genre. Unlike the devoutly spiritual and superstitious world of the early Tudors, Bacon's era stood at the brink of the Enlightenment. Bacon's support for scientific inquiry and inductive reasoning coloured his (unfinished) utopian account[14] *New Atlantis* (1627).[15] Morton described Bacon's outlook as one that 'confidently believed that the whole universe, from the solar system to the mind of man, was a vast complex machine and could be mastered absolutely by a sufficient understanding of the laws of mechanics'.[16] In *New Atlantis*, Bacon describes the mythical island of Bensalem,[17] on which was located Salomon's House, a scientific research institution that, naturally, employed a Baconian method to decipher the secrets of nature and applied that knowledge in bettering society.

A theme of enlightened self-interest endured from Bacon's era into the next century, where it was much in evidence in works such as Daniel Defoe's *Robinson Crusoe* (1719).[18] Here, 'utopia is a one-man colony where the individual owes everything to his own efforts and is neither helped nor hindered by anyone'.[19] Like other utopias of the eighteenth century, Defoe's – aside from its island setting – shares little in common with More's communal ethos, universal equality and insistence on pleasurable work. Indeed, it was not until the chimneys of industrial capitalism desecrated England's 'green and pleasant land' and the 'dark satanic mills' menaced most modes of handicraft that the English utopia returned sharply to its earlier humanistic aspirations.[20]

'The foundations of society were never so shaken as they are at this day', thundered John Ruskin. 'It is not that man is ill fed, but that they have no pleasure in the work by which they make their bread, and therefore look to wealth as the only means of pleasure.'[21] In *The Nature of Gothic*, published in the second volume of *The Stones of Venice*, Ruskin championed the creative freedom liberated by the arts and crafts in place of the soulless grind that plagued the nineteenth-century labourer. It was this essay in particular that deeply inspired his younger contemporary, William Morris.[22]

The central theme explored in Morris' seminal utopian work *News from Nowhere* (1890)[23] was precisely the relationship between work and pleasure. Here, utopia is set not on an island, but in a twenty-second-century Britain that has recovered its rural heritage and embraced a return to an agrarian economy and a medieval tradition of craftwork. Corrupt parliamentary politics have given way to a socialist form of decentralised popular democracy; money has been abolished; formal education has been replaced by experiential learning and apprenticeship, and useless, repetitive toil at industrial machines has been superseded by meaningful forms of work that dissolve partitions once constructed between intellectual and manual labour.

More specifically, *News from Nowhere* called for the revival of the medieval workshop with its small-scale, ecologically sustainable and high-quality craft production. This was in stark contrast to Edward Bellamy's *Looking Backward*, published two years earlier.[24] Bellamy's utopian vision was one of machines and industrial armies in which the United States is organised as one great business corporation run by the people and fulfilling their collective capitalist interests.

Because of his staunch defence of handwork and the artisanal workshop, Morris is often labelled a Luddite.[25] This categorisation is inaccurate, however. He was not adverse to machines that freed people from monotonous and mundane tasks. In the case of the 'great staple industries' of the time (e.g. textiles or iron and steel production), for example, Morris stated that automatic machinery had beneficially turned the worker who had been reduced to a machine into the 'tender of a machine'.[26] What he railed against most vehemently was not the 'tangible steel and brass machine', but the 'great intangible machine of commercial tyranny' built on the division of labour. This he held responsible for abolishing craftsmanship among the wage-earning classes and driving handwork to near-extinction.[27] He also lamented the displacement of handcrafted wares by mass-produced ones of inferior quality. Though 'wonders of invention', he wrote, the bulk of industrial machines merely serve the production of 'measureless quantities of worthless makeshifts'.[28]

Then, as now, the counterargument to Morris' vision was that handmade items are considerably more costly than mass-produced ones, which undermines hopes for a true democracy of craft. The cost differential is justified by the greater time, attention, risk and skilled expertise required in making bespoke things or operating small-batch assembly in comparison to factory production. Economies of scale are achieved in industrial processes by significantly reducing or eliminating those factors and by using cheaper, lower-grade raw materials, thereby cutting unit costs and maximising profits to producers and investors. Later on in this chapter, I discuss how that maxim applies somewhat differently to woodworking and furniture making than it does, for example, to ceramics, textiles, glass and many other handicrafts. In any case, Morris' revival of craft was censured for ultimately catering to indulgences of the elite, and his own designs for woven fabrics, wallpaper and wooden furnishings have remained markers of middle-class privilege.

Morris himself acknowledged the paradox, protesting that craftsmanship had become the preserve of 'the professional classes, who claim the position of gentleman'.[29] Indeed, the disjuncture between the real costs of 'handmade' and desires to democratise craft and widen public access to better-quality, more aesthetically pleasing wares, furnishings and architectural environments poses an ongoing challenge to many socially aware makers, including numerous fine-woodwork trainees at the College. Morris was fully attuned to the conundrum of 'affordable craft', and so in the utopian society conceived in *News from Nowhere*, demand and production are based on need, not excess or profit. And, without monetary exchange to drive the market, people choose to engage in work for the higher pursuits of pleasure and self-actualisation.

Having rejected the workings of industrial capitalism, Morris turned to romantic imagery of England's medieval past and innovatively reconstrued that into something new (as he did with his artistic designs) in order to project a future of alternative possibilities.[30] By rearticulating and propelling the nostalgia of John Ruskin and of Scottish historian and essayist Thomas Carlyle[31] into the future, and by supplementing Karl Marx with a dimension of the individual's sensibilities, values and desire for self-realisation, sociologist Ruth Levitas observed that Morris 'effected a synthesis between Romanticism and Marxism which enriched and transformed both'.[32] As a result, Morris' dream of a socialist transformation in life and labour was to be realised not through centralisation and state governance of regulations and communal principles, but through the willed and 'active participation of individuals in all aspects of the social process'.[33]

News from Nowhere thus offers a poignant critique of the alienating forces of capitalism and 'invites us to experience what it would mean to be in full possession of our humanity'.[34] Utopia, Levitas argued, is not a blueprint for change in the way that Marxist ideology is, but rather its key function is the education of desire and longing.[35] The imaginings it contains enable 'people to work towards an understanding of what is necessary for human fulfilment, a broadening, deepening and raising of aspirations in terms quite different to those of their everyday life'.[36] Paul Ricoeur likewise differentiated between ideology and utopia. He elaborated on the dialectical relationship between the two, whereby the former functions to preserve and legitimate the identity of a person or group, while the latter is a vehicle for challenging the status quo and exploring possible ideals towards which we are directed, but which we realise, at some level, we will never fully attain.[37] In sum, utopia fuels that exploration and it enlightens and gives form to our desires.

THE SPIRIT OF HANDICRAFT

The schedule of tea breaks structured our workday at the College. One morning, after tea, the fine woodworkers were directed from the canteen to a classroom. A shuffle of heavy work boots plodded in through the doorway and saw-dusted bodies settled into seats. One trainee grumbled to his neighbour about missing workbench time: tools idled and project deadlines loomed. The guest speaker flashed a smile at the small gathering, shifting nervously and making final inspections of his PowerPoint presentation. His entirely black attire contrasted smartly with the coif of silver hair, and the broken arm of his black-rimmed spectacles was mended neatly with tape. His look, to my mind, was more 'architect' than woodworker. The room quietened down and our programme convenor, David W., introduced the man before us as Philip Koomen, an esteemed furniture maker and an active figure in England's growing ecological movement for sustainable timber sourcing, use and design.

'Becoming a furniture maker', Koomen began, 'was a move toward a utopian ideal.'[38] The Craft Revival of the 1970s made that realisation more possible, and he considered himself fortunate to have played his part. At twenty-one years old, and just one year into a university degree in social science, Koomen left academia to seek the 'nature and purpose of work' and a 'practical approach to making a difference'. For him, furniture making would be a 'path to self-knowledge', bringing together 'the designer and the maker as one'. He recounted how the following year he set up a partnership with a fellow carpenter near Henley-on-Thames to repair furniture and make reproduction pieces.[39] As a self-taught craftsman, learning and experience came through patient practice with his tools and timber, and a spiritual outlook and code of ethics guided his professional engagement. What had begun as a search for an appropriate way of working became an ongoing evolution of self as a designer-maker.

Koomen described how, with the 1992 launch of *AGENDA 21* (the United Nations' declaration on environment and sustainable development for the twenty-first century), he and a small band of other British woodworkers responded keenly to the call for a grassroots approach to sustainability. In many respects, renowned furniture maker John Makepeace had started blazing that trail nearly a decade earlier when he purchased Hooke Park, a 350-

acre forest near Parnham House in Dorset, where 'he set out to reintegrate the growing of wood with its sustainable use'[40] and to 'combine craft practice with ecological concerns'.[41] According to design historian Tanya Harrod: 'His aim was to revive woodland crafts by training students to set up entrepreneurial woodland industries using roundwood thinnings, a by-product of good forestry.'[42]

For Koomen, the Rio Earth Summit further underscored the need to combat deforestation and develop sustainable forestry practices, and it drove home a UN-declared fact that 'the major cause of the continued deterioration of the global environment is the unsustainable pattern of consumption and production, particularly in industrialized countries'.[43] Koomen described how correcting the situation would require sensitising and educating both producers and consumers about the fragile relationship between economy, lifestyle and environment – an issue whose urgency has only increased year on year, month on month.

Koomen took on this challenge personally. 'I understood wood as a commodity, but I needed to understand the forestry debate and I had to develop a fitting business model', he told his audience of college trainees. The objective of his model was to reduce the distances that separated the forest resources he used, his place of work and processes of making, and the delivery of finished items to clients. Local sourcing and sustainable use of timber in his native Oxfordshire became the subject of a doctoral study, which led him to become an advocate for 'the craftsperson as educator'. 'Craftsmanship is a sort of universal language that connects the designer-maker with the client-consumer', he explained. Producers therefore have a responsibility to raise client awareness of the ethical dimensions as well as the aesthetic ones that determine their consumer choices. He believed that educating people effectively creates markets for sustainable furniture design. 'Craft is a model of sustainability', and we should be striving to 'build things that last, things for the future'.

Koomen's weave of sustainability, self-sufficiency, place-making through practice, ethical framework and contentment in work resonated strongly with a number of trainees in the audience. As budding designer-makers, they shared aspirations to be employed in something meaningful that contributed to making the world a better, greener place. Paramountly, they coveted the sense of autonomy and control that Koomen possessed for overseeing all stages of his creative enterprise. Together, these goals constituted a heady mix of More and Morris' collective socialism and Defoe's one-man colony.

Other trainees who were present at the lecture harboured similar ambitions to various degrees, but were less persuaded by Koomen when his talk turned to the role that spiritual growth, the Baha'i faith and Sufi Islam played in his professional life. He flatly rejected Morris' *News* for its secular socialism, devoid of religion. For a few of the young trainees who came directly from secondary school to the fine-woodwork programme, the spiritual message simply fell flat. All agreed, however, that Koomen was a master craftsman, and his business success offered a beacon of hope and a target to strive for.

JOURNEYS INTO WOODWORKING

John W.

Nearly a decade before my arrival at the Building Crafts College, when its operations were still on Great Titchfield Street, John W. had been a mature student on the fine-woodwork programme. John was now a designer-maker of furniture, as well as a part-time instructor, assisting in the College workshop two days each week. He conducted one-to-one tutorials at trainees' workbenches, accompanied them to the wood mill to machine components for their projects and, occasionally, gave dedicated lectures on practical topics, such as structural design for furniture or how to set up a workshop. Carpentry, however, was not where John began his working life. Like the trainees that I introduce below, he was a vocational migrant, and, like all the vocational migrants to the programme, he followed a unique path into the trade.

Since early childhood, John enjoyed working with his hands and building things, and he was especially captivated by tools. 'A well-designed tool is the peak of design', he told me. As a boy, he helped out on weekends at a small carpentry firm nicknamed 'The Factory', which was operated by a friend of his father. Nevertheless, he had never anticipated becoming a cabinet maker. The general expectation at that time, he recalled, was that you attend school, get your A levels and probably move on to university. If not, then you find a job with a company that will train you up. 'Having a trade never crossed my mind', he admitted, though, upon further reflection, he ventured that his parents would not have dissuaded him from that route. 'My father was a dentist, who always wished he had had the courage to do something else.' When John finally made his career change later in life, his father was fully supportive.

After finishing school, John studied civil engineering, graduating from university in 1968. He then enlisted in two years of formal training, after which he became a member of the Institution of Civil Engineers. For a civil engineer, 'design and function go hand-in-hand', he explained. 'Engineers tend to like useful things, but there is also beauty in a well-designed structure.' He stayed in that profession for nearly thirty years:

> The first chunk of my career was spent on construction sites where there was a significant amount of trade work going on, including carpentry. I learned a great deal about the various trades merely through observing since there was little opportunity to talk together on the big sites.

John said that he watched *how* the tradesmen were doing things, not just *that* they were doing things. 'It's amazing how you can learn by watching an experienced tradesman: how they behave, and the techniques they use. Unfortunately, I had never watched anyone using a wood plane ... So the first time I picked one up to use, it was a disaster!', he chuckled, remembering the start of his woodwork training.

The availability and steadiness of employment contracts in the construction industry typically fluctuate with the ebbs and flows of the national economy, so 'there was always the insecurity of not knowing how long a job was going to last', John said. After spending three years on a contract in Saudi Arabia, he returned to the United Kingdom in the early 1990s to discover that he was being made redundant. That cycle of events was becoming all too familiar. In addition to the stress caused by the precarious nature of employment in the sector, he also felt increasingly 'divorced from engineering': 'The more senior you get, the less you actually do of the profession. You end up doing more paperwork, management tasks, sitting in meetings, chasing costs – but *not* engineering!' A further push factor to quitting the profession was the growing body of legislation on health and safety, and 'seeing the potential of being made a scapegoat by the lawyers ... It was time to get out'. The lucrative contract in the Middle East had allowed him to save money for a career change, and John was determined to reclaim the pleasure that he had discovered as a boy in hands-on making.

One morning, while fingering through the pages of the *Daily Telegraph*, John's wife found an advertisement for the Building Crafts College. 'I gave them a ring, had an interview, and put my deposit down' to enrol on the fine-woodwork programme, he told me. When he trained in the mid-1990s, 'there was less emphasis on doing the architectural joinery and producing technical drawings', and so 'students progressed to making furniture projects in hardwoods more quickly', which was precisely what he wanted to do. In his time, fine-woodwork graduates received only a City & Guilds diploma and not the Intermediate Construction Award (ICA) in Wood Occupations or National Vocational Qualifications (NVQs). His understanding of the present situation, with its emphasis on set joinery projects and drawing, was to make students eligible for the ICA in addition to the City & Guilds diploma, thereby attracting funding for the programme from the government's Learning and Skills Council. Importantly, this funding allowed the College to keep tuition fees to a minimum. But, as far as John was concerned, students merely gained an 'irrelevant piece of paper'.[44]

After graduation from the Building Crafts College, John was among a small minority of trainees who would succeed as independent furniture makers. The combination of long experience in the world of work, a meticulous plan of action and, significantly, the available capital to launch a business as a sole trader allowed him to set up a workshop and accept commissions. 'The budget just for the necessary machines was £20,000. That's an impossible investment for most young students', he acknowledged. But, like a handful of graduates from furniture-making programmes around the country, John's modest earnings as a designer-maker were supplemented – at least for the present time – by the salary he earned as a college instructor. Becoming financially reliant on making bespoke furniture alone is a risky business, as I will explore in Chapter 9.

John W. was a popular instructor at the College because of the broad knowledge he possessed about craft techniques, his engineer's sagacity in problem solving and his calm, rational disposition. In addition to practical tutorials, he made the time to engage students in conversation about their plans for the future, and generously offered advice on the purchase of tools and machinery or the rental of workshop space. His gentlemanly manner also provided a model for good professional conduct. When I asked what qualities he thought were necessary for succeeding as a fine woodworker, his response was that 'an individual must be an excellent carpenter with good hand-tool and power-tool skills; they should have some expertise in design if they're going to make furniture – at least if they're going to make nice pieces! And they need a sense of aesthetics.' He paused thoughtfully before adding: 'But, I think most of all, they need to be self-critical of their own work.'

Six Trainees

Jens left school with dreams of being an oboist and opted to do a degree in music at Nottingham University. By the end of studies, however, he came to the unsettling realisation that he was unlikely to succeed as a performing musician, and soon after took a job with the British Broadcasting Corporation (BBC). He was employed there for five years as a programme researcher for radio before making the break to retrain as a fine woodworker.

'I wasn't happy with my work, being just a cog in a giant machine', Jens recalled with despondency. 'The BBC is a creative place, of course, but I felt completely removed from the audience. Some people might say "Oh, great bit of research", but most had no clue that I was working on the programme.' Having read a number of feature stories in the weekend newspapers about professionals who switched to vocational trades, Jens mused that he, too, would be better satisfied doing something more creative with his hands than tapping at a keyboard.

The financial risks were high, as were the social ones. Jens was nearly thirty with a mortgage and limited savings. 'I had never contemplated NVQs or manual work', he explained. 'My school pushed everyone toward university. If you're middle class, you go to university. That's the mentality. Most of my friends have safe jobs, earning big salaries. And now here I am, spending all my life's savings.' He paused briefly, before adding: 'But, it's on something I *really* want to do.' He recognised that the chances of reaping huge financial rewards from woodwork were highly unlikely, yet he had already discovered pride in being part of an historic profession and in possessing skills that he believed were relevant, but that had become increasingly rare over the past decades.

A second fine-woodwork trainee, Robert, told a different story. 'I had a complete lack of satisfaction with corporate, computer-based life', he said with antipathy. 'There were always bigger processes happening at higher levels over which I had little control. I had lots of responsibility, but little authority. I was always busy, always stressed.'

After receiving an MPhil in social sciences, Robert took a job at a London-based environmental consultancy: 'I joined, believing that I would be part of something that could make things better. But I discovered that, in reality, we were only making things less worse.' Stress-related illness forced him to resign at thirty-one and embark on a new path in terms of living and working. Becoming a carpenter promised scope for being autonomous and the freedom to seek a professional identity that need not conform to the dominant Western model of success.

'Working with wood and hand tools is like a retreat, almost in a religious sense', Robert explained. 'I feel that I can cut myself off from the negative manifestations of modernity – the noise, the constant material consumption – and return to being someone capable of completing something, from a thought to a finished product.' He articulated how woodworking gave him a sense of integrity and transformed work into a satisfying way of living day to day: 'I can turn up in any place and just be a carpenter, a woodworker. It's a skill that I think there'll always be a demand for, and to have it seems good and honest.'

Donna, who was in the second and final year of the programme, said that she had never quite known what she wanted to do professionally. She finished a university degree in marketing and later held posts in various business institutions. Her latest job before coming to the Building Crafts College was in the IT department of the British Home Office in Croydon, earning what she described as 'nice money' and saving it with a view to making the next move.

'I wanted to work with my hands, to make things. And, I liked wood because it's a natural material', Donna explained. 'It was probably in my head

Figure 6.1 A fine-woodwork student using a bevelled chisel, 2007.
© David Wheeler

for years, but not seriously. So, finally having a pot of cash, I put the idea to the forefront.' When she arrived at the College, she was keen on learning architectural joinery. However, as the course progressed into the second year, her interests, like those shared by most others on the programme, shifted to furniture making.

As opposed to some male trainees who considered the craft as 'manly', Donna believed that 'furniture making is carpentry's link to the female' and the domestic realm. 'I find working with wood a really feminine thing to do', she said. 'To be making things, to be creative with your hands, whether with a paintbrush or whatever, is seen to be a quite feminine quality. In no way does it make me feel "manly", that's for sure! Doors, windows and stairs might be quite "butch", but furniture is a girly thing', she jested provocatively, flashing a mischievous grin. 'They [i.e. the male trainees] just don't realise it. They're a bunch of big girls' blouses!' In a more serious tone, she added:

> A piece of furniture's like a little baby. You put all that love into making it and nurturing that wood to get it into the form that you want it. It's incredibly female. I don't understand how it can be seen as 'manly'. That's a very traditional view of carpentry,

being a man's thing, isn't it? But there's absolutely no reason for it, even physically, unless you're doing heavy construction-type work.[45]

For Donna, 'furniture making is, at the end of the day, about people-pleasing'. Her aim to fully integrate the client's vision into the production process was informed by her prior experience as a facilitator in the business world. 'People should have an input rather than buying it pre-made', she asserted with conviction. 'There needs to be some individuality in this mass-produced world of IKEA and Habitat. Furniture makers are in a position to help people realise their own art.'

In contrast to the hectic pace and sense of fragmentation she experienced in her previous career, Donna described woodworking as a practice that allowed her to focus in a calm and controlled manner. 'I don't see myself as a high-end artist making the next fabulous "one-off". But', she said with a sigh of satisfaction, 'putting all that energy into creating new and useful things is a nice place to be.'

On the subject of moving from 'headwork' to handwork, Donna countered: 'We're not academic failures. Many of us are high achievers who decided to take a left turn. Maybe we should be in firms, project managing for £30, £40 or £60K a year. But we ditched all that for something better.' A nagging uncertainty nevertheless lingered with her as to whether the livelihood she imagined was tenable or not. 'Most people probably think that wanting to be an independent furniture maker is a pipedream', she confided. 'And, I guess it remains to be tested.'

Shane, another final-year student, also addressed the uncertain economies of becoming a furniture maker:

> Gone are the days when we can really make much of a living. We've got a tough situation in fine woodwork. It's still a 'shed-in-the-backyard' industry. As a rule, people set up on their own and try to make it work. A few of us may be lucky enough to make our mark; become one of the top ten in the country, and make some serious money out of it.

Yet, despite his allusion to a financial measure of success, Shane regularly iterated that he was not in woodwork for the money. 'Never have and never will be!' he exclaimed. 'I don't want a huge factory or anything like that. I just want to be able to release what I want to release.'

Shane was a creative designer, a skilled carpenter and a fastidious perfectionist. Unlike Donna, he aspired to produce luxurious bespoke pieces for a privileged and art-savvy clientele. But, though he strove for recognition, he denied that material gain was his key motivator. 'Being able to create is what is vital', he told me, and being in that mode 'is where other people like me to be, because they like me best when I'm happy. Doing the fine woodworking makes me a better person'.

Art had been Shane's main passion in school, and creating things was the prime outlet for his emotions. He studied art in secondary school and was accepted into the interior design programme at London Guildhall University. Contrary to his expectations, however, he soon found that the course was stifling his artistic passions. 'Short bouts of freedom to think creatively were followed by what seemed like months of sitting at the drawing board', he recounted with exasperation. 'There was lots of paperwork and searching though books and trade magazines for products and finishes – just the sort of thing that didn't interest me.'

Shane struggled to finish the programme. Afterwards, he spent a few years drifting from one venture to the next before heading to Stafford, in the West Midlands, to enrol on a college art foundation course. He built props part-time for the college theatre, working under the direction of a senior carpenter, who Shane described as 'an old-school type'. 'When I got it wrong, the guy threw spanners and hammers at me', he exclaimed, only half-jokingly. 'But I learned lots from him.' After six years of 'earning a pittance', Shane deemed it time to get proper qualifications and to hone the carpentry skills he had amassed. Now, with his fine-woodwork diploma nearly complete, he proudly distinguished himself as a 'craftsman' and hoped to never find himself in a 'factory-type shop just knocking things out'. 'I need to be with people who are masters of their trades, who have passion. People similar to me', he concluded with a wry smile.

In contrast to Shane, his fellow trainee, Angela, had no background in woodworking when she started the programme. At forty-one, with nearly two decades of experience in nursing, she began her search for a career that would allow her to work artistically with her hands. 'That aspect was absolutely fundamental', she affirmed. 'It's when I'm lost in the moment of creating that I feel most comfortable.'

Angela regretted not having ventured into something 'arty' during her schooldays, but her secondary modern in North London 'tried to make everyone into something ready for a job in the bank'. There was no history of professional artists in her family and so 'it all seemed very dangerous'. She recalled that: 'Neither parent was particularly handy, so I normally came up with the solutions for fixing things. I knew this made me happiest, but I couldn't see how I could translate that into work.' Like many of the trainees, Angela insisted that money had never been her prime motive. So, with an educational grounding in science, a vocation in nursing seemed the logical choice. 'What I confused at the time was that just because something is "vocational" doesn't mean that it's necessarily going to satisfy you. What I really needed was a creative outlet.'

While working at a hospital in South Wales, Angela and her partner bought a house, which served as her testing ground for 'DIY' work. She also arranged with her hospital employer to spend one day a week doing a garden-design course:

> That was fantastic! I really enjoyed it, but I came to the conclusion that I didn't want to draw pictures of people's gardens and have the gardens made by someone else. I wanted to do the whole thing. But, in reality, that sort of work was just physically too challenging.

'When I started fine woodwork', Angela remembered, 'my partner was a bit sceptical. Not about me making money, but about whether I would ever *think* again. Would we ever have proper conversations again? Who would I be mixing with? How much intellectual stimulation was I going to get?' These concerns, she believed, reflected popular misconceptions in Britain that building and craft trades are for the intellectually and academically challenged. 'The truth is that an awful lot of people from educated backgrounds have thought carefully about why they want to do this', she said, referring to her fellow woodworkers. 'This is a profession that requires patience, dexterity, a degree of creativity, a holistic approach, and . . . yes, more patience!'

I've got so much pride!' Angela said elatedly. 'When I actually tell people, "I'm a carpenter", the reaction's amazing! "Oh, that's so unusual!" they say. I'm absolutely delighted with myself that I've done this. I'm almost smug about it. I don't feel the need to apologise for my profession in any way.'

Like Donna, Angela wasn't driven towards the superstar status enjoyed by some of Britain's elite designers: 'If I really wanted to make it as a top furniture maker in this country, I'd have to put so much of my time into advertising and promotion rather than being a craftsperson, and I really don't want that. It's not why I made the change.' She believed that there is enough work in the wood trades to make a decent income in London: 'I can make enough money doing carpentry and joinery work, and do fine woodwork on the side.' She hesitated briefly, giving shape to her future while narrating it: 'And, if I'm lucky, that will eventually become most of what I do.'

The final person introduced here is Russell. After completing a philosophy degree at University College London and taking a failed stab at entry to the Royal Military Academy Sandhurst, Russell took an interim job as an agent with a London real estate broker. The job was financially rewarding and he found himself surrounded by people in the building industry, including architects and developers. This sparked his interest in the building trades, and he soon realised that many contractors were doing poor work and that he could do better.

'I always had a leaning toward doing something creative', Russell told me. 'But, for some reason I put it off. Perhaps because it's not seen. . .' He paused. 'Well, there just aren't many of those sorts of careers that make financial sense', and so he allowed 'the pragmatic side of [his] mind to take control'.

He recollected the enthusiasm he had for artwork as a boy and professed: 'If you have that inside you, you'll always find an outlet for it. For years I was really into cooking.' During his search for a training facility, he came across the telephone number for the Institute of Carpenters, and from there was directed to the Building Crafts College. 'At first, I was interested in the whole building side of things.' During the first year in fine woodwork, he took an evening course in plastering: 'My idea was that I could run a more efficient business if I knew as many trades as possible. I wanted to buy places, do them up and sell them. The thought of working for other people just didn't appeal.'

Russell's introduction to furniture making during the second year of the programme changed all that, and he began rigorously exploring his potential as a designer. Importantly, he discovered that there is 'something quite magical' in realising an idea. Carpentry is not a fixed corpus of craft knowledge and techniques, but rather, as illustrated in Chapter 8 and as realised by Russell, woodworking continually involves 'creative, practical problem solving'. In the activity of woodworking, physical practice with tools and materials is tightly coupled with problem solving in an unfolding dialogue as a carpentry project progresses. 'That's the beauty of all practical disciplines: you can rely on your wits. There's a huge scope of possibilities, and maybe that's why so many engineers find their way into this field', he surmised.

Russell ranked 'personal satisfaction' tops, and declared that 'to succeed in life, you have to enjoy what you're doing. Financial success is not my main motivator, otherwise I would have stayed working as a property agent.' Making money, however, did figure more strongly in Russell's future goals than it did for many of his fellow vocational migrants. 'I'm a competitive person. Ambitious. And that's the sort of thing you relate with wealth. So, it's always been at the forefront of my mind. But', he qualified, 'money isn't my *main* driver.' He described his ideal situation as one in which he could generate enough income as a recognised furniture designer to invest in property for restoration, interior design work and future sale. 'In a world where everything's being homogenised, there'll always be people looking for something individual; something special and different from the rest', he concluded confidently.

SHARED IDEALS, SHARED GOALS

Through woodworking, John W. rediscovered his delight in well-crafted tools and in his ability to combine his structural knowledge with aesthetics. Jens valued the opportunities that carpentry offered to be creative with his hands, and Robert cherished control over all phases of his artisanal production and managing his own working environment. Donna underlined the importance of human relations and the need to bring clients into the design process. She also alluded to the appeal of working and shaping natural materials into functional and aesthetic artefacts. Shane spoke of channelling his passion and energies into the creation of unique objects that fuse art and technology, while Angela discovered self-esteem in possessing specialised skills and in being part of a craft tradition. Russell thrived on the constant challenges that woodworking presents and the spectrum of possibilities in making handcrafted furniture.

The values and assets cited by these men and women were representative of the sentiments expressed by a majority of vocational migrants to fine woodworking who I interviewed over the years. They conceived of carpentry as a wholesome profession, rooted in humankind's early cultural beginnings and meeting basic human needs: not merely in providing implements and furnishings, but also in fulfilling the need to engage in creative production. Psychological and emotional links were soldered between contemporary practice and imaginings of an ancient heritage that finds universal expression in the woodwork of all peoples at all times, as well as in the unique technologies and expressions that evolved in particular regions and places. In a Romantic, almost Jean-Jacques Rousseau-like sense,[46] the heart of the craft was construed by several interviewees as 'noble' and 'honest', uncorrupted by Western modernity's rationalised division of labour, technological abstraction, speed, placeless-ness, and alienation from the meaning and value of work.

Additionally, being 'in the flow' of craftwork invoked a gratifying connection: namely, that between subject and world. In the uninterrupted rhythm of work at their benches, the College fine woodworkers experienced a unity between their mindfully engaged bodies, the tools in their grasp, and the timber they worked. Ruskin eloquently expressed that unity in his writing on ironwork:

> All art worthy of the name is the energy – neither of the human body alone, nor of the human soul alone, but of both united, one guiding the other: good craftsmanship and work of the fingers joined with good emotion and work of the heart.[47]

In a carpenter's daily work, hand tools are pivotal to experiencing unity between self and the material world. American woodworker Jonathan Thornton remarked that woodworking hand tools 'have become probably the most complex, numerous and varied of all categories of hand-craft tools',[48] and the history of their invention is premised upon the constitution, abilities and practices of our human bodies. As I will discuss in greater detail in Chapter 7, hand tools in practice become as an extension of one's limbs, hands and fingers, and regular practice with them results in a coordinated integration

Figure 6.2 Portrait of a final-year fine-woodwork trainee with her bespoke chair project, 2006. © Trevor H.J. Marchand

of mind, body and tool. In turn, this integration forges direct and animated relationships between one's subjectivity and things-in-the-world.

Most vocational migrants, and younger trainees too, spoke of the need to connect their future practice to the natural environment from which their timber would be sourced and to the marketplace they would serve. In a series of coordinated efforts, trainees across both years of the programme insisted on guarantees from senior administrators that College timber supplies were being harvested from sustainable sources, and, whenever possible, from Western European forests to reduce carbon footprint and environmental impact. According to a World Wide Fund for Nature report published at that time, the United Kingdom was importing more illegally logged timber than any other European country, accounting for an estimated 28 per cent of its foreign timber imports.[49] A barrage of reports linking illegal timber sourcing with environmental degradation, global warming and 'Third World' poverty influenced many trainees in their careful selection of species for projects and in their choosing to use off-cuts from the timber racks when feasible.

There were, of course, divergent views on the importance of using sustainably sourced materials.[50] One former graduate, Mike, who had come to fine woodwork from a career in marketing and advertising, and was establishing himself as a furniture maker at the time of our interview in 2006, believed that:

> Many [furniture makers] use environmental talk as a marketing ploy, without real commitment to it. There's something sweet and nice about using English timber, but it's also nice to use imported woods. The look is important, and I'm not prepared to compromise on that. I'll use green products if I can, but I can't use them all the time. It's just not a driving force for me.

Donna, by contrast, was a robust advocate of sustainable practices. She evolved a method for glue-laminating off-cuts of oak to produce the chunkier components of a display unit that she was making for the College. She spoke ardently of immigrating after finishing college to Eastern Europe to start up a small furniture-making industry that would use salvaged timber from construction waste and demolitions. Her goal at the time was to propagate greater regional awareness of finite forestry resources.

Relatedly, numerous trainees associated their adopted trade with the production of high-quality 'heirloom' pieces that would ideally be passed down through generations, and possibly repurposed and reused. The goal to make things that were durable stood in stark contrast to items of furnishing sold in most high street stores, which were seemingly manufactured with inbuilt obsolescence or to be thoughtlessly disposed of when fashion trends changed. Reaction against those deeply ingrained economic strategies and cultural attitudes fed the growth of an environmental consciousness among vocational migrants at the College.

SHARED ANXIETIES

On his website manifesto, British avant-garde furniture maker Fred Baier posted these words of inspiration for neophytes:

> If you want to make it in the field of making things, you need single-mindedness, determination – preferably without arrogance – and an inner confidence in the face of nay-sayers ... It's frowned upon nowadays to choose a career for its life qualities rather than its pecuniary rewards, but that's the only real way to prevent work being something you don't like doing ... If you want to release your full creative potential, resist as far as possible, for as long as possible, the urge to be secure ... Deal with your customers very carefully. Don't let them dilute your ideas, and watch the lure of patronage.[51]

For vocational migrants at the College, however, strategies for revolutionising life and work were offset by a number of deep-seated anxieties and concrete obstacles. Pedagogical emphasis during the two short years of training was on acquiring carpentry skills and not on preparing for the job market or learning to manage a business. This is true of many college-based vocational training programmes. They offer the invaluable luxury of time to explore ideas about craftwork, experiment with different methods, make mistakes, absorb an array of hand skills and progress at a personal pace, but all this usually comes at the expense of not learning the ropes for successfully launching an enterprise and operating as a sole trader. The consequences of that lacuna in the curriculum are explored more fully in Chapter 9. In the words of a former graduate: 'The College is set apart from everything else, which I suppose is part of its appeal. But it's sort of like its operating in a little bubble.'

By contrast, in on-site apprenticeships such as those that I documented in Yemen and Mali, and described in Chapter 1, skill training is typically integrated with the economics of the workshop or worksite, and apprentices are directly exposed to daily interactions and negotiations with the full cast of actors, including other tradespeople, suppliers, brokers, merchants, accountants, tax officials and, importantly, clients, each with their individual expectations, demands, budgets, deadlines and idiosyncrasies.

Though all of the vocational migrants introduced in this chapter renounced money (to greater or lesser extents) as the prime motivator for their career change, many underlying concerns nevertheless revolved around practical money matters. Given the high costs of renting space in London and the prices for basic tools and machinery, the question of whether 'setting up shop' was feasible or not surfaced repeatedly at tea breaks, lunchtime and pub outings. 'Will I generate enough work to survive?', 'Is there a market for bespoke furniture?' or 'for my ideas?' And, perhaps most troubling: 'Will I have to go back to my old line of work?'

Another anxiety lurking beneath the surface was the uncertainty about one's competency as a designer and a maker. Good design requires conversance with historic styles and contemporary trends, a 'vision' and a propensity to innovate (or, at the very least, to create the illusion of doing so), aesthetic discernment, an 'eye' for proportion, an understanding of the materials, and an engineer's intuition about structural limits and possibilities. The art of fine woodworking demands exacting precision in marking out the timber and in cutting, chopping and planing it, minimal tolerances in fitting and joinery, and near-perfection in veneering, polishing and finishing. A designer-maker of architectural joinery or furniture must also be capable of sketching out ideas, drafting and reading plan, elevation and section drawings, producing full-scale rod drawings, and calculating quantities, costs and schedules. This represents a daunting skillset, even before throwing into the mix the social and business skills needed for running a viable workshop.

In spite of this formidable range of intellectual, embodied and social skills, nagging doubts nevertheless persisted among some vocational migrants as to whether woodworking was a 'worthy' pursuit. As mentioned earlier, that doubt was incubated in British schooling, and in British society more generally, where manual work was accorded low status. Worries were exacerbated by the concerns expressed by parents, partners or friends, as illustrated in Angela's case and by the need Donna felt to emphasise that fine woodworkers are 'not academic underachievers'.

The most pressing worry, and that to which all other anxieties ultimately related, was the prospect of failing to achieve autonomy over one's production. The longing for self-sufficiency over creative processes and livelihood was not a quest for isolation from the world, but to be part of a new order. That longing motivated searches for independence from the abstract economy generated by big finance, corporate power and shareholder interests, for separation from popular consumerism that is manipulated by marketing and puppeteered by advertising, and for liberation from the alienating working conditions of late capitalism. Craftwork held the kernel of a promise to unite mind, body and spirit in pleasurable activity, unleash creative potential and empower the maker within a circular economy – one that joins makers and clients in their shared desire for durable, handcrafted objects that are produced from sustainably sourced materials and that, at the end of their serviceable life, can be recycled or will return to the earth from which they came.

THE MARCH OF MACHINES

In 1973, economist Ernst Schumacher published the influential book *Small Is Beautiful*, which called for an entirely new way of life in Britain and the West. It laid out the prerequisites of 'a lifestyle designed for permanence', founded on alternative methods of production and new patterns of consumption.[52]

Schumacher's vision was unquestionably utopian, and its objective was to educate desire and human longing for something better. He disparaged the industrial methods and technological framework of the twentieth century, and advocated total reform of the agricultural and manufacturing sectors, modelling his ideas on small-scale, ecological, user-friendly technologies. In the socialist spirit of utopian thinkers, from More to Morris, Schumacher championed humankind's fundamental need to derive pleasure from daily work. Many machines of the modern age, he believed, had constricted or eliminated the need for skilled handwork that employed natural, rudimentary materials. He observed that 'such work has become exceedingly rare, and to make a decent living [at it] has become virtually impossible'. Craftwork, instead, had become a luxury. On that basis, he persuasively diagnosed modernity's 'neuroses' as stemming from our disengagement from satisfying, creative handwork.[53]

Emerging contemporaneously with Schumacher's publication was the British Craft Revival. The gradual replacement of traditional apprenticeships with college training after the Second World War had resulted by the 1970s in a loosely connected group of graduates who set up 'cottage workshops' and steadily formed a professional network. Two important catalysts for that network were the exhibition circuit, in which the Prestcote Gallery in the small village of Cropredy, Oxfordshire, played a seminal role,[54] and the growing media coverage of handicraft, including the new Crafts Council publication, *Crafts Magazine*.

Pioneers of the movement included furniture makers-in-wood Jeremy Broun, Fred Baier, David Colwell, Martin Grierson and John Makepeace. A common aim among these craftsmen was to partake in rewarding creativity and small-scale, bespoke production that tapped into the venerable traditions of quality woodworking. At the same time, they cleared the ground for a new and forward-looking tradition of British furniture making, which continues today.

The movement was reinforced throughout the 1980s and 1990s with graduates from various colleges around the country, and by rising numbers of self-taught furniture makers. In conversation with one of the few remaining furniture makers in the once-industrious village of West Wycombe in the Chilterns,[55] he conceded:

Some of today's best furniture makers are those older people who changed careers and chose carpentry. They're intelligent and usually self-trained. They're not making overly complicated pieces like craftsmen in the past, with carvings and cabriole legs, but they're making good quality, straightforward furniture with simple geometries and uncomplicated joints.[56]

Furniture makers' relations to machinery had also evolved. There was a general consensus that machines had their purpose, not just in batch production, but likewise in bespoke creations. Some, like Baier and Makepeace, had seized the opportunities that newly available technologies offered to their processes of both design and making. In Broun's writing about Alan Peters, who had apprenticed with the eminent Arts and Crafts figure Sir Edward Barnsley, he noted the vital role played by machines in the 'economic survival' of the craftsperson.[57] But it was also widely acknowledged that machines should be used on a scale that preserves the character of the craft and the significance of the artisan. It is not machines or power tools, but hand tools that remain instrumental to woodworkers' identities on both symbolic and practical levels. Essayist Donovan Hohn captured the essence of that relationship:

> Machines are both the rival and the antithesis of humanity. In their complexity, they resemble us. In their simplicity (all those parts, and yet no Oedipus complex, no withdrawal symptoms, no fear of death, no ecstasy), they are monstrous . . . Machines are largely autonomous and threaten us with obsolescence, whereas a [hand] tool is nothing without us.[58]

With similar sentiment, anthropologist Eugene Cooper, in his study of the art-carved furniture industry in China during the 1980s, remarked that the introduction of power-driven machines, in combination with a division of labour introduced by industrial capitalism, made 'man an extension of a machine, by taking out of his hand the tool that was an extension of himself'.[59] In large-scale furniture-making operations in Britain, too, factory owners often welcomed new mechanised technologies in place of traditional hand skills because, in the words of Roger Coleman, technology conveniently 'side-steps those awkward people who insist on making their own decisions about how a job should be carried out'.[60]

These perspectives on the fractious relationship between hand tools and machines, and the potential for machines to disrupt or capsize pleasurable craft, evoke Morris' version of utopia as opposed to that of Bellamy's, in which industrial processes are protagonists for a better world. Displacement by machines posed a less immediate threat to the independent designer-makers I met than it did to craftspeople employed by larger furniture-making operations. Nevertheless, the eventuality of displacement did factor in the anxieties some makers had over the future of the wood trades and their own livelihoods. Among the vocational migrants at the College, for example, machines were made potent symbols of the world they opposed and hoped to change. Handheld power tools were invested with that negative imagery to greater or lesser extents, but computer numerical control (CNC) machines of the kind we witnessed in operation during a field trip to a furniture factory were most definitely conceived as lying outside the margins of craft. Standard milling machinery, on the other hand, was more readily accommodated within utopian worldviews as a beneficial necessity that speedily and accurately prepared the timber, and thus freed-up time for the more gratifying tasks of handcrafting the finished lengths, joints and details.

In fact, the introduction of mechanisation in the fine-woodworking trades had a slow start during the Industrial Revolution and remained challenging and problematic in ways that the mechanisation of other crafts was not.[61] It therefore 'did not dispense with the need for either hand tools or handicraft skills' in carpentry.[62] This was in large part due to the variable nature of timber in comparison to cotton, wool, glass, clay or metals. Variability exists not only between species of timber, but also between one plank and the next of the same. A degree of unpredictability over the behaviour of a plank subject to fast-cutting blades made it difficult to homogenise machining processes and applications, which is the hallmark of efficient industrial production.

Marxist historian Raphael Samuel noted that the application of steam-power to sawmills during the nineteenth century affected sawyers, but had

Figure 6.3 Fine-woodwork trainees using the overhand planer in the small mill, 2013. © Trevor H.J. Marchand

little direct impact on woodworkers.[63] Sawmills did not obviate the need for handsaws, nor planing-machines the hand-plane, because the action of machines was 'too crude for the many hard woods and too indiscriminate for different lengths, breadths and thicknesses required' for making particular fine items. Even the application of steam-power to the turner's lathe did not eliminate the turner's skill in guiding the blades, and the powered band-saw was 'so constructed that it could be handled almost as dexterously as if it had been a chisel or a plane'.[64] However, the advent of computer numerical control machinery would redefine the terrain for craftwork in the late twentieth and twenty-first centuries.

CNC technology arrived shortly after the Second World War, when the blades of the earliest machines operated on instructions from punch tapes. Steep advancement in computing and digital technologies over the past half-century has resulted in CNC machinery and 3D printing and prototyping apparatuses that have revolutionised industrial production, and that have also encroached on the territory of traditional crafts, including fine woodworking. With blades and drills directed by coded programmes and without the need for manual operators, CNC machines and prototyping tools offer designers and makers new possibilities,[65] but they also pose new kinds of threats. Among my fellow woodworking trainees, several expressed grave concern that CNC technology might colonise the making of bespoke furniture.[66] The disappearance of or further reduction to the demand for hand skills would evidently foil the pursuits of pleasurable work I have documented. There was also fear that the faster, cheaper production would render fine furniture in the minds of consumers yet another disposable item, with all the environmental implications that has.

FINAL REFLECTIONS ON EDUCATING DESIRE AND PRESENT-DAY LONGING

We are right to long for intelligent handicraft to come back to the world.
—William Morris[67]

With a worsening climate crisis and the growing sense of urgency around environmental issues, increasing numbers of Britain's designer-makers, like Phil Koomen, have taken on board the need for sustainability in their practice. A green approach is deliberately marketed as integral to what they sell. It is argued that the demand for sustainably sourced timber is translating into more responsibly managed forests worldwide,[68] and that making furniture from wood requires far less energy consumption and produces a smaller carbon footprint than items produced from metal, glass and plastics. Not

only are these artisans producing and selling durable, serviceable and aesthetically pleasing wares, but they are also crafting values and lifestyles for
themselves and, hopefully too, for their clients. Ideally, clients will desire
original pieces infused with their author's pride-in-making and an authentic
narrative about quality and sustainability.

In striving to bolster both aesthetic appreciation and ethical consumerism in the broader public, such craftspeople have – knowingly or not –
adopted and adapted Morris' sense of duty to educate desire. Some communicate their philosophies and manifestos in words, either on websites,
brochures and publications or at seminars, conferences and craft fairs. But
perhaps every craftsperson best conveys their guiding ethos in their embodied practices, their selections of materials and the objects they make. As performance or artefact, these material manifestations of the craftsperson are
made available to others for contemplation, commentary and, possibly, em-
ulation. In particular, crafted objects take on a life of their own as they travel
out from the workshop or studio into the wider world as enduring signs of
the ingenuity and skilful intelligence that made them.

Designer-makers who consciously draw inspiration from the spirit of the
Arts and Crafts, the Craft Revival or other politically spirited craft movements recognise the need to breathe new life into those imagined pasts by
rearticulating the values and guiding principles within their own visions for
tomorrow. It was within this countercultural tradition of longing for radical
change and a more humane and sustainable future that most vocational migrants at the Building Crafts College positioned themselves. At tea and in the
pub, discussions and debates turned to world crises, the environment and
the precarious status of craftwork in the global economy. These present concerns, in combination with the pleasure that each had discovered in woodworking, allowed the vocational migrants to reappropriate the tradition of
utopian longing and animate it with contemporary relevance.

Utopia, as determined at the start of the chapter, is forever displaced,
both physically and temporally, and so too is its object of desire. The realisation of utopia is always postponed because its existence as a concept lies in
its dialectical relation to the present and is therefore in a perpetual state of
transformation. Consequently, longing produces a necessary and agonising
disjuncture between the subject and the possibility of attaining one's dream.

More concretely, countless craftspeople from the nineteenth century
onwards have longed for the recovery of place: an anchoring of practice
that nurtures personal or regional expression and a sense of belonging. The
current reality for fine woodworkers (and other craftspeople), however, is
complex and contradictory: tools and materials are regularly imported from
distant places; the timber on racks may be sourced illegally or from forests
that are not truly sustainable; ambitions to foster direct relations with in-

Figure 6.4 Fine woodworkers enjoying a tea break at the College, 2006.
© Trevor H.J. Marchand

dividual clients may succumb, by necessity, to a reliance on brokers and retailers; and the solvency of the workshop may become dependent upon commissions that compromise principles and cherished autonomy. In sum, the prospect that Morris identified more than a century ago of the craftsperson becoming alienated from their work and dislocated from place by the forces of a global capitalist economy continues to loom large.[69]

The phenomenon of dislocation likewise applies to the reproduction of fine woodworkers. With small student-instructor ratios and an emphasis on hand tools and professional comportment, the College environment succeeded in preserving traditional core values of craftwork and in scaffolding personal formation. However, the progressive transfer of on-site learning to training institutions over the past century has served to segregate craft theory and hand-skill development from the real operational challenges and learning opportunities found in the workshop or on site. In effect, the reproduction of fine woodworkers has been deterritorialised.

By contextualising my study of vocational migrants within a history of English utopian thought and writing, this chapter has illustrated that longing for a recovery of handicraft and its associated lifestyle is by no means unique to our present era; it has also demonstrated that utopian ideals are forever transforming. That dynamic nature imbues utopias with a magnetism, which continues to draw a small-but-steady flow of individuals to craftwork on quests for both self-actualisation and participation in a countercultural community. This occurs in spite of ever-evolving technologies that render hand skills superfluous; the marginal position of craft within national and global economies; the confinement of patronage to mainly elite, difficult-to-access niche markets; and the high costs and financial risks that establishing a workshop entails.

Decisions to abandon more conventional occupations in order to retrain in craftwork must therefore be duly recognised as an individual coping strategy and an attempt to reform subjectivity in the face of the disorientating flux of cultural, political and economic forces and a collapsing environment. By relocating the self within an imagined heritage of craft production and by embodying the ethos of a future utopia that promises purpose and pleasure, my fellow vocational migrants were striving to realise a unity of mind, body and spirit, an aesthetic integration of work with life, and a harmonious balance between individual, community and the natural world.

NOTES

An earlier and briefer version of this chapter was published as 'Vocational Migrants and a Tradition of Longing' in *Traditional Dwellings and Settlements Review: Journal of the International Association for the Study of Traditional Environments*, 19(1) (2007), 23–40. The material has been revised and the scope of discussion enlarged in preparing this book chapter.

1. Macdonald, 'Morris after Marcuse', 47.
2. In a 2012 report commissioned by the Crafts Council, a 'strong "localist" strain' among British craftspeople was noted. 'Many seek to build small businesses strongly rooted in particular places, emphasising authenticity and building on local traditions [i.e. choice of materials].' But although more than 70 per cent did not export outside the United Kingdom, many expressed wishes to take advantage of global business opportunities (Crafts Council et al., *Craft in an Age of Change*, 40).
3. Morris, 'The Revival of Handicraft', 341.
4. The earliest surviving copy of the celebrated Middle English (Irish English) poem is kept in the British Library, London, where it is also available as a digital manuscript, under the title *The Kildare Lyrics*, dated mid-fourteenth century (MS Harley 913, ff. 3r–6v). The poem, however, may have been written as early as the late thirteenth century. Alternatively spelled Cockaigne, the word is a Middle English name referring to the 'land of plenty' in medieval myth. The satirical poem was possibly penned by a Franciscan friar in Kildare and was intended to critique the cloistered life of a Cistercian monastery. *The Land of Cockaigne* is also the English title of a painting made by Pieter Brueghel the Elder in 1567, titled *Het Luilekkerland* in Dutch.
5. Lines 1–6; 27–30, and 44–45. The translation is from the edited text in Bennett and Smithers, 'The Land of Cockaygne', 136–44.
6. Morton, *The English Utopia*, 33.
7. From the Greek: *ou* ('not') + *topos* ('place'). The combination of the two terms, *utopia*, is thought to have been first used by Thomas More.

8. More, *Utopia*, 55.
9. Despite espousing notions of equality, the patriarchal perspective that More adopts relegates the 'weaker sex' to lighter jobs, while men perform the heavier ones, illustrating a persistent association between woodwork and 'manliness', which some male trainees at the Building Crafts College invoked and that female ones ardently challenged. A gendered division of labour is also strongly evoked by Ruskin, who wrote that 'a happy nation may be defined as one in which the husband's hand is on the plough, and the housewife's on the needle' (Ruskin, 'The Work of Iron', 81).
10. More, *Utopia*, 45.
11. Ibid., 59. Notably, American essayist Henry David Thoreau also praised the idea that at the end of the labourer's day, 'he is then free to devote himself to his chosen pursuit, independent of his labor', as opposed to the employer, who never finds respite from worry (Thoreau, 'Walden', 114).
12. More, *Utopia*, 73.
13. See White, 'Aristotle and Utopia', 650–53.
14. As outlined in Bacon, *The New Organon*.
15. Bacon, 'New Atlantis', 149–86.
16. Morton, *English Utopia*, 63.
17. From Hebrew, meaning 'The Son of Wholeness'.
18. Defoe, *Robinson Crusoe*.
19. Morton, *English Utopia*, 100.
20. References from William Blake, *And Did Those Feet in Ancient Times* (poem, 1804), also known as the hymm 'Jerusalem'. The 'satanic mills' refer to the Albion Flour Mills in Southwark, which was the first major factory in London. It was destroyed in 1791, possibly by an act of arson committed by traditional millers economically impacted by the Albion Mills. Ron Eglash noted that the revolt against the conflations made during the Enlightenment between technological and social progress began 'most famously in the writings of Emerson and Thoreau' (Eglash, 'Technology', 331).
21. Ruskin, 'The Nature of Gothic', 16–17.
22. Wilmer, 'Introduction', xii.
23. Morris, 'News from Nowhere'.
24. Bellamy, *Looking Backwards*.
25. A Luddite was a 'member of an organised band of nineteenth-century English handicraftsmen who rioted for the destruction of the textile machinery that was displacing them' (*Encyclopaedia Britannica*, https://www.britannica.com/event/Luddite, retrieved 2 June 2021).
26. Morris, 'Art and Its Producers', 348–49. For evidence of the influence of Marx's *Das Kapital* on Morris with respect to this passage, see Marx, *Capital*, Volume 1, Part 4, Chapter 15. Morris had studied *Das Kapital* and was influenced by Karl Marx's thinking on the history of industrialisation, but he nevertheless held a distinct view of that history and of the role of machinery. Alan K. Bacon concluded that 'Marx had in mind a picture of people working with machines, but although Morris did not advocate the abandonment of all machinery, the whole basis of his vision was that people would spend a great deal of time doing handwork, and as little time as possible working with machines' (Bacon, 'Morris's View', 8).
27. Morris, 'Art and Its Producers', 348–49.
28. Morris, 'News from Nowhere', 126.

29. Morris, 'Art and Its Producers', 349.
30. Medieval imagery and lore likewise provided the main source of inspiration for the Pre-Raphaelite artists, including Dante Gabriel Rossetti and Edward Burne-Jones, with whom Morris enjoyed close relationships. This was also shared by the architects of the neo-Gothic style of the Victorian era, whose circle included another of Morris' collaborators, Philip Webb. Roger Coleman noted that, like Morris but a half century later, Walter Gropius, founder of the Bauhaus, took inspiration from the Middle Ages, and in particular the building of the great cathedrals in which he saw 'precedents for a unity of the arts and crafts within an architectural whole, which he believed capable of shaping a humane world' (Coleman, *The Art of Work*, 80).
31. Of particular influence on Morris was Carlyle's *Past and Present* (1843), the author's major commentary on work and industrial England (Carlyle, *The Works of Thomas Carlyle*, Volume 10).
32. Levitas, *The Concept of Utopia*, 114. Here Levitas is discussing the views of E.P. Thompson (Thompson, *William Morris*). See also Morton, *The English Utopia*, 162–64 for a discussion of Morris' synthesis of history with the present in his projection of a socialist future.
33. Levitas, *The Concept of Utopia*, 108.
34. Ibid., 122.
35. However, it could be argued that French theorist Henri de Saint-Simon and philosopher Charles Fourier did endeavour to realise their pre-Marxist socialist utopias.
36. Levitas, *The Concept of Utopia*, 122.
37. Ricoeur, 'Ideology and Utopia'. See also Taylor, 'Editor's Introduction', xxi.
38. All quotes from Philip Koomen are taken from his lecture at the Building Crafts College, delivered on 15 June 2006.
39. Reproduction furniture is made in imitation or copy of an historic style (e.g. 'Georgian reproduction' or 'Victorian reproduction').
40. Crichton-Miller, 'Going against the Grain', W13.
41. Harrod, *The Crafts in Britain*, 460.
42. Ibid. 'Roundwood thinnings' refers to the efficient use of small-diameter timber that is cut when thinning forests as part of good woodland management.
43. United Nations Division for Sustainable Development, *AGENDA 21*, Chapter 4, Article 4.3.
44. According to John W., City & Guilds used to be both the curriculum provider and the awarding body of the Diploma. At the time of my fieldwork, however, City & Guilds awarded NVQs, ICAs and ACAs (Advanced Construction Awards) according to a curriculum set by the Construction Industry Training Board (CITB). The Diploma was issued jointly by City & Guilds and the Carpenters' Company, and was a unique diploma awarded to students of the Building Crafts College only. Furthermore, the ICA was a lower-level qualification than the C&G/Carpenters' Company Diploma. The ICA was academically equivalent to a GCSE or NVQ Level 2. The next level up from the ICA was the ACA, equivalent to an A level or NVQ Level 3. The ICA and ACA were issued to students who were training for employment, but who did not have access to the onsite training necessary for an NVQ.
45. For a description of the relation of American masculinity to the concept of handiness with tools, see Hohn, 'A Romance of Rust', 46.
46. Jean-Jacques Rousseau was an eighteenth-century philosopher whose essay, *Of the Social Contract* (1762), deliberates on how a political community with legitimate po-

litical power might be established different from that shaped by commercial interest and state control. He drew upon imagery of societies that exist in a 'state of nature' in developing his alternative model, in which the power of a monarchy is replaced by a direct democracy of free people (Rousseau, *Social Contract*, 1–133).

47. Ruskin, 'The Work of Iron', 69.
48. Thornton, 'How an Adze Is Like an Atlatl'.
49. Hickman, 'Britain Leads EU Imports'.
50. A survey commissioned in 2011 by the Crafts Council, Creative Scotland, the Art Council of Wales and Craft Northern Ireland found that just under one-third of makers in the United Kingdom had changed their practice during the previous three years in response to environmental concerns, the most popular change being to source more environmentally sustainable of sensitive materials and to reduce transport miles (Crafts Council et al., *Craft in an Age of Change*, 8.
51. Baier, 'Words by Fred', subsection 'Surviving'.
52. Schumacher, *Small Is Beautiful*, 9.
53. Ibid., 122–23.
54. Prestcote Gallery was opened by Ann Hartree in Prestcote Manor, which had been inherited by her friend Anne Crossman.
55. In the nineteenth century, West Wycombe was home to many wood turners and it contained the North & Sons furniture-making factory, which employed most of the village population. Factories making chairs, most famously the Windsor chair, would have been an even more common sight in nearby High Wycombe. Raphael Samuel states that in High Wycombe in the 1860s, Windsor chairs made with hand labour rather than machines were being produced at an astonishing rate of one a minute and all year round (Samuel, 'The Workshop of the World', 38).
56. In conversation with a head craftsman at Brown's Furniture Maker, West Wycombe, 22 April 2006.
57. Broun, 'Introduction', web publication.
58. Hohn, 'A Romance of Rust', 56.
59. Cooper, 'Mode of Production', 263.
60. Coleman, *The Art of Work*, 93.
61. See Ettema, 'Technological Innovation', 198. Ettema's essay supplies a fascinating history of woodworking machinery, beginning with Samuel Miller's invention of the circular saw in 1777, the 1793 landmark patent of Samuel Bentham (renowned mechanical engineer and brother of Jeremy Bentham) for a range of woodworking machines, and William Newberry's 1808 patent for the band-saw. Ettema's history proceeds into the nineteenth century with the introduction of power sanders (which corresponded with the advent of power transmission systems), reciprocating mortisers, tenoner machines and even dovetailers, which enjoyed little success. A machine specifically designed for cutting ornamental woodwork was patented in 1845, and used to carve woodwork for the new Houses of Parliament.
62. Samuel, 'The Workshop of the World', 37.
63. Ibid., 36.
64. Ibid., 37.
65. See, for example, Crafts Council et al., *Craft in an Age of Change*, 39.
66. For a thought-provoking contemporary study of the evolving relationship between humans and technology, see Michael Fisch's ethnographic study of Tokyo's over-

stretched commuter network and human interactions with the continually updating train traffic diagram (Fisch, *An Anthropology of the Machine*).

67. Morris, 'The Revival of Handicraft', 339.

68. The WWF-UK claimed that: 'More demand of products certified as coming from sustainably managed forests filters up the supply chain and creates increased demand and investment in forest certification in forests around the world' (WWF-UK, *Timber Scorecard 2017*, 50). See also Jurgens, *Learning Lessons*, 2–3. IKEA, which uses an estimated 1 per cent of the world's wood supplies, announced on its webpage that: 'Since 2017, 100% of the wood we source from countries with a history of challenges related to forest management comes from more sustainable sources' (IKEA, 'Wood').

69. Morris, 'News from Nowhere', 124.

CHAPTER 7

THE INTELLIGENT HAND

C on, the first-year instructor, encouraged complete immersion in our carpentry exercises by challenging us to tap into our perceptual awareness
of working with the tools and the timber. Many of my fellow trainees described working with wood as being 'pleasurably sensuous'. It stimulates and
heightens the senses of sight, touch and smell: the mellow hue of resinous
Redwood, the aromatic cedar of Lebanon, chocolaty American walnut and
the spicy tannins of oak that purple the fingertips. Every plank of timber
possesses distinct properties – direction of grain, figured patterns, texture,
density and hardness – and each behaves differently to the teeth of a saw or
under the blade of a plane or a chisel. As Walter Rose eloquently described
in his classic *The Village Carpenter*:

> To the woodworker the varied dispositions of woods are almost human: even in the
> same species they differ, some yielding to his wishes as though glad to co-operate,
> others stubborn and intractable.[1]

Rose's tribute to the village carpenter records a profession and way of life
in his native Buckinghamshire at the turn of the twentieth century.[2] He
descended from a line of master carpenters and apprenticed to his father
and grandfather, and to the small team of bench-hands in the family's employment. The chapters of Rose's slim book describe the impressive, but at
the time standard, variety of work that the shop undertook, manufacturing
everything from wooden water pumps to coffins, erecting door frames and
timber roofs, and repairing furniture and windmills.

Rose's reminiscences of the timber yard and workshop vividly portray
an environment animated by skilled handwork, a light-hearted exchange
of banter, the smell of freshly cut timber, and the rhythmic chorus of saws,

whispering bench planes and thundering mallets. Sounds enable the hearer to map out the corresponding activities within the workshop space, and thereby to judge distances and calibrate proximity without the need to pause work and take a look. Auditory senses, too, are critical to monitoring one's own performance and progress, and sound supplies 'information on the effectiveness or accuracy of a movement' and of the tool.[3] Again, in the words of Rose:

> The sound of tools properly used is a pleasing tune. The craftsman has no need to examine a saw to know if it is sharp, or if it is handled properly. Nor need he look at a plane to know if it functions at its best. The ill-used tool makes a discordant noise, which is agony to the trained ear.[4]

Woodworking, like any skilled practice, relies on an additional 'sixth sense'. This is the somatic system, which may be defined as interconnected bodily perceptions of the position, orientation, movement, and muscular contraction and release of our own torso, neck, head, limbs and digits. The somatic system plays a role in calibrating direction, angle, force and rhythm with the tool in hand; in correcting or modifying stance, posture or grasp; in signalling the achievement of a correct and economic performance; and, hopefully, in alerting the self to a wrong or dangerous practice in order to safely evade injury. Long practice and accumulated experiences progressively fine-tune the craftsperson's somatic perception to the present task, enabling the confident performance and the rapid, responsive recalibration of the tool-wielding body that qualifies the 'expert'. As college trainees, attuning our senses to the tasks, materials and working environment was critical to our formation as carpenters.

All the fine-woodwork instructors emphasised the importance of mastering hand tools and promoted their use over power tools whenever practicable. This was because hand tools gave us a more immediate feel for, and understanding of, the timber and the actions we performed on it. Instructor Cheryl M. told me: 'Before the students get into the "gadget side" of carpentry and start buying too many expensive tools, it's important to teach them to trust what their eyes and their fingertips are telling them. Timber is a living, breathing material.' She paused, rubbing the palm of her hand over the Formica table-top that separated us. 'Unlike this table, where you can feel nothing at all', she resumed, 'each piece of timber can talk to you.'

Proper care and maintenance of cutting edges was stressed, and trainees were encouraged to buy old tools and restore them to working condition for regular use at the bench. Jens and Robert were devoted to salvaging rebate planes, moulding planes, grooving planes, marking gauges, dovetail saws and mortise chisels, all of which they purchased from websites, flea markets and second-hand shops. Not only were there financial savings to be had, but equally both men appreciated the often-superior quality of the Sheffield steel and iron castings manufactured in the past. Restoring tools also contributed to the ethos around sustainability and green politics articulated by Koomen in Chapter 6.

Robert, in particular, derived satisfaction from the fact that the component parts and mechanical workings of hand tools can be plainly observed, studied and comprehended. He could therefore take them apart, clean or repair them, and then reassemble them for improved use. This was part of the overall control that many craftspeople yearn to have over all dimensions of their work. Notably, numerous parts of hand tools are anthropomorphised or metaphorically referred to by the names for anatomical features of familiar animals, which I will discuss later in the chapter. This renders them conceptually and physically familiar to the user and the repairer, and thereby more accessible, understandable and amenable to making one's own.[5] The close connections between the human body and the bodies and extremities of woodworking tools are indeed ancient and have played a significant part in the story of our evolution.

Rose, too, emphasised the need for the skilful handling and mindful maintenance of one's tools: 'Treat the plane as a human being, it will respond to good treatment, but will be ruined by careless, haphazard use.'[6] The intimate relationship between a craftsperson and their tools is eloquently captured in the following quote from Rose, which expresses the progressive manner in which carpenter and tool reciprocally form one another in shape and posture, and in performance and efficiency:[7]

> It is not possible to picture a carpenter or joiner apart from his tools . . . To such experienced bench-hands the tools were co-operators in the common service of life, the character of the tool becoming like that of the owner. There existed a subtle unity of disposition between the tools and their proper users, which was simply the outcome of much common use, a peculiarity in the working of the tool born of a corresponding peculiarity in the method of the user. The joiner became accustomed to handling it, to its distinctive shape and grip, its temper and weight.[8]

It is the nature of that relationship that I explore more fully in this chapter. More specifically, the chapter investigates the way that hand tools in general become an extension of the human body during the course of practical training and use. The evolution of our brain, our hands and the tools that we have creatively improvised or imaginatively invented throughout the history of our species has unfolded in the age-old interaction between all three.[9] Our tool-using abilities are foundational to the pleasure we can derive in work; indeed, they make working possible, and therefore make possible our ability to shape and change the world around us for the better – but sometimes, too, for the worse. For William Morris, hand tools in craftwork were seminal to the creation of a utopian way of life.

The inquiry framing this chapter grew out of my prior fieldwork with masons in Yemen and Mali discussed in Chapter 1. The focus of the present chapter is the vocational training in woodworking at the College and the practices of the English furniture makers whom I interviewed. I draw upon related literature on skill and craft, and upon research in the cognitive and neurosciences that explores the intricate connections between brain, hand and tools. Deeper thinking about this fascinating relationship promotes both a more informed understanding of the nature of craftwork and greater appreciation for the complex kinds of intelligence that constitute skilled handwork.

BRAIN, HAND AND TOOL

> The hand is not a thing appended, or put on, like an additional movement in a watch; but a thousand intricate relations must be established throughout the body in connection with it such as nerves of motion and nerves of sensation … But even with all this superadded organisation the hand would lie inactive, unless there were created a propensity to put it into operation.
>
> —Charles Bell[10]

The hand is the most effective body part for manipulating objects and for configuring and modifying our physical environment. Hands, too, are an important medium for communicating, expressing and even shaping ideas and emotions, either on their own or more typically in coordination with utterances, spoken language, facial expression or posture. 'Every motion of the hand in every one of its works carries itself through the element of thinking', wrote Heidegger, for: 'All the work of the hand is rooted in thinking.'[11] For that reason, it is unsurprising that the hand has influenced the language and imagery we use in thinking about the mind. In the words of philosopher Colin McGinn: 'We grasp the mind as a *grasping* organ – we apprehend it as *apprehensive.*'[12]

Hands perform an astounding array of functions. They point, gesture and sign; make fists, protect or express tenderness; support our body, head and other appendages; climb or break a fall; catch and throw; grasp, hold, carry, wield and manipulate external objects; and operate tools. My present concern is with the operation of tools, and more specifically with the nature of skilled hand-tool use, which might be defined at the outset as practised coordination between brain, hand and tool, acting in direct relation with the environment and with the intention of manipulating or reconfiguring objects or materials. But what does such 'coordination' entail?

Nearly two centuries of scientific progress separate the studies made by Scottish surgeon and anatomist Sir Charles Bell and American neurologist Frank Wilson, but their accounts of the hand converge on the same finding – namely, the existence of a special and intricate connection between brain and hand. Echoing the above quote from Bell, Wilson points out that brain and hand resist differentiation into neatly bounded categories and are instead intimately joined by the nervous system, each stimulating activity and development in the other. The nervous system connects brain, spinal cord, peripheral nerve, neuromuscular junction and onward 'down to the quarks' of our fingertips, and back again. Wilson astutely concludes that 'brain is hand and hand is brain'.[13]

A hand tool, by contrast, is an inanimate artefact that, seemingly, is plainly distinguishable from the brain-body that wields it. A hand tool can be generically defined as an implement or device that is grasped and employed to act upon another object or to alter the state of a material, lending greater efficiency to what can be achieved by hand (or other body part) alone. In action, however, a hand tool becomes an extension of the forearm, hands or fingers, and thereby integrated within a brain-hand-tool complex.

Already in 1949, British physical anthropologist Kenneth Oakley wrote that 'considered functionally, [tools] are detachable extensions of the forelimbs'.[14] American anthropologist Margaret Mead drew further attention to this phenomenon in a UNESCO report in 1953:

> Where technology is simple, the tool is an extension of the body; the shuttle elongates and refines the finger, the mallet is a harder and more powerful fist. The tool follows the rhythm of the body; it enhances and intensifies but it does not replace and does not introduce anything basically different.[15]

The experience of that union was poetically evoked by carpenter and columnist Jeff Taylor: 'At a certain point, upon a day, you almost become the work, a moving and cognitive part of the tool in your own hand.'[16] And artist Eric Sloane observed that hand tools are:

> so much an extension of a man's hand or an added appendage to his arm, that the resulting workmanship seem[s] to flow directly from the body of the maker and to carry something of himself into the work. True, by looking at . . . an old piece of furniture you can imagine the maker much more clearly than you can by beholding anything made today.[17]

How is the union between brain, hand and tool achieved? This question, which I set out to address, has remained equally fascinating to anthropologists, archaeologists, anatomists, neurobiologists, cognitive scientists and all who share an interest in the nature of human knowledge, learning, practice and material culture.

THE HAND IN ANTHROPOLOGY

It seems from the coalescing body of evidence from archaeology, physical anthropology, anatomy and neurology that our relationship with tools stretches back nearly two million years.[18] Evolution of the brain-hand was necessary for making and using tools. But, likewise, tool use played a pivotal role in the further evolution of the human hand[19] and the brain,[20] as well as in the development of gestural communication and language,[21] and of culturally defined notions of intelligence.[22]

Coevolution of brain, hand and tool endowed humans with the remarkable capacity for transferring a proximal goal (e.g. grasping a mallet) to a distal one (e.g. driving a wooden peg). This demands tight coordination between multiple cognitive domains and physical strategies. Our ability to conceptually identify and understand the uses of a wide variety of tools, to plan with tools and satisfy goals, and to manipulate tools with high levels of (manual) dexterity is a defining trait of our species.

Hands are our primary means for not only engaging with but also learning about the overwhelming majority of tools that humankind has invented and fashioned.[23] In any trade, whether masonry, carpentry, smithing, the culinary arts, medical surgery or others, learning the tools typically entails picking them up and giving them a try. Hand skills, however, are more complex than simply training the hands to perform a series of correct actions. They involve balanced posture and complementary movements of other body parts in synchrony with the dominant hand, a sophisticated coordination between sensory knowledge and motor activity, an ability to flexibly adjust and respond to the material being worked, and the knowhow to make corrections and repairs, often in ways that are invisible to all but the craftsperson.

This kind of mastery is normally developed through specialised training, and often within a community of practitioners. Craft training regimes focus on hand skills, although, as was discussed in Chapter 1, anthropology has revealed that training, especially within apprenticeship frameworks, results equally in the formation of values, ethos and social persona, and the learning of related professional competencies.[24] Nonetheless, the 'skilled hand' has long been *the* focal point of craftwork and, as reported by Wilson, 'for a great number of people, the hand ... becomes the critical instrument of thought, skill, feeling and intention for a lifetime of professional work'.[25]

Relatedly, Howard Risatti contends that 'the skilled hand must be understood as not only making, but also measuring, giving scale and proportion to craft forms so they will accommodate the body both physically and psychically'.[26] I would further add that skilled handwork lends practitioners a vital sense of agency to make, undo, repair and transform their world, and the world of others, in immediate, practical, hands-on ways.[27] The pursuit of pleasurable work is the pursuit of such agency. In spite of this, the hand, as an instrument and expression of knowledge and agency, had been largely overlooked by social and cultural anthropology, with a few noteworthy exceptions.

In 1888, Frank Baker, Professor of Anatomy at the University of Georgetown, published his essay 'Anthropological Notes on the Human Hand' in the very first issue of *American Anthropologist*.[28] Baker's aims were twofold: first, to describe the role of the hand as charm and fetish in warding off disease, changing fortunes and bringing luck; and, second, to propose a more rigorously scientific physiognomy that would illuminate the inextricable links between hand and mind, and supersede the quack's art of chirognomy. His animated explorations of 'curious superstitions' take the reader across time and space, from ancient Greece and medieval France, to the 'laying on of hands' by English monarchs, and to the rural counties of England and the Catholic communities of Baltimore where hands of the deceased were still being used for curative purposes.[29]

At the time of Baker's publication, Charles Bell's study of *The Hand* continued to be an authoritative source, and newly discovered empirical evidence was confirming the thorough integration of nervous with muscular systems. Baker cleverly employed the demonstrable anatomical connection between brain and hand to support his anthropological thesis that the hand is an enduring and universal symbol of human and divine power.

Four years later, anthropologist Frank Hamilton Cushing published his fascinating and detailed essay on the influence of hand usage on cultural development. Initially curator of ethnology for the National Museum in Washington DC, Cushing became a leading expert on indigenous Zuni culture, living for extended periods in a Zuni Pueblo and arguably founding the practice of participant observation, which came to denote the anthropological method. Cushing's essay opens with a description of the 'three great steps in the intellectual development of man' – namely, 'the biotic', referring to humankind's ability to walk erect and have free hands; 'the manual', or our capacity to make an environment by hand, which in turn gave rise to the ability for rational devising, and 'the mental', enabling humankind's quest for the 'ascertainment of *truth*'.[30] Following a series of crosscultural investigations into hand influence on the formation of spoken language terms, recorded numerals and ceremonial succession, Cushing determined that 'the hand of man has been so intimately associated with the mind of man that it has moulded intangible thoughts no less than the tangible products of his brain'.[31]

The topic of 'handedness', pursued only briefly by Baker and Cushing, was taken up more fully by French sociologist Robert Hertz in his essay 'The Pre-eminence of the Right Hand' published in 1909.[32] A student of sociologist Émile Durkheim, Hertz was the first to associate the religious polarities of sacred and profane with the symbolic powers of right and left respectively. His study, grounded mainly in available ethnographic data on the Maori, proposed that practices of suppressing the left hand are an attempt to restrain the sorcery and occult powers associated with it. Hertz notes at the outset the asymmetrical neurological connection between the 'preponderance of the right hand' and the 'greater development in man of the left cerebral hemisphere'.[33]

Subsequent structural and symbolic studies of handedness offered valuable insights into the constellation of relationships mapped between human bodies and religious beliefs, the complexity and contradiction inherent in collective representations, and evolving social status and power relations among neighbouring groups and castes in a changing world.[34] In his analysis of handedness, Warren Tenhouten claimed that Hertz's analogical association of right to left and sacred to profane exists in 'virtually every culture'.[35] However, taking a cue from Durkheim,[36] Tenhouten observed that the efficacy of dual classification systems erodes as societies experience increasing differentiation and specialisation. This, he argued, 'liberates' the left hand from culturally constructed forms of abhorrence, but the humiliating consequence for the left hand is that it is reduced to 'its biological reality as, what Hertz called, a "humble auxiliary" to the dominant right hand'.[37]

Despite these incursions into the symbolism of handedness, dedicated exploration by social and cultural anthropologists of the wondrous connection between hand and brain appears to have ceased somewhere near the turn of the twentieth century, the inquiry having been surrendered to physical anthropologists and the natural sciences.[38] It is therefore necessary for me, as a social anthropologist and craftsperson, to revisit the subject that was first expounded by Charles Bell and probed by Baker, Cushing and even Hertz, but to now bring the role of hand tools more squarely into the hand-brain puzzle and to take on board the available learning from other disciplines.

THE PHYSICAL HAND, GRASPS
AND BIMANUAL COORDINATION

The coupling of brain and hand within the weave of the nervous system makes it impossible in practice to draw any definitive functional boundary between them. Our fingertips have evolved to contain some of the densest concentrations of nerve endings in the body. Because of this, the sense of touch is most powerfully associated with the hand. Artist Tappio Wirkkala spoke of 'eyes at the fingertips' in reference to 'the subtlety and precision of the tactile sense of the hand'.[39]

In the evolutionary history of the brain-hand connection, the development of human bipedalism was arguably the most critical step. McGinn proposed that 'free hands were the engine of the entire cultural process'.[40] The freeing of our upper limbs and hands allowed for more complex manipulation of the physical environment. And with the evolution of the opposable thumb came the ability for articulated grasps and firmer grips of objects, and the manufacture of increasingly sophisticated artefacts and tools. These activities together multiplied and refined brain-hand links to the point that the hand became the most physically adept and nimble part of the human anatomy, capable of more intricate and precise manipulation than that in the comparable extremity of any other animal.

In *Homo sapiens*, the hand's skeletal structure contains twenty-seven bones. Remarkably, the two hands together account for a little over one-quarter of the total number of bones in the body. Beginning from the wrist (*carpus*), eight carpal bones are arranged in two successive rows of four, the lower of which is fitted into a shallow socket formed by the smaller ulna and larger radius bones of the forearm. The five metacarpals are joined along the upper row of carpal bones, making up the palm with its inner surface of strength and its weak backside, referred to as the hand's dorsum. The five extending digits are composed of phalanges. The three in each of the four long fingers are named the proximal, intermediate and distal phalanges, reflecting their respective distance from the palm. The design of the human thumb, containing just two phalanges, is among the most significant evolutionary features distinguishing us from our primate cousins. The metacarpal of the thumb is joined at the wrist's multifaceted trapezium-carpal in such a way that the thumb can be rotated 90 degrees perpendicular to the palm and can be brought opposite to the fingers in order to pinch and grasp objects. These capacities make the thumb the most mobile digit of the hand and a crucial component in the history of human tool use and skilled handwork.

Skeletal movement requires the support of muscles, which are animated by electrochemical exchanges of signals between neurons. Hand movement is initiated in the shoulder muscles. Shoulder movement automatically anticipates and supports hand movements, 'transporting' the hand to its intended target.[41] The basic mechanics of the arm and fingers are operated by two kinds of specialised muscles: one producing flexion (e.g. biceps and flexor digitorum) and the other extension (e.g. triceps and extensor digitorum) of a single joint. More specifically, the so-called extrinsic muscles of the hand consist of the long flexors originating on the underside of the forearm and extending through the palm into the fingers, and the extensors originating on the topside of the forearm and extending into the fingers along the hand's dorsum. Flexors and extensors allow for bending and straightening of the fingers respectively.

In combination, the extrinsic muscles are responsible for the wide range of possible hand motions, but their control over hand and digit movement is crude in comparison to the so-called intrinsic muscles of the hand. The intrinsics originate on the carpal and metacarpal bones, and are accountable for fine hand and precision finger movement, and for the coordination of such movement in parallel and sequence. In addition to extrinsics and intrinsics, the thumb is also comprised of other small, specialised muscles, lending it its 'opposable' abilities and making possible a number of sophisticated grasp formations.

Grasping is a prehensile action, in that it involves gripping and holding an object either partially or wholly with an extremity.[42] Wilson distinguishes between 'power grips' and 'precision grips', defining the former as 'any holding posture that uses the palm as a buttress' (e.g. using a mallet), and the latter as using 'any combination of thumb in opposition to fingers' (e.g. squeezing pliers).[43] Kinds of power grips include the 'three-jaw chuck' employed for such activities as hammering or throwing, and the 'pad-to-side' grip for performing tasks like sawing or cutting with a blade.[44] The three-jaw chuck can also take pronated or supinated forms, most commonly associated with overhand and underhand grips. These are used, for example, in weightlifting to execute presses and arm curls respectively. Swinging a cricket bat or making a slap-shot with an ice-hockey stick involves a simultaneous combination of both pronated and supinated grasps in order to secure and manipulate the sporting equipment. An important point to flag here is that grip is determined by task, not tool.

Grasping an object entails 'a highly precise registration of neurological preparations for the biomechanical requirement of the task'.[45] The arm must move the hand to the target guided by vision (or possibly by sound or touch), and the hand must orient itself, simultaneously forming the palm, fingers and thumb in a manner appropriate for grasping, then manipulating, the target object. As contact is made, the fingers and palm receive haptic information and responsively adjust and fine-tune the grip, and apply the necessary force to lift, then carry, manipulate or operate.

Touch is both reactive and proactive, seeking tactile data that informs the shape of the grip, the application of pressure and the subsequent hand movements.[46] The orientation of the hand, the configuration of the grip, and the adjustments of palm, fingers and thumb differ considerably, whether the target is a teacup or a hammer, or for that matter whether it is granny's dainty bone-china teacup, a sturdy coffee mug or a Chinese tea bowl.

Engage for a brief moment, if you will, in a mental exercise. Imagine *with your body* the biomechanics involved in grasping a screwdriver lying lengthwise in front of you on a workbench, its handle at six o'clock relative to your downward gaze. In reaching for the screwdriver, any of the following occurrences will result in a failed grasp: misjudging the spatial location of the tool relative to your body or your moving hand; misaligning the orientation of your hand in relation to the position of the tool's handle; producing the wrong formation of palm, fingers and thumb; or, once having made contact, failing to close your grasp and complete the grip by forming your palm and digits around the circumference of the handle with the necessary force. The marvel, however, is that the vast majority of us nearly always get it right.

The development of the arts and handicrafts, music, gardening, sport and countless other human activities entails the encoding of procedures, regulations and standards, and the proliferation of discrete discourses and bodies of knowledge. It also involves the invention and refinement of specialised tools and implements, coupled with the delineation of distinct tasks. Tools and tasks demand a diversity of grasps, grips and dexterous manipulations, each configuration dependent upon the goal of the exercise, and on the practice and experience of the individual. Hands, after all, are not merely 'generic organs', but are 'unique individuals'.[47] In his discussion of grips, Richard Sennett astutely noted that, with training and long hours of practice, 'grips develop in individuals just as they have developed in our species'.[48]

Such individual stylisation applies equally to dextrous manipulations, notably including the ways that we learn to coordinate and compliment the actions of our dominant and nondominant hands in bimanual activities. Coordination, Sennett remarked, is best achieved if both hands are engaged in learning the task from the start as opposed to incrementally mastering each segment and subsequently trying to suture the actions together in a seamless performance.[49] The reason for this, explained Wilson, is that the two unequal hands perform complimentary functions, whereby the nondominant hand counterbalances and 'frames' the activities of the dominant one, or continually adjusts the position and orientation of the material being worked or worked upon.[50] 'The spatial and temporal scales of movement of the two [roles] are different', he observed, 'the dominant being "micrometric" (i.e. lower in amplitude and faster in repetition) and the nondominant being "macrometric" ... [involving a wider] variety of improvised holds and move sequences.'[51]

Take, for example, a right-handed carpenter using a paring chisel to remove waste from a simple 'housing joint'.[52] With his dominant hand, he grips the chisel handle with a pad-to-side hold, index finger and thumb pointing downward along its hardwood shaft to maximise control over the sharp cutting edge. As he moves the tip of the chisel into position along the bottom of the rectangular channel of the housing joint, he takes hold of the long, flat metal blade with his nondominant left hand, applying a precision grip by lightly bracing its width between his thumb and four fingertips. Before be-

Figure 7.1 A woodworking student using a bevel-edged paring chisel to remove timber from a housing joint, 2013. © Trevor H.J. Marchand

ginning to pare away timber, he carefully aligns the chisel tip with the edges of the channel, relying on sight and the 'feel' conveyed by the tool to the hands, adjusting his posture, position and cutting angle accordingly.

Monitoring and adjusting the carpenter's body and tool will proceed in that way throughout the activity, responding also to the sound of the blade and 'feedback' from the timber. While paring away wood shavings, his dominant right hand and forearm control the angle, rhythm and force of the backward-and-forward thrust of the chisel's cutting edge along the wood surface, and his left lends increased command over the directionality of the cut and over the sequential application and relaxation of force applied to the timber. While the grip and movement performed by his right hand remain largely unchanged throughout the exercise, he transfers the fingers on his left up and down the length of the metal blade to balance force with accuracy. His left hand is also periodically employed to remove wood shavings from the channel (accompanied by a blast of warm air issued from pursed lips) and to check its surfaces for smoothness, shape and depth.

According to Wilson's account, the complex but generally repetitive muscular tasks performed by the carpenter's dominant hand are 'automised' by his brain, thereby requiring minimal sensory monitoring; his nondominant hand moves in 'supportive anticipation . . . conforming its movements both to the behaviour of an external object and to the action of the other hand, to ensure that the object and the handheld tool will intercept at the intended time and place'.[53]

INTRODUCING THE 'CORRESPONDENCE PROBLEM'

Skilled handwork involves fast and fluid exchanges of various kinds of sensory information, motor-action feedback, semantic knowledge, and reflective thought on goals, present actions and tasks completed. When this exchange of action, information and thought is synchronised, makers may experience a sense of harmony in what they see, hear, feel and do with tools, implements and materials. When a task at the workbench, for example, was progressing smoothly, trainees and seasoned woodworkers alike described their state of being as 'focused', 'meditative' and 'calming'. At the Building Crafts College, all claimed that regular tool work honed a sense of discipline over their train of thought and heightened the sense of coordination in their movements and activities.

My fellow trainees also referred to this experience as 'being in the zone' or as 'the Zen of woodworking', in which body, mind and soul were fully absorbed in the presentness of the task-event. Even when certain tool-wielding actions are mastered and the neuromuscular system performs them in a seemingly automatic way, they become 'routinised but not mindless',[54] for the woodworker is acting not merely *upon*, but *with* tools and *with* materials, whose properties respond to the actions made with them and upon them. Those 'responses' are perceived and processed by the senses, which in turn shape reflective thought and guide the woodworker's continual, and usually subtle, adjustments of posture, bimanual activity and exertions of force.

In discussing carpentry, educationalist and author Mike Rose wrote that the biomechanical skills involved in the craft 'build on and enhance basic sensory, kinaesthetic, and cognitive abilities that emerge through natural development'.[55] Building upon and enhancing these basic abilities demands considerable personal investment of motivation, dedicated practice, focused attention and time. Biomechanical mastery of one's art demands lengthy dedication,[56] but it also relies on nurturing patience and persistence. Every woodworking trainee, instructor and professional furniture maker whom I interviewed cited these as being necessary virtues of the trade. In both Yemen and Mali, the masons I worked alongside periodically uttered the standard Arabic proverb 'as-sabr jamil' (الصبرجمل, 'patience is beautiful') Patience and persistence are essential to achieving steady concentration and carefully planned actions, and to calmly accepting and creatively responding to arising errors and unforeseen challenges.

Figure 7.2 A fine-woodwork trainee using a tenon saw, 2007.
© Trevor H.J. Marchand

Patience and persistence are also key attributes to the development of disciplined perception, or what James Gibson has termed the 'education of attention'.[57] In anthropologist Cristina Grasseni's study of 'skilled vision' among northern Italian cattle breeders, she argued that the long apprenticeship beginning in childhood includes learning to actively search for certain kinds of information in the daily living environment and cultivating a distinct way of seeing both bovine and landscape.[58] Skilled vision is also coveted among woodworkers. 'Having a good eye is synonymous with being a good carpenter', reported Wendy Millroy, an ethnomathematician who became an apprentice furniture maker during fieldwork in South Africa.[59] Although woodworkers rely on touch, hearing and even smell to monitor and adjust their operations, skilled vision commonly comes into play while assessing the figure of timber, judging straightness, angles, symmetry and proportions, and approximating dimensions and volumes – or, as Millroy described it, 'mathematizing'.[60]

Additionally, skilled vision is critical to a carpenter's hand-eye coordination. The phenomenon of hand-eye coordination in tool-using activities gives rise to a number of related questions: how do we grasp what we see? How is information supplied by vision regarding '*what* a tool is' and '*where* it is located' integrated with our motor cognition?[61] More precisely, how does visual information serve as input to the coordinated motor operations involved, first, in delivering the hand to the tool and forming an appropriate grasp, and then transferring the hand, and, more to the point, the functional end of the tool to a precise location on the material or artefact being worked?

The short answer is that the brain-body must solve the 'correspondence problem', meaning that it must integrate signals from vision and haptics in a manner that combines information referring to the same object located in space in dynamic relation to the moving hand.[62] But, again, how does this occur? And how is this ability honed through a craftsperson's training and practice – or, conversely, diminished through injury, slackening regimes of practice, changes to design, technologies or procedures, or the inevitable fact of ageing and physical deterioration? I return to the correspondence problem in the next section, with an explanation for this seemingly mundane and recurrent, but in fact remarkable phenomenon.

EXTENDING THE BODY

Where the tool has its stories, the hand has its gestures ... But 'bringing into use' is not a matter of attaching an object with certain attributes to a body with certain anatomical features; it is rather joining a story to the appropriate gestures.

—Tim Ingold[63]

As discussed earlier in this chapter, hand tools in use supplement and extend, and are psychologically incorporated into, the physiology of limbs, hands and digits. Carpentry hand tools in particular enable woodworkers to execute a large number of actions with and upon wood more efficiently and with higher levels of precision than by hand and arm alone.[64] These actions include pounding, tapping, pulling, cutting, chopping, carving, bending, shaping, boring, scraping, smoothing, bracing, holding, pinching, cramping, joining and measuring.

Language contains preliminary clues to the embodied relations we have cultivated with carpentry tools. In English, for example, the proper names for a variety of specialised tools, tool parts or common wood joints refer metaphorically to human or animal anatomies, thereby inciting some level of somatic identification and abetting a more immediate, visceral understanding of their form, function or fit: for example, a snipe bill plane, shoulder plane, bullnose plane and granny's tooth plane; the head, striking face and claw of a hammer; the teeth of a saw, or cheek of a frame saw; the mouth, throat, frog, toe horn and sole of a bench plane; the neck of a chisel, or a swan-neck chisel; the jaws of a ratchet brace, jaws of a vice; the eye of an adze; a tusk peg, dovetail joint, tongue-and-groove joint, finger joints, and the 'male' and 'female' components of a mortise-and-tenon joint.

Regarding specifically the relation between tool names and tool functions, philosopher Gilbert Ryle commented that 'we do not often need to make explicit mention of the special functions of particular utensils and instruments; not because they have not got functions, but because the names of these utensils and instruments themselves generally tell us their functions'.[65] In woodworking, general category terms such as 'saw', 'hammer', 'chisel' and 'plane' are both noun and verb in a number of languages,[66] describing equally the kind of hand tool, its function and the action associated with using it. The fact that proper noun and functional verb share the same lexical term (or lexical root) may be a contributing factor to the fascinating neurological finding that an area in our brain's left temporal lobe associated with processing action words is also activated when naming tools.[67]

In a neurological experiment using functional magnetic resonance imaging (fMRI), it was confirmed that both 'seeing tools' and 'silently naming them' activate the left dorsal premotor cortex in equal measure.[68] Silently naming tool functions (e.g. hammering), however, increases activation of the left dorsal premotor cortex, and also activates another area in the premotor cortex as well as the supplementary motor area (SMA) associated with planning and coordinating complex movements like bimanual tool use.[69] It was concluded from these results that motor cognition plays a significant role in assisting our recognition, identification and understanding of objects that have a 'motor valence'. In other words, motor cognition is in fact part and parcel of our meaning-making processes, and the information that motor cognition supplies is incorporated into the mental representations we entertain about artefacts like tools. After all, the meaning of a tool is not fully accounted for by the object's appearance, but centrally includes its function, which is animated by a user in combination with the materials acted upon.

Therefore, to think of a smoothing plane implies not only thoughts of it as an object, but also as an *object-in-use*. 'No object considered purely in and for itself, in terms of its intrinsic attributes alone, can be a tool', insisted Ingold. 'To describe a thing as a tool is to place it in relation to other things within a field of activity in which it can exert a certain effect.'[70] Philosopher and feminist theorist Elizabeth Grosz similarly observed that 'it is only insofar as the object ceases to remain an object and becomes a medium, a vehicle for impressions and expressions, that it can be used as an instrument or tool'.[71]

According to eminent British psychologist Richard Gregory: 'Tools contain ready-made answers to practical problems.'[72] Tools are already a part of the world into which we are born: they have a history of use, and the basic properties and function of many have changed little since ancient times.[73] As cultural artefacts, they possess their own history of use and shared meaning, and through practice, users are, so to speak, 'socialised in the tool'.[74] A familiar tool whose 'story' we know invites us to take it up, becoming a 'vehicle for learning about the properties of materials themselves',[75] a means of problem solving or an enabler for modifying and transforming our physical and possibly our social worlds. This quality that invokes even the most fleeting urge to pick up and use is what has been identified as the 'motor valence' of a tool,[76] a property powerfully conjured by John Updike in several lines contained in his poem 'Tools'. 'Tools wait obliviously to be used', Updike observed, such as pliers, with their 'notched mouth agape', or the brace and bit 'fit to chew a hole in pine like a patient thought'.[77]

What additional insights might we gain from cognitive and neuroscience research into the unity of body and hand tools in use? Earlier, I introduced the correspondence problem, whereby the brain must integrate haptic and visual stimuli referring to the same object so that the hand reaches and grasps its target. This calculation presumably becomes more complex when a handheld tool is introduced (e.g. reaching with pliers to squeeze the head of a protruding nail to remove it from a plank) because visual information about the object (the nail head) is spatially separated from the hand (as biological effector) by the tool (as prosthesis).

Behavioural experiments have demonstrated that, during tool use, an actor's multisensory attention (i.e. tactile, visual and auditory) shifts to the side of space (left or right) corresponding to the dominant hand grasping the tool and, significantly, to where the tip or functional component of that tool is being wielded.[78] The results of cognitive-neuroscience experiments further indicated that when using a handheld tool, the brain treats the haptic signal as though it were coming from the operational end of the tool, not the hand.[79] This allows the brain to combine haptic and visual information coming from the very same distal location (e.g. the head of the nail being clasped by the jaws of the pliers), thereby solving the correspondence problem.

Close sensory engagement with tools can also result in their temporary incorporation into a sense of what belongs to our body, or 'body schema'. The body schema is a nonconscious system regulating the proprioceptive sense of our body's posture and movement, and dynamically updated by information supplied by all sensory modalities including visual, auditory, haptic and motor.[80] A changing sense of what constitutes the body has a corresponding effect on the body's relation to its surrounding space. Indeed, the brain's representation of peripersonal space (i.e. a sense of space within reaching distance) and extrapersonal space (i.e. the sense of space beyond reaching distance) are shown by cognitive experiments to be remapped when using a tool. The tool, as an extension of the mechanics of body in space, extends one's sense of 'nearness'.[81] Similarly, peri-hand space, in which vision and touch are integrated, is spatially extended during tool use in direct correlation with the length of the tool and, more specifically, with its functionally effective length.[82]

I conclude with a final example relevant to my inquiry into the brain-hand-tool complex. Results of neuroscience experiments on grasping implied that, when using a handheld tool such as pliers to grasp another object, motor representations of the way that we would grasp that object with our own hand are instantiated for guiding the grip orientation of the tool. fMRI data have indicated that the same areas of the motor cortex are activated when planning a grasp either with the hand or with the mechanics of a handheld tool. This strongly suggests that motor representations for manual actions (i.e. actions performed directly with our biological effectors) provide the operational basis for orienting and manipulating the clasping or gripping components of a tool, thereby facilitating the 'transfer of skill' between hand and tool.[83] During use, the tool therefore becomes one with the skilled practice of the craftsperson's mind-body.

CONCLUDING REMARKS ON THE 'EXTENDABLE BODY'

The relation between brain, hand and tool is at once evolutionary, physical, neurological, psychological, cultural and social in nature. This multifaceted relation holds the key to what makes us human. Continued engagement by social and natural scientists in exploring the everyday manifestations of this remarkable union is essential to understanding the intelligent hand

and better appreciating the depth and breadth of craft skills, as well as other tool-wielding activities. Mastering a tool, after all, modifies and expands our integrated cognitive and physical capacities.

Importantly, the intricacy of the brain-hand-tool relationship lays to rest any lingering credence in mind-body dualism, and goes one step further by disclosing the inseparable relation between mind, body and environment. It also makes plain the unfeasibility of a fully 'natural' or 'normal' body. The physical, neurological and psychological convergence of human and machine renders it difficult, if not impossible, to determine where the body begins and ends. In their *Assembling Bodies* exhibition catalogue, curators Anita Herle, Mark Elliot and Rebecca Empson observed that: 'Technologies intended to augment or enhance the body often extend the body [through time and space] beyond its corporeal boundaries. They do not make the body "whole", but add to it in a process that has no preordained end.'[84] The technologies referred to include prehistoric stone implements, modern-day craft and trade tools, handheld weaponry, spectacles, dentures, wooden legs and simple prosthetics. It also included external and internal attachments of advanced robotic prosthetics and the kinds of functionally sophisticated implants popularly associated with the creation of cyborgs.[85]

Over the past century, medicine, mechanical engineering, material sciences and nanotechnology have tightened the weave between human biology and technological creation. Major advances, for example, were made in plastic surgery during the First World War, setting the technological and procedural groundwork for modern cosmetic surgery that now employs a wide range of synthetic implants for body enhancement, 'correction' and alteration. Developments in artificial pacemakers witnessed transformation from the portable plug-in machines of the 1920s to the first external wearable pacemakers in 1957, followed a year later by a fully implantable device that has since undergone vast improvement in term of its design and function.

Prostheses, too, have evolved from purely aesthetic replacements for missing limbs, eyes and teeth, fashioned in wood, glass, plastics and other materials, to robotic prosthesis integrated with, and directly controlled by, the body's neuromuscular system.[86] Advances in prosthetic limbs, hands and feet have reached the point whereby prosthetics now offer arguably significant advantages over our real, fully functional body parts. Prosthetic technology also moved to the internal reaches of the body in the form of joint replacements, valves and operational components of organs.

Communities of researchers strive to develop cognitive prosthetics that will functionally replace missing, damaged or 'malfunctioning' parts of the brain. To this list of 'internal tools' that supplement and improve the workings of our body-mind can be added *in vitro* fertilisation,[87] customised stem cells for growing and replacing human organs, future designs for refashioning sight with 'video vision' and micro- and macro-bionic eye implants, installing built-in sensor devices, and embedding brain data or knowledge chips.[88]

Already three decades ago, anthropologist Emily Martin pointed out that in the era of late capitalism, characterised by 'technological innovation, specificity, and rapid, flexible change', the processes of labour were accelerating and the pace of deskilling and reskilling was intensifying.[89] While regimes of perpetual (re)training seemingly fulfil ideas of continual learning and work as a productive challenge resulting in personal growth, such regimes in fact power the neoliberal drive for a flexible workforce, short contracts, and diminished responsibility and obligations of employers.[90] Martin correctly identified the need for more dedicated studies of the experiences of labourers in relation to the pressures of time and the constant changes in tasks and tools. In Chapter 6, I addressed the advent and advance of computer numerical control (CNC) machinery and the practical and psychological impacts that it was having, and might have, on contemporary fine woodworkers. 'What does it mean for the future of our craft?' some pondered. What long-term implications will it and the expanding branches of related technologies have, I ask, for the 'intelligent hand' – the marker and maker of our species?[91]

If I dare to speculate about what the future trajectories might be, my guess is that forthcoming computing, digital, robotic, prosthetic and bionic discoveries have two possible outcomes. They could further diminish, or even extinguish, the practical and economic needs for skilled handwork. That result would, in the words of McGinn, 'cause a sickness of the soul far greater than any technological or social change yet inflicted on us'.[92] Or, alternatively and more optimistically, the new tools and technologies will be fashioned to incorporate and nurture our deeply human need to touch, exercise dexterity and propagate our ancestral brain-hand-tool connections.

Haptic technologies have progressed a long way from computer mice and joysticks to cutting-edge developments that produce cutaneous sensations in the user, allowing for virtual interaction with three-dimensional shapes and volumes. The future horizons in this field are vast. Human geographer Mark Paterson predicted the coming of 'software that gives the illusion of solidity, elasticity, texture and all touch-based properties of visual objects, in conjunction with force-feedback hardware . . . [thereby] feeling the force and resistance of tools and materials'.[93] The reality of this science is now on our doorstep. For craftspeople, it may create new opportunities for collaborative design, and potentially for collaborative making 'by hand'. If so, the evolution of the wondrous relationship between brain, hand and tools is set to continue.

NOTES

An earlier and briefer version of this chapter was published as 'Knowledge in Hand', in R. Fardon, O. Harris, T.H.J. Marchand, M. Nuttall, C. Shore, V. Strang and R.A. Wilson (eds), *The Sage Handbook of Social Anthropology*, Volume 2, Part 4: 'Futures' (London: Sage, 2012), 261–72. I also directed a short documentary film, *The Intelligent Hand*, with footage shot at the Building Crafts College during my second period of fieldwork in 2012–13. The subject material has been reworked and updated, and the scope of discussion and references to ethnographic material significantly expanded in preparing the text for this chapter.

1. Rose, *The Village Carpenter*, 40.
2. Within England's woodworking communities, references to the idealised 'village carpenter' continued for many decades after Rose's publication. In 1940, for example, the Vice President of the Institute of Carpenters described one member of its Western Section, Dom Christopher Batley, a monk of Princknash Abbey, as 'the living example' of Rose's village carpenter.
3. Thornton, 'How an Adze'.
4. Rose, *The Village Carpenter*, 55.
5. See also Hohn, 'A Romance of Rust', 49.
6. Rose, *The Village Carpenter*, 54–55.
7. Hohn suggests that tools, more strongly than any other human artefact, 'retain the traces of their owners' ('A Romance of Rust', 56).
8. Rose, *The Village Carpenter*, 49–50.
9. On the coevolution of brain, hand and tool, see also François Sigaut, whose main argument is that tools made humankind rather than the reverse (Sigaut, *Comment Homo Devint Faber*).
10. Bell, *The Hand*, 87.
11. Heidegger, 'What Calls for Thinking?', 357.
12. McGinn, *Prehension*, 73 (emphasis added).
13. Wilson, *The Hand*, 307.
14. Oakley, *Man the Tool-Maker*.
15. Mead, *Cultural Patterns*, 257.
16. Taylor, *Tools of the Trade*, 5.
17. Sloane, *A Museum*, 2.
18. See Leakey, *Olduvai Gorge*.
19. Marzke, 'Precision Grips'; and Marzke and Marzke, 'Evolution of the Human Hand'.
20. Washburn, 'Tools and Human Evolution'; and Peeters et al., 'The Representation of Tool Use'.
21. Greenfield, 'Language, Tools and Brain'; Frey, 'Tool Use'; McGinn, *Prehension*, 59–66.
22. Maynard, Greenfield and Childs, 'Culture, History, Biology, and Body'; and Maynard, Subrahmanyam and Greenfield, 'Technology'.
23. Exceptions include, for example, drinking straws, which are manipulated, at least in part, with the mouth. Upper-limb amputees also learn to use their feet and mouths to perform many of the tasks that handed individuals habitually execute with tools.
24. For classic examples in the anthropology of craft/sport and apprenticeship, see Coy, *Apprenticeship*; Dilley, 'Tukolor Weavers'; Downey, *Learning Capoeira*; Goody, 'Learning, Apprenticeship and the Division of Labour'; Gowlland, *Reinventing Craft in China*; Herzfeld, *The Body Impolitic*; Lave, *Apprenticeship*; Lave and Wenger, *Sit-*

uated Learning; Makovicky, 'Something to Talk about'; O'Connor, 'Embodied Knowledge'; Portisch, 'The Craft of Skilful Learning'; Rice, *Hearing and the Hospital*; Sinclair, *Making Doctors*; Stoller, *The Taste of Ethnographic Things*; and Wacquant, *Body and Soul*.

25. Wilson, *The Hand*, 277.
26. Risatti, *A Theory of Craft*, 109.
27. See also Rose, *The Mind at Work*; Crawford, *Shop Class*; and Paradise and Rogoff, 'Side by Side'.
28. Baker, 'Anthropological Notes'.
29. In support of historic attributions of supernatural powers to the hand, contemporary philosopher Colin McGinn states that 'the naturally evolved human hand is the nearest thing to magic in the known universe – though it is a perfectly natural biological organ that evolved from the fin of a fish' (*Prehension*, 125).
30. Cushing, 'Manual Concepts', 289–90, emphasis in original.
31. Ibid., 308.
32. Hertz, 'The Pre-eminence of the Right Hand'. Hertz originally published this essay in French in 1909.
33. Ibid., 336.
34. For example, Needham, 'The Left Hand of the Mugwe'; Needham, 'Right and Left in Nyoro Symbolic Classification'; and Mines, 'Models of Caste'.
35. Tenhouten, 'The Eclipse of the Sacred', 16.
36. Durkheim, *The Division of Labour*.
37. Tenhouten, 'The Eclipse of the Sacred', 22.
38. Exceptions include a number of excellent anthropological studies of the use of hand gesture and deictic pointing in communication, including, for example, Hutchins and Palen, 'Constructing Meaning'; Haviland, 'Pointing, Gesture Spaces, and Mental Maps'; and Endfield, 'The Body as a Cognitive Artifact'.
39. Cited in Pallasmaa, *The Thinking Hand*, 54.
40. McGinn, *Prehension*, 117.
41. Wilson, *The Hand*, 73.
42. Prehensility is displayed not only by hands, but also by toes, monkey tails, elephant trunks and the snouts of marsupials. In differentiation from prehensile movements, nonprehensile ones are hand and finger interactions with an object, instrument or material that do not involve grasping.
43. Wilson, *The Hand*, 120.
44. Ibid., 161. For a detailed clinical study of grasps, see Edwards, Buckland and McCoy-Powlen, *Developmental and Functional Hand Grasps*.
45. Wilson, *The Hand*, 120.
46. For a more detailed discussion of the proactive and reactive properties of touch, see Sennett, *The Craftsman*, 152.
47. Pallasmaa, *The Thinking Hand*, 26.
48. Sennett, *The Craftsman*, 152.
49. Ibid., 164–65.
50. Wilson, *The Hand*, 159.
51. Ibid., 160–62.
52. A housing joint is a simple rectangular channel cut across the grain of a board that 'houses' the end of another board slotted in perpendicularly (e.g. a shelf slotted into the vertical ends of a bookcase).

53. Wilson, *The Hand*, 162.
54. Rose, *The Mind at Work*, 78.
55. Ibid., 76.
56. Richard Sennett wrote that there is wide consensus among craftspeople, artists and musicians that mastery demands a minimum of 10,000 hours of practice (Sennett, *The Craftsman*, 172).
57. Gibson, *The Ecological Approach*.
58. Grasseni, 'Communities of Practice'.
59. Millroy, 'An Ethnographic Study', 173.
60. On embodied mathematising, see also Marchand, 'Toward an Anthropology'.
61. In my survey of the brain science literature, I discovered an underlying assumption that human spatial understanding is universally manifested from an egocentric perspective. Ethnographic studies of spatial relativity, however, reveal that some individuals or cultural groups display a strong propensity to calculate the location of an object or thing relative to neighbouring objects or to absolute frames of reference. See, for example, Levinson, 'Relativity in Spatial Conception and Description'; and Senft, *Referring to Space*.
62. Takahashi, Diedrichsen and Watt, 'Integration of Vision'.
63. Ingold, 'Walking the Plank', 73.
64. Rose, *The Mind at Work*, 78–79. See also Weber, Dixon and Llorente, 'Studying Invention', 485–86.
65. Ryle, 'Pleasure, Part I', 142.
66. In Arabic and French, for example, object noun and action verb are derived from the same root. For example, in Arabic, saw (n) منشر (v) نشر; hammer (n) مدقة (v) دق; chisel (n) منقاش (v) نقش; plane (n) مسحخ (v) سحخ. And in French, saw (n) *scie* (v) *scier*; hammer (n) *marteau* (v) *marteler*; chisel (n) *ciseau* (v) *ciseler*; plane (n) *rabot* (v) *raboter*.
67. Martin et al., 'The Neural Correlates'.
68. Grafton et al., 'Premotor Cortex Activation'.
69. The premotor cortex and supplementary motor area are part of the overall motor cortex located at the posterior of the frontal lobe.
70. Ingold, 'Walking the Plank', 71.
71. Grosz, *Volatile Bodies*, 80.
72. Cited in Rose, *The Mind at Work*, 79.
73. Mercer, *Ancient Carpenters' Tools*.
74. Preiss and Sternberg, 'Technologies for Working Intelligence', 204.
75. Rose, *The Mind at Work*, 79.
76. Grafton et al., 'Premotor Cortex Activation'.
77. Updike, 'Tools', 134.
78. Holmes et al., 'Tool-Use'.
79. Takahashi, Diedrichsen and Watt, 'Integration of Vision'.
80. Holmes and Spence, 'The Body Schema'.
81. Berti and Frassinetti, 'When Far Becomes Near'.
82. Farne, Iriki and Ladavas, 'Shaping Multisensory Action-Space'.
83. Jacob, Danielmeier and Frey, 'Human Anterior Intraparietal and Ventral Premotor Cortices'. See also Umilta et al., 'When Pliers Become Fingers'.

84. Herle, Elliot and Empson, *Assembling Bodies*, 77. The exhibition was held at the University of Cambridge Museum of Archaeology and Anthropology from March 2009 to November 2010.

85. NASA scientists Manfred Clynes and Nathan Kline coined the term 'cyborg' in 1960 to refer to a body altered by machines that would expand our human capacity for space exploration. Charles Laughlin observed that 'the emergence of the cyborg is a process of progressive technological penetration into the body, eventually replacing or augmenting the structures that mediate the various physical and mental attributes that we normally consider natural to human beings' (Laughlin, 'The Evolution of Cyborg Consciousness', 147 and 154).

86. See Nelson, 'Phantom Limbs'.

87. Classen, 'Touch and Technology'.

88. Harris, 'The Head of the Blue Chip II'.

89. Martin, 'The End of the Body?', 122–23.

90. See Deleuze, 'Postscript'.

91. Colin McGinn poses a similar question in the conclusion of his book *Prehension*, 147.

92. Ibid., 148.

93. Paterson, 'Digital Touch', 434.

CHAPTER 8

PROBLEM SOLVING AT THE WORKBENCH

⌒⌒⌒

'Being in the zone' and operating in oneness with tools, materials and fellow collaborators on a project is a source of profound pleasure, but it is only a part of the story of skilled handwork. Learning and practising a craft inevitably involves periodic ruptures to the 'flow' and making mistakes. Problem solving is therefore a core activity of craftwork – arguably *the* core activity – and one that gives rise to the pleasures of overcoming obstacles, learning new things and discovering greater self-sufficiency.

Even the most seasoned expert is susceptible to error when experimenting with different tools, methods or materials, or when confronting a novel design or an unforeseen challenge. Mistakes also occur when distracted, when mentally or physically fatigued, or when having an 'off day'. A degree of risk is inherent to all handwork. Craftsman and instructor David Pye correctly observed that craftsmanship 'depends on the judgement, dexterity and care which the maker exercises as he works', and 'the result is continually at risk during the process of making'.[1]

Risk in handwork extends beyond control of mind-body activities to encompass the variable quality and performance of tools and the properties of materials. The design or function of a tool, for instance, might not be entirely proficient for the task at hand. A tool might also malfunction during operation or become blunt, misaligned or defective in some other manner with use or through inadequate maintenance. Materials – especially natural ones such as timber, stone or clay – possess distinctive characteristics, inconsistencies and 'flaws' that behave and respond in sometimes unpredictable or unforeseen ways to applied actions with hand or tool. A plank of timber may contain hidden knots, patches of gummy resin, splits or shakes, inconsistent grain direction, complicated figure, or uneven density and hardness. Any of these can cause mishaps with the tool or misjudgement on the part of the woodworker, resulting in, for example, an imperfect cut, an uneven or flaked surface, a skewed drill hole or the removal of too much timber from the component being made.

Timber is a costly material and so too is the labour that goes into transforming it into architectural joinery or cabinetry. Discarding a piece of timber each time an error is made and beginning anew is economically unviable for a workshop and for a vocational college. Waste of timber resources also contravened the widely shared aspiration among trainees at the Building Crafts College and among the makers I met to practise in environmentally sustainable ways. It was understood that mastering the centuries-old methods of woodworking contributed significantly to minimising waste since, as explained by artisan and author Roger Coleman, they had evolved to 'accommodate the nature of the materials, stabilise and neutralise internal stresses and tensions, and produce sound durable piece[s] of work with deceptive ease'.[2]

Because carpentry, like all handicrafts, is a 'workmanship of risk' and the potential for slip-ups is persistently present, learning to quickly and correctly identify dangers or errors and to make corresponding adjustments or repairs is absolutely essential. In fine woodworking, for example, mistakes made in the shaping of individual components for a piece of architectural joinery or furniture are often not apparent until the project is dry-assembled (i.e. without glue) in a test run. At that point, the woodworker might notice that the fit between joints is too tight or too loose, that the assembly is 'out of square' or that there is a misalignment in depth between the finished surfaces of joined components. Identifying the exact location, cause and nature of the problem involves a little detective work, which may delay production, but progresses learning.

Speed, efficiency and accuracy in solving problems come with experience, and such experience is gained only through making mistakes in the first place and in setting them right. College instructor John W. actively encouraged students to develop their own problem-solving methods as they progressed through the fine-woodwork programme. 'By second year', he said, 'I expect them to come to me not with a problem but with a proposed solution. It might not be the right one, but at least we have a starting point for a discussion about planning a way forward.' John firmly believed that: 'If students come up with their own solutions, they'll remember them better.'

The previous chapters illustrated that accomplished craftsmanship demands a remarkable set of attitudes, postures and activities. These include patient perseverance, devotion to continuous learning and long hours of practice, critical self-awareness, acute attunement to one's total working environment, good bodily posture and steady balance, nimble grasp of the tool(s), quick hand-eye coordination, responsive application of force and pressure, and a feeling for fluid movement and a sense of rhythm. Perhaps most impressive is the craftsperson's dynamic ability to recalibrate all of these in a seamless dialogue with the constantly changing nature of the work undertaken. Unsurprisingly, achieving such synchronicity and efficiency of thought and movement is highly challenging for the neophyte, and the learning curve is steep. To master a craft, the challenge must be embraced and problems encountered along the way need to be reconceptualised as opportunities.

This chapter presents a detailed exploration of the ways that mistakes are identified, problems conceived and solutions found at the workbench, and of the pleasure gained and confidence won in doing so. From the viewpoint of 'situated cognition', any kind of problem – carpentry ones included – is anchored in a concrete setting and resolved by 'reasoning in situation-specific ways, making use of the material and cultural resources locally available'.[3] Drawing on his many years of experience as an instructor of bicycle mechanics, educator Tom Martin noted that: 'Pedagogical strategy should ensure that students relate to a subject with lived experience and learn something that is clearly situated in their larger understanding of the world.'[4] In arguing for the adoption of an 'alternative epistemology' in teaching approaches, he aptly observed that 'only in the messy process of examining how we know things can we design situations that respect the learner'.[5] The case study featured in this chapter illustrates how that epistemology in teaching might ideally play out in all places of learning, including school classrooms.

BACKGROUND TO THE STUDY

The observations and analyses I present focus on a single example from among the many one-on-one sessions between trainees and instructors that I video-recorded during my second period of fieldwork at the Building Crafts College. The daily practice of sorting out slip-ups and repairing gaffes is more often undertaken by a carpenter working on their own, and in silence (or possibly speaking aloud or silently to themself). But when problem solving unfolds between two individuals, their thoughts, ideas and strategies are verbally communicated as well as practically negotiated through their coordinated, and at times not-so-coordinated, activities. The processes entailed in solving a problem are thereby more immediately accessible to the researcher's observation, transcription and analysis.

Additionally, my recording of workbench sessions captured the dynamics of teaching and learning, and of communicating and interpreting techniques in spoken language and with the body. Trainees were not only supported in identifying their mistake(s) and devising suitable remedies, but, occasionally, they also benefited from the instructor's adept demonstrations of handling the timber and proper tool use. This was the case in the example presented in this chapter.

In 2012–13, I conducted ten video data capture sessions at the College with the assistance of a professional cameraman. The sessions were spread across year one of the fine-woodwork programme, starting on the first day of training for the new cohort. The study had two objectives. The first was to document the progression of four students (of a total of fifteen first-year trainees) in learning and mastering basic hand tools. Data capture involved the use of cameras at fixed front and side views of the trainees at their workbenches, while absorbed in sawing, planing and chiselling. Using motion-capture software, the video clips enabled me to execute a detailed analysis of postures, grasps, gestures and movements, to monitor rates of improvement (or not) and, in some cases, to identify the evolution of an individual's personal style of practice.

The second objective, and one pertinent to the subject of this book, was to video-record on-the-spot workbench tutorials between programme instructors and individual trainees. These unscheduled tutorials normally took place when instructors were making their rounds of the workshop and spotted a struggling student or if a trainee expressly requested assistance. Most workbench exchanges revolved around identifying and resolving problems encountered while carrying out basic carpentry exercises or more complex design-and-making projects.

The video clip selected for writing this chapter is of a one-to-one workbench tutorial session between Cheryl M., who, by that point, had replaced Con as first-year convenor, and Neil, a first-year trainee with no previous woodworking experience.[6] Neil was also one of the four trainees who volunteered to participate in my detailed study of tool-wielding practices. The tutorial between Cheryl and Neil lasted seven minutes and forty-six seconds, centring on an ill-fitting timber joint that Neil was making.

The detailed transcription I present contains more than merely the dialogue between the two protagonists and an account of the carpentry exercise in question. It includes a 'thick' description of postures and movements, as well as hand gestures and the ways in which either party investigated the timber and carpentry joints through touch. It reports how visual judgement was employed, the ways that sight lines and shared focal points were established, and how available light sources in the workshop were optimised for carrying out visual assessments of the timber components. Throughout the exchange, I note the selection of various carpentry tools and other utensils, and the ways these were used by either party to point, measure, compare and repair. I describe how the instructor scrutinised Neil's lines and the indentations made with pencil and marking gauge respectively while preparing his timber components. In doing so, Cheryl was able to 'excavate' and interpret the student's previous procedures, to judge the accuracy of his saw cuts and to detect where the trouble spots lay. The transcription also includes observations of the ways instructor and trainee tested the components using basic principles of physics in order to diagnose the joint trouble.

Finally, the transcription endeavours to capture the fluctuating rhythms of the exchange between Cheryl and Neil, and to record their use of humour, changing facial expressions and the mutability of emotional states, including feelings of frustration, bewilderment and accomplishment. Those details serve to more accurately identify the convergences and divergences in communication and understanding between the two woodworkers, as well as their struggles to speak, to do and to be heard.

Like my first fieldwork at the Building Crafts College, the second study involved in-depth audio-recorded interviews with the trainees and instructors. By interweaving material from Neil's interview with the transcription of the workbench tutorial, the chapter offers insights into the young man's educational background, individual ways of learning, attitudes towards different teaching methods, and his recent attraction to woodworking. Such insights flag up moments during the tutorial when the instructor successfully accommodated Neil's preferred mode of learning (or not) and, likewise, when Neil resisted or was less responsive to Cheryl's preferred methods of teaching.

Cheryl's professional experience and teaching philosophy were shared in Chapter 5, but I include here additional interview material that is directly relevant to the topic of problem solving. Ultimately, the detailed account aims to make apparent the complexity and thickness of exchange and knowledge making that unfolded between both parties in a short period of time, and in their collaborative efforts to resolve an elementary problem.

NEIL: REFLECTIONS ON LEARNING AND EDUCATION

At the time of our interview together, Neil was nineteen years old. He was tall, slim and broad-shouldered, with a mop of thick sandy-coloured hair, bright blue eyes and clear Nordic skin. He lived in Kentish Town, North London, with his mother and two younger brothers, aged ten and one. Neil went to secondary school at Haverstock in Chalk Farm where he also completed his A level exams, including one in art. 'I've always been quite into art', he told me. 'That was my thing. I liked painting and drawing. It was my way of being creative.' Though he was placed in the 'gifted and talented' programme, he confessed that reading and writing weren't his strengths, and though he 'did quite good in art', he failed to get an A-grade because he 'didn't do the essays'. 'I would get told off because I was doing my own thing', he recounted. 'I'd spend a week or two working on the same painting while the others were doing loads of things and writing.'

When his schoolmate Stephen applied to the art foundation course at Central Saint Martin's College of Arts and Design, Neil briefly contemplated doing the same. His father had been a student there, and both his parents, he told me, were 'quite arty'. But instead, he opted to continue working as a fashion model – something he had been doing since year ten. 'I was enjoying the modelling a lot. I wasn't really keen on Saint Martins. I would have been going to uni[versity] just to have a lot of fun, and I didn't think it was worth paying the 30 grand for that.' Modelling paid well and it allowed Neil to travel to new places and meet what he described as 'high-profile' people. Together, these things gave him 'a massive social life'.

Two years after A levels, Neil bumped into Stephen, who by that time had dropped out of the art foundation programme. Stephen enthusiastically shared his latest find: the fine-woodwork course at the Building Crafts College. As Neil discovered more information about the programme and drew the connection between training in joinery and a possible future as a furniture maker, it struck him for the first time that this was something he could really picture himself doing. 'Why didn't I know about this, or think about this before?' he asked himself. He described his newfound option of furniture making as a 'massive world of creativity waiting to happen'. The 'hands-on' aspect of the trade held great appeal: 'It's not like just making marks on paper or canvas', he mused, 'It's hands-on, with objects.' In addition, he spoke about the 'deep satisfaction' that he derived from following a project all the way through, from start to finish.

Like Stephen, Neil had no prior woodworking experience. 'I never sawed anything. Never held a chisel', he admitted. Nonetheless, after the first few weeks at the workbench, he was confident of having made the right choice. Weighing up the differences between his previous employment as a fashion model and carpentry work, he concluded: 'I read about friends from modelling in the newspaper, and I sometimes think I'm missing out. What I'm doing now is so different: I'm sawing and chiselling in a workplace. But, I'm definitely doing something I enjoy and something that I'm going to get more out of in the long run.'

The college training regime was considerably different and allegedly more challenging than the teaching-learning dynamics Neil had experienced during A levels. He claimed that students in his secondary school would get 'a hell-of-a lot of praise' merely for demonstrating interest in doing the work and wanting to learn, regardless of actually doing the work or the results they achieved. Reflecting on that situation, he resolved that: 'You don't get praise like that in the real world. You're supposed to do your work. And when you've done it, you're given more to do.' He viewed the College as an important step for him towards joining that 'real' world.

On their rounds between workbenches, the woodwork instructors pointed out mistakes and informed trainees when they were doing it wrong. 'At first, I was like "Where's my praise?" Not anymore, Neil! Slap in the face. You're in reality now!' Neil chuckled while describing the adjustments he was having to make in attitude and self-discipline. On the other hand, he added, 'I went to a school where we were all throwing chairs around the classroom, so this place is pretty relaxed by comparison'. In general, the workshop environment was conducive to Neil's preferred mode of creative learning and exploring, and to getting on with work.

Patience and concentration, according to Neil, were the two most essential aptitudes demanded by fine woodworking. A woodworker needs to 'enjoy being with their own thoughts and zone out', he told me. In my conversations with other woodworkers, the importance of 'zoning in' was underscored, or many spoke of the elation they experienced while being 'in the zone'. I therefore asked Neil to describe what he meant by 'zoning out'. 'Sometimes when I'm doing something creative, like here [at the College] or when I was doing my art', he explained, 'I'll be conscious of other things that I'm already thinking about. Instead, I just want to relax and stop "thinking" – just concentrate and let it flow.' His objective was to be immersed in tasks, such as cutting and chopping joints.

At first, Neil strained to describe 'zoning out', and more particularly to differentiate in words between a distractive kind of thinking *about* which displaces awareness from the present moment – spatially, temporally and eventfully – and thinking *in* the present activity. 'I don't know if you know what I mean?' he asked. 'But sometimes I'm really aware of what I'm thinking about, and other times, if I'm doing something, I don't even realise what I'm thinking. But then all of a sudden I've realised something; I've answered a question; I've done what I'm doing.' In referring to an extracurricular woodcarving course that he was taking in the evening, Neil added: 'I zone out of everything around me and tune in. I'm not really aware of what I'm thinking. I'm *in* my thoughts.' It emerged that his 'zoning out' was a complementary process to becoming 'attuned' to the job at hand, since achieving the latter demanded the former. His explanation candidly captured the idea that doing something 'mindlessly' does not equate to doing something without thinking, but rather quite the reverse: it implies full, undivided mind-body absorption in the task.

In order to achieve that absorption, Neil frequently relied on music to tune out distractions and other abrasive disturbances. The workshop environment was sometimes noisy, with the deafening screech of routers, jocular

bantering over workbenches and occasional bouts of boisterousness emanating from the ground floor below the fine-woodwork mezzanine, where
the bench-joinery apprentices trained. In the fine-woodwork cohort was a
grouping of three young men, their workbenches positioned side by side,
who regularly broke into song, *a cappella* style. Numerous other trainees, including Neil, complained that the 'merry chorus' was a nuisance, hindering
their efforts to focus.

Although students were not technically permitted to wear headsets,
Cheryl and her assistant Kate tolerated MP3 players at the workbench, as
long as the volume was kept reasonably low and earphone cords were concealed beneath clothing, safely out of snagging distance from tools, timber
planks and moving limbs. 'Music's a big mood changer for me', Neil commented. 'I put on Miles Davis. It's calming and I get on with my work.' He
listened to a variety of 'relaxing happy music', mainly blues, jazz and reggae,
but a little house music, too, especially on a Friday afternoon. 'Music gets me
in the rhythm. It keeps me in good, positive attitude. And sometimes I move
in time with the music as well' when tooling the timber. How this affected
his carpentry results, I cannot report. Nevertheless, when confronting obstacles while woodworking or discovering mistakes that are bound to thwart
progress, it is indeed important to hold on to a 'positive attitude'.

JOINT TROUBLE

In week nine of term one, Neil was working on a Redwood pine frame. The
objective of the assignment was to practice making various kinds of wood
joints along the length of a stile (i.e. the two vertical side members of a
frame-and-panel door). In addition to a bridle joint and a typical 'through'
mortise-and-tenon joint (in which the tenon passes 'through' the entire
width of the stile and its end-grain is revealed on the side from which it
exits), the exercise also included a more challenging 'stopped' (or 'stub')
mortise-and-tenon. In the 'stopped' version, the depth of the mortise is
chopped to about three-quarters the width of the stile so that the inserted
tenon does not pass all the way through and the joint is elegantly concealed
(see Chapter 4, Figure 4.3 for an illustration of basic timber joints).

After carefully marking out two pieces of timber, Neil picked up a tenon
saw to cut a tenon at the end of the timber component that would serve as
the rail (i.e. a horizontal structural member in a door frame with tenons at
either end that fit into the mortises of the stiles). Using a mortise chisel and
mallet, he chopped out the corresponding mortise at the midway point along
the stile. Neil snugly fitted the tenon into the mortise, but, when he laid the
T-shaped assembly flat on his workbench, he discovered that it rocked back

and forth very slightly. In some way, the two components were misaligned and he would need to identify the problem and correct it, or else begin the assignment all over again. Fine woodworkers are trained to strive for minimal tolerances of less than one millimetre, and such accuracy constituted a weighty criterion in project assessment at the College.

Neil disassembled the joint and carefully rechecked his measurements and the faint pencil traces of his marking lines on the surfaces of both components. To his eye they appeared correct, but the imperfect fit implied that a mistake had been made. Neil quietly studied the assembly for some time on his own, and without results, before summoning the courage to ask a workshop instructor for assistance.

Later, in conversation together, Neil complained that he wasn't getting the attention he had grown accustomed to in school:

> Sometimes I want to get help, but I can't get it. With me, if I'm stuck, I'll wait around. I'm really bad at asking for help. This is why I'm a bit behind. I would prefer [the instructors] to come around and ask, 'How's it going?' It was a big step – even now – for me to say: 'Can you help me here?'

Neil also spoke to me about a growing division in the workshop between those who were picking up the skills quickly and those, like himself, who were struggling to keep up and sensing that they weren't getting their fair share of attention. 'Now, I just do it for myself', he said:

> I'm not going to wait around all day. If I do it wrong, then I do it wrong. That's a bit of a downer, but, well … that's how you learn. I want to do it right the first time, but now I realise that I'm going to have to get things wrong.

Neil's burgeoning independence was precisely what Cheryl wanted for all her students. 'When they've looked and they can't find where the error is, that's when they call me over', she explained:

> They're gaining the confidence to try working things out for themselves, and they've got bench partners to talk to as well. But if there's something they think is crucially wrong and they can't quite put their finger on it, then it's my role to ask them questions: what have they checked for? How have they checked for it?

Cheryl's questions were aimed at scaffolding students in extending their grasp of both the source and the nature of an obstacle. She confirmed that teaching students to solve their problems is a two-way dialogue. 'They're learning nothing if I give them a list of things. It's not about me saying, "Yeah, do that, that, and that, and it'll be fine." That's the end of teaching, isn't it?' she asked rhetorically. 'It's about how you get the individual to learn. Getting them to understand what they need to look out for. Where do they need to look for it? What can they rule out? And where do they need to start?' In writing on the processes of transfer, educator Stephen Billett underscored the importance of a mentor's guidance for supporting learners to:

> understand what they do not know; to support them with the procedures that they have not yet developed, let alone honed; and also to represent and perhaps model the kinds of values and dispositions that underpin, support or direct the thinking and acting required for effective performance . . . in the workplace.[7]

Cheryl arrived and took up a stance at the centre of the workbench. Neil, a full foot taller, shuffled sideways to stand at Cheryl's left. Their relative positioning silently defined a shared focal space surrounding the carpentry project lying on the worktop in front of them. It also reaffirmed the instructor–student relationship that underpinned the tenor of the ensuing exchange. Cheryl took a small steel ruler from the breast pocket of her white lab coat, pressed it flush against the worktop and passed it beneath the T-shaped assembly to verify that, indeed, there was a tiny gap, likely resulting from a flawed joint between the rail and the stile. Grasping the assembly lightly with both hands while keeping it flat on the worktop, she then ran the tip of her right index finger over the seam of the joint:

Figure 8.1 Fine-woodwork instructor Cheryl and first-year trainee Neil collaboratively exploring the trouble with Neil's stopped mortise-and-tenon joint, 2012. © Trevor H.J. Marchand

'This piece feels like it's. . .' Without completing her utterance, Cheryl picked up the assembly and turned it over, setting it back down on the worktop on its opposite face to examine further.

Leaning with his elbows on the worktop and moving in closer to Cheryl, Neil reached with his left hand into the focal space and, while touching the seam between the two components, inquired softly 'Could it be on *this* side somewhere. . .?'

Absorbed in her own thinking, Cheryl interjected, redirecting Neil's attention to what she was examining: 'Right, have a look at *that*.' She placed her right hand on top of the stile, near to where it joined the rail. The instructor began: 'If we look at it from the other side. . .', and she completed her thought by physically demonstrating how the two joined components rocked back and forth.

Neil grunted understanding.

'So that's. . . that's lower down', she said, pointing to the bottom face of the rail where it joined the stile. 'And so when I press on *there*. . .' Cheryl moved her hand back to the top of the stile component and rocked it by pressing down with her middle finger, once again finishing her statement with the physical action. 'Remember?' she asked Neil, referring to an earlier conversation they had, 'I said this looks like it's tilting.'

'Yeah.' Neil leaned in closer to watch Cheryl's fingers pressing down on the top of the stile.

'It clearly is, isn't it?' Cheryl declared. 'So if we pull these apart', she continued, while teasing the tenon out of the mortise, 'let's make sure it isn't one wonky piece or another wonky piece; that it's just a wonky joint.' In other words, Cheryl wanted to ascertain that the timber components were neither bent nor twisted, and that the actual problem lay with Neil's mortise-and-tenon joint. She touched the top of each of the separated pieces of timber simultaneously, pressing down lightly to check for rocking movement. Satisfied, she confirmed: 'So the pieces on their own aren't moving.'

Neil shot a sideway glance at Cheryl and then returned his focused gaze to her hands on the timber components.

'The pieces together', Cheryl began, while easing the tenon slowly back into the mortise, 'are only OK up to *there*.' The approximate location was identified by the sudden stiffening of her movement with the tenon. 'Then they're having to be pushed a little.' She demonstrated this by applying greater force to wiggle the tenon into the mortise. She then lifted the joined assembly from the worktop to examine it and pressed the two components tightly together. 'That's why they're not coming together on the shoulder', she attested, as she turned the T-shaped assembly in narrow profile for both she and Neil to observe. 'Because, if you look at this bit', she said while tapping the end of the stile with her index finger, 'you can see it's twisting over.' She then proposed with a smile: 'So let's make them happier together.'

While explaining procedures or correcting students' techniques, Cheryl occasionally anthropomorphised timber components, as well as tools, by assigning them emotions. By suggesting to Neil that they make the mortise and tenon 'happier together', she was inviting the student to empathise with the joint, and more particularly with the 'discomfort' that the tenon was experiencing while being forced into the mortise.

Cheryl's analogy made between human social relations and the relationship between mortise and tenon was a prompt for Neil to draw connections between something he presumably already knew from life with his new experiences of the carpentry task and the nature of timber. The power of analogies can effectively assist students in organising both their situated thinking about and actions with tools, materials and design-and-making practices, as well as with their behaviour and emotional dispositions. Analogies may be 'indexical to the immediate material environment in which they are produced' or belong to 'broader cultural and historical realities'.[8] In any case, they are jointly elaborated and collectively negotiated between instructor and trainee, and therefore students, like Neil, may elect to either adopt or abandon the conceptual resource, or possibly later 'recycle' it in the context of an entirely different task.[9]

In the example discussed above, Cheryl's introduction of an emotional dimension to the logistical basis of problem solving in craft incited a stronger bond between the young woodworker and his tools and materials, and promoted a greater investment of care in getting things right. A master woodworker's 'feel' for the timber and for the tool-in-hand comes in large measure from the empathy they develop through regular tool maintenance, sharpening blades and their constant haptic, visual and olfactory engagement with the medium, as was discussed in Chapter 7.

Cheryl was now preparing to more accurately identify the source of the trouble. 'I teach students what to look out for', she told me. 'The only reason I know is because, one, I've made the mistakes myself and had to correct them. You always remember your own mistakes better. And, two, because I've taught the same joints enough times to know where the danger points lay and where most people struggle. So', she continued, 'we can look at those first, and if we rule those out, then we can look at what's left.'

Cheryl put the assembled components back down on the worktop and eased the tenon out of the mortise with a gentle side-to-side motion. 'Let's start off with where they stopped being happy', she half said to Neil, half to herself. Moving the rail in towards the stile again, this time at an angle, Cheryl tested a corner of the tenon to the mortise opening. 'That already isn't. . .', she began. But, without completing the thought, she launched into another: 'If you look. . .' She paused briefly to rotate the assembly on the worktop so that Neil could gaze straight along the line of the tenon entering the mortise. 'The problem with *this* joint', she stated (implying a comparison between the 'stopped' mortise they were examining with the regular 'through' version), 'is that you can't see through from the other side.' She tapped the timber with her fingertips on the side opposite the mortise opening to reinforce the point. 'So, it's not like the bridle [joint] where it's all very open', gesturing cursorily with her right hand to the existing bridle joint at one end of Neil's stile. 'It's all very closed-in', she continued, 'and difficult to judge.'

Picking up, handling and physically rotating the individual or assembled components – either on the worktop or in mid-air – affords the woodworker different visual perspectives from which to assess the nature of the problem. Regular handling and rotating also cultivates the cognitive ability to mentally rotate, assemble and disassemble three-dimensional objects in the 'mind's eye'. This is an essential skill for imagining, creating and making artefacts, whether it is a woven textile, a clay vessel, blown glass, a piece of jewellery, a stone carving or a carpentry project.[10] It is also vital for problem solving when it is discovered that something, somewhere, in the thing being made has not gone to plan.

Making architectural joinery or furniture typically involves the assembly of two or more (and sometimes many) components, each with their own specified dimensions, shape, profiles and function in the final assembly. A carpenter needs to be able to visualise not only each individual component, but also how they fit together to make the whole, and make the whole hold together. The challenge of picturing and rotating joints in the mind's eye can be especially acute because joints are often (but not always) concealed from view and, depending on the kind of joint, the angles and configurations of the interlocking parts may be geometrically highly complex.[11]

The stopped mortise-and-tenon that Neil was making is not an especially complicated joint, but he and Cheryl nevertheless needed to picture what was happening when the outer surfaces of the tenon (i.e. the face cheeks, edge cheeks and shoulders) were coming into contact with the inner ones of the mortise. With practice, and through gradual exposure to increasingly complex joints, Neil's three-dimensional 'grasp' of their interlocking geometries and his capacity to design with select joinery elements for a project 'in mind' would strengthen.

As discussed in Chapter 4, the processes of designing architectural joinery or a piece of furniture typically involve conceptually imagining the desired properties, form or style of the object or thing to be made in tandem with sketching and technical drawing, and sometimes with producing rough mock-ups or smaller-scale models (i.e. maquettes).[12] Sketching, drawing and making models allow the carpenter to bring shape and sharper focus to their ideas, while carefully working out and scrutinising proportions and details.

At the start of any new workshop exercise, Cheryl and her co-instructor Kate displayed and circulated good finished examples that had been produced by previous cohorts of trainees. Visual and haptic interaction with the examples helped students to better visualise and understand what they were setting out to make. Routinely, the students were required to first produce technical drawings of the assigned project, which included dashed-line representations of the geometries of the interlocking joint components that were concealed from view. Producing full-scale rod drawings of all the elevations, enlarged detail drawings of the joints, an axonometric drawing,[13] and occasionally a scale model of either the complete project or a complicated part of it served not only to inform the subsequent processes of full-scale making in timber, but also to hone the woodworkers' skills in thinking about and imagining their project three-dimensionally.

By this point, Cheryl had snugly introduced one corner of the tenon diagonally into the mortise: 'If you look at *that*', directing Neil's attention. 'Feel *that*', she instructed, keeping her right hand on the stile and removing her left from the rail so that Neil could grasp and manoeuvre it himself. 'And push that just lightly.' Neil gently tested the fit by sliding the tenon in and out of the mortise, keeping the rail at the same angle to the stile as his teacher had set up. 'It feels happy, doesn't it?' Cheryl inquired.

'Yeah, it does', Neil nodded in agreement with a fixed stare on the assembly. While keeping hold of the stile with his left hand, he removed his right hand from the rail to make room for Cheryl, who in turn grasped it with her left.

'It feels fairly happy', Cheryl repeated. Then, changing the position of the rail to align the opposite corner of the tenon with the mortise opening, she said: 'Now, feel *that* and see what that feels like.' Neil resumed fitting the two components while Cheryl kept her right hand on the stile. 'Can you feel that there's. . .?' Without completing her question, Cheryl glanced at Neil before returning her gaze to the pieces of timber.

From the immediate context, Neil deduced that the teacher was asking if he felt an obstruction as he eased the tenon into the mortise, and he replied: 'At the end, yeah.' He continued feeling for the fit while intently scrutinising the joint components.

Cheryl's regular questioning kept Neil actively involved in the process, and it allowed her to gauge the student's comfort in that process and his level of understanding. Cheryl also employed the inclusive pronoun 'we' and the corresponding cohortatives (i.e. first person plural imperatives of verbs, for example, 'let's' [let us]), to periodically reinforce that the present task was a shared one, and that it was not the responsibility of the instructor alone to resolve the issue. Indeed, Neil would be expected to take ownership of similar problems arising in the future, and to independently manage the processes in finding solutions.

For now, however, both parties were focused on identifying the trouble with the fit between mortise and tenon. Their shared context, comprising the bounded space on Neil's worktop, the two timber components in question and the collaborative activity in which they were both engaged, facilitated the flow of their verbal communication. As demonstrated in the preceding dialogue between instructor and trainee, there was no need for Cheryl to verbally complete all of her statements or questions. The shared context enabled Neil to incrementally build a conceptual interpretation of Cheryl's utterance up to the point that she had finished speaking, and to thereby complete her utterance in his own mind and respond to it accordingly.

Arguably, the phenomenon of shared utterance, whereby parties in dialogue complete one another's utterances by either verbally interjecting or silently completing in the mind, occurs with greater frequency when both (or all) parties are absorbed in the same activity and intent on the same goal. It can also be expected that such conditions increase the likelihood that the hearer will formulate an accurate interpretation of what the speaker had in mind to say – but this is not always the case. As we will see, Neil wrongly completed Cheryl's unfinished statements at later points in their dialogue, and so the instructor needed to interject and generate her intended conclusion in order to steer the dialogue (and their shared problem solving) back on course.[14]

'Yeah, there's some squashing, isn't it', suggested Cheryl. Neil grunted agreement. 'Whether it's the top bit. . .', Cheryl mused aloud, while taking over the fitting of components from Neil, 'or the bottom bit?' After a brief pause, Cheryl proposed an answer to her own question, while sliding the tenon in and out of the mortise: 'I would say – if you look at *that*. . .' She pointed with her right index finger to draw Neil in for a closer look at the point where the tenon and mortise met. 'It looks like it might be more the bottom bit, doesn't it?' Cheryl retrieved the small metal ruler from the breast pocket of her coat to point to the mortise opening. 'That looks like a bit of a gap.'

'Yeah, because it lifts upward', concurred Neil, referring to the rail. He gestured a rising motion with his left hand to emphasise his hypothesis.

'Yeah, so. . .', Cheryl disassembled the components and lifted the stile from the worktop. 'It could be *in there*', she ventured, pointing inside the mortise. She then exchanged the stile for the rail to study the cheeks of the tenon. 'Or, it could be on the bottom of *this*', referring to the tenon. 'Let's have a look at the bottom of this first. . .'

'Yeah'. Neil consented.

'. . . just because the bottom of *this* would be a whole lot easier', Cheryl reasoned. The instructor meant that it would be simpler to correct a problem on the surface of the tenon than amending one inside the deep and narrow mortise where it was more difficult to see, to verify and to access.

'Yeah, yeah', said Neil, looking back again to the two timber components.

Cheryl picked up a small steel engineer's square from the worktop. Eyeing the end of the tenon, she announced 'Looks good *there*, at the back', while gesturing with her index finger along the back edge on the top cheek of the tenon. 'It's slightly high *there*', she observed, pointing to another spot near the back of the tenon cheek. 'But that's right at the back where we know we don't have the problem.' Neil nodded. Cheryl ran the engineer's square along the tenon cheek to check the flatness of the surface: 'So we can see it's high at the back, *there*. That looks massive', she smiled. 'When you look at the light at this end', using her index finger to indicate the sliver of light emanating from between the blade of the engineer's square and the tenon cheek, 'you think, "God! That looks really massive." But in reality, what is that?' Neil leaned in more closely to see. 'It's probably about. . .', she continued.

Neil interjected, 'I wasn't sure if I. . .'

Cheryl interrupted, 'If you look at that pencil line in the back. . .'

Neil enjoyed and appreciated the instruction he was receiving at the College, but he was sometimes frustrated by not getting direct answers to his questions. This, he reflected, was a common problem throughout his education: 'I ask for help. The teacher will start talking, and I'll ask again. But they carry on until they've finished. I try and say something, but they'll speak a bit louder to imply, "I'm not finished talking yet!" But in my head, I'm like, "you're not actually answering my question".' While teachers were engrossed in a monologue, Neil often felt that he needed clarification on the points they were raising in quick succession and he would want to interrupt and ask: 'What did you mean by that?' But by the time he managed to formulate his question, 'they've already said three other sentences. Then they go off and my [original] question wasn't answered'.

Cheryl held the rail up, first gesturing with her index finger along the shoulder line of the tenon to the right, 'Can you see that there's a difference between *that* line. . .' – then gesturing along the shoulder line to the left – 'and a difference between *that* line?' She picked a mechanical pencil up from the worktop and identified the possible trouble spot by marking a dotted line across the tenon cheek. 'So, we could say, below that point here.' Neil leaned in again to look. 'But because it was already meeting resistance', Cheryl added while gesturing with her index finger to a location on the tenon cheek, 'quite early on. . .'

Neil pointed to a spot on the tenon cheek and interjected with a question: 'Is it that high up there?'

Cheryl resumed her unfinished statement: '. . . we know that's not the problem straight away.' She then pointed to the spot just referred to by Neil, and then continued to slide the engineer's square slowly along the cheek, adding: 'So it might be all the way along.'

'But if it is, then. . .', Neil tendered unsuccessfully.

Still carefully scrutinising with the engineer's square, Cheryl interjected with abbreviated accounts of her ongoing observations: 'Very slightly at the front . . . going to a bit more . . . and a bit more.' She picked up the pencil again to mark a spot, and Neil, with his chin resting on his right fist, watched attentively. 'So, we've got something higher here than we want it to be. And if we look *here*. . .', said Cheryl, showing her student the front face of the tenon and moving her left thumb along its top front edge to emphasise the spot. 'That's obviously a mistake, that line, isn't it?' she asked rhetorically with a patient smile.

'Yeah', Neil conceded.

While instructors and trainees esteemed the importance of learning through trial and error, there was a consensus that blatant mistakes in technique or procedure should be pointed out early to prevent them from becoming habit. During our conversation together, Neil acknowledged: 'Sometimes I need to be spoon-fed to understand. If someone tells me something, I can do it; but I won't be happy if I don't know *why* I'm doing it.' He stressed the need for the reasoning behind a practice or procedure because: 'If I'm not completely in the know, I get a bit confused.'

Now and then, 'out the corner of [his] eye', Neil surveyed how the two trainees at the adjacent bench were getting on with their tasks. Both were several years older than him and had prior woodworking experience. 'There are loads of questions I'd like to ask, but I don't like asking', he confided. 'Instead, I keep my business to myself.' On occasion, however, Neil did visit Stephen's bench to seek 'reassurance' that he was on track, or he consulted with fellow trainee Ian whom he deemed to be a competent carpenter and 'on the same wavelength' as a person. 'You're not on your own here', Neil explained, 'but how you choose to do things is your choice.' With a growing number of resources available on the internet, many trainees independently researched woodworking techniques after college hours, picking up 'tips' on technique and procedures from sites such as YouTube. However, Neil claimed that he didn't use the internet at home, so his learning was reliant on the resources available in the college workshop.

'Yeah.' Cheryl rotated the rail so that they could view its side profile. 'But if we look *here*', she continued, 'we've got a little bit of gauge line, which I would expect to see all the way around.' She was referring to the remaining lines on the timber that Neil had made with the marking gauge to guide his sawing of the tenon. Cheryl pivoted the rail 180 degrees to view the opposite side of the tenon in profile. 'Because I can't see a gauge line all the way around . . . a faint little bit *there* . . . and *there*', she said pensively, indicating with her thumb along the edges of the tenon. She then pivoted the rail 180 degrees back to the earlier side-view and, using the tip of her pencil to point, she noted: 'I can't see it *there*.' Exchanging the pencil for the engineer's square, she added: 'But we know that back to be higher than the front.' Holding the engineer's square to the tenon cheek, she pondered: 'So what do we do?' Now using her index finger to point to a spot on the tenon cheek, she began: 'If we look at it like that, that's definitely higher. . .'

'Yeah', said Neil.

'. . . at the back than the front', Cheryl concluded. Standing up straight and turning half-left towards Neil, she asked: 'So is it that your gauge lines are wrong?'

In response, Neil also assumed an erect posture and took a half-step back. His face turned serious. 'I don't think so', he said defensively.

'Could be', Cheryl stated flatly. Then, slowly and contemplatively: 'So what. . .' While judiciously studying the tenon, she suddenly modified her line of inquiry: 'Or is it that you've lost your gauge lines on *there*', referring to one side of the tenon. 'And so now you'll need to lose them on *there*. . .' She pinched the opposite side of the tenon between her left thumb and index finger to indicate the spot. 'Because it's not fitting', she added, while pointing to the mortise in the stile lying on the worktop in front of them, 'on *this* side?' And again, she pinched the side of the tenon between her thumb and index to make the location clear to Neil.

'Yeah, I didn't know. . .', Neil responded, moving in closer and leaning on his elbows. Cheryl placed the rail back on the worktop and began testing the tenon to the mortise again. 'I didn't do it. . .', Neil began. 'The lines I made are quite thin', he defended, closely spacing his two index fingers to emphasise the 'thinness'. He then followed on with a staccato of incoherent utterances: 'So they're . . . If not . . . Maybe too small.' At this point, Neil looked to Cheryl who had again lifted the rail to study the tenon at its end. 'So, I had to take them passed the lines', he continued, making a sweeping gesture with his right hand to simulate the activity of 'passing' the lines. Cheryl remained fully focused on her pursuit, returning the rail to the worktop and again fitting the tenon to the mortise in order to identify the trouble spot.

'Yeah', said Cheryl. With upright index finger, she motioned for Neil to stop talking while she studied the mortise and tenon. 'The funny thing is', she began, lifting the rail and pointing to a spot on the underside of the tenon, 'is it's high on *that* side.' She replaced the rail on the worktop and continued fitting the tenon to the mortise. 'If you look at *that* side', she directed Neil's attention to the topside of the tenon, 'that's the side that's going in OK. So, if it's meeting some resistance *there. . .*', she continued as she picked up the stile and pointed inside the mortise, 'it must be. . .' And, she picked up her pencil to point more delicately at the interior surfaces of the mortise, '. . . *in there* – where we don't want it to be.' Cheryl reached inside the mortise with the tip of the pencil and marked one of its interior surfaces.

In addition to making pencil marks directly on the timber during tutorials, Cheryl commonly used pencil on paper to teach, explain and resolve problems with the trainees. She was a fine drawer and possessed a sophisticated sense of spatial conceptualisation and reasoning. When pondering how two components might be joined, how the constituent parts of a window frame needed to be profiled or how an entire assembly would be glued up, she frequently developed her thoughts through sketching plan, section and axonometric drawings. For some trainees, this method helped them to better visualise the task and the solution. The drawings Cheryl left behind also served as a reminder of the lesson or as an artefact with which students could think creatively about alternative designs and procedures for executing the task.

Neil, on the other hand, and despite his experience as a painter, rarely found drawings and diagrams on paper to be useful. He said the instructors 'are often drawing something, but I'm not really sure what they're drawing'. The pencil marks that Cheryl made directly on Neil's pieces of timber, by contrast, better suited his preferred mode of learning. According to him, carpentry 'is a hands-on thing' and 'that's the way it should be shown', working directly with the tools and on the timber. Neil's preference for a hands-on approach in teaching and learning is explored further in the next section.

THE PROBLEM IDENTIFIED

Gesturing with the small finger of his right hand towards Cheryl's use of her pencil inside the mortise, Neil commented: 'That's a good way of finding out.'

'Yeah', Cheryl confirmed, stopping to study the thin, rigid metal tip of her mechanical pencil. Then, scanning Neil's worktop, she added: 'If you've got a pencil that's either really, really sharp or you've got one of these little skinny ones. . .' Cheryl started marking inside the mortise again: 'If you run it in like *that*, and it hits a bit of resistance. . .' She made a stabbing gesture in the air with the pencil. 'That's exactly what this is doing', she exclaimed, lifting the rail and executing the same stabbing motions with the tenon towards the mortise. 'Isn't it?'

'OK', Neil nodded in agreement.

Neil stared into the mortise as Cheryl probed its surfaces with her pencil tip. After a pause, she reported: 'Meeting some little bit of resistance . . . So, if I slide the pencil in like *that*. . .' She inserted the pencil tip along one of the inner faces of the mortise: 'I'm hitting what feels like a brick wall, but what is in fact only like a tiny bit of fluff.' Cheryl pinched together her thumb and index finger to illustrate the smallness of the obstruction that she detected with her pencil tip.

'You could use the ruler as well', Neil suggested, pointing with his small finger towards the small metal ruler on the worktop, 'because it's, like, wider. . .' He implied the width of the ruler by making a space between the tip of his thumb and index finger.

Intercepting Neil's suggestion, Cheryl picked up the metal ruler to use in place of the pencil. 'You could do it . . . Yeah, exactly, you can do it with a ruler.' She inserted the flat end of the ruler along the interior surfaces of the mortise. 'Because that's like using. . .', she paused briefly to lift the ruler out of the mortise to inspect its flat end, 'a completely blunt chisel, then. Isn't it?'

'Yeah, yeah!' Neil smiled with satisfaction.

Redwood pine is a 'temperamental' softwood species.[15] Planed surfaces of Redwood are easily marked or dented by applied pressure from implements, and when working with plane or chisel against, or perpendicular to, the grain, it tends to flake or splinter. Mortises are chopped into the board, perpendicular to the grain, and therefore the inner faces of a mortise in Redwood are often rough and 'splintery' compared to mortises chopped in, for instance, a plank of hard English walnut.

While interviewing Neil, I asked whether the properties of the timber had anything to teach him about the way he used his tools; and, if so, what. He replied in the affirmative, explaining that, when chiselling or planing, the wood will 'tell you, "Don't do that!" because it'll tear to pieces!' Grain direction, wood figure, knots and the hardness of the timber respond to the tool blade and signal to the attentive hand a need to recalibrate the pressure and force exerted or to change direction. As a first-year trainee, Neil's workshop experience so far was limited to Redwood pine, though he was being inducted in working with hardwoods in his extracurricular woodcarving course. His growing familiarity with Redwood pine told him that the sharp metal tip of the mechanical pencil was too fine an implement for the rough surfaces in the mortise, and this prompted his recommendation to use the broader, blunter end of the ruler.

Persisting with her examination, Cheryl affirmed, '[The ruler's] not doing any damage, but it is showing you. . .'
'Yeah', replied Neil.
'. . . where the pick-up point is', Cheryl concluded. She pointed with the metal ruler to a specific spot inside the mortise. 'And it's *there*, really.' Cheryl put the ruler back down on the worktop and held the stile out in front of her with both hands so that she and Neil could look straight into the mortise. 'To look down into *that*', she instructed while pointing into the mortise with her left index finger, 'and be able to say what's high or low at the back would be quite difficult, wouldn't it?'
'Hmmm', Neil pondered.
Cheryl now pointed into the mortise with the small finger of her right hand: 'Because we've got a load of shadow', and she glanced upward towards the light fixture above Neil's workbench. Putting the stile back onto the worktop directly beneath her, Cheryl peered straight down into the mortise. Neil's eyes initially swam over the worktop and then his gaze settled on the mortise into which his instructor was peering. 'And if we do it like that', she proposed, looking at Neil and pointing downward to indicate the direction of her sightline into the mortise, 'you can't tell what's *higher* or *lower* in that very easily.' While stating this observation, the instructor pivoted a flat outstretched hand above the mortise opening to spatially emphasise 'higher' and 'lower'. 'Can you?' she asked.
'No', Neil confirmed.
Cheryl picked the stile up again with both hands from the worktop and held it out in front at eye level so that she could peer into the mortise. 'You'd want it *that* way to be able to tell . . . But as soon as it's that way, you can't. . .', she started.
Attempting to complete his instructor's idea, Neil interjected, '. . . see into it', shaking his head in agreement at what he thought Cheryl was implying.
'. . . get any light', Cheryl corrected. 'So it's almost like you'd want to shine a light down there', she tendered while gesturing with bunched fingers on one hand to exemplify 'shining light' into the mortise opening.
'A head torch', Neil added humorously. He gestured a 'head torch' with the back of his hand pressed against his forehead and fingers 'beaming' outward.
'. . . to be able to see', Cheryl concluded.

Neil was grateful for advice offered by the instructors and by his small circle of workshop chums. He was amenable to 'having a look' at the proposed procedure and, if the reasoning resonated with him and he understood the potential advantages, he might 'add it to [his] technique'. Such was the case with Cheryl's recommended method for examining the inner surfaces of the mortise described in the preceding dialogue.

Like all the woodworkers in my study, Neil's learning demonstrated that skills are not acquired by submissively imitating the example of experts. Rather, developing a skill involves both conceptual and motor-based interpretation of what is seen,[16] and through practice a skill becomes bespoke tailored by, and for, the individual carpenter. A new skill, such as wielding a chisel with effect and efficiency, is generated by combining prior conceptual knowledge (i.e. background understanding of the purpose and function of the tool) and previous practical experience (i.e. biomechanical knowhow for grasping, positioning the body, moving in rhythm, and applying directional force and pressure) with new information parsed from a demonstration or an explanation. And, with practice and experimentation, the skill evolves. 'Everyone has their own feel', Neil said. 'Whether one's better than another. . .?' He astutely left that question dangling, inferring that that was something for the individual learner-practitioner to judge based on their personal 'feel' for the tool and the results they achieved with it.

At this point, Cheryl stood erect again and turned towards Neil. In reaction, the student's posture straightened and he took a step back. 'On the other hand', Cheryl continued confidently, 'we've picked it up', referring to the obstruction inside the mortise. She retrieved the ruler from the worktop and inserted it into the mortise: 'We know where it is. And now, if we use . . . If we can pick it up with *this*. . .', she said, glancing at Neil.

'Yeah', Neil responded, still standing erect with left hand on the worktop and right hand on his hip.

'. . . then we can pick it up with the chisel without even being able to see it', Cheryl resolved. The instructor clamped the stile in the workbench vice with the mortise opening facing out towards her. 'So, we know it's on this side, not too far in', she said while tapping the surface of the stile with her finger to indicate the trouble spot inside of the mortise. She picked up a bevel-edged chisel lying on the worktop in front of her. Neil repositioned himself behind his teacher to watch her work the inside of the mortise with the tool. Cheryl began, and then stopped to scan the worktop: 'Maybe something a little meaty?' she inquired, asking Neil for a wider chisel. The student reached across the worktop to open his chisel case for the instructor to choose. Cheryl selected one, verified with her fingertips that it was sharp, and then began working inside the mortise. As she applied pressure, the piece of timber slipped downward in the vice. Neil diplomatically swallowed a chuckle. Cheryl flashed a smile of self-consciousness. She repositioned the component and tightened the vice before continuing work inside the mortise. After a few moments, she removed the chisel and placed the backside of the steel blade flat against the top surface of the stile. Without announcing the fact, Cheryl was preparing to offer Neil a demonstration. She grasped the handle lightly in her right hand and pressed down on the bevel-edged blade with the index and middle fingers of her left hand. This kept the chisel perfectly flush with the timber surface. She proceeded to move the blade around in a clockwise pattern without paring any wood or making a mark. Neil watched closely. 'If I do it on here', Cheryl said, referring to the top surface of the stile, 'I can see what I'm doing.'

'Yeah', Neil concurred.

'Well, not that anything much is happening', Cheryl noted. 'I can see what I'm doing. But even if I don't look. . .' Her gaze turned away from the chisel tip towards Neil as she continued moving the tool around clockwise. 'It's still doing the same thing', she declared. Cheryl proceeded to let go of the handle and, with just one finger pressing down on the top of the blade, she kept the chisel in position and continued the circular motion. 'Because it can't scoop out', she added. The objective of Cheryl's demonstration was to teach Neil the importance of keeping the back of the chisel blade flush against the timber so that its bevelled tip removes only unwanted protrusions and does not gouge the finished surface.

'I don't do a lot of teaching in the classroom', Cheryl told me, weighing the differences between academic institutions and vocational ones. 'I think that 95 per cent of the valuable teaching that goes on here is practical, and *in* the immediate.' Neil, too, was resolute that he learned best by being shown and then monitored while he had a go. 'It's important to see someone do it right', he said. 'It's a mix of you seeing them and them seeing you do it', and receiving constructive feedback. He offered the example of learning to make dovetails:

> It works best when they show [you] how to do them: 'Like this and like that.' And [they say], 'Hold [your chisel] like this, for that reason.' 'Now you do it; and I'm going to watch you do it.' And then they'll say 'No, that's wrong' or 'It's good like that'.

But, referring to earlier experiences, Neil complained that 'sometimes they'll show you and go off . . . and then I'm left asking myself "Am I doing it right?"'

Concerning Cheryl's teaching style, Neil remarked that the verbal explanations, observations and exclamations that accompanied her demonstrations supplied vital information 'about how she's feeling; or about how she's *feeling* the instrument or tool'. Cheryl's words performed like gestures, directing Neil's attention to specific locations and to salient activities in, and qualities of, her demonstration. Her words also opened dialogue between instructor and trainee and created opportunities for Neil to seek clarification or to formulate and test his own suggestions and solutions.

In their study of interactional learning and instruction between attending medical surgeons and resident trainees, communications expert Alan Zemel and medical educator Timothy Koschmann examine the ways in which narrative provides an affordance in an experiential learning context.[17] While demonstrating a surgical procedure, the attending produces narratives of her tactile inspection of the 'worksite', thereby rendering her 'surgical reasoning' publicly available to the resident. The attending's language also served indexical functions, like Cheryl's, by 'pointing' the resident's attention and hands-on learning to the correct location: 'By removing her hand from the worksite and then calling on the resident to "feel there" . . . the attending makes relevant as a next action the resident's inspection of the site in the manner demonstrated.'[18]

'But you can't do *that*. . .', observed Neil, pointing to the movement Cheryl was making with the chisel on the outer surface of the stile, '. . . in there.' He pointed to the inside of the mortise.

To demonstrate, Cheryl returned the chisel blade inside the mortise: 'Well, we can a little bit. So, if I've got . . . if I've got my thumb *there*. . .' She positioned her hands and fingers on the tool to exhibit her grasp.

'Yeah', watched Neil.

'. . . and my fingers [are] underneath', she continued. Cheryl momentarily removed the chisel from the mortise again to show Neil her hand position. 'And I'm squashing the chisel down flat.'

'OK', Neil said, following his instructor's display closely.

Neil reckoned that learning to operate the succession of new tools that were introduced over the first year of training became exponentially easier with time and practice. 'After you get a grip of the movement and know how to hold a tool', he said, 'your hands know how to adapt to a completely new one.' To use psychologist James Gibson's term, hand tools possess 'affordances',[19] such as their overall length and size, shape of their handle, and width and position of their blade(s) or sharp point(s). These affordances of the tool, along with the carpentry experiences Neil had acquired to that point and his attunement to the workshop environment, made it possible for him to grasp and approximate the correct use with a newly introduced tool in the curriculum of learning. Though carpentry was a recent pursuit for Neil, he claimed that 'Because I've had my hands on other instruments [e.g. his paint brushes and drawing utensils], I've got that understanding of how to adapt'.

'You can a little bit', Cheryl confirmed. Neil's nod conveyed understanding. 'As long as you're holding the chisel down. . .', she slowly explained while removing the chisel again from the mortise and holding it up to display her hand and fingering position, '. . . as close as you can to the top. . .' She returned the chisel inside mortise, '. . . and pressing down as hard as you can, onto that surface. It will then pick up anything higher than that.' She removed the chisel one more time to emphasise the articulation of her grasp and firmness of her hold. She then handed the chisel to Neil and, standing to one side, told him: 'Try it! Try it and see.' The student moved quickly into position, approximated his teacher's grasp on the tool and placed it inside the mortise. 'You're looking for something about *there* inside', Cheryl instructed, and she scribbled lightly with her pencil on the top surface of the stile to indicate the location below and inside. She took a step back while Neil had a go: 'Can you feel it?' she asked.

'Yeah', he replied.

'Good!' Cheryl gestured with open arms as a token of resolve and relief. As she began to walk away, she reiterated '*It* is there', referring to the obstruction they discovered inside the mortise. 'We've seen that it's there. And the chisel can pick that up.' Cheryl took her leave and Neil carried on with the task.

'What I want is to be able to back away and nothing happens', Cheryl told me. 'And if I can do that, then they're more than ready for second year. They're working with each other; they're advising each other. Soon they'll be talking about the design bit, and they'll not even have to ask each other about the joinery bit. So that's "Job done!"'

NEIL'S MEDITATIONS ON SKILL-BASED KNOWLEDGE

In our discussion together, I invited Neil to elaborate upon his evolving relation with the carpentry tools he was striving to master. He began by telling me that the tool-in-hand helps to bring his mind-body to fuller concentration on the task, but that this didn't happen immediately. He recounted:

> At first, I'd hold one of the tools and think to myself: 'This is an object and I'm using this object to cut wood or chisel away.' It probably sounds a bit cheesy, but now it just feels more like an extended part of me. I can feel what I'm doing [to the timber] at the end of the chisel rather than, like, 'I'm just pushing this object into it'.

With growing experience, Neil claimed 'to know how the chisel is on the wood by the feel; not by looking'. He did not discount the importance of visually monitoring his results with the tools, but rather he emphasised his growing reliance on the haptic information received by his hand from the blade for controlling and modifying his activity:

> Beforehand, I'd be chiselling away and realise 'Oh no! I've gone passed the line!' Or think 'Why did that happen!' But now if I [make a mistake], I know at that exact moment that I'm doing it – not after – because I can *feel* myself doing it.

Neil made the comparison with learning a musical instrument:

> If you're a natural guitar player, for instance, all that means is that your hands can already make those movements. But if not, you teach your hands, and eventually you can. Carpentry tools are just like that. It's muscle training. At first you might not have such a smooth way about the way you move. But after a while your hands learn to move in a certain way, and more freely. Like drawing and painting: your hand might not be able to produce a certain stroke because it doesn't like that movement. But the more you try . . . Well, eventually you'll be able to do it. 'Practice makes perfect!'

Neil had concluded, chuckling at his use of that cliché. He then went on to thoughtfully explain how his appreciation for handicraft had developed since starting the programme:

> Before, I thought carpentry couldn't be hard. Anyone can do that sort of thing: sticking bits of wood together with a few nails, and so on. It's just a bit of labour. I think in society, generally, it's seen as either, 'You're book-smart, knowledgeable and academic' or 'You make things with your hands – duh!' Now I appreciate what people do with their hands. When I see a fine piece of woodwork, I look at what's gone into making it.

After just a few months on the course, Neil claimed that: 'It's opened my mind to considering the time and effort that's gone into making something: not just with wood, but with anything – even brickwork in building. It's opened my eyes to look at things in a different way.' But he believed that the manual trades needed 'positive marketing' as attractive options for young people in Britain. 'It's seen as: "Are you eighteen to twenty-five and not in a job? Try carpentry!"' he announced sardonically. As far as he was concerned, vocational training programmes were narrowly targeting 'people who feel like they haven't got any other options' and the manual trades were portrayed as 'a last resort'. Conversely, handicraft 'needs to open up to the world', he stated with conviction: 'It should be advertised to everyone. . . as really creative and something good to get into.'

CONCLUSION

The discussion and explorations in this chapter revolved around a thick transcription of a video-recorded workbench tutorial between woodworking instructor Cheryl and first-year trainee Neil. While carrying out a practice exercise for making a variety of basic wood joints, Neil discovered a problem with the fit of his 'stopped' mortise-and-tenon. Cheryl arrived at his workbench and, together, they engaged in a set of procedures for defining the parameters of the task, identifying the nature and location of the trouble, and determining a suitable course of action to rectify the mistake. Notably, the problem was identified and defined as it was being worked out.[20] During the tutorial session, a number of tools and implements were employed, and Cheryl offered Neil a technical demonstration of using a bevel-edged chisel to remove unwanted protrusions from finished timber surfaces, including the inner surfaces of the mortise that he had chopped. In the end, with the mistake identified, the solution in hand, and a new technique learned, Neil confidently assumed charge for making the repair and carried on independently with his project.

The detailed transcription allowed for a closer reading of the communication that unfolded between the two parties in solving the problem and for discovering the richness of its texture. The communication between Cheryl and Neil relied not merely on words alone, but on gestures, deictic pointing, posture and bodily comportment, facial expressions, and on the direction, focus and intensity of their gaze. It also incorporated active displays with the tools, the use of various implements to extend and amplify gestures and to refine pointing, and, notably, the information directly supplied by the timber components.

Jointly inspecting, handling and reorienting the position of the two pieces of shaped wood allowed instructor and student to communicate observations, thoughts and questions concerning the straightness of edges, condition of surfaces, and geometric relations between mortise and tenon. Pressing down upon the components – separated and joined – as they lay flat on the worktop enabled the instructor both to test and to demonstrate to Neil their behaviour when subject to physical forces. And the palimpsest of Neil's pencil lines, marking-gauge incisions, and cuts were directly referred to by either party to establish a shared understanding of the trainee's past actions upon the timber.

Verbal utterance, embodied practices and the artefacts-to-hand variously communicate thought, ideas, queries, emotions, ways of doing things, information and evidence. In the dialogue between Cheryl and Neil, all three vehicles of communication were employed in combination to negotiate and define a shared focal space and a shared goal, and to develop their collaborative thinking and understanding of the problem and its solution.

Importantly, verbal and nonverbal forms of communication were also periodically used to check parity of understanding that each was incrementally constructing during the course of dialogue. In the case study presented, this was best exemplified by the instructor. Cheryl looked Neil in the eyes to ascertain whether he was following her; she asked him to confirm his understanding, and she directed him to imitate her own handling, manipulation and testing of the timber components, and thereby discover equivalent results. At times, Neil did misinterpret what his instructor intended to communicate. When he interjected and completed her unfinished utterance with an idea different from that which she had in mind to say, Cheryl immediately responded by finishing her own statement or question. Clarifying her thought in this way was aimed at bringing Neil back into step with her evolving thinking about the issue, and re-establishing a shared focus and goal in the dialogue between them.

In several instances, Cheryl's utterances were seemingly less directed at conveying information to Neil than bringing narrative order to her own hands-on exploration of the timber components. These brief dialogues with the self – manifested in either spoken words or silent thought – can play an important role in practical problem solving. Observations and discoveries of 'evidence' made while handling the timber are sequentially marked by formulating accompanying words or statements. Problems or challenges detected with hands and eyes (or other perceptual senses) are given shape by formulating questions that can be conceptually entertained. In a woodworking context, a dialogue of questions and observations gives the carpenter's problem-solving task direction and enables them to ponder potential solutions and possible ways forward, either while continuing to engage with the timber or perhaps while spending time away from the physical work.

Additionally, in the workbench tutorial described, Cheryl's externalised narrative of discoveries and her self-generated dialogue of questions and answers rendered her conceptual thinking that accompanied her intelligent handling of the timber more readily available to the student. Indeed, it offered Neil a valuable demonstration of the critical examination-and-questioning procedures he would need to follow and hone when confronting the next woodworking challenge. Making good an error is a skill. It is as much a part of being a craftsperson as possessing expert knowledge of the materials and mastering practice with the tools.

A number of conclusions can be drawn from the problem-solving tutorials I have recorded (and partaken in) at the Building Crafts College, and these are applicable more generally to any kind of hands-on craftwork. Problem solving in craft relies, in the first instance, on having a critical eye to spot an upcoming challenge and a critical sense of touch to detect that something has gone amiss, and to make those observations as early in the design-and-making process as possible. Once challenge or trouble has been detected, a craftsperson must be prepared to patiently take time out to explore the precise nature of the problem and cogitate on the correct course of action. This variously involves systematic examination of the thing(s) being made, retracing steps and procedures, reviewing the methods of making, imagining alternative ways forward, and evaluating them, perhaps with the aid of sketches, drawings and mock-ups. In contrast to eliminating a mistake altogether, a craftsperson may purposefully choose to leave traces of it in the finished work or to positively incorporate it in the finished piece. Making errors and skilfully integrating them can become part of the overall creative design process.

Whether eliminating or integrating an error, the activity of problem solving is embedded in the maker's existing knowledge and experience. But, in the process, experimentation with the tools and materials and testing out new techniques to find solutions pushes boundaries and broadens horizons. Accomplished craftspeople possess a willingness to learn, and to learn in perpetuity. Designer and maker of furniture Peter Fleming persuasively expressed the delight in exploration and learning:

> When making, the ground shifts a bit with each discovery in relating one form to another, or seeing how a material can be transformed or pressed into a service previously unconsidered. This is indeed the starting point for an investigation, a groundless assumption made as a basis for reasoning, where the results have yet to be tabulated into theory.[21]

Posing problems and setting new challenges for oneself is therefore critical to a maker's growth and development, and to re-experiencing the triumphal pleasure that accompanies overcoming and moving forward. In problem-posing forms of learning, educator and philosopher Paulo Freire remarked that people 'come to see the world not as static reality, but as a reality in process, in transformation'.[22] The central case study showed that the task of resolving a simple mortise-and-tenon joint presented a rich learning opportunity not only for the trainee, but for the instructor as well. Problem solving, learning and transformation proceed hand in hand.

Problem solving is built into every stage of craftwork: design, quantifying, costing, budgeting, scheduling, making, delivering and installing a commission for a client. All of these activities present challenges to resolve and overcome. In sum, craftwork *is* problem solving, and the craft of carpentry, like any creative occupation, is defined by the distinct array of challenges it throws up for its trainees, instructors and seasoned practitioners.

NOTES

1. Pye, *The Nature and Art of Workmanship*, 20.
2. Coleman, *The Art of Work*, 89.
3. Kirsch, 'Problem Solving', 264.

4. Martin, 'Femi, Brake Mechanic', 370.
5. Ibid., 373.
6. Numerous video clips of problem-solving sessions between instructors and train-ees were recorded and transcribed. The analysis of this particular clip with Neil was selected because the session was of suitable duration, the audio quality was consis-tently good, which made possible a complete and detailed transcription, and it was a representative example of all the filmed sessions in terms of its content, dialogue, interaction and process.
7. Billett, 'Recasting Transfer', 12.
8. Filliettaz, de Saint-Georges and Duc, 'Skiing, Cheese Fondue and Swiss Watches', 137.
9. Ibid.
10. See also Roger Coleman's example of the need for a bricklayer to 'have a mental picture of the entire building or at least the section under construction' by the time they begin laying the first course (Coleman, *The Art of Work*, 94).
11. See, for example, Klaus Zwerger's classification and drawings of wood joints used in European and Japanese building traditions (Zwerger, *Wood and Wood Joints*, 85–97).
12. See Coleman (*The Art of Work*, 26–27) on the 'two distinct, but not separate stages', in making a window: the one conceptual and the other practical. Being a carpenter himself, he argues that: 'The conceptual part of the process is as much a part of the trade of joinery as is the craft of the productive part.'
13. An axonometric drawing is 'an orthographic projection of an object on a plane in-clined to each of the three principal axes of the object' (*New Oxford Dictionary*).
14. For a detailed analysis of shared utterance, see Marchand, 'Embodied Cognition and Communication'; and Purver and Kempson, 'Incrementality'.
15. Coleman, *The Art of Work*, 89.
16. See Marchand, 'Embodied Cognition and Communication'.
17. Zemel and Koschmann, '"Put Your Fingers Right in Here"'.
18. Ibid., 170.
19. Gibson, *The Ecological Approach to Visual Perception*.
20. See Kirsch, 'Problem Solving', 268.
21. Fleming, 'Wood Practice', 66.
22. Freire, *Pedagogy of the Oppressed*, 64. Also quoted in Martin, 'Femi, Brake Mechanic', 370.

CHAPTER 9

MANAGING PLEASURABLE PURSUITS

> A great deal of intelligence can be invested in ignorance when the need for illusion is deep.
>
> —Saul Bellows[1]

Utopian ideals and longings for alternative ways of living are formulated in juxtaposition to the messy circumstances of real times and places. Chapter 6 examined the ways in which the utopian literature of different periods served variously as charters for the 'good life and plenty', sagacious politics, social equality, a balanced education of mind and body, and pleasurable work. All such tales of hope were devised in dialectical relation to the select and usually polemical versions of the real worlds in which their authors lived. In cultivating imagery of what exists in *potentia*, utopian thinkers wilfully and temporarily suspended their knowledge of the fuller spectrum of often-contradictory forces at play in daily life. Real and complex social, political, religious and economic regimes were typically flattened into two-dimensional caricatures of all that was wrong, and that could thereby be easily toppled by pen and paper and supplanted by new idyllic orders.

Notably, arriving at a clear utopian vision demands the luxury of being able to take time out from the disorientating flux of quotidian demands and pressures. This means discovering a safe haven from where it is possible to ignore what is unwanted and to renew energies, reflect on what is desirable and redirect aspirations in ways that will hopefully have lasting beneficial consequences.

In the same way that a utopia is concocted in direct resistance to some version of reality, strategic ignorance might likewise be enacted in direct resistance to knowing. Acts of ignorance (or choosing not to know) and acts of knowledge procurement therefore exist in a mutually constitutive partnership,[2] as do utopia and the 'real world'. Furthermore, both utopia and ignorance imply and produce kinds of absence, manifested respectively as a nonplace and the banishment or suspension of knowledge. By contrast, their counterparts (i.e. the real world and active knowing) are conceived as presence and tangible existence.

Grounded in my studies at the Building Crafts College, this chapter considers the matrix of relationships between all four terms and, more specifically, the variety of positions taken up by trainees, instructors and administrators in the discursive spaces produced when the continuum between knowing and ignoring was intersected by that between 'real world' and utopia.

For all the fine-woodwork trainees and instructors whom I came to know at the College, the choice of carpentry was integral to their pursuits of pleasurable work and a satisfying life. By the time they graduated from the programme, a majority of trainees dreamed of becoming designer-makers of fine furniture or bespoke cabinetry, operating autonomously or in communal workshops and, crucially, exercising control over the creation and sale of their handcrafted wares.

The College importantly provided an incubation space for an assortment of personalised, but usually compatible, utopian visions of work and life. The sentiments expressed by fellow trainee Robert resonated strongly with other narratives I documented:

> I've never been happy with settling with what's there. I've always had an urge to be autonomous; a desire to live separately from those aspects of life that I don't like – crime, cars, traffic, noise and constant material consumption. As a craftsman, I hope to be able to work when I want and how I want.

Robert justified his ambitions as being entirely relevant to the contemporary world, insisting that: 'My utopia is *not* rooted in the past.' Rather, he hoped to set an example through his practices of 'what might be' when the mindful energy of the body is mobilised in place and in the present moment. He continued:

> Increased mechanisation, increased mobility: both have been a turn for the worse. In some ways the world is devalued by being able to get to places more and more quickly. I don't ignore the technical benefits [of our age], but there are more of us wanting more and more. My instinct is to stop, find a better way to live, and hope some people take notice.

This chapter features the ambitions and utopian visions of four of my fellow trainees. Their concerns as both mature students and aspiring craftspeople, and the complexities and contradictions of their shifting positions and perspectives were regularly aired in conversations with one another and in dialogue with me. Explorations of 'not knowing' and the arts of ignoring are made in the context of four key issues and events that profoundly marked our collective experiences at the College. Each is discussed under a separate section heading, which follow one another in a loosely chronological sequence that begins in the final weeks of our first year of training and finishes with our graduation from the programme.

The first section examines the ways that 'not knowing' was employed in both teaching and learning at the College, and it sets the groundwork for the remainder of the chapter. The next considers the ways in which the conceptual division made between traditional hand tools and power tools, as well as machinery, served to buttress ideals of 'true' or 'authentic' craft and craftsmanship, and to distinguish fine woodwork from site carpentry. Maintaining the divide relied on actively ignoring the merits of machinery, as well as the very real hand-eye skill involved in deftly operating power tools.

The third section confronts the lack of tuition in business management and its impacts. College promotional literature stated that the programme would prepare graduates for setting up as sole traders. A handful of one-off lectures were offered, but, in general, trainees were disappointed by the absence of a dedicated course. In fact, however, their desire for that knowledge was often contradicted by the effort they were willing to expend in attaining it. Trainees treasured their bench time above all else, and, as one accurately noted, most students would have been reluctant to attend a classroom module. In effect, they passively colluded with instructors and administrators in ignoring the critical importance of basic business and marketing knowhow to succeed as a sole trader. The sanctuary of the College also made it easy to keep at bay the challenging realities of the UK marketplace for makers of bespoke furniture.

The final section supplies an account of my cohort's participation in the annual *New Designers* show in Islington. The stark contrast between the safe and intimate atmosphere of the College workshop and the competitive bustling enormity of the outside world of design and making rattled utopian dreams of Morris' pleasurable work or of comfortably settling down in Thoreau's *Walden* as 'the village carpenter'.[3] Issues that had been conveniently put to one side while training at the workbench now loomed large and could no longer be ignored. In that rapid realisation (or admission), the short-lived workshop community fractured and utopias were tainted by real demands and obligations to make a living on the tools.

'NOT KNOWING' IN TEACHING

The final architectural joinery assignment in year one was a half-scale staircase in Scots pine (*Pinus sylvestris*), with a balustrade, bullnose treads and a curtail step (i.e. the bottom-most step with a flared, semi-circular end) to support a newel post. When I completed my staircase in late May, my instructor Con suggested that I make a traditional hanging sign in American oak (*Quercus robur*). The hanging sign had been a Carpenters' Craft Competition piece sometime in the early 1990s and had been made by competing carpentry and joinery trainees from around the country. The project comprised an elegantly curved bracket with chamfered edges and a horizontal arm from which the framed sign hung on brass eye-hooks.

As I proceeded, I discovered that the bracket was far more complicated than I had initially gathered from the official project description, concealing a number of conceptually challenging geometries and joints, including a so-called 'mason's mitre joint'. In my workshop log, I glibly recorded that: 'This project is a little daunting, but there'll be much to learn.' In fact, I made a variety of blunders along the way that forced me to recut tenons and remake entire components. Naturally, this was part and parcel of the at-times frustrating learning process, which, with patience and perseverance, would hopefully result in the sense of elation that comes with solving a problem and extending one's capabilities.

Part-time instructor John W., who was introduced in Chapters 4 and 6, brought to his craftwork and his teaching the discipline, clarity, methodical precision and structural understanding that he had amassed as an engineer. When John was available in the workshop, I eagerly welcomed his input in resolving my latest troubles with the hanging sign. According to John, teaching something practical, like carpentry, is a straightforward case of 'explanation, demonstration, watching and correcting'. Together, we explored a variety of options for cutting the tenons located at either end of the curved bracket and, though he made his preferred methods known, he encouraged me to get on with the solution that I felt most comfortable with and confident about.

Con likewise encouraged us to explore options and make informed choices, but his approach was distinctly different. 'My teaching method hasn't really changed over the years', he told me in conversation. 'My mentors never gave me a straight answer. If you were interested in something, you'd find it.' Con regularly feigned 'not knowing' when students sought advice on selecting tools for a task, inquired about the physical properties of a timber species or asked how to resolve a technical problem. He did so by turning their questions directly back on them. His contrived ignorance was an effective strategy to make us think for ourselves. With a little effort and patience, the answers could be discovered by reading the photocopied handouts that Con regularly distributed or by referring to the manuals and periodicals in the College library. We were also at liberty to search for what we needed in the workshop tool cabinet and to experiment with different methods.

Nevertheless, Con's 'not knowing' was occasionally construed by trainees as an exercise of power, since clearly he was electing to withhold information and coercing us to labour for it. His persistent method was in fact productive of his mentees' cumulative knowledge and problem-solving skills, which, over time, instilled confidence and built self-esteem. 'By doing this, I try to get across to the students that this is a *long* process', he explained. 'But I also try to put them at ease by reminding them that, while in college, they have the time, and that I have the patience – if they have.'

With the College year drawing to a close, those who had finished making their architectural joinery projects were authorised to make a start on the first of the year-two assignments, namely a bedside cabinet of their own design. This was our initial foray into furniture making and the first large-scale project in hardwood. The bedside cabinet project also allowed trainees to explore and begin defining their individual aesthetic preferences. For many of us, our search for a personal style as designers and makers would intensify over the course of the second year, which in turn would heighten the sense of competition between us. All trainees were keen to leave behind casement windows and frame-and-panel doors, and to test their tool blades on hardwoods and hone their skills in furniture making.

Tony and the young-and-talented Tariq led the pack, making rapid progress with their bedside cabinets. I seized the opportunity to play 'apprentice' to both men, assisting them with the dry assembly and the gluing-up of their projects, and thereby harvesting practical tips before reaching those stages in my own project. Unlike Con's feigning 'not to know' as a pedagogical strategy, my 'not knowing' how to proceed with present and forthcoming steps in making the bedside cabinet I had designed stemmed from an authentic lack of knowledge and experience. This was typically the case for all trainees, including Tony and Tariq on occasion. Frank admissions or declarations of 'not knowing' were rarely derided by others in the workshop and were more usually repaid with opportunities to garner knowhow from more experienced others – and in ways far more expedient than experimenting on one's own.

'Not knowing' where to locate technical information or how to execute a task were the premise for asking peers to lend a hand. Teenager Josh, for example, regularly took up a stool at the side of Tony's bench, silently watching, assisting when appropriate, and learning. But when Josh's more direct requests for information or assistance with his projects were refused, Josh cunningly played to Tony's pride in his technical skill and he humorously appealed to Tony's seniority in age: 'I'm just a boy!' Josh would say with a devilish smirk. 'I haven't a clue how it's done!' Such tactics exposed vulnerability on the part of the less-experienced party and reinforced the hierarchy in skill within the cohort, but if effectively deployed, they also resulted in shortcuts to knowledge. Whereas Con's 'not knowing' was an (albeit productive) exercise of power, a student's sometimes exaggerated admissions of 'not knowing' created relations of dependency and subordination, but with a tactical eye on advancing their knowledge and possibly their status within the pecking order.

In my own example, by exposing, and even embellishing, the uncertainties I had regarding the making of my bedside cabinet, I invoked a temporary mentee–mentor relationship with Tariq or Tony, despite the considerable difference in our ages. In doing so, I hoped that Tony would impart some of his precious joinery expertise that he had gained as a door and window manufacturer. More significantly, I also hoped that his words of wisdom would confirm the partial knowhow I already possessed, thereby incrementally building my confidence to push on with my project and tackle more challenging tasks.

On the last Friday of term, Robert, Tony, Jens and I visited the Jerusalem Tavern pub in Clerkenwell for an extended 'carpentry theory session', and we animatedly talked about new design ideas and summer plans. A burgeoning topic of discussion over the first year was how we might perpetuate the dynamism, enjoyment and camaraderie that the four of us valued beyond the end of the College programme. Serious talk about establishing a communal workshop, however, typically regressed to jovial ribbing about one guy's slow pace, another's clumsy designs, or someone else's lack of focus or ambition.

Later that evening, Robert rose from the hardwood settle to buy the next round, returning sometime later with four overflowing pints and an ebullient air. He announced with a wide grin that, during the course of casual banter with the barman, he secured a commission to repair a damaged stair tread in the pub. Successfully accomplishing this first paid contract boosted Robert's self-confidence in his hands-on, 'hand-tools-only' method, emboldening the maverick approach that he would cultivate in his furniture designs during year two and later in his professional work.

During the short summer break, Robert gained further on-site experience by assisting a handyman with a host of odd jobs. Alex set up a back-garden workshop in his native Swindon, Tony reluctantly returned to manufacturing doors and windows in Potters Bar, and several other trainees, including Jens, grudgingly took up temporary posts in their former places of work.

In preparation for next session's focus on furniture, David W., the second-year convenor, assigned a summer project that involved writing a short illustrated report on two established designer-makers of our choice. We were to investigate the maker's inspirations, the ways they built up a portfolio of work, the venues where they sold their pieces, and the timbers they favoured. David's aim was to inspire in us a holistic view of the world of craftsmanship, including an understanding of the business of bespoke furniture making. Most of the cohort, however, didn't make the time or have the inclination to arrange a meeting with an established maker. At the time, this struck me as curious given that the exercise provided an opportunity to network within the professional community and to increase one's knowledge about marketing and financial survival strategies among self-employed artisans. I return to issues of business and marketing, and of ignoring this field of learning, later in the chapter.

MAN VERSUS MACHINE

When training resumed in year two, the fine woodworkers were obliged to participate weekly in a machining course. The classes were convened on Tuesday mornings by a highly experienced machinist and affable gentleman, John A., whose objective, aside from introducing us to the workings of basic milling machinery, was to prepare us for possibly engaging in small to medium-scale batch production of items of furniture or architectural joinery.

In his introductory talk, John A. urged us to think carefully about how the machines might best serve our practices and our future business interests. His calm and patient demeanour was ideally suited to training novices to safely use the big, noisy and potentially hazardous machinery in the mills. As described in Chapter 4, the large mill housed the crosscut saw, the overhand planer, the thicknesser, a spindle moulder, a large tenoner, a mortiser and a band-saw. When the machines were in full operation, the large mill was an intensely clamorous – and, initially, an intimidating – space. The busy facility was shared between the fine woodworkers and the troops of bench-joinery apprentices who attended the College in rotation on block release from their places of work.

Simmering tensions between the bench-joiners and the fine woodworkers were made starkly apparent in their muted and disinterested encounters in the mill. The physical scales of their respective course projects differed considerably: the joiners were being trained to erect doorframes and staircases, while the fine-woodworkers' curriculum moved progressively away from architectural joinery to smaller, more tightly detailed pieces of furniture. Relatedly, the tools of choice amongst the former tended to be handheld power tools, with a penchant for the quick and efficient router; whereas the soundscape of the fine-woodwork studio, situated on a mezzanine overlooking the bench joiners, was more often suffused with the wisp of planes, the rhythm of saws and the tap of wooden mallets on the tops of chisels – although the serenity was sporadically shattered by the screech of a router.

More significantly, there was a general difference in circumstances between the two groups, and in their expectations for work or labour. Although the average age of the bench-joinery apprentices was just sixteen
to eighteen years old, they were already rooted in the workplace, earning
a wage for their labour, and enrolled on the government's Apprenticeship
training scheme to receive National Vocational Qualifications (NVQs) and
secure a future in the construction industry. In this sense, they were *of* the
world outside the College. Each time they arrived on rotation, they carried
that world of labour with them, in their comportment, language, interests
and pastimes.

By contrast, none of the fine woodworkers were presently employed in
a workshop, with the exception of Tony, who occasionally returned to the
door and window manufacturer to earn quick cash. Daily life at the College
became our world for the two years we spent there. In Robert's words: 'I'm
passionate about working and creating here. The course projects aren't just
an exercise, and it doesn't feel like I have to divide work from life when doing
this.' Indeed, trainees conceived of fine woodworking as 'work', not 'labour'.
Their distinction matched that made by philosopher and political theorist
Hannah Arendt. For Arendt, labour is constituted by the endless, repetitive
activities necessary for sustaining life, whereas work is an 'unnatural' function that elevates us above the repetitious cycle of nature and through which
humans create meaningful, durable worlds in which we can live. Where
labour produces consumables that are used up in consumption, work produces an objective world that underpins a shared human reality.[4]

For the majority of trainees, it was hoped that craftwork would be a way
of living, not merely the means to make a living. However, thoughts about
the commerce of craftwork and its related pressures and competition were
kept at bay. Their knowledge about the true circumstances of life and work
among self-employed designer-makers, operating out there in the 'real
world', was riddled with gaping holes. An underlying awareness of their
own ignorance provoked pangs of anxiety – especially among the vocational
migrants – over the real costs of taking two years out with no definite future
prospects and the risk of failing in the pursuit.

The bedside cabinet project, which was resumed at the start of year two,
combined the basic joinery elements that we had learned during the first
year with new methods and techniques. While honing existing skills, we
expanded our repertoire by experimenting with new hand tools, handheld
power tools and the machines in the mill. Despite having initially deplored
the idea of spending more time in the mill and less at the workbench, a few of
the students quickly arrived at the realisation that the machining course was
opening new horizons for solving woodworking challenges and, perhaps
most importantly, it was strengthening the connections between their de-

sign and making processes. Ideas developed on paper needed to be achievable in timber and with the tools and machinery available, and, in turn, a progressive familiarity and greater dexterity with the tools and machinery informed what could be imagined in the mind's eye, sketched on paper and tested with maquettes.

In other ways, however, the machining course was at odds with the central tenets of our fine-woodwork instructor, who cultivated strong loyalties among some trainees. David ardently advocated an almost-exclusive use of classic hand tools and an engagement in handwork reliant on the immediate tactile relation between a maker's hand, the tool blade and the material being worked. In that traditional way of woodworking, the senses of sight, hearing, smell, kinaesthesia and proprioception combine with touch to produce a whole-bodied experience in the task and an intimate, multilayered dialogue with the grain, figure, density and olfactory properties of the wood.

When machining, by comparison, one's vision is often obscured by scratched and dust-coated protective eyewear and the auditory senses are impaired by ear guards and numbed by the deafening drone of motors and spinning blades. Perhaps most significantly, the sense of touch is largely dissociated from the process except when feeding a length of timber to the blades. The direct 'brain-hand-tool-material' connection that is experienced with a tenon saw, bevelled chisel or smoothing plane, for example, is extinguished when processing and shaping a plank on a thicknesser, over-hand planer or spindle moulder. That connection is also much diminished when using a handheld power tool: a router, for instance, merely cuts through the timber, knot or not, regardless of the direction of the grain or the patterning of the figure.

The desire for control over design and making that most woodwork trainees shared extended to control over the tools that they owned and used. With a little time and patience, and a sprightly curiosity in mechanical functions, hand tools can be taken apart, sharpened, repaired, modified and reassembled (as could the old-fashioned milling machinery). By contrast, the average carpenter has limited knowledge of the internal workings, electrics and computer chips of the portable power tools in their workshop. For many, the inability to manually manipulate power tools in combination with the absence of 'sensible' contact with the timber when using them produces an aura of alienation (or separation) from craftwork. Alienation was precisely what vocational migrants to woodworking had longed to avoid.

The misfit between the aims of John A.'s machining course and David's Arts and Crafts ethos hampered the full benefits we might have derived by more seamlessly suturing these two essential skillsets in our practice. Not all trainees, however, subscribed to David's philosophy of woodworking. 'With all due respect', Alex started, 'David's ideas are those of a cabinet maker of a

Figure 9.1 Fine-woodwork trainees using a handheld router in the workshop, 2013. © Trevor H.J. Marchand

bygone era. Hand tools are what David uses, and that makes him happy. But', he added with zeal, 'if there's a power tool or a machine that can do the job, I'm having it!' For Alex and like-minded trainees, John's machining course shone light on a multitude of viable career paths and more lucrative possibilities in the wood trades.

While still at college, Alex began purchasing his own power tools and investing in small-scale milling machinery for his workshop back home in Swindon. He regularly perused the trade magazines and carefully scrutinised the details in manufacturers' catalogues. Using machinery and power tools safely and optimally demands a thorough understanding of their purpose, potential and limitations, and plenty of hands-on practice. In preparing to cut holes, make grooves or finely contour the edge of a timber component with a handheld router, for example, a carpenter must select the appropriate router bit for the task, design and construct a jig to control the cutter, and accurately calibrate the depth of the plunge. Alex was a master at this. He controlled a router with poise, balanced posture, steady hand-eye coordination, correct velocity of movement and an even application of pressure. Trainees like Alex and Tony appreciated the merits of power tools and, in their hands, the level and complexity of skill involved was apparent.[5]

In the opposite camp, Robert was the most vocal proponent of the merits of classic hand tools. Remembering the start of the course, he recalled:

'When I first picked up most of the tools, I twizzled them around in my hand searchingly. But now I just pick up the combination square, for example, and use it almost unthinkingly.' Mastering a tool was empowering for Robert, as it was for all the trainees. 'It makes me so much more confident; carefree in some ways; more complete, and. . .', here he paused to chuckle, 'even more "manly" – whether that's a good thing or a bad thing!'

'Machines', Robert believed, 'represent a "wrong time", when we rushed headlong towards efficiency of production and manufacture and lost some of the person along the way.' Similarly, agronomist and historian François Sigaut wrote, that 'the whole history of technology in modern times largely appears as an endeavour to capture skill and convert it into knowledge'.[6] Robert preserved an unshakeable commitment to being 'part of something that helps find a way of living that isn't dependent on economic success, but on true happiness'. Central to this approach was minimising the amount of machining he had to do as part of his work, 'partly from an environmental point of view, partly from hating the noise'. And, he added, 'because a thing of great benefit can be made from an offcut of timber that is just about the right size and only needs a bit of jiggling and tweaking with a hand plane'.

Indubitably, the fine-woodwork programme, like craftwork more generally, nurtured a counterculture to mainstream capitalism, mass production, mindless consumption, environmental degradation, speed and the placeless-ness of global markets. But this politicisation of craft was certainly not representative of all trainees or all craftspeople. In his drive for efficiency, Alex's blunt retort to Robert was: 'You can use a plane if you want. If it comes out, you're lucky. If it doesn't, you're not. I want a financially viable career. If power tools make the job twice as quick, I'll use them!'

The majority of trainees, however, occupied sliding positions between the two poles and were (reluctantly) prepared to acquiesce after graduation to the structural demands of the 'commercial world out there'. Jens spoke of 'the deep satisfaction of doing something with your hands' and of being able to say: 'I've made this!' But, in a later conversation, Jens struck a more nuanced perspective, saying: 'Though I want to know in my own mind that I'm a craftsman and I can do everything by hand, I completely appreciate that, in the real world, we're going to be doing things more and more by machine.' Machines, he acknowledged, have their place: 'If it takes two days to handcut your dovetails by saw and half an hour by machine, then perhaps I'll have to keep the handiwork as a side line.'

This cautious and tempered admission of the machine into the world of handwork closely aligned with William Morris' thoughts on the matter in the late nineteenth century:

I have spoken of machinery being used freely for releasing people from the more mechanical and repulsive part of necessary labour; and I know that to some cultivated people, people of the artistic turn of mind, machinery is particularly distasteful, and they will be apt to say you will never get your surroundings pleasant so long as you are surrounded by machinery. I don't quite admit that; it is the allowing machines to be our masters and not our servants that so injures the beauty of life nowadays.[7]

On occasion, when the shriek of a router broke the concentration of those working quietly with hand tools, the normally jocular exchange of banter between workbenches turned to abrasive remarks, and the operator risked being publicly lampooned as a 'wood butcher', or worse. These attacks were launched in spite of the fact that all trainees, at one point or another, had to use a router to carry out certain tasks for the assigned projects. The bitter commentary nevertheless divided those who used that power tool habitually from those who did so only when hand tools were deemed impractical or impossible for the task. At a deeper level, the snide quips served to fortify the ideology of a 'priestly caste' that defended the craft status of fine woodwork, and abided by the principle that a craftsperson is defined first and foremost by the 'purity' of skilled handwork. Handwork, after all, was conceived as the path to a utopian self-sufficiency, mind-body integration and pleasurable work.[8]

A small handful of trainees across the various cohorts during my research chose not to learn how to use handheld power tools for as long as they could possibly get away with it; some feigned disinterest in integrating them with their workbench methods, while others used them, but held them in contempt. They elected to ignore the fact that the controlled, efficient and optimal operation of a handheld power tool is a practised skill, as is programming a CNC router for a series of complex procedures, or accurately setting up and operating a tenoner or spindle moulder. I surmise that these conscious decisions to 'not know' or to circumscribe learning were acts of defiance against a real or perceived encroachment of machines upon the territory of makers. Hand tools were made emblems of the counteroffensive against alienating modes of production, and the threat of being (re)absorbed into the fog of global market forces that were amorphous and over which one had no control.

MARKETING IGNORANCE

I met with Betty Norbury one sunny afternoon for tea at the elegant Queen's Hotel in Cheltenham. Betty owned a shop in an upmarket quarter of the Regency spa town, and she was the undisputed doyenne of the United Kingdom's handcrafted furniture market. Though not a maker herself, she exuded in equal measure a passion for fine timbers and skilled woodwork, and an antipathy towards the general public who, she charged, were overwhelmingly ignorant of the craft. She had a steadfast determination to promote the industry and provide Britain's top furniture makers with a venue for exhibiting and selling. She therefore curated her first furniture show in 1981, and from 1994 onwards she organised the annual *Celebration of Craftsmanship & Design*.

Betty was also invested in raising awareness among craftspeople of the importance of business acumen to surviving in the trade. With reference to her instructive, straight-talking book on marketing and promotion,[9] she told me: 'I make it very clear that I'm not telling you how to get rich. I'm telling you how to make a success of what you do, so that you can live in a way that you want to live.' According to her, the key ingredient to success in the field is 'to hang in there' and build a reputation. The opening lines of her book spell this out plainly: 'To succeed as a craftsman it is not enough to be good at your work . . . You have got to be a mixture of craftsman, salesman, public relations officer and packager.'[10] This mixture also includes cultivating the necessary social graces and communication skills for gaining access to the small and often elite target market and win their patronage.

Having worked closely with bespoke furniture makers over many years, Betty observed that many were incapable of marketing their own wares. 'They're obsessed', she began, before pausing to amend the generalisation: '*Some* are obsessed with the way it's made. There's no good them making something with the most wonderful dovetails in the world if somebody isn't going to cross the room to look at it. You've got to capture their imagination with the piece.' She carried on while handing me a copy of her newest book, *Bespoke*.[11] 'When I put this together, you won't believe the number of photographs of dovetails I got sent. And a lot of the makers won't even invest in proper photographs!' she exclaimed.

Colin E.-E., who succeeded David as convenor of the College's fine-woodwork course in 2008 and was previously editor of *Furniture & Cabinet Making* magazine, concurred wholeheartedly with Betty Norbury's assessment. In his words: 'Most craftspeople are useless businesspeople, and can't promote themselves to save their lives. They might be brilliant at what they make, but absolute crap at getting it out there in the market.'[12] Indeed, my own conversations with numerous designer-makers confirmed that only a minority of practitioners had any formal training in business management,[13] and many loathed the marketing side of enterprise,[14] dismissing it as a distraction from their real work of creating furniture and cabinetry.

As keenly noted by anthropologist Laurie Kain Hart: 'The ideology of artisans . . . is grounded in the concepts of individual production and use value', as opposed to exchange value, 'even if they well know that value can never be determined by the isolated process of production.' The value of the things that artisans make, Hart wrote (following Arendt), is created when it appears in the public realm and is transformed into a commodity: 'The producers in the end, with their ideas of autonomy, are subverted by the operations of the market.'[15]

Betty's frank pronouncements on makers' intentional disregard for effectively marketing their production in many ways reflected the College's continuing failure to incorporate elementary business training into the fine-woodwork programme. While excelling in technical tuition, Building Crafts College trainees complained that the programme sorely lacked an elementary module in business management and marketing. For the vast majority of those I worked alongside and interviewed over the years, money was not the prime motivator in taking up the trade. Nevertheless, they acknowledged that a grasp of basic business skills was essential to realising autonomy and control over what and how they would produce.

Though the prospectus professed to equip students with such knowledge,[16] the actual shortfall in this area of training was routinely pointed out to senior management by the elected student representatives, and with a rising sense of urgency as their respective cohorts progressed through the second and final year.[17] However, student pleas and their offers of constructive suggestions had little impact on the curriculum contents. At the end of our first year, the College Director offered an hour-long talk on 'setting up a business'. All attendees conceded that it was informative and that the Director covered impressive ground, but the single hour of general tuition was judged to be no more than a taster session.

During the second year, instructor David made earnest attempts to remedy the lack of connection between our college experience and the business of furniture making. He scheduled two lectures by established English designer-makers and one by a mature graduate of the College who had formerly worked in corporate marketing. These events succeeded in putting trainees into direct contact with contemporary practitioners, but many felt that the talks served a limited purpose. Following the first lecture, Jens remarked: 'The thing I'm *really* interested in is how people make that transition from training to actual furniture making for a living. The guy didn't go into that at all.' He continued with note of frustration: 'He talked mainly about high-end furniture that gets shown in flash galleries. I felt completely detached from that.'

A letter was written and sent by the fine-woodwork trainees to the Clerk and Master of the Carpenters' Company, politely requesting that the Livery consider establishing a 'nursery' workshop where recent graduates might continue to hone skills, build a clientele, make commissions and gradually transition to their own sustainable workshop and businesses. The Company thoughtfully considered the letter that had been signed by the full complement of fifteen students in the programme, and the Clerk responded that they were fully aware of the benefits that such a transitional space would provide, but that they were not yet in a position to realise such a venture.

David arranged a fieldtrip for all students on the programme to visit the famous ERCOL factory located in Princes Risborough. The purpose was to witness quality furniture making on an industrial scale. The factory visit, in combination with the talks by independent craftsmen, gave trainees a clearer idea of the spectrum of employment options, from the cottage workshop to industrial manufacturing. David's agenda, however, consistently revolved around furniture making. General carpentry and architectural joinery, both of which offered greater prospects for employment, were left behind after year one. Despite the impressively sophisticated machinery at ERCOL and the factory's seemingly congenial working atmosphere, the trainees, without exception, pined to emulate the 'independent craftsman' model, Alex included. Assembly-line production and a punch-clock culture held no attraction. Alex articulated his antipathy to factory work with a bite:

> Got to a point in life where I thought I had to do something for me. Got fed up of working for other people; being a small cog in a big machine; having no voice in how things work, and just being told what to do by people who were half my intelligence, if that!

On a separate occasion, assistant instructor John W. delivered a pragmatic talk on the practicalities and costs of setting up a workshop. Notably, John was the only member of staff at the time actively running a furniture-making business, and so the advice he offered was grounded in first-hand experience. His lecture reviewed the essential tools and machines required for a workshop and then briefly enumerated other basic necessities for setting up as a sole trader, including finding affordable and appropriate workshop space. John cautioned that monthly rents varied wildly, depending not only on square footage, but also on whether the space was in central London, a shop along a village high street or a unit tucked away in an industrial estate. Visibility and proximity to potential markets also had to be factored into the choice of location.

Other salient items from the long list that John rattled off included: securing adequate financing to cover start-up costs; installing dust extractors, basic milling equipment and a good quality bench; buying a suitable vehicle for transporting raw materials and finished items; purchasing liability insurance; creating a website and devising a marketing strategy. To paraphrase John's message about marketing: 'Prospective clients aren't likely to just turn up at your workshop and commission a bespoke chair or a table. They need to know you're out there, and they need to be able to see the quality of your workmanship.'

Trainees' thoughts, however, became fixated at an earlier point in John W.'s lecture: namely on his presentation of estimated start-up costs. For the basic tools and machinery alone, it was recommended that we budget at least £10,000 (John had spent twice that sum in setting up shop). That figure would pose a steep investment for many on the course, especially given that they had already incurred the cost of two years' tuition fees, compounded by lost earnings over that period.[18]

The real costs of starting up for a woodworker had increased exponentially over the past 150 years. Citing figures supplied by Victorian journalist Henry Mayhew,[19] Marxist historian Raphael Samuel wrote that 'The value of a good cabinet-maker's chest of tools' in mid-1850s London was £10.[20] This is equivalent to approximately £900 in 2007 money (when the cohort graduated),[21] which is less than one-tenth of the minimum tool budget John W. had calculated. In large measure, the substantial increase is accounted for by the high costs of machinery and power tools, which were not available to the Victorian cottage carpenter, but which are now deemed essential for the contemporary workshop. In 2007, as in the 1850s, owning one's own means of production was a potent signifier of a woodworker's independence and self-sufficiency,[22] but achieving that status would sadly prove impossible for some.

Failure to progress from training to becoming a fully qualified and active member of the trade is in fact a recurring theme in the history of carpentry and other craft trades in London. Historian Doreen Sylvia Leach noted that in the fifteenth and sixteenth centuries, few carpentry apprentices named in the Carpenters' Company accounts appear later in the records as having paid for their Freedom or as having taken on their own apprentices. Possible reasons for this, she speculated, were that the price of the Freedom was beyond the reach of many, while others may have remained in the trade, but practising at a low level.[23]

John W. had geared his talk to inspire positive planning for postgraduation, but the dispiriting reality of the high costs, professional responsibilities and the vast skillset (beyond actual woodworking) that is required to survive as a sole trader flummoxed most thinking about the future. It was not that trainees had been entirely clueless to the fact that realising their dreams would entail financial investment, further learning and enormous effort, but rather most had deferred these unpalatable realities, choosing instead to channel their attention towards the tools and the workbench. It was that tactical deferment, or active ignoring, of the complete picture and the real risks of failure that is especially noteworthy. In effect, it amounted to a form of resistance that was ultimately self-defeating.

John had made a commendable job of setting out the key issues, but, yet again, students deemed one hour to be far too little. There was no additional tuition on managing and marketing a small business. The other workshop instructors were skilled in their craft, but their workplace experience was either minimal or long outdated, and so they were poorly equipped to mentor on the subject. In the woodworking projects, trainees were regularly required to produce cutting lists for the timber needed, but only rarely were we required to price the materials, and never the costs of labour. This contributed to the marginalisation of labour value in the minds of most fine woodworkers from their central pursuit of pleasurable, meaning-making work.

For the bench-joinery and shop-fitting apprentices, they skilled up on the ground floor of the College, and those with the opportunity and inclination learned the business of construction from senior colleagues, line managers or the site foreman when they rotated back to work. However, the structure and nature of the fine-woodwork programme and the profile of its average student were considerably different. There was no work-placement component and only a small minority of trainees had either been previously employed in the wood trades or had family connections in that line of work. The Edward Barnsley Workshop succinctly summarised the dilemma: 'Furniture making is a specialised field and it's hard to find work without experience but hard to gain experience without finding work.'[24] Over the decades, the programme at the Building Crafts College had also attracted a growing proportion of mature 'vocational migrants', who now constituted the majority. Although they entertained high hopes of leaving college with both carpentry skills and business knowhow, at some level they also recognised that the combination was perhaps too tall an order for so short a course.

The missing business management module nevertheless remained a source of discontent. Halfway through the programme, Robert confided that: 'It's an area where I'm really lacking confidence in terms of knowing where to start.' Perhaps ironically, Robert was the only member of our cohort to create a website for marketing his services before graduating from the programme. When playfully baited by the others for becoming commercially minded, he defended his decision by insisting that he had no ambitions of becoming a 'designer' or 'a known craftsperson', but he did need 'to earn a living'. He qualified his plans to sell his works by asserting that he would do so 'on [his] own terms'.

By the end of the course, Jens wrestled with the overpowering feeling that he was still incapable of accurately estimating the costs of materials and labour for an item that he might make. 'I've got a vague idea of what it should sell for', he said, 'but no idea what profit I'd be making.'

Alex, too, expressed disappointment:

Like most educational institutions, the College didn't fill all the promises it makes in the prospectus. I had understood that we'd be able to come off the street with no carpentry and leave here with the ability to start our own business. That was my main agenda – to be my own boss.

Offering a somewhat more nuanced perspective, Tony observed from experience that:

Like other things they tried offering us, we would have moaned about having to take a couple of days or a week to go and listen to someone talking boring stuff. I'll bet you some of us wouldn't have turned up. It's a bit of a catch-22 situation.

A couple of weeks after graduating, Tony had to formulate a detailed business plan to secure a bank loan and he was forced to seek guidance and assistance from friends and family with appropriate knowhow. At that point, he complained that this should have been part of the curriculum, 'But', he quickly added, 'I'm really not sure there was enough time.' The strength of the course, Tony believed, was its emphasis on the practical: 'I don't get on with theory, or the writing-up bit.' This sentiment was widely shared and time on the tools was universally cherished. I therefore concur with Tony that, despite the grievances, any bid by the College to substitute bench time for more classroom instruction, including business training, would have met with staunch resistance.[25]

To be sure, college administrators, workshop convenors and woodwork trainees colluded in selectively ignoring the realities of the UK marketplace for bespoke furniture and the limited opportunities for qualifiers to secure gainful employment in this specialised and arguably elitist vocation. The College continually deferred inclusion of a business management module and it kept no database on job placement or the career trajectories of its graduates. Understandably, resourcing such a database would have been costly, but perhaps another reason for its non-existence was that it would have been too dispiriting to keep tabs on the plight of graduates in a national job market where craftsmanship is undervalued and where, as Betty Norbury observed, consumers remain fundamentally ignorant of the excellence in UK design and making.

In truth, the reality is somewhat more complicated. Mass-produced wooden fittings for the home, imported furniture from Eastern Europe and Asia (which is often of sound quality), and flat-pack DIY kits are readily available at affordable prices from Britain's favourite home stores. This merchandise satisfies the needs and tastes of the vast majority of us. High-quality hardwood joinery and bespoke furniture making, on the other hand, are trades relatively isolated from the wider economy. The time and effort that goes into designing and crafting handmade objects keeps their pricing in a band of its own. Regrettably, many individuals and institutions with the capital to afford such items may be hesitant to commission and invest because of the risks associated with owning something entirely unique that doesn't comply with a recognisable trend or hasn't been sanctioned by popular taste.

Without the right social connections, accessing patrons with the means and the daring to be 'taste-makers' is difficult at best. At the high end, bespoke furniture is detached from market logics and, like an artwork, the value is indexed to the author's name as they become established and cultivate a reputation among the small and exclusive circle 'in the know'. The pieces of some makers in fact become collectibles, surpassing their functional use and consumed instead as aesthetic objects for contemplation and display. This, too, presents a dilemma to the craftsperson aspiring to a socialist utopia.

NEW DESIGNERS AND UTOPIA CAPSIZED?

In November of year two, a brief meeting was organised between instructor David and trainees Robert, Jens, Tony and myself to discuss participation in the forthcoming *New Designers* exhibition. This important annual event was held each July at the Business Design Centre in Islington, showcasing the talent of thousands of new design graduates from across the United Kingdom. Alex opted out, claiming to be unconcerned with the 'designer-y side of woodworking', and the three teenage members of our cohort – Josh, Tariq and Liam – were lacking in either confidence or initiative.

Early in the new year, we received official news that the Building Crafts College had been allotted a prime spot in the main exhibition hall.[26] Robert, Jens, Tony and I collectively decided to display our selected furniture creations against wallpaper backdrops whose style, pattern and colours would complement the individual designs we had been developing during year two. Alongside the strengthening alliance between us was a growing sense of excitement and anticipation about publicly displaying our work, but feelings of rupture, fragmentation and anxiety were also taking root.

Robert authored our blurb for the *New Designers* programme, titling the submission *Modern Design with Medieval Roots*. He wrote:

> Our four graduating students exhibiting this year have all demonstrated exceptional talent in both designing and making. All four have exemplary craft skills. They can all make a beautifully dovetailed drawer, but that's just a starting point. Where they take their learning is up to them, and their outputs are as different as the people themselves – as you will see.

As the year progressed, individual design and stylistic preferences crystallised, and each of us progressed from methods of random experimentation to aesthetic convictions. Tony looked to bold landscapes and curvilinear forms in nature for inspiration, Jens resurrected his Scandinavian heritage in the clean lines and elegant proportions of his furniture, inspired in particular by Danish designer Hans Wegner, Robert brought his *bricoleur*'s eye to collecting and assembling his woodwork designs, and I pursued contemporary explorations of the geometries and 'honest joinery' of the English Arts and Crafts tradition in oak.

Most trainees had had no previous tuition in the history of art, design or aesthetics. With the exception of a single class outing to the London Design Museum to visit the furniture collection, design was not a formal element of the college curriculum. A few of the students made strident efforts to educate themselves and to discover and develop a more discriminating palette, while others embraced their 'not knowing' about design and narrowed their focus onto the technical aspects of woodworking. Displaying 'too much interest' in design challenged some students' ideals of masculinity or of 'straightforward' craftsmanship, both of which were routinely invested with notions of practicality, functionality and a lack of fussiness.

For some, it was advantageous to 'not know' too much about their own design sensibilities and approach. In describing his design process, Robert said: 'It's a compromise, I suppose. I always have half an eye on scavenging and half an eye on my design idea. But it's really hard to pin point. I can't say I've got strong...' He paused briefly before continuing: 'I'm not conscious of having a strong design ethos. This will sound absolutely pompous, but it's almost like it's sort of happening through me rather than my trying. It feels almost too ridiculous', he chuckled, 'but I honestly can't tell you where the designs come from. I think they've been percolating through my subconscious while sitting for the last ten years in office jobs that I've hated. And, there's just been this outpouring of creativity in the past year, particularly in doing the furniture.'

Prior to the official opening of *New Designers*, exhibitors were invited to a 'Prepare Day'. 'Good presentation is vital for a successful event and can be achieved through careful thought and preparation', stated the opening paragraph of the Prepare Day programme. 'Be sure to have business cards.' 'Understand implications of royalties, licensing and copyright.' 'Be confident about writing invoices and sales agreements.' And 'Smile!' A page of handy tips for managing journalists and the press, and ways to spot potential buyers or commissioners was distributed. We were offered suggestions for getting our wares online, creating webpages and working with eBay. The bottom line was: 'Sell yourself!'

New Designers ran for four days in July attracting an estimated 17,000 visitors. Jens, Robert, Tony and I each displayed several pieces of furniture at the designated Building Crafts College stand. These comprised our bedside

Figure 9.2 The author and fellow fine-woodwork trainees setting up at the *New Designers* exhibition, 2007. © David Wheeler

cabinets, coffee tables and chairs. Having initially been apprehensive about what we might gain from the experience, Jens concluded at the close of the show that 'It was fantastic!' and Tony proclaimed that we had 'held our own' and that we had attracted 'interest from the right people'. 'The biggest comment was how well it's made', Tony continued, 'and that all the design has come from us.' For Jens, the positive reception of his work gave him 'a huge boost of confidence'. 'I was approached by employers saying that I should give them a call!' he beamed momentarily, then added: 'But it would have been much nicer if I could've had some firm orders and money changing hands.'

While also relishing the attention, Robert was more pointedly sceptical about the flattery and fleeting promises: 'I'm here in the rarefied atmosphere of *New Designers* and I want it to be a success, but there's a whole lot more to making a success of it than just having a few positive comments at a design show.' Later in our conversation, he reflected: 'There are people there who try to build you up, and, I suppose by being there, you're asking to be built up.' Determined not to be swept away in the euphoria of the event, Robert vexedly asserted: 'I don't want to be pressured by some man who selfishly wants to commission me to make something, and then we start arguing whether I get 50 per cent or 60 per cent. I'd rather just hang a back door for someone – someone who I like – and be happy with it.'

The conflicting sentiments expressed by my three colleagues encapsulated an inner turmoil that we, and our fellow trainees and instructors who visited the show, experienced at *New Designers*. We were simultaneously dazzled by the buzz of the crowds and accosted by the enormity of the world of design and making beyond the College. It quickly became apparent to all that the event marked a threshold between the security, camaraderie and creative indulgence that we had enjoyed for two years, and the brutal, brazen reality of the competitive marketplace into which we now stepped, still clutching the hopes we had nurtured. Was the pursuit of pleasurable work over or just beginning?

Shortly after our departure from the College workshop, pressing responsibilities, new uncertainties and fresh hopes engulfed the lives of each graduate. The fellowship was ruptured, the community dissipated, and planning for the future once again became an individual affair.

'When I leave here', Alex told me:

> I'm going to spend one, maybe two years being a 'wood butcher!' Just doing site furniture and kitchen fitting to get a serious amount of cash behind me so that I can go on to do what I want to do: to build bespoke furniture for audiovisual systems. Produce big expensive stuff. All custom made; built-in. There's a good market and people make a phenomenal amount of money. Lots of the people doing it can knock together a cabinet, but they're not real carpenters, whereas I can make stuff that will command premium dough.

Tony, too, had his eyes set on starting a business: 'I'm not afraid of getting up early and working weekends if I have to. But, my biggest worry is getting a workshop and making the payments until I've got enough work.' He hoped that by negotiating a space-sharing arrangement with his former employer in Potters Bar, it would reduce rental costs and the outlay for new tools and machines. Tony was banking on family, word-of-mouth and his existing network of contacts in the trade for his first commissions. If need be, he would return temporarily to manufacturing doors and windows, but only to 'make ends meet and pay off the business loan' that he was waiting to receive.

For Jens, our time at the College had been 'the most enjoyable two years of [his] life'. 'It's been a positive change', he added. Thinking back to a time before the course, he recalled: 'I couldn't have said what I would be doing in the next five years because I had been stuck in a rut for so long. But now I know that, in some shape or form, I'll be woodworking for the rest of my life.' Like his fellow graduates, Jens was deeply invested in 'being happy' with the things that he made and in 'having an important role rather than a small part' in the process. Unlike Alex and Tony, however, he had no immediate plans to 'go down the route of independent work just yet'. In his view, two years had not been sufficient for getting a firm grip on the technical side of things: 'If I work with somebody, I can pick up tips on how to work faster and make better joints.' Jens was also unwilling to dedicate the sizeable resources that one guest lecturer said we would need for promoting our work: 'For the time being, I want to keep away from all that marketing and self-promotion. I'm still building confidence, I guess.'

'I'm constantly reminding myself', said Robert thoughtfully, 'that I'm not in this to be a fine furniture maker. I'm in this to have a good quality of life. So my ambitions in terms of status and financial position are minimal.' He confessed to being nervous about starting out on his own mainly because:

> I feel I know hardly anything. All I've learned is a bit of confidence to tackle things, and maybe get them wrong, and to think my way around problems. And I've learned the basics of joining timber together. I'm fighting the scary knowledge that there's a huge amount that I don't know. I need to put that to the back of my mind and march forward regardless, because I don't think I could work for anyone again, and certainly not full time. I haven't got it in me anymore.

This spoke volumes to both the state of 'not knowing' and the conscious act of ignoring that is strategically employed to manage knowledge,[27] clear a pathway through the thicket of information and unknowns, and bring full attentiveness to the immediate task at hand.

One thing about which Robert was fully confident was his newly acquired ability to earn a living on the tools. Impressively, he already had a busy rota of jobs scheduled on the heels of *New Designers*: 'I have to refurbish two brush-scrubbing tables and hang a new back door for someone. And, I take up my workshop in Forest Hill on the first of August.' Reflecting on his experience at the College and pondering the future, he told me:

> It's been the most remarkable and rapid two years of my life. It's been a process of learning I've enjoyed more than any other I've embarked upon – and I've done quite a few, though mainly academic. That said, I'm also ready to move on. My time is up. I'm ready to become the next thing that I am, being on my own.

He paused before reinforcing the divide between his future and the recent past: 'You realise that people go off their own way. And people you liked and worked well with, you may no longer work well with. It's just what happens. You develop new networks as you develop new skills.'

New Designers had been a major catalyst in growing new networks and broadening horizons, as well as in fomenting new challenges and exposing greater unknowns. It marked our 'banishment' from the college refuge where the actual costs of setting up, the business of craftwork, rapidly changing operating technologies and the real scarcity of commissions for fine furniture could all be safely ignored. In the aftermath, graduates were forced to redefine their relationships with one another and to scramble for new positions in the world of work. In doing so, they also had to recalibrate ambitions and develop more flexible expectations. For those who remained committed to the pursuit of personal fulfilment and pleasurable work, utopias now needed to be reimagined, reinterpreted and narrated anew.

SOME FINAL REFLECTIONS

In contrast to the previous chapters that explore ways of knowing, writing this chapter demanded my more careful deliberation upon the unknowns and the act of ignoring. In doing so, it became apparent that, in my role as anthropologist, I too had been ignoring important issues in the field site: namely, absences, conscious and unconscious concealments, and the marginalisation of certain kinds of knowledge. Indeed, relegating certain thoughts or activities outside thinking and doing, and excluding certain skills and technologies from the repertoire, played fundamental parts in constructing and protecting precious ideals of craft, craftwork and what it is to be a craftsperson.

I commenced my exploration of 'not knowing' and the art of ignoring during the first year, at the point when the programme emphasis shifted from architectural joinery to furniture. A few exemplary accounts of teaching and learning revealed how declarations of 'not knowing' were strategically employed by one workshop instructor to promote independent learning among his students, and how claims to 'not knowing' were tactically used by trainees, including myself, to garner assistance, gain speedier access to knowhow, and get assurances from others that we were woodworking correctly.

The story then proceeded to the second year, beginning with the compulsory milling and machining course. A variety of stances – both economic and political – were taken up on the nature of the relation of machines and power tools to craftwork. A minority endeavoured to ignore their role in woodworking altogether, but concessions were gradually, if grudgingly, made. An oppositional faction embraced them for their economy, speed and efficiency, while choosing to ignore that some carpentry tasks are in fact achieved more accurately and efficiently with a well-maintained traditional hand tool.

Both of those polemical positions were grounded in a form of mind-body ignorance, characterised by a refusal or reluctance to learn the skills and to recognise the advantages and benefits of either machines or hand tools. As I discussed, most trainees took more moderate and pragmatic views, making

use of the full gamut of tools according to the needs of the task. But nevertheless, a large number continued to deny that, like wielding a hand tool,
the safe and accurate operation of machinery and handheld power tools demands full concentration and deftness of eye-hand coordination. While machining and power tooling were accepted as necessary activities, they were
simultaneously excluded from ideals of pure craftwork. In this rivalry, hand
tools proffered the heraldry of an 'uncorrupted' tradition, whereas the boisterous handheld router bore the badge of efficiency (and masculinity) within
the smaller opposition camp.

The penultimate section of the chapter demonstrated that the real need
to market what one produces was neglected or actively ignored by many fine
woodworkers – trainees and qualified practitioners alike. Unsurprisingly,
the art of making was heavily prioritised over the business of trade, since
handwork constitutes the core pleasure and is conceived as the defining activity of the craftsperson. The majority of mature 'vocational migrants' to
the trade had sought to escape, among other things, the alienating effects of
'exchange value' and the brassy, boastful 'trumpet blowing' (in Jens' words)
of the marketing world. Their 'business' as craftspeople was producing, not
selling. At the same time, they conceded that business skills were needed to
realise their desires to be self-sufficient and to retain control over what they
created, from start to finish.

While requests for a dedicated business management module were unre-
ciprocated by the College, closer examination of the conflict revealed that
trainees would have likely resisted this additional tuition because it would
have infringed upon bench-time. The expectation of leaving the course with
business knowhow was therefore unmatched by commitment to acquiring
it, and this observation was corroborated by the fact that none pursued outside tuition in the subject while at the College.

While absorbed in producing flawless dovetail joints, steam-bending timber into exquisite forms and carving cabriole legs, trainees and instructors
ignored the mushrooming competition for handmade furniture from imports of cheaper, mass-produced and in some cases elegantly designed hardwood furniture. Conveniently ignored, too, was the obvious impact that an
economic recession might have on job prospects and potential earnings in a
trade producing superfluous, luxury items. Little did we know of the ticking
subprime-mortgage time bomb and the 'Great Recession' it would unleash
across Britain and the world shortly after we graduated.

Equally unpopular to ponder was the factual scarcity of clients willing
to risk commissioning a unique piece of furniture, or with pockets deep
enough to pay and the patience to wait for it to be designed, made, polished
and delivered. As I described, accessing that small and typically elite market

of 'taste-makers' is more critically dependent on the craftsperson's existing social and cultural capital than on their flair for design or technical accomplishment. The salience of social class to success remained unspoken since, in contrast to the world of commerce and finance, craftwork was popularly conceived as a leveller: a way of working and living that eliminated 'useless toil' and conquered forms of economic and social disparity among its practitioners with an overriding sense of fulfilment and contentment.

In sum, ignoring and 'not knowing' were regularly employed to manage or evade what was either too much or discomforting knowledge.[28] By circumventing inconvenient truths, ringfencing awkward topics or avoiding certain activities, woodwork trainees were attempting to defer anxieties about the world of work and disengage from its noisy, disorientating messiness. Doing so enabled them to remain anchored in skill learning and creative making, while profiting from the time and tranquillity in the *Nowhere* of the college workshop to imagine alternative, idealised futures.

Actively 'not knowing' and ignoring therefore need to be acknowledged as practical and practised skills in their own right. They comprise conceptual, emotional and embodied activities that select, conceal, order, suture, shape, reconfigure and style raw stimuli, experiences and information into manageable ways of being and knowing. And some individuals master it much better than others. However, that carefully tended realm of being and knowing is fragile. When the context changes and security is unplugged, utopian visions crack and rupture ensues.

Rupture to the camaraderie that had been steadily built over the two years of intensive training together was witnessed most dramatically during the *New Designers* show at the end of the course. That exposure to the frenetic marketing and business of design and production, and the sheer size of this commercial sector inflicted lasting tensions and new competitions between the once-tight cohort of fine woodworkers, fracturing social relations and demolishing shared goals. As observed by anthropologist Rudi Colloredo-Mansfeld in his study of indigenous artisans in Ecuador, competition is not simply derivative of capital; it imputes a structural relationship among competing artisans whereby they 'require each other to devise the signs and styles from which they all create themselves and their enterprises'.[29]

In the aftermath, actors were forced to take up new positions, mobilise new social alliances, renegotiate long-term goals and aspirations, and reinterpret or reinvent the utopias that they had authored for themselves. Encroachment of the world did not necessarily extinguish idyllic aspirations; rather, it modified them. Arguably, this recurring process is vital for individual growth and development, and for crafting livelihoods that are viable, resilient and hopefully pleasurable.

NOTES

An earlier and briefer version of this chapter was published as 'Managing Pleasurable Pursuits: Utopic Horizons and the Arts of Ignoring and "Not Knowing" among Fine Woodworkers', in R. Dilley and T. Kirsch (eds), *Regimes of Ignorance: Anthropological Perspectives on the Production and Reproduction of Non-knowledge* (New York: Berghahn Books, 2015), 70–90. Dilley and Kirsh's volume of ethnographically grounded chapters explores the mutually constitutive relations between knowledge and ignorance (and public knowledge and secrecy) within political and social contexts. Ignorance and non-knowledge are recognised as being not merely the absence of knowledge; rather, they are produced and reproduced by 'a constellation of discursive practices and power relations giving rise to epistemological gaps and forms of unknowing that have generative social effects and consequences' (Kirsch and Dilley, 'Regimes of Ignorance', 2).

1. Bellows, *To Jerusalem and Back*, 127.
2. See Hobart, 'Introduction'; and Dilley, 'Reflections on Knowledge Practices', 176.
3. References to Morris, *News from Nowhere*; Thoreau, 'Walden'; and Rose, *The Village Carpenter*.
4. Arendt, *The Human Condition*.
5. For an interesting comparison, see anthropologist Jamie Cross' study with workers in a factory in India that mass-manufactured consumer diamonds: 'At the heart of a seemingly endless repetition of movements and gestures lay aesthetic and non-instrumental embellishments in technique, flourishes of superior skill and judgement that expressed an individual's ability to control his machines and tools' (Cross, 'Technological Intimacy', 137).
6. Sigaut, 'Learning, Teaching, and Apprenticeship', 109.
7. Morris, 'How We Live', 25.
8. There is an interesting comparison to be made here with the stonemasons working on Glasgow Cathedral. According to anthropologists Thomas Yarrow and Siân Jones, the masons 'celebrate hand tools as symbols of a more engaged, slower, more responsive "traditional" way of working. However, they are also sceptical of the external imposition of "traditional" methods in conservation contexts, including policies that prescribe hand-tool use to the exclusion of power tools and machines. Though hand tools are symbolically invested as a locus of tradition, resistance is not to specific tools or machines but to the determination of working practices in accordance with externally imposed standards and processes' (Yarrow and Jones, 'Stone Is Stone', 269).
9. Norbury, *Marketing and Promotion*.
10. Ibid., 9.
11. Norbury, *Bespoke*.
12. In an interview conducted at the Building Crafts College, 20 October 2009.
13. A study of nearly 2,000 'makers' across the United Kingdom published in 2012 reported that although '89% met at least some of their general business skill needs' (i.e. bookkeeping, web design, marketing), just '43% had some training in business skills since starting their business' and 'almost half felt they needed to develop additional business skills' (Crafts Council et al., *Craft in an Age of Change*, 25).
14. In the same report, it was stated that just 25 per cent of makers surveyed across the United Kingdom wanted training in marketing.
15. Hart, 'Work, Labor, and Artisans', 600.

16. Like the Building Crafts College, prospectuses for furniture making courses at Buck-inghamshire Chilterns University College, London Metropolitan University and Rycote College assured applicants that they would be equipped with the necessary skills to design and make furniture, and the knowhow to run a small independent business.

17. From copies of a letter written by students in 2001 and staff student meeting minutes in 2002, it was apparent that trainees on the fine-woodwork programme had been requesting provision of tuition from experts in industry, tool companies and guest lecturers since at least the time that the College moved from Great Titchfield Street to Stratford. Graduates from cohorts prior to 2005 informed me of the same.

18. It is important to note that numerous students on the fine-woodwork and stone-masonry diploma courses at the College were the beneficiaries of generous support from the Carpenters' Company, which partially or fully covered tuition fees.

19. H. Mayhew, co-founder of the satirical magazine *Punch*, compiled his publications about working people in London in the *Morning Chronicle* and published the book *London Labour and the London Poor* in 1851.

20. Samuel, 'The Workshop of the World', 38.

21. I calculated this figure using the Consumer Price Index (CPI) UK inflation calculator.

22. Cf. Samuel, 'The Workshop of the World', 38.

23. Leach, 'Carpenters in Medieval London', 145–46.

24. https://www.barnsley-furniture.co.uk (retrieved 8 June 2021).

25. Likewise, a report commissioned by the Crafts Council and published in 2020 noted with regard to the demand for business training among early-career professional makers that: 'Historically, the Crafts Council have offered training courses in many of the topics tested in the makers' survey, and have experienced makers' reporting a need for this training, but then not necessarily taking advantage of it when it was available' (Morris Hargreaves McIntyre, *The Market for Craft*, 75).

26. That year, exhibition spaces for furniture design were granted to twenty-four differ-ent higher education institutions across England. Of these programmes, only a very small number focused on fine woodwork or offered intensive training in traditional bench methods.

27. For a discussion of this phenomenon at work in another social and cultural con-text, see Roy Dilley's fascinating exploration of the ways that French colonial officers and institutions in West Africa worked to produce ignorance and nonknowledge as 'positive absences' in the fabric of colonial understanding (Dilley, 'Problematic Reproductions').

28. Festinger, *A Theory of Cognitive Dissonance*.

29. Colloredo-Mansfeld, 'An Ethnography of Neoliberalism', 125–26.

CHAPTER 10

SKILL AND AGEING

How different everything is for the craftsman who transforms a part of the world with his own hands, who can see his work as emanating from his being and can step back at the end of a day or lifetime and point to an object – whether a square of canvas, a chair or a clay jug – and see it as a stable repository of his skills and an accurate record of his years, and hence feel collected together in one place, rather than strung out across projects which long ago evaporated into nothing one could hold or see.

—Alain de Botton[1]

From a meadow seedling, an English oak matures, thickening into an immense, deeply furrowed trunk that bears a sprawling canopy of gnarled, twisting branches. After decades, or possibly centuries, it is felled with a logger's chainsaw. The branches are removed and its mighty bole is trucked to a mill where it is converted into planks. Air-dried in a shed and stamped at one end with 'FSC' to certify sustainable sourcing,[2] the planks of timber are then exchanged between brokers and merchants. Several eventually find their way to a furniture maker's bench. In their hands, selected planks are thicknessed and planed, marked-up, cut to length and prepared for joining.

Natural growth ceased when the oak was felled, but the shape, form and colouring of the planks continue to change with changing humidity, temperature and exposure to sunlight. The anatomy of each board's grain, golden medullary rays, and knots respond in sometimes-erratic ways to the carpenter's tools. The oak timber is progressively transformed into four sturdy legs, two broad arms and the ladder back of a comfy fireside chair. In the home of its new owner, the chair's wooden surfaces are sat upon, leaned against, polished and dusted, stained with a ring of red wine and chewed by the family's puppy. Years later, the chair is willed to the children, invaded briefly by woodworm, restored, damaged by water and salvaged from a fire. And then it is passed along once again.

Like the oak, a carpenter's skills and their dedication to the trade may extend beyond the working life of that individual. This chapter explores the growth, development and deterioration of craft skill over a lifespan from the perspectives of four generations of woodworkers. It begins and ends with George,[3] a carpenter whose memories of apprenticeship and practice take the starting point for my chapter back to the 1930s in southeast England, and whose acts of generosity have made training possible for future generations in the trade. The accounts in between from carpenters Josh, Tony and James investigate in turn the early education of a teenage woodworker, the experience and growing confidence of a young man setting out as a furniture maker, and the professional practice of an established middle-aged designer-maker whose initial role as apprentice has, with the passing years, turned to mentor.

As attested by the previous chapters, woodworking presents a constant challenge, and mastering the craft demands persistence and willingness to learn and continually develop. This theme has been central to my investigation throughout. A woodworker's skilfulness is a measure of their ability to respond creatively, solve problems and incorporate new information into their working processes. Design and making are interrelated skills that grow in response to, and in tight relation with, the craftsperson's total working environment and life experiences, and therefore evolve in unforeseen ways, producing unique solutions that progressively come to be associated with an individual's method and style.

However, skill-based knowledge does not merely grow and develop. Like the organic properties of the timber they work, the skills of woodworkers, too, are susceptible to damage, deterioration and decline. The final section of the chapter returns to George in order to explore the impact of ageing, injury and illness on tool-wielding practices, and the reskilling and restructuring strategies devised by those determined to remain active in their beloved trade. Jim O. described his own personal strategy in Chapter 5. It may be recalled that, after having badly 'tweaked his back', Jim retrained in order to successfully transfer his carpentry skills from construction sites to workshop teaching. In discussing George's circumstances, I reference literature from the neurosciences that examines transformation in the nervous system as the body grows, practises and ages.

Grounded in their field study findings, anthropologists claim that self and identity are not fixed, but rather are constantly in the making. Neuroscientific literature lends support to that claim by illustrating how our brains and nervous systems, too, are ever-changing. Engaging with issues of ageing and transformation from an interdisciplinary perspective can deepen our understanding of the factors entailed in processes of growth and making.

In this chapter, I weave background history, analysis and theory into the ethnography of life stories. The four woodworkers featured reflected carefully on their creative processes, choices and personal development as craftspeople, and articulated their thinking on these matters as fluidly as they wielded their tools. I therefore include detailed quotations from their accounts alongside my own explanations, through which I bring narrative order to the events we discussed and the things that I learned from them.

GEORGE: A WOODWORKER'S TRAINING IN DECADES PAST

There was a great deal of unemployment in the 1930s, so you did what you could.[4] I left school, at fourteen of course, which you had to do in those days. A year later my sister married a carpenter whose father had a workshop in Croydon, and so I went there. He had quite a good place, though the machinery was old-fashioned and wouldn't be allowed today. My first job every morning was to start up the gas-engine, which drove a series of shafts with pulleys that came down to each machine. The fly-wheel on the machine was bigger than I was and had a great big handle. Legally speaking, I wasn't allowed to work machinery until I'd gone past sixteen. That was a law. In fact, once a year the government would send an inspector around. It was always a big laugh because the inspector would come to see if you were physically fit. They'd ask: 'Are you deaf, dumb, daft or dippy?' 'Yes Sir, we are', we'd say. 'That's alright then. You're fit!' We didn't know much then about health and safety, or what-not.

—George Pysden

I visited George Pysden at his home in leafy Woldingham, Surrey, on 22 January 2008. George, aged ninety, was a widower and capably looked after himself. He graciously offered me a cup of tea on arrival before taking me on a tour of the spacious reception rooms on the ground floor to view examples of furniture that he made during his long career as a woodworker. The cabinets and tables were classical in form, proportion and detail, and their highly polished surfaces displayed intricate inlaid geometries of precious woods – a skilled art for which George was renowned. I had first been introduced to George's workmanship at the Carpenters' Livery Hall in the City of London, where several of his elegant tables furnished the grand reception rooms. George was admitted to the Freedom in 1982 and to the Livery in 1984.[5]

We proceeded to the conservatory where we sat together chatting for much of that sunny afternoon, overlooking a lawn that sloped steeply away from the house down to a small garage-cum-workshop along the main road. George told me about his life and work:

When I was a young boy, people didn't look at computers and what-not. They had hobbies. I got pleasure from making things. I bought an old treadle-lathe for making candlesticks and we did a bit of woodwork at school. There are so many different things you can do with a piece of timber. That's why I think wood and forests are our greatest blessing! So I got interested in carpentry. From an early age, without saying 'Yes this is what I'd like to do', I knew instinctively that I was going to do it.

This childhood fascination with making things by hand was commonly cited by woodworkers as a key influence in their later career choices. A small minority of those interviewed came from families with a history in the trade, and some had their first introduction to carpentry at school, albeit in usually elementary ways.[6] Most of the 'vocational migrants' introduced in previous chapters came to the Building Crafts College fine-woodwork programme with some basic level of DIY experience, but not necessarily in carpentry. Wood, perhaps more than any other material, possesses widespread allure for those wanting to make or build useful objects. Historian and woodworker Harvey Green observed that: 'Ordinary people assume that they know or can readily discover how to work with wood, whereas working with metals and plastic is mysterious, dangerous and requires tools that are too expensive and too large for most people to acquire or use.'[7]

Wood and woodworking also appeal to the senses. Different varieties of timber have distinct colour, odour, density, grain and figure, and every plank responds differently to the teeth of a saw or the cutting blade of a plane. Notably, the processes of working with hand tools and giving shape and form to a plank of timber also serve to *re-form* the maker.[8] Focused practice and repetition gradually bring about new configurations in perceptual awareness,[9] physiology and neural circuitry,[10] as well as changes to one's emotional state, disposition and sense of self.[11] A history of past hobbies, sport and play regularly form the backdrop to the more intensive training that, in effect, grows the body and mind of the learner into a full-fledged craftsperson. I asked George to tell me more about a woodworker's training in the past:

> In the days before I was born, if your dad wanted you to be a woodworker, you would be 'articled'. It probably cost your dad about £25, which was a lot of money then. If you work it out, £2 was a week's wage, so that's more than ten weeks' wages to get his son articled to a firm of woodworkers.[12] But then that firm was obliged by law to train the boy until the age of twenty-one. In any case, articling was gradually phased out because there wasn't much affluence in the 1920s and 30s. There were expensive [vocational] colleges that those at my end of the spectrum had no hope of attending. It was all pie in the sky.

George was from a working-class background and his father had been a train driver for Southern Railway:[13]

> If you wanted to be a woodworker you had to get a job with a woodworking firm. And if you were really keen, you'd attend night school, which was much more affordable at about £1 a term. Of course, one wanted to go to night school – which unfortunately I never did – to learn maths and geometry, since they're important in the trade.[14]

According to George, there was no standardised form of learning when he was a lad:

> You worked with the governor all the time. He told you what to do and you had to do it, otherwise you might get a thick ear. It was like that in those days. You learned your job the hard way. We bought the timber in ready-planed and then set it out by hand, cut it and mortised-and-tenoned it, by hand. To start off, I was given a cutting list and it was my job to find the right sizes of timber. We never threw the small pieces away. We had a place where all the short ends were stacked up. I measured them up to see what we could get out of them, and then I stood next to my governor while he set it out for the cuts. As I progressed, he put me on more advanced work. After all, he couldn't do everything, and that's why he employed me. An apprentice has to be taught, of course; but then they have to learn it themselves.[15] I was brought up, not in mass production, but in small-scale individual work – what we would call 'short runs'. You know, perhaps twenty-off or thirty-off, or something like that.

English woodworker and local historian Walter Rose noted that the traditional seven-year apprenticeship, codified during the Elizabethan period and still the standard in his father's day, had been shortened to just four or five years by the time he was a youth in the late nineteenth century. By the late 1930s, at the time when George had entered the trade, the duration was further reduced to the point where 'there is a general disinclination for any apprenticeship at all, and a sad misconception as to the amount that has to be learned'.[16]

As has already been discussed more fully in Chapter 3, the status of craft and building-trade apprenticeships in Britain declined over the course of the twentieth century. In comparison with its European industrial competitors, the level of government investment in vocational training was meagre, and responsibility of training was relegated to industry and individual employers.[17] By the 1970s and 1980s, however, many construction firms, small and large alike, came to favour flexible contracts over directly employing their labour, and, with that change of practice, employer investment in training diminished yet further.[18] Numbers of apprentices fell sharply during these decades, and again most dramatically in the early and mid-1990s.[19] In the government's attempt to address Britain's widening skills gap, the Modern Apprenticeship scheme was implemented, combining workplace training with periods of block release at vocational colleges or the equivalent and leading to National Vocational Qualifications (NVQs).

George believed that today's college training is inferior to the tuition his generation received before the Second World War and that now 'they're too keen on these NVQs':

> When we did woodwork at school, the mindset was that you might very well do this for a living, whereas today that's not the case. In fact, parents don't want their children

to become woodworkers. They want them to be computer engineers, or designers, or what-not. Woodworking just isn't upper-crust enough. Yet, what would they do if they didn't have a woodworker?

On 6 January 1940, George took an oath in the Royal Air Force and served his country during the Second World War. 'After nearly six years in service, your mind wasn't organised like it was when you started out', he told me, and it took a great deal of effort to rebuild a normal civilian life. He soon found jobs in different places, and later that year he married, put a deposit on a house and started his own business, 'moonlighting as a carpenter' in his spare time. The volume of commissions grew steadily, and by the start of the 1950s, he had set up a workshop in Croydon. Six months later, he took on his first apprentice, Fred, a young man in his mid-twenties. Fred had originally served an apprenticeship to a bookbinder, but after two years of national service his sights were fixed on woodworking and he approached George for employment and training.

George gradually purchased second-hand machinery, which was scarcely available after the War. He and Fred accepted any commissions that came their way 'to pay the bills'. 'But every so often I got something that was really fascinating to make', George recounted. 'And as I got more interested in [finer woodwork], I gradually changed over to making furniture, like the pieces you've seen here', gesturing to the interior rooms we had visited. George soon outgrew his premises and so purchased a bombsite on the opposite side of the road where he erected a brand new workshop. He later moved again to a larger piece of land, which he profitably developed over the years to include his own large workspace and a multistorey commercial unit that he rented out.

Fred stayed for four years at George's workshop before embarking on his own business venture, but he continued to pay regular social calls to his former mentor. Over the course of his career, George estimated that he trained nearly ten people on the tools. 'It's a trade where young people come and go. Some, like Fred, stayed a long time before going off to promote their own lives, while others were gone after just a few months', he told me:

> You've got the type of person who likes the 'outdoor life', working on building sites. It's freedom, isn't it. But when winter comes, they want to be indoors, and before spring they're gone. You've also got young people who come in thinking they want to be a woodworker: 'I'll work with my hands! It'll be easy.' They perhaps do it for eighteen months, two years; then they're off wanting to do something else.

I asked George what sorts of ideal qualities he looked for in a trainee:

> Woodwork is a trade where you've got to think – really think. There's nothing automatic. I say to the youngsters who come to me: 'Any fool can get a big hammer

and smash things up. It don't require brains. But can you take a hammer and make something worthwhile?' You've got to want to create something and to be able to say 'I made that'. You've got to have pride.

If a young person knocked at his door today, George would recommend that 'they find a small workshop that does varied work, and start there'. A small workshop doing bespoke joinery and furniture offers trainees the best opportunity to 'learn it themselves'.

JOSH: LEARNING THE BASICS

Josh was among the youngest members of the fine-woodwork cohort at the Building Crafts College, arriving straight from secondary school and supported by a grant from the Carpenters' Company. He was a tall and lanky sixteen-year-old boy with bright blue eyes, a sprinkle of freckles on his pale nose and cheeks, and a faint shadow of downy hair over his upper lip. Josh's family lived in Aldersbrook, an Edwardian housing estate in northeast London, and his older twin sisters and both parents were engaged in artistic occupations. Josh readily acknowledged that growing up in a creative household motivated his career choice, but he also conceded that he was better at 'making practical things' than doing art and design.

Figure 10.1 Portrait of fine-woodwork trainee Josh, 2006. © Trevor H.J. Marchand

Josh was first introduced to carpentry in year seven at school and was immediately drawn to working with his hands: 'I also tried metalwork and electronics, but I kept burning my fingers in electronics and things moved too slowly in metalwork.' Sitting across the table from me in the College library and fidgeting with his collection of fraying festival wristbands, Josh told me:

> Kids who went to my primary school just moved on to the [local] secondary school. That's what people from my neighbourhood do. My school friends are all jealous that I've jumped ship and I'm out there doing something I enjoy. They're just stuck in school doing something they hate. So, it's quite pleasing to know that I'm doing something to get where I want to be.

In the beginning, however, the full days at college dragged on for what seemed like an eternity to Josh. By mid-afternoon, he was counting down the minutes, and he routinely had his tools stored away and his work area swept long before official leaving time. Con, our first-year instructor, would gently but firmly reprimand Josh and delegate small tasks to keep his mind and hands occupied until 4:30 PM. Punctual timekeeping, along with accurate diary keeping and general tidiness of working areas, was rigidly reinforced.

By his own admission, Josh was impatient and careless, preferring to be active with his hands and tools and less concerned with the end result. Indeed, eagerness was one of his defining characteristics, in large part due to the exuberance of youth, but also owing to a certain intensity of spirit. 'I would like this carpentry thing better if things were quicker', he told me. 'If I get it wrong, I'll just start again and catch up. It doesn't bother me.' But he also possessed an impressive level of critical awareness regarding his own actions and decisions, and of the social dynamics in the workshop: 'I get annoyed with myself when I make a mistake. I start working faster and the mistakes build up, and I try to cover them up.'

Josh executed his early projects with haste and a degree of recklessness. Con, with ample experience in taming youthful zeal, tailored the project specifications to alleviate some of the time pressure for Josh, allowing him to bring greater concentration to improving the basic hand skills. The first project to combine what we had so far learned in term one about standard joinery was the making of a small tool cabinet in Redwood pine. We would use those finished cabinets to store our tools and workbooks for the remainder of the programme. We therefore had licence to design our individual cabinet as we pleased, but the project specifications insisted on the inclusion of dovetail joints (see Chapter 4, Figure 4.3). We would need to be practised in producing those by the time the curriculum came to making hardwood items of furniture.

As mentioned in Chapter 4, Redwood pine is ideally suited to learning carpentry because it is affordable, easily worked and sufficiently challenging for developing skills. With a little poetic licence, intriguing parallels may be drawn between the growth and properties of Redwood pine and the early stages of the college training regime. Fast-growing Redwood is planted at tight, regular spacing in managed forests. This protects young trees from the full brunt of winds and weather, but deprives them of optimal sunlight and precipitation, thereby producing straighter, denser wood. This fast, straight growth might be metaphorically compared to the steep and largely linear nature of every novice's learning trajectory during the first six months. The heavily structured college curriculum was aimed at cultivating conscientious attitudes, sensitising judgement and perception, and equipping students with a basic skillset that each would build upon and progressively expand over the duration of the programme and throughout their working lives.

Comparisons might also be drawn between the figure of Redwood pine and the relatively homogeneous level of experience shared by new trainees. It may be recalled that a timber's figure refers to the combination of natural features displayed on the face of a cut board, including streaks of colour, grain pattern, medullary rays, conspicuous growth rings, knots and other natural 'defects', all of which may be deliberately accentuated with planing, scraping, oiling and polishing. Though Redwood pine exhibits colour variation between the heartwood and sapwood, its figure is limited, revealing none of the character of a plank milled from the bole of an old English oak that bent to the sunshine, bowed in the wind or accrued a long history of twists and burls.[20] Likewise, the novice's early knowledge of woodworking lacks dimensionality, and the disciplined regimen and brisk pace of the college curriculum was calculated to restrain early development within narrow margins. By year two, however, the rapid rate of learning would gradually ease, broadening the scope for individual meanderings along the learning path and for taking detours into novel problem-solving exercises in design and with tools and materials. This would ultimately yield richer, more entangled histories of personal discovery and, if successful, more resilient and resourceful methods of practice.

After marking out the dovetail joints for his Redwood tool cabinet, Josh asked Con what kind of chisel he should use to chop them out. 'Good question Josh', the instructor replied in a deadpan tone, before strolling away. 'I didn't have a clue what to do', Josh confessed. 'Just had to make a decision and do it. So I followed my instinct of what's best.' Con's Socratic method of instruction encouraged us to creatively exploit the available workshop resources in order to plan or improvise solutions to our problems. In addition to the common tool cupboard, resources included a shelving unit of reference material and, significantly, one's community of peers, who might offer a diversity of perspectives and approaches to any carpentry challenge.

Josh struggled, however, with carpentry manuals and photocopied hand-outs. It was the abstract nature of book learning that had driven him away from the school classroom to handwork in the first place. He insisted that demonstrations worked best, but then qualified his statement by adding: 'Sometimes it goes on for too long. I need to be shown quickly. If something's repeated more than once, I just get distracted.' He regularly abandoned his workbench to pay social visits. He pulled up a stool at a neighbour's bench, nestled in comfortably, struck up casual conversation while watching them work and sometimes offered to lend a hand. 'I pick up things that way', he told me, 'especially from Tony.' That dynamic between Josh and Tony was described in the previous chapter. Josh especially appreciated Tony's tips on making jigs,[21] which helped to 'speed up the whole process of getting things done'. Josh also kept a regular eye on his age-mate Liam, who was stationed at the adjoining bench:

> With Liam, I'm generally ahead of him in the projects so I get to see a different way of how I might have done things. But sometimes he doesn't have a clue what he's doing, so I just show him. I've picked it up from Con or Tony, so I teach Liam.

Josh explicitly recognised that instructing others, either verbally or through demonstration, and sometimes merely with straightforward encourage-ment, was integral to his own learning processes. When he eventually completed his tool cabinet, dovetails and all, he did so with a deep sense of satisfaction: 'When I'm doing something nice, and I do it well, I just get a happy feeling from it. Forty-eight dovetails! I feel like I've achieved some-thing. And that's the main reason I came here.'

I sat down with Josh again at the end of the first year to review the past months and listen to the ambitions he had for the future. 'I've learnt a lot', he began. 'Considering what I learnt from five years at school and what I've learnt here. . .' He paused a moment before continuing:

> It's done what I wanted it to do. I've learnt to think about what I'm doing and how I should do it, and about how I come to a decision. I know now that I need to come up with an action plan for how I'm going to make something, otherwise I get muddled up. But what I need to change is my attitude that 'It's time to go!' when it comes three o'clock, because I know if I start doing that now, that'll be my attitude for the rest of my life.

I asked Josh what knowhow he was hoping to leave with by graduation. 'With the knowledge that I can make things', he responded without hesita-tion. 'I want to have the confidence to see something and say, "I can make

that", and just know that not many people can do the stuff I'm able to do.'
He beamed.

'What do you plan to do with your life when you finish here?' I probed. 'I
know I don't want to go into full-time work at eighteen or nineteen, making
doors and windows for the rest of my life', Josh replied. 'That's what Tony's
left behind, isn't it. I could do that for a while, but I'll get bored.' He conceded that in order to become a furniture maker, he would probably need
additional training in design. Reflecting deeply as he narrated the script for
his future, he concluded:

> By twenty-one-ish, after a BA in furniture making, I could have those qualifications
> and a better idea about what I can do. It'll give me that little bit more to be first in the
> queue for a nicer job, a bit more money and, best of all, the freedom to do what I want
> to do. It'll be a good investment.

Like all craftspeople I met over the years, Josh was seeking control over his
working life and satisfaction from the quality and kind of things he would
produce. By growing and diversifying his skillset, he was strategically mapping out a plan for achieving those goals.

TONY: PUSHING THE LIMITS

By Christmastime in year two, growing numbers of fine-woodwork trainees
were cutting short the tea and lunch breaks to return to their benches and
make progress with their projects. The shift from architectural joinery to
furniture making sparked enthusiasm and invigorated the friendly, productive competition amongst us. Competition extended beyond mere technical
skills to include the ways that we had come to individually inhabit idealised
notions of the 'fine woodworker' in our actions and demeanour.[22]

Trainees were motivated not only to explore design as an expression of
personal interest and aesthetic taste, but also to test their evolving abilities
to make functional objects in hardwood timbers. In general, slow-growing
hardwoods occur in a greater range of hue and colour than softwoods, and
with a superior depth of character and more pronounced figure: classic European oak (*Quercus robur*) is coarsely textured, and its distinctive growth
rings and broad, golden medullary rays are exquisitely revealed when quar-
ter-sawn; American walnut (*Juglans nigra*) is sought for its chocolate-brown
heartwood, while paler English walnut (*Juglans regia*) is prized for its varied
grain and dark streaks; European beech (*Fagus sylvatica*) is fine and even-
textured, mellowing in colour from pale to golden-brown after cutting;
the dark heartwood of rosewood timber (*Dalbergia latifolia*) is luxuriously
streaked with black and deep purple, and its narrow bands of interlocking

grain produce a delicate ribbon pattern; tulipwood (*Liriodendron tulipifera*) has a finely textured, straight-grained heartwood ranging in colour from olive-green to brown, with distinctive blue streaks; and the reddish, flecked heartwood and fine finish of black cherry (*Prunus serotina*) makes this an ever-popular timber with furniture makers.[23] These represent only a small sample of the hardwoods commonly used in making fine furniture, musical instruments and luxury items, and for turnery and architectural joinery.

The College timber rack was regularly stocked with the more plentiful American varieties of oak and walnut, as well as tulipwood, cherry, ash and beech. Giving the trainees free rein to select hardwoods for their first furniture project – a bedside cabinet – was like unleashing novice sommeliers in a fine wine cellar, armed with corkscrews. Some of the resulting cabinets exhibited a giddy assortment of timbers selected to maximise colour contrasts, and others were made from timber varieties with hardness and grain patterns far too challenging for our present levels of experience.

However, timber selection was progressively tempered and cultivated by budding interests in exhibition catalogues and reference volumes,[24] as well as by the illustrated lectures delivered by visiting furniture makers and the group outings we made to museums and exhibitions. Deliberation and consultation among trainees on aesthetic and stylistic choices became more regular. Casual conversation was increasingly peppered with references to the history of furniture and exchanges of opinion on contemporary design trends. Banter, too, conveyed critical commentary or expressed veiled praise for another's design decisions or woodworking techniques. In effect, these everyday interactions raised awareness among trainees that they were actively participating in a craft with multiple histories and aesthetic traditions. Each of those traditions was the product of discrete methods and philosophies, which in turn gave rise to distinct expressions of form and structure.

Students variously investigated the English Arts and Crafts, unadorned Shaker furniture, Japanese joinery, vintage Scandinavian design, clean Modernism and crisp Bauhaus lines, while others sought inspiration from Surrealism or de Stijl art, or from the form and texture of natural objects. Individuals variously subscribed to, or reacted against, particular traditions in developing their own proclivities and staking out positions within the vast territory of craftsmanship.

Our final and most challenging assignment was the chair project, which required trainees to make use of their full spectrum of existing skills and to refine and develop these in response to the new challenges posed by their individual designs. By this point, our standard skillset comprised the ability to execute technical scale drawings; quantify materials needed, prepare a cutting sheet and estimate costs; select, mill and machine the timber; mark out, make simple jigs and adeptly handle a wide array of carpentry tools;

cramp and glue up the final assembly; and finish the surfaces of our furniture pieces with a scraper or spokeshave and polish them up with oil or wax. The legs of Josh's chair design needed to be turned on the lathe with a selection of chisels, gouges and parting tools, and so he needed to spend additional time learning and practising operations on that machine. The seats for two other projects involved simple upholstering, which also had to be added to the skillsets of those trainees.

Design, of course, is not a singular, isolated and individual event of 'genius', but rather a multifaceted activity that is stretched over time and generated by, among other things, viewing images, reading about styles, interacting with exemplars, dialoguing and debating with other people, imagining with the 'mind's eye', sketching, producing measured drawings or models, physically making, and making mistakes and resolving them. The finished creation becomes progressively defined as the project ensues, but the processes of design may continue with rethinking and remaking that object.

In the case of chairs, good design demands careful consideration of their loadbearing components, and their resistance to tension, compression, sheer, torsion or bending when the chair is sat upon or moved about. It also demands deliberation on the anatomy, posture and ergonomic comfort of a generic (or sometimes a particular) future sitter. Peter Nicholson, a polymath of the late eighteenth and early nineteenth centuries who had originally apprenticed as a cabinet maker, exalted the 'art of chair making'. In his view, chairs, like other pieces of furniture, should be 'adapted to the beautiful curved lines of the human figure'.[25] Unsurprisingly, chair making in Britain became a distinct craft by the eighteenth century. Architectural historian Galen Cranz noted that chair making combines 'the skills of turner, carver, joiner and upholsterer', and requires the chair maker to refine and codify 'the best rules for chair design . . . from both the physiological and the aesthetic point of view'.[26] Together, this long list of considerations described the remit of our assignment to design and make a functional and pleasing chair.

Chairs with sinuously curved components, such as cabriole legs or curved splats, demand the additional design and making of (sometimes complex) jigs, and meticulous planning for safely and effectively shaping the components on the whirling cutter-heads of the spindle moulder or cutting them out on the band-saw. Designing the chair and designing the jigs are not discrete activities; instead, one informs the other of possibilities and limitations to what can be made.

The chair project offered a welcome challenge for Tony in particular. The first-year joinery tasks had largely replicated his working knowledge as a door and window manufacturer, and his carpentry skills had not been significantly expanded during the bedside cabinet or coffee table projects. Tony's precision with the saw, the tight fit of his joinery, and the flawless finish of his projects were unsurpassed by any other in the cohort. While chopping mortises, for example, his stance and posture were relaxed, his gaze fully directed to the spot he was working, and his swing with the mallet was fluid and rhythmic, perfectly meeting the top of the chisel handle each time with a resounding 'thump'. By comparison, the carriage of Tony's neighbouring colleague was tense and almost confrontational towards the task. He stood awkwardly at his bench, grasping his chisel and mallet in a somewhat alien manner, and his torso and limbs wrestled to execute the chop.

However, what Tony possessed in technical skill, he lacked in design experience. His fellow trainees playfully derided his previous projects for their allegedly unimaginative form and clumsy proportions. With admirable maturity, he translated the message of their banter into a personal challenge and embarked on the final chair project with the goal to improve his design skills and extend his abilities as a maker.

Tony was thoughtful and articulate, and usually generous with woodworking tips and guidance when others requested assistance. In our first one-to-one interview at the start of the programme, he was already fixed on becoming a furniture maker, while the plans of fellow classmates at that time ranged from vague to not-yet-crystallised. 'My plan is to own a workshop specialised in bespoke pieces: tables, chairs, cabinets – though not necessarily kitchens. Making kitchens is getting onto the same track as making windows and doors. It gets repetitive and you're always working to deadlines', he cautioned. 'I want to create stuff from my own designs and with my own tools that I can send to exhibitions and galleries.' He paused to reflect before adding:

> I guess I'm more interested in the artistic and imaginative side of woodworking, even though it might not be as lucrative. Money's needed, of course, but it's not the 'be-all and end-all'. I'd prefer to make what I enjoy for a living than slave away in someone else's workshop. A good lifestyle is most important.

Tony signed on at the Building Crafts College to supplement his skillset and to secure the time and space needed to explore his potential. We spoke about skill learning and development, which, according to him, had to be 'first-and-foremost practical'. 'The stuff we're learning is hard to explain', he told me. 'You'll never understand it from a book or pictures as well as you can by watching it. It's even more important to have the chance to do it yourself, to make a mistake, to try it again, and to do it until you get it right. You won't get it until you've made the mistake and learned from it. Then it clicks!' he exclaimed with a broad, knowing smile.

I pushed Tony for his reflections on that moment of epiphany. 'When you're using a new tool', I asked, 'how do you know when you've "got it

right"?' 'You get the right feel', he replied directly. 'It just goes so much better, more efficiently. There's one way to use a tool properly, and that's the way
you've got to do it. Once you've got the feel, you just can't use it wrongly.'

In addition to making and amending mistakes and honing technique,
Tony also named 'challenge' as integral to learning. 'It's exciting as well', he
added. 'It's nice making easy stuff, but a challenge makes you think. That's
how your mind grows.' Other ingredients that he listed as essential to mastering woodwork were patience, discipline, drive and a certain measure of
stubbornness to see one's idea through to its logical conclusion. Stubbornness, he proposed, comes with age: 'You're easy about it all when you're
fifteen. But we're not fifteen anymore, and we have an idea in mind of what
we're going for.'

The series of challenges Tony set for himself with the chair would indeed
test the limits of his skill and his generally calm nature. His first and most
difficult hurdle was to move conceptually beyond the basic archetype: 'A
picture of a typical bloody chair gets stuck in my head, and "It's gotta have
four legs, a back and two arms!" I find it really hard to rubbish that and start
afresh. So I have to build on it to make it different.' Solo visits to the Victoria
& Albert Museum failed to inspire, and so he perused furniture catalogues –
'Not to copy', he said, but 'just to get shapes'. The icons of twentieth-century
design that had stirred the motivations of fellow trainees left Tony unmoved.
'My ideas have always come from the shapes of natural objects and trees', he
explained, and so he began drawing sweeping curves on a sheet of paper:

> The overall shape started coming in my trying to get away from the straight lines of a
> normal chair. The design literally emerged in seconds. And from there it was a matter
> of coming up with something that could work and that I could actually make.

Tony's chair design was composed of a single sinuous line of bent wood that
formed the legs and backrest, and that supported a seat. Not only would
bending be a new procedure for Tony, but doing so with hardwood timber
to replicate the set of tight curves he had drawn on paper posed a formidable
challenge. Until that point, he had worked only with solid, squared pieces
of timber to assemble architectural joinery and furniture. But 'By exploring
different avenues', he commented, 'you evolve a skill, and then more things
become viable. And your thinking broadens, as well as your design.'

Tony judiciously elected to use European ash (*Fraxinus excelsior*), which is
a dense, strong wood with good natural lustre and normally pale 'ash-blond'
in colour. In *Sylva*, a classic Enlightenment discourse on forestry, writer
and gardener John Evelyn praised the universal use of ash by 'the carpenter, wheelwright, cartwright ... the cooper, turner and thatcher' because
of its remarkable strength and beauty.[27] Historically, ash wood was used
during the Neolithic period for making the handles of stone hatchets;[28] the

North American Iroquois favoured it for making false facemasks,[29] and oil extracted from the wood was used in seventeenth-century England to cure a variety of ailments.[30] Its mystical and curative properties may well have been attributed to its peculiar sexual nature, for, though ash is nominally dioecious, 'some trees change sex yearly, some carry branches of the wrong sex, some are hermaphrodite and some produce dual-sex ("perfect") flowers'.[31] In modern times, ash, of which there are sixty species, has been popularly used in the production of tool handles, ladder rungs, sporting equipment and cabinet making. Importantly for Tony, the properties of ash also make it an excellent timber for steam-bending and other forms of bending.

After investigating different ways of bending timber in consultation with workshop tutors and published material, Tony determined that the most feasible method for achieving the tight curves and the required structural stability would be to laminate layers of ash veneer. He first produced a small jig in order to run a series of bending trials with various thicknesses of timber made up of layers of veneer and wet glue. He recalled being surprised at the supple pliability of the ash, which, when soaked with cascamite glue, became 'almost like cardboard'. Cascamite was chosen in part for its bonding strength, but also because its consistency and pot life can be easily regulated by adding water. Tony deemed this a crucial quality since extended pot life would afford him the necessary time to apply the glue, neatly stack the layers of veneer, and transfer the length of moist, laminated timber to the jig that would press it into the desired form. 'I managed to bend a curve far tighter than what was needed for the chair, answering any doubts I might have had', he told me. Trials with the prototype jig also informed the subsequent design and construction of the more complex full-scale model.

The resulting jig was, in itself, a splendid work of craftsmanship. It comprised two massive blocks, each made from six layers of one-inch-thick MDF board and a top layer of heavy birch plywood, all sturdily bolted together. The inner edges of the blocks were symmetrically profiled to match the chair's curves, and they could be cramped firmly together using an improvised system of wooden braces and steel connecting rods that spanned the width of the jig. As soon as a long narrow strip of the laminated ash was prepared with glue, it was positioned immediately between the smoothly contoured edges of the blocks, and the gap between them was closed. Bolts at the end of the steel rods were tightened in synchrony, slowly squeezing the formwork together and thereby pressing the laminated timber into shape.

The job required assistance from several pairs of volunteering hands. Producing the tightest radial curves at either end of the chair's bent profile while keeping the laminated veneers intact necessitated innovative thinking. 'The idea to use some kind of roller was the result of one of many useful brainstorming conversations I had with [instructor] David W.', Tony recounted.

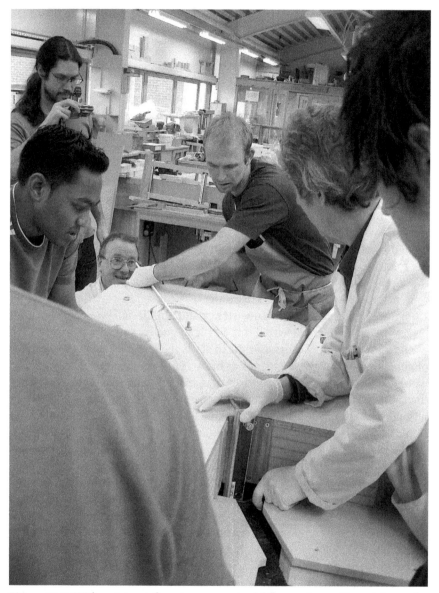

Figure 10.2 With assistance from instructors and fellow trainees, Tony tightens the jig that he created for moulding the curved components of his chair design, 2007.
© David Wheeler

The ingenious and elegant solution involved a simple plate of sheet metal bolted to the jig and a pivoting wooden lever fitted with a steel roller. When the lever arm was manually pulled, the roller applied even pressure to the sheet metal with the laminated veneer below, neatly folding it around the circumference of the profile, and then clamping it in place. The final process was impressively smooth. The glue was left to dry and the bent chair component was removed displaying excellent results.

Two identical bentwood components were made in this manner and joined together, side by side, with thick, polished steel dowels. Tony manufactured a separate seat in solid ash, and this was supported directly on the bentwood 'knees' of the chair and attached to the chair back using traditional tusk-tenon joints. The decision to use tusk-tenons was a calculated one: 'The design for my chair is all modern, so I wanted to incorporate a traditional joint to connect with the carpentry, yeah. Otherwise you're just a sculptor. And I'm not a sculptor, I'm a furniture maker', he declared, thereby negotiating the craft boundaries as much for himself as for his audience. The final addition of an upholstered leather seat pad and headrest completed the project.

Several months later, while reflecting on the progress he had made both technically and in design, Tony affirmed that: 'At college, you're always trying to better your last project, and you want something that stands out and gets that "second glance" from people.' In making his chair, he discovered an affinity for furniture with clean, curved lines and he set himself the challenge to convey his developing tastes using the sparest number of components: 'My chair's just three bits of timber wedded together. I like that. It's simple, yet complicated enough to make people wonder how I did it.'

In exploring that sense of 'wonder' elicited by an accomplished piece of carving or cabinetry, historian and woodworker Harvey Green observed that Grinling Gibbons' Baroque lime-wood garlands dazzle not only because of their technical precision, but also because they are 'feats of the mind and the hand . . . so beyond the boundary of normal humans'.[32] Through the ages, fine woodworkers have strived to conjure that sense of wonderment, illusion or *trompe l'oeil* through the hyper-naturalistic representations, intricate details, seductive geometries and daring structural configurations they created by hand. Prime examples in contemporary English furniture making include John Makepeace's *Mollusc Desk*, Fred Baier's *1/2 Cone = Cube – Cylinder = Table*, and Martin Grierson and George Mkrtichian's *Falling Water* cabinet.[33]

Tony now spoke with confidence about the relation between good design and strong lines, relaying how 'the chair's sweeping curves should draw the eye, more so than its actual function. So, in the end, it's more than one thing'. Viewers and sitters, he hoped, would appreciate not only the fastidious craftsmanship, but would also discern a unique aesthetic in his work. 'I want to give my pieces that individual quality so people can always see that I made it', he explained. 'You need to be able to separate yourself out, at least that little bit, to get the market no one else is getting.' Like his fellow graduates who were mentally and emotionally preparing to leave behind the security of the College workshop and set out into professional practice, competition for patronage would drive Tony's future efforts to develop and market a distinctive personal style.

The year after graduating, Tony was invited to attend the highly prestigious City & Guilds Lion Awards Ceremony, where the Master of the Carpenters' Company presented him with the first-ever Carpenters' Award for Excellence. The award has subsequently been made annually to a graduate demonstrating exceptional creative craft skills. The *Carpenters' Company Broadsheet* reported that: 'Tony was praised for the intricacy of his cabinet making, laminating and machine-based work, and commended for his innovation and originality in problem solving.'[34] He was subsequently admitted to the Freedom of the City, thereby formally being awarded a place in the ancient history of London's carpenters.

JAMES: FROM APPRENTICE TO MENTOR

I met with bespoke furniture maker James Verner at his workshop in the tranquil Devon village of Hawkchurch, where we discussed his personal experiences of apprenticeship and training. James' first exposure to the world of furniture making was on a visit to Parnham House in Dorset, where John Makepeace had set up the renowned School for Craftsmen in Wood in 1977.[35] But, like most British middle-class children, his parents and schoolteachers never intimated the possibility of going to vocational college to learn woodworking. After completing joint honours in psychology and art history at the University of St Andrews, James found itinerant work making steeplechase fences at racecourses around England and Ireland, doing what he described as his 'finest work with a chainsaw'.

At twenty-five years of age, James decided to get serious about woodworking and become a furniture maker. He proffered free labour in return for an apprenticeship and, following a long string of polite refusals, he was taken on by Nick Smith, whose workshop specialised in furniture restoration, but also accepted occasional commissions for new pieces. 'When there weren't things being made, I was dismantling and restoring the most wonderful bits of furniture, which is a great way to learn how to build new ones', James told me. He described his training with Nick as 'entirely informal', a model he would later adopt for training his own apprentices.

The first task that Nick assigned James was to plane a plank square, cut it in half, and join the two pieces at a right angle with three dovetails, before repeating the exercise with more refined lapped dovetails. 'I found it satisfying', James reminisced. 'I was good at it, and faster than others [in the workshop], so very soon I was moved onto making things.' In his view, Nick's workshop provided a 'superb learning environment' where trainees were 'able to learn without undue pressure'. 'He gave us enough rope to hang ourselves but not enough to ruin the whole piece.' The workshop also instilled traditional values, both in design and craftsmanship, and it took time for James to realise that perhaps 'there were alternative ways more appropriate to furniture making in the twenty-first century'. James' own contemporary designs combined sleek, modern elegance with traditional joinery, and he employed a mixture of hand tools, machinery and jigs to produce them.

Since opening his own workshop in 1996, James had trained more than a dozen young men and women. He felt a certain responsibility to pass on the skills, but more importantly he enjoyed teaching – and, through teaching, learning. 'I love what I do and I enjoy sharing it with others by providing a good, interesting workplace where people can develop and grow', he told me. That ethos became part of the furniture that his team produced. According to James:

> A beautifully crafted object can't be forged in a crucible of misunderstanding, pressure or unpleasant working conditions. It has to grow out of a space of understanding, communication and resources. The more you put around its base, the better it's going to be. Without becoming too mystical, I do believe that objects embody the energies that are put into their making.

James' personal satisfaction came from the 'immersion and focus' he experienced at the bench. For him, woodworking 'is a mixture between writing and yoga. There's a little bit of ballet, movement, smell, touch, sound – the whole thing. When you're actually working, every sense is focussed on what you're doing'. Regardless of one's level of expertise, woodworking is a process of constant learning and discovery. For James, that process ought to be 'like going for a walk. You enjoy the process, you enjoy the journey, but it's not a forced march'.

Like his former mentor, James strived to make the process of learning, discovery and personal development available to those he employed. 'Historically', he mused, 'apprenticeships were so much more than just learning the trade. They were really about learning how to make the transition from youth to adulthood.' That transition is achieved mainly through learning to think for oneself, and, by doing so, nurturing self-respect. He offered a recent example of self-directed learning, pointing to a young man busily assembling a cabinet component at a bench across the workshop:

Figure 10.3 Portrait of furniture maker James Verner at his workshop, 2008.
© Trevor H.J. Marchand

> I was talking to Warren just this morning. He needed to join one piece of wood to another, so I started going into great detail about a jig that might be made for the job. But, in the end I said to him: 'You're actually the person doing the task, so it's up to you to work out a way to do it.'

Like all experienced woodworkers, James recognised that making mistakes is essential to learning and growing, but, equally, exploration and experimentation need to be kept in check with the real financial costs of errors and lost time. He didn't need to be watching to judge whether his carpenters were getting it right – he had only to listen to their tools and materials. 'If something sounds harmonious, the work is flowing. If it doesn't, I need to go over and have a chat.'

Over the years, James became acutely aware of the time needed to help someone develop their skills, and therefore increasingly cautious about taking on school-leavers who possessed no prior training or experience. 'To have someone turn up and take away your time from bench or business is really limiting', he explained:

> In bespoke furniture, the biggest factor in the cost of the piece is the time spent at the workbench. Materials are about 10 per cent of the total; all the rest is labour. So any limitations on time are going to affect the bottom line.

When hiring new trainees, James claimed he could gauge an applicant's aptitude by what they could tell him about timber and, more significantly, by the way they moved:

> A woodworker needs to have an awareness of what they're doing in an environment. A natural gesticulator, for instance, would be dangerous around machinery and a hazard around a piece of furniture that's had hundreds of hours put into it.

Elaborating on the importance of good proprioceptive and kinaesthetic awareness, he added: 'In a way, it's a form of intelligence – to know where one's body is in space and to be aware of one's surroundings.'

Social competence and enthusiasm were other essential attributes that James looked for in an applicant. He needed to be confident that the individual would integrate with the team and be sympathetic to the kind of furniture he designed: 'They must convey that they're passionate – frankly, they're going to have to be passionate because they're getting paid bugger all.' So far as technical competence was concerned, he was certain that he could teach almost anybody to cut timber, but that wasn't his ambition. 'I want to help people become exceptional woodworkers', he said.

When trainees reached that stage of development, however, they typically moved on to start their own businesses. James took a philosophical perspective on that cyclical loss of in-house expertise and of the resources put into training: 'As long as I get my pound of flesh, that's OK. After all, life's about a great deal more than money.' He derived greater pleasure, he told me, from observing the growth in an apprentice's skillset and in their sensitivity to the medium. 'And maybe', he added, 'they grow in other ways as well – as people.'

GEORGE: FINAL YEARS

In November, two months prior to our meeting, George Pysden had humbly received the Master Craft Certificate in Joinery at Carpenters' Hall.[36] He shared his thoughts about achieving mastery in the trade. 'When I make a piece of furniture now', he said animatedly, 'even before I cut a plank of timber, I know what I'm going to do. I can see every part of it in my mind. That ability has developed over the last fifteen or twenty years.' He nodded in the direction of a delicate inlaid table where a tray of fresh tea and biscuits sat waiting, and continued: 'I could make that without a drawing as long as I've got some measurements for the height, width and centre. I've got it so ingrained, that I can see every joint I'm going to make.'

George conceded to making sketches on paper to which he could revert during the process 'because', he added almost apologetically, 'you can't remember everything'. But, again he insisted: 'I can see every bit of that in my mind before I start it.' George's *seeing in his mind* involved more than the mere ability to visualise what the overall design would look like. As a minimum, his *seeing* was a multifaceted ability to conceptualise the joints connecting the legs to the table top, the width of the rails, and the pattern of the inlay; to imaginatively compare and contrast varieties of timber, and select pieces appropriate to the task; to think viscerally about the processes of physically making and assembling the table; and to calculate the costs of labour and materials. If George were making the table for a client, knowledge of that

Figure 10.4 Portrait of furniture maker George Pysden sporting a Carpenters' Company necktie, 2005. © Don Stevens

individual's personal tastes, needs and budget would also enter the equation. His accretion of interconnected practical, conceptual, sensory and social experiences endowed him, as it does other seasoned craftspeople, with a skill for 'envisioning' a new project as a whole and in all its complexity. The ability to imaginatively anticipate and simultaneously plan for the design, the making and the business of craft is what qualifies a 'Master' craftsperson.[37]

Growth and development into mastery are equally marked by an ability to respond in effectual ways to the unexpected and to creatively improvise in face of the unforeseen. For the woodworker, the material nature and performance of their tools is continually at risk of changing, as described in earlier chapters. In handwork, the orchestration of grasp, stance and posture, and of applied pressure, motion and direction, is in constant need of often subtle calibration. New projects and designs introduce new kinds of problems demanding novel solutions, which are typically arrived at by recombining and reconfiguring the knowhow, resources and technologies to hand. But an ability to respond and improvise is vital not only to daily mastery with tools and materials; it is also critical when incremental, or occasionally sudden, changes are experienced by the ageing or injured craftsperson in their physical health, mental wellbeing or perceptual abilities. In order to persist in one's trade and execute the necessary tasks, the body-mind must compensate for temporary impairments or permanent losses by reconfiguring its muscular, neurological and sensory resources. This is often achieved in correspondence with physical reorganisation of, and adaptations made to the working environment in which they operate – a subject to which I will return shortly.

Like the trajectory of a craftsperson's skills over their lifetime, the wooden furniture that a carpenter makes also transforms, deteriorates and perishes over its useful life.[38] In recounting a story about a client's fine cherry-wood dining table that was warped by radiators, George exclaimed with exasperation: 'Since the War, more expensive furniture has been ruined by central heating!'

A tree dies when felled, but its timber continues to absorb and exude moisture with changing atmospheric conditions, causing swelling, shrinkage, splitting, cupping or bending. The colour and durability of timber are also susceptible to a host of damaging factors including heat, light, rot and insect infestation. Many of these alterations can be minimised or delayed through an appropriate selection of timber for the purpose and location, by using veneers in place of solid hardwoods, by applying polish, wax or lacquer, or through restorative intervention, which may include the use of fungicides or chemical preservatives, or grafting new wood onto perished components.

Some defects and forms of deterioration in timber, however, are actually desirable to woodworkers and clients. Burrs, burls and abnormal growths in trees may yield timber with prized character, frequently used for turning bowls or handles, or for producing costly, exotic veneers. Diseased wood, too, might present a unique figure that can be accentuated under the sharp iron of the smoothing plane. The squiggly traces of long-departed woodworm, a deepening or mellowing hue of the timber; the crackle of old lacquer and even a discernible history of wear and tear contribute to the prized patina of antique furniture and family heirlooms. In such cases, ageing and deterioration are positively conceptualised, valued and accommodated within a set of narratives that restore purpose and usefulness to the furniture, and salvage it from the trash heap or fireplace.

Through restoring old furniture, George, like James Verner, had learned a great deal about the behaviour of timber and about earlier woodworking techniques, which, in turn, informed his own design and making practices. While being interviewed for a story published in *The Independent* newspaper in 1998, George explained that 'The basics have stayed much the same' in furniture making, though 'there's been a great improvement in the tools and machinery'. And, he added humorously, 'everything's electric now and I wish I was too'.[39] He was eighty-one years old at the time with sixty-five years of hands-on experience in the trade, but he nevertheless continued to work every day in his Croydon carpentry shop from 7:30 AM to 2:30 PM.

Over the next decade, George's pace steadily declined, and notably so after the death of his wife Joan in 2000. With no children, he was alone in the house. His last trainee, Bob, a middle-aged man who had lately taken up carpentry, visited George regularly and lent a hand with small woodworking tasks. George no longer had the physical strength to move large planks or to operate heavy machinery, and the fingers of his once strong, large hands were bent and their joints swollen. With age, his eyesight deteriorated and he now wore thick-lensed glasses, but his hearing was surprisingly sharp despite having worked for so many decades engulfed by the thunderous noise of machines.

Bob assisted in reconfiguring the height of George's workbench and the positions of lighter machinery to suit his mentor's changing needs. He moved timber to where George was woodworking at a given time, and to where the ageing carpenter might manipulate it more easily and safely. He carried out machining tasks according to George's instructions, and was thereby learning at the same time. Bob assisted, too, in keeping the workshop hazard-free and tidy. While physically getting on with his craft in the best way possible, George was also channelling his project planning and preparation, carpentry knowhow, and sense of orderliness and safe practice into the actions and activities of Bob. Thus, in a similar manner to the way that George's eyeglasses had become an extension of his body, enabling him to see and to visually discern his work, so too had Bob become an extension of George's craftworking.

A life in woodworking exercises, disciplines, forms and eventually strains the body. Ageing carpenters frequently suffer from arthritic joints and worn cartilage, and these afflictions are typically compounded by more general kinds of age-related deterioration, including diminished muscular strength, decreased flexibility and dexterity, and a gradual loss of bone mass. The perceptual senses of sight, hearing, smell and touch, all of which play significant roles in the processes and pleasures of woodworking, become impaired at varying rates with old age and in various combinations. Accidents and injury, including repetitive strain disorders, incurred over the span of a woodworker's career may also result in chronic pain, loss of sight or hearing, or missing digits. But ageing and injury are not simply stories of fragility and decay.[40] Loss can entail the generation of new coping mechanisms, the growth of alternative ways of sensing and processing environmental stimuli, or the development of novel methods and embodied strategies for performing tasks and achieving goals. I use the term 'embodied' here to include the brain and nervous system, as well as viscera, muscle tissues and sensory organs.

Until recently, it was believed that, by early adulthood, the brain and nervous system were fully formed, resulting in a brain that is organised into fixed function-specific regions.[41] Although neuroscientists and cognitive scientists had generally acknowledged the functional plasticity of the adult brain in response to, for instance, the acquisition of new motor skills, it was not believed that repeated practice could result in structural changes to the central nervous system. The possibility of structural plasticity was therefore essentially denied.

Some of the earliest experiments to challenge that prevailing doctrine used magnetic resonance imaging (MRI) techniques to study the brains of keyboard and string musicians. Results indicated that the 'human motor cortex can exhibit functionally-induced and long-lasting structural adaptations'.[42] Subsequent research on 'adaptive plasticity' (i.e. plasticity associated with learning new tasks and skills) proved that structural changes in the brain do indeed occur with neuronal plasticity. By using advanced MRI techniques, a now-famous study published in 2000 showed that the size of the posterior hippocampus, a region associated with spatial representation, was larger among London taxi drivers than participants in the control group.[43] It was also shown that the posterior hippocampus of cabbies grew in proportion to the duration of their driving experience.[44]

Four years later, a study of young adults learning to juggle importantly established that there is a transient and selective structural change in brain areas that are associated with the processing and storage of complex visual motion.[45] A later study confirmed these findings, discovering that synaptic organisation in the motor cortex associated with the learning of a new task is both rapid and enduring, and that practice serves to strengthen the dendritic spines (spinogenesis) of the new synaptic organisation, thereby providing 'a potential cellular mechanism for the consolidation of lasting, presumably permanent, motor memories'.[46]

Of direct relevance to my account of George Pysden, it is now broadly accepted that brain plasticity occurs throughout one's lifetime and into old age.[47] Plasticity (defined as 'the brain's continuous embryogenetic potential to induce new nervous tissue, and thereby to change its form')[48] is deemed to be an inherent property that enables our brains to react to both internal and external stimuli at a structural level.[49] Our brain, like our sense of self, is therefore in a state of ongoing and dynamic change in relation to our total environment and physical body. Neurological studies suggest that the potential for reorganisation within the primary sensorimotor areas of the ageing brain not only allows for the acquisition of new skills, but also serves as a compensatory mechanism, making possible the formation of alternative neural circuits for achieving a particular goal when the original synaptic arrangements break down or deteriorate.[50]

As George's eyesight weakened and the dexterity and strength in his fingers, hands and the rest of his body declined, the pace of his work slowed and the scale of his projects decreased. However, he did not stop woodworking. He found other carpentry jobs to do and his brain-body organised alternative ways of realising them, including the extension of his tasks through Bob, his workshop mentee.

At the close of my interview with George, having learned about his long and successful career, I asked what he still hoped to achieve as a carpenter and furniture maker. 'Well, I actually wish I could go back to full-time work again', he replied somewhat regretfully:

> I retired in 2000. That's eight years ago now, and I was already quite old then. As people left me, I didn't hire anyone else and gradually I was left on my own, except for the visits from Bob. In any case, I've kept my workshop and that's full of machinery, of course. Planers, a spindle moulder, a massive belt sander, a vertical sander, a lathe that I fiddle around with. But I suppose what I'd love to do – but at my age I'm not going to spend the money – I would love to have what they call a 'copy lathe' so I could make a barley twist![51]

With the mention of the copy-lathe and making 'barley twists', George's eyes brightened. In the past, the ability to manufacture that decorative feature by hand was the mark of a highly accomplished turner or carver, and a comprehensive apprenticeship training once included turning and carving alongside joinery, cabinet making and shop fitting. George still exhibited a determination to learn new skills and master new dimensions of his trade.

Two months after my pleasant visit to Woldingham, I received an email message from Carpenters' Hall. George Pysden had died peacefully at his home on Easter Monday, aged ninety. Just a couple of weeks earlier, he had reportedly attended lunch at the Hall in London and was 'in good form'. The full-page obituary published in the *Carpenters' Company Broadsheet* announced that: 'In an act of typical generosity, George willed 75 per cent of his residuary estate to the Company's College . . . for young people wishing to enter or study the trade.'[52] It was later revealed that an impressive sum of three-quarters of a million pounds sterling had been willed to the Charitable Trust in annual support of two 'Pysden Scholars' embarking on the fine woodwork programme at the Building Crafts College.[53] George's legacy in his beloved trade was secured.

CONCLUSION

In this chapter I investigated the growth and the deterioration of skill through personal accounts offered by four woodworkers. Although Josh, Tony, James and George were at different stages of their lives and careers, their individual motivations coalesced around a desire for further learning and enskilment, and for progressively attaining mastery in their chosen vocation. All four men had embarked upon their carpentry careers by joining existing communities of practice, affording them access to workshops, mentors and role models. The luxury of time for experimenting with tools and materials, making mistakes and resolving them within a supportive environment was deemed essential to evolving the combination of motor ability and sensory awareness that comprise a woodworker's competence.

Josh, Tony, James and George also listed the requisite virtues of patience, disciplined focus and, importantly, self-respect. As James explained, self-respect breeds the confidence to confront new challenges and improvise solutions, thereby growing one's skillset and propagating one's transformation from trainee to mentor. Young Josh noted that he improved his own techniques by regularly taking on the mentor's role, demonstrating standard carpentry procedures to his fellow trainee, Liam. Tony had turned the teasing about his designs into a learning opportunity and a personal challenge, which augmented his skills and, as a result, bolstered his self-respect and bestowed newfound confidence in his own aesthetic preferences. James and George, with greater experience, had successfully scaffolded and guided the enskilment of aspiring furniture makers of all ages. In doing so, and by founding their own workshops, both men gained a fuller, more complex mastery of not only the craft of fine furniture making, but also the operational and business dimensions of the trade.

As already explored in Chapter 9, staying financially afloat as a furniture maker is a constant challenge, calling for regular upskilling, revitalising client networks, refreshing the business profile and rethinking goals. In time, and with perseverance, James and George established steady patronage for what they created, and George won status among his peers and eventually earned institutional recognition from the Carpenters' Livery Company. George's long hands-on experience of making and running a business had cultivated the capacity of his 'mind's eye' to imagine a new project in its totality – not merely in terms of what it would look like, but also how it would be made and how much it might cost to make it.

By that point, however, the deterioration and decline in George's motor skills, physical strength, endurance and the acuity of his perceptual senses had become more apparent, and these changes were hampering his craftwork. George nevertheless continued to work and to set new goals for himself. His failing eyesight was compensated over the decades by both stronger prescriptions for his spectacles and a progressive transfer of reliance on sight to greater confidence in touch, hearing and possibly smell for discerning and orientating his activities within the workshop environment. His determination to carry on was sensibly balanced by shortening his work day, accepting commissions for fewer and smaller-scale items, and adapting his carpentry methods accordingly. He harnessed the assistance of a former apprentice, who made physical modifications to the workshop setting and performed basic tasks in compliance with George's wishes, and in the interests of his safety. The ageing carpenter's ongoing activity in a progressively changing workplace slowly reconfigured his muscular, neurological and sensory resources in ways that allowed him to carry out old tasks in new ways.

The growth and the deterioration of skill are not mutually exclusive processes, but rather the development of one skillset may result in the simultaneous decline of others, and, significantly, vice versa. Young men and women who take up woodworking and devote considerable time and energy to perfecting their skills inevitably neglect or possibly abandon other activities in which they once partook. The embodied skills related to those past activities will therefore stagnate or regress. In Josh's case, his promise as a talented footballer was relegated to the sidelines, as were Tony's esteemed rock-climbing pursuits, when both men immersed themselves deeply, and with dedication, in the vocational training at college. As for James, when demand for his furniture increased, he expanded his workforce and invested in machinery. Consequently, a greater proportion of his time was now spent managing the business operations and less 'on the tools'. The skilled use of hand tools insists on a regular regime of practice, without which dexterity declines and the 'feeling' for efficient and 'ballet-like' movements at the bench recedes.

In the event of injury or illness, or through the processes of ageing, muscular, neurological and sensory abilities are impaired or deteriorate at varying rates, affecting the woodworker's skilled operations. In response, alternative pathways, methods and means for realising tasks may grow and develop, resulting in new skills. Following on from this observation, it is important to underscore the fact that realising a given task can be achieved in a variety of different ways, each one enlisting a distinct array of physical, cognitive and sensory resources, and the way that individuals continue to accomplish that task over their lifetime is likely to change in response to changes in the resources available. Future studies of craftwork therefore need to diligently account for the diversity of resources that are drawn together in producing a personal skillset and to record, analyse and theorise the ways that such configurations change over time and in accordance with the events and changing circumstances over a craftsperson's lifetime.

The observations made in this chapter reflect in some ways my own experiences as an ageing anthropologist. When conceiving of this study with woodworkers, I had already accepted that I was no longer quite up to the task of hauling armloads of bricks and bucketloads of mortar all day long and up and down the steep and winding staircases of Yemeni minarets, or of transporting stacks of spiny palm-wood timbers, tossing and catching weighty mud bricks, and enduring brutal temperatures on West African construction sites. I had become more susceptible to lower back pain, my vision had deteriorated somewhat, and the decline in my hearing made it more challenging to pick up new vocabulary and detect nuance in languages that weren't mine. It was time to pursue fieldwork in a craft that would be gentler to my body and to learn a trade that, like George, I might continue practising until – and if – I make it to the ripe age of ninety.

NOTES

An earlier and briefer version of this chapter was published as 'Skill and Aging: Perspectives from Three Generations of English Woodworkers', in E. Hallam and T. Ingold (eds), *Making and Growing: Anthropological Studies of Organisms and Artefacts* (Farnham: Ashgate, 2014), 183–202. The chapters in Hallam and Ingold's groundbreaking volume critically explore the ways that things are made or grown, and the similarities and distinctions between these processes and the resulting artefacts/lifeforms. The editors and contributing authors examine the nature of materials and the situated activities of design and creativity in order to shift our thinking about growing 'not as something that takes place in the space intermediate between God-given nature and man-made society . . . but as the very ground of becoming from which the forms of the artificial take shape' (Ingold and Hallam, 'Making and Growing', 4–5).

1. De Botton, *The Pleasures and Sorrows*, Chapter VI, 'Painting', 182.
2. FSC is the Forest Stewardship Council. Other major certification programmes include the Programme for the Endorsement of Forest Certification (PEFC) and the Sustainable Forestry Standard (SFI).
3. This chapter is dedicated to the memory of George Pysden, a true gentleman and craftsman.
4. The UK unemployment rate in the early 1930 reached 22 per cent (Benjamin and Kochin, 'Unemployment', 434, Table 6).
5. For a discussion of the Freedom of the City (of London), see Chapter 2. Becoming a Freeman (or Freewoman) is achieved by nomination, patrimony or being presented by a Livery Company. Freedom of the City remains strongly associated with the Liveries.
6. Technology training in British schools throughout much of the twentieth century was centred on woodworking, metalwork and engineering. With the demise of the UK's manufacturing sector, however, secondary school Design and Technology departments expanded their remit to reflect the changing career opportunities for students, including courses in such subjects as food technology.
7. Green, *Wood*, xx–xxi.
8. Marchand, 'Muscles, Morals and Mind'.
9. Grasseni, *Developing Skill*; and Rice, 'Learning to Listen'.
10. Downey, 'Practice without Theory'; Johnston, 'Plasticity'; Landi and Rossini, 'Cerebral Restorative Plasticity'; Rees, 'Being Neurologically Human Today'; and Xu et al., 'Rapid Formation'.
11. Damasio, *Descarte's Error*; and Downey, 'The Importance of Repetition'.
12. For example, the annual earnings for a skilled male in the building trades in 1911 (six years before George Pysden was born) was £105, or roughly £2 per week.

13. Carpenters' Company, 'Obituaries: George Pysden', 3.

14. For a detailed study and discussion about the role of maths and geometry in carpentry work, and the ways that mathematical problems are recognised and solved in practice, see Millroy, 'An Ethnographic Study'. Interestingly, late eighteenth/early nineteenth-century cabinet-maker-cum-architect Peter Nicholson noted that 'with the exception of a knowledge of perspective, and of a few simple methods of drawing common curves, geometry is of little use to [the cabinet maker]; and, when it is studied too closely, it leads to a harsh and mechanical mode of designing' (Peter, *Practical Carpentry*, 2).

15. The importance of the learning side of the equation was emphasised by anthropologist Jean Lave, who challenged the classic teaching-learning dichotomy that imputes hierarchy, ignores the seminal role of context and reproduces the notion that knowledge is somehow 'transmitted' from one individual to another (Lave, *Apprenticeship*).

16. Rose, *The Village Carpenter*, 135. In the construction industry, the length of apprenticeship was 'reduced from five years in 1945, to four years in 1964, to three years by 1963' (Clarke, 'The Changing Structure', 36).

17. For more detailed discussion of the history of vocational training and apprenticeship in the United Kingdom, see Aldrich, 'The Apprentice in History'; Clarke, 'The Changing Structure'; and Lane, *Apprenticeship In England*.

18. See Clarke, 'The Changing Structure', 37.

19. Gospel, 'The Revival of Apprenticeship', 439–40.

20. See, for example, Green, *Wood*, 133–34; and Zwerger, *Wood and Wood Joints*, 12.

21. A jig is 'a device that holds a piece of work and guides the tools operating it' (*New Oxford Dictionary*). Jigs are normally designed and made by the individual carpenter to accomplish the task at hand, and may range in form and construction from very simple to complex, with multiple components.

22. Cf. Colloredo-Mansfeld, 'An Ethnography of Neoliberalism', 123.

23. For further descriptions of the characteristics and qualities of timbers popularly used in carpentry, see Bridgewater et al., *Woodwork*; Jackson and Day, *Collins Complete Woodworker's Manual*; and Johnson and More, *Tree Guide*.

24. Among the reference books popularly referred to by trainees were Tanya Harrod's comprehensive historical overview of British craft, including furniture making, and its developments through the twentieth century (*The Crafts in Britain*); Edwards et al.'s overview of British furniture from 1600 to 2000 (*British Furniture*); and Judith Miller's tome on world styles of furniture through the ages (*Furniture*).

25. Peter, *Practical Carpentry*, 1.

26. Cranz, *The Chair*, 45.

27. Evelyn, *Sylva*, 91–92.

28. Max Gschwend, cited in Zwerger, *Wood and Wood Joints*, 119.

29. Green, *Wood*, 216.

30. Evelyn, *Sylva*, 92.

31. Johnson and More, *Tree Guide*, 436.

32. Green, *Wood*, 209.

33. For images of these particular Makepeace and Baier pieces, see Miller, *Furniture*, 519; and for the Grierson and Mkrtichian cabinet, see https://www.martingrierson.co.uk/gallery/falling-water (retrieved 10 June 2021).

34. Neal, 'First Carpenters' Award', 9.

35. In 1976, Makepeace bought the Tudor-period Parnham House and set up a residential school of furniture making. Parnham house was sold in 2001, and Makepeace returned to full-time designing and making furniture (Crichton-Miller, 'Going against the Grain', W13).

36. The Master Craft Certificate is a scheme sponsored by the Worshipful Company of Carpenters, the Worshipful Company of Joiners and Cealers, the City & Guilds London Institute and the Institute of Carpenters. It offers official and independent recognition of the holder's superior mastery of their craft beyond NVQ Level 3.

37. For further detailed discussion of this masterly ability to envision a new design-and-build project in its entirety, see Marchand, *Minaret Building*, 202–39.

38. For a colourful description of the ways that various species of timber rot and deteriorate, see Anonymous, 'Wood and Its Deterioration', 64.

39. Lacey and Yiasoumi, 'Away in a Manger'.

40. Dengen, 'Back to the Future', 224.

41. Amunts et al., 'Motor Cortex'; Landi and Rossini, 'Cerebral Restorative Plasticity', 350; and Rees, 'Being Neurologically Human', 155.

42. Amunts et al., 'Motor Cortex', 206. See also Elbert et al., 'Increased Cortical Representation', 305–7.

43. Maguire et al., 'Navigation-Related Structural Change', 4398–403.

44. Johnston, 'Plasticity', 97.

45. Draganski et al., 'Neuroplasticity', 311–12.

46. Xu et al., 'Rapid Formation', 917. In addition to adaptive plasticity associated with learning a new skill or task, other forms of plasticity include developmental plasticity, induced mainly by environmental experience in the maturing brain, restorative plasticity in response to brain damage or injury, and cross-modal plasticity involving the recruitment of one region of the cortex normally associated with a specific function (e.g. vision) for the processing of sensory information of another sensory modality (e.g. tactile) (Johnston, 'Plasticity'; and Landi and Rossini, 'Cerebral Restorative Plasticity').

47. Boyke et al., 'Training-Induced Brain Structure Changes'.

48. Rees, 'Being Neurologically Human', 151.

49. Landi and Rossini, 'Cerebral Restorative Plasticity', 350.

50. Ibid., 353 and 359.

51. A 'barley twist' in furniture making is a double-helix spiral on a chair or table leg, and is regularly found on antique furniture of Tudor to Edwardian vintage.

52. Carpenters' Company, 'Obituaries: George Pysden', 3. George Pysden's long-term commitment to encouraging young people to enter the woodworking trades was expressed by him in an interview published in *The Independent* newspaper ten years earlier, in which he was quoted as saying: 'These days people think that working with their hands is downmarket but it's a quality craft industry and I love it. I help to run a competition each year for schools and colleges, to encourage young people' (Lacey and Yiasoumi, 'Away in a Manger').

53. Mead, 'Report by the Charities Administrator', 12.

EPILOGUE
Towards a Hands-On Curriculum

At the end of our first year of training, fellow fine-woodwork trainee Robert conducted an interview with me.[1] By that point, I had already recorded several rounds of interviews with all first and second-year students in the programme, and with several instructors and a number of the Modern Apprentices who trained at the College. Robert insisted that I take a turn to reflect on my own experiences as a trainee and on my current thinking about life and work. It was a fruitful exercise, producing a record of 'where I was at' midway through my fieldwork. After just a few weeks into the study, the distinction between my roles as anthropologist and woodwork trainee began to blur and only became woollier as my membership within the community of practice solidified. In anthropology speak, I had 'gone native'.

This epilogue begins with contents extracted from the longer interview. Robert's prefacing of the questions he posed and his periodic contribution of perspectives and experiences to our discussion are highly indicative of his own thinking at that time, and corroborate his ideas and values expressed in Chapter 6. The principles, plans and concerns to which he alludes resonated closely with other fine-woodwork trainees included in both my studies at the Building Crafts College and with the numerous British craftspeople I have encountered and interviewed since.

Following the abridged interview, I reflect on my dual positions as researcher and member of the community that I was studying, and discuss some of the complications involved in doing fieldwork on a subject close to one's heart. The allure of the 'workshop ideology' – characterised by work-life harmony, autonomy and environmentally responsible practice – was powerful. I review a number of key countercultural movements that formed the backdrop to that thinking before turning to a contrasting examination of 'stardom' in the world of furniture design and making. An overview of the hopes and the hardships associated with that exclusive world of high-end bespoke furniture making introduces my discussion of the more daunting and immediate challenges that arose with the Great Recession. The financial crash in 2008 had lasting repercussions for the entire British craft sector, including my fellow woodworkers who had only just graduated. The penultimate section of the Epilogue recounts the trajectories of many of the newly qualified carpenters who were introduced in the earlier chapters.

The Epilogue concludes with the exploration of an issue that has driven my academic and personal interests in craftwork from the start; namely, the need to radically reform the educational curriculum by placing hands-on making at its heart. Craftwork nurtures the development of the whole person – intellectually, physically and spiritually – and is therefore elemental to cultivating an informed democracy and an empowered civil society. Creative hands-on problem solving offers real hope for dismantling the persistent mind-body hierarchy that blinkers popular understandings of intelligence, and perpetuates a reward system that venerates 'mindwork' and debases the work of the hand. Achieving parity in the ways that the two are appreciated and valued, I argue, rests on the coordinated efforts of academic researchers, government, the education sector and the media, but also on parents whose attitudes colour those of their children. I ultimately conclude that craftwork endows individuals with the skillset to engage practically and thoughtfully with the world, and to make it a better place.

IN INTERVIEW WITH ROBERT

Robert and I sat comfortably across a worktable from one another in the quiet of the College library, insulated from the clamour of the wood mill machinery and buzz of power tools. We had the library to ourselves, without disturbance. This was where I had conducted the majority of my interviews with trainees and instructors.

Robert (R): Do you see yourself pursuing carpentry as a living?

Trevor (T): I'm seriously considering the possibility. [Pause] I suppose the worry is whether I could make a living from it.

R: I suppose it depends on what your living consists of? If you choose not to have much in terms of material possessions, then you can probably live your life fairly comfortably. You probably already have possessions that will do you throughout life, and therefore enable you to do what you want.

T: Yes, true.

R: Do you feel differently about yourself, one year in? I mean, I know I do, and I know Jens does. For me, there's a greater confidence about who I am and what I can offer to people. I really enjoyed that commission last month to replace a wooden step in the Jerusalem Tavern. It allowed me to become part of a place that I already loved. And for the first time in my life I can say 'I'm a carpenter', when people ask, rather than 'I'm a sort of nameless, nebulous, corporate thing'. Has it helped you to define who you are?

T: I think it's actually done the opposite. It's dropped me into a state of flux ... [pause] which isn't bad, and is somehow exciting, I guess. Before now, I could easily define myself by my profession. So, in a way, this fieldwork has muddled things.

R: So, it sounds that your confidence has been shaken?

T: Hmmm. No, not exactly ... But, it has thrown up a lot of personal questions beyond the research ones that I'm investigating. I've become one of the subjects in my study. I don't feel like an 'outsider' or an observer here at the College. I'm part of it, and I find myself sharing the ambition to become a craftsman.

R: In all this, is there a search for your 'self' as more complete? As something more than just developing the manual skills? A bit like [William] Morris, I suppose, where the goal is to take pleasure in work – even of the most mundane kind?

T: Yes, and that's been ongoing. All my previous fieldwork was with builders. The majority of tasks they assigned to me were mundane: lifting, hauling, stacking. I was a labourer, not one of the craftsmen. But the work *felt* good. I enjoyed being part of making beautiful buildings and having achieved a tangible result at the end of each day.

R: You share some of my preferences for doing things by hand. Where did that come from?

T: That's a terrific question. I suppose the handwork fits with my general attitude to life. I like doing things under my own steam: engaging with objects in ways that I can reason about and understand – understand why they're broken, for example, and how I might fix them. I resent being surrounded by 'invisible' technologies that I can't get my hands on. I want that direct interface between my body and the materiality of whatever it is I'm making – like that first mark I make on a sheet of paper when beginning a drawing, or that shaving I take away from the timber with a plane. Those actions and the material they're made upon 'feed back' to me. They reform the way I'm using my body and the tool [in hand]. That immediacy – that dialogue with things – is incredibly satisfying. It makes me feel alive – in the now – if you know what I mean.

R: Yes. But how do you feel about the fact that, commercially, you'll likely have to use machines to survive?

T: Well, that dialogue between maker and material that I just mentioned doesn't happen quite the same way with the machines, does it? But machines and power tools have their function in the workplace, like they do here at the College. They give us time to focus on the more creative tasks. I am wary, though, of *too many* gadgets. Why do we chase after complexity? Isn't there elegance in simplicity?

R: Yes. I was having that discussion with a friend who argues that: 'Being human is about being curious, and therefore it's natural that we strive to develop more and more complex technology.' My feeling is the total opposite: that the way forward is to simplify life by weaning ourselves off the unnecessary technology while keeping the bits that actually assist with what we need to do.

T: There's something to be said, too, about keeping the relations of production simple – anchored in a 'sense of place'. As a furniture maker, I'd want to meet the people who commission my work and help them to appreciate all that's gone into making what they're buying. I'd also want to know – and I'd want the buyer to know – where the wood's coming from: Is it sustainably sourced?

R: I'm reading a good book at the moment called *The Secret Life of Trees*, written by a man who's clearly in love with trees.[2] So, there's an environmental aspect to the way you would practise as a carpenter: a concerted stewardship of resources?

T: Certainly. It's a simple fact that if we don't change the ways we produce and consume, our precious planet is doomed. Most politicians are far too invested in economic growth by whatever means possible and in clinging to power. They're not leading a Green Revolution. So, absolutely, we must take it into our own hands and make whatever small differences we can. I believe craftspeople have a responsibility to enlighten clients about quality and the sustainability of resources used in what they buy.

R: On another matter, how are you coping with your fellow trainees? Are you picking up as much from them as you are from the instructors?

T: Yeah. I've learned an enormous amount from sharing tips at the bench. But, beyond the skills, I've learned more about English culture in the past year than I did during my previous twelve on this island! And, I've learned heaps about English banter and sarcasm, and how to survive it! The workshop has been a fantastic learning environment.

R: It has. And, it's also been the fastest year of my life.

T: Holy Toledo, it's been fast! That gives me a bit of anxiety, because I'm that much closer to having to decide what's next. Am I going to take this train beyond the research project?

R: [With frankness] I don't think you will. You need to combine your academic pursuits and your carpentry in some realistic way.

TOO CLOSE TO GRASP

Robert was correct, of course. I did not leave the university (at least not immediately) and I did not become a furniture maker. Five years after graduating from the Building Crafts College, I returned there to conduct a second research project. I published articles, made a short documentary film, and delivered dozens of academic lectures and public talks based on the two studies with fine woodworkers. It nevertheless took more than a decade to complete this book. A string of momentous life events, new research projects, competing deadlines and other book publications were all factors in the delay. There was, however, another, perhaps more significant, reason: I had become too close to my subject of study and had embraced the contemporary politics of craftwork as my own.

I made plain in the Prologue that, even before starting the carpentry fieldwork, I longed to break away from the managerial bureaucracy, bloating administration, sinking esteem and dispiriting audit culture that was plaguing the British university system. That desire predisposed me to more fully embrace the ideals of life and work that were incubated within my woodworking community, and that had also been foundational to the modern history and politics of Western European and North American craftwork.

Taking up and taking part in shaping worldviews in the workshop afforded penetrating insight into values, social politics and aspirations. But, in doing so, I also risked ignoring inconvenient truths and omitting unpalat-

Figure 11.1 The author at his workbench at the Building Crafts College, 2007.
© David Wheeler

able realities from my anthropological thinking and writing. It was therefore necessary to create distance – politically and emotionally. Only by disengaging was I able to take stock of the structural issues, inconvenient contradictions and real challenges that lurked and operated within the wider, messier context.

Anthropologist Rebecca Prentice published a candid essay on this not-so-uncommon phenomenon.[3] Prentice carried out fieldwork on the shop floor of a Trinidadian garment factory, where learning to sew as a factory worker was central to her participant observation methods. She astutely observed that embodying the skills of sewing also instilled in her the ideologies that made that work meaningful to her co-workers. Prentice recalls being 'enthralled' by her informants' visions of skill as 'independence, autonomy and pleasure', and those visions became hers. It took considerable time after fieldwork for Prentice to 'disembody' the shop-floor ideology and to develop an objective understanding of the situation. She came to recognise that, in fact, the individualisation of garment workers was 'a complex but localised feature of neoliberal development in Trinidad', which served the economic interests of factory owners.[4] The agency that Prentice had initially attributed to her fellow seamstresses was confounded by this admission.

Like Prentice, it took considerable effort for me to disembody the ideologies of the workshop – at least to the extent that I could begin thinking critically about them as independent from my own convictions and beliefs. During my years at the Building Crafts College, I had shared in the dream of becoming a designer-maker. I also shared with the majority of vocational migrants a desire to reduce the scale of our worlds to one more immediately manageable: to transform the impotence we experienced in the face of global forces and events into a confident capacity to bring about change through the things of beauty and worth that we would produce and the ways we would produce them. Like them, I believed, too, that the mode of production that characterised studio craft held promise of living authentically and earning an honest wage.

Unlike Prentice, who joined an already-established community of seamstresses and absorbed an existing (but presumably not static) shop-floor ideology, I had joined a fine-woodwork community that was newly formed by the fresh cohort of trainees. All members, including myself, actively contributed to articulating the form and content of our largely compatible workshop ideologies. Visions for the future emerged progressively in our training together and in social exchanges, but our pursuits of pleasurable work were also informed by our regular interactions with the cohorts immediately ahead and behind ours, by the College instructors and the visiting furniture makers, as well as by what we read, the media we consumed, the places we visited and the broader politics of craftwork.

It would therefore be misleading to suggest that aspirations and visions were incubated wholly within the workshop environment, and without influence from popular cultural and social currents. Chapter 6 traced a brief history of utopian thinking in Britain and its present-day incarnation in the politics of many vocational migrants and of contemporary craftwork more generally. In the next section, I enumerate an array of other movements, expressions of popular resistance and public events that inspired and shaped the workshop ideologies.

DISCONTENTS AND COUNTERDISCOURSES

The month before my cohort arrived at the College, Hurricane Katrina made landfall in Florida and Louisiana with devastating impact. The Kyoto Protocol had come into force earlier that year,[5] and grassroots environmental awareness and activism gained momentum in 2006 with the release of Al Gore's documentary film *An Inconvenient Truth*.[6] The environmental movement, with its early beginnings in the nineteenth century, was becoming ever more urgent,[7] and a prominent force in the minds of woodworkers who planned to pursue sustainable place-centred practices.

As mentioned in previous chapters, a core of college trainees were persistent in their demands to administrators that the timber on the racks be Forest Stewardship Council (FSC)[8] certified and be supplied by ecologically responsible timber merchants. Programme convenor David W. gave full backing to those demands and was a vocal advocate for using locally grown timber. Some students deliberately selected British or European-sourced hardwoods for making their furniture projects and others recycled off-cuts from the bins in the wood-mill or repurposed exotic hardwoods salvaged from demolition sites. All students described the items they created as being 'built to last' or 'heirloom pieces', in explicit contrast to the 'mass-produced', 'flat-pack', 'assemble-it-yourself' furniture sold on the high street, which one colleague proposed is 'ultimately destined for landfill'.[9]

The idea that craftwork could and should be a vehicle for sound environmental and social practices endured across successive cohorts of fine-woodwork trainees, and seemingly grew stronger.[10] In an interview in 2012, vocational migrant Emily asserted:

> The relevance of the craftsmanship we're learning here [at the College] is largely political. Lots of designers in the 1950s and 60s were instructed to make things that would wear out and break in order to fuel consumption. From the vantage point of human nature, going down the route of mass consumption is like self-harm. It's where the disillusion in society comes from. We've been led into a cynical way of living that is destroying society by not allowing people to be resourceful or to understand how things are made. It's giving people crap; churning out more and more rubbish. The consequences are fairly devastating, both socially and environmentally. On that basis alone, it's a shame we can't train everybody to make things that they need.

Emily's stress on the social value to be derived from people learning to make and becoming more resourceful dovetailed with the ideologies of well-established grassroots movements that promote self-reliance and cyclical economies, and emphasise the importance of locality, quality and environmental stewardship. Some of the best organised of these at the time were in the agricultural and food sectors, including the international Slow Food association and the Common Ground project in Britain, both founded in the 1980s. Such schemes had bearing on the provenance and quality of fresh food and produce sold in London's busy street markets, as well as on the growth of local seed-swapping communities and the resurgent interest in allotment gardening. For my fellow fine-woodwork trainees, this translated into valuing the patience and the time that it takes to produce unique, well-made things.

Those students whose concerns extended to sustainable building construction knew of, or had visited, the long-established Centre for Alternative Technology (CAT) in mid-Wales, with its motto 'inspire, inform, enable'. They also paid visits to the Building Centre in Bloomsbury to survey the displays of timber products and discover the latest innovations in green technologies.[11] By the time I began my second study at the College, the internet was hosting dedicated sites where carpenters shared best practice and YouTube was being populated with countless videos on everything from tool sharpening to sophisticated cabinet-making techniques. Not only did these websites and videos serve as popular skill-learning resources for motivated woodwork trainees, but many also incited broader participation in the new craft movement and raised awareness of sustainable practices and alternative politics.[12]

As suggested by Emily, and evoked by the Slow Food manifesto and CAT's mission,[13] self-reliance and handwork can be harnessed for political ends and as a means to social reform. In particular, craftwork has been an engine of grassroots countercultural movements since at least the nineteenth century, as I described in the Introduction to this book. Up to the present day, craft, as a fully embodied practice in dialogue with materials, retains its capacity as a social movement of resistance and opposition to a range of issues,[14] including crass capitalism, mainstream throwaway consumerism, the threats posed by artificial intelligence and robotisation to human agency, creativity and employment, homogenization (and degradation) of high streets and city centres, a proliferation of surveillance and recognition technologies, and the sense of disembodiment precipitated by phones, apps, social media, the internet and gaming.

In an interview,[15] Colin E.-E., successor to David W. as convenor of the fine-woodwork programme, captured craft's promise as a liberating force at the turn of the millennium:

> During my ten years as editor [of *Furniture and Cabinetmaking* magazine], I knew most of the established makers, but I kept stumbling across new ones who were doing good work in little workshops tucked up some country lane – and I keep coming

across them now. There was a sea change in people's thinking [in the 1990s], and I think it was the beginning of something that's still happening: partly the tech revolution, partly people's dissatisfaction with mass production. It's like the modern equivalent of . . . maybe not the Arts & Crafts movement – not as big a sea change as that, with William Morris. But I think it's people becoming dissatisfied with the soullessness of working in big corporate organisations; everybody being slotted into little pockets of existence, and the routine of it all. Take Jackson for example, our 'maker-in-residence'.[16] He was a computer programmer who was fed up with typing in code, solving people's problems, and nobody actually realising what he was doing for them. He might have been earning good money, but the job satisfaction just wasn't there. That's a key reason why we've seen lots of people coming into [the programme].

It was indisputable that a general malaise with standard working conditions was reorientating professional women and men, like Jackson, towards craftwork and skilled trades. When discussing their former office environments in interview or casual conversation, vocational migrants expressed palpable discontent with the limitations imposed on personal creativity and individual learning, the invisibility of their contributions, the low social or ecological value of what they produced, the persuasive power of shareholder interests over corporate governance and direction, and the growing disparity in income between the few at the top and the rest. Their discontents closely resembled those shared by the British population at large and across job sectors. This had spawned a vibrant counterdiscourse of positive thinking and self-help that addresses 'work-life balance' (or, alternatively, 'work-life harmonisation'),[17] stress management and problem solving through personal coaching, peer support groups, therapy, meditation, mindfulness, yoga, pilates or other mind-body techniques.

A shift away from owning things to having embodied experiences was also taking root, most prominently among the demographic cohort of millennials, to which Josh, Liam and Tariq belonged.[18] Craftwork, with its continuous stream of challenges and triumphs, was ranked as a supreme experience, and one that could be pursued over a lifetime. The swap of things for experiences was a form of resistance to materialist capitalism and, for many, a strategy to securing more personal control over achieving contentment, fulfilment, connectedness or happiness. While interviewing me, Robert tidily summarised that view: 'If you choose not to have much in terms of material possessions, then you can probably live your life fairly comfortably.'

THE ALLURE OF STARDOM

There was an alternative prospect on the radar of the College's aspiring fine woodworkers. In sharp contrast to the ideal of owning a workshop 'tucked up some country lane', escaping the rat race and focusing on quality versus quantity in both life and work was the alluring world of high-end, bespoke furniture making. This niche is inhabited by a competitive league of star craftspeople, skilled not only at the workbench but also at marketing their wares, ideas and artisan identities. Social connections, networking, creating websites and personal narratives, and actively exhibiting on the circuit of fairs and galleries around the country and overseas are essential to drawing and retaining a clientele with a palate for novel items and the cash to pay.

The names of elite makers have dominated the official story of English furniture for the past three centuries, but only a small handful became household names, most notably the eighteenth-century masters Thomas Chippendale, Thomas Sheraton and George Hepplewhite. Late nineteenth and early/mid-twentieth-century designer-makers of furniture in wood, such as Ernest Gimson, the Barnsley brothers, Gordon Russell and Alan Peters, are well known to scholars and collectors, but not to a general public. With the possible exception of John Makepeace, the same holds true for today's avant-garde makers, despite the vibrancy of the contemporary bespoke furniture industry.[19] As woodwork instructor Cheryl M. shrewdly remarked:

> Everybody in the country knows who Andy Murray is.[20] But, name a furniture maker? Most people couldn't. Most people don't know anything about any of the trades, really, apart from the name of someone who came round the house to fix something. Broadly speaking, furniture making isn't regarded as any higher than that.

As makers-in-the-making, however, it was our duty to become acquainted with the names and styles of leading English furniture makers who emerged during the 1960s and 1970s Craft Revival and the following two decades. The list of early names reveals the extent to which the craft was dominated by white men.[21] The roster of up-and-coming stars at the turn of the millennium displayed better gender balance, but, notably, not greater ethnic diversity.[22]

The 'big name' makers we had read about or who visited the College were operating what appeared to be viable businesses, exhibiting their furniture at prestigious venues and winning prizes. They had managed to push the boundaries of furniture design and develop signature styles while remaining true to the natural properties of wood and the traditions of the craft. In the wise words of furniture maker Jeremy Broun: 'Tradition without innovation is stagnant, and innovation without tradition is frivolous.'[23] Pieces created by a select few have been acquired by national collections held by, for example, the Crafts Council, the Victoria & Albert Museum, the Fitzwilliam Museum and other institutions in Britain and around the world.

The status and success of these makers were inspiring to the trainees. For some, however, thoughts of chasing fame wrestled uncomfortably with their motives to simplify life and work. There was also an unwanted awareness that the English market for one-of-a-kind pieces was miniscule, and that the risks and costs involved in striving to become the 'artist-craftsperson' were high. Colin E.-E. put his finger on this dilemma:

> There have always been a few enlightened collectors who have money and can see what the maker's on about. But, generally speaking, when it comes to design, there's a tendency in this country to be conservative, with a small 'c'. It's always been the case. So, a 'traditional' craftsman has always been more likely to survive [than an avant-garde maker]. Being a [John] Makepeace or someone with an edgy approach to design is much harder here [in England] than it might be in Central Europe.

Continuing on a more optimistic note, however, Colin remarked on progressive changes in consumer tastes for 'more contemporary and daring' home furnishings, which he attributed to 'the advent of the Conran Shop and IKEA'. Flat-pack, mass-produced furniture was more usually conceived as the nemesis of designer-makers, but exhibition curator Betty Norbury, too, praised IKEA for moving the market on from its obsession with antiques, second-hand and reproduction furniture.[24] Furniture maker Johnny Hawkes expounded on this phenomenon with panache:

> The UK is saturated with eighteenth-century furniture. Our heritage is second to none: Chippendale, Hepplewhite, Sheraton and [Robert] Adams. What they made is incredible. Old money – from the nineteenth century all the way up to Thatcher – could go out and get the real stuff, and the rest [of the population] were happy with the repro[duction] shit – the gutter of all furniture. But, in the 80s, it wasn't old money but 'new flash' that was leading the way. City traders didn't give a shit for history, didn't want old stuff in their houses. They wanted new. So, a new market for modern furniture was created. The spin-off from that was Conran and Habitat – cool furniture on a commercial basis. IKEA is a company from God! It got the public out of a rut and into modern furniture. Some of it is really good design. It's been a fantastic thing for the market. Now, the first-time house buyer skips the repro shit and shops at IKEA. They get used to living with modern furniture. And then, when they accumulate money, they can commission and buy better-quality, bespoke pieces. IKEA is my marketing! We're not good at marketing. We [craftspeople] haven't a fuckin' clue.[25]

Another weighty contributor to changing consumer tastes for 'edgier' furniture and to a growing appreciation for skilled handwork and well-made, quality items was the proliferation of craft exhibitions in London and around the country. For those trainees who ventured to them, the exhibitions offered windows onto the latest design trends and innovations in making methodologies, and they ignited personal ambition. As discussed in Chapter 9, our participation in the *New Designers* show as exhibitors brought the College and its trainees into lively dialogue with furniture-making programmes from around the country and with leaders in design and manufacturing.[26]

Key exhibiting events during the period of my research that motivated trainees and honed aesthetic discernment included curator Betty Norbury's long-running annual *Celebration of Craftsmanship & Design* in Cheltenham (mentioned in Chapter 9). This was one of the nation's largest selling events promoting handcrafted furniture by British makers.[27] In 2004, the Crafts Council inaugurated *Collect* (see the Introduction to this volume), which also became an annual exhibition but on a much grander scale, featuring handmade furniture as well as textiles, ceramics, glass and jewellery created by a top tier of contemporary designer-makers from the United Kingdom and beyond. *Collect* was hosted at prestigious London venues and plugged as one of the world's leading fairs for contemporary applied arts.[28] In 2006, and in partnership with Somerset House, the Crafts Council initiated a second annual event, *Origin: The London Craft Fair*, which also featured furniture makers.[29] An important component of the Craft Council remit was, and continues to be, to make works of fine craftsmanship, including original furniture in wood, accessible to the public in England and Wales. This aim was satisfied with *Collect* and other shows, but 'accessibility' for most visitors was regrettably restricted to spectatorship, while buying what was on offer remained the prerogative of a well-healed minority.[30]

The craftworld inhabited by the vast majority of British makers is considerably different from that of the select few who exhibit nationally and internationally and enjoy the patronage of elite markets. The bulk of craftspeople typically create high-quality functional items that appeal to the aesthetic tastes, requirements and budgets of average middle-class consumers, and they eke out a living in doing so. The results of a survey conducted with nearly 2,000 British makers published in 2012 reported that more than half were earning net profits of less than £5,000 annually.[31] Low earnings were also reported as being a 'central problem' to the sustainability of the heritage craft sector.[32] As remarked by sociologist Doreen Jakob, 'crafting provides personal rewards but rarely sustainable, fulltime incomes'.[33] While just one in four craftspeople earned their total income from making and selling contemporary craft objects, the remainder were engaged in second occupations to make a living.[34]

Perhaps more problematic than meagre earnings is that most individual makers working from home or in studios scattered across Britain lack formal support and cohesive political representation to address and resolve the operational, economic and marketing challenges they face.[35] The reality for most fine woodworkers and furniture makers is no different. Despite sparkling ambitions harboured by some at college and the Herculean efforts they made, only a tiny minority will ever make the starring line-up.

In 2009, esteemed craftsman Martin Grierson organised what would become for a brief period a biannual show at the Millinery Works in Islington. Its title, *21ˢᵗ-Century Furniture: The Arts & Crafts Legacy*, explicitly underscored the homage paid by many contemporary makers to the late nineteenth and early twentieth-century masters. Like Betty Norbury's Cheltenham exhibition, Grierson's event feted handcrafted furniture in wood created by Britain's leading designer-makers, and it, too, was directed at an elite market of consumers and collectors. Among the seventy items exhibited in Grierson's third show was a two-drawer desk by Jackson, the former computer programmer and vocational migrant to the trade mentioned earlier by Colin E.-E.[36] His inclusion was a triumph for the Building Crafts College. For trainees, he was living proof that they, too, might one day have a place at the high table.

HURDLES TO SUCCESS

A month after my cohort graduated with high hopes, the subprime mortgage crisis erupted in the United States. By the following year, it had become a full-blown global financial catastrophe, precipitating what has been dubbed the 'Great Recession' (2008–13) and instigating a seemingly incessant programme of fiscal austerity measures in Britain.

Despite sharp falls in consumer spending and growth in unemployment figures, the Great Recession had insignificant impact on markets for personal luxury goods,[37] including exclusive, high-end handcrafted objects. By 2011, it was reported that Europe's market for luxury goods had in fact grown.[38] Evidently the '1 per cent' had been far better insulated against the economic downturn than the average citizen. 'While high street retailers are going to the wall', reported *The Guardian* in 2013, 'the world's most luxurious brands are reporting booming sales.' This was due in large part to increased demand in China and the Asia-Pacific region more generally, which by that year had become the world's largest market for luxury goods.[39]

In the United Kingdom, established producers of handcrafted items that carried marks of prestige and exclusivity were also largely shielded from the economic fallout. Two years into the recession, Proskills, which had been established by the British government to assist industry in upskilling employees (including furniture makers),[40] reported that 'many traditional bespoke, craft-based companies operating in niche markets have managed to maintain a good level of business'.[41]

This was not the case, however, for the broader UK craft sector, which was bruised by significant transformations in consumer habits. The wider societal trend was to reduce inessential consumption and live within one's means. In this day and age, few handcrafted items can any longer be considered essential. A study commissioned by the Crafts Council predicted that the tightening of wallets might 'constrict further market growth for craft and the entry of new buyers into the marketplace'.[42] By 2012, it was clear that 'the domestic market for low- and middle-end creative products of many kinds' had been 'affected by imports of cheap goods of reasonable quality', suggesting that the 'future market for UK craft [would] become increasingly concentrated at the higher end'.[43]

Regarding the 'disconnect between the ideology of crafting and capitalism', Doreen Jakob correctly observed that 'designing and making crafts takes a long time and many crafters are unable to price their items in such a way that their efforts are being fairly rewarded'.[44] While sales were in fact up for suppliers of craft materials in response to a growth in hobbyists and part-time professional crafting during the postrecession period,[45] the economic prospects for the majority of British craftspeople had become increasingly precarious and their livelihoods insecure.

On a more optimistic note, the 2012 Crafts Council study proclaimed craft's capacity to respond robustly to several key consumer trends that emerged in the immediate postrecession period. These included consumer demand for items that were personalised, had 'authenticity', had added ethical value in terms of provenance and reduction of environmental impact, signalled new kinds of connoisseurship (i.e. ethically motivated objects or those with a 'story' or that were 'conversational pieces') and offered an 'experiential' dimension.[46]

By 2020, the Crafts Council reported that those emergent consumer trends had indeed been translated into burgeoning popular interest in the activity of making and in owning handmade objects.[47] Britain's craftworld was becoming more buoyant once again. Craft had 'entered the mainstream market' in England, with 73 per cent of the surveyed population allegedly buying craft. Most purchases, however, were for 'craft at a lower value'[48] or from online platforms such as Etsy and Folksy.

Despite the uplifting news about the flourishing interest in things handmade, the present income levels of craftspeople remain low in comparison with the annual median salary in Britain.[49] As noted by Jakob, the challenge for today's craft movement is to 'grapple with its economic and social realities and find new ways to overcome its intrinsic dichotomy of efficiency and exclusivity'. The 'movement' (in whichever way that might be constituted) is compelled to do so if craft is 'to thrive and to transform the "nice work" it creates into "good jobs"'.[50] The conundrum identified by Jakob, however, has deep roots that are not easily disentangled. This was poignantly summarised by wood joiner Roger Coleman already in the 1980s. Torn between hopes for a 'fulfilling and unalienated way of working' and the structural forces of the capitalist economy in which he operated, Coleman conceded that:

We appear to gain control over our lives only to lose it in the process. When I behaved as a creative craftsman, as an artist of sorts, I lost money and could not afford to work. Lacking a private income, I had to choose between lowering my standards to compete with shoddy mass-produced goods, which still set price levels, even for handwork, and going stoically bankrupt.[51]

In the decades since Coleman's book was published, the number of British makers has actually swelled year-on-year and the pursuit of pleasurable work persists. Lamentably, however, the struggle he described to achieve a fulfilling and financially sustainable work-life harmony in the prevailing market conditions has remained unchanged.

WOODWORKERS' JOURNEYS

Of the two dozen fine woodworkers who trained at the Building Crafts College between 2005 and 2007 while I was enrolled on the programme, only a tiny minority managed to immediately establish themselves as sole traders making bespoke furniture. Individual artisanal skill played its part, but the accomplishment rested more heavily on the independent financial means of those graduates to take the plunge and weather the long and risky start-up period required for building business networks and a clientele.

To the best of my knowledge, the majority of others persisted in the wood trades in one form or another for at least a few years after graduating. They hired bench space in existing workshops or found employment with firms specialised in batch production, fitting kitchens or doing architectural joinery and site carpentry. Some occasionally landed private commissions to create the kind of furniture they had designed and made at college. Over the following years, several graduates left carpentry behind altogether and moved on to other pursuits, while a tenacious few progressively established themselves as sole traders, producing a mix of fine woodwork, cabinetry or furniture.

Chapter 9 registered the numerous obstacles to setting up and succeeding as a sole trader in high-end architectural joinery or furniture making. Students in creative arts, crafts and vocational programmes throughout Britain, and not merely those at the Building Crafts College, graduate and move into the world of work with inadequate (or no) business training for making a living at what they do. For many, that lacuna in their education represents the highest hurdle to achievement. The Crafts Council's 2020 study reported that the need for business start-up, management and marketing training among early-career professional makers and emerging craftspeople has remained acute over the past two decades.[52] In spite of the fact that it is makers who identify the need, enrolment figures on short courses offered by institutions like the Crafts Council have remained meagre.[53]

The steady fact is that most craftspeople channel their emotional, physical and intellectual energies into design and making, and into the constant creative problem solving that those combined tasks entail. Business planning, accounting, client networking, promotional campaigning and social media marketing, though recognised as necessary, are perceived by most as a distinct enterprise that steals valuable time, resources and focus away from what they do best. That antagonistic relationship between creative making and the business of selling has arguably always existed to varying degrees for most craftspeople in all times and places. In centuries past, however, when the typical English workshop was a household enterprise as opposed to being managed by the lone artisan, as is so often the case today, a division of labour between family members, apprentices or other household residents would have satisfied the full gamut of business needs more efficiently.[54]

For the graduating woodworkers, and especially for those living and wishing to remain in London, finding affordable workshop space posed another major impediment. Unlike crafts that can be executed almost entirely at a small workbench or in a confined space, carpentry practice, with its array of costly tools, noisy and cumbersome machinery, and racks of timber, necessitates a spacious interior that is separated from one's home and neighbours, and is fitted with mechanical dust extraction. The price of real estate and exorbitant rental costs make it almost impossible to operate a workshop in or around the capital for most career-starters, and their inability to demonstrate consistent and adequate earnings simply puts bank mortgages out of reach. Without a loan, the basic necessary machinery, too, is often unobtainable. Cash or credit is also required for a host of other start-up tasks, including preparing and disseminating marketing material or building a business website.

Two further issues confound the ambitions of many of those who, in particular, want to be furniture makers. In order to lure commissions for bespoke items, a maker needs an attractive portfolio of existing creations to hand. However, the cost of producing experimental prototypes of furniture in hardwoods is high, and while such pieces remain unsold, they represent frozen assets and consume valuable space in the workshop or in storage. Second, in comparison to the sheer number and variety of venues for showcasing and selling compact and easily portable crafts, such as ceramics, glasswork, woodcarving, woodturning, jewellery, textiles or artisanal items, events and locations for marketing bespoke furniture are far more limited in England. Relatively speaking, bespoke furniture is a 'big-ticket' item that demands considerably more room for display than most other crafts. Relatedly, entering one's creations into the handful of dedicated annual shows around the country is highly competitive, and exhibiting normally entails entry fees and transport costs, as well as the risk of no sales and time lost at the bench.

I conclude this penultimate section of the Epilogue with brief accounts of the journeys – to the extent that I know them – taken by, in the first instance, Donna, Shane, Russell and Angela after graduation. These four vocational migrants to fine woodworking were in the cohort senior to mine and their aspirations for work and life were introduced in Chapter 6. I then follow with short biographies of my fellow trainees.

Upon completing her training, Donna was given a commission by the College to design and make an awards-display cabinet in oak for the public area on the ground floor. Carrying out the project at her old bench gave her access to college materials, machinery and mentoring while offering the opportunity to develop methods for efficiently laminating off-cuts to create the chunkier components of her design. This allowed her to put into practice her ecological and sustainable visions for carpentry. Upon completing the cabinet, she eagerly took up a contract to work with the team of specialised carpenters conserving the *Cutty Sark*. Dry-docked since 1954 along the Thames embankment at Greenwich, the *Cutty Sark* was one of the last and one of the most elegant tea clippers ever built (1869). With its fascinating history of international travel and ownership, the vessel is considered to be part of Britain's nautical heritage. Joining the conservation efforts therefore carried considerable prestige for Donna. Tragically, as the project was nearing completion, a fire broke out on the *Cutty Sark* on the night of 21 May 2007, causing extensive damage.[55] The conservation work was halted and the carpentry team disbanded, at which point I lost track of Donna.

Shane graduated from the College with a number of Carpenters' Company prizes for his skilled workmanship and received a scholarship to attend the City & Guilds of London Art School in Kennington to study woodcarving.[56] I am uncertain of where his creative talents took him afterwards. Shane's classmate Russell, who had previously studied philosophy, had a trial period with a carpentry workshop in Wiltshire. He quickly discovered, however, that the work was repetitive and unsatisfying, the pay poor and the location too distant from his native London. He therefore put his entrepreneurial mind to being self-employed and his hands to a number of other building trades before finally launching an architectural soundproofing and acoustical design company. Since 2010, Shane's enterprise has thrived, attracting impressive commissions for high-end commercial, public and residential work.

As for Angela, she worked for a couple of years in and around London as a carpenter and cabinet maker, securing good commissions from the growing number of women who preferred to employ female tradespeople for new projects, maintenance and renovations in their homes. Angela later followed her partner to settle in the Netherlands, where she continued to work as a furniture maker until 2011, after which she left woodworking for an advisory position with Royal Dutch Shell.

As I became rapidly reabsorbed into academic work and writing following our grandiose graduation at Carpenters' Hall, nearly every other man in my cohort pursued his dream. Soon after our end-of-year show at *New Designers*, Tony, Jens and Robert pursued their individual paths, but the three men employed one another from time to time to assist with unwieldy commissions.

Tony was the recipient of the first-ever Carpenters' Award for Excellence at the City & Guilds Lion Awards in 2008, where he was praised for his innovation and originality in problem solving. The award formally recognised the exceptional creative craft skills that went into his final bentwood-chair project, which was described in Chapter 10. Tony was subsequently awarded the Freedom of the City of London by the Livery. Despite these esteemed accolades, he grudgingly returned to the door-and-window manufacturer in Potters Bar to accrue savings for starting up his own business, managing to manufacture several private commissions while there.

Towards the end of 2008, Tony jubilantly announced that he had received an offer of work from a firm in Auckland specialised in luxury yacht interiors. Robert organised a merry send-off celebration at a City pub, but Tony's arrival in New Zealand was not so merry. Having shipped all his tools and sundry supplies overseas, he was grimly informed on the first day of work that he was being laid off. 'The recession is biting just as hard over here', Tony discovered, 'and mainly on my ass!' His work permit was restricted to cabinet making and, with just five weeks remaining before deportation, he signed a contract with a small firm that kept him employed in Auckland for several months.

When Tony returned to England in the spring of 2010, the recession was still 'biting' at home. The difficulty in finding carpentry work led him to briefly consider moving into forestry, but instead he persisted with woodworking and succeeded in establishing a workshop in his hometown of St Albans and setting up a marketing website for his services. He eventually relocated his growing business to the Isle of Purbeck in Swanage, and now operates a buoyant fine-woodwork and furniture-making workshop with his wife. On occasion, he still collaborates on projects with Jens.

Jens remained in Hackney after graduation, working for a number of different carpentry firms and independent craftspeople. The latter included the innovative designer-maker Gareth Neil, until Gareth's output contracted with the recession. Like Tony, Jens nevertheless persisted in woodworking and he gradually established himself as a sole trader specialised in producing built-in furniture, shelving and cabinetry for clients across London. The clean, modernist Scandinavian aesthetic that he explored at the College continues to characterise his professional work.

Soon after *New Designers*, Robert won a prestigious commission to design and make a lectern for the historic Dutch Church at Austin Friars in the City of London. He did so at a bench hired in an existing carpentry shop. The success of that project led to additional contracts from the same church to make scores of chairs and an oak cabinet in what Robert coined 'Modern English Folk' and 'Mid-century Medieval' style. He later secured a small commission from Guildhall and an impressive contract to produce wood furnishings for the headquarters of Bestival, an annual music festival that supports environmental and social causes. Despite the recession, he reported doing 'a brisk business', though 'not necessarily profitable'. 'I don't think I'm charging enough', he wrote to me. 'I've also been about 25 per cent out in estimating the time it takes to do things.' Nevertheless, he discovered that his 'speed of work and confidence improved with each job'.

Longing to escape the city, Robert and his wife sold their home in South London and moved to a tranquil rural location in North Wales, which offered ample workshop space. He continued to make architectural joinery and furniture in his hallmark whimsical fashion, using off-cuts, native timbers and other natural materials in playful, inventive combinations. A selection of these was exhibited at a local gallery where he was invited as 'guest maker'. Several years later, however, he returned to South London. Not presently making furniture, he contentedly earns a living as a freelance writer and part-time bicycle mechanic.

Alex launched a business from the fully equipped workshop that he built in his Swindon back garden. He specialised, as planned, in producing bespoke cabinetry for home entertainment systems. As he generated more work, he transferred his practice to larger premises, while gaining 'real enjoyment from the woodwork'. Regrettably, personal circumstances threw his advancements into reverse, forcing Alex to relocate to the north of England, where he found a flat but no workshop. When we last corresponded, his driving ambition was to return to cabinet making.

Tariq found good employment immediately after graduation with a high-end shop-fitting firm in London. Unfortunately, he disappeared from my radar without a trace, but I have no doubts that his talents as a carpenter have taken him onwards to success. I also lost track of Liam after college, but, with any luck, he followed in his father's footsteps as he had hoped and is now a futures trader in southeast England.

Josh was our only fellow trainee to pursue further education after the fine-woodwork programme. He proudly completed an undergraduate degree in design at Lincoln University, finishing with a very respectable upper second. While at university, he continued to attend music festivals, collect wristbands and enjoy teenage life. He also attended the *Milan Furniture Fair* as part of his studies, opening his mind to making things with an array of different contemporary materials. After university, he sent an email to report that he landed work as a cabinet maker with a high-end joinery firm in West London, where Jens, too, had worked for a short time. Josh signed off, writing: 'I've got to jump back on the spindle moulder now and make some more dust!' A decade later, he was no longer 'on the tools' or 'making dust'. He shared the news that he had been promoted to project coordinator within the same joinery firm and was now discovering new challenges in his office-based work.

Every woman and man who arrived at the Building Crafts College to become a craftsperson did so from a unique background of experiences, as described in Chapter 4. After two intense years of learning and growing together, sharing aspirations and building relationships, they parted to make their own paths into the world of work. Some paths occasionally crossed, but most diffused, travelling along separate trajectories. Regardless of whether graduates remained active in the wood trades or became entrepreneurs in business, employees of companies, or bike mechanics, each one will surely have carried in themselves a greater measure of patience, attentiveness, curiosity, problem-solving skills and appreciation for the creative wonders of the hand. It is not for me to say whether the men and women introduced in my book found the pleasurable work they pursued, nor is it for me to judge.

TOWARDS A NEW CURRICULUM

As noted earlier, it took time to gain a critical perspective on the politics of craftwork and a nuanced understanding of the matrix of mutable forces at play in contemporary craftworlds. Nevertheless, my belief in the pursuit of pleasurable work and my quest to put embodied learning at the heart of mainstream education remain steadfast. In this concluding section, I reiterate that commitment.

By September 2007, after my cohort's graduation, student numbers at the Building Crafts College had risen to more than 300 and plans were under way for an extension of the College that would increase floor space by 30 per cent. With London's bid for the 2012 Olympics secured, grand designs were rolled out for creating the Queen Elizabeth Olympic Park on a mix of greenfield and brownfield land in Stratford. The park would contain the Olympic Village and several of the major sporting facilities, including the main stadium, aquatics centre and velodrome. The choice of site spurred the redevelopment of the Thames Gateway, the construction of a new Westfield Shopping Centre and the regeneration (read 'gentrification') of Stratford's town centre.

The Building Crafts College was ideally located to benefit from all four of these gargantuan projects by negotiating training partnerships with firms that employed construction and shop-fitting apprentices. It also devised and managed a network of Building One-Stop Shops that gave local East London residents the skills and confidence to find employment in the booming construction sector in the adjoining boroughs of Newham, Tower Hamlets, Hackney and Waltham Forest.

As a private training provider, however, the College faced considerable funding challenges during the era of austerity that followed the 2008 financial crisis. These troubles were compounded by a convoluted nationwide qualifications system and the constant scramble to interpret and satisfy its ever-shifting criteria.[57] Nevertheless, at the start of the academic year in 2019 (and six months before the outbreak of the COVID-19 pandemic), the College reported 500 enrolments on its by-then greatly expanded range of courses.[58] Growth of the institution since 2001 had kept step with changing regulations and curricular demands set by the Department of Education and various skills councils. The College had also been proactive in seeking new opportunities and in responding to the pressing need to generate income.[59]

The College Principal avowed that: 'Recruitment of willing students is not a problem.' But, he added, 'the challenge is to access and match funding to those who wish to develop a career in the crafts'.[60] Privately run vocational colleges that were on the frontlines in the nation's battle to shrink its longstanding skills gap were in fact squeezed by a lack of financing from government funding bodies throughout the postrecession period.[61] Facilities at further education colleges across Britain that offered wood machining, shop-fitting and joinery tuition were reported to be deteriorating as a result.[62] Additionally, the government's introduction of the new Apprenticeship Levy in 2017 was evidently a 'cost-cutting, procurement-simplifying exercise' destined to have detrimental impact on 'small, quality providers', like the Building Crafts College, as well as on 'small and medium building contractors who normally send their apprentices' to such colleges.[63]

The Executive Director of the Crafts Council likewise clocked the Tory's contradictory stances and its contraction of support for craft-related design and technology education. While the Departments of Business and Culture heralded the impressive growth of the creative industries sector during Britain's economic recovery, the Department of Education narrowed the school curriculum, 'keen to emphasise traditional academic subjects over the arts', including crafts.[64]

As a consequence, schools that had managed to preserve their precious woodworking, metalworking and other technology departments through the decades of cuts finally witnessed their closure. 'With the pressure on school budgets', commented the Chief Executive Officer of the British Woodworking Federation, 'if the choice is fixing the roof or upgrading or servicing the woodworking machines, then direction of travel is set.'[65] Schools also experienced drastic declines in the enrolment of pupils on creative courses.[66]

These major setbacks were compounded by the fact that school appraisals in the United Kingdom are narrowly based on proportions of students attaining A levels and gaining admission to university. Incentives and rewards for preparing school leavers to follow routes into vocational and craft training or Apprenticeships are, by contrast, negligible.

In its *Education Manifesto for Craft and Making*, the Crafts Council set out a clear vision, calling on government, business and educators to ensure that:

> every child has a chance to discover their practical abilities, develop their creative talents, and become a maker of the future. This vision is rooted in the knowledge that craft skills lead to diverse careers and creative satisfaction throughout life.[67]

It is not merely government, business and educators who need to be brought on board this agenda for sweeping educational reform. The country needs a sea change in thinking among parents and guardians too. Many judge the vocational route as inferior to the academic one, and far less prestigious. Craft and other kinds of creative skilled handwork are perceived as poor and unfulfilling career options for their children. In short, manual trades, including the arts and crafts, are denigrated as a refuge for the academically less capable.

The demise of hand-skills and craftwork in the United Kingdom is explained in large part as a consequence of rapid industrialisation and exponential population growth in the nineteenth century, hastened in the twentieth century by technological advancement, globalisation and Britain's shift to a service economy. The resulting low status of manual trades persists in the post-industrial era. In combination, parents' dismissive attitudes, mainstream schooling, the economic system and the political class prioritise and reward intellectual work over physical skill (with the notable exception of elite professional sport). While it would be unrealistic to suppose that the march of technology can be stemmed or the impacts of globalised mass production reversed to restore some idealised world of craftsmanship, it is entirely possible to alter the ways that we, as a society, appreciate and value handwork.

In popular discourse on intelligence, the 'mind' prevails while the body continues to be underestimated, undervalued or misrepresented as being subservient to mind. Today, however, anthropology, cognitive studies, the neurosciences, philosophy of mind, craft studies and education studies are providing fresh insights into the nature of skill learning, tool use, and the interconnectedness of language, conceptual thought, sensory apparatus and motor cognition. Careful cross-disciplinary studies of how the body learns and knows are essential to undermining entrenched stereotypes and cultivating fuller appreciation of skilled practice. Promisingly, contemporary research is supplying the basis for more encompassing and empirically based understandings of knowledge and intelligence. Discoveries and new theories are disseminated in academic outputs, but if general attitudes towards handwork are to be enlightened, then findings also need to be channelled through Parliament and the media, and embraced by the education sector and translated into new pedagogies.

As the book chapters reveal, absorption in creative handwork broadens cognitive development; unifies body, mind and spirit by strengthening coordination between brain, hand and perceptual senses; sharpens problem-solving skills; hones patience, concentration, focused awareness and dedication to tasks; nurtures a sense of ownership and responsibility; and engages us mindfully with the natural world that gives us life, and with the material world that gives it meaning. Creatively solving problems, making things and sharing them with others are not only pleasurable; they are culturally, socially and economically productive. They are also at the very core of what makes us human and what endows us with humanity. For these reasons, education of 'the hand' should be valued on a par with that of 'the mind'. In fact, the indissoluble link between the two must be formally recognised as the basis for revolutionary educational reform.

In 1880, at the time when William Morris was railing against the predominant utilitarian ethos of public education and the commercial opportunism that had infiltrated the university,[68] the school-leaving age in England was just ten years old. By the mid-twentieth century, it was fifteen years old and increased to sixteen by 1972. At present, young men and women may choose to leave school at sixteen, but recent legislation requires that they either stay in full-time or part-time education or enrol on an Apprenticeship (or preparatory traineeship) until the minimum age of eighteen. Surely the increased length of statutory schooling and training offers a unique occasion for radically rethinking the basic curriculum for all students – from primary school through secondary and postsecondary education. A new and progressive curriculum must address physical and emotional intelligences as well as conceptual thinking in order to nurture the whole person. In doing so, schooling can become the democratic enabler it should be, supplying supportive mentoring and a diversity of instruction that fosters skills for independent critical thinking and empowers each individual to choose, pursue and realise their full potential.

Morris rejected the division made between academic learning and practical training, believing that education should cultivate the powers of the mind as well as those of the eye and hand.[69] He energetically advocated for a liberal education that would provide students with opportunity to:

> have [their] share of whatever knowledge there is in the world according to [their] capacity or bent of mind, historical or scientific; and also to have [their] share of skill

of hand which is about in the world, either in the industrial handicrafts or in the fine arts.[70]

A true education, Morris believed, should stoke the quest for knowledge and the creation of beauty for its own sake. Phillippa Bennett, scholar and trustee of the William Morris Society, proposed that Morris' vision for a rounded education still holds promise to 'transform our relationship' to whatever work we do by helping us to discover 'interest in it, and perhaps even beauty'.[71] This would lead not only to individual self-actualisation, but likewise to a more diverse and resilient economy and a happier, more inclusive and egalitarian society. There should exist no obligation for boys and girls – or for women and men – to choose between a future of mindwork or handwork. Viable options to engage in both, and in unison, need to be made available. This, of course, can arise only if learning frameworks at school and in the workplace are engineered to scaffold lifelong pursuits of physical, intellectual and spiritual development.

In the spirit of both Morris and American philosopher and educational reformer John Dewey,[72] contemporary educationalist Mike Rose argued that:

> To acknowledge our collective capacity is to take the concept of variability seriously. Not as slots along a simplified cognitive continuum or as a neat high-low distribution, but as a bountiful and layered field, where many processes and domains of knowledge interact.[73]

I agree wholeheartedly with Rose.

Creating a more level playing field that prizes a plurality of intelligences must begin at school and in the home. Defusing the dichotomy and dismantling the hierarchy between mind and body need not diminish the importance of 'book-smarts'; rather, a level playing field hinges on raising the profile of skill-based knowledge and suturing the plurality of intelligences into a pioneering curriculum of learning activities.

Craftwork proffers the ideal curricular activity for synthesising diverse ways of knowing and for elegantly bridging learning with our immediate material surroundings and the wider world of which we are a part. It is a pathway to intellectual and physical discovery that elicits skilful improvisation and, on occasion, innovation. At the nucleus of practical hands-on making is problem solving, which drives imaginations and fosters abilities to predict, plan, weigh options and carefully strategise solutions. Creatively working things out with materials and tools, and often in collaboration with others, emplaces learners and seasoned practitioners alike in the immediacy of the present, while simultaneously engaging them with rich histories of practice and prompting them to anticipate and shape possible futures.

For certain, not every pupil who engages in craftwork at school will become a craftsperson in the traditional sense, but each young person who

Figure 11.2 The author's *Djenné Fireside Chair*, in American white oak (*Quercus alba*) and gold-leaf detailing. Italian cinnabar upholstery created by Barbara Heywood, 2007. © Trevor H.J. Marchand

undergoes a hands-on curriculum will be equipped for carrying a measure of the sagacity of craftsmanship into whatever work they do, and into novel realms of research, design and making that we cannot yet even imagine. In short, craftwork prepares people for social citizenship and endows them with the skills for making the world a better place for all.

NOTES

1. Conducted on 25 July 2006.
2. Tudge, *The Secret Life of Trees*.
3. Prentice, 'Knowledge, Skill, and the Inculcation of the Anthropologist'. See also Downey, Dalidowicz and Mason, who note that being an apprentice in the field 'is often constrained in ways that do not affect less deeply embedded ethnographers' ('Apprenticeship as Method', 184).

4. Prentice, 'Knowledge, Skill, and the Inculcation of the Anthropologist', 59.
5. The 1997 Kyoto Protocol is an international treaty that extends the 1992 United Nations Framework Convention on Climate Change. It came into force on 16 February 2005.
6. Directed by Davis Guggenheim, 2006.
7. The Alkali Act, passed in 1863 to reduce muriatic acid gas emissions from Leblanc alkali works in Britain, is considered the first major environmental act in modern times.
8. Established in 1993, the FSC is an international nonprofit, multi-stakeholder organisation that promotes responsible management of the world's forests.
9. These were terms regularly used by my fellow trainees.
10. The Crafts Council at al. reported in 2012 that 'just under a third (thirty-one per cent) of makers had changed their practice in the previous three years in response to environmental concerns. The most popular change was to source more environmentally sustainable or sensitive materials' (Crafts Council et al., *Craft in an Age of Change*, 8).
11. The Building Centre was established in 1931.
12. An eminent example of this is *The Craftsmanship Initiative* website, with its motto 'Create a World Built to Last': https://craftsmanship.net (retrieved 9 June 2021).
13. See Slow Food, *Good, Clean and Fair*; and Centre for Alternative Technology, 'Mission Statement'.
14. See Metcalf, 'Contemporary Craft', 16.
15. Conducted at the Building Crafts College, 20 October 2009.
16. The Maker-in-Residence programme for fine woodworkers was initiated at the College in September 2008. This allowed for one or two of the top graduates from each cohort to spend an additional year at the College, with a dedicated bench and access to the resources. Makers-in-residence spent the year making either their own commissions or ones received by the College, and they served as mentors for the current cohorts of trainees. Though the number of graduates benefiting from the programme was necessarily limited, it was nevertheless an important step made by the College in providing the necessary incubation space for graduates to prepare for becoming independent makers.
17. Links between work and family have been a subject of policy research since the 1960s, but sociologists Gregory and Milner note that: 'Work-life balance has come to the forefront of policy discourse in developed countries in recent years [i.e. the early 2000s], against a backdrop of globalization and rapid technological change, an ageing population and concerns over labour market participation rates, particularly those of mothers at a time when fertility rates are falling' (Gregory and Milner, 'Editorial', 1).
18. See, for example, Hamblin, 'Buy Experiences'; and Morgan, 'NOwnership'.
19. John Makepeace is recognised as one of the most significant figures of the British Craft Movement of the 1970s. In 2011, Somerset House hosted the first solo retrospective of his work.
20. At the time of writing, Andy Murray was a top-ranking British professional tennis player from Scotland.
21. For example, prominent names of Craft Revival furniture makers include Richard La Trobe-Bateman, Fred Baier, Martin Grierson, Jeremy Broun, Rupert Williamson, Johnny Hawkes, Andrew Varah and Phil Koomen. Later entrants to the trade's top

rank included Richard Williams and the husband-and-wife teams Rod and Alison Wales, and Justin Williams and Jane Cleal.

22. A sample of top contemporary makers includes Katie Walker and Sarah Kay, as well as Gareth Neil and David Gates. In the early 2000s, furniture making and carpentry in general continued to attract few female applicants. In 2003, 'a survey of 1,000 people, carried out for the [Equal Opportunities] Commission by BMRB International, suggested that about half – 54% of women and 47% of men – thought the advice they were given on leaving school was influenced by their sex' (BBC, 'Gender Bias'). In 2006, inspectors from the watchdog Ofsted reporting on the government's Young Apprenticeship programme (introduced in 2004), said that more must be done to encourage ethnic minority youngsters to take up apprenticeships and to counter gender stereotyping (BBC, 'Apprenticeship Scheme Praised'). Regarding UK craft makers more generally (but not including heritage sector crafts), it was noted in the 2012 report that though 'the sector is largely female', the 'percentage of black and Asian makers remains low' (Crafts Council et al., *Craft in an Age of Change*, 7; see also 18–20 for a statistical breakdown). This remained unchanged in 2020, with 75 per cent of makers identifying as female, but only between 2 and 4 per cent of makers identifying as being from BAME communities (Morris Hargreaves McIntyre, *The Market for Craft*, 8).

23. See Jeremy Broun's webpage, http://www.jeremybroun.co.uk (retrieved 9 June 2021).

24. Interview at the Queens Hotel, Cheltenham, 16 November 2007.

25. Interview at his studio in Pewsey, 17 August 2006. Regarding the issue of 'marketing', the Crafts Council et al. report stated in 2012 that 'a significant minority of makers' felt that they lacked skills in this domain, and that almost half felt they needed to develop additional business skills (*Craft in an Age of Change*, 9 and 25).

26. The annual *New Designers* show in Islington has showcased the work of top graduates from British design courses around the country since 1985. In 2006, four second-year fine-woodwork trainees took the initiative to enter their furniture projects for the first time, and this subsequently became a regular event at which Building Crafts College graduates publicly exhibit their finest creations. The Carpenters' Company announced in 2018 that Building Crafts College students had won several design awards at the 2017 show and that the College 'is becoming more widely known as a college that can compete with university programmes in both design and making across the country' (Austen, 'New Designers Exhibition', 4–5).

27. Launched by Norbury in 1994 at the Thirlestaine Long Gallery in Cheltenham, the summer exhibition continued to run annually at the time of writing. In 2009, furniture maker Jason Heap took over the organisation and curation of *Celebration of Craftsmanship & Design* from Betty Norbury.

28. *Collect* was staged for the first five years at the Victoria & Albert Museum and for the next decade at the Saatchi Gallery. In 2020 it opened at Somerset House, closing just before the COVID-19 pandemic lockdown in the city.

29. Running for four years only, *Origin* brought together hundreds of the most innovative and influential international designer-makers, who were on hand to meet and speak with the visiting public and to sell their wares. In 2015, two years after the end of my second fieldwork project at the College, the Crafts Council, in partnership with Platform Gallery (located at Habitat, King's Road) staged *Inside out: An exhibition of Furniture from the Crafts Council Collection*. The show featured twenty-four

pioneering pieces by significant makers, spanning four decades from Alan Peters to Sarah Kay. Although not all of the objects displayed were made in wood, many were, and the exhibition evinced the Crafts Council's efforts to promote (knowledge about, but arguably not accessibility to) innovative handcrafted furniture to the general public.

30. Charlotte Abrahams reported in 2008: 'Craft pieces by leading makers are far from cheap (you won't get much for under £1,000), but as this is an expanding market, prices have still not peaked and so there's a lot of potential for investment' (Abrahams, 'Hands That Do Dishes').

31. Crafts Council et al., *Craft in an Age of Change*, 3.

32. Creative & Cultural Skills et al., *Mapping Heritage Craft*, 6.

33. Jakob, 'Crafting Your Way out of the Recession?', 127.

34. Crafts Council et al., *Craft in an Age of Change*, 25.

35. See, for example, Creative & Cultural Skills et al., *Mapping Heritage Craft*, 6. In the 2012 Crafts Council et al. report, it is noted that 88 per cent of makers are sole traders and almost two-thirds work from home, 'most usually in a formal workshop on their home premises' (*Craft in an Age of Change*, 4 and 22).

36. Jackson (not his real name) graduated from the fine-woodwork programme at the Building Crafts College and received a City & Guilds Medal for Excellence in 2010.

37. Arnett, 'What Happens to Luxury'.

38. Friedman, 'Why Luxury Is Recession-Proof'.

39. Neate, 'Recession Bypasses Market'.

40. Proskills was set up as a Sector Skills Council in 2003 and was fully funded by the government. The government withdrew its funding in 2011, after which Proskills became self-financing. It worked with employers and industry bodies to develop and review more than 2,500 National Occupational Standards, including development of the Furniture Manufacturer Apprenticeship Standard. Proskills ceased trading in 2016 due to 'ever-changing skills environment which has made it more difficult than ever to create the desired level of sustainability' (Farley, 'Proskill UK Closes').

41. Lightfoot, 'Pencil, Ruler, Fretsaw', 49.

42. Morris Hargreaves McIntyre, *Consuming Craft*, 45. This study, commissioned by the Crafts Council, was based on survey responses from more than 4,000 adults in England and 416 in-depth surveys with people who bought or were predisposed to buying crafts.

43. Crafts Council et al., *Craft in an Age of Change*, 9.

44. Jakob, 'Crafting Your Way out of the Recession?', 138.

45. Ibid., 128–29.

46. Morris Hargreaves McIntyre, *Consuming Craft*, 41–43.

47. Morris Hargreaves McIntyre, *The Market for Craft*, 5.

48. Ibid., 6.

49. Ibid., 8.

50. Jakob, 'Crafting Your Way out of the Recession?', 139.

51. Coleman, *The Art of Work*, 144.

52. Morris Hargreaves McIntyre, *The Market for Craft*, 72 and 74–75.

53. Ibid., 75.

54. We know from historical records of medieval England, for example, that the wives of craftsmen sometimes played active roles in running the business (C. Phythian-Adams, quoted in Leach, 'Carpenters in Medieval London', 148–49).

55. Originally suspected to be a case of arson, it was later determined by forensic investigators that the fire may have been caused by an industrial vacuum cleaner that was left switched on. The *Cutty Sark* was again restored at great cost and opened to the public in 2012, but was damaged by a smaller fire in 2014.

56. Opened in 1879 and receiving assistance from the Fish Mongers and other London liveries, the School provides training in wood and stone carving, as well as architectural decoration and gilding, and encourages the retention of traditional skills.

57. Augar, *Independent Panel Report*, especially Chapter 4 (114–41).

58. Conway, 'Building Crafts College' (2019).

59. See the Building Crafts College website for a comprehensive overview of the courses offered: http://www.thebcc.ac.uk/about-the-college (retrieved 9 June 2021).

60. Conway, 'Building Crafts College' (2011), 3.

61. Conway, 'Building Crafts College' (2017), 3.

62. McIlwee, 'The Emerging Skills Crisis', 8.

63. Bower, 'Message from the Master', 2. On the negative impacts of the Apprenticeship Levy, see also McIlwee, 'The Emerging Skills Crisis'.

64. Greenlees, 'Making a Manifesto'.

65. McIlwee, 'The Emerging Skills Crisis'.

66. Between 2007 and 2013, there was a 25 per cent drop in take-up of craft-related GCSEs. In higher education, the number of craft-related courses fell by 46 per cent (Crafts Council, *Education Manifesto*, no pagination). See also Brown, 'Arts and Culture'.

67. Crafts Council, *Education Manifesto*, no pagination.

68. See Morris, 'Thought on Education' and 'The Aims of Art'.

69. Bennett, 'Educating for Utopia', 64.

70. Morris, 'How We Live', 18.

71. Bennett, 'Educating for Utopia', 67.

72. Especially Dewey, *Democracy and Education*.

73. Rose, *The Mind at Work*, 216.

BIBLIOGRAPHY

◠◡◠

Abrahams, C. 'Hands That Do Dishes'. *The Observer*, 20 January 2008. Retrieved 9 June 2021 from https://www.theguardian.com/artanddesign/2008/jan/20/design.homes.

Adamson, G. *Thinking through Craft*. Oxford: Berg, 2007.

———. 'Section Introduction: Contemporary Approaches' in G. Adamson (ed.), *The Craft Reader* (Oxford: Berg, 2010), 585–87.

Aikin, L. *Memoirs of the Court of King James the First*, vol. 1. London: Longman, Hurst, Rees, Orme, Brown and Green, 1822. Digitised in 2007: https://books.google.co.uk/books/about/Memoirs_of_the_Court_of_King_James_the_F.html?id=jjI2AA AAMAAJ&redir_esc=y (retrieved 9 June 2021).

Aldrich, R. 'The Apprentice in History', in P. Ainley and H. Rainbird (eds), *Apprenticeship: Towards a New Paradigm of Learning* (London: Kogan Page, 1999), 14–24.

Alford, B.W.E., and T.C. Barker. *A History of the Carpenters' Company*. London: George Allen & Unwin, 1968.

Amunts, K., G. Schlaug, L. Jancke, H. Steinmetz, A. Schleicher, A. Dabringhaus and K. Zilles. 'Motor Cortex and Hand Motor Skills: Structural Compliance in the Human Brain'. *Human Brain Mapping*, 5(3) (1997), 206–15.

Annas, J. 'Epicurus on Pleasure and Happiness'. *Philosophical Topics*, 15(2) (1987), 5–21.

Anonymous. 'Wood and Its Deterioration'. *Journal of the British Institute of Certified Carpenters* (October 1923), 64. Reprinted in *Cutting Edge*, November/December 2013, 21.

Arendt, H. *The Human Condition*. Chicago: University of Chicago Press, 1969 [1958].

Aristotle. *Nicomachean Ethics*. Translated by J.A.K. Thomson; revised with notes and appendices by H. Tredennick. Introduction and Further Readings by J. Barnes. London: Penguin, 2004.

Arnett, G. 'What Happens to Luxury during a Recession'. *Vogue Business*, 16 August 2019. Retrieved 9 June 2021 from https://www.voguebusiness.com/companies/luxury-recession-saks-bond-yield.

Ashbee, C.R. *The Guild of Handicraft, Its Deed of Trust and Rules for the Guidance of Its Guildsmen*. Broad Campden: Essex House Press, 1909.

Association of University Teachers. 'Memorandum Submitted by the Association of University Teachers', in *Select Committee on Science and Technology Minutes of Evidence*,

7 March 2002. Retrieved 9 June 2021 from https://publications.parliament.uk/pa/cm200102/cmselect/cmsctech/507/2012311.htm.

Atlas, J. 'Oxford versus Thatcher's England'. *New York Times*, 24 April 1988. Retrieved 9 June 2021 from https://www.nytimes.com/1988/04/24/magazine/oxford-versus-thatcher-s-england.html.

Augar, P. *Independent Panel Report to the Review of Post-18 Education and Funding*, May 2019. UK: APS Group on behalf of the Controller of Her Majesty's Stationery Office.

Austen, N. 'New Designers Exhibition'. *The Carpenters' Company Broadsheet*, 57 (2018), 4–5.

Bachman, I. 'New Craft Paradigms', in J. Johnson (ed.), *Exploring Contemporary Craft: History, Theory and Critical Writing* (Toronto: Coach House Books with the Craft Studio at Harbourfront Centre, 2002), 45–50.

Bacon, A.K. 'Morris's View of the History of Industrialism'. *Journal of William Morris Studies*, 5(1) (1982), 2–8.

Bacon, F. 'New Atlantis', in S. Bruce (ed., with Introduction and notes), *Three Early Modern Utopias: Utopia, New Atlantis, and the Isle of Pines* (Oxford: Oxford University Press, 1999 [1620]), 149–86.

———. *The New Organon*. Cambridge: Cambridge University Press, 2008.

Baier, F. 'Words by Fred: Vision and Reality'. Retrieved 9 June 2021 from http://www.fredbaier.com/words/by-fred/p/vision-reality.

Baker, F. 'Anthropological Notes on the Human Hand'. *American Anthropologist*, A1(1) (1888), 51–76.

Barnett, C. *The Verdict of Peace: Britain between Her Yesterday and the Future*. London: Macmillan, 2001.

BBC. 'Education: Blair Wants Student Boom'. *BBC News*, 8 March 1999. Retrieved 9 June 2021 from http://news.bbc.co.uk/1/hi/education/292504.stm.

———. 'Blair's University Targets Spelt out'. *BBC News*, 30 January 2002. Retrieved 9 June 2021 from http://news.bbc.co.uk/1/hi/education/1789500.stm.

———. 'Charles Promotes Apprenticeships'. *BBC News*, 14 November 2002. Retrieved 9 June 2021 from http://news.bbc.co.uk/1/hi/education/2474583.stm.

———. 'Where Next for School-Leavers?' *BBC News*, 20 August 2003. Retrieved 9 June 2021 from http://news.bbc.co.uk/1/hi/education/3167447.stm.

———. 'Increase in Student Numbers Not Needed'. *BBC News*, 29 March 2004. Retrieved 9 June 2021 from http://news.bbc.co.uk/1/hi/education/3578827.stm.

———. 'Gender Bias in Training Scheme'. *BBC News*, 5 May 2004. Retrieved 9 June 2021 from http://news.bbc.co.uk/go/pr/fr/-/1/hi/education/3684369.stm.

———. 'Skills Gap Threatens UK Future'. *BBC News*, 5 December 2005. Retrieved 9 June 2021 from http://news.bbc.co.uk/1/hi/education/4501346.stm.

———. 'Apprenticeship Scheme Praised'. *BBC News*, 20 October 2006. Retrieved 9 June 2021 from http://news.bbc.co.uk/go/pr/fr/-/1/hi/education/6070712.stm.

———. 'Promise of a Skills Revolution'. *BBC News*, 18 July 2007. Retrieved 9 June 2021 from http://news.bbc.co.uk/go/pr/fr/-/1/hi/education/6904298.stm.

———. 'Half of New Jobs Go to Migrants'. *BBC News*, 30 October 2007. Retrieved 9 June 2021 from http://news.bbc.co.uk/go/pr/fr/-/1/hi/uk_politics/7069779.stm.

———. 'Skills Drive to Boost Workforce'. *BBC News*, 16 November 2007. Retrieved 9 June 2021 from http://news.bbc.co.uk/1/hi/education/7097125.stm.

———. 'University of Bath Replaces "Highest Paid" Vice Chancellor'. *BBC News*, 4 September 2018. Retrieved 9 June 2021 from https://www.bbc.co.uk/news/uk-england-somerset-45406697.

Bell, C. *The Hand: Its Mechanisms and Vital Endowments as Evincing Design*. Breinigsville, PA: General Books LLC, 2009 [1833].

Bellamy, E. *Looking Backwards: 2000–1887*. Boston: Houghton Mifflin & Co., 1888.

Bellows, S. *To Jerusalem and Back: A Personal Account*. New York: Viking Press, 1976.

Bence, V., and C. Oppenheim. 'The Evolution of the UK's Research Assessment Exercise: Publications, Performance and Perceptions'. *Journal of Educational Administration and History*, 37(2) (2005), 137–55.

Benjamin, D.K., and L.A. Kochin. 'Unemployment and Unemployment Benefits in Twentieth-Century Britain: A Reply to Our Critics'. *Journal of Political Economy*, 90(2) (1982), 410–36.

Bennett, J.A.W., and G.V. Smithers (eds). 'The Land of Cockaygne', in *Early Middle English Verse and Prose*, 2nd edn (Oxford: Clarendon Press, 1968), 136–44.

Bennett, P. 'Educating for Utopia: William Morris on Useful Learning versus "Useless Toil"'. *Journal of William Morris Studies*, 20(2) (2013), 54–72.

Bentham, J. *An Introduction to the Principles of Morals and Legislations*, Mineola, NY: Dover Publications, 2007.

Berti, A., and F. Frassinetti. 'When Far Becomes Near: Remapping of Space by Tool Use'. *Journal of Cognitive Neuroscience*, 12(3) (2000), 415–20.

Billett, S. 'Recasting Transfer as a Socio-personal Process of Adaptable Learning'. *Educational Research Review*, 8 (2013), 5–13.

Blair, T. 'Leader's Speech, Brighton 1997'. Speech Archive, *BritishPoliticalSpeech*. Retrieved 9 June 2021 from http://www.britishpoliticalspeech.org/speech-archive.htm?speech=203.

———. 'UK Politics: Tony Blair's Speech in Full', *BBC News*, 28 September 1999. Retrieved 9 June 2021 from http://news.bbc.co.uk/1/hi/uk_politics/460009.stm.

Bloom, C. *Violent London: 2,000 Years of Riots, Rebels and Revolts*. London: Palgrave Macmillan, 2003.

Bower, R. 'Message from the Master'. *The Carpenters' Company Broadsheet*, 58 (2018), 2–3.

Boyke, J., J. Driemeyer, C. Gaser, C. Büchel and A. May. 'Training-Induced Brain Structure Changes in the Elderly'. *Journal of Neuroscience*, 28(28): 7031–35.

Boyson, R. *Wordsworth and the Enlightenment Idea of Pleasure*. Cambridge: Cambridge University Press, 2012.

Brehony, K.J., and R. Deem. 'Challenging the Post-Fordist/Flexible Organisation Thesis: The Case of Reformed Educational Organisations'. *British Journal of Sociology of Education*, 26(3) (2005), 395–414.

Brewer, T. 'Savouring Time: Desire, Pleasure and Wholehearted Activity'. *Ethical Theory and Moral Practice*, 6(2) (2003), 143–60.

Bridgewater, A., G. Bridgewater, G. Bridgewater, C. Eden-Eadon, S. Francis, J. Lloyd, J. Tibbs and J. Wilkie. *Woodwork: The Complete Step-by-Step Manual*. London: Dorling Kindersley Ltd, 2010.

Broun, J. 'Introduction', in *Alan Peters: The Maker's Maker*. Retrieved 9 June 2021 from http://www.jeremybroun.co.uk/ebooks/HTML5/makersmaker/files/assets/common/downloads/publication.pdf?uni=67d5c48fede5378ceed0b115fbfd9a9c.

Brown, G. 'Speech on Expansion of Apprenticeships: 28 January 2008'. *UK National Archives*. Retrieved 9 June 2021 from https://webarchive.nationalarchives.gov.uk/20080908231316/http://www.number10.gov.uk/Page14414.

Brown, M. 'Arts and Culture Being Systematically Removed from UK Education System'. *The Guardian*, 17 February 2015. Retrieved 9 June 2021 from https://www.theguardian.com/education/2015/feb/17/arts-and-culture-systematically-removed-from-uk-education-system.

Buckley, M. 'Burning Issues'. *The Carpenters' Company Broadsheet*, 55 (2017), 7–8.

Burnette, J. *Gender, Work and Wages in Industrial Revolution Britain*. Cambridge: Cambridge University Press, 2009.

Buszek, M.E. (ed.). *Extra/Ordinary: Craft and Contemporary Art*. Durham, NC: Duke University Press, 2011.

Bynner, J. 'Youth Transitions and Apprenticeships: A Broader View of Skill', in T. Dolphin and T. Lanning (eds), *Rethinking Apprenticeships* (London: Institute for Public Policy, 2011), 17–28.

Callaghan, J. 'A Rational Debate Based on Fact', speech at Ruskin College, Oxford, 18 October 1976. Retrieved 9 June 2021 from http://www.educationengland.org.uk/documents/speeches/1976ruskin.html.

Cann, R., R. Kempson and L. Marten. *The Dynamics of Language: An Introduction*. Amsterdam: Elsevier, 2005.

Caplan, A., A. Aujla, S. Prosser and J. Jackson. *Race Discrimination in the Construction Industry: A Thematic Review*. Manchester: Equality Research and Consulting Ltd., prepared for the Equality and Human Rights Commission, 2009.

Carlyle, T. *The Works of Thomas Carlyle*, vol. 10, *Past and Present*. Cambridge: Cambridge University Press, 2010.

Carpenters' Company. *Records of the Worshipful Company of Carpenters*, vol. I, *Apprentices' Entry Books, 1654–1694*, Book 3: 1692.

———. *The Carpenters' Company: Building Crafts College and Institute of Carpenters*. London: Carpenters' Company, pamphlet, no date.

———. 'Obituaries: George Pysden'. *Carpenters' Company Broadsheet*, 38 (2008), 3.

———. 'Administrative/Biographical History', in *Worshipful Company of Carpenters, 1438–1958*. AIM25, Archives in London and the M25 Area, reference code 0074 CLC/L/CC, Retrieved 9 June 2021 from https://aim25.com/cgi-bin/vcdf/detail?coll_id=14150&inst_id=118&nv1=search&nv2.

———. *Estates, Charities and Gifts of the Carpenters' Company, 1357–2003*. AIM25, Archives in London and the M25 Area website, reference code GB 2812 G. Retrieved 9 June 2021 from https://aim25.com/cgi-bin/vcdf/detail?coll_id=7272&inst_id=91&nv1=search&nv2.

Cassels, Sir J. *Modern Apprenticeships: The Way to Work*. Report of the Modern Apprenticeship Advisory Committee, September 2001. London: Department for Education and Skills, and Learning and Skills Council.

Centre for Alternative Technology. 'Mission Statement: What We Do'. Retrieved 9 June 2021 from https://www.cat.org.uk/about-us/what-we-do.

Chaucer, G. 'General Prologue', in Jill Mann (ed.), *The Canterbury Tales* (London: Penguin, 2005), 3–34. Originally written 1387–1400.

Chew, H.M., and W. Kellaway (eds). 'Introduction', in *London Assize of Nuisance, 1301–1431: A Calendar*. London: London Record Society, vol. 10, 1973, ix–xxxiv. *Brit-*

ish History Online. Retrieved 9 June 2021 from http://www.british-history.ac.uk/london-record-soc/vol10/ix-xxxiv.

Clark, L. *Carpenters' Hall: A Short Account and Tour of the Hall of the Worshipful Company of Carpenters, London*. London: Carpenters' Company, 1997.

Clarke, L. 'The Changing Structure and Significance of Apprenticeship with Special Reference to Construction', in P. Ainley and H. Rainbird (eds), *Apprenticeship: Towards a New Paradigm of Learning* (London: Kogan Page, 1999), 25–40.

Clarke, L., and C. Wall. 'Omitted from History: Women in the Building Trades', in M. Dunkeld, J. Campbell, H. Louw, M. Tutton, B. Addis, C. Powell, and R. Thorne (eds), *Proceedings of the Second International Congress on Construction History*, vol. 1 (Exeter: Short Run Press, 2006), 35–59.

———. 'Are Women "Not up to" Working in Construction – at All Times and Everywhere?', in M. Munn (ed.), *Building the Future: Women in Construction* (London: Smith Institute, 2014), 10–19.

Clarke, L., E. Michielsens, S. Snijders, C. Wall, A. Dainty, B. Bagilhole and S. Barnard. *No More Softly-Softly: Review of Women in the Workforce*. London: ProBE Publication, 2015.

Classen, C. 'Touch and Technology', in C. Classen (ed.), *The Book of Touch* (Oxford: Berg, 2005), 401–8.

Clifford Collard, N. 'Crafting Livelihood, Negotiating Challenges and Realising Opportunities: An Ethnography of Life, Learning and Work amongst Young Ghanaian Weavers' (unpublished Ph.D. thesis, SOAS, 2017). Retrieved 9 June 2021 from https://ethos.bl.uk/OrderDetails.do?uin=uk.bl.ethos.722871.

Coleman, R. *The Art of Work: An Epitaph to Skill*. London: Pluto Press, 1988.

Collini, S. 'HiEdBiz'. *London Review of Books*, 25(21) (2003), 3–9.

———. *What Are Universities for?* London: Penguin, 2012.

———. 'Kept Alive for Thirty Days'. *London Review of Books*, 40(21) (2018), 35–38.

Colloredo-Mansfeld, R. 'An Ethnography of Neoliberalism: Understanding Competition in Artisan Economies'. *Current Anthropology*, 43(1) (2002), 113–37.

Conway, L. 'Building Crafts College'. *The Carpenters' Company Broadsheet*, 41 (2010), 3–4.

———. 'Building Crafts College'. *The Carpenters' Company Broadsheet*, 43 (2011), 3.

———. 'Women at the College'. *The Carpenters' Company Broadsheet*, 50 (2014), 5.

———. 'Building Crafts College'. *The Carpenters' Company Broadsheet*, 55 (2017), 3.

———. 'Building Crafts College'. *The Carpenters' Company Chronicle 2019* (2019), 6–9.

Cooke, E., G. Ward and K. L'Ecuyer. *The Maker's Hand: American Studio Furniture, 1940–1990*. Boston: Museum of Fine Arts, 2003.

Cooper, E. 'Mode of Production and Anthropology of Work'. *Journal of Anthropological Research*, 40(2) (1984), 257–70.

Corporation of London, *The Livery Companies of the City of London*. London: Perivan Colour Print, 2001.

Coughlan, S. 'Education, Education, Education'. *BBC News*, 14 May 2007. Retrieved 9 June 2021 from http://news.bbc.co.uk/1/hi/education/6564933.stm.

———. 'The Symbolic Target of 50% at University Reached'. *BBC News*, 26 September 2019. Retrieved 9 June 2021 from https://www.bbc.co.uk/news/education-49841620.

Coy M.W. (ed.). *Apprenticeship: From Theory to Method and Back Again*. Albany, NY: State University of New York Press, 1989.

Crace, J. 'Business Lament Lack of Bright Trainees'. *The Guardian*, 20 April 2004.

Crafts Council. *An Education Manifesto for Craft and Making*. London: Crafts Council, 2014. No pagination.

Crafts Council, Creative Scotland, Art Council of Wales and Craft Northern Ireland. *Craft in an Age of Change*, 2012. Retrieved 28 June 2021 from https://www.craftscouncil .org.uk/documents/866/Craft_in_an_age_of_change_2012.pdf.

Cranz, G. *The Chair: Rethinking Culture, Body, and Design*. London: W.W. Norton and Company Ltd., 2000.

Crawford, M. *Shop Class as Soulcraft: An Inquiry into the Value of Work*. London: Penguin, 2009.

Creasey, A. 'Training, Mentoring and Assessing in the 21st Century'. *Cutting Edge*, March 2019, 9–10.

Creative & Cultural Skills and Crafts Council. *The Craft Blueprint*. London: Creative and Cultural Industries Ltd., 2009.

Creative & Cultural Skills, TBR and Pomegranate. *Mapping Heritage Craft: Focus Group Briefing Paper*. 2013. Retrieved 9 June 2021 from https://www.ccskills.org.uk/ articles/mapping-heritage-craft-4.

Crichton-Miller, E. 'Going against the Grain'. *Wall Street Journal*, 18 March 2011, W13.

Cross, J. 'Technological Intimacy: Re-engaging with Gender and Technology in the Global Factory'. *Ethnography*, 13(2) (2012), 119–43.

Csikszentmihalyi, M. *Flow: The Psychology of Optimal Experience*. New York: Harper & Row, 1990.

Cushing, F.H. 'Manual Concepts: A Study of the Influence of Hand-Usage on Cultural Growth'. *American Anthropologist*, 5(4) (1892), 289–318.

Dale, R. 'The Thatcherite Project in Education: The Case of the City Technology Colleges'. *Critical Social Policy*, 9(27) (1989), 4–19.

Damasio, A. *Descarte's Error: Emotion, Reason and the Human Brain*. New York: G.P. Putnam's Sons, 1994.

Daniels, G.W. *The Early English Cotton Industry*. Manchester: Manchester University Press, 1920.

De Botton, A. *The Pleasures and Sorrows of Work*. London: Penguin, 2010.

Defoe, D. (1719). *Robinson Crusoe*. London: Penguin Classics, 2012.

Deissinger, T. 'Apprenticeship Systems in England and Germany: Decline and Survival', in W-D. Greinert and G. Hanf (eds), *Towards a History of Vocational Education and Training in Europe in a Comparative Perspective*, vol. I (Luxembourg: Cedofop Panorama Series, 2002), 28–45.

Deleuze, G. 'Postscript on the Societies of Control'. *October*, 59 (1992), 3–7.

Dengen, C. 'Back to the Future: Temporality, Narrative and the Ageing Self', in E. Hallam and T. Ingold (eds), *Creativity and Cultural Improvisation* (Oxford: Berg, 2007), 223–35.

Department for Education and Skills. *21st Century Skills: Realising Our Potential: Individuals, Employers, Nation*, Policy Paper. Norwich: TSO, 9 July 2003.

Dewey, J. *Democracy and Education*. London: Macmillan, 1916.

Dewey, K. 'The Rise, Fall, Rise, Fall and Rise Again of Apprenticeships'. *Paper Technology* (Autumn 2016), 47–49.

Dilley, R. 'Tukolor Weavers and the Organisation of Their Craft in Village and Town'. *Africa: Journal of the International African Institute*, 56(2) (1986), 123–47.

————. 'Reflections on Knowledge Practices and the Problem of Ignorance', in T.H.J. Marchand (ed.), *Making Knowledge* (Oxford: Blackwell, 2010), 176–92.

————. 'Problematic Reproductions: Children, Slavery and Not-Knowing in Colonial French West Africa', in T.G. Kirsch and R. Dilley (eds), *Regimes of Ignorance: Anthropological Perspectives on the Production and Reproduction of Non-knowledge* (New York: Berghahn Books, 2015), 138–58.

Dolton, P.J., G.H. Makepeace and J.G. Treble. 'The Youth Training Scheme and the School-to-Work Transition'. *Oxford Economic Papers, New Series*, 46(4) (1994), 629–57.

Dormer, P. (ed.) *The Culture of Craft*. Manchester: Manchester University Press, 1997.

Downey, G. *Learning Capoeira: Lessons in Cunning from an Afro-Brazilian Art*. Oxford: Oxford University Press, 2005.

————. 'Practice without Theory: A Neuroanthropological Perspective on Embodied Learning'. *Journal of the Royal Anthropological Institute*, special issue 'Making Knowledge', edited by T.H.J. Marchand (2010), S22–S40.

————. 'The Importance of Repetition: Ritual as an Extension of Mind', in M. Bull and J. Mitchell (eds), *Cognition, Performance and the Senses* (London: Bloomsbury, 2014), 45–62.

Downey, G., M. Dalidowicz and P. Mason. 'Apprenticeship as Method: Embodied Learning in Ethnographic Practice'. *Qualitative Research*, 15(2) (2015), 183–200.

Draganski, B., C. Gaser, V. Busch, G. Schuierer, U. Bogdahn and A. May. 'Neuroplasticity: Changes in Grey Matter Induced by training'. *Nature*, 427 (2004), 311–12.

Dunlop, O.J., and R. Denman. *English Apprenticeship and Child Labour: A History*. London: Unwin, 1912.

Durkheim, É. *The Division of Labour in Society*. London: Palgrave Macmillan, 1984 [1893].

Edwards, C., P. Brewer, T. Rosoman, J. Meyer, M. Barrington and C. Claxton Stevens. *British Furniture 1600–2000*. London: Intelligent Layman Publishers Ltd., 2005.

Edwards, D.S. 'The History and Politics of the Youth Opportunities Programme, 1978–1983' (unpublished Ph.D. thesis, UCL, 1985). Retrieved 9 June 2021 from https://discovery.ucl.ac.uk/id/eprint/10019227.

Edwards, S., D. Buckland and J. McCoy-Powlen. *Developmental and Functional Hand Grasps*. Thorofare, NJ: Slack, 2002.

Eglash, R. 'Technology as Material Culture', in C. Tilley, W. Keane, S. Küchler, M. Rowlands and P. Speyer (eds), *Handbook of Material Culture* (London: Sage, 2006), 329–40.

Elbert, T., C. Pantev, C. Wienbruch, B. Rockstroh and E. Taub. 'Increased Cortical Representation of the Fingers of the Left Hand in String Players'. *Science*, 270 (1995), 305–7.

Ellis, G. *Modern Practical Joinery*. London: Stobart Davies, 1989. Originally published 1902.

Elmes, J. 'History of Architecture in Great Britain: A Brief Sketch or Epitome of the Rise and Progress of Architecture in Great Britain'. *Civil Engineer and Architect's Journal*, 10 (1847), 166–70 and 209–10.

Emerson, R.W. 'Nature 1836', in *Nature and Selected Essays* (London: Penguin, 2003), 35–82.

Endfield, N. 'The Body as a Cognitive Artifact in Kinship Representations: Hand Gesture Diagrams by Speakers of Lao'. *Current Anthropology*, 46(1) (2005), 51–80.

Epstein, S.R. 'Transferring Technical Knowledge and Innovating in Europe, c.1200–c.1800'. Working Papers on the Nature of Evidence, No. 01/05. London: LSE Department of Economic History, 2005.

Ericson, K.A., R.T. Krampe and C. Tesch-Romer. 'The Role of Deliberate Practice in the Acquisition of Expert Performance'. *Psychological Review*, 100(3) (1993), 363–406.

Ettema, M.J. 'Technological Innovation and Design Economics in Furniture Manufacture'. *Winterthur Portfolio*, 16(2/3) (1981), 197–223.

Evans, K. 'Competence and Citizenship: Towards a Complementary Model for Times of Critical Social Change'. *British Journal of Education and Work*, 8(2) (1995), 14–27.

Evelyn, J. *Sylva, or, A Discourse of Forest Trees: With an Essay on the Life and Works of the Author by John Nisbet*. Milton Keynes: Biblio Life, 2009 [1664].

Farley, P. 'Proskill UK Closes'. *Furniture News*, 1 July 2016. Retrieved 9 June 2021 from https://www.furniturenews.net/news/articles/2016/07/2044647021-proskills-uk-closes.

Farne, A., A. Iriki and E. Ladavas. 'Shaping Multisensory Action-Space with Tools: Evidence from Patients with Cross-modal Extinctions'. *Neuropsychologia*, 43(2) (2005), 238–48.

Fergusson, R., and L. Unwin. 'Making Better Sense of Post-16 Destinations: A Case Study of an English Shire County'. *Research Papers in Education*, 11(1) (1996), 53–80.

Ferris, M. 'Making Futures: Craft as Change-Maker in Sustainably Aware Cultures', in *Making Futures*, vol. 2 (Plymouth: Plymouth College of Art, 2011) (no pagination).

Festinger, L. *A Theory of Cognitive Dissonance*. Palo Alto: Stanford University Press, 1957.

Filliettaz, L., I. de Saint-Georges and B. Duc. 'Skiing, Cheese Fondue and Swiss Watches: Analogical Discourse in Vocational Education'. *Vocations and Learning*, 3 (2010), 117–40.

Finegold, D., and D. Soskice. 'The Failure of Training in Britain: Analysis and Prescription'. *Oxford Review of Economic Policy*, 4(3), (Autumn 1988), 21–53.

Fisch, M. *An Anthropology of the Machine: Tokyo's Commuter Train Network*. Chicago: University of Chicago Press, 2018.

Fleming, P. 'Wood Practice', in J. Johnson (ed.), *Exploring Contemporary Craft: History, Theory and Critical Writing* (Toronto: Coach House Books with the Craft Studio at Harbourfront Centre, 2002), 63–67 and 119.

Fletcher, B., and B.F. Fletcher. *A History of Architecture on the Comparative Method*. London: B.T. Batsford, 1896.

Fletcher, B.F., and H.P. Fletcher, *Carpentry and Joinery: A Text-Book for Architects, Engineers, Surveyors and Craftsmen*. London: D. Fourdrinier, 1897.

Foley, N. *Apprenticeship Statistics*. House of Commons Library Briefing Paper, number 06113, 2020.

Freire, P. *Pedagogy of the Oppressed*. London: Penguin, 1970.

Freud, S. 'Beyond the Pleasure Principle', in J. Strachey (ed.), *The Standard Edition of the Complete Psychological Works of Sigmund Freud, Volume 18 (1920–1922): Beyond the Pleasure Principle, Group Psychology and Other Works* (London: Vintage, 2001), 7–64.

Frey, S. 'Tool Use, Communicative Gesture and Cerebral Asymmetries in the Modern Human Brain'. *Philosophical Transactions of the Royal Society B-Biological Sciences*, 363(1499) (2008), 1951–57.

Friedman, M. 'The Methodology of Positive Economics', in *Essays in Positive Economics*. Originally published 1953. (Chicago: University of Chicago Press, 1966), 3–43.

Friedman, V. 'Why Luxury Is Recession-Proof'. *Financial Times*, 17 October 2011. Retrieved 9 June 2021 from https://www.ft.com/content/e319c5f3-126e-3814-912c-00695d3ff3c4.

Fuller, A., and L. Unwin. 'Reconceptualising Apprenticeship: Exploring the Relationship between Work and Learning'. *Journal of Vocational Education and Training* 50(2) (1998), 153–71.

———. 'Learning as Apprentices in the Contemporary UK Workplace: Creating and Managing Expansive and Restrictive Participation'. *Journal of Education and Work*, 16(4) (2003), 408–26.

———. 'Does Apprenticeship Still Have Meaning in the UK? The Consequence of Voluntarism and Sectoral Change', in G. Hayward and S. James (eds), *Balancing the Skills Equation: Key Issues and Challenges for Policy and Practice* (Bristol: Policy Press, 2004), 101–15.

———. 'The Content of Apprenticeship', in T. Dolphin and T. Lanning (eds), *Rethinking Apprenticeships* (London: Institute for Public Policy, 2011), 29–39.

Gallie, W.B. 'Pleasure, Part II', in G. Ryle and W.B. Gallie, 'Symposium: Pleasure'. *Proceedings of the Aristotelian Society*, Supplementary Volumes, vol. 28, *Belief and Will* (1958), 147–64.

Garrett, H. *The Handplane Book*. Newtown, CT: Taunton Press, 1997.

Gibson, J. *The Ecological Approach to Visual Perception*. Boston: Houghton Mifflin, 1979.

Gillard, D. 'Thatcher and the New Right', in *Education in England: A History*. Published online 2018. Retrieved 9 June 2021 from http://www.educationengland.org.uk/history/chapter15.html.

Gladwell, M. *Outliers: The Story of Success*. New York: Little, Brown and Company, 2008.

Gleeson, D., D. Glover, G. Gough, M. Johnson and D. Pye. 'Reflections on Youth Training: Toward a New Model of Training Experience?' *British Educational Research Journal*, 22(5) (1996), 597–613.

Glynn, S.R. 'The City of London and Higher Education', in R. Floud and S. Glynn (eds), *London Higher: The Establishment of Higher Education in London* (London: Athlone Press, 1998), 122–50.

Goody, E. 'Learning, Apprenticeship and the Division of Labour', in M.W. Coy (ed.), *Apprenticeship: From Theory to Method and Back Again* (Albany, NY: SUNY Press, 1989), 233–56.

Gospel, H.F. 'Whatever Happened to Apprenticeship Training? A British, American, Australian Comparison'. *A Centre for Economic Performance Discussion Paper, LSE*, 1994. Retrieved 9 June 2021 from http://eprints.lse.ac.uk/20909.

———. 'The Revival of Apprenticeship Training in Britain?' *British Journal of Industrial Relations: An International Journal of Employment Relations*, 36(3) (1998), 435–57.

Gowlland, G. *Reinventing Craft in China: The Contemporary Politics of Yixing Zisha Ceramics*. Canon Pyon: Sean Kingston, 2017.

Grafton, S.T., L. Fadriga, M.A. Arbib and G. Risolatti. 'Premotor Cortex Activation during Observation and Naming of Familiar Tools'. *NeuroImage*, 6 (1997), 231–36.

Grasseni, C. 'Communities of Practice and Forms of Life: Towards a Rehabilitation of Vision', in M. Harris (ed.), *Ways of Knowing: New Approaches in the Anthropology of Experience and Learning* (Oxford: Berghahn Books, 2007), 203–21.

———. *Developing Skill, Developing Vision: Practices of Locality at the Foot of the Alps*. Oxford: Berghahn Books, 2009.

Gray, D., and M. Morgan. 'Modern Apprenticeships: Filling the Skills Gap?' *Journal of Vocational Education & Training*, 50(1) (1998), 123–34.

Green, H. *Wood: Craft, Culture, History*. London: Penguin, 2007.

Greenfield, P. 'Language, Tools and Brain: The Ontogeny and Phylogeny of Hierarchically Organized Sequential Behavior'. *Behavioral and Brain Sciences*, 14(4) (1991), 531–51.

Greenhalgh, P. 'Introduction: Craft in a Changing World', in P. Greenalgh (ed.), *The Persistence of Craft: The Applied Arts Today* (London: A & C Black, 2002), 1–17.

———. (ed.). *The Persistence of Craft: The Applied Arts Today*. London: A & C Black, 2002.

Greenlees, R. 'Making a Manifesto'. *Crafts Council Newsletter*, September 2014.

Gregory, A., and S. Milner. 'Editorial: Work-Life Balance: A Matter of Choice?' *Gender, Work and Organization*, 16(1) (2009), 1–13.

Griffin, E. *Liberty's Dawn: A People's History of the Industrial Revolution*. New Haven: Yale University Press, 2014.

Grosz, E. *Volatile Bodies: Towards a Corporeal Feminism*. Bloomington: Indiana University Press, 1994.

Hallam, E., and T. Ingold (eds). *Making and Growing: Anthropological Studies of Organisms and Artefacts*. Farnham: Ashgate, 2014.

Hamblin, J. 'Buy Experiences, Not Things'. *The Atlantic*, 7 October 2014. Retrieved 9 June 2021 from https://www.theatlantic.com/business/archive/2014/10/buy-experiences/381132.

Hanawalt, B. *Growing up in Medieval London: The Experience of Childhood in History*. New York: Oxford University Press, 1995.

Harris, D. 'The Head of the Blue Chip II', in A. Herle, M. Elliot and R. Empson (eds), *Assembling Bodies: Art, Science and Imagination* (Cambridge: Museum of Archaeology and Anthropology, University of Cambridge, 2009), 84–86.

Harris, M. *Modern Apprenticeships: An Assessment of the Government's Flagship Training Programme*. Institute of Directors Policy Paper, August 2003, London.

Harrod, T. *The Crafts in Britain in the 20th Century*. New Haven: Yale University Press, 1999.

Hart, L.K. 'Work, Labor, and Artisans in the Modern World'. *Anthropological Quarterly*, 77(3) (2004), 595–609.

Harvey, D. *A Brief History of Neoliberalism*. Oxford: University of Oxford Press, 2007.

Haviland, J. 'Pointing, Gesture Spaces, and Mental Maps', in D. McNeill (ed.), *Language and Gesture* (Cambridge: Cambridge University Press, 2000), 13–46.

Hayes, J. '"The Craft So Long to Lerne": Skills and Their Place in Modern Britain'. Speech delivered on 26 October 2010 for Department for Business, Innovation & Skills. Retrieved 9 June 2021 from https://www.gov.uk/government/speeches/the-craft-so-long-to-lerne-skills-and-their-place-in-modern-britain.

Heidegger, M. 'What Calls for Thinking?', in D. Farrell Krell (ed.), *Basic Writings* (New York: HarperCollins, 1977), 341–68.

Henley, J. 'Heritage Crafts at Risk'. *The Guardian*, 22 March 2010. Retrieved 9 June 2021 from https://www.theguardian.com/uk/2010/mar/22/heritage-crafts-at-risk.

Herbert, W. *The History of the Twelve Great Livery Companies of London*, 2 vols. Self-published by the author in 1836–37. Republished by David & Charles Reprints, Newton Abbot, 1968.

Herle, A., M. Elliot and R. Empson (eds). *Assembling Bodies: Art, Science and Imagination*. Cambridge: Museum of Archaeology and Anthropology, University of Cambridge, 2009.

Hertz, R. (translated by R. Needham and C. Needham). 'The Pre-eminence of the Right Hand: A Study of Religious Polarity'. *HAU: Journal of Ethnographic Theory*, 3(2) (2013), 335–57.

Herzfeld, M. 'It Takes One to Know One: Collective Resentment and Mutual Recognition among Greeks in Local and Global Contexts', in R. Fardon (ed.), *Counterworks: Managing the Diversity of Knowledge* (London: Routledge, 1995), 127–45.

———. *The Body Impolitic: Artisans and Artifice in the Global Hierarchy of Value*. Chicago: University of Chicago Press, 2004.

———. 'Deskilling, "Dumbing Down" and the Auditing of Knowledge in the Practical Mastery of Artisans and Academics: An Ethnographer's Response to a Global Problem', in M. Harris (ed.), *Ways of Knowing: New Approaches in the Anthropology of Experience and Learning* (Oxford: Berghahn Books, 2007), 91–110.

Hickman, M. 'Britain Leads EU Imports of Wood Logged Illegally'. *The Independent*, 22 November 2005. Retrieved 9 June 2021 from https://www.independent.co.uk/environment/britain-leads-eu-imports-of-wood-logged-illegally-516380.html.

Hobart, M. 'Introduction: The Growth of Ignorance?', in M. Hobart (ed.), *An Anthropological Critique of Development: The Growth of Ignorance* (London: Routledge, 1993), 1–30.

Hohn, D. 'A Romance of Rust: Nostalgia, Progress, and the Meaning of Tools'. *Harper's Magazine*, January 2015, 45–63.

Holmes, N., and C. Spence. 'The Body Schema and the Multisensory Representation(s) of Peripersonal Space'. *Cognitive Processing*, 5(2) (2004), 94–105.

Holmes, N., D. Sanabria, G. Calvert and C. Spence. 'Tool-Use: Capturing Multisensory Spatial Attention or Extending Multisensory Peripersonal Space?' *Cortex*, 43(3) (2007), 469–89.

Hoppus, E. *Mr. Hoppus's Measurer Greatly Enlarged & Improved*. London, 1790.

Howes, D. 'Charting the Sensorial Revolution'. *The Senses and Society*, 9(1) (2006), 113–128.

Hume, D. *A Treatise of Human Nature*. London: Penguin, 1985.

Hung, S., and J. Magliaro (eds). *By Hand: The Use of Craft in Contemporary Art*. New York: Princeton Architectural Press, 2007.

Hutchins, E., and L. Palen. 'Constructing Meaning from Space, Gesture, and Speech', in L. Resnick, R. Säljö, C. Pontecorvo and B. Burge (eds), *Discourse, Tools, and Reasoning: Essays on Situated Cognition* (Berlin: Springer, 1993), 23–40.

Huxley, T.H. 'Professor Huxley's Inaugural Address on Education at the Opening of the South London Working Men's College'. *Quarterly Journal of Education*, 1(4) (1868), 145–55.

IKEA, 'Wood: A Material with Many Qualities'. Retrieved 9 June 2021 from https://www.ikea.com/gb/en/this-is-ikea/about-us/wood-a-material-with-many-qualities-pubd4deffde.

The Independent. 'Youth Training Scheme a Failure and a Disgrace, Labour Says'. 13 February 1995. Retrieved 9 June 2021 from https://www.independent.co.uk/news/youth-training-scheme-a-failure-and-a-disgrace-labour-says-1572820.html.

Ingold, T. 'Walking the Plank: Meditations on a Process of Skill', in J.R. Dakers (ed.), *Defining Technological Literacy: Towards an Epistemological Framework* (New York: Palgrave Macmillan, 2006), 65–80.

Ingold, T., and E. Hallam. 'Making and Growing: An Introduction', in E. Hallam and T. Ingold (eds), *Making and Growing: Anthropological Studies of Organisms and Artefacts* (Farnham: Ashgate, 2014), 1–24.

Institute of Carpenters, *Annual Report*, for the period ending 31 December 2008.

Jackson, A., and D. Day. *Collin's Complete Woodworker's Manual*. London: Collins, 2005.

Jacob, S., C. Danielmeier and S. Frey. 'Human Anterior Intraparietal and Ventral Premotor Cortices Support Representations of Grasping with the Hand or a Novel Tool'. *Journal of Cognitive Neuroscience*, 22(11) (2010), 2594–608.

Jakob, D. 'Crafting Your Way out of the Recession? New Craft Entrepreneurs and the Global Economic Downturn'. *Cambridge Journal of Regions, Economy and Society*, 6 (2013) 127–40.

Jakob, D., and N.J. Thomas. 'Firing up Craft Capital: The Renaissance of Craft and Craft Policy in the United Kingdom'. *International Journal of Cultural Policy*, 23(4) (2017), 495–511.

Johnson, J. (ed.) *Exploring Contemporary Craft: History, Theory and Critical Writing*. Toronto: Coach House Books with the Craft Studio at Harbourfront Centre, 2002.

Johnson, O., and D. More. *Tree Guide: The Most Complete Field Guide to the Trees of Britain and Europe*. London: HarperCollins, 2004.

Johnston, M. 'Plasticity in the Developing Brain: Implications for Rehabilitation'. *Developmental Disabilities Research Reviews*, 15 (2009), 94–101.

Joseph, K. 'Keith Joseph – 1985 Speech Higher Education'. 21 May 1985. Retrieved 9 June 2021 from http://www.ukpol.co.uk/keith-joseph-1985-speech-on-higher-education.

Jupp, E.B. *An Historical Account of the Worshipful Company of Carpenters of the City of London*. London: William Pickering, 1848.

Jupp, E.B., and W.W. Pocock. *An Historical Account of the Worshipful Company of Carpenters of the City of London: Compiled Chiefly from Records in Their Possession*, 2nd edn. London: Pickering & Chatto, 1887.

Jurgens, E. *Learning Lessons to Promote Certification and Combat Illegal Logging in Indonesia: September 2003 to June 2006*. Jakarta: Center for International Forestry Research, 2006.

Kempson, R., W. Meyer-Viol and D. Gabbay. *Dynamic Syntax: The Flow of Language Understanding*. Oxford: Blackwell, 2001.

Kennedy Melling, J. *Discovering London's Guilds and Liveries*. Princes Risborough: Shires Publications Ltd., 2003.

Kirsch, D. 'Problem Solving and Situated Cognition', in P. Robbins and M. Ayded (eds), *The Cambridge Handbook of Situated Cognition* (Cambridge: Cambridge University Press, 2009), 264–306.

Kirsch, T.G., and R. Dilley. 'Regimes of Ignorance: An introduction', in T.G. Kirsch and R. Dilley (eds), *Regimes of Ignorance: Anthropological Perspectives on the Production and Reproduction of Non-knowledge* (New York: Berghahn Books, 2015), 1–29.

———. *Regimes of Ignorance: Anthropological Perspectives on the Production and Reproduction of Non-knowledge*. New York: Berghahn Books, 2015.

Knoop, D., and G.P. Jones. 'Masons and Apprentices in Mediæval England'. *Economic History Review*, 3(3) (1932), 346–66.

———. 'The Impressment of Masons in the Middle Ages'. *Economic History Review*, 8(1) (1937), 57–67.

Lacey, H., and V. Yiasoumi. 'Away in a Manger in Frosty'. *The Independent*, 20 December 1998.

Laërtius, Diogenes. 'Epicurus', in D. Laërtius, *Lives of the Eminent Philosophers*, translated by P. Mensch, edited by J. Miller (New York: Oxford University Press, 2018), 491–544.

Lancaster, H. 'Message from the Master'. *The Carpenters' Company Broadsheet*, 46 (2012), 1–2.

Lancy, D.F. '"First You Must Master Pain": The Nature and Purpose of Apprenticeship'. *Society for the Anthropology of Work Review*, 33(2) (2012), 113–26.

Landi, D., and P.M. Rossini. 'Cerebral Restorative Plasticity from Normal Ageing to Brain Disease: A "Never Ending Story"'. *Restorative Neurology and Neuroscience*, 28 (2010), 349–66.

Lane, J. *Apprenticeship in England, 1600–1914*. London: Routledge, 1996.

Lanning, T. 'Why Rethink Apprenticeship?', in T. Dolphin and T. Lanning (eds), *Rethinking Apprenticeships* (London: Institute for Public Policy Research, 2011), 6–16.

Laughlin, C. 'The Evolution of Cyborg Consciousness'. *Anthropology of Consciousness*, 8(4) (1997), 144–59.

Lave, J. *Apprenticeship in Critical Ethnographic Practice*. Chicago: University of Chicago Press, 2011.

Lave, J., and E. Wenger. *Situated Learning: Legitimate Peripheral Participation*. Cambridge: Cambridge University Press, 1991.

Leach, D.S. 'Carpenters in Medieval London c. 1240–c. 1540' (unpublished Ph.D. thesis, Royal Holloway, University of London, March 2017).

Leakey, M.D. *Olduvai Gorge: Excavations in Beds I and II, 1960–1963*. Cambridge: Cambridge University Press, 1971.

Leitch, Lord S. *The Leitch Review of Skills: Prosperity for All in the Global Economy of Skills*. London: The Stationery Office, 2006.

Leunig, T., C. Minns and P. Wallis. 'Networks in the Premodern Economy: The Market for London Apprenticeships, 1600–1749'. *Journal of Economic History*, 17(2) (2011), 413–43.

Levene, A. 'Parish Apprenticeship and the Old Poor Law in London'. *Economic History Review*, 63(4) (2010), 915–41.

Levinson, S. 'Relativity in Spatial Conception and Description', in J. Gumperz and S. Levinson (eds), *Rethinking Linguistic Relativity* (Cambridge: Cambridge University Press, 1996), 177–202.

Levitas, R. *The Concept of Utopia*. Hemel Hempstead: Syracuse University Press, 1990.

Lewcock, R. 'Early and Medieval Sanaa: The Evidence on the Ground', in T.H.J. Marchand (ed.), *Architectural Heritage of Yemen* (London and Chicago: Gingko Press and University of Chicago Press, 2017), 30–39.

Lightfoot, L. 'Pencil, Ruler, Fretsaw: The New National Furniture School Hopes to Provide Skilled Graduates for Britain's Craft Industry', *The Independent*, 9 December 2010, 49.

Lindenbaum, S. 'City and Oligarchy: The London Midsummer Watch', in B. Hanawalt and K. Reyerson (eds), *City and Spectacle in Medieval Europe* (Minneapolis: University of Minnesota Press, 1994), 171–88.

London Department of Planning and City Development, *East Marylebone Conservation Area Audit*. London: City Hall, 2006.

Luckman, S. *Craft and the Creative Economy*. New York: Palgrave Macmillan, 2015.

Macdonald, B.J. 'Morris after Marcuse: Art, Beauty, and the Aestheticist Tradition in Ecosocialism'. *Journal of William Morris Studies*, 19(3) (2011), 39–49.

Maguire, E.A., D.G. Gadian, I.S. Johnsrude, C.D. Good, J. Asburner, R.S. Frackowiak and C.D. Frith. 'Navigation-Related Structural Change in the Hippocampi of Taxi Drivers'. *Proceedings of the National Academy of Sciences of the United States of America*, 97 (2000), 4398–403.

Maguire, M. 'Modern Apprenticeships: Just in Time, or Far Too Late?', in P. Ainley and H. Rainbird (eds), *Apprenticeship: Towards a New Paradigm of Learning* (London: Kogan Page, 1999), 163–75.

Makovicky, N. 'Something to Talk about: Notation and Knowledge Making among Central Slovak Lace-Makers'. *Journal of the Royal Anthropological Institute*, special issue 'Making Knowledge', edited by T.H.J. Marchand (2010), S80–S99.

Marchand, T.H.J. 'Gidan Hausa: Report to the Canadian International Development Agency' (unpublished report, 1993).

———. 'Walling Old Sanaa: Re-evaluating the Resurrection of the City Walls', in *Terra 2000: 8th International Conference on the Study and Conservation of Earthen Architecture* (London: James & James Science Publishers Ltd, 2000), 46–51.

———. *Minaret Building and Apprenticeship in Yemen*. London: (Curzon) Routledge, 2001.

———. 'Process over Product: Case Studies of Traditional Building Practices in Djenné, Mali, and San'a', Yemen', in J.M. Teutonico and F. Matero (eds), *Managing Change: Sustainable Approaches to the Conservation of the Built Environment* (Los Angeles: Getty Conservation Institute, 2003), 137–59.

———. 'Crafting Knowledge: The Role of Parsing & Production in the Communication of Skill-Based Knowledge among Masons', in M. Harris (ed.), *Ways of Knowing: New Approaches in the Anthropology of Experience and Learning* (Oxford: Berghahn Books, 2007), 173–93.

———. 'Vocational Migrants and a Tradition of Longing'. *Traditional Dwellings and Settlements Review: Journal of the International Association for the Study of Traditional Environments*, 19(1) (2007), 23–40.

———. 'Muscles, Morals and Mind: Craft Apprenticeship and the Formation of Person'. *British Journal of Educational Studies*, 56(3) (2008), 245–71.

———. *The Masons of Djenné*. Bloomington: Indiana University Press, 2009.

———. 'Negotiating License and Limits: Expertise and Innovation in Djenné's Building Trade'. *Africa*, 79(1) (2009), 71–91.

———. 'Embodied Cognition and Communication: Studies with British Fine Woodworkers'. *Journal of the Royal Anthropological Institute*, special issue on 'Making Knowledge', edited by T.H.J. Marchand (2010), S100–S120.

———. 'Embodied Cognition, Communication and the Making of Place & Identity: Reflections on Fieldwork with Masons', in N. Rapport (ed.), *Human Nature as Capacity* (Oxford: Berghahn Books, 2010), 182–206.

———. 'Making Knowledge: Explorations of the Indissoluble Relation between Minds, Bodies, and Environment'. *Journal of the Royal Anthropological Institute*, special issue 'Making Knowledge', edited by T.H.J. Marchand (2010), S1–S21.

———. 'Negotiating Tradition in Practice: Mud Masons and Meaning-Making in Contemporary Djenné', in J.M. Teutonico (ed.), *Terra 2008 Proceedings* (Los Angeles: Getty Conservation Institute and Trust Publications, 2011), 23–28.

———. 'Knowledge in Hand: Explorations of Brain, Hand and Tool', in R. Fardon, O. Harris, T. Marchand, M. Nuttall, C. Shore, V. Strang and C. Wilson (eds), *Handbook of Social Anthropology* (London: Sage, 2012), 260–69.

————. 'The Djenné Mosque: World Heritage and Social Renewal in a West Africa town', in O. Verkaaik (ed.), *Religious Architecture: Anthropological Perspectives* (Amsterdam: Amsterdam University Press, 2013), 117–48.

————. 'For the Love of Masonry: Djenné Craftsmen in Turbulent Times'. *Journal of African Cultural Studies*, 26(2) (2014), 155–72.

————. 'Skill and Ageing: Perspectives from Three Generations of English Wood Workers', in E. Hallam and T. Ingold (eds), *Making and Growing: Anthropological Studies of Organisms and Artefacts* (Farnham: Ashgate, 2014), 183–202.

————. 'A Diary of Filmmaking with Djenné Masons: From "Studies of" toward "Studies with"'. *Visual Anthropology*, 28(4) (2015), 308–23.

————. (director). *The Intelligent Hand* (documentary film). 2015. Retrieved 9 June 2021 from https://www.youtube.com/watch?v=73VwgChjTyo.

————. 'Managing Pleasurable Pursuits: Utopic Horizons and the Arts of Ignoring and "Not Knowing" among Fine Woodworkers', in R. Dilley and T. Kirsch (eds), *Regimes of Ignorance: Anthropological Perspectives on the Production and Reproduction of Non-knowledge* (Oxford: Berghahn Books, 2015), 70–90.

————. (director) *The Art of Andrew Omoding* (documentary film). 2016. Retrieved 9 June 2021 from https://www.youtube.com/watch?v=zi13kf5rLpA.

————. 'Explorations in Creativity with Andrew Omoding: Artist, Maker and Raconteur', in *Radical Craft: Alternative Ways of Making* (Birmingham: Craftspace, 2016), 48–59.

————. 'Introduction: Craftwork as Problem Solving', in T.H.J. Marchand (ed.), *Craftwork as Problem Solving: Ethnographic Studies of Design and Making* (Farnham: Ashgate, 2016), 1–29.

————. 'The Minarets of Sanaa', in T.H.J. Marchand (ed.), *Architectural Heritage of Yemen: Buildings That Fill My Eye* (London and Chicago: Gingko Press and University of Chicago Press, 2017), 118–27.

————. 'Ducks and Daughters: Story-Making with Andrew Omoding'. *Art + Reading: A journal of Reading and Making*, 1(1) (2018), 45–50.

————. 'Toward an Anthropology of Mathematizing'. *Interdisciplinary Science Reviews*, special issue 'From Science to Art and Back Again: The Anthropology of Tim Ingold', 43(3–4) (2018), 295–316.

————. 'Dwelling in Craftwork: The Art of Andrew Omoding'. *Journal for European Ethnology and Cultural Analysis*, special issue 1, 'Ways of Dwelling' (2019), 46–72.

————. 'Review Essay: "Building a World Heritage City – Sanaa, Yemen" by Michele Lamprakos'. *British Foundation for the Study of Arabia (BFSA) Bulletin*, 24 (2019), 50–53.

Marsh, B. 'Introduction', in B. Marsh (ed.), *Records of the Worshipful Company of Carpenters Volume I: Apprentices' Entry Books 1654–1694* (Oxford: Oxford University Press, 1913), v–xiii.

————. (ed.). *Records of the Worshipful Company of Carpenters*, 7 vols. Oxford and London: University of Oxford Press, 1913–68.

Martin, A., C. Wiggs, L. Ungerleider and J. Haxby. 'The Neural Correlates of Category-Specific Knowledge'. *Nature*, 379(6566) (1996), 649–52.

Martin, E. 'The End of the Body?' *American Ethnologist*, 19(1) (1992), 121–40.

Martin, T. 'Femi, Brake Mechanic: Kinesthetic Learning and Mike Rose's "Remedial" Education'. *Mind, Culture, and Activity*, 19(4) (2012), 368–75.

Marx, K. *Capital: A Critique of Political Economy*, vol. 1. London: Penguin, 1990.

Marzke, M.W. 'Precision Grips, Hand Morphology, and Tools'. *American Journal of Physical Anthropology*, 102(1) (1997), 91–110.

Marzke, M.W., and R.F. Marzke. 'Evolution of the Human Hand: Approaches to Acquiring, Analysing and Interpreting the Anatomical Evidence'. *Journal of Anatomy*, 197 (2000), 121–140.

Matthews, M. 'Message from the Master'. *The Carpenters' Company Broadsheet*, 38 (2008), 1.

May, M. 'Message from the Master'. *The Carpenters' Company Broadsheet*, 33 (2006), 2.

Maynard, A., P. Greenfield and C. Childs. 'Culture, History, Biology, and Body: Native and Non-native Acquisition of Technological Skill'. *Ethos*, 27(3) (1999), 379–402.

Maynard, A., K. Subrahmanyam and P. Greenfield. 'Technology and the Development of Intelligence: From the Loom to the Computer', in R. Sternberg and D. Preiss (eds), *Intelligence and Technology: The Impact of Tools on the Nature and Development of Human Abilities* (London: Lawrence Erlbaum Associates, 2005), 29–54.

McCormack, S. 'Rewards for Early Starters'. *The Independent*, 11 March 2004.

McCutchan, J.W. 'A Solémpne and a Greet Fraternitee'. *Publications of the Modern Language Association of America*, 74(4) (1959), 313–17.

McGinn, C. *Prehension: The Hand and the Emergence of Humanity*. Cambridge, MA: MIT Press, 2015.

McIlwee, I. 'The Emerging Skills Crisis in Joinery'. *Cutting Edge* (March 2016), 8.

Mead, A. 'Report by the Charities Administrator'. *The Carpenters' Company Broadsheet*, 40 (2009), 11–12.

Mead, M. (ed.). *Cultural Patterns and Technical Change*. Paris: UNESCO, 1953.

Mercer, H.C. *Ancient Carpenters' Tools*. Mineola, NY: Dover Publications, 2003 [1929].

Metcalf, B. 'Contemporary Craft: A Brief Overview', in J. Johnson (ed.), *Exploring Contemporary Craft: History, Theory and Critical Writing* (Toronto: Coach House Books with the Craft Studio at Harbourfront Centre, 2002), 13–23.

Metcalf, S. 'Neoliberalism: The Idea That Swallowed the World'. *The Guardian*, 18 August 2017. Retrieved 9 June 2021 from https://www.theguardian.com/news/2017/aug/18/neoliberalism-the-idea-that-changed-the-world.

Middleton, N. 'The Education Act of 1870 as the Start of the Modern Concept of the Child'. *British Journal of Educational Studies*, 18(2) (1970), 166–79.

Miller, J. *The Foundations of Better Woodworking: How to Use Your Body, Tools and Materials to Do Your Best Work*. Blue Ash, OH: Popular Woodworking Books, 2012.

Miller, J. *Furniture: World Styles from Classical to Contemporary*. London: DK Publishing, 2005.

Millroy, W.L. 'An Ethnographic Study of the Mathematical Ideas of a Group of Carpenters'. *Journal for Research in Mathematics Education*, 5 (monograph) (1992), 1–210.

Mines, M. 'Models of Caste and the Left-Hand Division in South India'. *American Ethnologist*, 9(3) (1982), 467–84.

Mirza-Davies, J. 'Apprenticeships Policy, England Prior to 2010', Briefing Paper 07266, 2015. London: House of Commons Library.

More, T. *Utopia*. Translated and introduction by P. Turner. London: Penguin, 2003.

Morgan, B. 'NOwnership, No Problem: An Updated Look at Why Millennials Value Experiences over Owning Things'. *Forbes*, 2 January 2019. Retrieved 9 June 2021 from https://www.forbes.com/sites/blakemorgan/2019/01/02/nownership-no-problem-an-updated-look-at-why-millennials-value-experiences-over-owning-things.

Morris Hargreaves McIntyre. *Making it to Market: Developing the Market for Contemporary Craft*, A strategic report commissioned by Arts Council England, 2006.

———. *Consuming Craft: The Contemporary Craft Market in a Changing Economy*. A report commissioned by the Crafts Council. Manchester: Morris Hargreaves McIntyre, 2010.

———. *The Market for Craft*. A report commissioned by the Crafts Council and partners, May 2020. Retrieved 9 June 2021 from https://www.craftscouncil.org.uk/stories/market-craft-report-launched.

Morris, W. 'Thought on Education under Capitalism'. *Commonweal*, 30 June 1888.

———. 'News from Nowhere', in W. Morris, *News from Nowhere and Other Writings*, edited and with an introduction by C. Wilmer (London: Penguin, 2004), 41–226.

———. *News from Nowhere and Other Writings*, edited and with an introduction by C. Wilmer. London: Penguin, 2004.

———. 'Useful Work versus Useless Toil', in W. Morris, *News from Nowhere and Other Writings*, edited and with an introduction by C. Wilmer (London: Penguin, 2004), 285–306.

———. *The Relations of Art to Labour*, edited by A. Bacon and L.C. Young. London: William Morris Society, 2004.

———. 'The Aims of Art', in W. Morris, *The Collected Works of William Morris*, with introductions by his daughter May Morris, vol. 23 (Cambridge: Cambridge University Press, 2012), 81–97.

———. 'Art and Its Producers', in W. Morris, *The Collected Works of William Morris*, with introductions by his daughter May Morris, vol. 22 (Cambridge: Cambridge University Press, 2012), 342–55.

———. 'How We Live and How We Might Live', in *The Collected Works of William Morris*, with introductions by his daughter May Morris, vol. 23 (Cambridge: Cambridge University Press, 2012), 3–26.

———. 'The Revival of Handicraft: An Article in the *Fortnightly Review*, November 1888', in W. Morris, *The Collected Works of William Morris*, with introductions by his daughter May Morris, vol. 22 (Cambridge: Cambridge University Press, 2012), 331–41.

———. 'The Arts and Crafts of Today'. Retrieved 9 June 2021 from https://www.marxists.org/archive/morris/works/1889/today.htm.

Morris, W., with P. Webb and other founder members of SPAB. 'Manifesto for the Society for the Protection of Ancient Buildings (SPAB)', 1877. Retrieved 9 June 2021 from https://www.spab.org.uk/about-us/spab-manifesto.

Morton, A.L. *The English Utopia*. London: Lawrence & Wishart, 1952.

Moss, J. 'Pleasure and Illusion in Plato'. *Philosophy and Phenomenological Research*, 72(3) (2006), 503–35.

Murphy, M. 'Bureaucracy and Its Limits: Accountability and Rationality in Higher Education'. *British Journal of Sociology of Education*, 30(6) (2009), 683–95.

National Heritage Training Group England. *Traditional Building Crafts Skills: Assessing the Need, Meeting the Challenge*. Research report, 2005. Retrieved 9 June 2021 from https://historicengland.org.uk/content/docs/research/traditional-building-craft-skills-skills-needs-analysis-of-the-building-heritage-sector-in-england-2005.

NCVQ Working Party. 'The National Council for Vocational Qualifications'. *British Journal of Occupational Therapy*, 52(4) (1989), 145–47.

Neal, M. 'First Carpenters' Award Presented at City & Guilds Lion Awards Ceremony'. *The Carpenters' Broadsheet*, 38 (2008), 9.

Neate, R. 'Recession Bypasses Market for Luxury Goods'. *The Guardian*, 15 February 2013. Retrieved 9 June 2021 from https://www.theguardian.com/business/2013/feb/15/recession-bypasses-luxury-goods-market.

Needham, R. 'The Left Hand of the Mugwe: An Analytical Note on the Structure of Meru Symbolism'. *Africa: Journal of the International African Institute*, 30(1) (1960), 20–33.

———. 'Right and Left in Nyoro Symbolic Classification'. *Africa: Journal of the International African Institute*, 37(4) (1967), 425–52.

Nelson, D. 'Phantom Limbs and Invisible Hands: Bodies, Prosthetics, and Late Capitalist Identifications'. *Cultural Anthropology*, 16(3) (2001), 303–13.

New Oxford Dictionary, 2001 edn, edited by J. Pearsall. Oxford: Oxford University Press.

Nicholson, P. *Practical Carpentry, Joinery and Cabinet-making; being a new and complete system of lines for the use of workmen*, revised by T. Treadgold. London: Thomas Kelly, 1847 [1826].

Noorthouck, J. 'Appendix: Charters (Henry VII to Elizabeth)', in *A New History of London Including Westminster and Southwark*. London: R. Baldwin, 1773, 799–811. *British History Online*. Retrieved 9 June 2021 from http://www.british-history.ac.uk/no-series/new-history-london/pp799-811.

Norbury, B. *Marketing and Promotion for Crafts*. Ammanford: Stobart Davies, 1995.

———. *Bespoke: Source Book of Furniture Designer Makers*. Ammanford: Stobart Davies, 2007.

Northrop, B.G. *Education Abroad and Other Papers*. New Haven: Tuttle, Morehouse and Taylor, 1874.

Novembre, G., and P.E. Keller. 'A Grammar of Action Generates Predictions in Skilled Musicians'. *Consciousness and Cognition*, 20(4) (2011), 1232–43.

Oakley, K.P. *Man the Tool-Maker*. London: British Museum, 1949.

O'Connor, E. 'Embodied Knowledge: The Experience of Meaning and the Struggle towards Proficiency in Glassblowing'. *Ethnography*, 6(2) (2005), 183–204.

Orwin, M. 'Dynamic Syntax as a Basis for Modelling Meaning in Music?' in M. Orwin, C. Howes and R. Kempson (eds), *Language, Music and Interaction*. London: College Publications, 2013, 51–65.

Osborne, G. 'Budget 2011 Speech, Chancellor George Osborne'. *The Telegraph*, 23 March 2011. Retrieved 9 June 2021 from https://www.telegraph.co.uk/finance/budget/8401022/Budget-2011-Chancellor-George-Osbornes-speech-in-full.html.

Oulton, N., and H. Steedman. 'The British System of Youth Training: A Comparison with Germany', in L.M. Lynch (ed.), *Training and the Private Sector* (Chicago: University of Chicago Press, 1994), 61–76.

Page, W. (ed.). 'Houses of Military Orders: St Thomas of Acon', in *A History of the County of London: Volume 1, London within the Bars, Westminster and Southwark*. Originally published by Victoria County History, London, 1909, 491–95. *British History Online*. Retrieved 9 June 2021 from http://www.british-history.ac.uk/vch/london/vol1/pp491-495.

Pallasmaa, J. *The Thinking Hand: Existential and Embodied Wisdom in Architecture*. Chichester: John Wiley & Sons, 2009.

Paradise, R., and B. Rogoff. 'Side by Side: Learning by Observing and Pitching in'. *Ethos*, 37(1) (2009), 102–38.

Paterson, M. 'Digital Touch', in C. Classen (ed.), *The Book of Touch* (Oxford: Berg, 2005), 431–38.

Peeters, R., L. Simone, K. Nelissen, M. Fabbri-Destro, W. Vanduffel, G. Rizzolatti and G.A. Orban. 'The Representation of Tool Use in Humans and Monkeys: Common and Uniquely Human Features'. *Journal of Neuroscience*, 29(37) (2009), 11523–39.

Plato. *Philebus*, translated with an introduction by R.A.H. Waterfield. London: Penguin, 1982.

———. *The Republic*, translated with an introduction by D. Lee. London: Penguin, 1987.

Portisch, A. 'The Craft of Skilful Learning: Kazakh Women's Everyday Craft Practices in Western Mongolia'. *Journal of the Royal Anthropological Institute*, special issue 'Making Knowledge', edited by T.H.J. Marchand (2010), S62–S79.

Preiss, D., and R. Sternberg. 'Technologies for Working Intelligence', in R. Sternberg and D. Preiss (eds), *Intelligence and Technology: The Impact of Tools on the Nature and Development of Human Abilities* (London: Lawrence Erlbaum Associates, 2005), 183–208.

Prentice, R. 'Knowledge, Skill, and the Inculcation of the Anthropologist: Reflections on Learning to Sew in the Field'. *Anthropology of Work Review*, 29(3) (2008), 54–61.

———. '"No One Ever Showed Me Nothing": Skill and Self-Making among Trinidadian Garment Workers'. *Anthropology and Education Quarterly*, 43(4) (2012), 400–14.

Preston, A. 'The War against Humanities at Britain's Universities'. *The Guardian*, 29 March 2015. Retrieved 9 June 2021 from https://www.theguardian.com/education/2015/mar/29/war-against-humanities-at-britains-universities.

Purver, M., and R. Kempson. 'Incrementality, Alignment and Shared Utterance', in *Proceedings of the 8th Workshop on the Semantics and Pragmatics of Dialogue* (Catalog), 2004, 85–92.

Pye, D. *The Nature of Design*. London: Littlehampton Book Services Ltd., 1964 (republished in 1978 as *The Nature of Aesthetics of Design*. London: Herbert Press).

———. *The Nature and Art of Workmanship*. London: Herbert Press, 1968.

Racz, I. *Contemporary Crafts*, Oxford: Berg, 2009.

Raffe, D. 'Education, Employment and the Youth Opportunities Programme: Some Sociological Perspectives'. *Oxford Review of Education*, 7(3) (1981), 211–22.

Raithby, J. (ed.). 'Charles II, 1666: An Act for Rebuilding the City of London', in *Statutes of the Realm: Volume 5, 1628–80* (s.l, 1819), 603–12. *British History Online*. Retrieved 9 June 2021 from http://www.british-history.ac.uk/statutes-realm/vol5/pp603-612.

Randall, E. 'The TOPS Preparatory Course: A Pilot Scheme'. *The Vocational Aspect of Education*, 28(69) (1976), 7–10.

Rappaport, S. *Worlds within Worlds: Structures of Life in Sixteenth-Century London*. Cambridge: Cambridge University Press, 1989.

Rees, T. 'Being Neurologically Human Today: Life and Science and Adult Cerebral Plasticity (an Ethical Analysis)'. *American Ethnologist*, 37(1) (2010), 150–66.

Renard, G. *Guilds in the Middle Ages*. Translation from the French by D. Terry and edited with an introduction by G.D.H. Cole, Kitchener, Ontario: Batoche Books, 2000 [1918].

Rice, T. 'Learning to Listen: Auscultation and the Transmission of Auditory Knowledge'. *Journal of the Royal Anthropological Institute*, special issue on 'Making Knowledge', edited by T.H.J. Marchand (2010), S41–S61.

———. *Hearing and the Hospital: Sound, Listening, Knowledge and Experience*. Canon Pyon: Sean Kingston, 2013.

Ricoeur, P. 'Ideology and Utopia as Cultural Imagination'. *Philosophic Exchange*, 7(1) (1976), Article 5. Retrieved 9 June 2021 from https://digitalcommons.brockport.edu/cgi/viewcontent.cgi?article=1193&context=phil_ex.

Ridley, J. *A History of the Carpenters' Company*. London: Carpenters' Hall, 1995.

Risatti, H. *A Theory of Craft: Function and Aesthetic Expression*. Chapel Hill: University of North Carolina Press, 2007.

Roberts, K. 'Career Trajectories and the Mirage of Increased Social Mobility', in I. Bates and G. Riseborough (eds), *Youth and Inequality* (Buckingham: Open University Press, 1993), 229–45.

Rose, M. *The Mind at Work: Valuing the Intelligence of the American Worker*. London: Penguin, 2004.

Rose, W. *The Village Carpenter: The Classic Memoir of the Life of a Victorian Craftsman*. Ammanford: Stobart Davies, 2009 [1937].

Rosenbaum, S. 'Epicurus on Pleasure and the Complete Life'. *The Monist*, 73(1) (1990), 21–41.

Rousseau, J.-J. *Of the Social Contract and Other Political Writings*, edited by C. Bertram. London: Penguin, 2012.

Ruskin, J. 'The Two Paths', in A.T. Cook and A. Wedderburn (eds), *The Complete Works of John Ruskin*, Library Edition, vol. XVI (London: George Allen, 1905), 245–411.

———. 'The Nature of Gothic', in J. Ruskin, *On Art & Life* (London: Penguin, 2004), 1–56 (first published in J. Ruskin, *The Stones of Venice*, vol. 2. London: Smith, Elder & Co., 1851–53).

———. 'The Work of Iron', in *Nature, Art and Policy*, reprinted in J. Ruskin, *On Art & Life* (London: Penguin, 2004), 57–98.

Ryle, G. *The Concept of Mind*. London: Routledge, 2009 [1949].

———. 'Pleasure, Part I', in G. Ryle and W.B. Gallie, 'Symposium: Pleasure'. *Proceedings of the Aristotelian Society*, Supplementary Volumes, vol. 28, *Belief and Will* (1958), 135–46.

Ryle, G., and W.B. Gallie. 'Symposium: Pleasure'. *Proceedings of the Aristotelian Society*, Supplementary Volumes, vol. 28, *Belief and Will* (1958), 135–64.

Samier, E. 'Weber on Education and Its Administration: Prospects for Leadership in a Rationalized World'. *Educational Management and Administration*, 30(1) (2002), 27–45.

Samuel, R. 'The Workshop of the World: Steam, Power and Hand Technology in Mid-Victorian Britain'. *History Workshop Journal*, 3(1) (1977), 6–72.

Schumacher, E. *Small Is Beautiful*. London: Vintage, 1993.

Schwerdtfeger, F. *Traditional Housing in African Cities: A Comparative Study of Houses in Zaria, Ibadan and Marrakesh*. Chichester: John Wiley & Sons, 1982.

Senft, G. *Referring to Space: Studies in Austronesian & Papuan Languages*. Oxford: Clarendon Press, 1997.

Senker, P., H. Rainbird, K. Evans, P. Hodkinson, E. Keep, M. Maguire, D. Raffe and L. Unwin. 'Working to Learn: A Holistic Approach to Young People's Education and Training', in P. Ainley and H. Rainbird (eds), *Apprenticeship: Towards a New Paradigm of Learning* (London: Kogan Page, 1999), 191–205.

Sennett, R. *The Craftsman*. London: Allen Lane, 2008.

Sennitt, J. 'Message from the Master'. *The Carpenters' Company Broadsheet*, 39 (2009), 1–2.

Sharp, K., and M. Kinder. 'The New Workforce Dilemma'. *The Craftsmanship Initiative*, Spring 2018/Fall 2019. Retrieved 9 June 2021 from https://craftsmanship.net/the-workforce-dilemma.

Sharpe, K. *The Personal Rule of Charles I*. New Haven: Yale University Press, 1996.

Shoemaker, R. *The London Mob: Violence and Disorder in Eighteenth-Century England*. London: Hambleton Continuum, 2004.

Shore, C., and S. Wright. 'Audit Culture and Anthropology: Neo-liberalism in British Higher Education'. *Journal of the Royal Anthropological Institute*, 5(4) (1999), 557–75.

Sigaut, F. 'Learning, Teaching, and Apprenticeship'. *New Literary History*, 24 (1993), 105–14.

——. *Comment* Homo *Devint* Faber. Paris: CNRS Éditions, 2012.

Simonton, D. 'Gendered Work in Eighteenth Century Towns', in M. Walsh (ed.), *Working out Gender: Perspectives from Labour History* (Aldershot: Ashgate, 1999), 29–47.

Sinclair, S. *Making Doctors: An Institutional Apprenticeship*. Oxford: Berg, 1997.

Sizer, L. 'The Two Facets of Pleasure'. *Philosophical Topics*, 41(1) (2013), 215–36.

Sloane, E. *A Museum of Early American Tools*. New York: Dover Publications, 1964.

Slow Food. *Good, Clean and Fair: The Slow Food Manifesto for Quality*. Retrieved 9 June 2021 from https://n4v5s9s7.stackpathcdn.com/wp-content/uploads/2015/07/Manifesto_Quality_ENG.pdf.

Smith, A. *An Inquiry into the Nature and Causes of the Wealth of Nations*, 2 vols. London: W. Strahan and T Cadell, 1758.

Smuts, A. 'The Feels Good Theory of Pleasure'. *Philosophical Studies: An International Journal for Philosophy in the Analytic Tradition*, 155(2) (2011), 241–65.

Snell, K.D.M. *Annals of the Labouring Poor: Social Change and Agrarian England, 1660–1900*. Cambridge: Cambridge University Press, 1985.

Steedman, H., H. Gospel and P. Ryan. *Apprenticeship: A Strategy for Growth*. A special report published by the Centre for Economic Performance, London School of Economics and Political Science. October 1998.

Steinmann, S. 'The Vocational Education and Training System in England and Wales'. *International Journal of Sociology* 28(4) (Winter, 1998/1999), 29–56.

Stoller, P. *The Taste of Ethnographic Things: The Senses in Anthropology*. Philadelphia: University of Pennsylvania Press, 1989.

Strathern M. (ed.). *Audit Cultures: Anthropological Studies of Accountability, Ethics and the Academy*. London: Routledge, 2000.

Strathern, M. 'The Tyranny of Transparency'. *British Educational Research Journal*, 26(30) (2000), 309–21.

——. 'A Community of Critics? Thoughts on New Knowledge'. *Journal of the Royal Anthropological Institute*, 12(1) (2006), 191–209.

Streeck, W. 'Through Unending Halls'. *London Review of Books*, 7 February 2019, 29–31.

Sturt, G. *The Wheelwright's Shop*. Cambridge: Cambridge University Press, 1993 [1923].

Sweett, W.T. 'Commentary'. *Journal of the Incorporated Institute of Certified Carpenters* (April 1940) (no pagination).

Takahashi, C., J. Diedrichsen and S. Watt. 'Integration of Vision and Haptics during Tool Use'. *Journal of Vision*, 9(6) (2009), 1–13.

Tancell, J. 'The Tree of Life in Carpenters' Hall'. *The Carpenters' Company Broadsheet*, 43 (2011) 16–17.

——. 'The Stratford Estate: A Brief History'. *The Carpenters' Company Broadsheet*, 47 (2013), 18–21.

———. 'Carpenters' Company Charities 1333–1700'. *The Carpenters' Company Broadsheet*, 52 (2015), 9–11.

———. 'Carpenters' Company Charities from 1700'. *The Carpenters' Company Broadsheet*, 53 (2016), 16–18.

———. 'Plague, Fire and the Carpenters' Company 1665–1666'. *The Carpenters' Company Broadsheet*, 54 (2016), 20–22.

———. 'The Carpenters' Company in World War One'. *The Carpenters' Company Broadsheet*, 55 (2017), 16–17.

———. 'The Carpenters' Tudor Wall Paintings'. *The Carpenters' Company Broadsheet*, 58 (2018), 12–14.

———. 'Women and the Carpenters' Company'. *The Carpenters' Company Broadsheet*, 57 (2018), 18–20.

———. 'Company History: Celebrating Excellence – 125 Years of the Building Crafts College'. *The Carpenters' Company Chronicle 2019*, October 2019, 32–35.

Taylor, C.C.W. 'Pleasure'. *Analysis*, 23(1) (1963), 2–19.

Taylor, G.H. 'Editor's Introduction', in G.H. Taylor (ed.), *Lectures on Ideology & Utopia: Paul Ricoeur*. New York: Columbia University Press, 1986.

Taylor, J. 'Building Crafts College'. *The Carpenters' Company Broadsheet*, 37 (2008), 4–12.

Taylor, J.D. *Tools of the Trade: The Art and Craft of Carpentry*. San Francisco: Chronicle Books, 1996.

Tenhouten, W. 'The Eclipse of the Sacred and the Paradoxical Liberation of the Right Hand'. *Anthropology of Consciousness*, 6(2) (1995), 15–26.

Thiel, D. *Builders: Class, Gender and Ethnicity in the Construction Industry*. London: Routledge, 2013.

Thomas, A.H. 'Introduction: Apprenticeship', in A.H. Thomas (ed.), *Calendar of the Plea and Memoranda Rolls of the City of London: Volume 2, 1364–1381*, xxx–xlvii. Originally published by His Majesty's Stationery Office, London, 1929. *British History Online*. Retrieved 9 June 2021 from http://www.british-history.ac.uk/plea-memoranda-rolls/vol2/xxx-xlvii.

Thomas N. 'Modernity, Crafts and Guilded Practices: Locating the Historical Geographies of 20th Century Craft Organisations', in L. Price and H. Hawkins (eds), *Geographies of Making, Craft and Creativity* (London: Routledge, 2018), 60–77.

Thompson, E.P. *William Morris: Romantic to Revolutionary*. London: Merlin Press, 1955.

Thoreau, H.D. 'Walden', in *Walden and Civil Disobedience* (London: Penguin, 1986), 43–382.

Thornton, J. 'How an Adze Is Like an Atlatl and Other Aspects of Paleo-Woodworking' (unpublished paper presented to the American Institute for Conservation, 2005).

Thorogood, G. *One Hundred Years: History of the Institute of Carpenters, 1890–1990*. London: Institute of Carpenters, 1990.

Tudge, C. *The Secret Life of Trees: How They Live and Why They Matter*. London: Allen Lane, 2005.

UK Parliament. *House of Commons Hansard*, vol. 67, 14 November 1984. Retrieved 9 June 2021 from https://hansard.parliament.uk/commons/1984-11-14/debates/82707f83-24eb-44a8-8d9a-8a249871883e/SchoolsAndFurtherEducation.

Umilta, M., L. Escola, I. Intrskirveli, F. Grammont, M. Rochat, F. Caruana, A. Jezzini, V. Gallese and G. Rizzolatti. 'When Pliers Become Fingers in the Monkey Motor System'. *Proceedings of the National Academy of Sciences of the United States of America*, 105(6) (2008), 2209–13.

United Nations Division for Sustainable Development. *AGENDA 21: United Nations Conference on Environment and Development, Rio de Janeiro, 3–14 June 1992*. Retrieved 9 June 2021 from http://sustainabledevelopment.un.org/index.php?page=view&nr=23&type=400&menu=35.

Unwin, L. 'Employer-Led Realities: Apprenticeship Past and Present'. *Journal of Vocational Education and Training*, 48(1) (1996), 57–68.

———. 'Twenty-First Century Vocational Education in the United Kingdom: What Would Dickens Think?' *Pedagogy, Culture and Society*, 12(2) (2004), 175–200.

Updike, J. 'Tools'. *Poetry*, 182(3) (2003), 134.

Venkatesan, S. 'Learning to Weave; Weaving to Learn. . . What?' *Journal of the Royal Anthropological Institute*, special issue on 'Making Knowledge', edited by T.H.J. Marchand (2010), S158–S175.

Wacquant, L. *Body and Soul: Notebooks of an Apprentice Boxer*. Oxford: Oxford University Press, 2004.

———. 'Habitus as Topic and Tool: Reflections on Becoming a Prizefighter'. *Qualitative Research in Psychology*, 8(1) (2011), 81–92.

Wade, J. *History of the Middle and Working Classes*. London: Effingham Wilson, 1833.

Walford, C. 'Fires and Fire Insurance Considered under their Historical, Financial, Statistical, and National Aspects'. *Journal of the [Royal] Statistical Society*, 40 (1877), 347–424.

Wall, C. 'The Building Industry during War and Reconstruction', in *An Architecture of Parts: Architects, Building Workers and Industrialisation in Britain, 1940–1970* (London: Routledge, 2013), 32–50.

Wallis, P. 'Apprenticeship and Training in Premodern England'. *Journal of Economic History*, 68(3) (2008), 832–61.

Wallis, P., C. Webb and C. Minns. 'Leaving Home and Entering Service: The Age of Apprenticeship in Early Modern London'. *LSE Working Papers*, no. 125/09 (2009), 1–32. Retrieved 9 June 2021 from http://www.lse.ac.uk/Economic-History/Assets/Documents/WorkingPapers/Economic-History/2009/WP125.pdf.

Ward, L. 'Tough Choices Are Looming on Student Fees.' *The Independent*, 15 May 1997. Retrieved 9 June 2021 from https://www.independent.co.uk/news/tough-choices-are-looming-on-student-fees-1261496.html.

Warner, M. 'Learning My Lesson: Marina Warner on the Disfiguring of Higher Education'. *London Review of Books*, 37(6) (2015), 8–14.

Washburn, S. 'Tools and Human Evolution'. *Scientific American*, 203(3) (1960), 63–75.

Weber, M. 'The Alleged "Academic Freedom" of the German Universities', in *Max Weber on Universities: The Power of the State and the Dignity of the Academic Calling in Imperial Germany*. Translated, edited and introductory note by E. Shils (Chicago: University of Chicago Press, 1974), 14–23.

Weber, R.J., S. Dixon and A.M. Llorente. 'Studying Invention: The Hand Tool as a Model System'. *Science, Technology and Human Values*, 18(4) (1993), 480–505.

Weir, S. *Qat in Yemen: Consumption and Social Change*. London: British Museum Publications, 1985.

White, T.I. 'Aristotle and Utopia'. *Renaissance Quarterly*, 29(4) (1976), 635–75.

Wilmer, C. 'Introduction', in W. Morris, *News from Nowhere and Other Writings* (London: Penguin, 2004), ix–xli.

Wilson, D.R. 'The Institute of Carpenters Examinations'. *The Cutting Edge: Journal of the Institute of Carpenters* (2006), 10–11.

Wilson, F.R. *The Hand: How Its Use Shapes the Brain, Language and Human Culture*. New York: Pantheon Books, 1998.

Woodward, D. 'The Background to the Statute of Artificers: The Genesis of Labour Policy, 1558–63'. *Economic History Review*, New Series, 33(1) (1980), 32–44.

Woolf, V. *A Room of One's Own*. London: Hogarth Press, 1929.

Woollacott, A. *On Her Their Lives Depend: Munitions Workers in the Great War*. Berkeley: University of California Press, 1994.

World Economic Forum. 'Chapter 1: The Future of Jobs and Skills', in 'Part 1: Preparing for the Workforce of the Fourth Industrial Revolution', in *The Future of Jobs Report*, 2016. Retrieved 9 June 2021 from https://reports.weforum.org/future-of-jobs-2016/chapter-1-the-future-of-jobs-and-skills/#view/fn-1.

Worshipful Company of Carpenters. *The Carpenters' Company: General Information*. London: Carpenters' Company, 2010.

WWF-UK, *Timber Scorecard 2017: Sustainability Progress among Buyers of Timber and Wood Products*. Retrieved 9 June 2021 from https://www.wwf.org.uk/sites/default/files/publications/Jul17/WWF_Timber_Scorecard_2017_0.pdf.

Xu, T., X. Yu, A. Perlik, W. Tobin, J. Zweig, K. Tennant, T. Jones and Y. Zuo. 'Rapid Formation and Selective Stabilization of Synapses for Enduring Motor Memories'. *Nature*, 462 (2009), 915–20.

Yarrow, T., and S. Jones. '"Stone Is Stone": Engagement and Detachment in the Craft of Conservation Masonry'. *Journal of the Royal Anthropological Institute*, 20(2) (2014), 256–75.

Yeomans, D.T. 'Early Carpenters' Manuals'. *Construction History*, 2 (1986), 13–33.

Zemel, A., and T. Koschmann. '"Put Your Fingers Right in Here": Learnability and Instructed Experience'. *Discourse Studies*, 16(2) (2014), 163–83.

Zwerger, K. *Wood and Wood Joints: Building Traditions of Europe and Japan*. Basel: Birkhäuser, 2000.

INDEX

Printed in the USA
CPSIA information can be obtained
at www.ICGtesting.com
LVHW021350050424
776490LV00014B/187